SMITHSONIAN HANDBOOKS

BIRDS

— OF —

FLORIDA

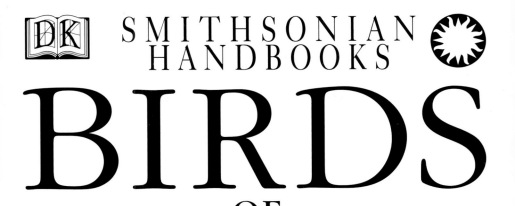

SMITHSONIAN
HANDBOOKS

BIRDS

— OF —
FLORIDA

Fred J. Alsop III

LONDON, NEW YORK, MUNICH,
MELBOURNE AND DELHI

Editor-in-Chief Russell Greenberg, PhD
Director of the Migratory Bird Center at the National Zoological Park

Senior Editor Jill Hamilton
Art Editors Gus Yoo, Megan Clayton
Editorial Director Chuck Wills
Creative Director Tina Vaughan
Publisher Sean Moore
Production Manager Chris Avgherinos
DTP Designer Russell Shaw
Picture Research Martin Copeland, Mark Dennis

Produced by Southern Lights Custom Publishing
Editorial Director Shelley DeLuca
Production Director Lee Howard
Graphic Design Miles Parsons, Tim Kolankiewicz, Scott Fuller
President Ellen Sullivan

First American Edition, 2002
2 4 6 8 10 9 7 5 3 1

Published in the United States by
DK Publishing, Inc.
95 Madison Avenue
New York, New York 10016

DK Publishing, Inc. offers special discounts for bulk purchases for sales promotions
or premiums. Specific, large-quantity needs can be met with special editions, including
personalized covers, excerpts of existing guides, and corporate imprints. For more information,
contact Special Markets Department, DK Publishing, Inc.; Fax: 800-600-9098.

Library of Congress Cataloging-in-Publication Data

Alsop, Fred.
Birds of Florida / Fred J. Alsop III.-- 1st American ed.
p. cm. -- (Smithsonian handbooks)
ISBN 0-7894-8387-4 (alk. paper)
1. Birds--Florida--Identification. I. Title. II. Series.

QL684.F6 A68 2002
598'.09759--dc21

2001047630

Printed and bound by Kyodo in Singapore.
Color reproduction by Colourscan, Singapore.

See our complete product line at
www.dk.com

CONTENTS

INTRODUCTION • 6
How this Book Works 8
Guide to Visual References 10
Anatomy of Birds 12
Topography of a Bird 14
Variations within Species 16
How to Identify Birds 18
Identifying Birds in Flight 20
Bird Silhouettes 22
Behavior 24
Abundance and Distribution 26
Watching Birds in the Backyard 28
Watching Birds in the Field 30
How to Be a Better Birder 32
Conservation 34
Extinction 35

SPECIES PROFILES • 38
ACCIDENTAL, VAGRANT
AND CASUAL SPECIES • 370

Glossary 385
Index 391
Acknowledgments 399

INTRODUCTION

Birdwatching, or birding as it is now commonly called, is practiced by more than 60 million North Americans – making it the single largest hobby on the continent. North America is an exciting place to go birding because it contains birds representing more than 920 species that are permanent or summer residents, visit regularly, or stray occasionally to the continent.

AVIAN DIVERSITY

Having attained the power of flight more than 150 million years ago, birds might be expected to be uniformly distributed in every corner of the Earth. But they are not. They are bound to the earth by the habitats to which they have adapted, and they are limited by geographical barriers as well as the history of their lineage.

Different species are often associated with major plant communities, or biomes, that provide them with critical habitat requirements for part or all of their annual cycle. Polar regions of permanent ice and snow are home to

The BARN OWL hunts in areas cleared for agriculture.

Ivory Gulls; the arctic tundra to Snowy Owls, ptarmigans, jaegers, Gyrfalcons, and countless shorebirds in summer. The great block of northern coniferous forests provide seeds for crossbills, grosbeaks, finches, and nuthatches; in summer, insects for flycatchers, vireos, and warblers abound. Deciduous forests, southern pine forests, grasslands, and deserts all hold particular species of birds different from those in other biomes. Other species, such as herons, are adapted for freshwater ponds, lakes, rivers, and streams; still others for marshes and seashores as well as the open ocean.

The GREAT BLUE HERON has adapted to freshwater habitats.

BIRDWATCHING IN NORTH AMERICA

The incredible diversity of North America's avian population is evidenced by the more than 920 species of birds that are now accepted as having occurred in North America. These species can be found in a wide variety of habitats, from spectacular mountain ranges, vast grasslands, hot and cold deserts, chaparral, deciduous and coniferous forests, swamps and pine forests, tundra, glaciers, and ice fields. Inhabiting this vast area are billions of individual birds.

The widespread YELLOW WARBLER is common along woodland edges.

Many birdwatchers practice their hobby close to their own backyards. They learn to recognize the species they see most often and occasionally identify a "new" species for the yard, perhaps even photograph the birds they see. Many take their birding to the field. Some are so passionate that they travel North America identifying as many species as they can, often covering many miles on short notice to observe a newly discovered vagrant.

Not even the most ardent birder has seen all of the species recorded on the North American continent. But that is part of the fun and challenge of birding. It holds something for every level of interest, and the amateur birder stands as much chance as the professional of making a discovery that sheds important light on the field of ornithology.

AMERICAN COOTS thrive in hardwood swamps.

HOW THIS BOOK WORKS

Until now, no tool for identifying birds has also provided access to information on behavior, nesting, flight patterns, and similar birds in a compact and user-friendly format. Written for the novice as well as the experienced birder, this book showcases in individual page profiles each of the 331 species of birds documented as occurring in the state of Florida. The species

The CANADA GOOSE can be found almost anywhere in North America at some point during the year.

are in taxonomic order and include all those known to breed in Florida and adjacent islands and seas within two hundred miles of the coast, as well as all species documented as regular visitors by the American Ornithologists' Union (AOU) and the American Birding Association (ABA). Species recorded as casual, vagrant, or accidental visitors are listed in a separate section beginning on page 370. Only those species listed on the current AOU *Check-list of North American Birds* (7th edition, 1998 and its 42nd Supplement, 2000) and the ABA 1998–99 ABA *Check-list Report, Birding* 31: 518–524 are included. Other species that have been seen but not yet accepted by the AOU or ABA are not included. Excluded also are a host of introduced exotic species that are living in the wild, mostly in southern Florida, that are not yet recognized by either the AOU or the ABA as having viable breeding populations there.

FINDING YOUR BIRD

To find a bird, scan the pages of the book, or look up its scientific or common name in the index. The species are in taxonomic order, beginning with the non-passerines such as grebes, ducks, hawks, owls, doves, hummingbirds, and woodpeckers. They are followed by the passerines, the perching or songbirds, which begin on page 234. The species profiles will help you identify a bird as well as learn about its natural history.

LEAST GREBE (non-passerine)
Birds that do not perch and sing are in the first part of this book.

TOWNSEND'S WARBLER (passerine)
Birds that do perch and sing are in the second part of this book.

Scientific family name •

Scientific name of species •

Average length from tip of bill to tip of tail •

Average length between tips of open wings •

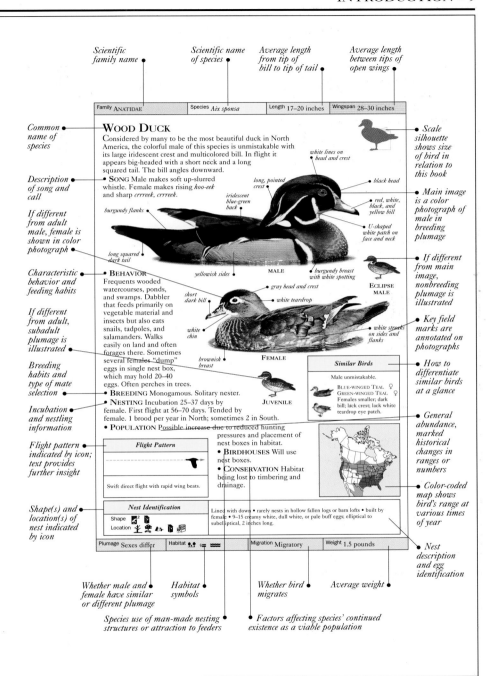

Family ANATIDAE | Species *Aix sponsa* | Length 17–20 inches | Wingspan 28–30 inches

Common • name of species

WOOD DUCK

Considered by many to be the most beautiful duck in North America, the colorful male of this species is unmistakable with its large iridescent crest and multicolored bill. In flight it appears big-headed with a short neck and a long squared tail. The bill angles downward.

Description • of song and call

• **SONG** Male makes soft up-slurred whistle. Female makes rising *hoo-eek* and sharp *crrreek, crrreek.*

If different from adult male, female is shown in color photograph •

Characteristic • behavior and feeding habits

• **BEHAVIOR** Frequents wooded watercourses, ponds, and swamps. Dabbler that feeds primarily on vegetable material and insects but also eats snails, tadpoles, and salamanders. Forages easily on land and often forages there. Sometimes several females "dump" eggs in single nest box, which may hold 20–40 eggs. Often perches in trees.

If different from adult, subadult plumage is illustrated •

Breeding • habits and type of mate selection

• **BREEDING** Monogamous. Solitary nester.

Incubation • and nestling information

• **NESTING** Incubation 25–37 days by female. First flight at 56–70 days. Tended by female. 1 brood per year in North; sometimes 2 in South.

• **POPULATION** Possible increase due to reduced hunting pressures and placement of nest boxes in habitat.

Flight pattern • indicated by icon; text provides further insight

• **BIRDHOUSES** Will use nest boxes.

• **CONSERVATION** Habitat being lost to timbering and drainage.

Flight Pattern

Swift direct flight with rapid wing beats.

Shape(s) and • location(s) of nest indicated by icon

Nest Identification

Shape
Location

Lined with down • rarely nests in hollow fallen logs or barn lofts • built by female • 9–15 creamy white, dull white, or pale buff eggs; elliptical to subelliptical, 2 inches long.

Plumage Sexes differ | Habitat | Migration Migratory | Weight 1.5 pounds

Scale • silhouette shows size of bird in relation to this book

Main image • is a color photograph of male in breeding plumage

If different • from main image, nonbreeding plumage is illustrated

Key field • marks are annotated on photographs

How to • differentiate similar birds at a glance

General • abundance, marked historical changes in ranges or numbers

Color-coded • map shows bird's range at various times of year

Nest • description and egg identification

Annotations on images:

white lines on head and crest
long, pointed crest •
black head •
iridescent blue-green back
red, white, black, and yellow bill
burgundy flanks •
U-shaped white patch on face and neck
long squared dark tail •
yellowish sides • **MALE**
burgundy breast with white spotting
gray head and crest •
short dark bill •
white teardrop •
ECLIPSE MALE
white • chin
white streaks on sides and flanks
brownish breast • **FEMALE**

JUVENILE

Similar Birds

Male unmistakable.

BLUE-WINGED TEAL ♀
GREEN-WINGED TEAL ♀
Females smaller; dark bill; lack crest; lack white teardrop eye patch.

Whether male and • female have similar or different plumage

Habitat • symbols

Whether bird • migrates

Average weight •

Species use of man-made nesting • structures or attraction to feeders

Factors affecting species' continued • existence as a viable population

GUIDE TO VISUAL REFERENCES

PHOTOGRAPHS

Because users of this guide will be viewing these birds in backyards, woodlands, and other natural environments, realistic photographs are used as visual reference. Some rare and seldom-photographed species are illustrated. Unless otherwise noted, the primary image shows the male bird in breeding plumage. If the adult female has significantly different plumage from the male a second image depicts the female in breeding plumage. If field marks are not visible in a photograph they are described in the accompanying text.

squared blackish tail with slight cleft

chestnut sides of face extend to sides of nape

blue-black crown

whitish forehead

short black bill

chestnut throat with black center patch

CLIFF SWALLOW

blue-black wings and back

whitish underparts with dusky gray-brown sides and flanks

ILLUSTRATIONS

Many birds also have other plumages, including the winter plumage, which are depicted in illustrations. The plumage of the immature if different from both adults also is illustrated. Some species have different color morphs, which are also illustrated.

LIGHT MORPH JUVENILE　　**WINTER PLUMAGE**　　**WHITE MORPH**

SIMILAR BIRDS

In many cases it can be difficult to distinguish between certain birds in the field. Therefore, the species accounts feature a list of similar birds with accompanying text that identifies distinct features and behavior that clearly set them apart. Male and female symbols indicate the sex of the bird that could be mistaken for the species being profiled.

Similar Birds

CAVE SWALLOW
Pale cinnamon-buff throat; cinnamon forehead; richer cinnamon-rust rump.

DISTRIBUTION MAP

Each species profile has a map showing where the bird is likely to be seen either all year long (permanent resident), in the breeding season (summer resident), or in the winter (winter resident). The maps depict only those parts of each species' range within North America and up to approximately 100 miles offshore north of central Mexico to the northern borders of Canada.

permanent resident　　　summer resident　　　winter resident

SCALE SILHOUETTES

These show the silhouette of the bird overlaid proportionally on a copy of this book.

NEST IDENTIFICATION

The Nest Identification box provides icons describing nest shape and location.

Flight Pattern	

Swift graceful flight alternating several deep, rapid wing beats with long elliptical glides with sharp sweeping upturns at the end. Soars on thermals and updrafts.

FLIGHT PATTERN

Each bird's flight pattern is shown in its species profile by an icon. For more information on flight patterns, see page 20.

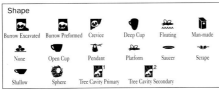

Nest Identification	Pellets of clay or mud, with lining of grasses, down, and feathers • usually under eaves of buildings or under dams or bridges; sometimes on ridges of canyons; rarely on trunk of conifer tree under overhanging branch • built by both sexes • 3–6 white, cream, or pinkish eggs, marked with browns; oval to long oval, 0.8 x 0.5 inches.
Shape	
Location	

Shape

Burrow Excavated, Burrow Preformed, Crevice, Deep Cup, Floating, Man-made, None, Open Cup, Pendant, Platform, Saucer, Scrape, Shallow, Sphere, Tree Cavity Primary, Tree Cavity Secondary

Location

Bank, Building, Bridge, Cave, Chimney, Cliff, Conifer, Decidous, Floating, Grass, Gravel Roof, Hollow Log, Man-made, Pebbles, Reed/Cattails, Shrub, Snag, Bare Soil, Stump

HABITAT

At the bottom of each species account is a set of icons representing all the habitat types in the order in which the bird is found, from the most to the least likely.

forest: coniferous, broadleaf, temperate, or tropical

open forest; more space between the trees, tundra forest, semiopen areas

forest edge, oak and riparian

grassland with scattered trees (includes farmland, citrus groves, orchards)

bushes, shrubs, thickets and undergrowth; tropical lowland

areas of scrub vegetation, frequently with thorns

open landscapes: grassland, tundra, savanna, coastal ponds/sloughs – salt, brackish or freshwater, coastal marshes, coastal wetlands, salt marshes, prairie potholes

semidesert

desert

lakes, rivers and vicinity, sandspits, mudflats, ponds

upland streams and vicinity

open sea, low flat islands

rocky or sandy seashore, bay islands, coastal islands, shallow coastal habitats, coastal bays, coastal mangroves, tidal flats, sand spits, mudflats

freshwater marshes, swamps

rocky places or cliffs (both on the coast and inland)

mountains, wooded canyons

ANATOMY OF BIRDS

Birds are the most diverse terrestrial vertebrates with more than 9,800 extant species. Mammals are the only other homeothermic group with whom they share the planet. Yet, although mammal species number less than half that of birds, the mammals are much more varied in body shape and size. Mammals vary in form from primates to giraffes to armadillos, with specialists in running, hopping, flying, swimming, burrowing, digging, and climbing. Birds, however, all look like birds – with the same basic architecture, a body shape dictated by the demands of flight.

FEATHERS

Birds have three basic types of feathers: down, contour, and flight (wing and tail) feathers. Down feathers are next to the bird's skin for insulation. The contour is the most commonly recognized feather and the one that covers most of the bird's body. Typical contour feathers consist of a central shaft or quill and the flattened portion or vane. Contour feathers that extend beyond the wings and tail are the flight feathers.

DOWN

CONTOUR

FLIGHT
(**WING AND TAIL**)

BONES

In most species both the wings and the legs must be strong enough to transport the full weight of the bird, yet light enough to fly. Some bones have been fused and some bear internal struts. Ribs are overlapped for strength; others are hollowed, thinned, and reduced in numbers for lightness. In flying birds, and those flightless birds like penguins that use flipperlike forelimbs to "fly" underwater, the sternum, or breastbone, bears a thin knifelike keel to which the large flight muscles of the breast, the pectoral muscles, are attached.

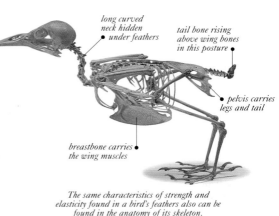

long curved neck hidden under feathers

tail bone rising above wing bones in this posture

pelvis carries legs and tail

breastbone carries the wing muscles

The same characteristics of strength and elasticity found in a bird's feathers also can be found in the anatomy of its skeleton.

BILLS

Birds' bills are composed of a horny sheath overlying a bony core. The entire lightweight structure has evolved in countless ways to the specialized needs of its owner, from seed-cracking to nectar probing and from fish-catching to fruit-picking. Birds also use their bills to build nests, preen, and court. Bills may change in size and/or color in breeding season.

The ROSEATE SPOONBILL uses its spoon-shaped bill to scoop food from water.

The EVENING GROSBEAK uses its conical bill to crunch seeds.

The BUFF-BELLIED HUMMINGBIRD uses its long needlelike bill to probe into flowers for nectar.

The RED CROSSBILL's bill features mandibles crossed at the tips that are ideal for digging the seeds out of pinecones.

LEGS AND FEET

The legs of birds are thin, strong, and springy, and in most species lack feathers on their distal parts where they are instead covered with scales. Muscles, which are concentrated on the portion of the leg nearest the body, control the extremities with a series of tendons. Toes generally number four with three forward and one opposable toe pointed backward, but some North American birds have only three. Toes are covered by scales and have claws at their tips which in birds of prey are enlarged into strong talons.

The AMERICAN ROBIN has a typical bird's foot: four toes with three forward and one back.

Some, like the HAIRY WOODPECKER, have two toes forward and two back.

The MALLARD has three webbed toes and one vestigial toe in back.

The DOUBLE-CRESTED CORMORANT has four webbed toes.

The BALD EAGLE has claws enlarged and elongated into talons.

WINGS AND TAILS

The shapes of wings and tails are an adaptation to where and how a bird flies. Look carefully at flight silhouettes: forest raptors (a) have rounded wings for living in dense vegetation; swallows (b) have narrow tapering wings. The tapering wings and narrow tail of a falcon (c) contrast with the broad splayed wings and broad tail of an eagle (d), which allow an eagle to soar. Terns (e) have long elegant wings; albatross wings (f) are very long, with an extended inner section for flying over water like a sailplane.

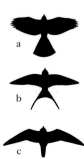

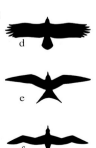

TOPOGRAPHY OF A BIRD

A s you consult the species profiles in this book you will encounter a number of ornithological terms that describe the "landscape," or groups of feathers, of a bird's body. Learning these terms will help you use your field guide and, when you look at living birds, prompt you to see more detail with each sighting.

TIPS FOR THE FIELD
1. Start by looking at the bird's head. Note its bill and the markings on its face.
2. Get a feel for the bird's overall shape and size and note body markings.
3. Note shapes and markings of tail and wings.
4. Watch it fly and note markings visible in flight.

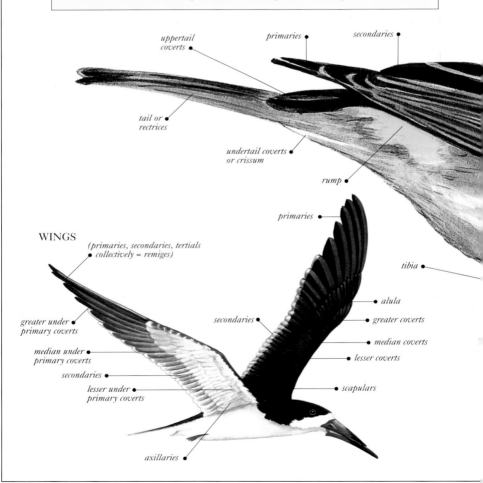

uppertail coverts

primaries

secondaries

tail or rectrices

undertail coverts or crissum

rump

primaries

WINGS
(primaries, secondaries, tertials collectively = remiges)

tibia

greater under primary coverts

secondaries

alula

greater coverts

median under primary coverts

median coverts

lesser coverts

secondaries

lesser under primary coverts

scapulars

axillaries

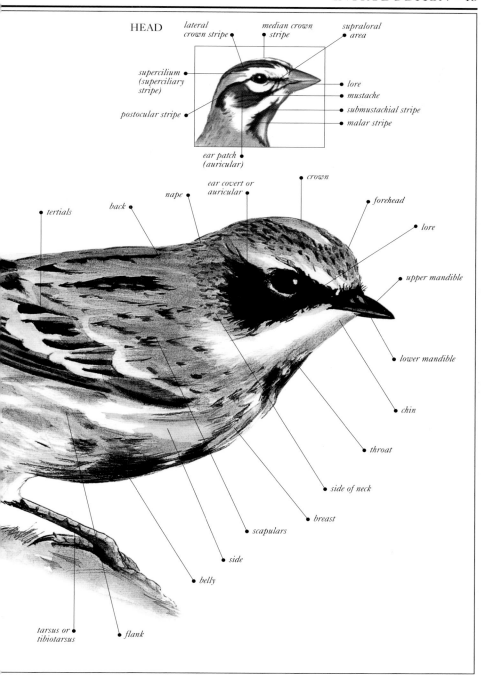

HEAD

lateral crown stripe

median crown stripe

supraloral area

supercilium (superciliary stripe)

lore

mustache

submustachial stripe

malar stripe

postocular stripe

ear patch (auricular)

crown

ear covert or auricular

forehead

nape

lore

back

tertials

upper mandible

lower mandible

chin

throat

side of neck

breast

scapulars

side

belly

tarsus or tibiotarsus

flank

VARIATIONS WITHIN SPECIES

Birds are the most colorful of all terrestrial vertebrates. Their coloration varies widely not only from species to species but within species. Often plumage colors differ between the sexes, between adults and their young, and from season to season. All of these different color patterns increase the challenge of identification for the birder.

MALE/FEMALE VARIATIONS

Within a species, adult males often differ in color and pattern of plumage, and sometimes in size, from adult females.

MALE

FEMALE

JUVENILE

PAINTED BUNTINGS have three distinct plumages.

JUVENILE PLUMAGE VARIATIONS

On an individual bird, color changes occur when feathers molt, or drop from their follicles to be replaced by new feathers. In its life span a bird will molt many times. After its first molt, when it loses its natal down, the bird will attain its *juvenile plumage*. This will be its first plumage with contour and flight feathers. This plumage often does not resemble that of either adult and is worn briefly for a few weeks or months. For the purposes of this book the term "juvenile" is used to refer to subadult plumaged birds that may, or may not, be sexually mature.

MALE

FEMALE

JUVENILE

Male and female NORTHERN CARDINALS have different plumages, while juveniles resemble females.

OTHER SUBADULT PLUMAGES

Although in many species, such as the bunting and cardinal, the juvenile attains adult plumage after its first year, there are species in which it takes the juvenile longer to do this. It may take juveniles of some species two years or more. These individuals may experience what are known as first, second, or even third winter or summer plumages before attaining the plumage of adult birds. The Ring-billed Gull is one such example.

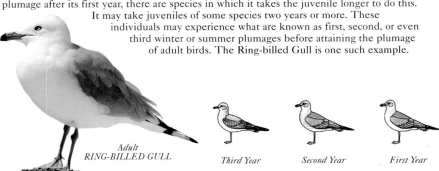

Adult
RING-BILLED GULL

Third Year

Second Year

First Year

SEASONAL VARIATIONS IN ADULT BIRDS

Most adult birds have two molts a year with a complete molt of all feathers after the breeding season and a partial molt in late winter/early spring in which only the head and body feathers are replaced.

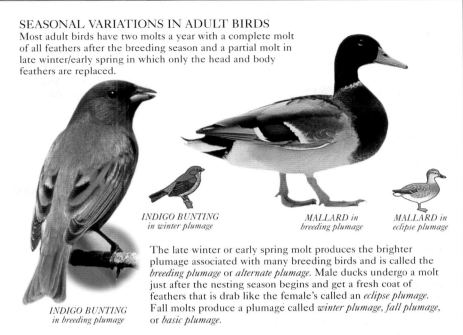

INDIGO BUNTING
in winter plumage

MALLARD in
breeding plumage

MALLARD in
eclipse plumage

INDIGO BUNTING
in breeding plumage

The late winter or early spring molt produces the brighter plumage associated with many breeding birds and is called the *breeding plumage* or *alternate plumage*. Male ducks undergo a molt just after the nesting season begins and get a fresh coat of feathers that is drab like the female's called an *eclipse plumage*. Fall molts produce a plumage called *winter plumage, fall plumage*, or *basic plumage*.

OTHER VARIATIONS

Some genetic variations in color and pattern can be seen among populations representing different geographical races of a species. These races are also referred to as subspecies.

*SLATE-
COLORED
JUNCO*

*OREGON
JUNCO*

*PINK-SIDED
JUNCO*

*WHITE-WINGED
JUNCO*

*GRAY-HEADED
JUNCO*

The DARK-EYED JUNCO has five adult plumage variations associated with different geographical regions.

Hybrids between species may produce birds that share some characteristics of each parent but still have a very different appearance.

Some species have two or more color phases or morphs.

*LAWRENCE'S
WARBLER*

*BREWSTER'S
WARBLER*

*Results from crosses between Golden-winged Warblers and
Blue-winged Warblers and their offspring.*

*The EASTERN SCREECH-OWL has red, gray,
and brown morphs.*

HOW TO IDENTIFY BIRDS

Birds that come to backyard feeders often stay long enough for you to study them in detail, but not all birds are so cooperative and often a fleeting glimpse is all you get. Learn to get the best look you can under the conditions and to see the entire bird well. First impressions of a bird, especially a new species for you, will give you clues for comparing it with birds you already know. What you are looking for are field marks, those physical clues that include size, shape, color patterns, and behavior, and also the habitat the bird is in and the sounds it may make.

Learn to routinely and quickly look at the details of the head; markings on the body, wings, and tail; and the shapes of the bird's parts.

HEAD
Is the crown:

striped   streaked   capped   crested

Look for other markings on the face such as:

superciliary stripes   eye lines   eye rings   spectacles

mustache marks   malar marks   ear patches   a mask through the eye

BODY PLUMAGE
Are the underparts:

plain and unmarked   streaked   spotted

TAIL
Is the tail:

forked

rounded

fan-shaped

wedge-shaped

pointed

notched

square

short

long

MARKINGS
Does it have distinctive wing or tail markings such as:

bars

bands

spots

contrasting colors

BILL
Is the bill:

cone-shaped

needlelike

hooked

decurved

spatulate

long or short

SONG
Many expert birders rely on their ears as much as their eyes to identify birds. Any of the many cassette tapes, CDs, or videos can help you learn the songs, calls, and other sounds birds make.

BEHAVIOR
The behavior of the bird will also provide clues to its identity. Does it bob, wag, or pump its tail either up and down or back and forth? Note its flight pattern. Does it back down a tree or go headfirst? For more information on Behavior, see page 24.

IDENTIFYING BIRDS IN FLIGHT

How a bird flies – the speed of the wing stroke as well as the pattern – can often help you recognize a species.

Direct – steady flight with regular wing beats, along a constant line; typical of most species, including waterfowl, herons, doves, crows, shorebirds, and many songbirds.

Dynamic soaring – glides over water "downhill" with the wind to its back and when close to the surface quickly turns 180 degrees back into the wind. There the bird is lifted back up to near the original height upon which it turns back and soars "downhill" again. Characteristic of many pelagic species, including albatrosses, shearwaters, and petrels.

Flap and glide – alternates a burst of several wing beats with a short or long level glide. Many birds of prey, both hawks and owls, use this flight pattern as do Black Vultures, ibis, and pelicans.

Flightless – many species living in environments free of predators have given up the energy-demanding activity of flight. The only flightless North American species, the Great Auk, was hunted to extinction in 1844.

Glide – wings are held fully or partially extended as the bird loses altitude. Many birds glide down to a landing, or from perch to perch. Hawks may glide from the top of one thermal to the bottom of the next in migration.

Hawking – flying up from the ground or down from an aerial perch to seize a flying insect and looping back down to the same or nearby perch. Characteristic of flycatchers and other small, active insect-eating birds such as warblers, the Cedar Waxwing, and several species of woodpeckers.

Hovering – rapid wingbeats while the bird remains suspended in one spot over the ground or water. Typical of hummingbirds, kingfishers, American Kestrel, Osprey, Rough-legged Hawk and many small birds that hover briefly to glean food from vegetation.

Mothlike – an erratic, sometimes bouncy, slow flight seen in nightjars, a few storm-petrels, and in the display flights of some small birds.

Skims – the flight pattern of the Black Skimmer in which the bird flies a steady course with its lower mandible cleaving the surface of still water as it feeds.

Static soaring – requires about a twentieth of the energy of flapping flight. Birds soar on rising heated columns of air, thermals, or on deflected currents and updrafts. Large hawks, eagles, vultures, storks, White Pelicans, and gulls soar this way.

Straight line formation – an energy-saving style of flight used by some larger birds such as cormorants, pelicans, ibis, some waterfowl, and others. Birds may fly one behind the other, or abreast as do some scoters and eiders.

Undulating – some small birds conserve energy by rising on one or more wing beats and then folding the wings to the body and swooping down to the next wing beat. Characteristic of woodpeckers, finches, and chickadees.

V formation – an energy-saving flight style used by some larger birds, including ducks, geese, cranes, and cormorants.

Zigzag – a pattern used by birds flushed from the ground as a way to elude predators. The Common Snipe and several species of quail are good examples.

BIRD SILHOUETTES

The first step in identifying a bird is to narrow down the possibilities to one or two families. Most species in a family share a unique combination of physical traits, such as the size and shape of the bill, that gives the family a distinctive silhouette. Some larger families are broken into subfamilies. For example, buteos and accipiters, both hawks in the family Accipitridae, have very different flight silhouettes. Identification becomes easier once you have learned the characteristic shape of each family and subfamily. The silhouettes shown here will help you place birds into their family groupings.

SWIMMING BIRDS

DUCK
medium length neck
spatulate-shaped bill

CORMORANT
elongated body
long, thin neck
thin, hook-tipped bill

LOON
elongated body
short, thick neck
moderately long, thick bill

GREBE
long, thin neck
head small in
proportion to body

PERCHING BIRDS

WREN
small
tail often cocked
upward at an angle
thin bill slightly decurved

WARBLER
small bird
small, thin bill

ORIOLE
conical, pointed bill

OWL
very upright posture
large head
no apparent neck

FINCH
thick bill for
cracking seeds

FLYCATCHER
upright posture
appears a little
large-headed

WOODPECKER
clings upright to side
of tree trunk
uses stiff tail as a prop

NUTHATCH
clings to tree trunks
and large branches
no apparent neck
straight, needlelike bill

STANDING BIRDS

THRASHER
thrushlike but with
longer tail
medium length bill

PEEP
thin bill
dumpy body
moderately long legs

HERON
long neck and legs
daggerlike bill

THRUSH
thin bill
plump body
relatively long legs

CORVID
short neck
strong bill
heavy body

FLYING BIRDS

GOOSE
heavy body
small head
long, outstretched neck

ACCIPITER
broad wings
long, relatively
narrow tail

BUTEO
broad wings and tail
individual primary
feathers visible on wing

SWIFT
long, very thin,
swept-back wings
almost no visible tail

SWALLOW
long, pointed,
swept-back wings

GULL
long, angular wings
spread tail
moderate bill

FALCON
narrow tail
relatively
narrow,
pointed wings

VULTURE
large bird
small head
long, broad-based wings
with visible primaries

BEHAVIOR

A large portion of the bird behavior we admire is instinctive and associated with particular species and families. So as you look for field marks, notice the bird's body language. It will give you many clues to its identity.

TAIL MOVEMENT
Some birds flip their tails as they move or perch. The tail may be cocked at an angle over the back, fanned open or closed, wagged, bobbed, or pumped up or down. Some birds constantly bob their bodies up and down as they walk or stand; others bob or jerk occasionally, while others sway back and forth as they walk.

BODY MOVEMENT
Some birds hop like a sparrow. Some run or walk. They may climb trees straight up, hitch up or back down them, walk headfirst down them, or cling upside down. Many birds wade like herons and egrets, or swim like ducks and geese. Some aquatic species feed by dabbling or tipping up their bodies with their heads and necks beneath the surface. Others dive completely below the surface.

BEWICK'S WREN holds its tail high above its back as it hops, often flicking it from side to side.

The PAINTED REDSTART spreads its tail, flashing the white outer tail feathers.

The BLUE-WINGED TEAL dabbles for food.

The TRICOLORED HERON wades.

FORAGING

Notice whether the bird forages on the ground, in the treetops, or at the mid-story level. Shorebirds may stay on the dry sand or away from the water's edge on a mudflat, or they may wade in the shallows, while some species may wade up to their bellies. Some shorebirds pick at their food while others drill and probe rapidly in the mud.

A juvenile WHITE IBIS probes with its bill for food in shallow water.

These MOURNING DOVES are foraging on the ground.

DISPLAY BEHAVIORS

Many species exhibit distinctive display behaviors during breeding season. They may dance like Prairie-Chickens, cranes, or Western Grebes; "skylark" like sparrows or buntings; or put on the aerial shows of woodcock and snipe. Many species, especially ground-nesters, will try to lead intruders away from the nest with distraction displays including the broken-wing or crippled-bird act.

The GREAT EGRET flashes its long white plumes in courtship display.

ABUNDANCE AND DISTRIBUTION

What does it mean when someone says a bird is "common" or that a species is "abundant" or "rare?" To appreciate a bird species' presence (or lack of it) in a given region you need to consider the factors of habitat, geographical range, and season of the year. Keep in mind that the distribution and abundance of birds, among the most mobile of the earth's creatures, are not static and the boundaries of populations often change. Birds are easily impacted by changes in climate and habitat brought about by natural or human causes, with seasonal migrations being the most obvious result. Thus knowing the seasonal occurrence of a bird is important in confirming its identification. The range maps in this guide are color-coded to provide you with this information. You can get even more specific information from local checklists, local bird books, websites, and local birders.

Abundant means a species is so conspicuous that birders usually observe more than 25 individuals daily in proper habitat and season.

EUROPEAN STARLING

Common means birders are likely to see 5–25 individuals daily in proper habitat and season.

BLACK-CAPPED CHICKADEE

Uncommon species can be widespread but may not be observed by birders searching for it in proper habitat and season.

Fairly common means a species is common enough that birders should observe at least one individual daily in proper habitat and season.

YELLOW-THROATED VIREO

LONG-EARED OWL

Casual means a bird that wanders into North America at infrequent intervals and is not observed annually, but exhibits a pattern of occurrence over several decades.

Rare can mean either that the species is widely distributed outside North America but exists in low numbers here, or that the entire population is small and local.

ANTILLEAN NIGHTHAWK

WHITE-THROATED ROBIN

Irruptive means the species is erratic in its movements – present and even numerous in a region in one year and absent the next.

SNOWY OWL

Vagrant is a migrant that has strayed off its usual route.

WHITE-EYED VIREO

RING-NECKED PHEASANT

Introduced means a non-native species deliberately released in a legal effort to establish a population.

Exotic means a non-native species illegally released or escaped, such as the many parrot species in south Florida, or a non-native species that has arrived in the region on its own like the Cattle Egret, or with passive human assistance (such as hitching a transoceanic ride on a ship).

CATTLE EGRET

Permanent residents live in the same geographic region all year.

NORTHERN CARDINAL

Summer residents breed and raise their young in one region and leave to winter in another region, usually to the south.

CEDAR WAXWING

SHY ALBATROSS

Accidentals are species that have occurred fewer than ten times in a region.

Transients pass through a region only once or twice a year during their spring and/or fall migrations.

AMERICAN TREE SPARROW

Winter residents arrive in a region only during the winter months after their breeding season, and usually breed to the north of it.

SEMIPALMATED SANDPIPER

WATCHING BIRDS IN THE BACKYARD

If you provide suitable food, shelter, and water, birds will come to your backyard. If you offer a variety of these necessities you will attract a greater diversity of birds. Place your feeders, nesting boxes, and birdbaths where the birds will feel safe from people and animals and where you can see the birds as you go about your daily routine.

FOOD AND FEEDERS

Many people enjoy feeding birds year-round. Basic types of feeders include platform feeders, hopper feeders, tube feeders, ball feeders, window feeders, fruit feeders, nectar feeders, and suet feeders. Standard foods include black (oil) sunflower seed (the best single seed), striped sunflower seed, hulled sunflower (chips/hearts) seed, niger (called "thistle") seed, safflower seed, white proso millet seed, red millet seed, milo seed, corn (whole kernel, shelled, and cracked), peanuts, peanut butter, suet and suet mixes, fruits, and nectar.

HOUSE FINCHES and a NORTHERN CARDINAL find food and shelter.

AMERICAN GOLDFINCHES at a tube feeder

A female RED-BELLIED WOODPECKER finds suet in a wire cage feeder.

WATER

Birds need water as much as they need food. If you include even one dependable source of water in your yard you will attract a great variety of birds to drink, bathe, and cool off. If there is a running water or dripping water element even more species will come. There are many styles of water containers to choose from but the only requirement is: Maintain a stable supply of clean water in a shallow container no deeper than three inches.

NORTHERN CARDINAL at a traditional birdbath

"Hotel" for PURPLE MARTINS

Two types of nest boxes you can make yourself

SHELTER AND NEST BOXES

Planting trees, shrubs, and other vegetation not only provides food for birds but shelter and nesting places. Many species will use nest boxes. Others will use nesting shelves or ledges, and larger species will use raised nesting platforms. Nesting boxes can be made of wood, aluminum, or plastic; natural gourds are often used for martins and swallows.

Urban nest for MOURNING DOVES

WATCHING BIRDS IN THE FIELD

Very little gear is needed to watch birds, other than your own curiosity. Two indispensable items are a good pair of binoculars and a good field guide. Birding with experienced birders who know the area is also valuable in getting you off to a good start. It is a good idea to keep a small notebook handy. Later you may want to add a camera and telephoto lens; a spotting scope with tripod becomes a good investment for the more serious birder.

A long-lens camera and binoculars allow birders to photograph and see birds that might otherwise be missed.

BINOCULARS
Look for magnifying ranges
of 7x to 10x power

BINOCULARS

Look for magnifying ranges from 7x to 10x power. The outside diameter of the lenses that are farthest from your eyes (the objective lenses) should range from 35mm to 50mm. The power of magnification and the diameter of the objective lenses (the latter helps determine light-gathering ability) are combined and stamped on the binoculars as two numbers such as: 7 x 35, 7 x 50, or 8 x 42. Small compact binoculars such as 8 x 23 are lightweight and tempting to carry in the field, but the small size of the objective lenses limits the amount of light they can gather, making birdwatching under low light difficult.

BASIC PHOTOGRAPHY EQUIPMENT

The best camera body for bird photography is a 35mm single lens reflex (SLR). This camera allows you to view the subject directly through the lens. Many birds move quickly so your camera should have a fast shutter speed of at least 1/500 sec or higher, and the films you use with natural light should have high exposure speeds in the range of 200–400 ISO (ASA). A telephoto lens will allow you to photograph a larger image; you will need one in the 300mm to 500mm range. A sturdy tripod is required for sharp exposures. Use blinds to conceal yourself from the bird and let you get much closer. Automobiles will work as long as you stay inside.

TRIPOD
To improve the sharpness
of your exposures

CAMERA
35mm single lens reflex (SLR)

TELEPHOTO LENS
Look for a lens in the 300mm to
500mm range

A temporary moveable blind in the form of a simple tent can conceal birders enough to put wary birds at ease

HOW TO BE A BETTER BIRDER

There are many ways to improve your birding skills and increase your enjoyment of birdwatching.

STUDY AT HOME
Time spent at home studying your field guide will make a big difference. Find local checklists of birds, or state and regional bird books, that provide even more specific information about the birds in your area. Listen to recordings of bird songs and calls.

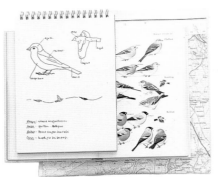

Patience is one of a birder's most important skills.

IMPROVE YOUR FIELD SKILLS
Birds have keen color eyesight and hearing. They are frightened by sudden movements, loud noises, and bright clothing that does not "blend" with the background. Experienced birders move deliberately, stalking quietly. They converse in low tones and stand patiently.

Birds are curious and attracted to sounds. When you make "pishing" noises (forcing air out through clenched teeth as if saying "pish, pish, pish"), or "squeaking" (making a high-pitched squeak by sucking air through closely pursed lips, a sound that can be amplified by "kissing" the back of your hand) many birds' curiosity will be piqued and they will come closer. Often they produce alarm notes or assembly calls, causing even more birds to come out where you can see them.

KEEP A RECORD
Keeping good records of the birds you see will help you learn when seasonal species are present and how abundant they may be. There is still much science does not know about birds, particularly about behavior and abundance in some habitats, and the amateur birder can make valuable contributions.

PRACTICE BIRDING ETHICS

Birding is not without its responsibility to the welfare of the bird. The American Birding Association has compiled a Code of Ethics for its members. (Copies can be obtained by writing to the ABA at the address below.) Their basic message is that birders' actions should not endanger the welfare of birds or other wildlife; they should not harm the natural environment; and birders must always respect the rights of others, especially their rights to privacy and private property rights.

A female feeds baby BLUEBIRDS

The welfare of fledgling SCREECH-OWLS like these depends on birders who practice good ethics.

BIRD PROTECTION IN BREEDING SEASON

Remember that birds are sensitive to disturbance. Nothing should be done that will frighten them or alter the surroundings of their nest. Once frightened, they may abandon the nest, and this could set their breeding back a whole year.

RUBY-THROATED HUMMINGBIRD feeds her young

JOIN A CLUB

Every state and province has established bird clubs. Many local clubs are associated with state, provincial, or regional ornithological societies that network activities, have regular meetings, and publish newsletters. You can locate your nearest bird clubs on the internet, or though the Conservation Directory of the National Wildlife Federation, your state conservation or wildlife department, local library, or newspaper.

Birding organizations exist on the national and international level as well. Some national organizations and their publications are:
• American Birding Association, PO Box 6599, Colorado Springs, CO 80934; *Birding.*
• American Ornithologists' Union, *The Auk;* Association of Field Ornithologists, *Journal of Field Ornithology;* Cooper Ornithological Society, *The Condor;* Wilson Ornithological Society, *Wilson Bulletin.* All can be contacted c/o Ornithological Societies of North America, 810 E. 10th Street, Lawrence, KS 66044.
• Laboratory of Ornithology at Cornell University, 159 Sapsucker Woods Road, Ithaca, NY 14850; *Living Bird* quarterly.
• National Audubon Society, 700 Broadway, New York, NY 10003; *Audubon.*

CONSERVATION

We are lucky that here in North America we have lost relatively few bird species to extinction. Laws to protect some species were passed as early as the late 1700s, but even then some came too late or were not enforced. Today, all species of birds native to North America are protected by state, provincial, and federal laws and cannot be collected or held in captivity without a legal permit (introduced, non-native species are not so protected). Some species, considered game species, are managed and can be legally harvested during hunting seasons.

The WOOD STORK is declining due to habitat destruction and the disruption of water flow through southern Florida.

Some populations of LEAST TERN are endangered due to human disturbance of nesting areas.

Still, many species of North American birds are in decline. Several species require management because their populations have become dangerously low. These species are given additional protection and listed by state, provincial, or federal authorities as "threatened" or "endangered." The bird conservation effort across America is joined by organizations such as the National Audubon Society, the American Bird Conservancy, and Partners in Flight.

The latter group is an Americas-wide coalition of more than 160 organizations and government agencies. Many of our continent's birds have not fared well at the hands of man. They have been persecuted as pests, victimized by wanton shooting, deprived of habitat, subjected to poisons, forced into competition by introduced species, and preyed upon by brood parasites. Many of the species that nest in North America, particularly songbirds and shorebirds, are neotropical migrants wintering in other countries where they are exposed to similar stresses, often with less protection.

BROWN PELICANS live side by side with America's offshore oil industry.

EXTINCTION

The North American continent north of Mexico hosts more than 700 species of native nesting birds. Direct persecution and indirect population stresses caused by loss of required habitat – both factors generated by humans – have resulted in a small percentage that are now either extinct or on the very brink of extinction. Likewise, many other species are declining and some are in serious trouble. The first to go was the Great Auk, the only flightless species on the continent, after centuries of unregulated exploitation. Many of these species were abundant, and some, like the Passenger Pigeon, were among the most numerous species in North America. Often sheer numbers made them easy to kill in quantity and their marketing profitable. Improvements in firearms and transportation, plus the conversion of the vast eastern forests into farmland, hastened the decline of these species.

Today we are more enlightened. We have enacted laws and extended efforts to save species. There are preservation success stories with species like Peregrine Falcons, Bald Eagles, Brown Pelicans, Ospreys, Whooping Cranes, and Trumpeter Swans. But, there is still much to do as human populations continue to alter critical habitats.

The Ivory-billed Woodpecker and Bachman's Warbler are considered probably extinct. Shown on the following pages, the Great Auk, Passenger Pigeon, and Carolina Parakeet, are now classified as extinct.

Family PICIDAE	Species *Campephilus principalis*	Length 19.5 inches	Wingspan 30–32 inches

IVORY-BILLED WOODPECKER

The largest woodpecker north of Mexico depended on large tracts of primeval bottomland and swamp forests to sustain its feeding habits. The head and bill were used by Native Americans for trade items and early settlers valued them for good luck, but it was the felling of the large southern forests and the loss of its food supply that doomed this woodpecker. Once it became rare, people hunted the remaining birds for museum and private collections. An estimated twenty-two birds existed in the US in 1938; the last records were in the 1940s. Unverified sightings are still being reported from the South, and a Cuban subspecies was confirmed to be alive in the late 1980s.

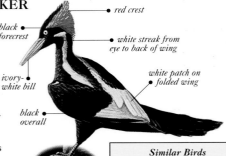

red crest

black forecrest

white streak from eye to back of wing

ivory-white bill

white patch on folded wing

black overall

- **SONG** Nasal clarinet-like *yank, yank, yank*, often in a series like a large White-breasted Nuthatch.
- **BEHAVIOR** In pairs, mated for life, or in small family groups just after nesting season. Fed on wood-boring insects under bark of dead or dying trees, some fruits and berries. Ranged from Ohio River Valley to east Texas, Gulf Coast, and also to the state of Florida.

Similar Birds

PILEATED WOODPECKER Smaller • male has red crest and mustache mark; black mask extends from lores to nape; white supercilium begins behind eye; white chin; white line extends from base of bill to sides of breast • female has black forehead and mustache.

| Family PARULIDAE | Species *Vermivora bachmanii* | Length 4.25–4.75 inches | Wingspan 6.75–7.5 inches |

BACHMAN'S WARBLER

Possibly never very numerous, this songbird lived in bottomland forests and swamps and their canebrakes along the coastal plain from southern Kentucky and Missouri to South Carolina. It was found in the Gulf coastal states in migration on its way to and from wintering grounds in Cuba and in some locations along the Suwannee River in Florida. The clearing of these forests for timber and agricultural drainage hastened the decline. The last certain US record was near Charleston, South Carolina, in 1962; and the last individual seen was a wintering female in Cuba in 1981.

- **SONG** Buzzy trill of 6–8 notes on a single pitch; similar to Worm-eating Warbler or Chipping Sparrow but higher pitched. Persistent singer on breeding grounds.
- **BEHAVIOR** Solitary or in pairs. Foraged at middle to high level in trees. Nested in thickets within 3 feet of ground in briers, canebrakes, or bushy tangles. Gleaned insects from foliage and branches.

black forecrown

gray hindcrown and nape

yellow forehead and supercilium

olive upperparts

large black bib on breast

yellow underparts

MALE

white undertail coverts

white tail patches

Similar Birds

HOODED WARBLER ♂
Similar to male but has yellow face; black hood from crown to throat; white outer tail feathers.

NASHVILLE WARBLER ♂
Similar to female but has yellow chin, throat, and underparts; gray head, crown, and nape.

| Family ALCIDAE | Species *Pinguinus impennis* | Length 28–30 inches | Wingspan 23–25 inches |

GREAT AUK

The largest alcid was the original penguin and the only flightless species on the continent in historical times. Widespread in the 16th and 17th centuries, it was recorded as breeding on islands from Scotland and Sweden to the Gulf of St. Lawrence and the Canadian Maritimes. Once numerous, centuries of raids on its colonies by sailors and fisherman who took adults and young for food brought it to extinction. Wintering along the Atlantic Coast occasionally as far south as Florida, the last known pair was captured at their nest on Eldey Rock off the coast of Iceland on June 3, 1844.

- **SONG** Generally silent except when alarmed in breeding colonies. Croak or guttural gurgling.
- **BEHAVIOR** Flightless. Gregarious; in flocks or small groups at sea. Nested in large colonies on isolated rocky islands in North Atlantic. Widespread at sea in the nonbreeding season in winter. Walked upright on land standing erect. Used short wings to move swiftly underwater, steering with its feet, diving down to an estimated 250 feet to feed on fish.

short white postocular spot

brownish black wings with white tips to secondaries

brownish black tail and upperparts

large arched black bill crossed by numerous vertical white lines

large white oval in front of eye

white underparts from upper breast to tip of undertail coverts

Similar Birds

RAZORBILL
Much smaller; single vertical line near tip of bill; white line from base of bill to eye; white underparts ascend to point on throat; black upperparts, tail, and wings; white trailing edge on secondary feathers.

Family COLUMBIDAE	Species *Ectopistes migratorius*	Length 16 inches	Wingspan 24–25.5 inches

PASSENGER PIGEON

The most abundant bird in North America at the time of European settlement may have made up a quarter of its bird population. The Passenger Pigeon and the eastern deciduous forest upon which it depended were destroyed simultaneously. John James Audubon described migrating flocks that stretched for miles in the sky and took three days to pass over, and which he estimated to contain over a billion birds. As the forest was reduced to farmland, the birds were hunted throughout the year. The last known wild specimen was shot in 1898; and the last surviving bird, Martha, a captive reared individual, died at age 29 in the Cincinnati Zoo in 1914.

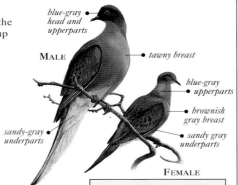

blue-gray head and upperparts

MALE

tawny breast

blue-gray upperparts

brownish gray breast

sandy-gray underparts

sandy gray underparts

FEMALE

• **SONG** Loud grating croaking, chattering, or clucking notes. Not dovelike.

• **BEHAVIOR** Highly gregarious; lived, foraged, wandered, and nested in large groups. Fed on tree seeds, fruits, berries, buds, and invertebrates. Nomadic; went where food was plentiful. Nested from Missouri, Kentucky, and Virginia northward into southern Canada and west to Kansas. Wintered south to Gulf Coast.

Similar Birds

MOURNING DOVE
Smaller; pinkish fawn head and underparts; brownish gray upperparts; white-tipped outer tail feathers; black spots on upper inner wing; black spot on lower cheek.

Family PSITTACIDAE	Species *Conuropsis carolinensis*	Length 16 inches	Wingspan 24–26 inches

CAROLINA PARAKEET

Once abundant in the East from eastern Nebraska to New York and south to the Gulf Coast, this beautiful parakeet was hunted for its feathers, the pet trade, for sport, and as a pest of orchards, cornfields, and gardens. Flocks had such strong bonds that when some of their numbers were killed the remainder of the flock returned to their bodies repeatedly until all were shot. By the late 1870s it existed only in remote Florida swamps; the last known birds were shot in the early 1900s, and the last reported individual of the only endemic US parrot died in the Cincinnati Zoo in the year 1914.

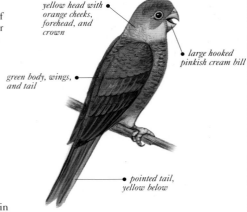

yellow head with orange cheeks, forehead, and crown

large hooked pinkish cream bill

green body, wings, and tail

pointed tail, yellow below

• **SONG** Loud quarrelsome screams given in flight.

• **BEHAVIOR** Social. Gregarious, occurring in flocks except in breeding season when pairs nested in dense colonies. Mated for life. Roosted communally in hollow trees. Fed in bottomland forests, riverbanks, and cypress swamps on tree seeds, thistle, cocklebur, grass seeds, fruits, and berries.

Similar Birds

No similar native species.

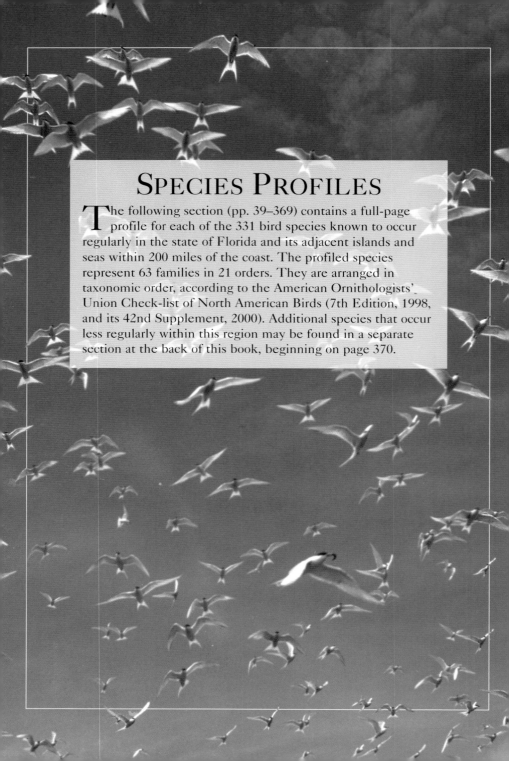

SPECIES PROFILES

The following section (pp. 39–369) contains a full-page profile for each of the 331 bird species known to occur regularly in the state of Florida and its adjacent islands and seas within 200 miles of the coast. The profiled species represent 63 families in 21 orders. They are arranged in taxonomic order, according to the American Ornithologists' Union Check-list of North American Birds (7th Edition, 1998, and its 42nd Supplement, 2000). Additional species that occur less regularly within this region may be found in a separate section at the back of this book, beginning on page 370.

Family GAVIIDAE	Species *Gavia stellata*	Length 24–27 inches	Wingspan 42–45 inches

RED-THROATED LOON

This is the smallest loon and the only one without profuse white spotting on its upperparts in the breeding plumage. When the bird is on the water, its slender bill appears upturned and is often held pointed upward by the swimming bird. In juvenile and winter plumage both sexes have a gray crown and hindneck, dark gray back with many small white spots, pale upturned bill, and a white face, sides, foreneck, and underparts.

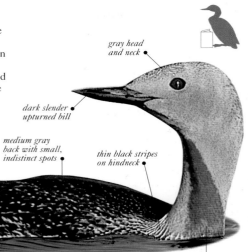

gray head and neck

dark slender upturned bill

medium gray back with small, indistinct spots

thin black stripes on hindneck

dull red patch on foreneck

• **SONG** Usually silent. On breeding ground, prolonged wails and gooselike *kwuk-kwuk-kwuk*.
• **BEHAVIOR** Flies with neck drooping. Only loon to leap directly into flight from water or land. Feeds primarily on fish, which it catches in dives down to 90 feet. Solitary except on wintering grounds and in migration, when hundreds may congregate in bays along the coast.
• **BREEDING** Usually a solitary nester. Sometimes forms loose colonies.
• **NESTING** Incubation 24–29 days by both sexes. Precocial young leave nest and take to water about 1 day after hatching, then fly at about 49–60 days. 1 brood per year.
• **POPULATION** Common to fairly common on breeding grounds; fairly common on coast in winter; casual to very uncommon inland in winter. Populations stable.
• **CONSERVATION** Vulnerable to loss of habitat due to development in high Arctic and to pollution, particularly oil spills, in wintering areas. Many drown in gill nets.

WINTER PLUMAGE

Similar Birds

ARCTIC LOON
PACIFIC LOON
Breeding adults have dark throat; dark flanks; large white spots on back • in winter plumage, lack white spots on back; bill not upturned; dark gray of crown and hind neck contrast sharply with white face and foreneck. • Arctic Loon in the West only.

Flight Pattern

Direct flight with swift rapid wing beats.

Nest Identification

Shape ⌒ Location ▬ ✦✦✦

Moist depression or heap of damp vegetation mixed with mud • male sometimes constructs copulation platform away from nest • 1–3 olive-green to dark brown eggs, sometimes with blackish brown spots.

Plumage Sexes similar	Habitat 〰️ 〰️	Migration Migratory	Weight 3.4 pounds

DATE _____ TIME _____ LOCATION _____

Family GAVIIDAE	Species *Gavia immer*	Length 28–36 inches	Wingspan 50–58 inches

COMMON LOON

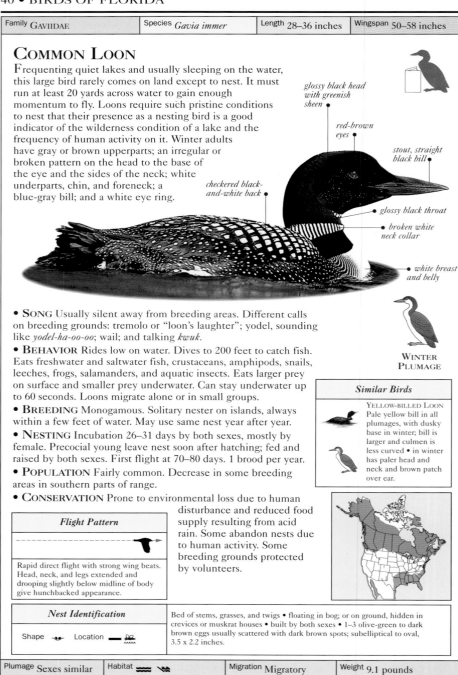

Frequenting quiet lakes and usually sleeping on the water, this large bird rarely comes on land except to nest. It must run at least 20 yards across water to gain enough momentum to fly. Loons require such pristine conditions to nest that their presence as a nesting bird is a good indicator of the wilderness condition of a lake and the frequency of human activity on it. Winter adults have gray or brown upperparts; an irregular or broken pattern on the head to the base of the eye and the sides of the neck; white underparts, chin, and foreneck; a blue-gray bill; and a white eye ring.

glossy black head with greenish sheen

red-brown eyes

stout, straight black bill

checkered black-and-white back

glossy black throat

broken white neck collar

white breast and belly

WINTER PLUMAGE

- **SONG** Usually silent away from breeding areas. Different calls on breeding grounds: tremolo or "loon's laughter"; yodel, sounding like *yodel-ha-oo-oo*; wail; and talking *kwuk*.
- **BEHAVIOR** Rides low on water. Dives to 200 feet to catch fish. Eats freshwater and saltwater fish, crustaceans, amphipods, snails, leeches, frogs, salamanders, and aquatic insects. Eats larger prey on surface and smaller prey underwater. Can stay underwater up to 50 seconds. Loons migrate alone or in small groups.
- **BREEDING** Monogamous. Solitary nester on islands, always within a few feet of water. May use same nest year after year.
- **NESTING** Incubation 26–31 days by both sexes, mostly by female. Precocial young leave nest soon after hatching; fed and raised by both sexes. First flight at 70–80 days. 1 brood per year.
- **POPULATION** Fairly common. Decrease in some breeding areas in southern parts of range.
- **CONSERVATION** Prone to environmental loss due to human disturbance and reduced food supply resulting from acid rain. Some abandon nests due to human activity. Some breeding grounds protected by volunteers.

Similar Birds

YELLOW-BILLED LOON Pale yellow bill in all plumages, with dusky base in winter; bill is larger and culmen is less curved • in winter has paler head and neck and brown patch over ear.

Flight Pattern

Rapid direct flight with strong wing beats. Head, neck, and legs extended and drooping slightly below midline of body give hunchbacked appearance.

Nest Identification

Shape ⌣ Location ▬ ≈

Bed of stems, grasses, and twigs • floating in bog; or on ground, hidden in crevices or muskrat houses • built by both sexes • 1–3 olive-green to dark brown eggs usually scattered with dark brown spots; subelliptical to oval, 3.5 x 2.2 inches.

Plumage Sexes similar	Habitat ≈≈ ⌇	Migration Migratory	Weight 9.1 pounds

DATE _____ TIME_____ LOCATION _____

Family PODICIPEDIDAE	Species *Podilymbus podiceps*	Length 12–15 inches	Wingspan 22.5 inches

PIED-BILLED GREBE

The most widespread and best-known grebe in North America sometimes hides from intruders by sinking until only its head shows above water or by diving like other members of the group. This stocky grebe has a large head and short thick bill that gives it a chickenlike profile, easily distinguishing it from other grebes, even at a distance. The bill is light-colored and has a black ring around it during the breeding season but lacks the ring in winter.

large head
dark eye
eye ring
brownish gray body
short neck
dark ring on short thick bill

WINTER PLUMAGE

- **SONG** Loud, cuckoolike call, *cuck, cuck, cuck, cow-cow-cow, cow-ah-cow-ah.*
- **BEHAVIOR** Forages by diving from the surface and swimming underwater, propelled by its feet. Feeds some on vegetation, but about half of the diet is made up of aquatic insects with the remainder split almost equally between small fish and crustaceans.
- **BREEDING** Monogamous. Solitary nester.
- **NESTING** Incubation 23–27 days by both sexes, but female does more. Young move from nest to adult's back less than an hour after hatching. Nest use stops in 24–42 days. First flight at 35–37 days. Young fed by both sexes. 1–2 broods per year.
- **POPULATION** Very common in range.
- **CONSERVATION** May be declining due to habitat loss.

Similar Birds

LEAST GREBE
Smaller with golden (not dark) eye; slender, dark bill; much more restricted North American range.

Flight Pattern

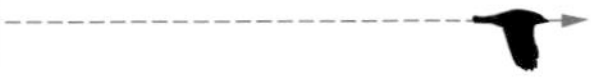

Direct flight with rapid wing beats.

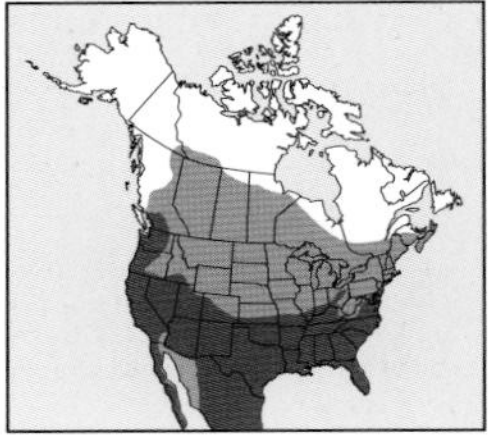

Nest Identification

Shape Location

Platform of decaying vegetation • inconspicuously anchored to vegetation in open water among reeds or rushes • built by both sexes • 2–10 pale bluish white or nest-stained eggs; elliptical to subelliptical, 1.7 inches long.

Plumage Sexes similar	Habitat	Migration Some migrate	Weight 15.6 ounces

DATE 7/17/09 TIME ______ LOCATION ______

Family PODICIPEDIDAE	Species *Podiceps auritus*	Length 12–15 inches	Wingspan 24 inches

HORNED GREBE

The "horns" for which this bird is named are actually tufts of golden feathers above and behind the eyes, which are present only during the bird's breeding season. In summer the reddish neck of the Horned Grebe distinguishes it from the Eared Grebe, which shares much of the breeding range. The Horned Grebe's life is tied to water, breeding in freshwater habitats and often spending the winter both in freshwater and in saltwater.

• **SONG** This grebe gives an abrasive *keark, keark* or *yark, yark*. It also makes a repeated prattling sound followed by shrill screams.

golden "horns"

black head

reddish neck

dark straight bill

short tail

• **BEHAVIOR** The Horned Grebe eats as its primary diet mostly fish and some crustaceans as well as aquatic insects. Tamer than other grebes, it often allows a close approach by humans. Its nests are often built so that they are concealed poorly or not at all.

WINTER PLUMAGE

• **BREEDING** Monogamous. Most often a solitary nester; sometimes in loose colonies of 4–6 pairs.

• **NESTING** Incubation 22–25 days by both sexes. Precocial young fed by both sexes. First flight at 45–60 days. 1 brood per year, sometimes 2.

• **POPULATION** Common.

• **CONSERVATION** Declining apparently due to oil spills and habitat loss.

Similar Birds

EARED GREBE
More triangular head; has black neck in summer • dusky neck and black cheeks in winter.

WESTERN GREBE
CLARK'S GREBE
Black above and white below; much larger; much longer necks and bills.

Flight Pattern

Direct flight with rapid wing beats.

Nest Identification

Shape ⌒⌒   Location ⌊⌊⌋

Floating heap of wet plant material, including underwater plants, rotting vegetation, rubbish, and mud • often anchored to vegetation • 3–7 whitish to very pale green eggs, usually nest-stained; 1.7 inches long.

Plumage Sexes similar	Habitat ⬎ ≈ ⌇	Migration Migratory	Weight 1 pound

DATE _____ TIME_____ LOCATION _____

Family PROCELLARIIDAE	Species *Pterodroma hasitata*	Length 16 inches	Wingspan 35–40 inches

BLACK-CAPPED PETREL

This poorly known "gadfly" petrel, which is found well offshore in the Gulf Stream, holds its broad wings bent at the wrist in flight. Its dark tail is long and wedge-shaped, contrasting with the rump, uppertail coverts, and tail base, all of which are white on most birds, although a few atypical individuals have a dark rump. Above its white forehead and hooked dark bill, the black cap is separated from the brownish gray upperparts by a broad

white collar, although this field mark is lacking in some birds. It is possible to mistake very dark-plumaged individuals for the very rare Bermuda Petrel well off the Atlantic Coast. The Black-capped Petrel is fairly common off the western edge of the Gulf Stream off North Carolina, and as many as 100 birds have been recorded on some days.

- **SONG** Noisy at night on breeding grounds. Generally remains silent at sea.
- **BEHAVIOR** Noted for its high, erratic, roller coaster–like arcing flight at sea, especially in steady winds. Springs lightly from the water into flight.
- **BREEDING** Little is known about breeding habits. Nests on mountains and cliffs on a few islands in the Caribbean.
- **NESTING** Incubation 51–54 days by both sexes. Semialtricial young remain in nest 90–100 days, and are fed by both sexes.
- **POPULATION** Declining due to disturbance by humans as well as predation by mongooses and rats.
- **CONSERVATION** Little protection has been established over much of its breeding range.

Similar Birds

BERMUDA PETREL Much rarer; lacks white color; shorter bill; narrower white rump patch.

GREATER SHEARWATER Larger; hooked black bill; black cap extends below eye; white collar, underparts, and U-shaped band on uppertail coverts; dusky smuge on belly; black tail; flight pattern differs.

Flight Pattern

Often swoops upward in great arcs above horizon.

Nest Identification

Shape ▨ ▨   Location ▥

No lining in either excavated or preformed burrow on sea cliffs • 1 white egg.

Plumage Sexes similar	Habitat ≈≈≈	Migration Migratory	Weight 9.8 ounces

DATE _____ TIME_____ LOCATION _____

Family PROCELLARIIDAE	Species *Calonectris diomedea*	Length 18–21 inches	Wingspan 44 inches

CORY'S SHEARWATER

The largest shearwater found along the Atlantic Coast skims the surface of the ocean with slow wing beats and a buoyant flight similar to that of the albatross. When this bird is seen flying straight ahead, its wings show a distinctive downward bow from wrist to wing tip. The large pale bill as well as the way the brown upperparts blend gradually with the white underparts without producing a capped appearance is distinctive. Cory's is the only Atlantic shearwater that occasionally soars.

brownish gray upperparts

narrow pale tips of uppertail coverts contrast with dark tail

large pinkish yellow bill with dusky tip

white underparts

• **SONG** Generally silent except on breeding grounds.
• **BEHAVIOR** Gregarious, often forming flocks that number in the hundreds or thousands. Frequently follows predatory fish to feed on the bait fish they drive to the water's surface. Feeds at night on crustaceans and large squid it takes from the surface. Has a keen sense of smell.
• **BREEDING** Monogamous. Colonial.
• **NESTING** Incubation 52–55 days by both sexes. Semialtricial young stay in nest about 90 days, although parents abandon young while still in nest. Young are fed by both sexes at night.
• **POPULATION** Numerous, but showing some decline.

dusky trailing edge on underwing

dusky primaries

Similar Birds

GREATER SHEARWATER
Dark bill; distinct dark cap with white collar across nape; clear white rump band; smudge of dusky color on belly; clear contrast between dark upperparts and white underparts.

Flight Pattern

Soars if wind is up, looping and circling on fixed wings. Or, deep wing beats with wings bowed downward in long low glide.

Nest Identification	
Shape ◐ ◑ ◒ Location 🪨 🏠	Both sexes work together to either dig a new burrow or clean out a previously used burrow • sometimes under a rock • no material added • 1 white egg; blunt oval or subelliptical, 2.8 inches long.

Plumage Sexes similar	Habitat 〰〰 🐚	Migration Migratory	Weight 1.2 pounds

DATE _____ TIME_____ LOCATION _____

Family PROCELLARIIDAE	Species *Puffinus gravis*	Length 18–20 inches	Wingspan 39.5–48 inches

GREATER SHEARWATER

This large powerful shearwater is fairly common off the Atlantic Coast of the US in spring migration where it remains well out to sea on its way to its south Atlantic breeding grounds. Party fishing boats and sports fishermen know this strong heavy-bodied bird well, for it often comes to their boats and may try to take the bait off their hooks as the lines are lowered to the bottom or retrieved close to the surface. The bird sometimes takes fish that are tossed back overboard. Although it appears gull-like at a distance, the bird is easily distinguished by its stiff straight wings. A dark brownish black cap extends beneath the eyes and is often separated from the brownish gray back by a white nape collar. A dusky smudge on its belly and pinkish legs and feet are visible from below when the bird is in flight.

U-shaped white band on uppertail coverts

black tail

dark cap extends below eye

hooked dark bill

white collar

white underparts

- **SONG** Noisy with catlike squalls when aggressively feeding around fishing trawlers.
- **BEHAVIOR** Attracted to boats and tame on water near them. Attends fishing boats where it competes for food in a hostile manner. Dives to 20–30 feet in pursuit of fish.
- **BREEDING** Monogamous. Colonial.
- **NESTING** Incubation by both sexes. First flight at 84 days. Semialtricial young fed by both sexes at night.
- **POPULATION** Total well over 5 million and seems to be increasing. From the Gulf of Maine northward it is common in the summer.
- **CONSERVATION** Many are killed by severe storms in North Atlantic; carcasses sometimes found on beaches.

Similar Birds

BLACK-CAPPED PETREL
Smaller; different flight pattern; different under wing pattern; white forehead; larger white rump patch.

CORY'S SHEARWATER
Pale bill; lacks distinctive cap, white nape collar, white U-shaped rump patch, and smudge on belly.

Flight Pattern

In strong winds soars in high arcs, often banking to change direction. Or, deep wing beats with a long glide near water.

Nest Identification

Shape ☒ ☒   Location 🪺 ⁂

Lined with grass • sharply angled • about 3 feet long • sometimes in crevice among rocks • 1 white egg.

Plumage Sexes similar	Habitat 〰 ⚓	Migration Migratory	Weight 1.9 pounds

DATE _____ TIME_____ LOCATION _____

Family PROCELLARIIDAE	Species *Puffinus griseus*	Length 18–20 inches	Wingspan 37–43 inches

SOOTY SHEARWATER

A common summer visitor off both the Atlantic and Pacific Coasts, this stocky short-necked sooty brown bird is probably the best-known shearwater in North American waters. It normally feeds well offshore, but during strong onshore winds hundreds of birds may be seen by observers from the shoreline. Look for the long slender dark wings with silvery gray underwing coverts. Some birds may have a white underwing lining. Legs and feet are blackish.

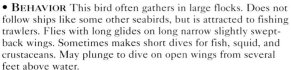

silvery gray underwing coverts

long slender dark wings

long dark bill

dark sooty brown plumage, darkest on tail and primaries

• **SONG** The Sooty Shearwater is silent except for noisy squeals when squabbling for food. Also makes inhaled and exhaled *koo-wah-koo-wah-koo-wah* when on breeding grounds.

Similar Birds

SHORT-TAILED SHEARWATER Shorter bill; less contrasting grayer underwing linings often restricted to a panel on the median secondary coverts and extending slightly onto the inner median primary coverts; underwings may be dark overall, lacking pale panels • only in the West.

• **BEHAVIOR** This bird often gathers in large flocks. Does not follow ships like some other seabirds, but is attracted to fishing trawlers. Flies with long glides on long narrow slightly swept-back wings. Sometimes makes short dives for fish, squid, and crustaceans. May plunge to dive on open wings from several feet above water.

• **BREEDING** Colonial. The Sooty Shearwater nests on various isolated islands in the southern oceans.

• **NESTING** Incubation 52–56 days by both sexes. Semialtricial young remain in nest for about 97 days. Adults usually leave at night. Young fed by both sexes at night.

• **POPULATION** The Sooty Shearwater is an abundant bird, with a total population of more than 10 million.

Flight Pattern
Strong direct flapping alternating with long glides.

Nest Identification	
Shape	Location

Made of leaves and grass • up to 10 feet long • built by both sexes • 1 white egg; elliptical, 1.9 x 3 inches.

Plumage Sexes similar	Habitat	Migration Migratory	Weight 1.8 pounds

DATE _____ TIME_____ LOCATION _____

| Family PROCELLARIIDAE | Species *Puffinus puffinus* | Length 12–15 inches | Wingspan 33–35 inches |

MANX SHEARWATER

From a distance in flight, this medium-sized shearwater appears simply black above and white below. The white undertail coverts extend almost to the tip of the short tail, and the underwing linings are white. Some rare East Atlantic races are not as white below. In all plumages note how the dark cap extends onto the face and auriculars below

black cap extends below eye

blackish upperparts

black hooked bill

white of chin and throat extends to side of head behind ear coverts

white undertail coverts

white underparts

pinkish gray feet and legs

the eye, bordered below and behind by a whitish crescent that extends from chin and throat to the side of the head behind the auriculars, or ear coverts. Manx Shearwaters seem to be increasing in numbers, with more birds being recorded on pelagic birding trips off the North Carolina coast.

- **SONG** Generally silent at sea.
- **BEHAVIOR** Gregarious. This shearwater is excellent on the wing with stiff rapid wing strokes followed by shearing glides low over the water. Banks from side to side, showing black upperparts first, then the snow-white underparts. Good swimmer; sometimes goes underwater for fish and squid. Adults may forage more than 600 miles from nesting burrow, returning to it at night. Does not follow ships, but is attracted to smaller fishing boats and trawlers.
- **BREEDING** Monogamous. Colonial.
- **NESTING** Incubation 47–63 days by both sexes. Semialtricial young fed by both sexes. Parents abandon young at 60 days. Young leave nest 8–9 days later. 1 brood per year.
- **POPULATION** Apparently increasing off the East Coast.

Similar Birds

AUDUBON'S SHEARWATER
Similar but smaller; dark undertail coverts; different flight pattern with more rapid, fluttering wing beats.

BLACK-VENTED SHEARWATER
In the West only • dark mottling on sides of face, neck, and breast; dusky to dark undertail coverts.

Flight Pattern

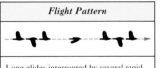

Long glides interrupted by several rapid wing beats.

Nest Identification

Shape 　Location

Lined with grass and leaves • on ground • on isolated islands • built by both sexes • 1 white egg; broad or blunt ovate or subelliptical, 2.35 x 1.6 inches.

| Plumage Sexes similar | Habitat | Migration Migratory | Weight 1.0 pound |

DATE _____ TIME_____ LOCATION _____

Family PROCELLARIIDAE	Species *Puffinus lherminieri*	Length 12 inches	Wingspan 27 inches

AUDUBON'S SHEARWATER

The smallest shearwater regularly seen off the Atlantic beats its wings more rapidly than any other Atlantic shearwater. This stocky bird with broad wings has dark brown upperparts, matching its tail, which is long for a shearwater. Pinkish legs and feet, dark undertail coverts, and dark tail are visible from below.

• **SONG** Generally this shearwater is silent. However, it has been heard to emit a variety of sounds including squeals, grunts, and cooing produced on its breeding grounds and during confrontations with other birds.

dark upperparts

dark tail and undertail coverts

hooked dark bill

white underparts

• **BEHAVIOR** Away from its breeding areas, Audubon's Shearwater is often seen in flocks that may number up to hundreds of birds. As a rule, this shearwater does not usually follow ships. It tends to spend most of its time on the water, where it may dive for its primary diet of marine organisms and animals, especially fish and squid.

• **BREEDING** This shearwater nests in colonies on small isolated islands, usually in rock crevices or under clumps of dense vegetation.

• **NESTING** Incubation 51 days by both sexes. Semialtricial young stay in nest 71–73 days. Fed by both sexes at night. 1 brood per year.

Similar Birds
LITTLE SHEARWATER More white in face and under wings; white undertail coverts; grayish legs and feet; different flutter-and-glide flight.
MANX SHEARWATER Larger; different flight pattern with more soaring and less flapping.

• **POPULATION** Declining.

• **CONSERVATION** Protected in only part of its breeding range. Caribbean populations disturbed by humans; adults and young taken from nest burrows for food.

Flight Pattern
Flap and glide flight with rapid wing beats.

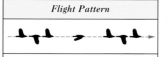

Nest Identification	
Shape 🦅 🦅 🦅 Location 🌿 🌊	No lining • on ground or in rock crevice • built by both sexes • 1 white egg, 2 inches long.

Plumage Sexes similar	Habitat 〰〰	Migration Migratory	Weight 5.9 ounces

DATE _____ TIME_____ LOCATION _____

Family HYDROBATIDAE	Species *Oceanites oceanicus*	Length 6–7.5 inches	Wingspan 16–17 inches

WILSON'S STORM-PETREL

This is the storm-petrel that is most commonly seen off the Atlantic Coast, and it may be one of the most abundant birds in the world. It is the smallest storm-petrel seen off the Atlantic Coast. Few pelagic birds are easily identified from a rocking boat at sea, but this species can be identified by its short squared tail and feet extending beyond the tip of the

dark sooty brown plumage

dark bill

paler bar on upper surface of inner wings

squared to slightly rounded tail

broad U-shaped white band on rump extends to undertail coverts

dark legs

yellowish green webbing between toes

tail, its rather short rounded wings, and its large U-shaped white rump patch. These birds often come very close to boats, crisscrossing the wake of the boat and providing excellent views and easier confirmation of their identity.

• **SONG** Usually silent at sea, but makes noisy chattering sounds around nesting colonies.

• **BEHAVIOR** Generally flies close to water surface with purposeful shallow wing beats similar to those of a swallow or small tern. Frequently patters feet on water while holding wings above the body as it feeds on small marine organisms, often "dancing" on the surface and almost hovering in one place as the winds lift it kitelike a few inches off the surface of the water. Frequently follows ships and chum lines (slicks of fish oils); attends fishing boats and whales as it forages.

Similar Birds
LEACH'S STORM-PETREL Larger; longer forked tail without feet protruding beyond tip; mothlike flight pattern.
 BAND-RUMPED STORM-PETREL Larger; longer tail; flight pattern is with shallow wing beats followed by stiff-winged glides similar to those of a shearwater.

• **BREEDING** Colonial.

• **NESTING** Incubation 40–50 days by both sexes. Semialtricial young fed by both sexes. Young leave nest at 46–97 days.

• **POPULATION** Large and apparently stable.

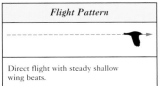

Flight Pattern
Direct flight with steady shallow wing beats.

Nest Identification	
Shape ▨ Location ▬	No built nest • hides egg in hole or crevice • 1 white egg, usually with reddish brown spots on larger end.

Plumage Sexes similar	Habitat 〰〰 ⌂	Migration Migratory	Weight 1.1 ounces

DATE _____ TIME_____ LOCATION _____

Family HYDROBATIDAE	Species *Oceanodroma leucorhoa*	Length 8–9 inches	Wingspan 18–19 inches

LEACH'S STORM-PETREL

This slender long-winged storm-petrel can be seen off both coasts of North America. Some of the birds found off the Pacific Coast have dark rumps, rather than the more common and conspicuous white rump broken in the middle by a gray-brown stripe. Besides the rump, this bird's plumage is entirely dark brown. The tail is long and forked, but the fork is not always easily seen. It has short legs and feet that do not reach or protrude beyond the tip of its tail.

ATLANTIC

• *long narrow pointed wings*

• *lighter grayish inner wing bar on upperwing*

• *forked tail*

• *dark brown plumage*

PACIFIC

• **SONG** Short sharp ticking notes ending in a slurred trill.

• **BEHAVIOR** Strictly nocturnal on breeding grounds. Does not follow ships. Feeds on surface of water on small squid, crustaceans, and fish. Often feeds with wings held above horizontal while it patters on water surface. Its characteristic flight is slow, erratic, and mothlike, or similar to that of a nighthawk.

white rump patch broken by a gray-brown stripe

• **BREEDING** Monogamous and colonial.

• **NESTING** Incubation 38–46 days by both sexes. Semialtricial young remain in nest 63–70 days. Fed at night through regurgitation by both sexes. First flight at 63–70 days. 1 brood per year.

Similar Birds

WILSON'S STORM-PETREL Shorter, rounded wings; feet extend beyond squared, not forked, tail; has swallowlike flight pattern.

ASHY STORM-PETREL BLACK STORM-PETREL Both lack the erratic flight pattern • both range off Pacific Coast.

BAND-RUMPED STORM-PETREL Larger; shorter wider wings; conspicuous large white rump patch; stiff-winged glides and zigzag flight like a small shearwater • ranges off Atlantic Coast.

• **POPULATION** Slight decline, although total population is in the millions.

• **CONSERVATION** Some declines are showing on islands where humans have introduced predator species.

Flight Pattern

Bounding and erratic; mothlike with frequent changes of direction and speed.

Nest Identification	Lined with leaves and grass • under grass, rocks, or tree roots, or on bank • may be built by both sexes, although some literature states only the male digs burrow • 1 creamy white egg, often nest-stained and occasionally marked with reddish purple; subelliptical to oval, 1.3 inches long.
Shape 🐚 🐚 Location ⛰ ⸬	

Plumage Sexes similar	Habitat 〰 〰	Migration Migratory	Weight 1.2 ounces

DATE _____ TIME_____ LOCATION _____

Family HYDROBATIDAE	Species *Oceanodroma castro*	Length 7.5–8.5 inches	Wingspan 16.5–18 inches

BAND-RUMPED STORM-PETREL

This tropical bird spends its time alone or in small groups at sea. It is seen in summer off the Atlantic Coast of North America. It seldom walks on the water. Often in the company of other storm-petrels, it can be separated from them by its flight pattern, which resembles that of a tiny shearwater. In flight the white rump patch is clear, and the black legs and feet do not project beyond the blackish tail, which in fresh adults has a slight notch.

faint pale gray-brown upperwing bar

sooty blackish brown overall

bold white band on rump and uppertail coverts

Juveniles resemble adults but paler greater coverts create a more distinct bar on the upperwing.

short stubby black bill

- **SONG** High-pitched squeak around nest. Silent at sea.
- **BEHAVIOR** Solitary, in pairs or small groups away from nests in nonbreeding season. Feeds at sea but does not follow ships. Eats crustaceans, small fishes, and other marine animals. Nocturnal around nesting burrow.
- **BREEDING** Monogamous. Colonial. Mates for life.
- **NESTING** Incubation 40–48 days by both sexes. Semialtricial young remain in nest 53–95 days, fed by both sexes through regurgitation. 1 brood per year.
- **POPULATION** Rare off North Atlantic; casual to uncommon in Gulf of Mexico; fairly common on mid-Atlantic Coast off North Carolina and Virginia. Storm-driven birds accidental inland.
- **CONSERVATION** Vulnerable to introduced predators in nesting areas and to pollution from oil spills.

Similar Birds

WILSON'S STORM-PETREL
Smaller in size; larger U-shaped white rump patch; longer black bill; yellow-webbed black feet project beyond squared tail; prominent diagonal secondary wing bar; more erratic and fluttery flight.

LEACH'S STORM-PETREL
Smaller; more distinct diagonal upperwing bar; longer more pointed wings; more deeply forked tail; ragged-edged white rump patch with central dividing line; bounding nighthawklike flight.

Flight Pattern
Buoyant zigzag with several rapid wing strokes followed by glide on horizontal or slightly downward-bowed wings.

Nest Identification	
Shape ▨ ◪　Location 🐦 ◧	No nest materials • burrows or crevices of rocky areas, 2–3 feet deep • dug by both sexes or cleaned out from previous year • 1 white egg; elliptical to subelliptical, 1.3 inches long.

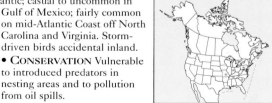

Plumage Sexes similar	Habitat ≋ ⸺ ⚶ ▲ 🦅	Migration Migratory	Weight 1.5 ounces

DATE _____ TIME_____ LOCATION _____

Family PHAETHONTIDAE	Species *Phaethon lepturus*	Length 28–32 inches	Wingspan 35–38 inches

WHITE-TAILED TROPICBIRD

This bird nests in Bermuda, the Bahamas, and throughout the Caribbean. It is the smallest of the tropicbirds, and the one most likely to be spotted off North America's Atlantic Coast. It also is the only tropicbird with a long black bar on the upperwing coverts. The white tail streamers can be up to sixteen inches long. Legs and feet are yellowish; toes have black webbing.

JUVENILE

• **SONG** In flight, a piercing scream *keek*

white overall

black loreal mask extends through and past eye

long white streamers on tail

orange to yellowish bill

black bar on outer primaries and upperwing coverts

or *keck*, often rapidly repeated. Call is a guttural squawk.

• **BEHAVIOR** Solitary or in noisy pairs or small groups. Ranges widely over oceans in nonbreeding season. Spots food from 50–100 feet above water, hovers, then makes direct dive. Eats small fish, crabs, and squid. Floats high in water with tail cocked upward. Attracted to ships, it may hover before landing in rigging. Comes farther inland than other tropicbirds.

• **BREEDING** Monogamous. Semicolonial.

• **NESTING** Incubation 40–42 days by both sexes, sometimes shorter period. Young altricial; first flight at 70–85 days; fed by both sexes. 1 brood per year.

• **POPULATION** Uncommon but regular in the Gulf Stream off North Carolina; rare and inconsistent on Dry Tortugas. Rare elsewhere on the Atlantic Coast to the Maritimes; one record in California.

• **BIRDHOUSES** Will nest in artificial in-ground chambers.

• **CONSERVATION** Vulnerable to introduced predators at nesting sites.

Similar Birds

RED-BILLED TROPICBIRD Larger; mostly white crown; narrower black bars on upperparts; black eye stripe; black primaries and primary coverts; red bill
• juvenile has black eye stripe, usually meeting around nape; fine barring on upperparts; large black primary patch; yellow bill; lacks long streamers.

Flight Pattern

Buoyant graceful pigeonlike flight with fluttering wing strokes alternated with soaring glides; hovers briefly over prey or perch before dipping down to it.

Nest Identification

Shape

Location

No nest • on ground in ridges of cliffs, crevices, caves, or sheltered by grasses or bush • 1 whitish to pale buff egg, flecked with brownish and purple spots; ovoid, 2.28 x 1.6 inches.

Plumage Sexes similar	Habitat	Migration Migratory	Weight 15.3 ounces

DATE _____ TIME_____ LOCATION _____

| Family PHAETHONTIDAE | Species *Phaethon aethereus* | Length 30–44 inches | Wingspan 40–42 inches |

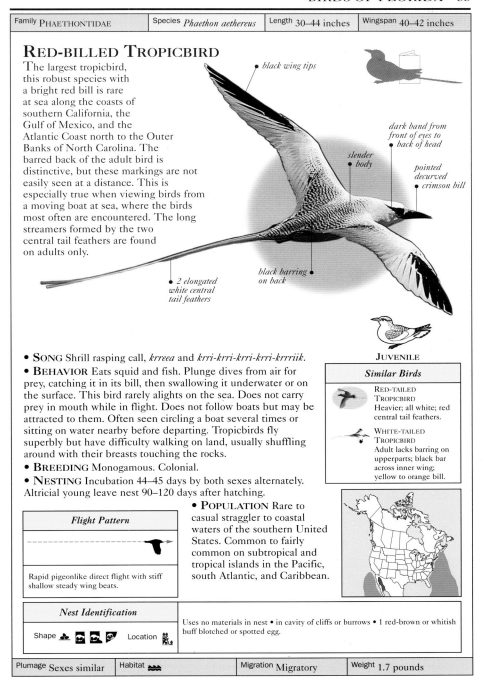

RED-BILLED TROPICBIRD

The largest tropicbird, this robust species with a bright red bill is rare at sea along the coasts of southern California, the Gulf of Mexico, and the Atlantic Coast north to the Outer Banks of North Carolina. The barred back of the adult bird is distinctive, but these markings are not easily seen at a distance. This is especially true when viewing birds from a moving boat at sea, where the birds most often are encountered. The long streamers formed by the two central tail feathers are found on adults only.

black wing tips

dark band from front of eyes to back of head

slender body

pointed decurved crimson bill

2 elongated white central tail feathers

black barring on back

JUVENILE

- **SONG** Shrill rasping call, *krreea* and *krri-krri-krri-krri-krrriik*.
- **BEHAVIOR** Eats squid and fish. Plunge dives from air for prey, catching it in its bill, then swallowing it underwater or on the surface. This bird rarely alights on the sea. Does not carry prey in mouth while in flight. Does not follow boats but may be attracted to them. Often seen circling a boat several times or sitting on water nearby before departing. Tropicbirds fly superbly but have difficulty walking on land, usually shuffling around with their breasts touching the rocks.
- **BREEDING** Monogamous. Colonial.
- **NESTING** Incubation 44–45 days by both sexes alternately. Altricial young leave nest 90–120 days after hatching.
- **POPULATION** Rare to casual straggler to coastal waters of the southern United States. Common to fairly common on subtropical and tropical islands in the Pacific, south Atlantic, and Caribbean.

Similar Birds

RED-TAILED TROPICBIRD
Heavier; all white; red central tail feathers.

WHITE-TAILED TROPICBIRD
Adult lacks barring on upperparts; black bar across inner wing; yellow to orange bill.

Flight Pattern

Rapid pigeonlike direct flight with stiff shallow steady wing beats.

Nest Identification

Shape | Location

Uses no materials in nest • in cavity of cliffs or burrows • 1 red-brown or whitish buff blotched or spotted egg.

| Plumage Sexes similar | Habitat | Migration Migratory | Weight 1.7 pounds |

DATE _____ TIME_____ LOCATION _____

Family SULIDAE	Species *Sula dactylatra*	Length 26–34 inches	Wingspan 60–62 inches

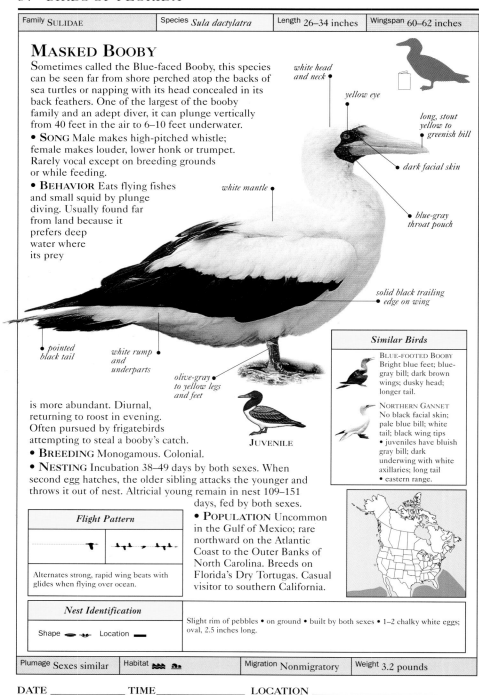

MASKED BOOBY

Sometimes called the Blue-faced Booby, this species can be seen far from shore perched atop the backs of sea turtles or napping with its head concealed in its back feathers. One of the largest of the booby family and an adept diver, it can plunge vertically from 40 feet in the air to 6–10 feet underwater.

• **SONG** Male makes high-pitched whistle; female makes louder, lower honk or trumpet. Rarely vocal except on breeding grounds or while feeding.

• **BEHAVIOR** Eats flying fishes and small squid by plunge diving. Usually found far from land because it prefers deep water where its prey

white head and neck

yellow eye

long, stout yellow to greenish bill

dark facial skin

white mantle

blue-gray throat pouch

solid black trailing edge on wing

pointed black tail

white rump and underparts

olive-gray to yellow legs and feet

JUVENILE

is more abundant. Diurnal, returning to roost in evening. Often pursued by frigatebirds attempting to steal a booby's catch.

• **BREEDING** Monogamous. Colonial.

• **NESTING** Incubation 38–49 days by both sexes. When second egg hatches, the older sibling attacks the younger and throws it out of nest. Altricial young remain in nest 109–151 days, fed by both sexes.

• **POPULATION** Uncommon in the Gulf of Mexico; rare northward on the Atlantic Coast to the Outer Banks of North Carolina. Breeds on Florida's Dry Tortugas. Casual visitor to southern California.

Similar Birds

BLUE-FOOTED BOOBY
Bright blue feet; blue-gray bill; dark brown wings; dusky head; longer tail.

NORTHERN GANNET
No black facial skin; pale blue bill; white tail; black wing tips • juveniles have bluish gray bill; dark underwing with white axillaries; long tail • eastern range.

Flight Pattern

Alternates strong, rapid wing beats with glides when flying over ocean.

Nest Identification

Shape ●—◡ Location ▬

Slight rim of pebbles • on ground • built by both sexes • 1–2 chalky white eggs; oval, 2.5 inches long.

Plumage Sexes similar	Habitat 〰〰 〰	Migration Nonmigratory	Weight 3.2 pounds

DATE _____ TIME_____ LOCATION _____

Family SULIDAE	Species *Sula leucogaster*	Length 26–29 inches	Wingspan 52–59 inches

BROWN BOOBY

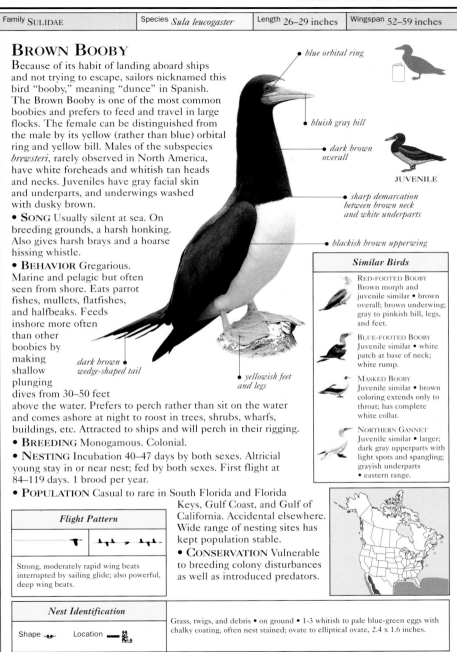

blue orbital ring

bluish gray bill

dark brown overall

JUVENILE

sharp demarcation between brown neck and white underparts

blackish brown upperwing

dark brown wedge-shaped tail

yellowish feet and legs

Because of its habit of landing aboard ships and not trying to escape, sailors nicknamed this bird "booby," meaning "dunce" in Spanish. The Brown Booby is one of the most common boobies and prefers to feed and travel in large flocks. The female can be distinguished from the male by its yellow (rather than blue) orbital ring and yellow bill. Males of the subspecies *brewsteri*, rarely observed in North America, have white foreheads and whitish tan heads and necks. Juveniles have gray facial skin and underparts, and underwings washed with dusky brown.

• **SONG** Usually silent at sea. On breeding grounds, a harsh honking. Also gives harsh brays and a hoarse hissing whistle.

• **BEHAVIOR** Gregarious. Marine and pelagic but often seen from shore. Eats parrot fishes, mullets, flatfishes, and halfbeaks. Feeds inshore more often than other boobies by making shallow plunging dives from 30–50 feet above the water. Prefers to perch rather than sit on the water and comes ashore at night to roost in trees, shrubs, wharfs, buildings, etc. Attracted to ships and will perch in their rigging.

• **BREEDING** Monogamous. Colonial.

• **NESTING** Incubation 40–47 days by both sexes. Altricial young stay in or near nest; fed by both sexes. First flight at 84–119 days. 1 brood per year.

• **POPULATION** Casual to rare in South Florida and Florida Keys, Gulf Coast, and Gulf of California. Accidental elsewhere. Wide range of nesting sites has kept population stable.

• **CONSERVATION** Vulnerable to breeding colony disturbances as well as introduced predators.

Similar Birds

RED-FOOTED BOOBY Brown morph and juvenile similar • brown overall; brown underwing; gray to pinkish bill, legs, and feet.

BLUE-FOOTED BOOBY Juvenile similar • white patch at base of neck; white rump.

MASKED BOOBY Juvenile similar • brown coloring extends only to throat; has complete white collar.

NORTHERN GANNET Juvenile similar • larger; dark gray upperparts with light spots and spangling; grayish underparts • eastern range.

Flight Pattern
Strong, moderately rapid wing beats interrupted by sailing glide; also powerful, deep wing beats.

Nest Identification	
Shape ⤸ Location ▬	Grass, twigs, and debris • on ground • 1-3 whitish to pale blue-green eggs with chalky coating, often nest stained; ovate to elliptical ovate, 2.4 x 1.6 inches.

Plumage Sexes differ	Habitat	Migration Nonmigratory	Weight 2.4 pounds

DATE _____ TIME_____ LOCATION _____

Family SULIDAE	Species *Sula sula*	Length 26–28 inches	Wingspan 53–60 inches

RED-FOOTED BOOBY

Preferring to feed at night far offshore, this tropical bird is the smallest of the boobies and has more color variations than perhaps any other seabird. It has at least four color morphs in two general forms: white and gray-brown. The white morphs show an overall white color, with black primaries, median primary coverts below and secondaries that occur in either a white-tailed or black-tailed form. The brown morphs have either a brown rump and tail or a white rump and tail. Juveniles of all morphs are brownish gray overall with a gray-blue bill, brownish underwings, and pinkish legs and feet.

• **SONG** A low throaty braylike chatter.

light blue bill
pink at base

JUVENILE

WHITE MORPH

red feet and legs

DARK MORPH

• **BEHAVIOR** Gregarious. Seminocturnal and crepuscular. Highly pelagic and rarely seen from mainland. May forage several hundred miles from land. Eats fish and squid. Plunge-dives for most food in deep waters. Also catches flying fish in air. Attracted to ships and lands on them. Often feeds in large flocks and returns to land to roost at night.

• **BREEDING** Monogamous. Colonial.

• **NESTING** Incubation 43–49 days by both sexes. Altricial young stay in or around nest 15 weeks; fed by both sexes. 1 brood per year.

• **POPULATION** Casual along the California coast, Gulf Coast, Dry Tortugas, and in Florida. Accidental elsewhere on Atlantic Coast.

Similar Birds

BLUE-FOOTED BOOBY
Bright blue feet; smaller; blue bill; white underparts; brown wings and mantle with white patches on back and neck; white axillars and wing linings • juvenile dark overall with white neck patch.

NORTHERN GANNET
Larger; white secondaries; dark gray feet and legs • juvenile speckled white • eastern range.

• **CONSERVATION** Population reduced due to destruction of habitat (principally the trees they require for nesting) by land clearing, herding of goats, and tourism development.

Flight Pattern

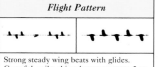

Strong steady wing beats with glides. Graceful, agile; skims low over water. 5 or more may form line dipping up and down.

Nest Identification

Shape 🐚   Location 🌿 🍃 🌾

Sticks and twigs • in trees, shrubs, or on thick grass tufts • built by both sexes; female does most of building while male gathers material • 1 chalky white egg; long elliptical or long to short subelliptical, generally broader at one end; 2.5 x 1.6 inches.

Plumage Sexes similar	Habitat 〰️ 〰️	Migration Nonmigratory	Weight 2.1 pounds

DATE _____ TIME_____ LOCATION _____

Family SULIDAE	Species *Morus bassanus*	Length 35–40 inches	Wingspan 65–71 inches

NORTHERN GANNET

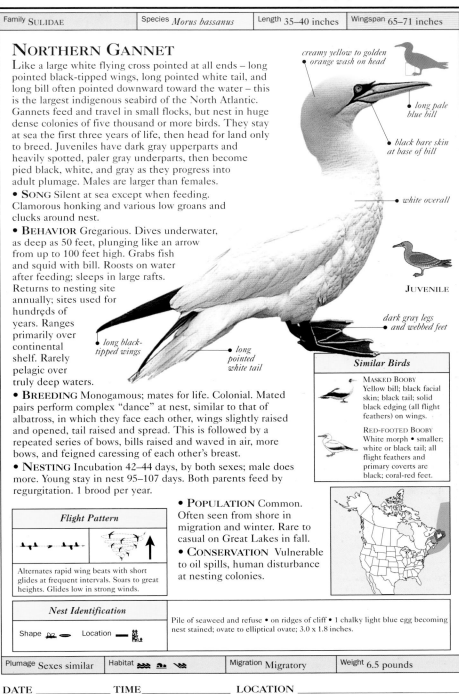

creamy yellow to golden orange wash on head

long pale blue bill

black bare skin at base of bill

white overall

JUVENILE

dark gray legs and webbed feet

long black-tipped wings

long pointed white tail

Like a large white flying cross pointed at all ends – long pointed black-tipped wings, long pointed white tail, and long bill often pointed downward toward the water – this is the largest indigenous seabird of the North Atlantic. Gannets feed and travel in small flocks, but nest in huge dense colonies of five thousand or more birds. They stay at sea the first three years of life, then head for land only to breed. Juveniles have dark gray upperparts and heavily spotted, paler gray underparts, then become pied black, white, and gray as they progress into adult plumage. Males are larger than females.

• **SONG** Silent at sea except when feeding. Clamorous honking and various low groans and clucks around nest.

• **BEHAVIOR** Gregarious. Dives underwater, as deep as 50 feet, plunging like an arrow from up to 100 feet high. Grabs fish and squid with bill. Roosts on water after feeding; sleeps in large rafts. Returns to nesting site annually; sites used for hundreds of years. Ranges primarily over continental shelf. Rarely pelagic over truly deep waters.

• **BREEDING** Monogamous; mates for life. Colonial. Mated pairs perform complex "dance" at nest, similar to that of albatross, in which they face each other, wings slightly raised and opened, tail raised and spread. This is followed by a repeated series of bows, bills raised and waved in air, more bows, and feigned caressing of each other's breast.

• **NESTING** Incubation 42–44 days, by both sexes; male does more. Young stay in nest 95–107 days. Both parents feed by regurgitation. 1 brood per year.

Similar Birds

MASKED BOOBY
Yellow bill; black facial skin; black tail; solid black edging (all flight feathers) on wings.

RED-FOOTED BOOBY
White morph • smaller; white or black tail; all flight feathers and primary coverts are black; coral-red feet.

• **POPULATION** Common. Often seen from shore in migration and winter. Rare to casual on Great Lakes in fall.

• **CONSERVATION** Vulnerable to oil spills, human disturbance at nesting colonies.

Flight Pattern

Alternates rapid wing beats with short glides at frequent intervals. Soars to great heights. Glides low in strong winds.

Nest Identification

Shape —— Location ——

Pile of seaweed and refuse • on ridges of cliff • 1 chalky light blue egg becoming nest stained; ovate to elliptical ovate; 3.0 x 1.8 inches.

Plumage Sexes similar	Habitat	Migration Migratory	Weight 6.5 pounds

DATE _____ TIME_____ LOCATION _____

Family PELECANIDAE	Species *Pelecanus erythrorhynchos*	Length 60–63 inches	Wingspan 96–110 inches

AMERICAN WHITE PELICAN

pale yellow crest

black wing tips and outer trailing edge of wing

graduated plates on upper mandible

oversized orange-salmon bill

short orange-red legs and feet

One of the most distinctive birds in North America, this huge pelican, with its immense bill and vast wingspan, is one of the largest waterbirds. Making their summer home near inland lakes, breeding birds shed the upper mandible plate after the eggs are laid and show a dull grayish crown and nape. In flight the head is drawn back on the shoulders with the bill resting on the breast, and the black primaries and outer secondaries contrast sharply with the white plumage. Young have a dull grayish bill and a brownish wash on the head, neck, and upper wing coverts.

• **SONG** Mostly silent. On nesting grounds guttural croaks.

• **BEHAVIOR** Entire flock may work communally to catch fish by "herding" them into shallow water or an enclosed area, then scooping the fish out of the water with pouches that can hold up to 3 gallons of water. Eats fish of little or no commercial value.

• **BREEDING** Monogamous. Colonial.

• **NESTING** Incubation 29–36 days by both sexes. Young stay in nest 17–28 days; fed by both sexes. Gather in groups called pods after fledging and continue to be fed by adults. First flight at 9–10 weeks. 1 brood per year.

• **POPULATION** Fairly common to common. Breeds in western lakes; winters in southwest and Gulf Coast states. Casual wanderer in migration.

• **CONSERVATION** Some decrease due to habitat loss and pesticide poisoning; however, has increased since 1970s. Despite legal protection most deaths due to shooting.

WINTER PLUMAGE

Similar Birds

WOOD STORK
Black trailing edge to wing (all flight feathers); black tail; dark head and bill; long legs trail beyond tail in flight.

BROWN PELICAN
Gray-brown upperparts; dark wings; darker bill; plunge dives for fish while flying.

Flight Pattern

Strong slow deep wing beats. Soars high on thermals. Flies in straight line or V formation.

Nest Identification

Shape ⚬ Location ▬

Made of built-up dirt and rubbish • on flat ground • 1–2 dull or chalky white eggs; ovate to elongate-ovate with some nearly elliptical–oval, 3.5 x 2.2 inches.

Plumage Sexes similar	Habitat 〰️ 〰️ 〰️	Migration Migratory	Weight 15.4 pounds

DATE _____ TIME_____ LOCATION _____

Family PELECANIDAE	Species *Pelecanus occidentalis*	Length 48–50 inches	Wingspan 78–84 inches

BROWN PELICAN

Louisiana's state bird is the smallest of the world's pelicans. Strictly a marine bird, it almost faced extinction because of pesticides and hydrocarbons that led to the thinning of its eggshells and reproductive failure in many colonies in the 1960s and 1970s. The population is now recovering, although it is still listed as threatened. It is rarely seen inland except around the Salton Sea. The color of its gular pouch varies from red in the West to blackish in the East. Young birds are brownish with a whitish belly.

- **SONG** Adults are silent except for occasional low croaking. Young make snakelike hiss.
- **BEHAVIOR** Coastal and pelagic. Eats fish taken near the surface by plunge-diving from air and scooping up prey with pouch. Sometimes attended by gulls that attempt to steal the catch before it can be swallowed. Gregarious. Often flies in long lines close to the water, with each bird closely following the flight path of the one ahead and all flapping and gliding in unison.
- **BREEDING** Monogamous. Colonial.
- **NESTING** Incubation 28–30 days by both sexes. Young begin to walk out of nest at 35 days if nest site is on ground, but do not leave nest until 63–80 days, when able to fly, if nest is elevated in shrub or tree. Tended and fed by both sexes. 1 brood per year.
- **POPULATION** Fairly common to common on Pacific Coast from central California southward, on the Atlantic Coast from Maryland southward around the tip of Florida, and westward along the entire Gulf Coast. Wanders north along coast in spring and summer. Rare inland, but common in Salton Sea.
- **CONSERVATION** Listed as threatened. Declined in mid-1900s due to pesticides; currently recovering in number.

white head and neck

pale yellow forecrown and forehead

dark chestnut hindneck

streaked gray-brown upperparts

pale yellow eyes

blackish pouch

yellowish gray bill with scarlet cast on distal portion and yellow tip

blackish brown breast and belly

JUVENILE

black legs and webbed feet

Similar Birds

AMERICAN WHITE PELICAN
Black wing tips and outer secondaries; white body; huge salmon bill; orange-red legs and feet; does not plunge dive for food.

NORTHERN GANNET
Juvenile has dark gray upperparts with pale speckling; paler underparts; pointed, straight pale bill; pointed tail with white U patch at base; long dark-tipped wings
- Atlantic and Gulf Coast range.

Flight Pattern

Graceful, powerful flight with deliberate wing beats alternating with short glides. Flies in straight line formation.

Nest Identification

Shape ___   Location ___

Sticks, reeds, and grass • in vegetation 6–20 feet high or on ground built up 4–10 inches • built by female with materials gathered by male • 2–4 white eggs often nest-stained; long oval, 2.8 x 1.8 inches.

Plumage Sexes similar	Habitat	Migration Migratory	Weight 8.2 pounds

DATE _____ TIME_____ LOCATION _____

Family PHALACROCORACIDAE	Species *Phalacrocorax auritus*	Length 32 inches	Wingspan 52 inches

DOUBLE-CRESTED CORMORANT

The most widespread cormorant in North America appears blackish overall from a distance, but may appear to have a green sheen in certain lighting. During breeding season it shows two small tufts of feathers; they are black in eastern birds, but larger and mostly white in western birds. Its wings are not completely waterproof, so upon leaving the water the bird often perches on exposed objects with its wings held out to catch the sun's rays and dry its feathers. This cormorant swims low in the water with its bill tilted slightly upward. In flight it has a distinct crook in its neck. Immature birds are brown with white face, foreneck, and breast.

- **SONG** Deep guttural grunt.
- **BEHAVIOR** Gregarious. Dives for fish, crustaceans, and amphibians from surface. Excellent diver, using feet for propulsion. Able to stay at 5–25 feet below surface for 30–70 seconds.
- **BREEDING** Monogamous. Colonial.
- **NESTING** Incubation 28–30 days by both sexes. Altricial young may leave nest at 21–28 days but may return to be fed by both sexes. First flight at 35–42 days. Independent at 63–70 days. 1 brood per year.
- **POPULATION** Common. Fluctuates because of persecution at nesting colonies, although increasing and expanding range, particularly in interior, in last 2 decades of the 20th century.
- **CONSERVATION** Often killed by fishermen who believe birds compete with them. Many populations hit hard, especially on California coast, in 1960s and 1970s by DDT, causing reproductive failures.

bright orange-yellow facial skin

long pale hooked bill

bright orange-yellow gular skin

green sheen on neck, head, and underparts

brown upperparts with black scaling

blackish overall

JUVENILE

black legs and feet

Similar Birds

NEOTROPIC CORMORANT Smaller; longer tail; posterior edge of gular skin often pointed with whitish border.

BRANDT'S CORMORANT Dark face; blue throat patch with buff border; shorter tail; flies with head and neck held straight • strictly coastal and pelagic western range.

GREAT CORMORANT Larger throat pouch bordered by white feathers; white cheeks and flank patches (breeding) • East Coast range.

Flight Pattern

Strong powerful direct flight. Sometimes soars briefly on thermals. Groups fly in straight line or V formation.

Nest Identification

Shape ⌒⌒   Location 🌿 🪨 ▬

In trees made of sticks and debris and lined with leafy twigs and grass • on rocks often made of seaweed and trash gathered at water's edge • near water • built by female • 2 nest-stained bluish white eggs; long subelliptical, 2.4 x 1.5 inches.

Plumage Sexes similar	Habitat 〜〜 🦆 🐚	Migration Migratory	Weight 4.0 pounds

DATE ___7|04___ TIME_____ LOCATION _____

Family PHALACROCORACIDAE	Species *Phalacrocorax carbo*	Length 35–40 inches	Wingspan 63 inches

GREAT CORMORANT

The largest North American cormorant is able to carry water in its throat pouch to pour over its chicks when they have been exposed to high temperatures. A proficient swimmer and diver, this bird has been found as deep as a hundred feet below the surface. Its large size, large bill, pale yellow chin, and white throat patch distinguish it from the Double-crested Cormorant, the only other cormorant sharing its northern Atlantic range. In breeding season short white plumes appear on the side of the neck, and white patches are visible on its flanks while in flight. Juveniles have brown upperparts and a white belly.

heavy hooked bill

bright yellow throat pouch with large border of white feathers

blocklike head

JUVENILE

- **SONG** Usually silent. Low throaty groans on breeding grounds.
- **BEHAVIOR** Excellent swimmer. Rides low in water, holding bill slightly angled above horizontal; uses webbed feet to swim. Dives for fish and crustaceans. When perched wet, holds wings in spread eagle position to dry.
- **BREEDING** Monogamous. Colonial. Breeds on cliffs or rocks.
- **NESTING** Incubation 28–31 days by both sexes. Altricial young stay in nest 50 days. Fed by both sexes. First flight is at 50 days. Fledged young may return to nest at night until they achieve independence in 30–40 more days. 1 brood per year.
- **POPULATION** Fairly common. Increased dramatically; range has spread southward. Thought to be limited by interactions with more numerous and well-established Double-crested Cormorant. Winters in small numbers from the Maritime Provinces south to South Carolina; rare farther south.
- **CONSERVATION** Vulnerable to disturbance at colonial nesting sites as well as the pollution of its marine environment.

short tail

Similar Birds

DOUBLE-CRESTED CORMORANT
Smaller; orange throat patch; no flank patches
- juveniles have slimmer bill, deep orange facial skin, pale breast and darker belly.

Flight Pattern

Strong direct flight with steady wing beats, but slow to reach full flight speed. Flies in V or straight line formation.

Nest Identification

Shape ⌒ Location 🪨 🌿 ▬ ▬

Twigs, seaweed, and bits of refuse • lined with grasses and moss • on ground in moderately elevated area • built by both sexes • 3–5 pale blue-green eggs, often nest-stained; long oval, 2.6 inches long.

Plumage Sexes similar	Habitat 🏖 🌊 ≈	Migration Migratory	Weight 5.0 pounds

DATE _____ TIME_____ LOCATION _____

Family ANHINGIDAE	Species *Anhinga anhinga*	Length 35 inches	Wingspan 45–48 inches

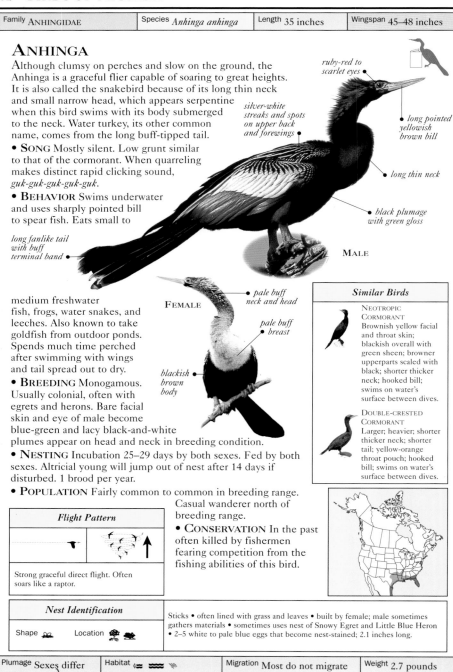

ANHINGA

Although clumsy on perches and slow on the ground, the Anhinga is a graceful flier capable of soaring to great heights. It is also called the snakebird because of its long thin neck and small narrow head, which appears serpentine when this bird swims with its body submerged to the neck. Water turkey, its other common name, comes from the long buff-tipped tail.

• **SONG** Mostly silent. Low grunt similar to that of the cormorant. When quarreling makes distinct rapid clicking sound, *guk-guk-guk-guk-guk*.

• **BEHAVIOR** Swims underwater and uses sharply pointed bill to spear fish. Eats small to medium freshwater fish, frogs, water snakes, and leeches. Also known to take goldfish from outdoor ponds. Spends much time perched after swimming with wings and tail spread out to dry.

• **BREEDING** Monogamous. Usually colonial, often with egrets and herons. Bare facial skin and eye of male become blue-green and lacy black-and-white plumes appear on head and neck in breeding condition.

• **NESTING** Incubation 25–29 days by both sexes. Fed by both sexes. Altricial young will jump out of nest after 14 days if disturbed. 1 brood per year.

• **POPULATION** Fairly common to common in breeding range. Casual wanderer north of breeding range.

• **CONSERVATION** In the past often killed by fishermen fearing competition from the fishing abilities of this bird.

ruby-red to scarlet eyes

silver-white streaks and spots on upper back and forewings

long pointed yellowish brown bill

long thin neck

black plumage with green gloss

MALE

long fanlike tail with buff terminal band

pale buff neck and head

FEMALE

pale buff breast

blackish brown body

Similar Birds

NEOTROPIC CORMORANT
Brownish yellow facial and throat skin; blackish overall with green sheen; browner upperparts scaled with black; shorter thicker neck; hooked bill; swims on water's surface between dives.

DOUBLE-CRESTED CORMORANT
Larger; heavier; shorter thicker neck; shorter tail; yellow-orange throat pouch; hooked bill; swims on water's surface between dives.

Flight Pattern	

Strong graceful direct flight. Often soars like a raptor.

Nest Identification	
Shape 🪹 Location 🌳🌿	Sticks • often lined with grass and leaves • built by female; male sometimes gathers materials • sometimes uses nest of Snowy Egret and Little Blue Heron • 2–5 white to pale blue eggs that become nest-stained; 2.1 inches long.

Plumage Sexes differ	Habitat 🌊〰️🌾	Migration Most do not migrate	Weight 2.7 pounds

DATE __7\04__ TIME_____ LOCATION _____

Family FREGATIDAE	Species *Fregata magnificens*	Length 37–41 inches	Wingspan 82–94 inches

MAGNIFICENT FRIGATEBIRD

The male has a most striking courtship display when he inflates his throat sac into a huge brilliant red balloon. In flight it looks almost sinister with its black plumage, long thin crooked wings, and deeply forked tail often folded into a point. Juveniles are black without gloss and have a white head, neck, sides, breast, and belly. Even when not nesting, flocks of these birds often gather at their permanent roosts in treetops, or on high cliffs.

straight hooked gray bill

entirely black with purple gloss on back and head

bright red pouch usually shows as red patch on throat when not distended

MALE

- **SONG** Clacks bill; nasal *kack* or *ka-ack*; soft chippering at nesting grounds. Silent at sea.
- **BEHAVIOR** Soars over sea to find food. Dives for prey and catches it in bill from surface. Eats fish, crustaceans, and jellyfish. Attacks other large seabirds in flight until they drop or disgorge their catch, which the frigatebird then catches in midair. Roosts communally and is gregarious.
- **BREEDING** Monogamous. Colonial.
- **NESTING** Incubation 40–50 days by both sexes. Fed by both sexes. First flight at 20–24 weeks. Young never left unguarded because other birds in colony may eat eggs and hatchlings. Most females do not breed every year.
- **POPULATION** Total difficult to monitor. Rare to casual on Salton Sea and along California coast to Washington. Breeds on Dry Tortugas off Florida Keys. Fairly common to casual along Gulf of Mexico, Florida coasts, and north to North Carolina. Rare straggler north to Maritimes and inland, especially after storms.

JUVENILE

straight hooked gray bill

white breast and sides

FEMALE

black without gloss

long, narrow pointed wings

long deeply forked tail

Similar Birds

♂ **GREAT FRIGATEBIRD**
Male has pale brownish alar bar; scalloped pale grayish axillars; green gloss on head and back
• female has gray-white throat, breast, and upper belly; red orbital ring; broader black belly patch • juvenile has white head, neck, and breast; neck and head tinged with rust-brown.

♀

Flight Pattern

Very high effortless soaring flight. Extremely graceful and buoyant in the air.

- **CONSERVATION** Frigatebirds are legally protected, but they are still killed in the nest by local people, who hunt at night with flashlights and clubs. Some years no young survive.

Nest Identification

Shape   Location

Sticks, twigs, grass, and reeds • in mangroves, trees, or bushes, 2–20 feet above ground • built by female with materials gathered by male, which often steals from neighbors' nests • 1 white egg; rarely 2.

Plumage Sexes differ	Habitat	Migration Nonmigratory	Weight 2.8 pounds

DATE _____ TIME_____ LOCATION _____

Family ARDEIDAE	Species *Botaurus lentiginosus*	Length 23 inches	Wingspan 42–50 inches

AMERICAN BITTERN

When it senses danger, the American Bittern hides by standing motionless with its bill pointed upward and its body tightly contracted. Thus it can be mistaken for a wooden stake in the marshes, saltwater and freshwater bogs, and wetland ponds it inhabits. The dark and light vertical streaks blend with shadows and highlights cast by surrounding vegetation, so the bird often goes unnoticed even from a few feet away. In flight the somewhat pointed dark outer wings contrast sharply with the inner wings and body.

dark brown crown

pointed yellowish bill

white throat

streaked brown and buff upperparts

long black strip or patch on each side of neck

pointed wings with contrasting dark tips

streaked brown and white underparts

JUVENILE

• **SONG** *Oonk-a-lunk* or *punk-er-lunk*, often heard at dusk; it is one of the strangest sounds produced by any bird; sounds like someone driving a stake into the mud with a wooden mallet.

• **BEHAVIOR** Stands motionless, often hidden by marsh vegetation, on ground or in water to search for prey. Eats frogs, small eels, small fish, small snakes, salamanders, crayfish, small rodents, and water bugs.

• **BREEDING** May be polygamous. Solitary nester.

• **NESTING** Incubation 24–29 days by female. Young stay in nest 14 days. Fed by both parents. 1 brood per year.

• **POPULATION** Fairly common. Declining in the South from marshland drainage.

• **CONSERVATION** Protected by law. Wetland conservation is critical for this species.

Similar Birds

♂ **LEAST BITTERN** Much smaller; black crown and back; shows buff wing patches in flight.

YELLOW-CROWNED NIGHT-HERON
BLACK-CROWNED NIGHT-HERON Juveniles have more heavily spotted upperparts; lack black mustache lines on face.

Flight Pattern

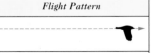

Strong direct flight with deep rapid wing beats.

Nest Identification

Shape 🪹 Location 🌾

Grasses, reeds, and cattails • lined with fine grasses • on dense marsh ground, dry ground above water, or mud in tall vegetation • built by female • 2–7 pale brown to olive-buff eggs, 1.9 inches long.

Plumage Sexes similar	Habitat 〰️ 〰️	Migration Migratory	Weight 1.6 pounds

DATE _____ TIME _____ LOCATION _____

Family ARDEIDAE	Species *Ixobrychus exilis*	Length 11–14 inches	Wingspan 16–18 inches

LEAST BITTERN

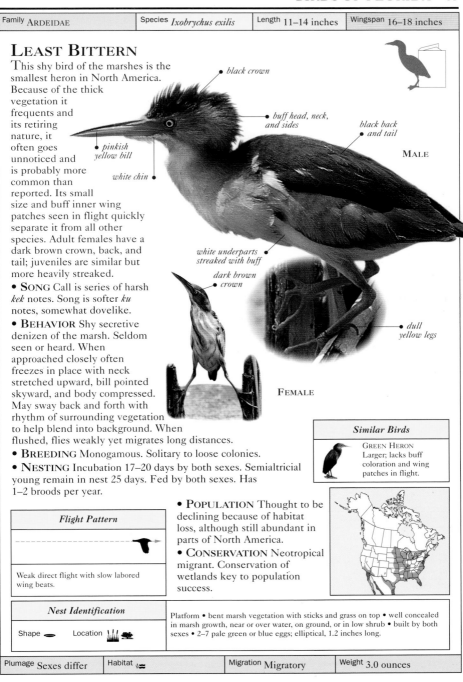

This shy bird of the marshes is the smallest heron in North America. Because of the thick vegetation it frequents and its retiring nature, it often goes unnoticed and is probably more common than reported. Its small size and buff inner wing patches seen in flight quickly separate it from all other species. Adult females have a dark brown crown, back, and tail; juveniles are similar but more heavily streaked.

- **SONG** Call is series of harsh *kek* notes. Song is softer *ku* notes, somewhat dovelike.
- **BEHAVIOR** Shy secretive denizen of the marsh. Seldom seen or heard. When approached closely often freezes in place with neck stretched upward, bill pointed skyward, and body compressed. May sway back and forth with rhythm of surrounding vegetation to help blend into background. When flushed, flies weakly yet migrates long distances.
- **BREEDING** Monogamous. Solitary to loose colonies.
- **NESTING** Incubation 17–20 days by both sexes. Semialtricial young remain in nest 25 days. Fed by both sexes. Has 1–2 broods per year.

black crown

buff head, neck, and sides

black back and tail

MALE

pinkish yellow bill

white chin

white underparts streaked with buff

dark brown crown

dull yellow legs

FEMALE

Similar Birds

GREEN HERON
Larger; lacks buff coloration and wing patches in flight.

- **POPULATION** Thought to be declining because of habitat loss, although still abundant in parts of North America.
- **CONSERVATION** Neotropical migrant. Conservation of wetlands key to population success.

Flight Pattern

Weak direct flight with slow labored wing beats.

Nest Identification

Shape ⬤   Location 🌾🪺

Platform • bent marsh vegetation with sticks and grass on top • well concealed in marsh growth, near or over water, on ground, or in low shrub • built by both sexes • 2–7 pale green or blue eggs; elliptical, 1.2 inches long.

Plumage Sexes differ	Habitat 〰	Migration Migratory	Weight 3.0 ounces

DATE _____ TIME_____ LOCATION _____

Family ARDEIDAE	Species *Ardea herodias*	Length 46–52 inches	Wingspan 77–82 inches

GREAT BLUE HERON

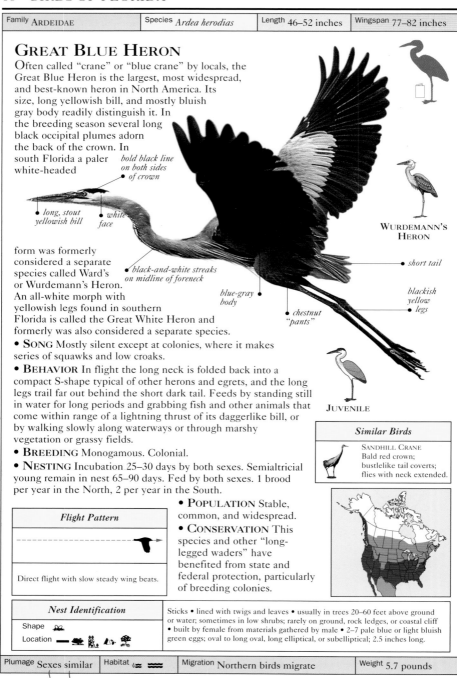

Often called "crane" or "blue crane" by locals, the Great Blue Heron is the largest, most widespread, and best-known heron in North America. Its size, long yellowish bill, and mostly bluish gray body readily distinguish it. In the breeding season several long black occipital plumes adorn the back of the crown. In south Florida a paler white-headed

bold black line on both sides of crown

long, stout yellowish bill *white face*

WURDEMANN'S HERON

form was formerly considered a separate species called Ward's or Wurdemann's Heron. An all-white morph with yellowish legs found in southern Florida is called the Great White Heron and formerly was also considered a separate species.

black-and-white streaks on midline of foreneck

blue-gray body

chestnut "pants"

short tail

blackish yellow legs

• **SONG** Mostly silent except at colonies, where it makes series of squawks and low croaks.

• **BEHAVIOR** In flight the long neck is folded back into a compact S-shape typical of other herons and egrets, and the long legs trail far out behind the short dark tail. Feeds by standing still in water for long periods and grabbing fish and other animals that come within range of a lightning thrust of its daggerlike bill, or by walking slowly along waterways or through marshy vegetation or grassy fields.

JUVENILE

• **BREEDING** Monogamous. Colonial.

• **NESTING** Incubation 25–30 days by both sexes. Semialtricial young remain in nest 65–90 days. Fed by both sexes. 1 brood per year in the North, 2 per year in the South.

Similar Birds
SANDHILL CRANE Bald red crown; bustlelike tail coverts; flies with neck extended.

• **POPULATION** Stable, common, and widespread.

• **CONSERVATION** This species and other "long-legged waders" have benefited from state and federal protection, particularly of breeding colonies.

Flight Pattern
Direct flight with slow steady wing beats.

Nest Identification	
Shape	Sticks • lined with twigs and leaves • usually in trees 20–60 feet above ground or water; sometimes in low shrubs; rarely on ground, rock ledges, or coastal cliff • built by female from materials gathered by male • 2–7 pale blue or light bluish green eggs; oval to long oval, long elliptical, or subelliptical; 2.5 inches long.
Location	

Plumage Sexes similar	Habitat	Migration Northern birds migrate	Weight 5.7 pounds

DATE 7\7\04 _____ TIME_____ LOCATION _____

Family ARDEIDAE	Species *Ardea alba*	Length 37–41 inches	Wingspan 55 inches

GREAT EGRET

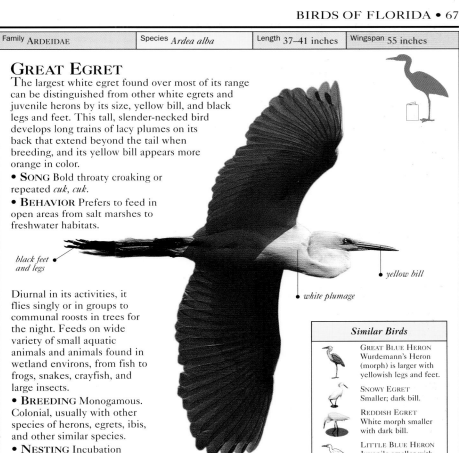

The largest white egret found over most of its range can be distinguished from other white egrets and juvenile herons by its size, yellow bill, and black legs and feet. This tall, slender-necked bird develops long trains of lacy plumes on its back that extend beyond the tail when breeding, and its yellow bill appears more orange in color.

- **SONG** Bold throaty croaking or repeated *cuk, cuk*.
- **BEHAVIOR** Prefers to feed in open areas from salt marshes to freshwater habitats.

black feet and legs

yellow bill

white plumage

Diurnal in its activities, it flies singly or in groups to communal roosts in trees for the night. Feeds on wide variety of small aquatic animals and animals found in wetland environs, from fish to frogs, snakes, crayfish, and large insects.

- **BREEDING** Monogamous. Colonial, usually with other species of herons, egrets, ibis, and other similar species.
- **NESTING** Incubation 23–26 days by both sexes. Young stay in nest 21 days. Fed by both sexes. 1 brood per year.
- **POPULATION** Decimated by plume hunters in late 1800s. Protected since early 20th century. In recent decades breeding range has expanded northward.
- **CONSERVATION** With full protection in North America, species is increasing. Still, factors such as polluted waters, coastal development, and draining of wetlands negatively impact egrets.

Similar Birds

GREAT BLUE HERON Wurdemann's Heron (morph) is larger with yellowish legs and feet.

SNOWY EGRET Smaller; dark bill.

REDDISH EGRET White morph smaller with dark bill.

LITTLE BLUE HERON Juvenile smaller with dark bill.

CATTLE EGRET Much smaller; yellow legs and feet.

Flight Pattern

Buoyant direct flight with deep steady wing beats.

Nest Identification

Shape   Location

Made of sticks • unlined or lined with fine material • in tree or shrub, usually 10–40 feet above ground • built by both sexes • 1–6 pale blue-green or light blue eggs, 2.2 inches long.

Plumage Sexes similar	Habitat	Migration Some migrate	Weight 2.0 pounds

DATE 7/17/04   TIME_____   LOCATION _____

Family ARDEIDAE	Species *Egretta thula*	Length 22–27 inches	Wingspan 38–45 inches

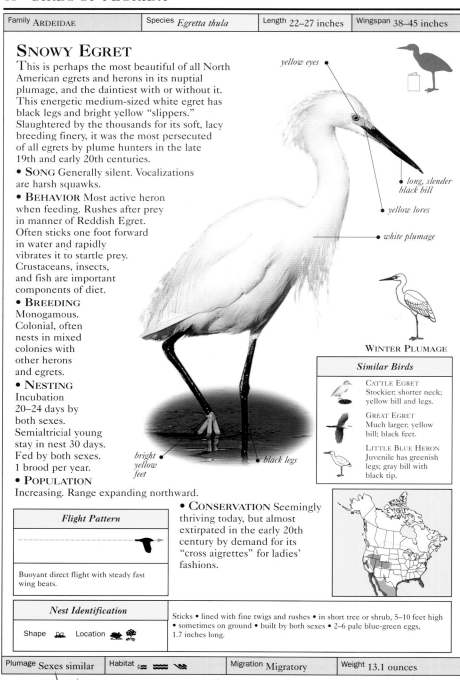

SNOWY EGRET

This is perhaps the most beautiful of all North American egrets and herons in its nuptial plumage, and the daintiest with or without it. This energetic medium-sized white egret has black legs and bright yellow "slippers." Slaughtered by the thousands for its soft, lacy breeding finery, it was the most persecuted of all egrets by plume hunters in the late 19th and early 20th centuries.

• **SONG** Generally silent. Vocalizations are harsh squawks.

• **BEHAVIOR** Most active heron when feeding. Rushes after prey in manner of Reddish Egret. Often sticks one foot forward in water and rapidly vibrates it to startle prey. Crustaceans, insects, and fish are important components of diet.

• **BREEDING** Monogamous. Colonial, often nests in mixed colonies with other herons and egrets.

• **NESTING** Incubation 20–24 days by both sexes. Semialtricial young stay in nest 30 days. Fed by both sexes. 1 brood per year.

• **POPULATION** Increasing. Range expanding northward.

• **CONSERVATION** Seemingly thriving today, but almost extirpated in the early 20th century by demand for its "cross aigrettes" for ladies' fashions.

yellow eyes

long, slender black bill

yellow lores

white plumage

WINTER PLUMAGE

Similar Birds

CATTLE EGRET
Stockier; shorter neck; yellow bill and legs.

GREAT EGRET
Much larger; yellow bill; black feet.

LITTLE BLUE HERON
Juvenile has greenish legs; gray bill with black tip.

bright yellow feet

black legs

Flight Pattern

Buoyant direct flight with steady fast wing beats.

Nest Identification

Shape   Location

Sticks • lined with fine twigs and rushes • in short tree or shrub, 5–10 feet high • sometimes on ground • built by both sexes • 2–6 pale blue-green eggs, 1.7 inches long.

Plumage Sexes similar	Habitat	Migration Migratory	Weight 13.1 ounces

DATE ⁊\०ʮ ___ TIME _____ LOCATION _____

Family ARDEIDAE	Species *Egretta caerulea*	Length 24–29 inches	Wingspan 40–41 inches

LITTLE BLUE HERON

Adults appear entirely dark at a distance, but at closer range they are slate-colored with a purplish maroon head and neck. This is the only dark heron species in North America in which the juvenile is white. The juvenile begins molting into adult plumage in its first spring and gradually acquires more blue-gray feathers, achieving a calico appearance in the transition from white to slate gray.

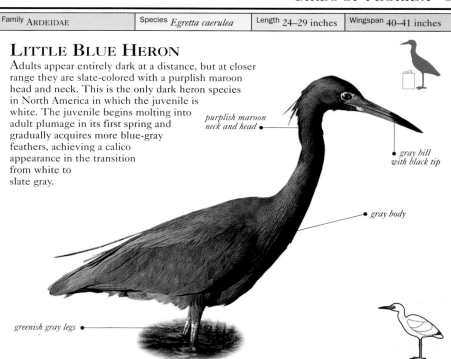

purplish maroon neck and head

gray bill with black tip

gray body

greenish gray legs

JUVENILE

• **SONG** Breeding male makes *eh-oo-ah-eh-eh*. Both sexes make loud nasal *skea* or *scaah* and low clucking notes.
• **BEHAVIOR** Prefers fresh water but can be found in brackish water and salt marshes. A stealthy stalker, it moves slowly as it wades in shallow water or along water's edge for prey. Feeds on a variety of small vertebrates, crustaceans, and large insects. Roosts in trees and shrubs at night.
• **BREEDING** Monogamous. Colonial; often nests in heronries with other species.
• **NESTING** Incubation 20–24 days by both sexes. Semialtricial young stay in nest 42–49 days. Fed by both sexes. Has 1 brood per year.
• **POPULATION** Increasing and expanding.
• **CONSERVATION** Responding to protection of nesting colonies.

Similar Birds

REDDISH EGRET
Dark morph similar to adult; rufous head and neck; pink bill with black tip • white morph similar to juvenile.

TRICOLORED HERON
White underparts.

Flight Pattern

Direct flight with steady quick wing beats.

Nest Identification

Shape
Location

Sticks and twigs • unlined or lined with finer material • usually in tree or shrub, 3–15 feet high • occasionally on ground • built by both sexes • 1–6 pale blue-green eggs; elliptical to subelliptical, 1.7 inches long.

Plumage Sexes similar	Habitat	Migration Migratory	Weight 12.9 ounces

DATE 7/17/04 TIME_____ LOCATION _____

Family ARDEIDAE	Species *Egretta tricolor*	Length 24–26 inches	Wingspan 36 inches

TRICOLORED HERON

Our only large dark heron with white underparts can be found in salty coastal marshes to inland freshwater. Its long, slender neck and long, thin bill make it seem larger and skinnier than other medium-sized herons. *Tricolored* refers to the dark upperparts, white underparts, and reddish brown stripes on the foreneck. In breeding plumage there are white plumes on the back of the crown and shaggy purplish or tan feathers on the lower neck, crown, and back.

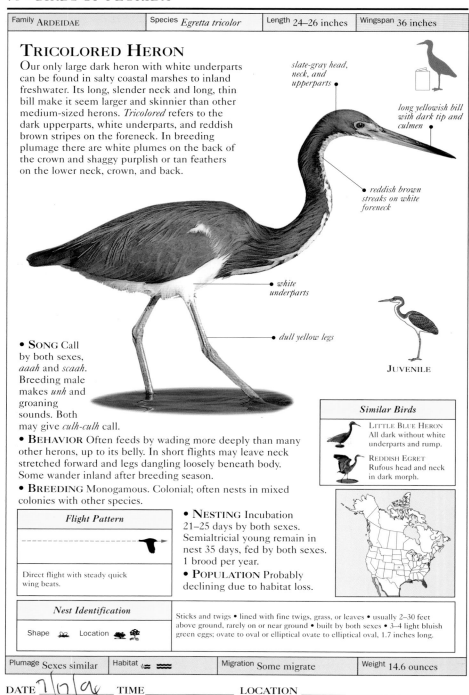

slate-gray head, neck, and upperparts

long yellowish bill with dark tip and culmen

reddish brown streaks on white foreneck

white underparts

dull yellow legs

JUVENILE

• **SONG** Call by both sexes, *aaah* and *scaah*. Breeding male makes *unh* and groaning sounds. Both may give *culh-culh* call.

• **BEHAVIOR** Often feeds by wading more deeply than many other herons, up to its belly. In short flights may leave neck stretched forward and legs dangling loosely beneath body. Some wander inland after breeding season.

• **BREEDING** Monogamous. Colonial; often nests in mixed colonies with other species.

Similar Birds

LITTLE BLUE HERON
All dark without white underparts and rump.

REDDISH EGRET
Rufous head and neck in dark morph.

Flight Pattern
Direct flight with steady quick wing beats.

• **NESTING** Incubation 21–25 days by both sexes. Semialtricial young remain in nest 35 days, fed by both sexes. 1 brood per year.

• **POPULATION** Probably declining due to habitat loss.

Nest Identification	
Shape 🐚 Location 🌿🌳	Sticks and twigs • lined with fine twigs, grass, or leaves • usually 2–30 feet above ground, rarely on or near ground • built by both sexes • 3–4 light bluish green eggs; ovate to oval or elliptical ovate to elliptical oval, 1.7 inches long.

Plumage Sexes similar	Habitat 〰️ 〰️	Migration Some migrate	Weight 14.6 ounces

DATE 7/17/04   TIME_____   LOCATION_____

Family ARDEIDAE	Species *Egretta rufescens*	Length 27–32 inches	Wingspan 46 inches

REDDISH EGRET

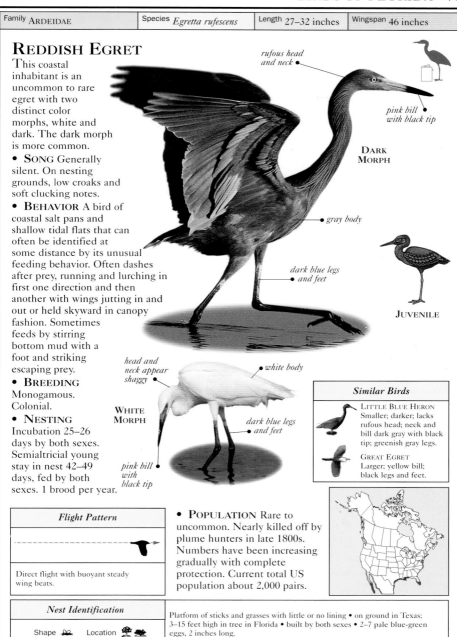

rufous head and neck

pink bill with black tip

DARK MORPH

gray body

dark blue legs and feet

JUVENILE

This coastal inhabitant is an uncommon to rare egret with two distinct color morphs, white and dark. The dark morph is more common.

• **SONG** Generally silent. On nesting grounds, low croaks and soft clucking notes.

• **BEHAVIOR** A bird of coastal salt pans and shallow tidal flats that can often be identified at some distance by its unusual feeding behavior. Often dashes after prey, running and lurching in first one direction and then another with wings jutting in and out or held skyward in canopy fashion. Sometimes feeds by stirring bottom mud with a foot and striking escaping prey.

• **BREEDING** Monogamous. Colonial.

• **NESTING** Incubation 25–26 days by both sexes. Semialtricial young stay in nest 42–49 days, fed by both sexes. 1 brood per year.

head and neck appear shaggy

white body

WHITE MORPH

dark blue legs and feet

pink bill with black tip

Similar Birds

LITTLE BLUE HERON Smaller; darker; lacks rufous head; neck and bill dark gray with black tip; greenish gray legs.

GREAT EGRET Larger; yellow bill; black legs and feet.

• **POPULATION** Rare to uncommon. Nearly killed off by plume hunters in late 1800s. Numbers have been increasing gradually with complete protection. Current total US population about 2,000 pairs.

Flight Pattern
Direct flight with buoyant steady wing beats.

Nest Identification	
Shape Location	Platform of sticks and grasses with little or no lining • on ground in Texas; 3–15 feet high in tree in Florida • built by both sexes • 2–7 pale blue-green eggs, 2 inches long.

Plumage Sexes similar	Habitat	Migration Most do not migrate	Weight 15.9 ounces

DATE _____ TIME_____ LOCATION _____

Family ARDEIDAE	Species *Bubulcus ibis*	Length 19–21 inches	Wingspan 36–38 inches

CATTLE EGRET

This is the only small white egret with the combination of a yellow bill and yellow legs and feet. Breeding adults have patches of buff-orange on crown, nape, lower foreneck, and back. Nonbreeding adults and immature birds lack the buff-orange patches and have yellow bill, legs, and feet. A big-headed, thick-necked, short-legged egret of the Old World (originally found in Spain, Portugal, and Africa), it introduced itself to South America in the 1880s and to Florida by the early 1940s. From there it moved over most of the US and into southern Canada.

- buff-orange patches on crown, nape, and back
- yellowish orange bill
- short thick neck
- buff-orange patches on lower foreneck
- white plumage
- yellowish orange feet
- short yellowish orange legs

JUVENILE

- **SONG** Various croaking sounds at breeding colonies; otherwise silent.

- **BEHAVIOR** Associates with cattle, horses, or other livestock in moist or dry pastures, where it feeds primarily on large insects disturbed by feeding livestock. Several birds may accompany a single cow, often riding on its back. Also follows tractors plowing fields to feed on the exposed insects and grubs. Largely diurnal, flying at dusk to communal roosts with other egrets, herons, and ibis to spend the night perched in trees or shrubs. They often form the nucleus of nesting colonies of other species of heron and egrets, and their presence may encourage the nesting of these birds in the heronries.

- **BREEDING** Monogamous. Colonial; often found in mixed breeding colonies with other species.

- **NESTING** Incubation 21–26 days by both sexes. Semialtricial young remain in nest about 45 days. Fed by both sexes. 1 brood per year.

- **POPULATION** North American population increasing.

- **CONSERVATION** Nesting colonies protected.

Similar Birds

SNOWY EGRET
Longer, more slender neck; black bill and legs.

LITTLE BLUE HERON
Juvenile is larger with longer, more slender neck; greenish gray legs and feet; black-tipped grayish bill.

GREAT EGRET
Larger; black legs and feet.

Flight Pattern

Direct flight with steady, rather rapid wing beats.

Nest Identification

Shape  Location

Sticks and reeds • lined with leafy green twigs • in tree or shrub • built by female from materials gathered by male • 1–9 pale blue or light bluish green eggs; subelliptical or elliptical, 1.9 inches long.

Plumage Sexes similar	Habitat	Migration Migratory	Weight 11.9 ounces

DATE 7/04 _____ TIME _____ LOCATION _____

Family ARDEIDAE	Species *Butorides virescens*	Length 18–22 inches	Wingspan 26 inches

GREEN HERON

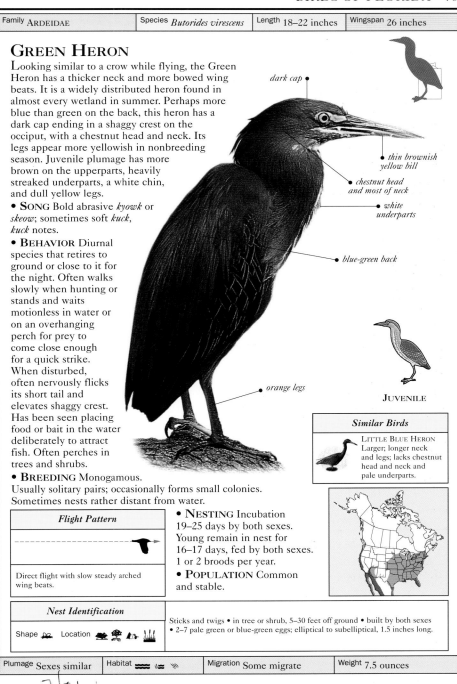

Looking similar to a crow while flying, the Green Heron has a thicker neck and more bowed wing beats. It is a widely distributed heron found in almost every wetland in summer. Perhaps more blue than green on the back, this heron has a dark cap ending in a shaggy crest on the occiput, with a chestnut head and neck. Its legs appear more yellowish in nonbreeding season. Juvenile plumage has more brown on the upperparts, heavily streaked underparts, a white chin, and dull yellow legs.

• **SONG** Bold abrasive *kyowk* or *skeow*; sometimes soft *kuck, kuck* notes.

• **BEHAVIOR** Diurnal species that retires to ground or close to it for the night. Often walks slowly when hunting or stands and waits motionless in water or on an overhanging perch for prey to come close enough for a quick strike. When disturbed, often nervously flicks its short tail and elevates shaggy crest. Has been seen placing food or bait in the water deliberately to attract fish. Often perches in trees and shrubs.

• **BREEDING** Monogamous. Usually solitary pairs; occasionally forms small colonies. Sometimes nests rather distant from water.

dark cap

thin brownish yellow bill

chestnut head and most of neck

white underparts

blue-green back

orange legs

JUVENILE

Similar Birds

LITTLE BLUE HERON Larger; longer neck and legs; lacks chestnut head and neck and pale underparts.

Flight Pattern

Direct flight with slow steady arched wing beats.

• **NESTING** Incubation 19–25 days by both sexes. Young remain in nest for 16–17 days, fed by both sexes. 1 or 2 broods per year.

• **POPULATION** Common and stable.

Nest Identification

Shape ⌒ ⌒   Location 🌿 🌳 🐦 🌾

Sticks and twigs • in tree or shrub, 5–30 feet off ground • built by both sexes • 2–7 pale green or blue-green eggs; elliptical to subelliptical, 1.5 inches long.

Plumage Sexes similar	Habitat 〰️ 🌿 🍃	Migration Some migrate	Weight 7.5 ounces

DATE ___7 / 01 __   TIME_____   LOCATION _____

7/04

Family ARDEIDAE	Species *Nycticorax nycticorax*	Length 25–28 inches	Wingspan 44–45 inches

BLACK-CROWNED NIGHT-HERON

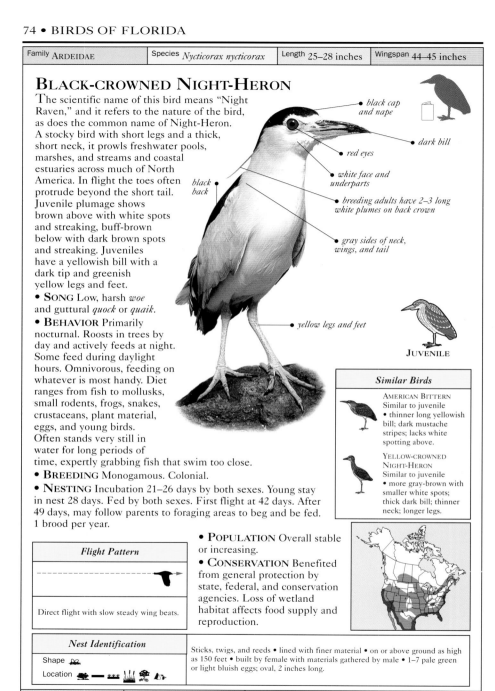

The scientific name of this bird means "Night Raven," and it refers to the nature of the bird, as does the common name of Night-Heron. A stocky bird with short legs and a thick, short neck, it prowls freshwater pools, marshes, and streams and coastal estuaries across much of North America. In flight the toes often protrude beyond the short tail. Juvenile plumage shows brown above with white spots and streaking, buff-brown below with dark brown spots and streaking. Juveniles have a yellowish bill with a dark tip and greenish yellow legs and feet.

- **SONG** Low, harsh *woe* and guttural *quock* or *quaik*.

- **BEHAVIOR** Primarily nocturnal. Roosts in trees by day and actively feeds at night. Some feed during daylight hours. Omnivorous, feeding on whatever is most handy. Diet ranges from fish to mollusks, small rodents, frogs, snakes, crustaceans, plant material, eggs, and young birds. Often stands very still in water for long periods of time, expertly grabbing fish that swim too close.

- **BREEDING** Monogamous. Colonial.

- **NESTING** Incubation 21–26 days by both sexes. Young stay in nest 28 days. Fed by both sexes. First flight at 42 days. After 49 days, may follow parents to foraging areas to beg and be fed. 1 brood per year.

Labels on illustration:
black cap and nape
dark bill
red eyes
white face and underparts
breeding adults have 2–3 long white plumes on back crown
gray sides of neck, wings, and tail
black back
yellow legs and feet

JUVENILE

Similar Birds

AMERICAN BITTERN
Similar to juvenile
- thinner long yellowish bill; dark mustache stripes; lacks white spotting above.

YELLOW-CROWNED NIGHT-HERON
Similar to juvenile
- more gray-brown with smaller white spots; thick dark bill; thinner neck; longer legs.

- **POPULATION** Overall stable or increasing.

- **CONSERVATION** Benefited from general protection by state, federal, and conservation agencies. Loss of wetland habitat affects food supply and reproduction.

Flight Pattern

Direct flight with slow steady wing beats.

Nest Identification

Shape

Location

Sticks, twigs, and reeds • lined with finer material • on or above ground as high as 150 feet • built by female with materials gathered by male • 1–7 pale green or light bluish eggs; oval, 2 inches long.

Plumage Sexes similar	Habitat	Migration Migratory	Weight 1.9 pounds

DATE ___7 | 01___ TIME_____ LOCATION _____

Family ARDEIDAE	Species *Nyctanassa violacea*	Length 22–28 inches	Wingspan 42–44 inches

YELLOW-CROWNED NIGHT-HERON

At home in coastal mangroves, inland swamps, and riparian woodlands, this short-necked, stocky heron has a gray body and a large black head boldly marked with a white cheek patch and white crown with yellowish tints on the forehead. During breeding season adult males and females have long white occipital plumes on the back of the head. The long yellow legs protrude well beyond the short tail in flight.

- **SONG** Short *woe* or *wok*. Its *quak* is higher and less harsh than that given by the Black-crowned Night-Heron.
- **BEHAVIOR** While mostly nocturnal, it is often active during the day. Exhibits strong preference for crustaceans, although it eats a variety of other aquatic organisms from fish to shellfish.
- **BREEDING** Monogamous. Solitary nester or forms small loose colonies. Also joins large nesting colonies with other herons and egrets, often chooses nesting site located on periphery of the colony.

thick dark bill

long white occipital plumes

large black head with yellowish white crown and white cheek patches

slender neck

JUVENILE

long yellow legs

Similar Birds

BLACK-CROWNED NIGHT-HERON
Black back; white head with black cap; short yellowish legs
- juvenile has brown crown; brown upperparts with large white spots and streaks; whitish-tan underparts with brown streaking; short yellow-green legs and feet; yellowish bill with black tip.

- **NESTING** Incubation 21–25 days by both sexes. Semialtricial young remain in nest 25 days, fed by both sexes. Probably 1 brood per year.
- **POPULATION** Stable.

Flight Pattern
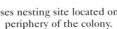
Direct flight with steady deep wing beats.

Nest Identification	
Shape 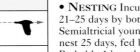 Location 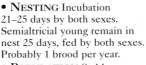	Sticks • lined with twigs or sometimes leaves • either on ground or in tree 30–40 feet high • built by both sexes • 2–8 pale blue-green eggs; oval to long oval, 2 inches long.

Plumage Sexes similar	Habitat	Migration Migratory	Weight 1.6 pounds

DATE _____ TIME_____ LOCATION _____

Family THRESKIORNITHIDAE	Species *Eudocimus albus*	Length 21–27 inches	Wingspan 38 inches

WHITE IBIS

The all-white plumage and long reddish decurved bill are distinctive. The color of the bill blends into the scarlet face of breeding birds; nonbreeding adults show a pink to red face. In flight the black wing tips are conspicuous. The juvenile White Ibis is the only dark ibis with white underparts and rump.
• SONG Male emits advertising call of *hunk-hunk-hunk-hunk*. Female squeals.

white plumage

black wing tips show in flight

scarlet face

reddish legs

decurved reddish bill with black tip

FIRST FALL PLUMAGE

Feeding birds give soft grunting *croo, croo, croo* frequently as they forage.
• BEHAVIOR Like other ibis, flies with neck and legs outstretched, often in long, loose lines. Seems to prefer marshes and pools near the coast, where it feeds by probing. Primarily diurnal like other ibis. Flies to communal roosts in shrubs and trees in evening for the night.
• BREEDING Monogamous. Colonial. Usually nests in mixed colonies with other wading species.
• NESTING Incubation 21–23 days by both sexes. Altricial young remain in nest 28–35 days. Fed by both sexes. Probably 1 brood per year.
• POPULATION Common to abundant in coastal marshes but local. Range has increased, but Florida population much lower than previous levels. Some heavy losses after major hurricanes destroy roosts/rookeries.

Similar Birds

GLOSSY IBIS
WHITE-FACED IBIS·
Similar to juvenile but differ in all plumages by white underparts and rump • Glossy Ibis range only in the East.

Flight Pattern

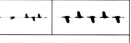

Rapid wing beats followed by short glide. Flies in straight line formation.

Nest Identification

Shape ▭ ⬤   Location 🌿 🌾 🌱

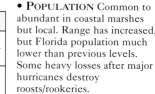

Sticks and sometimes cordgrass or reeds • near water, occasionally in shrub or on low, matted vegetation • usually 7–15 feet above ground or water • built by female from material gathered by male • 2–4 pale blue to green-white eggs with blotches of brown; subelliptical to long elliptical, 2.3 inches long.

Plumage Sexes similar	Habitat 〰 〰	Migration Some migrate	Weight 2.3 pounds

DATE ⁷/₁₇/⁰⁴   TIME _____   LOCATION _____

Family THRESKIORNITHIDAE	Species *Plegadis falcinellus*	Length 19–26 inches	Wingspan 36–38 inches

GLOSSY IBIS

From a distance this large bird with a dark decurved bill appears dark overall in the freshwater or saltwater marshes it frequents, but closer observation reveals deep chestnut plumage glossed with metallic greens and purples. The species occurs widely in the Old World and evidence suggests that perhaps it introduced itself to North America in the 1800s. Its North American range may be limited due to its recent arrival on the continent, as well as competition with the already established White Ibis. Breeding plumaged birds show intense green patches in their wings, greenish legs with red joints, pale blue around the face and blue-gray facial skin in the loral region.

- *dark iris*
- *metallic green and purple gloss on back, wings, head, and neck*
- *dark gray lores bordered with pale blue*
- *brownish black decurved bill*
- *chestnut plumage*

• **SONG** Guttural, grating croak, *ka-onk*.
• **BEHAVIOR** Gregarious. Flies in lines or groups, with individuals often changing position in the flock. In flight the head, neck, and legs are extended. Highly prone to wandering, thus turns up at great distances from breeding range, especially in spring. Uses long bill to probe for food, particularly crayfish and crabs in their holes. Also readily eats water snakes. Often feeds with other large wading birds, including the White Ibis. Flies to roost late in the day and frequently is seen roosting with other species of ibis, herons, and egrets.
• **BREEDING** Monogamous. Colonial; often nests in mixed colonies with other ibis, herons, and egrets.
• **NESTING** Incubation about 21 days, mostly by female. Semialtricial young remain in nest for about 28 days, fed by both sexes. 1 brood per year.
• **POPULATION** Common but local. Greatly increased and expanded during 20th century.

Similar Birds

WHITE-FACED IBIS
Reddish legs and lores bordered with white; white line around lore encircles eye; red iris.

WHITE IBIS
Juvenile • white underparts and rump.

Flight Pattern

Several shallow rapid wing beats followed by a short glide. Flies in straight line formation.

Nest Identification

Shape ⌒⌒ Location 🌿 🪴 🌱 🌳

Platform of sticks and marsh plants with depression in center • occasionally lined with leaves • in shrubs or low trees; on the ground on islands • built by both sexes • 1–5 pale blue or green eggs, 2 inches long.

Plumage Sexes similar	Habitat 🌾 〰	Migration Migratory	Weight Undetermined

DATE _____ TIME_____ LOCATION _____

Family THRESKIORNITHIDAE	Species *Ajaia ajaja*	Length 30–40 inches	Wingspan 50–53 inches

ROSEATE SPOONBILL

The only spoonbill native to North America, this is also the only large pink wading bird normally found on our southern coasts. Adults and juveniles alike are unmistakable with large spatulate bills. In flight the adult bird looks almost entirely pink and flies with its neck and legs extended. During breeding season the head sometimes becomes a copper-buff color. Juveniles are pale whitish overall.

- **SONG** Soft quacking sounds when disturbed.
- **BEHAVIOR** Feeds while wading in shallow water by rhythmically sweeping its spoonbill back and forth. Sensitive nerve endings snap bill shut

bare greenish head

white back

gray-green spatulate bill

white neck and breast

red coverts form red bar on folded wing

pink wings, rump, and underparts

pinkish red legs and feet

on any prey encountered. Often quite tame. Individuals and flocks frequently found in company of other wading birds.

- **BREEDING** Monogamous. Colonial; often nests in mixed colonies with other wading birds.
- **NESTING** Incubation 22–24 days by both sexes. Young stay in nest 35–42 days. Fed by both sexes. Capable of strong flight in 49–56 days. 1 brood per year.
- **POPULATION** Fairly common but local. Virtually eliminated from US in 1860s as water colonies were destroyed. Recolonization began in Texas and Florida in early 20th century. Still vulnerable to degradation of feeding and nesting habitats.
- **CONSERVATION** Drainage for development and mosquito control threatens foraging habitat.

Similar Birds

GREATER FLAMINGO
Much larger in size; entirely pink; longer legs and neck.

SCARLET IBIS
Much deeper red; slender decurved bill.

Flight Pattern

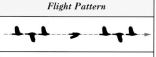

Steady flapping wing beats with short glides in between.

Nest Identification

Shape ➤ Location 🪹 🌳

Platform with deep hollow in center • made of sticks • lined with twigs and leaves • in mangroves, trees, and shrubs • usually 5–15 feet above ground or water • built by female with material from male • 1–5 white eggs, spotted with brown and occasionally wreathed, 2.6 inches long.

Plumage Sexes similar	Habitat 🪶 ᨆ	Migration Some migrate	Weight Undetermined

DATE _____ TIME_____ LOCATION _____

Family CICONIIDAE	Species *Mycteria americana*	Length 35–45 inches	Wingspan 65 inches

WOOD STORK

Numbers of the only stork that breeds in North America are much reduced from their former levels. This large bird of southern wetlands and swamps appears all white on the ground, except for its bare grayish "flinthead" and upper neck, blackish gray legs with pink feet, and black tail. In flight the trailing edge of the wings is black. Storks fly with legs and neck extended. Some wander northward after the breeding season in late summer and are irregularly recorded north to California, Tennessee, and Massachusetts; casually as far north as southern Canada. Many retreat to Florida in winter.

- **SONG** Usually silent. Adults clatter and snap bills during courtship and copulation. Adults also infrequently produce airy, low, rasping fizz or hiss reminiscent of Turkey Vulture.
- **BEHAVIOR** Walks or wades in shallow water up to its belly with head down when feeding. Reproductive cycles triggered by drying up of waterholes that concentrate fish in sufficient numbers for efficient feeding of young.
- **BREEDING** Monogamous. Colonial.
- **NESTING** Incubation 27–32 days by both sexes. Young stay in nest 55–60 days. Fed by both sexes. 1 brood per year likely.
- **POPULATION** Fairly common. Destruction of habitat and disruption of water flow through south Florida major causes of decline. Recently shifted range to South Carolina.
- **CONSERVATION** Endangered in US due to loss of breeding habitat.

bare gray head and upper neck

thick gray-brown decurved bill

white body

JUVENILE

blackish gray legs

Similar Birds

GREAT EGRET
Slender white neck; feathered head; yellow beak.

AMERICAN WHITE PELICAN
Short legs do not trail behind white tail; much longer orange beak; shorter neck.

WHITE IBIS
Smaller; entirely white except for red legs, feet, face, and decurved bill with black tip • in flight, body appears white with black wing tips; red features may look dark • flight pattern differs, with several rapid wing beats alternating with a glide.

Flight Pattern

Alternates between strong flapping flight and gliding. Masterful at soaring, riding high on thermals.

Nest Identification

Shape ⬚ ⬤   Location 🌳

Large sticks • lined sparsely with fine materials and green leaves • 50–80 feet above ground in large cypress trees standing in water • built by both sexes • 2–5 whitish eggs, elliptical to subelliptical, 2.7 inches long.

Plumage Sexes similar	Habitat 〰	Migration Nonmigratory	Weight 6.0 pounds

DATE ___7__|_04_____ TIME_____ LOCATION _____

Family CATHARTIDAE	Species *Coragyps atratus*	Length 23–27 inches	Wingspan 54–60 inches

BLACK VULTURE

Alternating between several quick flaps and a short sail on flat wings, this bird seems to labor on the wing more than the Turkey Vulture that it superficially resembles. In flight the wings are wide, with the six outermost primaries showing white bases beneath. The tail of this vulture is short and squared, barely extending beyond the wing, and the feet often protrude beyond it.

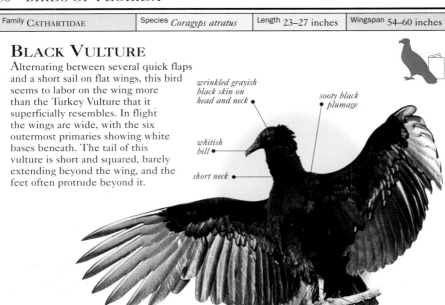

wrinkled grayish black skin on head and neck

sooty black plumage

whitish bill

short neck

white outer primaries

long gray-white legs and gray-white feet

- **SONG** Usually silent, but when competing for food it makes grumbling, barking, and hissing noises.
- **BEHAVIOR** Solitary or found in small to large groups. Often roosts communally. Diet consists primarily of carrion. Aggressive in nature for a vulture, it often dominates carrion when other species are present. Sometimes attacks and kills prey. It spreads its wings when on the roost, especially in the morning, to catch the ultraviolet rays of the sun.
- **BREEDING** Monogamous. Colonial.
- **NESTING** Incubation 37–48 days by both sexes. Semialtricial young remain in nest 80–94 days, and are fed by both sexes. 1 brood per year.
- **POPULATION** Fairly common to common. Decline in the Southeast has been due to the loss of safe nesting habitat. Overall, there has been a slight increase in the Northeast as range has expanded.

Similar Birds

TURKEY VULTURE Bare red head (black on juvenile); long rectangular tail; 2-toned wings from below (black in front, silver-gray trailing edge); holds wings in dihedral when soaring.

Flight Pattern

Several quick deep wing beats followed by a glide; soars on thermals.

Nest Identification

Shape

Location

No nest • lives in dark recesses or under cover in caves, hollow logs, stumps, tree trunks, or abandoned buildings • 2 light grayish green or bluish white eggs, usually marked with brown or lavender; elliptical ovate or elongate ovate, 3 inches long.

Plumage Sexes similar	Habitat	Migration Some migrate	Weight 4.8 pounds

DATE _____ TIME _____ LOCATION _____

Family CATHARTIDAE	Species *Cathartes aura*	Length 26–32 inches	Wingspan 68–72 inches

TURKEY VULTURE

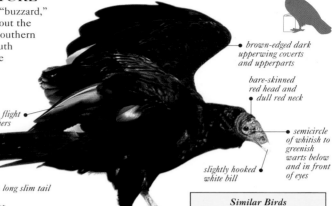

Commonly known as a "buzzard," this bird ranges throughout the United States and into southern Canada and south to South America. It gets its name from the red skin on its head and dark body feathers that resemble a turkey. This carrion feeder is perhaps most often seen in flight, when its two-tone wings, black in front and silver-gray flight feathers behind, are most visible. Soaring birds hold their wings above their backs in a shallow V called a dihedral and rock from side to side as if unsteady in the air.

brown-edged dark upperwing coverts and upperparts

bare-skinned red head and dull red neck

gray flight feathers

semicircle of whitish to greenish warts below and in front of eyes

slightly hooked white bill

long slim tail

pale pinkish white legs

• **SONG** Usually silent. Makes hisses, grunts, or growls around food.
• **BEHAVIOR** Circles just above treetops and up to 200 feet high, searching for prey by smell and sight. Birds gather quickly after an animal dies. Feeds primarily on fresh or rotten carrion. Also eats roadkill (many become victims to autos themselves); stillborn livestock and afterbirth; and dead young of egrets, herons, ibis, and similar species, at heronries. Has been known to eat vegetables and even pumpkins if shortage of food. Master at soaring. Often roosts communally at night.
• **BREEDING** Monogamous.
• **NESTING** Incubation 38–41 days by both sexes. Semialtricial young stay in nest 66–88 days; both sexes feed by regurgitating. 1 brood per year.
• **POPULATION** Common. Very slight overall increase.
• **CONSERVATION** Remarkably resistant to most diseases, especially those likely to be present in carrion.

JUVENILE

Similar Birds

BLACK VULTURE
Very black, including head and stubby tail; longer whiter legs often protrude beyond tail in flight; white primaries under wing tip; flaps and glides more.

GOLDEN EAGLE
Much larger; looks heavier; shorter fan-shaped tail; larger feathered head; large strongly hooked yellow beak; flies with wings held in flat plane.

ZONE-TAILED HAWK
Black; feathered head; bold white tail bands; barred black flight feathers; yellow cere, legs, and feet.

Flight Pattern
Circles with wings in shallow V and rocks unsteadily; moderately slow steady wing beats when not soaring.

Nest Identification	
Shape Location	Bare floors of caves, rock outcroppings, hollow trees, empty buildings, and rocks on cliffs • 1–3 white or cream eggs, often splashed with brown; subelliptical, long oval, or elliptical, 2.8 inches long.

Plumage Sexes similar	Habitat 	Migration Migratory	Weight 3.2 pounds

DATE 7/17/04 TIME_____ LOCATION _____

Family PHOENICOPTERIDAE	Species *Phoenicopterus ruber*	Length 36–50 inches	Wingspan 60 inches

GREATER FLAMINGO

Also known as the American Flamingo, this shy bird is distinguished by its unique bill, long neck, long legs, and brilliant pink color. The brightest pink coloring can be found on the undersurface of the wing, on the axillars and underwing coverts. The flamingo is an excellent swimmer, but it usually is observed on extensive mudflats or wading in the shallows adjacent to them, with its bill, and sometimes head, submerged as it slowly walks ahead filtering food from the ooze.

- **SONG** Honking and cackling. Low *onk* and *ohrn* and higher *aah AAH aah*. A flock sounds gooselike or like a group of frogs calling.
- **BEHAVIOR** Feeds in water of any wading depth. Immerses bill in water and sucks up organically rich bottom ooze from which it filters out edible content with its bill and tongue. Feeds primarily on planktonlike macroscopic organisms, including algal material, bacteria diatoms, plankton, tiny fish, and brine fly larvae.
- **BREEDING** Monogamous. Social and colonial.
- **NESTING** Incubation 28–32 days by both sexes. Fed by both sexes 3–4 days with nutritious red liquid secreted by glands in parents' digestive tract. Chicks then are herded into a group called a creche. Young have short straight bills for the first 40 days. First flight at 75–77 days.
- **POPULATION** Casual in south Florida; accidental elsewhere, principally on Texas coast. Most records in US may be escapees from captivity, especially those in Florida, but there is a very small nesting population of unknown origins in Florida Bay. Caribbean population rose from 12,000 birds in 1971 to 26,000 in the mid-1980s, probably due to protection of the primary nesting and wintering grounds.
- **CONSERVATION** Some protection in Caribbean breeding areas, but much greater efforts are needed.

flattened, bent pink bill with black tip and creamy pink base

bright pink overall

very long neck

pale scapulars

long pink legs with darker joints

JUVENILE

Similar Birds

ROSEATE SPOONBILL
Long, straight greenish gray spatulate bill; greenish gray bare head; white back, neck, and breast; shorter legs and neck.

Flight Pattern

Direct flight with rapid wing beats in long lines with neck extended forward and legs trailing. Flies in straight line formation.

Nest Identification

Shape ⬯ ⬯   Location ▬

Raised cone-shaped nest of mud on mudflats • built by female with assistance from male • cone usually 6–18 inches high and 17–20 inches in diameter at base with hollowed top • may be 2 feet apart or closer • usually 1 chalky white egg.

Plumage Sexes similar	Habitat ▬ 🦐	Migration Nonmigratory	Weight 7.8 pounds

DATE _____ TIME_____ LOCATION _____

| Family ANATIDAE | Species *Dendrocygna bicolor* | Length 18–21 inches | Wingspan 36 inches |

FULVOUS WHISTLING-DUCK

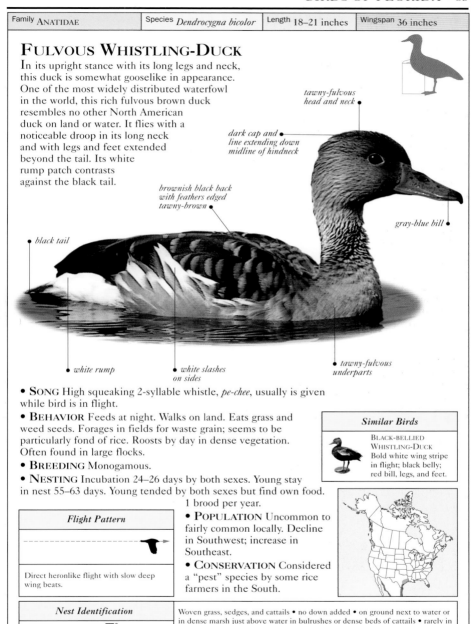

In its upright stance with its long legs and neck, this duck is somewhat gooselike in appearance. One of the most widely distributed waterfowl in the world, this rich fulvous brown duck resembles no other North American duck on land or water. It flies with a noticeable droop in its long neck and with legs and feet extended beyond the tail. Its white rump patch contrasts against the black tail.

tawny-fulvous head and neck

dark cap and line extending down midline of hindneck

brownish black back with feathers edged tawny-brown

gray-blue bill

black tail

white rump

white slashes on sides

tawny-fulvous underparts

• **SONG** High squeaking 2-syllable whistle, *pe-chee*, usually is given while bird is in flight.
• **BEHAVIOR** Feeds at night. Walks on land. Eats grass and weed seeds. Forages in fields for waste grain; seems to be particularly fond of rice. Roosts by day in dense vegetation. Often found in large flocks.
• **BREEDING** Monogamous.
• **NESTING** Incubation 24–26 days by both sexes. Young stay in nest 55–63 days. Young tended by both sexes but find own food. 1 brood per year.
• **POPULATION** Uncommon to fairly common locally. Decline in Southwest; increase in Southeast.
• **CONSERVATION** Considered a "pest" species by some rice farmers in the South.

Similar Birds
BLACK-BELLIED WHISTLING-DUCK Bold white wing stripe in flight; black belly; red bill, legs, and feet.

Flight Pattern
Direct heronlike flight with slow deep wing beats.

Nest Identification	
Shape	Woven grass, sedges, and cattails • no down added • on ground next to water or in dense marsh just above water in bulrushes or dense beds of cattails • rarely in tree cavity • built by female • 12–14 white or buff-white eggs; bluntly ovate, short ovate, or oval; 2.1 inches in diameter.
Location	

| Plumage Sexes similar | Habitat | Migration Migratory | Weight 1.6 pounds |

DATE __7 04__ TIME_____ LOCATION _____

Family ANATIDAE	Species *Chen caerulescens*	Length 25–31 inches	Wingspan 53–60 inches

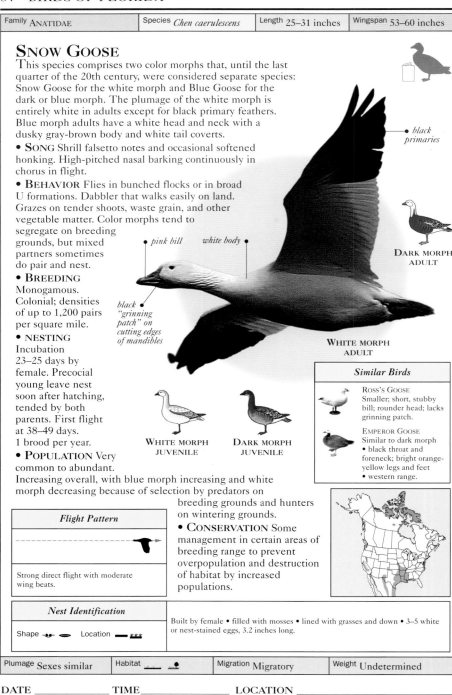

SNOW GOOSE

This species comprises two color morphs that, until the last quarter of the 20th century, were considered separate species: Snow Goose for the white morph and Blue Goose for the dark or blue morph. The plumage of the white morph is entirely white in adults except for black primary feathers. Blue morph adults have a white head and neck with a dusky gray-brown body and white tail coverts.

- **SONG** Shrill falsetto notes and occasional softened honking. High-pitched nasal barking continuously in chorus in flight.
- **BEHAVIOR** Flies in bunched flocks or in broad U formations. Dabbler that walks easily on land. Grazes on tender shoots, waste grain, and other vegetable matter. Color morphs tend to segregate on breeding grounds, but mixed partners sometimes do pair and nest.
- **BREEDING** Monogamous. Colonial; densities of up to 1,200 pairs per square mile.
- **NESTING** Incubation 23–25 days by female. Precocial young leave nest soon after hatching, tended by both parents. First flight at 38–49 days. 1 brood per year.
- **POPULATION** Very common to abundant. Increasing overall, with blue morph increasing and white morph decreasing because of selection by predators on breeding grounds and hunters on wintering grounds.
- **CONSERVATION** Some management in certain areas of breeding range to prevent overpopulation and destruction of habitat by increased populations.

black primaries

pink bill   *white body*

DARK MORPH ADULT

black "grinning patch" on cutting edges of mandibles

WHITE MORPH ADULT

WHITE MORPH JUVENILE   **DARK MORPH JUVENILE**

Similar Birds

ROSS'S GOOSE
Smaller; short, stubby bill; rounder head; lacks grinning patch.

EMPEROR GOOSE
Similar to dark morph • black throat and foreneck; bright orange-yellow legs and feet • western range.

Flight Pattern

Strong direct flight with moderate wing beats.

Nest Identification

Shape — Location —

Built by female • filled with mosses • lined with grasses and down • 3–5 white or nest-stained eggs, 3.2 inches long.

Plumage Sexes similar	Habitat	Migration Migratory	Weight Undetermined

DATE _____ TIME_____ LOCATION _____

Family ANATIDAE	Species *Branta canadensis*	Length 25–45 inches	Wingspan 75 inches

CANADA GOOSE

Found in every province and state at some time of the year, this is the most common, familiar, and widespread goose in North America. Breeding programs in the 20th century established or reestablished populations in the southern part of the range. Size varies tremendously over the vast range, from 22-inch Mallard-sized arctic birds to giant geese reaching 45 inches and weighing 24 pounds.

- **SONG** Small races make high rapid cackle; large races make deep, musical *honk-a-lonk*.
- **BEHAVIOR** Mates for life. Unlike most waterfowl but like most other geese, family units remain together through winter and until they return to breeding grounds. Dabblers and grazers; walk well on land. Feeds on variety of aquatic and terrestrial plants.
- **BREEDING** Monogamous.
- **NESTING** Incubation 25–30 days by female. Precocial young leave nest at 1–2 days. First flight at 42–49 days for smaller races, 56–63 days for larger races. Young feed themselves with parents' help.
- **POPULATION** Common to abundant. Species as a whole probably still increasing.
- **CONSERVATION** Widely harvested as a game bird; highly managed on breeding grounds, wintering areas, and migratory staging areas. Widely introduced to establish new populations or restore extirpated ones.

black head and neck

blackish bill

white "chin strap" wraps from ear to ear under throat

brownish gray upperparts

paler gray-brown breast and sides

white undertail coverts

light to dark underparts, depending on race

black tail

Similar Birds

BRANT
Lacks white chin strap; black breast.

BARNACLE GOOSE
Entirely white face; black breast; white sides • eastern range.

Flight Pattern

Strong direct flight with deep wing beats. Flies in V formation.

Nest Identification

Shape

Location

Sticks, grass, weeds, and moss • lined with down • on slightly elevated dry ground near water • will nest on man-made structures and nest platforms • built by female • 4–7 white, nest-stained eggs, 2.9 inches in diameter.

Plumage Sexes similar	Habitat	Migration Migratory	Weight 8.4 pounds

DATE _____ TIME_____ LOCATION _____

Family ANATIDAE	Species *Aix sponsa*	Length 17–20 inches	Wingspan 28–30 inches

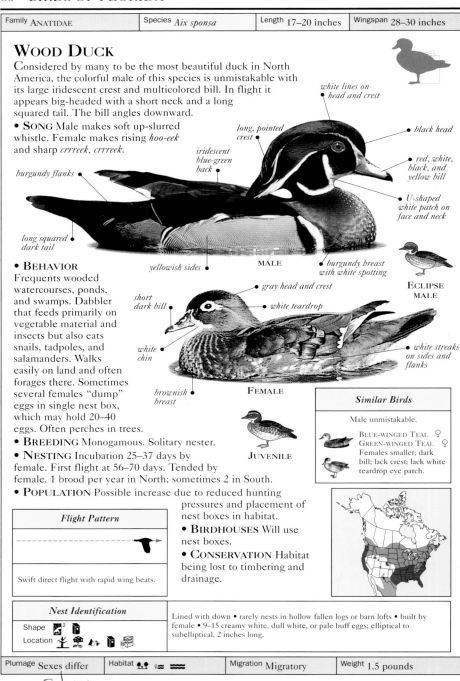

WOOD DUCK

Considered by many to be the most beautiful duck in North America, the colorful male of this species is unmistakable with its large iridescent crest and multicolored bill. In flight it appears big-headed with a short neck and a long squared tail. The bill angles downward.

• **SONG** Male makes soft up-slurred whistle. Female makes rising *hoo-eek* and sharp *crrreek, crrreek.*

white lines on head and crest

long, pointed crest

black head

iridescent blue-green back

red, white, black, and yellow bill

burgundy flanks

U-shaped white patch on face and neck

long squared dark tail

yellowish sides

MALE

burgundy breast with white spotting

ECLIPSE MALE

• **BEHAVIOR** Frequents wooded watercourses, ponds, and swamps. Dabbler that feeds primarily on vegetable material and insects but also eats snails, tadpoles, and salamanders. Walks easily on land and often forages there. Sometimes several females "dump" eggs in single nest box, which may hold 20–40 eggs. Often perches in trees.

gray head and crest

short dark bill

white teardrop

white chin

white streaks on sides and flanks

brownish breast

FEMALE

JUVENILE

• **BREEDING** Monogamous. Solitary nester.
• **NESTING** Incubation 25–37 days by female. First flight at 56–70 days. Tended by female. 1 brood per year in North; sometimes 2 in South.
• **POPULATION** Possible increase due to reduced hunting pressures and placement of nest boxes in habitat.
• **BIRDHOUSES** Will use nest boxes.
• **CONSERVATION** Habitat being lost to timbering and drainage.

Similar Birds

Male unmistakable.

BLUE-WINGED TEAL ♀
GREEN-WINGED TEAL ♀
Females smaller; dark bill; lack crest; lack white teardrop eye patch.

Flight Pattern

Swift direct flight with rapid wing beats.

Nest Identification

Shape
Location

Lined with down • rarely nests in hollow fallen logs or barn lofts • built by female • 9–15 creamy white, dull white, or pale buff eggs; elliptical to subelliptical, 2 inches long.

Plumage Sexes differ	Habitat	Migration Migratory	Weight 1.5 pounds

DATE 7\04   TIME_____   LOCATION _____

Family ANATIDAE	Species *Anas strepera*	Length 18–23 inches	Wingspan 31–36 inches

GADWALL

The male Gadwall is the grayest dabbling duck. Its gray body contrasts with the black rear and blends into the brown back, neck, and head. In flight both sexes show a white speculum. On water or land the white secondaries often appear as a narrow white patch in the folded wing. The male has yellowish legs and feet.

• **SONG** Female makes series of loud quacks that fall in pitch, *kaaak, kaaak-kak-kak-kak*. Male makes single low quack and shrill whistling sound.

brown head and neck

dark bill

brownish back

MALE

black tail coverts

gray body

gray upper mandible with orange sides

mottled brown back and sides

FEMALE

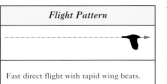

ECLIPSE MALE

• **BEHAVIOR** Dabbler. Feeds in shallows primarily on plant material. Often forages in grain fields and into wood lots for acorns. Walks well on land compared to most ducks. Flies in small flocks. Usually shy and wary; sociable and gregarious. Often feeds by dabbling with head underwater instead of tipping up like many other puddle ducks.

• **BREEDING** Monogamous. Solitary nester.

• **NESTING** Incubation 24–27 days by female. Young precocial; first flight at about 48–56 days. Tended by female. 1 brood per year.

• **POPULATION** Uncommon. Increasing due to expansion of nesting habitat because of unusually wet conditions in breeding range in late 1990s.

Similar Birds

MALLARD ♀
Blue speculum bordered with white; orange legs and feet.

Flight Pattern

Fast direct flight with rapid wing beats.

Nest Identification

Shape ⬬ ⬬ Location ⬩⬩⬩ ⱵⱵ

Grasses and weeds • lined with down • near water or dry land, surrounded by dense weeds or grass • built by female • 7–15 white to dull cream eggs.

Plumage Sexes differ	Habitat 〜 〜	Migration Migratory	Weight 2.2 pounds

DATE _____ TIME_____ LOCATION _____

Family ANATIDAE	Species *Anas americana*	Length 18–23 inches	Wingspan 30–35 inches

AMERICAN WIGEON

This species is identified in flight by the bold white patches on its forewings, which are gray on females, and the white underwing linings. The male has a conspicuous white forehead and crown, leading hunters to nickname it "baldpate." Both males and females are more rusty brown on their breast and sides than other dabbling ducks. Legs and feet are gray. In flight females show a white belly and undertail coverts and a green speculum.

• **SONG** Throaty whistle, *whew, whew, whew*. Female makes weak guttural quack.

gray head with wide green postocular stripe

white forehead and crown

black tail and undertail coverts

MALE

black-tipped blue-gray bill

white of underparts extends onto flanks

gray bill with black tip

gray head and neck

brown back with rusty shoulders

reddish brown breast and sides

ECLIPSE MALE

rufous-brown breast, sides, and flanks

FEMALE

• **BEHAVIOR** Dabbler. Flies in tight flocks that may twist and turn like those of teals. Eats plant material. Will graze on shore and in fields. Often feeds in shallow water with other duck species. Wary; takes flight quickly when it is disturbed.

• **BREEDING** Monogamous. Solitary. Nests on dry land, sometimes far from water; often on small islands.

• **NESTING** Incubation 22–25 days by female. Precocial young stay in nest 45–63 days. Fed by female. 1 brood per year.

• **POPULATION** Common and apparently stable. Breeding range expanding eastward in Canada and northeastern US. Increase has been due to wet conditions as well as increase in nesting sites.

• **CONSERVATION** No issues at present; carefully monitored and managed.

Similar Birds

EURASIAN WIGEON
♂ Rufous-brown head; creamy buff forehead and crown; gray sides and back • female shows dusky underwing linings in flight; gray-morph has brownish gray head, throat, and breast; rufous morph has rufous head, neck, throat, and breast.

Flight Pattern

Swift direct flight with strong wing beats.

Nest Identification

Shape — Location

Grasses and weeds lined with down • on dry land, sometimes on island • built by female • 6–12 white to creamy white eggs; elliptical, 2.1 inches in diameter.

Plumage Sexes differ	Habitat	Migration Migratory	Weight 1.7 pounds

DATE _____ TIME_____ LOCATION _____

Family ANATIDAE	Species *Anas rubripes*	Length 19–24 inches	Wingspan 33–36 inches

AMERICAN BLACK DUCK

The darkest dabbling duck on the water looks almost black at a distance, with a paler head and foreneck. In flight the white wing linings contrast boldly with the dark body and wings. The purplish blue speculum is bordered with black, and the posterior border often has a narrow white edge. It is as large as a Mallard. Into the 1940s this was the most abundant duck in eastern and central North America and was the most heavily hunted without noticable decline in numbers. Today it seems to be losing steadily to years of heavy hunting preasure and increasing displacement by Mallards.

brownish black body

pale brownish gray head and foreneck

MALE

yellow bill

greenish bill with black flecking

FEMALE

brownish black body

- **SONG** Typical female gives loud duck quack; male makes lower croak.
- **BEHAVIOR** Dabbler. Very alert and wary; one of the quickest ducks into the air when disturbed, thrusting upward energetically off water or land. Feeds in shallow water, taking mostly plant materials in winter and a variety of aquatic insects in summer.
- **BREEDING** Monogamous. Solitary nester. Sometimes hybridizes with Mallard.
- **NESTING** Incubation 23–33 days by female. Precocial young stay in nest 58–63 days. Fed by female. 1 brood per year.
- **POPULATION** Fairly common.
- **CONSERVATION** Management warranted due to decline in numbers, which may be caused by changes to its habitat and deforestation. Both of these circumstances seem to favor Mallards, which tend to replace Black Ducks where the two species coexist.

Similar Birds

MALLARD ♀
Female lacks contrast between head and body; paler brown; yellow-orange bill with blackish mottling; bright orange feet; metallic blue speculum bordered with a white front and back; white tail.

Flight Pattern
Swift direct flight with strong wing beats.

Nest Identification	
Shape	Shallow depression with plant material added • lined with down • on ground among clumps of dense vegetation • sometimes in raised situation, as on top of stump • built by female • 6–12 creamy white to greenish buff eggs.
Location	

Plumage Sexes differ	Habitat	Migration Migratory	Weight 3.1 pounds

DATE _____ TIME_____ LOCATION _____

Family ANATIDAE	Species *Anas platyrhynchos*	Length 23 inches	Wingspan 30–40 inches

MALLARD

One of the best-known waterfowl in the world, the Mallard can be found almost anywhere shallow freshwater occurs. Some even reside in salt marshes and bays. The male is larger than the female. Many domesticated forms are entirely white with an orange bill, legs, and feet.

• **SONG** Female makes loud *quack-quack-quack, quack, quack-quack,* descending in scale. Male sounds double note and low reedy *kwek-kwek-kwek.*

• **BEHAVIOR** Generally found in shallow freshwater, where it dabbles primarily for plant food, also taking insects, mollusks, and crustaceans. Sometimes dives underwater. Walks well and often forages on shore in fields and woodlots. Leaps directly into flight from water. Frequently hybridizes.

• **BREEDING** Monogamous. Solitary nester.

• **NESTING** Incubation 26–30 days by female. Precocial young leave nest soon after hatching. 1 brood per year.

• **POPULATION** Common to abundant.

• **FEEDERS** Corn or grains. In city parks some are tame enough to be hand-fed by humans.

• **CONSERVATION** One of the ducks harvested in greatest numbers by waterfowl hunters. Prone to lead poisoning from ingesting spent lead shot with food from bottom ooze.

yellow bill • • shiny green head
• gray-brown back
• metallic blue-violet speculum with white borders
white collar •
• 2 curled-up black tail feathers
purple-chestnut breast
white sides and underparts •
• orange feet and legs
• white tail
orange and brown mottled bill •
MALE

ECLIPSE MALE

• metallic blue-violet speculum with white borders
• white tail
orange feet and legs •
FEMALE

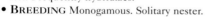

Similar Birds

Female resembles many other female ducks, but blue speculum bordered white is unique.

NORTHERN SHOVELER ♂
Long dark bill; white breast; chestnut sides.

COMMON MERGANSER ♂
Narrow red bill; puffy or crested head.

RED-BREASTED MERGANSER ♂
Narrow red bill; puffy or crested head.

Flight Pattern

Swift direct flight with strong wing beats.

Nest Identification

Shape 🦆 🥚

Location 🌿 🌾 🪶

Shallow pool of plant material gathered at the site, lined with down • may be more than 1 mile from water, usually on ground among concealing vegetation • built by female • 5–14 greenish buff or grayish buff eggs, 2.3 inches long.

Plumage Sexes differ	Habitat 〰️ 🦆 🔆	Migration Migratory	Weight 2.4 pounds

DATE __7/04__ TIME_____ LOCATION _____

Family ANATIDAE	Species *Anas fulvigula*	Length 21 inches	Wingspan 30–33 inches

MOTTLED DUCK

A large resident duck of southern marshes and coastal prairies, this bird is paler than the American Black Duck but also shows white wing linings in flight that contrast with its darker body. In flight it shows a metallic greenish purple speculum that is bordered on both sides by a black bar, and the trailing bar is also bordered with a narrow white line. Although the current population is stable, it is not as large as it was in the beginning of the 20th century as the toll from civilization's expanding development and agriculture's draining of southern marshlands has outweighed the toll from hunting.

fine dark streaking on back of head and sides of neck

brown body with buff mottling

yellow-orange bill without mottling

• **SONG** Male makes a low, raspy *kreeeb, kreeeb, kreeeb.* Female's quack similar to that of a female Mallard.

• **BEHAVIOR** Usually in pairs or small groups. Pairs persist for most of the year except during the postbreeding season molt. A somewhat tame dabbling duck that eats more animal food than the closely related Mallard. Feeds primarily on mollusks, crustaceans, and insects, but also eats vegetable matter. Courtship and pair formation for this species take place on the wintering grounds while Mallards, American Black Ducks, and other duck species are still present.

• **BREEDING** Monogamous. Solitary nester.

• **NESTING** Incubation 24–28 days by female. First flight at about 60–70 days. Fed by female. 1 brood per year.

• **POPULATION** Common. Stable. Introduced on South Carolina coast.

• **CONSERVATION** Heavily hunted in season.

Similar Birds
AMERICAN BLACK DUCK Much darker blackish brown with streaked cheeks and throat.
MALLARD ♀ Female has orange and brown bill with dark mottling; white borders on both sides of blue-purple speculum.

Flight Pattern

Direct flight with strong rapid wing beats.

Nest Identification	
Shape 🪶 ⬬ 🪶 Location ⚮⚮⚮ 🌿🌿 🪴	Shallow bowl of grasses and reeds • lined with down and breast feathers • in dense growth in marsh, usually within 600 feet of water, supported in dense clumps of grass • may be several inches above ground • built by female • 8–12 creamy white to greenish white eggs; elliptical, 2.2 inches long.

Plumage Sexes similar	Habitat ⌇⌇⌇	Migration Nonmigratory	Weight 2.3 pounds

DATE _____ TIME_____ LOCATION _____

Family ANATIDAE	Species *Anas discors*	Length 14–16 inches	Wingspan 23–31 inches

BLUE-WINGED TEAL

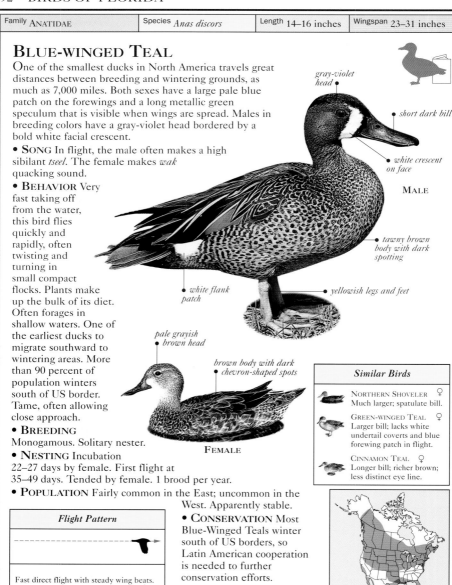

One of the smallest ducks in North America travels great distances between breeding and wintering grounds, as much as 7,000 miles. Both sexes have a large pale blue patch on the forewings and a long metallic green speculum that is visible when wings are spread. Males in breeding colors have a gray-violet head bordered by a bold white facial crescent.

• **SONG** In flight, the male often makes a high sibilant *tseel*. The female makes *wak* quacking sound.

• **BEHAVIOR** Very fast taking off from the water, this bird flies quickly and rapidly, often twisting and turning in small compact flocks. Plants make up the bulk of its diet. Often forages in shallow waters. One of the earliest ducks to migrate southward to wintering areas. More than 90 percent of population winters south of US border. Tame, often allowing close approach.

• **BREEDING** Monogamous. Solitary nester.

• **NESTING** Incubation 22–27 days by female. First flight at 35–49 days. Tended by female. 1 brood per year.

• **POPULATION** Fairly common in the East; uncommon in the West. Apparently stable.

• **CONSERVATION** Most Blue-Winged Teals winter south of US borders, so Latin American cooperation is needed to further conservation efforts.

gray-violet head

short dark bill

white crescent on face

MALE

tawny brown body with dark spotting

yellowish legs and feet

white flank patch

pale grayish brown head

brown body with dark chevron-shaped spots

FEMALE

Similar Birds

NORTHERN SHOVELER ♀
Much larger; spatulate bill.

GREEN-WINGED TEAL ♀
Larger bill; lacks white undertail coverts and blue forewing patch in flight.

CINNAMON TEAL ♀
Longer bill; richer brown; less distinct eye line.

Flight Pattern
Fast direct flight with steady wing beats.

Nest Identification	
Shape 〜 〜 ⬤ Location ▬ ✿ ⟘⟘	Shallow depression with some grass or weeds added • lined with down • on ground in prairie, hayfield, or coastal meadow • built by female • 6–15 white, olive-white, dull white, or tinged olive eggs; ovate to elliptical ovate, 1.8 inches in diameter.

Plumage Sexes differ	Habitat ⤳ ≈≈	Migration Migratory	Weight 14.4 ounces

DATE _____ TIME_____ LOCATION _____

Family ANATIDAE	Species *Anas clypeata*	Length 17–20 inches	Wingspan 27–33 inches

NORTHERN SHOVELER

No duck in North America has a bigger bill. The large, spatulate bill is longer than the head, giving the bird a front heavy look. In flight both sexes show large powder-blue patches on the forewing and a metallic green speculum. Both males and females have bright orange legs and feet.

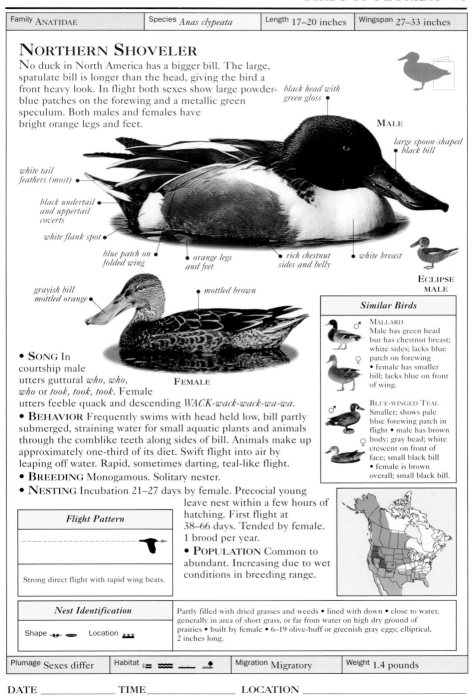

black head with green gloss

MALE

large spoon-shaped black bill

white tail feathers (most)

black undertail and uppertail coverts

white flank spot

blue patch on folded wing

orange legs and feet

rich chestnut sides and belly

white breast

ECLIPSE MALE

grayish bill mottled orange

mottled brown

FEMALE

Similar Birds

MALLARD
Male has green head but has chestnut breast; white sides; lacks blue patch on forewing • female has smaller bill; lacks blue on front of wing.

BLUE-WINGED TEAL
Smaller; shows pale blue forewing patch in flight • male has brown body; gray head; white crescent on front of face; small black bill • female is brown overall; small black bill.

• **SONG** In courtship male utters guttural *who, who, who* or *took, took, took*. Female utters feeble quack and descending *WACK-wack-wack-wa-wa*.

• **BEHAVIOR** Frequently swims with head held low, bill partly submerged, straining water for small aquatic plants and animals through the comblike teeth along sides of bill. Animals make up approximately one-third of its diet. Swift flight into air by leaping off water. Rapid, sometimes darting, teal-like flight.

• **BREEDING** Monogamous. Solitary nester.

• **NESTING** Incubation 21–27 days by female. Precocial young leave nest within a few hours of hatching. First flight at 38–66 days. Tended by female. 1 brood per year.

• **POPULATION** Common to abundant. Increasing due to wet conditions in breeding range.

Flight Pattern

Strong direct flight with rapid wing beats.

Nest Identification

Shape ⚬⚬ ⚬ Location ⚬⚬⚬

Partly filled with dried grasses and weeds • lined with down • close to water, generally in area of short grass, or far from water on high dry ground of prairies • built by female • 6–19 olive-buff or greenish gray eggs; elliptical, 2 inches long.

Plumage Sexes differ	Habitat	Migration Migratory	Weight 1.4 pounds

DATE _____ TIME_____ LOCATION _____

Family ANATIDAE	Species *Anas acuta*	Length 21–29 inches	Wingspan 29–35 inches

NORTHERN PINTAIL

No other North American duck has the body shape of a pintail, either on the water or in the air. It holds its long slender neck erect and its long pointed tail at an upward angle on the water. In flight pintails are long and slender with a white trailing edge on the inner wing.

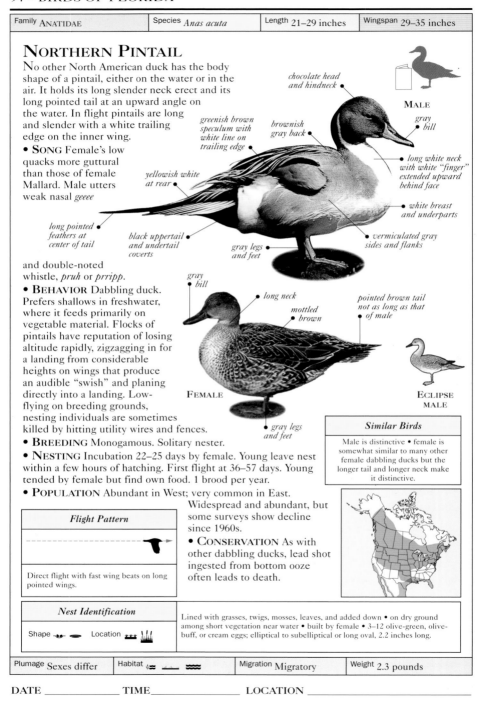

chocolate head and hindneck

MALE

greenish brown speculum with white line on trailing edge

brownish gray back

gray bill

long white neck with white "finger" extended upward behind face

white breast and underparts

yellowish white at rear

vermiculated gray sides and flanks

long pointed feathers at center of tail

black uppertail and undertail coverts

gray legs and feet

• SONG Female's low quacks more guttural than those of female Mallard. Male utters weak nasal *geeee* and double-noted whistle, *pruh* or *prripp*.

gray bill

long neck

mottled brown

pointed brown tail not as long as that of male

FEMALE

ECLIPSE MALE

gray legs and feet

• BEHAVIOR Dabbling duck. Prefers shallows in freshwater, where it feeds primarily on vegetable material. Flocks of pintails have reputation of losing altitude rapidly, zigzagging in for a landing from considerable heights on wings that produce an audible "swish" and planing directly into a landing. Low-flying on breeding grounds, nesting individuals are sometimes killed by hitting utility wires and fences.

• BREEDING Monogamous. Solitary nester.

• NESTING Incubation 22–25 days by female. Young leave nest within a few hours of hatching. First flight at 36–57 days. Young tended by female but find own food. 1 brood per year.

• POPULATION Abundant in West; very common in East. Widespread and abundant, but some surveys show decline since 1960s.

• CONSERVATION As with other dabbling ducks, lead shot ingested from bottom ooze often leads to death.

Similar Birds

Male is distinctive • female is somewhat similar to many other female dabbling ducks but the longer tail and longer neck make it distinctive.

Flight Pattern

Direct flight with fast wing beats on long pointed wings.

Nest Identification

Shape ⚬ ⚬   Location 🌾

Lined with grasses, twigs, mosses, leaves, and added down • on dry ground among short vegetation near water • built by female • 3–12 olive-green, olive-buff, or cream eggs; elliptical to subelliptical or long oval, 2.2 inches long.

Plumage Sexes differ	Habitat	Migration Migratory	Weight 2.3 pounds

DATE _____ TIME_____ LOCATION _____

Family ANATIDAE	Species *Anas crecca*	Length 12–16 inches	Wingspan 20–25 inches

GREEN-WINGED TEAL

The smallest dabbling duck in North America, the Green-winged Teal is also one of the most agile and fastest on the wing. Small compact flocks of Green-winged Teals often wheel and bank like Rock Doves in flight. Flying birds show no pale wing patches but rather a metallic green speculum bordered in front with chestnut and behind with white.

• **SONG** In courtship a *KRICK-et* note, from which species name is derived; it has been likened to the voice of the Spring Peeper. Female makes a faint *quack*.

• **BEHAVIOR** Forages in shallows by tipping up. Walks easily on land. Feeds in fields, wood lots, and agricultural areas. Primarily feeds on vegetable materials.

• **BREEDING** Monogamous with forced extra pair copulation. Solitary nester.

• **NESTING** Incubation 20–24 days by female. First flight at about 34 days. Precocial young are tended by female but find their own food.

dark glossy green patch from eye to nape with narrow white border below

MALE

rich chestnut head

black bill

vermiculated gray sides and back

buff-white breast with dark spotting

yellowish undertail coverts

vertical white bar separates breast from side

gray legs and feet

dusky brown body with buff mottling

EURASIAN RACE MALE

whitish belly

white undertail coverts with brown mottling

FEMALE

Similar Birds

BLUE-WINGED TEAL ♂
In flight shows white belly and pale blue forewing patches.
• female has longer bill.

CINNAMON TEAL ♀
Female is darker brown with longer bill.

Flight Pattern
Swift, sometimes erratic, direct flight.

• **POPULATION** Common. Increasing.

• **CONSERVATION** Vulnerable to ingesting spent lead shot from bottom mud while feeding.

Nest Identification	Grass, twigs, feathers, and leaves • lined with down • usually among grasses and weeds of meadows, sometimes in open woodlands or brush within 200 feet of water • built by female • 6–18 cream, light olive, buff, or dull white eggs; elliptical to subelliptical, 1.8 inches long.
Shape ꒰ Location ᐧᐧᐧ	

Plumage Sexes differ	Habitat ～～ ⩔	Migration Migratory	Weight 12.8 ounces

DATE _____ TIME _____ LOCATION _____

Family ANATIDAE	Species *Aythya valisineria*	Length 19–24 inches	Wingspan 28–36 inches

CANVASBACK

A sloping profile from the front of its crown to the tip of its long dark bill distinguishes this bird. It is one of the largest and heaviest ducks in North America. At a distance the male appears white with a black rear and breast. The long neck and head are rich rust-red. The female is grayer with a rusty tint to the neck and head.

- **SONG** Male makes grunt or croak; female makes quack.
- **BEHAVIOR** A wary species that often rafts well away from the shoreline. Flies high, frequently in formations.

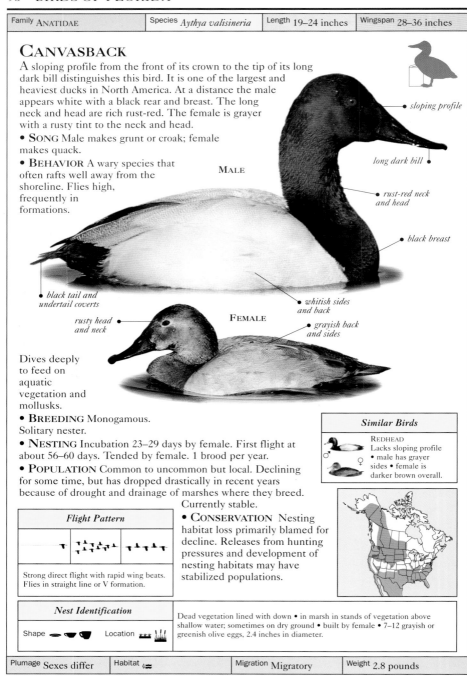

sloping profile

long dark bill

MALE

rust-red neck and head

black breast

black tail and undertail coverts

whitish sides and back

rusty head and neck

FEMALE

grayish back and sides

Dives deeply to feed on aquatic vegetation and mollusks.

- **BREEDING** Monogamous. Solitary nester.
- **NESTING** Incubation 23–29 days by female. First flight at about 56–60 days. Tended by female. 1 brood per year.
- **POPULATION** Common to uncommon but local. Declining for some time, but has dropped drastically in recent years because of drought and drainage of marshes where they breed. Currently stable.
- **CONSERVATION** Nesting habitat loss primarily blamed for decline. Releases from hunting pressures and development of nesting habitats may have stabilized populations.

Similar Birds

REDHEAD
Lacks sloping profile • male has grayer sides • female is darker brown overall.

Flight Pattern

Strong direct flight with rapid wing beats. Flies in straight line or V formation.

Nest Identification

Shape ● ◗ ◖   Location 🌾 🌿

Dead vegetation lined with down • in marsh in stands of vegetation above shallow water; sometimes on dry ground • built by female • 7–12 grayish or greenish olive eggs, 2.4 inches in diameter.

Plumage Sexes differ	Habitat 🌊	Migration Migratory	Weight 2.8 pounds

DATE _____ TIME_____ LOCATION _____

Family ANATIDAE	Species *Aythya americana*	Length 18–22 inches	Wingspan 29–35 inches

REDHEAD

A diving duck of freshwater marshes in summer, this bird congregates in large numbers on marine bays, estuaries, and big lakes in winter. The male's golden yellow eye is the most striking of North American waterfowl. In flight both sexes show a broad gray trailing edge to the wing.

round rufous-brown head

• **SONG** Silent most of year. During courtship male utters mewing sounds, *whee-ough* or *keyair*. Also makes low trilling *rrrrrr*. Female has grating *squak*.

• **BEHAVIOR** Diving duck. Crepuscular activities, including flight and feeding. Some feeding at night.

smoky gray upperparts and sides

black upper and lower tail coverts

black breast

MALE

blue-gray bill with black tip and white subterminal ring

pale at base of bill and on chin

rounded head

Primary diet of aquatic vegetation. Female appears to take initiative in courtship, often chasing males.

• **BREEDING** Monogamous. Brood parasite.

FEMALE

• **NESTING** Incubation 23–29 days by female. Young leave nest about 1 day after hatching. First flight at 56–73 days. Young tended by female but find own food. 1 brood per year.

• **POPULATION** Locally common. Declining in East. Far fewer than historical levels. Decrease due to loss of nesting habitat to agriculture, draining of wetlands, and drought.

• **CONSERVATION** Strictly regulated with hunting bag limits; some regions have no harvesting.

Similar Birds	
	CANVASBACK Male is whiter on sides and back; longer all-dark bill; sloping profile.
	GREATER SCAUP **LESSER SCAUP** Pale color on wings of female does not extend to primaries.
	RING-NECKED DUCK Female has peaked head.

Flight Pattern
Rapid direct flight with strong wing beats. Flies in V formation.

Nest Identification	
Shape ⬭ 🥚 Location 🌱🌱🌱	Dead vegetation and down anchored to standing growth • on bed of reeds and cattails connected to vegetation or set in thick marsh grasses above water • built by female • 9–14 pale olive, buff, or dull white eggs, 2.4 inches long • number of eggs hard to determine because Females lay eggs in nests of other Redheads.

Plumage Sexes differ	Habitat 〰️ 〰️〰️	Migration Migratory	Weight 2.6 pounds

DATE _____ TIME _____ LOCATION _____

Family ANATIDAE	Species *Aythya collaris*	Length 14–18 inches	Wingspan 24–30 inches

RING-NECKED DUCK

This puffy-headed diving duck with a peaked crown prefers small freshwater ponds, wooded lakes, and swamps. On water the male appears dark with whitish gray sides separated from the black breast by a white crescent that is clearly discernible at a distance. Both sexes have a white ring on the bill, white bellies, bluish gray legs and feet, and show a gray wing stripe in flight. The cinnamon ring at the base of the neck, which gives the duck its name, is a poor field mark, seen only at close range in good light.

peaked black head with purplish gloss

MALE

blue-gray bill with black tip and broad white subterminal ring

pale gray sides and flanks

black tail and back

black breast and neck

peaked head

white eye ring and thin postocular stripe

FEMALE

pale face at base of bill, chin, and throat

• **SONG** Generally silent. Male makes a faint wheezy whistle; female makes harsh *deeeer*.

• **BEHAVIOR** Swims lightly with head up. Excellent diver. Aquatic plants more than 80 percent of diet. Feeds on bottom as deep as 40 feet below surface.

• **BREEDING** Monogamous. Solitary nester.

• **NESTING** Incubation 25–29 days by female. Young leave nest in 12–24 hours. First flight after 49–56 days. Young tended by female but find own food. 1 brood per year.

• **POPULATION** Fairly common and widespread. Stable or increasing.

• **CONSERVATION** As with other ducks that feed on the bottom, may ingest lead shot and be susceptible to lead poisoning.

Similar Birds

♂ ♀ **GREATER SCAUP**
LESSER SCAUP
White wing stripe • male has gray back • female has white ring around bill.

♂ ♀ **TUFTED DUCK**
Males have white flanks • head rounded with tuft on back of crown; both sexes lack broad white band on bill • female lacks pale eye line; has shorter tuft on crown.

Flight Pattern

Direct flight with rapid wing beats in loose flocks.

Nest Identification

Shape ____ Location ____

Grasses, sedges, and weeds • lined with down and marsh plants • on dry hammock, clump of brush, or floating mat of vegetation, close to open water or just above water in marsh border of pond or slough • built by female • 6–14 olive, gray, olive-brown, or green-buff eggs; elliptical to oval, 2.3 inches long.

Plumage Sexes differ	Habitat	Migration Migratory	Weight 1.6 pounds

DATE _____ TIME _____ LOCATION _____

Family ANATIDAE	Species *Aythya marila*	Length 15–20 inches	Wingspan 30–34 inches

GREATER SCAUP

Breeding farther north than related species, this large diving duck prefers ponds and lakes in summer. It winters primarily along the coast, often in floating flocks or "rafts" of tens of thousands. The color of the gloss on the male's head usually greenish. From a distance on the water males appear black in front, white in the middle, and black behind. In flight the white wing stripe extends onto the primaries.

rounded black head with greenish gloss

blue-gray bill

MALE

- **SONG** Usually quiet. Common note is loud *scaup*. Courting males make soft whistled *week-week-whew*; female makes low *harrrr*.

finely barred gray flanks and back

black neck and breast

black tail and tail coverts

white sides and belly

- **BEHAVIOR** Diving duck. Often winters in huge flocks. Dives to 20 feet below surface to feed on variety of insects, plants, and vertebrates in summer. Diet at sea primarily mollusks and vegetable matter.

white around face at base of bill

dark brown upperparts

JUVENILE

- **BREEDING** Monogamous. May nest in colonies.

white belly

- **NESTING** Incubation 24–28 days by female. Precocial young led to water shortly after hatching. First flight at 35–42 days. Young tended by female but find own food. 1 brood per year.

gray legs and feet

FEMALE

Similar Birds

LESSER SCAUP
Smaller • male has grayer sides; more pointed head with usually purplish gloss
• females similar; white on wing does not extend onto primaries

- **POPULATION** Common to uncommon. Abundant in winter, with most individuals wintering along seacoasts.

- **CONSERVATION** Heavy winter concentrations in coastal bays may be vulnerable to oil spills and other pollution.

Flight Pattern
Direct flight with strong rapid wing beats.

Nest Identification	
Shape ⚬ Location	Lined with dead plant material and down • usually very close to water on an island, shoreline, or mats of floating vegetation • built by female • 5–11 dark olive-buff eggs, 2.5 inches long.

Plumage Sexes differ	Habitat	Migration Migratory	Weight 2.1 pounds

DATE _____ TIME_____ LOCATION _____

| Family ANATIDAE | Species *Aythya affinis* | Length 15–18 inches | Wingspan 24–33 inches |

LESSER SCAUP

Like the very similar Greater Scaup, at a distance the male appears dark in front, white in the middle, and dark behind. The Lesser Scaup has a more pointed head. The gloss on the male's head is usually purplish. In flight the white wing stripe confined to the secondaries. The Lesser Scaup is more commonly seen inland in winter than the Greater Scaup and is perhaps the most abundant diving duck in North America.

pointed black head with purple gloss

MALE

bluish gray bill

medium gray barring on back and flanks

- **SONG** Courting males utter low, whistled *whew*. Females make odd

black tail and tail coverts

black breast and neck

white at base of bill

dark brown head, neck, breast, and upperparts

rattling purr, *kwuh-h-h-h*.

mottled brown sides

- **BEHAVIOR** Diving duck. Behavior similar to closely related Greater Scaup. Diet varies with habitat but fairly evenly distributed between plant and animal materials.

FEMALE

- **BREEDING** Monogamous. Solitary nester.
- **NESTING** Incubation 21–28 days by female. Precocial young leave nest shortly after hatching. First flight after 45–50 days. Young tended by female but find own food.
- **POPULATION** Common. Slight decrease in 20th century.

Similar Birds
GREATER SCAUP Larger; white wing stripe extends through secondaries and onto primaries • male has whiter sides; more rounded head.

- **CONSERVATION** Deaths due to fishing nets and lines may be significant. Like many other waterfowl, ingests lead shot on bottom while feeding, often resulting in death. Increased use of steel shot intended to eliminate this.

Flight Pattern
Swift direct flight with strong wing beats.

Nest Identification	
Shape · Location	Addition of some grasses • lined with down • on dry land close to water, often on islands, in tall prairie grass • built by female • 6–15 olive or olive-buff eggs; elliptical to nearly oval, 2.3 inches long.

| Plumage Sexes differ | Habitat | Migration Migratory | Weight 1.9 pounds |

DATE _____ TIME_____ LOCATION _____

Family ANATIDAE	Species *Melanitta perspicillata*	Length 17–21 inches	Wingspan 30–36 inches

SURF SCOTER

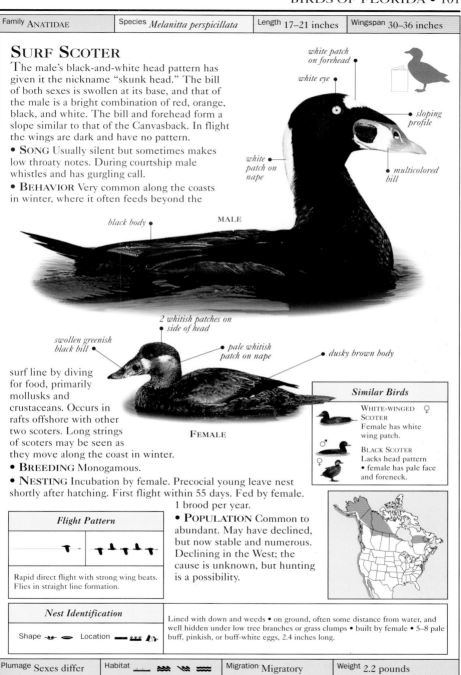

The male's black-and-white head pattern has given it the nickname "skunk head." The bill of both sexes is swollen at its base, and that of the male is a bright combination of red, orange, black, and white. The bill and forehead form a slope similar to that of the Canvasback. In flight the wings are dark and have no pattern.

- **SONG** Usually silent but sometimes makes low throaty notes. During courtship male whistles and has gurgling call.
- **BEHAVIOR** Very common along the coasts in winter, where it often feeds beyond the

white patch on forehead

white eye

sloping profile

white patch on nape

multicolored bill

black body

MALE

2 whitish patches on side of head

swollen greenish black bill

pale whitish patch on nape

dusky brown body

surf line by diving for food, primarily mollusks and crustaceans. Occurs in rafts offshore with other two scoters. Long strings of scoters may be seen as they move along the coast in winter.

FEMALE

- **BREEDING** Monogamous.
- **NESTING** Incubation by female. Precocial young leave nest shortly after hatching. First flight within 55 days. Fed by female. 1 brood per year.
- **POPULATION** Common to abundant. May have declined, but now stable and numerous. Declining in the West; the cause is unknown, but hunting is a possibility.

Similar Birds

WHITE-WINGED ♀ SCOTER
Female has white wing patch.

BLACK SCOTER ♂♀
Lacks head pattern
• female has pale face and foreneck.

Flight Pattern

Rapid direct flight with strong wing beats. Flies in straight line formation.

Nest Identification

Shape ⚬ ⚬   Location ▬ ⚬⚬⚬ 🌲🌳

Lined with down and weeds • on ground, often some distance from water, and well hidden under low tree branches or grass clumps • built by female • 5–8 pale buff, pinkish, or buff-white eggs, 2.4 inches long.

Plumage Sexes differ	Habitat ▬ ≈≈ ⌇≈ ≈≈	Migration Migratory	Weight 2.2 pounds

DATE _____ TIME_____ LOCATION _____

Family ANATIDAE	Species *Melanitta nigra*	Length 17–21 inches	Wingspan 30–35 inches

BLACK SCOTER

One of the large sea ducks, most birds of this species are seen on wintering grounds along both coasts. The male is the only all-black duck in North America. In flight both sexes show a silvery gray sheen on the flight feathers that contrasts with the black linings of the underwings. Wings make a whistling sound in flight. Males often winter further north than females, keeping in tight-knit flocks on the water. Adult males have brownish black feet and legs.

all-black plumage

yellow-orange knob on black bill

MALE

sooty brown cap

dark bill

center line to hindneck and body

pale brownish gray cheeks, sides of head, and foreneck

brownish black legs and feet

FEMALE

• **SONG** Usually silent. Male's melancholy mellow *cour-loo* thought by some to be the most musical duck call. In courtship male whistles; female has abrasive *cour-loo*.

• **BEHAVIOR** Diving duck. Usually feeds in shallower more protected waters about 25 feet deep. Primary diet is mollusks.

• **BREEDING** Monogamous.

• **NESTING** Incubation 27–28 days by female. Precocial young; first flight at about 46 days. Female tends young but leaves after 7-21 days. 1 brood per year.

• **POPULATION** Common to fairly common; casual to uncommon in the winter in interior. Declining.

• **CONSERVATION** Vulnerable to coastal oil spills.

Similar Birds
♂ WHITE-WINGED SCOTER SURF SCOTER
♂ Both sexes show white patches on head in all plumages.

Flight Pattern
Strong direct flight with rapid wing beats. Flies in straight line and V formation.

Nest Identification	
Shape ⌣ ⬭ Location	Coarse grass • lined with feathers • on ground hidden in standing grass or under shrub • built by female • 5–8 buff to pink-buff eggs; elliptical to oval, 2.5 x 1.7 inches.

Plumage Sexes differ	Habitat	Migration Migratory	Weight 2.4 pounds

DATE _____ TIME_____ LOCATION _____

Family ANATIDAE	Species *Bucephala albeola*	Length 13–16 inches	Wingspan 20–24 inches

BUFFLEHEAD

The name of this large-headed duck, which means buffalo-headed or ox-headed, belies the Bufflehead's agility in flying, swimming, and diving. It is the smallest diving duck, but it is one of the best divers. In flight the male's pink legs and feet are bright against white underparts, and a white patch crosses the entire inner wing; female shows white in the secondaries only. These birds nest only in North America.

• **SONG** Squeaky whistle and low squealing or growling call.

large white patch from eye to crown

large dark head with green to purple gloss in good light

black back

mostly white body

small bill

MALE

In courtship makes loud grating or chattering noise. Female has a harsh quack, *ec-ec-ec* and buzzy *cuc-cuc-cuc*.

• **BEHAVIOR** Can take off directly from water unlike other diving ducks. Uses feet to swim underwater. Dives in groups for safety, leaving "lookouts" on surface. Eats aquatic insects, larvae, snails, small fish, and aquatic plant seeds. On saltwater eats shrimp and other crustaceans, shellfish, and snails. Male performs head-bobbing display in courtship.

small white cheek patch

gray-brown body

FEMALE

white underparts

• **BREEDING** Monogamous. Solitary nester.

• **NESTING** Incubation 28–33 days by female. Precocial young leave nest by jumping out of tree cavity within 1 day of hatching. Tended by female. First flight at 50–55 days. 1 brood per year.

Similar Birds

HOODED MERGANSER ♂
Larger; brown sides; spikelike bill; large crest that can be fanned or lowered.

RUDDY DUCK ♂
Winter male resembles female Bufflehead
• longer bill and tail; large white cheek patch.

Flight Pattern

Swift direct flight with rapid wing beats.

• **POPULATION** Common but has declined.

• **BIRDHOUSES** Will use nest boxes located near water.

• **CONSERVATION** Much less numerous now due to unrestricted shooting in the 20th century and loss of habitat.

Nest Identification

Shape ▨² Location

No material added to nest • will use wooden box placed in tree • 8–10 ivory-yellow, light olive-buff, or cream to pale buff eggs; elliptical to oval in shape, 2 x 1.5 inches.

Plumage Sexes differ	Habitat ～～	Migration Migratory	Weight 1.0 pound

DATE _____ TIME_____ LOCATION _____

| Family ANATIDAE | Species *Bucephala clangula* | Length 16–20 inches | Wingspan 25–32 inches |

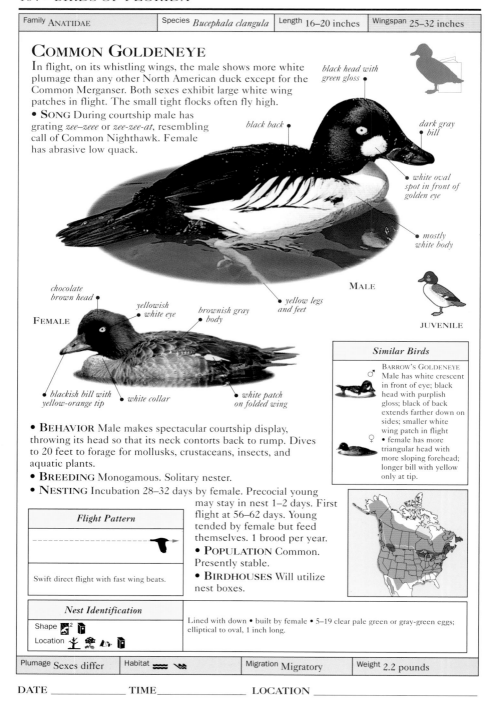

COMMON GOLDENEYE

In flight, on its whistling wings, the male shows more white plumage than any other North American duck except for the Common Merganser. Both sexes exhibit large white wing patches in flight. The small tight flocks often fly high.

black head with green gloss

- **SONG** During courtship male has grating *zee–zeee* or *zee-zee-at*, resembling call of Common Nighthawk. Female has abrasive low quack.

black back

dark gray bill

white oval spot in front of golden eye

mostly white body

MALE

chocolate brown head

yellowish white eye

brownish gray body

yellow legs and feet

FEMALE

JUVENILE

blackish bill with yellow-orange tip

white collar

white patch on folded wing

Similar Birds

BARROW'S GOLDENEYE
♂ Male has white crescent in front of eye; black head with purplish gloss; black of back extends farther down on sides; smaller white wing patch in flight
♀ • female has more triangular head with more sloping forehead; longer bill with yellow only at tip.

- **BEHAVIOR** Male makes spectacular courtship display, throwing its head so that its neck contorts back to rump. Dives to 20 feet to forage for mollusks, crustaceans, insects, and aquatic plants.
- **BREEDING** Monogamous. Solitary nester.
- **NESTING** Incubation 28–32 days by female. Precocial young may stay in nest 1–2 days. First flight at 56–62 days. Young tended by female but feed themselves. 1 brood per year.
- **POPULATION** Common. Presently stable.
- **BIRDHOUSES** Will utilize nest boxes.

Flight Pattern

Swift direct flight with fast wing beats.

Nest Identification

Shape

Location

Lined with down • built by female • 5–19 clear pale green or gray-green eggs; elliptical to oval, 1 inch long.

| Plumage Sexes differ | Habitat 〰 〰 | Migration Migratory | Weight 2.2 pounds |

DATE _____ TIME_____ LOCATION _____

| Family ANATIDAE | Species *Lophodytes cucullatus* | Length 16–19 inches | Wingspan 24–26 inches |

HOODED MERGANSER

The smallest native North American merganser has the largest crest. The male's crest is a vertical white fan bordered with black that can be raised and lowered during display. When the crest is folded, the head appears puffy. Flying birds of both sexes show a white wing patch on the secondaries. On water the male's white breast broken by two black lines in front of the chestnut sides serves as a good field mark.

- **SONG** Hoarse grunts and chatters. Displaying male gives rolling froglike *crrrroooo*; sometimes utters hollow pop.
- **BEHAVIOR** Male raises and lowers crest frequently in display. Excellent diver.

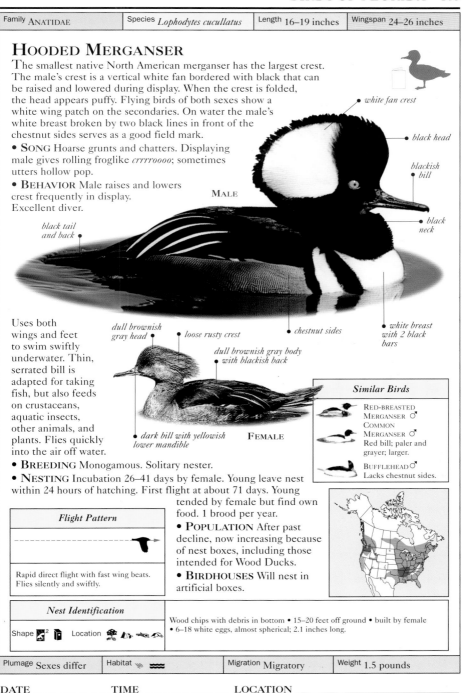

white fan crest

black head

blackish bill

black neck

MALE

black tail and back

dull brownish gray head

loose rusty crest

chestnut sides

white breast with 2 black bars

dull brownish gray body with blackish back

dark bill with yellowish lower mandible

FEMALE

Uses both wings and feet to swim swiftly underwater. Thin, serrated bill is adapted for taking fish, but also feeds on crustaceans, aquatic insects, other animals, and plants. Flies quickly into the air off water.

- **BREEDING** Monogamous. Solitary nester.
- **NESTING** Incubation 26–41 days by female. Young leave nest within 24 hours of hatching. First flight at about 71 days. Young tended by female but find own food. 1 brood per year.
- **POPULATION** After past decline, now increasing because of nest boxes, including those intended for Wood Ducks.
- **BIRDHOUSES** Will nest in artificial boxes.

Similar Birds

RED-BREASTED MERGANSER ♂
COMMON MERGANSER ♂
Red bill; paler and grayer; larger.

BUFFLEHEAD ♂
Lacks chestnut sides.

Flight Pattern

Rapid direct flight with fast wing beats. Flies silently and swiftly.

Nest Identification

Shape ▨² ▯ Location 🦆 🔥 🪶

Wood chips with debris in bottom • 15–20 feet off ground • built by female • 6–18 white eggs, almost spherical; 2.1 inches long.

| Plumage Sexes differ | Habitat 〰 〜 | Migration Migratory | Weight 1.5 pounds |

DATE _____ TIME_____ LOCATION _____

Family ANATIDAE	Species *Mergus merganser*	Length 22–27 inches	Wingspan 31–37 inches

COMMON MERGANSER

The Common Merganser is the largest merganser in North America. The male's mostly white body, dark head, and red bill easily distinguish it from the other mergansers at a distances or in flight. This is the only merganser in North America in which the female is crested and the male is not.

• **SONG** Male makes harsh croaks; female makes loud harsh *karr karr*.

• **BEHAVIOR** Expert diver pursues small fish under water. Also feeds on mollusks,

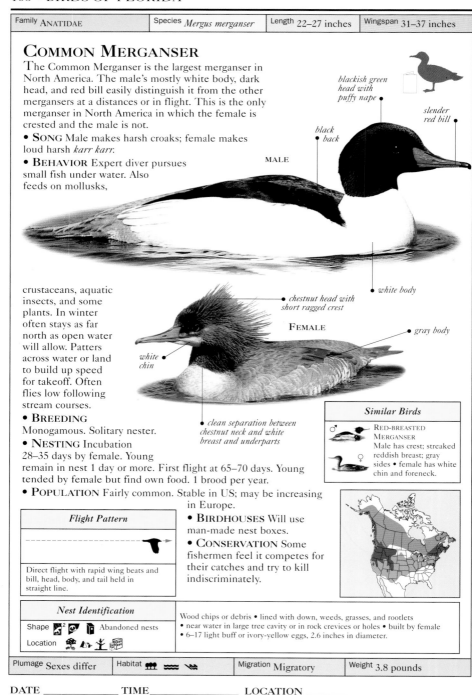

blackish green head with puffy nape

slender red bill

black back

MALE

white body

crustaceans, aquatic insects, and some plants. In winter often stays as far north as open water will allow. Patters across water or land to build up speed for takeoff. Often flies low following stream courses.

chestnut head with short ragged crest

FEMALE

gray body

white chin

• **BREEDING** Monogamous. Solitary nester.

• **NESTING** Incubation 28–35 days by female. Young remain in nest 1 day or more. First flight at 65–70 days. Young tended by female but find own food. 1 brood per year.

clean separation between chestnut neck and white breast and underparts

Similar Birds

♂ **RED-BREASTED MERGANSER** Male has crest; streaked reddish breast; gray sides • female has white chin and foreneck.

• **POPULATION** Fairly common. Stable in US; may be increasing in Europe.

• **BIRDHOUSES** Will use man-made nest boxes.

• **CONSERVATION** Some fishermen feel it competes for their catches and try to kill indiscriminately.

Flight Pattern

Direct flight with rapid wing beats and bill, head, body, and tail held in straight line.

Nest Identification

Shape ▨² ▧ ▨ Abandoned nests

Location ▦ ▲ ⚘ ▥

Wood chips or debris • lined with down, weeds, grasses, and rootlets • near water in large tree cavity or in rock crevices or holes • built by female • 6–17 light buff or ivory-yellow eggs, 2.6 inches in diameter.

Plumage Sexes differ	Habitat ⚏ 〰 ⤳	Migration Migratory	Weight 3.8 pounds

DATE _____ TIME_____ LOCATION _____

Family ANATIDAE	Species *Mergus serrator*	Length 16–26 inches	Wingspan 31–35 inches

RED-BREASTED MERGANSER

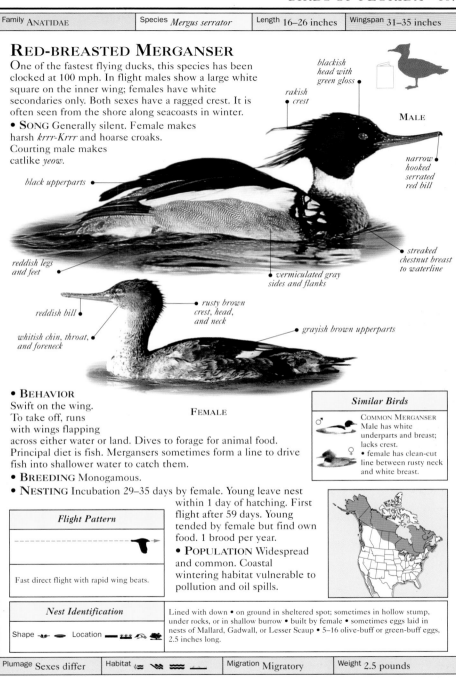

One of the fastest flying ducks, this species has been clocked at 100 mph. In flight males show a large white square on the inner wing; females have white secondaries only. Both sexes have a ragged crest. It is often seen from the shore along seacoasts in winter.

- **SONG** Generally silent. Female makes harsh *krrr-Krrr* and hoarse croaks. Courting male makes catlike *yeow*.

blackish head with green gloss

rakish crest

MALE

narrow hooked serrated red bill

black upperparts

streaked chestnut breast to waterline

reddish legs and feet

vermiculated gray sides and flanks

rusty brown crest, head, and neck

reddish bill

grayish brown upperparts

whitish chin, throat, and foreneck

FEMALE

- **BEHAVIOR**
Swift on the wing. To take off, runs with wings flapping across either water or land. Dives to forage for animal food. Principal diet is fish. Mergansers sometimes form a line to drive fish into shallower water to catch them.

- **BREEDING** Monogamous.

- **NESTING** Incubation 29–35 days by female. Young leave nest within 1 day of hatching. First flight after 59 days. Young tended by female but find own food. 1 brood per year.

- **POPULATION** Widespread and common. Coastal wintering habitat vulnerable to pollution and oil spills.

Similar Birds

♂ COMMON MERGANSER Male has white underparts and breast; lacks crest.

♀ • female has clean-cut line between rusty neck and white breast.

Flight Pattern
Fast direct flight with rapid wing beats.

Nest Identification	
Shape ⚬ ⬯ Location ▬ ▦ ◭ ⬭	Lined with down • on ground in sheltered spot; sometimes in hollow stump, under rocks, or in shallow burrow • built by female • sometimes eggs laid in nests of Mallard, Gadwall, or Lesser Scaup • 5–16 olive-buff or green-buff eggs, 2.5 inches long.

Plumage Sexes differ	Habitat	Migration Migratory	Weight 2.5 pounds

DATE _____ TIME_____ LOCATION _____

Family ANATIDAE	Species *Oxyura jamaicensis*	Length 14–16 inches	Wingspan 21–24 inches

RUDDY DUCK

This big-headed chunky duck has a long stiff tail that is often cocked and fanned forward. Wings are uniform in color. In winter males become gray-brown with a gray bill. In breeding season found in pairs or small loose groups on freshwater lakes and ponds. After nesting, may occur in large flocks; in winter it can be found on salt bays.

• **SONG** Usually silent. In courtship male utters continual *chuck-chuck-chuck-chuck-churrr*.

• **BEHAVIOR** Diving duck that can sink slowly beneath the surface like a grebe. When disturbed often swims away underwater instead of flying away. Gray legs and feet are placed so far beneath the body that it cannot walk upright. Primary diet of vegetable materials. A relatively tame bird.

• **BREEDING** Monogamous.

• **NESTING** Incubation 23–26 days by female. Young leave nest within a day of hatching. First flight at 42–48 days. Young tended by female but feed themselves. 1 brood per year, sometimes 2 in the South.

• **POPULATION** Fairly common to common. Current levels are lower than in the past.

• **CONSERVATION** Reasons for decline unknown, but this bird is very tame and easily killed by hunters. Shallow-water nesting areas are subject to draining for agriculture and droughts.

blackish cap reaches below eye

long stiff black tail

blue bill

white cheeks

MALE

rust-red body

whitish belly with light brown barring

WINTER PLUMAGE

blackish gray bill

white cheek with dark brown horizontal streak

brown-gray upperparts

pale underparts with fine brown barring

FEMALE

Similar Birds

♂ MASKED DUCK
Male lacks white cheek
♀ • female has 2 dark lines across face
• population very local.

♂ CINNAMON TEAL
Lacks stiff tail and white cheeks; large
♀ pale blue forewing patch in flight
• female lacks line through face.

Flight Pattern	
Jerky direct flight with rapid wing beats.	

Nest Identification	
Shape	Location

Grasses and cattails • lined with down • in dense marsh vegetation over shallow water • sometimes uses abandoned nests • built by female • 5–17 creamy white or nest-stained eggs, 2.5 inches long • eggs huge compared to body size and similar in size to those laid by much larger ducks.

Plumage Sexes differ	Habitat	Migration Migratory	Weight 1.3 pounds

DATE _____ TIME_____ LOCATION _____

Family ACCIPITRIDAE	Species *Pandion haliaetus*	Length 21–24 inches	Wingspan 54–72 inches

OSPREY

A kindred of other diurnal birds of prey, the Osprey is so distinctive it is sometimes placed in it own family. Its large size and uniquely curved claws allow the Osprey to carry a large fish a considerable distance to feed to its young in the nest. Occasionally an eagle dives upon an Osprey carrying a fish, forces a release, and catches the fish for itself before the fish hits the water.

mostly white head

dark brown upperparts with purplish gloss

broad black mark through cheeks and sides of neck

clear white belly

long tail with narrow black bars

toes equal in length on claws curved into one-third of a circle

- **SONG** Series of loud whistled *kyews* or melodious whistle of *chewk-chewk-chewk* or *cheap-cheap-cheap*.

- **BEHAVIOR** Eats mainly fish. Dives into water to catch prey from 30–100 feet above surface. Holds fish with both feet, stops to shake water out of feathers, points fish head forward to decrease wind resistance, and carries to perch or to feed young. Often flies with distinctive crook or kink in wing bent at wrist, which has a black patch.

- **BREEDING** Monogamous. Colonial or solitary nester.

- **NESTING** Incubation 32–43 days by both sexes; however, female does more, while male brings food. Semialtricial young stay in nest 48–59 days. Fed by both parents. 1 brood per year.

- **POPULATION** Uncommon inland; species is fairly common in its coastal range.

- **BIRDHOUSES** Osprey will build nest on man-made cartwheel on pole or on platforms built in marshes.

JUVENILE

Similar Birds

BALD EAGLE
Entirely white head and tail; crown held flat; dark underparts and underwings • juvenile has entirely dark head and patchy tannish white underwings.

- **CONSERVATION** Endangered in 1950s because of chemical pollution (especially DDT), but has since made a comeback, at least partly by transplanting young into areas where entire populations had been extirpated.

Flight Pattern
Deep, slow wing beats alternate with glides; sometimes soars on thermals.

Nest Identification	
Shape ⌒⌒ Location 🌳 ⛰ 📮 ⚓🏠	Sticks, sod, cow dung, seaweed, rubbish, and similar material • up to 200 feet above ground in dead or live trees near or over water, or atop telephone poles or bridges • built by both sexes • usually 3 white or pinkish eggs marked with brown and olive; 2.4 x 1 inches long.

Plumage Sexes similar	Habitat 〰〰 🦆	Migration Migratory	Weight 3.1 pounds

DATE 07/04 _____ TIME _____ LOCATION _____

| Family ACCIPITRIDAE | Species *Elanoides forficatus* | Length 19–25 inches | Wingspan 45–50 inches |

SWALLOW-TAILED KITE

Flying swiftly with its wings cleaving the air and its forked tail opening and closing like scissors, the Swallow-tailed Kite is a breathtaking sight. The largest of the North American kites, this bird resembles a huge Barn Swallow. The black upperparts contrast sharply with the white head and underparts. Never taking time to hover, it will drop down to skim the surface of water to bathe or drink and then swoop suddenly up over the treetops. A tropical species that in North America is normally found only in the Southeast in the spring and summer, during spring migration individuals may "overshoot" and appear as far north as New England.

• **SONG** Utters shrill *ee-ee-ee* or *pee-pee-pee.* When several fly together they make sweet shrill cries of *peat, peat, peat; klee, klee, klee;* or soft whistles.

• **BEHAVIOR** Forms flocks in winter or migration. Catches and eats food while flying. Feeds on insects such as bees, dragonflies, crickets, cicadas, and beetles. Also consumes small snakes, lizards, frogs, and small birds, which often are taken from the treetops.

• **BREEDING** Monogamous. Forms loose colonies.

• **NESTING** Incubation 24–28 days by both sexes, but mostly by female. Semialtricial young stay in nest 36–42 days. Fed by both sexes. Probably only 1 brood per year.

• **POPULATION** Common.

• **CONSERVATION** Listed as endangered in South Carolina. Disappeared from many areas in early 20th century. Population now apparently stable and slowly expanding range.

long pointed wings with black flight feathers and white wing linings

snow-white head and hind neck

black bill

dark brown to red eyes

snow-white underparts

15–16-inch-long black tail with deep fork

Similar Birds

MISSISSIPPI KITE
Slightly notched black tail; gray underparts and head.

Flight Pattern

Buoyant flight with deep slow wing beats and glides; a master at soaring on thermals and updrafts.

Nest Identification

Shape   Location

Sticks, twigs, moss, and pine needles • lined with leaves and lichen • usually in treetop, 60–130 feet above ground, concealed by thick foliage • built by both sexes • 2–3 white or creamy white eggs marked with brown, sometimes lavender, often concentrated at end; elliptical to short subelliptical, 1.8 x 1.25 inches long.

| Plumage Sexes similar | Habitat | Migration Migratory | Weight 15.6 ounces |

DATE 07/01   TIME_____   LOCATION _____
07/04

Family ACCIPITRIDAE	Species *Elanus leucurus*	Length 15–17 inches	Wingspan 40–42 inches

WHITE-TAILED KITE

Sometimes called the white hawk, the White-tailed Kite soars and glides like a small gull. When seen from a distance, this gregarious bird appears completely white. Previously called the Black-shouldered Kite, the white linings of the underwing are broken distally by a black "thumb" mark on the wrist. It is the only North American kite to hover while hunting, with tail down and often with legs dangling, over savanna, riparian woodland, marshes, grassy foothills, or the cultivated fields it searches for food. It is a master at soaring on thermals and glides long distances after reaching considerable heights. Juveniles' underparts and head are lightly streaked with rufous.

orange to reddish brown eyes

black bill

pale gray upperparts

black patch on shoulders

white underparts

- **SONG** Brief whistled *keep, keep, keep.*
- **BEHAVIOR** Active hunter. Pauses to hover and study ground before swooping on prey. Eats voles, field mice, pocket gophers, ground squirrels, shrews, small birds, small snakes, lizards, frogs, grasshoppers, crickets, and beetles. Often roosts communally.

buff-yellow feet and legs

long white tail

JUVENILE

- **BREEDING** Monogamous. Nests built close together, sometimes in loose colonies.
- **NESTING** Incubation 30 days by female. Young stay in nest 35–40 days. Fed by both sexes. Male hunts for food and drives away crows and other hawks. Up to 2 broods per year.

Similar Birds

MISSISSIPPI KITE
Lacks black shoulders and black "thumb" mark under wing; has black tail.

- **POPULATION** Common but local. Expanded in last half of 20th century.
- **CONSERVATION** Some concern about the spraying of pesticides and insecticides in open environments frequented by this species.

Flight Pattern

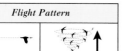

Hunts by flying slowly, gracefully, gull-like, with slow measured deep wing beats. Soars on thermals and updrafts.

Nest Identification		
Shape 🪹 Location 🌳 🌲	Sticks and twigs • lined with grasses, dry stubble, weed stems, and rootlets • in oaks, cottonwood, or eucalyptus, about 15–60 feet above ground • built by both sexes • 3–6 white eggs, heavily blotched with rich brown; ovate to oval, 1.7 x 1.3 inches.	

Plumage Sexes similar	Habitat 🌾〰️〰️	Migration Nonmigratory	Weight Undetermined

DATE _____ TIME_____ LOCATION _____

Family ACCIPITRIDAE	Species *Rostrhamus sociabilis*	Length 16–18 inches	Wingspan 45 inches

SNAIL KITE

Also known as the Everglades Kite, this resident of subtropical freshwater marshes has one of the most specialized diets of all birds. It eats only snails of the genus *Pomacea*, also called the green or apple snail, which lays its tiny white eggs on plant stems a few inches above water. This gregarious bird flies slowly up to 30 feet above the marshes while hunting, always keeping its bill pointed downward in search of freshwater snails. In flight the white tail with broad dark tip is easily seen. The juvenile looks like the female but is heavily streaked below.

- **SONG** Greeting call is grating *kor-ee-ee-a, koree-a*. If disturbed at nest, alarm call is cackling notes resembling those of Osprey.
- **BEHAVIOR** Glides slow and low over marsh, dropping to pick up snail with one foot; flies to perch and uses bill to extract snail from shell. Roosts communally on low bushes often over water.
- **BREEDING** When courting, flies high and then dives repeatedly in short sudden dips with wings folded. Loose colonies or solitary nester.
- **NESTING** Incubation 26–30 days by both sexes. Semialtricial young stay in nest 23–28 days, tended by one parent or the other. 1 brood per year; often 2 when food abundant.
- **POPULATION** Rare to uncommon. Local.
- **CONSERVATION** Florida population endangered. Droughts and man-made canals have drained marshes, reducing snail population. Widespread in tropics, but vulnerable to habitat loss.

extremely hooked thin black bill with reddish base

dark blue-black overall

MALE

long bright orange or red legs

broad dark distal band and narrow gray terminal band

white tail coverts

white over each eye

white chin and cheeks

JUVENILE

dark brown overall

FEMALE

Similar Birds

NORTHERN HARRIER ♂ White patch on rump, not on tail; narrower pointed wings in flight, not paddle-shaped, and held above back in dihedral.

Flight Pattern
Flies on slow shallow wing beats interrupted by short glides.

Nest Identification	
Shape 🐚 Location 🌿🌿	Green or dry sticks and leafy twigs • 3–9 feet above ground in low tree or hammock of marsh grass • built by both sexes, but male does most of work • 2–4 white eggs, sometimes marked with brown; oblong, oval, or short subelliptical, 1.7 inches long.

Plumage Sexes differ	Habitat ⌇	Migration Nonmigratory	Weight 13.3 ounces

DATE _____ TIME_____ LOCATION _____

Family ACCIPITRIDAE	Species *Ictinia mississippiensis*	Length 13–17 inches	Wingspan 34–37 inches

MISSISSIPPI KITE

Far from shy, the Mississippi Kite has been seen chasing bats into caves and flying around horseback riders and cattle to catch insects. This bird is not territorial; several might perch together in trees, even during nesting season. They also gather at communal perches and foraging areas, and often soar communally while hunting insects. As many as 20 birds have been recorded following a herd of livestock for flushed insects. The Mississippi Kite never hovers and has a smooth graceful flight with its white secondary feathers showing.

deep red eyes

pale ash-gray head

gray overall

yellow to red legs

- **SONG** Usually silent. Has alarm call of whistled *kee-e-e*. Also whistles *phee-phew*, *phee-phew*, resembling that of the Osprey.
- **BEHAVIOR** Gracefully catches large flying insects, often eating them in midair. Hunts with flock.
- **BREEDING** Monogamous. Colonial. Little courtship activity occurs on the US breeding grounds as the birds are already paired when they return from wintering in the neotropics.

JUVENILE

solid black tail

Similar Birds

WHITE-TAILED KITE Lighter tail; black shoulder patches; black "thumb" mark under wing.

NORTHERN HARRIER ♂ Male hovers and is larger; dark secondary feathers; white rump patch; facial disk.

- **NESTING** Incubation 31–32 days by both sexes. Young remain in nest 34 days, fed by both sexes. 1 brood per year.
- **POPULATION** Common to fairly common. Expanding range, particularly west of the Mississippi River. Regularly strays as far north as the southern Great Lakes region.

Flight Pattern
Buoyant flight with steady wingbeats; sometimes alternates several wing strokes with short to long glides.

Nest Identification	
Shape Location	Sticks and twigs • lined with green leaves and Spanish moss (where available) • in upper branches, small forks, and occasionally on horizontal lines, 30–135 feet above ground • built by both sexes • 1–3 white or bluish white eggs, unmarked or faintly spotted, often nest-stained.

Plumage Sexes similar	Habitat	Migration Migratory	Weight 12.6 ounces

DATE _____ TIME_____ LOCATION _____

| Family ACCIPITRIDAE | Species *Haliaeetus leucocephalus* | Length 34–43 inches | Wingspan 6–8 feet |

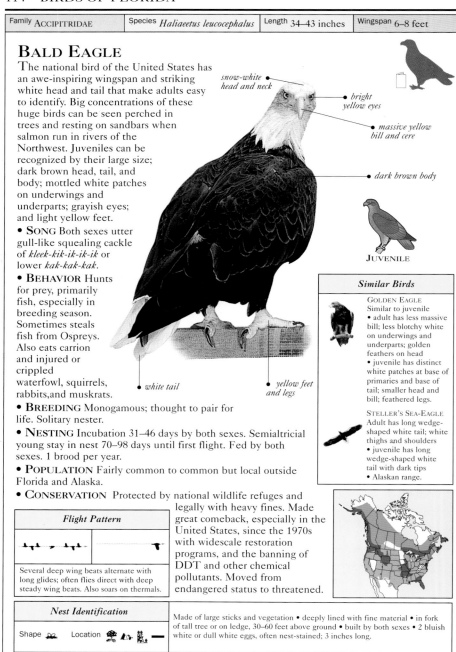

BALD EAGLE

The national bird of the United States has an awe-inspiring wingspan and striking white head and tail that make adults easy to identify. Big concentrations of these huge birds can be seen perched in trees and resting on sandbars when salmon run in rivers of the Northwest. Juveniles can be recognized by their large size; dark brown head, tail, and body; mottled white patches on underwings and underparts; grayish eyes; and light yellow feet.

snow-white head and neck

bright yellow eyes

massive yellow bill and cere

dark brown body

JUVENILE

- **SONG** Both sexes utter gull-like squealing cackle of *kleek-kik-ik-ik-ik* or lower *kak-kak-kak*.

- **BEHAVIOR** Hunts for prey, primarily fish, especially in breeding season. Sometimes steals fish from Ospreys. Also eats carrion and injured or crippled waterfowl, squirrels, rabbits, and muskrats.

white tail

yellow feet and legs

Similar Birds

GOLDEN EAGLE
Similar to juvenile
- adult has less massive bill; less blotchy white on underwings and underparts; golden feathers on head
- juvenile has distinct white patches at base of primaries and base of tail; smaller head and bill; feathered legs.

STELLER'S SEA-EAGLE
Adult has long wedge-shaped white tail; white thighs and shoulders
- juvenile has long wedge-shaped white tail with dark tips
- Alaskan range.

- **BREEDING** Monogamous; thought to pair for life. Solitary nester.

- **NESTING** Incubation 31–46 days by both sexes. Semialtricial young stay in nest 70–98 days until first flight. Fed by both sexes. 1 brood per year.

- **POPULATION** Fairly common to common but local outside Florida and Alaska.

- **CONSERVATION** Protected by national wildlife refuges and legally with heavy fines. Made great comeback, especially in the United States, since the 1970s with widescale restoration programs, and the banning of DDT and other chemical pollutants. Moved from endangered status to threatened.

Flight Pattern

Several deep wing beats alternate with long glides; often flies direct with deep steady wing beats. Also soars on thermals.

Nest Identification

Shape — Location

Made of large sticks and vegetation • deeply lined with fine material • in fork of tall tree or on ledge, 30–60 feet above ground • built by both sexes • 2 bluish white or dull white eggs, often nest-stained; 3 inches long.

| Plumage Sexes similar | Habitat | Migration Migratory | Weight 9.1 pounds |

DATE _____ TIME_____ LOCATION _____

Family ACCIPITRIDAE	Species *Circus cyaneus*	Length 16–24 inches	Wingspan 38–48 inches

NORTHERN HARRIER

Its owl-like facial disk and white rump patch, which is prominent in flight, set the Northern Harrier apart from all other North American falconiformes. Males take several years to acquire their gray-plumaged upperparts. Their wings are long with black-tipped trailing edges, and the outermost four or five primaries are black.

gray upperparts

chestnut spotting on breast and throat

MALE

whitish underparts

- **SONG** Shrill calls *kek, kek, kek* or *keee, keee, keee*, especially around the nest.
- **BEHAVIOR** Hunts using low slow flight that consists of alternately flapping and gliding with the wings held in a shallow V above the back. Often quarters back and forth over low vegetation and can turn and drop rapidly on prey that it may detect initially by sound. Feeds on small mammals, especially rodents up to the size of a small rabbit, frogs, snakes, small birds, carrion, and large insects. Sometimes hunts the edges of grass fires to capture prey driven out by the flames. Courtship flight of males is thrillingly acrobatic.

black wing tips and secondary tips

very long tail

JUVENILE

- **BREEDING** Some pairs monogamous; some males are polygamous with up to 3 mates. Solitary nester. Both sexes very vocal with high-pitched screams when defending nest.
- **NESTING** Incubation 31–32 days by female. Semi-altricial young stay in nest 30–35 days, fed by both sexes. 1 brood per year.
- **POPULATION** Common but declining.

disk of feathers around face

brown upperparts

FEMALE

Similar Birds

ROUGH-LEGGED HAWK ♀
Base of tail (not rump) white; broad blackish subterminal band on tail • does not course low over fields but hunts from perch or by hovering.

- **CONSERVATION** Populations have declined everywhere on its breeding range because of the loss of marshland habitat as well as pesticides. Formerly, many were lost to shooting.

Flight Pattern

Several deep wing beats alternate with glides.

Nest Identification

Shape ⬚ ⬚   Location ⚘ ⚘

Sticks and grass lined with fine material • usually placed on the ground • may be 5 feet above water or marshy terrain • built by both sexes, but female does most construction • 3–9 bluish white eggs, sometimes spotted with brown, 1.8 inches long.

Plumage Sexes differ	Habitat	Migration Some migrate	Weight 12.6 ounces

DATE _____ TIME_____ LOCATION _____

Family ACCIPITRIDAE	Species *Accipiter striatus*	Length 10–14 inches	Wingspan 20–28 inches

SHARP-SHINNED HAWK

A territorial bird, the Sharp-shinned Hawk occasionally strikes humans in defense of its nest. Its name describes its flattened, thin tarsus or shank. This is the smallest of the North American accipiters; the female is larger than the male. The head and neck seem small for its long, slender body. Its long tail has three to four narrow black crossbars, and is squared or notched at the tip. Juveniles have brown upperparts and white underparts with heavy brown streaking.

• *finely streaked red-brown throat*

blue-gray upperparts

red-brown bars across chest and belly

white undertail coverts

long bright yellow legs with "sharp shins"

JUVENILE

• **SONG** When disturbed utters *kek-kek-kek* or *kik-kik-kik*. Call is melancholy cry.

• **BEHAVIOR** Eats mostly small birds, including songbirds, taken off ground or twigs, or in air. Also eats small mammals (including bats), reptiles, grasshoppers, and other larger insects.

• **BREEDING** Monogamous. Solitary nester.

• **NESTING** Incubation 32–35 days by female. Semialtricial young stay in nest 23–27 days. Fed by both sexes. 1 brood per year.

• **POPULATION** Common to fairly common.

• **FEEDERS** Often attracted to concentrations of small birds

square or slightly forked tail

• *narrow white tip on tail*

Similar Birds

COOPER'S HAWK Rounded tail; larger (but female Sharp-shinned approach male Cooper's in size); larger head; more contrast between black crown and face; wide white band on tip of tail (can be tricky because of feather wear); sometimes lightly streaked undertail coverts.

at bird feeders, especially in winter.

• **CONSERVATION** Decline during 1950s through 1970s due to pesticides and heavy metal pollutants in environment. Some comeback in 1980s but is perhaps declining again.

Flight Pattern

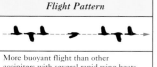

More buoyant flight than other accipiters with several rapid wing beats between glides.

Nest Identification

Shape ⌒ ⌒   Location 🌲🌳

Made of sticks and twigs • lined with strips of bark, grass, and coniferous needles • sometimes in deciduous trees but usually conifers, 10–60 feet above ground, next to trunk • 4–5 white or bluish eggs marked with browns, 1.5 inches long.

Plumage Sexes similar	Habitat 🌿 🌱 🌾	Migration Some migrate	Weight 3.6 ounces

DATE _____ TIME_____ LOCATION _____

Family ACCIPITRIDAE	Species *Accipiter cooperii*	Length 14–21 inches	Wingspan 27–36 inches

COOPER'S HAWK

Sometimes called the Blue Darter or Chicken Hawk by farmers; however, studies show poultry are only a small portion of the Cooper's Hawk's diet. It is named after William Cooper, who was the first person to collect one of these birds and have it identified. Like most hawks, the juvenile has heavily streaked underparts and brown upperparts, whereas adults show blue-gray upperparts. Females are larger than males, and both show a blue-gray back. In flight the long tail appears rounded.

JUVENILE

dark gray or black on top of head

deep red to yellow eyes

yellow cere

white undertail coverts

rounded tail with dark bars and a white band on tip

reddish bars across breast and belly

yellow legs and feet

- **SONG** Alarm call is *kac-kac-kac* or *kuck, kuck kuck, kuck.*
- **BEHAVIOR** Territorial; will not allow similar Sharp-shinned Hawk in same woodland. Attacks poultry, other birds, small mammals, and takes songbirds out of nest. Occasionally eats fish. Sometimes carries prey to water and kills it by drowning. Hunts by waiting in ambush or by dashing in swift low flight through wooded lot; surprises prey and catches it with talons.
- **BREEDING** Monogamous. Solitary nester.
- **NESTING** Incubation 32–36 days by both sexes, but more by female. Semialtricial young stay in nest 27–34 days, fed by both sexes. 1 brood per year.
- **POPULATION** Uncommon to rare. Steadily increasing after bottoming out in 1970s.
- **CONSERVATION** Decline in mid-20th century principally due to pesticides. Stable or increasing in most areas.

Similar Birds

SHARP-SHINNED HAWK Shorter tail with notched or squared end; smaller head; less contrast between back and crown; narrower white band at tip of tail • male much smaller, but female approaches size of male Cooper's.

Flight Pattern

Rapid wing beats followed by short glide; often circles in flight on thermals.

Nest Identification	
Shape ⌒ Location 🌲 🌳	Sticks and twigs • lined with chips, outer bark strips, and occasionally green conifer needles • in crotch of conifer near trunk or in deciduous tree, 10–60 feet above ground • built by both sexes, but male does more • 4–5 bluish white or greenish white eggs, spotted with browns and usually nest-stained; elliptical to subelliptical, 1.5 inches long.

Plumage Sexes similar	Habitat 🌾 🌳	Migration Some migrate	Weight 12.3 ounces

DATE _____ TIME_____ LOCATION _____

Family ACCIPITRIDAE	Species *Buteo lineatus*	Length 17–24 inches	Wingspan 32–50 inches

RED-SHOULDERED HAWK

This bird uses the same territory for years, and even succeeding generations may return to the same territory. The longest recorded continuous use of the same territory is forty-five years. Five races (*lineatus, alleni, extimus, elagans,* and *texanus*) show variations in color and size but all have barred rusty underparts, reddish wing linings, and shoulders with banded tails. In flight the long black tail displays numerous narrow white bands on adults and juveniles. Flight feathers are spotted and barred black and white and show a pale "window" at the base of the outer primaries. Male is larger than female.

• **SONG** Evenly spaced series of clear high loud and often rapidly repeated *kee-ah* or *clee-u clee-u clee-u* notes. Blue Jays can mimic the call perfectly.

• **BEHAVIOR** Stalks prey from perch. Catches and eats small to medium-sized mammals, small reptiles, amphibians, large insects, spiders, earthworms, snails, and an occasional bird. Prefers wet woodlands, often near water and swamps. Often perches low to hunt on posts, utility poles, and low to mid level in trees.

• **BREEDING** Monogamous. Solitary nester.

• **NESTING** Incubation 28 days by both sexes. Semialtricial young stay in nest 35–45 days. Fed by both sexes. 1 brood per year.

• **POPULATION** Fairly common in range.

• **CONSERVATION** Some decline due to habitat loss and human encroachment particularly in West. Pesticides in Midwest interfered with reproduction during the 1970s.

yellow cere

reddish shoulders

extensive pale spotting on upperparts

rust-red barring on underparts

JUVENILE

FLORIDA RACE

yellow feet and legs

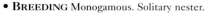

long black tail with numerous narrow white bands

Similar Birds

BROAD-WINGED HAWK Smaller; shorter tail; lacks barring in flight feathers; fewer, wider white tail bands; lacks reddish shoulders; lacks wing windows; peweelike call.

Flight Pattern	

Flies with fairly rapid stiff wing beats; soars on flat wings and glides on slightly drooped wings. Soars on thermals.

Nest Identification	
Shape ⌣⌣ Location 🌳🌿	Made of sticks, twigs, inner bark strips, dry leaves, moss, lichen, and coniferous needles • usually by a tree trunk 10–200 feet above ground • built by both sexes • 2–6 white or bluish white eggs, often nest-stained and marked with brown; short elliptical, 2.1 inches long.

Plumage Sexes similar	Habitat 🐾 🌾 🏡 🌳	Migration Some migrate	Weight 1.1 pounds

DATE 7 7 04 TIME_____ LOCATION _____

Family ACCIPITRIDAE	Species *Buteo platypterus*	Length 13–19 inches	Wingspan 32–39 inches

BROAD-WINGED HAWK

The smallest of the North American buteos is similar in size to a stocky crow. These birds, which migrate in flocks of thousands, make up the bulk of hawk flights in September in the East. This peaceful bird is one of the tamest hawks. In flight the tips of the flight feathers appear dark, producing a black border along the trailing edge of the wing, and the underwing linings vary from white to rusty-buff. The black-and-white bands in the tail are approximately equal in width. Juveniles are similar to adults but appear more washed out and have fainter tail bands; underparts are pale with heavy dark streaking.

dark brown upperparts

red barring on underparts

- **SONG** Thin shrill whistle, *peeteeee* or *peweeeeeeeeee*, often given in flight and similar to the high plaintive whistled note of an Eastern Wood-Pewee.
- **BEHAVIOR** Perches to watch for prey from utility poles and wires or near water along edge of woods. Hunts along wooded roads under the tree canopy. Swoops down to grab prey with talons. Eats amphibians, reptiles, small rodents, shrews, rabbits, some small birds, large insects, and insect larvae.
- **BREEDING** Monogamous. Solitary nester.
- **NESTING** Incubation 28–32 days by both sexes, but mostly by female. Semialtricial young stay in nest 29–35 days, fed by both sexes. 1 brood per year.
- **POPULATION** Common in eastern US and southern Canada west to a portion of eastern British Columbia. Rare in winter in California and Florida.
- **CONSERVATION** Large numbers once shot during migration, particularly along mountainous ridges in the East. Now protected by law. Neotropical migrant.

JUVENILE

large black-and-white bands on tail

Similar Birds

RED-SHOULDERED HAWK
Larger in size; narrower, more rounded wings with barred and spotted black-and-white flight feathers; buff to rusty-red wing linings; longer, narrower tail with white bands much narrower than dark ones.

Flight Pattern

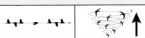

Several rapid shallow wing beats followed by a glide. Soars on thermals and updrafts.

Nest Identification

Shape [symbol]   Location [symbol]

Sticks, twigs, and dead leaves • lined with inner bark strips with lichen, outer bark chips, evergreen sprigs, and green leaves • in crotch of deciduous tree, 30–50 feet above ground • built by both sexes in slow process that takes 3–5 weeks • 2–4 white or bluish white eggs sometimes marked with brown; short elliptical, 1.9 inches long.

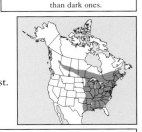

Plumage Sexes similar	Habitat [symbols]	Migration Migratory	Weight 14.8 ounces

DATE _____ TIME_____ LOCATION _____

| Family ACCIPITRIDAE | Species *Buteo brachyurus* | Length 15–17 inches | Wingspan 35 inches |

SHORT-TAILED HAWK

This crow-sized buteo is a rare to uncommon resident of the mangrove and cypress swamps of Florida and a rare to casual visitor in spring and summer to southern Texas. Most often observed while flying, this hawk rises out of the wooded lots in which it roosts on midmorning thermals, about the time the vultures do, and often spends much of the day high in the sky. In Florida the light morph, which has white underparts from chin to tail, is less common than the dark morph.

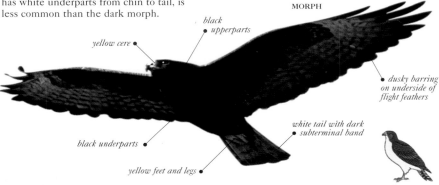

DARK MORPH

black upperparts

yellow cere

dusky barring on underside of flight feathers

white tail with dark subterminal band

black underparts

yellow feet and legs

LIGHT MORPH

- **SONG** High-pitched squeal and scream similar to that of the Red-shouldered Hawk, but the second part can be extremely piercing, *ssheeeeeeerrrrrreeeea*.
- **BEHAVIOR** Rarely hunts from a perch; principally hunts from high in the air and swoops down to treetops to snatch large insects, small birds, lizards, and snakes. Known to eat various other bird species, this small raptor was once observed eating a Sharp-shinned Hawk.
- **BREEDING** Monogamous. Solitary nester. Male attracts female with display of aerial acrobatics.
- **NESTING** Incubation about 34 days by female; male feeds female during incubation. Altricial young are fed by female, but male brings food. First flight at about 40 days.
- **POPULATION** Rare to uncommon and local in southern and central Florida; casual to rare in southeastern Texas; fairly common in Mexico, Central America, and South America.
- **CONSERVATION** Population appears to be stable, but only about 500 birds are recorded in Florida.

Similar Birds

SWAINSON'S HAWK Similar to dark morph but larger; wings and tail are narrower and longer; has dark flight feathers • also similar to light morph but has blackish gray barring on flight feathers that contrasts with white wing linings; brown head, neck, and band across chest.

Flight Pattern

Series of rapid wing beats followed by a glide. Soars on rising thermals and updrafts.

Nest Identification

Shape — Location —

Fresh green sprigs, twigs, leaves, bits of moss, and lichen • at top of cypress or other tree, 8–100 feet above ground • built by female with materials gathered by male • 2–3 off-white or bluish white eggs, occasionally marked with brown, 2.1 inches long.

| Plumage Sexes similar | Habitat | Migration Migratory | Weight 1.0 pound |

| Family ACCIPITRIDAE | Species *Buteo jamaicensis* | Length 19–25 inches | Wingspan 46–58 inches |

RED-TAILED HAWK

This hawk is found in more habitats than any other North American buteo and, consequently, is the most common hawk on the continent. This species has five races: a pale pink-tailed Great Plains race known as "Krider's Red-tailed," *krideri;* the eastern *borealis*, the southwestern *fuertesi*; the western, *calurus*; and the rare "Harlan's Hawk" or *harlani*, once considered a separate species, which is very dark with a white-based tail. All adults show a dark brownish mantle in flight and dark brown bar on leading edge of underwing. All juveniles have a dark brown tail with a black band. Because it perches low on woodland edges and along roadsides this is one of the most conspicuous and easily observed hawks.

reddish tail ranges from pale buff-pink to deep rufous-red

whitish flight feathers with pale barring

pale wing linings

large bill with yellow cere

white belly with broad band of dark streaking

EASTERN ADULT
BOREALIS

- **SONG** Harsh descending slurred *keeeeer-r-r*. Also rasping hissing screamy, *p-s-s-s, kree-kree ree-e-e.*
- **BEHAVIOR** Across its vast range takes a wide variety of prey Eats small to medium mammals, reptiles, amphibians, grasshoppers, spiders, earthworms, crustaceans, some fish, and an occasional small bird or bat. Carries small prey to perch; partially eats large prey on ground.
- **BREEDING** Monogamous; may mate for life. Solitary nester.
- **NESTING** Incubation 28–35 days by both sexes; more by female. Semialtricial young stay in nest 42–46 days. Fed by both sexes. 1 brood per year.

HARLAN'S HAWK

KRIDER'S RED-TAILED

Similar Birds
ROUGH-LEGGED HAWK Smaller bill and feet; feathered legs; white rump; white tail with multiple dark bands; black belly (light morph).
SWAINSON'S HAWK Multiple tail bands; dark flight feathers; pale wing linings; brown chest (light morph).

- **POPULATION** Very common. Some decline due to habitat loss.
- **CONSERVATION** Some eggshell thinning. Many still killed illegally, and some are accidentally killed by cars.

Flight Pattern

Several rapid strong wing beats followed by a glide. Soars well on thermals and sometimes hangs on updrafts.

Nest Identification	
Shape	Location	Sticks and twigs • lined with inner bark strips, evergreen sprigs, and green leaves • in crotch of large tree, on cliff ledge, or on artificial structure, as high as 120 feet above ground • built by both sexes • 2–3 white or bluish white eggs sometimes spotted brown, 2.4 inches long.

| Plumage Sexes similar | Habitat | Migration Migratory | Weight 2.3 pounds |

DATE _____ TIME_____ LOCATION _____

Family ACCIPITRIDAE	Species *Buteo regalis*	Length 22–28 inches	Wingspan 56 inches

FERRUGINOUS HAWK

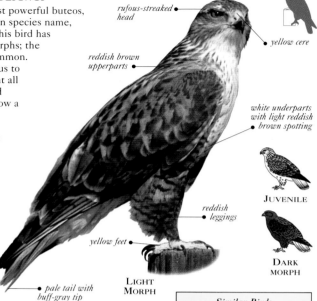

rufous-streaked head

yellow cere

reddish brown upperparts

white underparts with light reddish brown spotting

JUVENILE

reddish leggings

yellow feet

LIGHT MORPH

pale tail with buff-gray tip

DARK MORPH

One of the largest and most powerful buteos, this hawk is true to its Latin species name, meaning kingly or royal. This bird has light, dark, and reddish morphs; the light morph is the most common. Dark morphs are dark rufous to dark brown overall. In flight all three hold the long pointed wings in a dihedral, and show a white patch at base of primaries from above. The light morph appears almost completely white from below except for the reddish legs, which form a rusty red V beneath the body.

• **SONG** Alarm call of *kree-a* or *kaah kaah*.

• **BEHAVIOR** Eats mainly ground squirrels; spots them from perch, flies high in air, and swoops down to catch them. Also hunts prairie dogs, rabbits, small rodents, snakes, lizards, small to medium birds, and large insects. One of the few large hawks that hovers. Prefers open country, where it often hunts from low perches on fence posts, utility poles, or small trees.

• **BREEDING** Monogamous. Solitary nester.

• **NESTING** Incubation 31–33 days by both sexes, but female does more. Semialtricial young stay in nest 40–50 days; for first 21 days female stays on nest while male hunts, then both sexes hunt. First flight at 38–50 days. 1 brood per year.

• **POPULATION** Uncommon to fairly common. Rare to casual in migration or winter bordered by the Mississippi River and occasionally Florida.

• **CONSERVATION** Threatened and declining due to illegal shooting and loss of habitat. Some are accidentally killed by cars.

Similar Birds

ROUGH-LEGGED HAWK Dark morph has banded tail with broad dark subterminal band; no rusty leggings.

"KRIDER'S RED-TAILED" HAWK Juvenile is shorter; more rounded wings; dark subterminal tail band to tip; unfeathered tarsus.

Flight Pattern

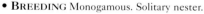

Quarters back and forth close to ground; alternates several deep flaps with glides similar to Northern Harrier. Soars on thermals and hovers.

Nest Identification

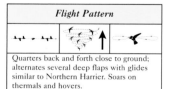

Shape   Location

Sticks and debris • lined with finer materials, including cow dung • usually on top of tree, 6–50 feet above ground; in treeless areas may build on cliffs or ground • built by both sexes • 2–6 pale bluish white eggs blotched with pale to dark browns and buffs; between spherical and elliptical, 2.5 inches long.

Plumage Sexes similar	Habitat	Migration Migratory	Weight 2.3 pounds

DATE _____ TIME_____ LOCATION _____

Family ACCIPITRIDAE	Species *Aquila chrysaetos*	Length 33–38 inches	Wingspan 6–8 feet

GOLDEN EAGLE

yellow cere

tawny-golden feathers on crown

tawny-golden feathers on nape and sides of neck

black bill

dark brown overall

feathered tarsus

yellow feet

JUVENILE

Like most other birds of prey, the female Golden Eagle is considerably larger than the male. This large dark eagle is fairly common in the West and rare to uncommon in the East. It has been clocked in a steep glide at 120 miles per hour and is estimated to swoop on prey in dives at more than 150 miles per hour. Juveniles in flight display "ringtail" plumage (a broad white tail band with a terminal band of black) and a broad white patch at the base of the primaries. Large birds of prey require large territories, and home ranges for a pair of this species have been recorded as large as 60 square miles.

- **SONG** Generally silent. Around nest makes yelping bark, *keya*, and whistled notes. During soaring courtship flight yelps or mews.
- **BEHAVIOR** Favors rabbit, ground squirrel, marmot, grouse, and ptarmigan. Also eats large insects, other small mammals, carrion, and reptiles, including turtles. Has been known to attack full-grown deer, antelopes, and birds as large as Great Horned Owls and cranes. Returns to the same nest yearly or every other year.
- **BREEDING** Monogamous; may pair for life. Solitary nester.
- **NESTING** Incubation 43–45 days by both sexes; female does more. Young stay in nest 66–70 days, dependent on parents for first 30 days. First flight at 65–70 days. Usually has 1 brood every 2 years.
- **POPULATION** Uncommon to rare in the East but fairly common in the West. A total of only 4,000–5,000 pairs were estimated in 1964. Circumpolar.
- **CONSERVATION** Protected by law. Thousands once killed by ranchers in efforts to protect livestock from potential predation. Also killed in collisions with aircraft. Protected areas established.

Similar Birds

BALD EAGLE Juvenile has larger head; shorter tail; mottled white patches on underparts make tail more blotchy; underwing pattern; bare tarsus.

Flight Pattern

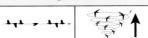

Alternates deep slow powerful wing beats with glides or rides easily on thermals.

Nest Identification	
Shape	Location

Sticks woven with brush and leaves • lined with fine material • located 10–100 feet high in trees • 8–10 feet across and 3–4 feet deep • built by both sexes • 2 white or creamy buff eggs marked with brown or reddish brown, 2.9 inches long.

Plumage Sexes similar	Habitat	Migration Some migrate	Weight 3.5 pounds

DATE _____ TIME_____ LOCATION _____

Family FALCONIDAE	Species *Caracara cheriway*	Length 20–25 inches	Wingspan 45–48 inches

CRESTED CARACARA

This large vulturelike raptor often walks on the ground on long legs in search of prey. Its black crown and short crest above the red to yellowish bare skin of the face are distinctive. In flight its flat profile, broad wings, and fanned tail are ravenlike. Flying birds also show white patches at the wing tips, a white head and breast, and a white tail with a broad black terminal band.

• **SONG** In breeding season makes loud *wick-wick-wick-wick-querrr*, throwing its head backward over its back on the last note. Harsh grating rattle. Usually silent.

• **BEHAVIOR** Makes head-throwing display. Only member of Falconidae that actually collects materials and builds nest. Often scavenges with vultures, where it may dominate the carcass. Feeds on variety of animal material, from large insects, reptiles, mammals, birds, amphibians, and fish to carrion.

• **BREEDING** Monogamous. Solitary nester.

• **NESTING** Incubation 28–33 days by both sexes. Semialtricial young stay in nest 30–60 days. Fed by both sexes. 1–2 broods per year.

• **POPULATION** Fairly common in Texas; rare to casual and local in Arizona; rare in Louisiana; fairly common and local in Florida. Has declined throughout its range. Florida and Arizona populations stable; Texas population increasing and expanding.

• **CONSERVATION** Considered threatened federally and in Florida.

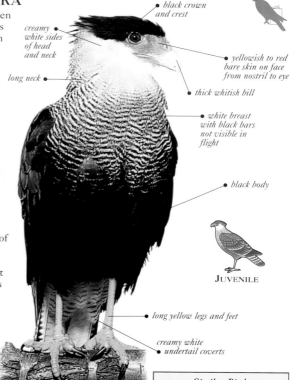

black crown and crest

creamy white sides of head and neck

long neck

yellowish to red bare skin on face from nostril to eye

thick whitish bill

white breast with black bars not visible in flight

black body

JUVENILE

long yellow legs and feet

creamy white undertail coverts

Similar Birds

BLACK VULTURE
Black head and beak; only creamy white on wing tips.

Flight Pattern
Strong steady deep wing beats; often alternates series of wing beats with long to short glides. Sometimes soars on thermals.

Nest Identification	
Shape Location	Sticks, vines, and twigs • lined with fine material • 15–30 feet above ground in palmetto or giant cacti • built by both sexes • 1–4 white or pinkish white eggs marked with browns, rarely unmarked; ovate to broadly oval or subspherical, slightly pointed at one end; 2.3 inches long.

Plumage Sexes similar	Habitat	Migration Nonmigratory	Weight 2.1 pounds

DATE 12/7/04 TIME_____ LOCATION _____

Family FALCONIDAE	Species *Falco sparverius*	Length 9–12 inches	Wingspan 20–25 inches

AMERICAN KESTREL

The smallest most common North American falcon is found all over the continent and north to the tree line in summer. It is sometimes called the Sparrow Hawk, a misnomer as the bird is neither a hawk nor does its diet include a significant amount of sparrows or other small birds. In flight it shows the typical long tail and long pointed wings of a falcon. A bird of the open country, it often is seen perched on wires along roadsides.

• **SONG** Alarm call a loud quick *klee-klee-klee* or *killy, killy, killy*.

• **BEHAVIOR** When perched bobs tail. Hunts rodents and insects from perch or hovers. Also eats bats, small birds, small reptiles, and frogs. Not dependent on drinking water in desert because it extracts water from its diet.

• **BREEDING** Monogamous. Solitary nester. During courtship male brings food and feeds female in the air.

• **NESTING** Incubation 29–31 days by both sexes, mostly by female. Semialtricial young stay in nest 30–31 days, fed by female. Male calls female from nest to feed. 1 brood per year, sometimes 2 in the South.

• **POPULATION** Common.

• **BIRDHOUSES** Readily nests in bird boxes built especially for kestrels. Occasionally attracted to bird feeders to prey on birds.

black-and-white pattern on head

rufous back with dark barring

2 vertical dark facial lines

spotted tawny-buff breast

MALE

long slender pointed wings

rufous-red tail without barring

blue-gray wings and wing coverts

2 vertical dark facial lines

streaked pale underparts

rufous tail with brown barring, black band, and narrow white tip

FEMALE

Similar Birds

SHARP-SHINNED HAWK Blue-gray upperparts; red-brown streaked and barred underparts; square or notched barred tail; short rounded wings.

MERLIN ♂ Larger; variegated head; lacks facial bars, blue-black tail and back; heavily streaked underparts • male has blue-black wings.

• **CONSERVATION** Migratory counts suggest recent decline in the Northeast; other populations seem stable. Expanded establishment of nest boxes in some areas, especially along highways, seems to have encouraged recovery.

Flight Pattern

Several rapid wing beats followed by a glide; often hovers on rapidly beating wings. Also soars on thermals.

Nest Identification	
Shape ▢ ▢ Location 🏠 🪺 ▢ ▢ 🪹 🌿	Little, if any, nest material • in old flicker tree holes, niches in walls, and holes under gables, 12–80 feet above ground • 3–7 white to cream or pale pink eggs, heavily blotched with browns, sometimes unmarked; 1.4 inches long.

Plumage Sexes differ	Habitat 	Migration Migratory	Weight 3.9 ounces

DATE _____ TIME_____ LOCATION _____

Family FALCONIDAE	Species *Falco columbarius*	Length 11–13 inches	Wingspan 23–26 inches

MERLIN

This medium-sized falcon of northern coniferous forests hunts the openings in parklike grasslands, bogs, and shrubby barrens. In flight it shows the distinctive falcon "jizz" of long pointed wings and a long tail with a big-headed, powerful look, and it displays impressive bursts of speed when in pursuit of prey. Geographic variation in color exists, from pale prairie birds to dark Pacific Northwest forms.

• **SONG** *Ki-ki-kee, kek-kek-kek* rapidly repeated.

• **BEHAVIOR** A relatively tame bird, allowing close approach. Defensive of nest; often attacks intruders, including humans. The Merlin flies close to the ground and catches prey with bursts of speed while in pursuit, rather than by diving or hovering. It is a bird that often hunts from an open perch. Primary diet of small birds, mammals, and large insects. May frequent cities in winter.

• **BREEDING** Monogamous. Solitary nester.

• **NESTING** Incubation 28–32 days mostly by female. Semialtricial young stay in nest 25–35 days. Fed by both sexes. 1 brood per year.

• **POPULATION** Uncommon.

blue-gray crown

yellow enlarged area at base of bill

white chin and throat with streaking

whitish buff head and nape

narrow black mustache

blue-gray back and wings

whitish buff underparts heavily streaked brown to black

yellow legs and feet

MALE

blue-black tail with gray barring and white tip

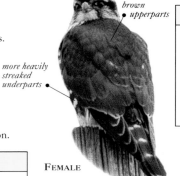

brown upperparts

more heavily streaked underparts

FEMALE

Similar Birds

AMERICAN KESTREL ♂
Smaller; bobs tail and hovers; barred rufous back and tail.

PEREGRINE FALCON
Larger; indistinct barring on tail; dark hood on head extends beneath eye like broad sideburn.

• **CONSERVATION** Some declines attributed to pesticides and heavy metals in food chain.

Flight Pattern

Swift direct flight with rapid powerful wing beats.

Nest Identification

Shape

Location

Uses old tree nests of crows, magpies, and hawks, relined with bark and feathers • 15–35 feet above ground • built by female • 2–7 white eggs, some marked with reddish brown; short elliptical, 1.6 inches long.

Plumage Sexes differ	Habitat	Migration Most migrate	Weight 5.7 ounces

DATE _____ TIME _____ LOCATION _____

Family FALCONIDAE	Species *Falco peregrinus*	Length 16–20 inches	Wingspan 43–46 inches

PEREGRINE FALCON

A peregrine in a stoop is one of the fastest birds in the world, reaching speeds of 175 mph or more.

- **SONG** Usually silent. On breeding grounds makes loud *witchew, witchew, witchew*. When disturbed gives loud repeated *cack, cack, cack, cack*.
- **BEHAVIOR** Prefers open areas with good vantage points on which to perch, often near water. Feeds almost exclusively on birds it takes in the air after a steep swift dive from above them. Wanders widely after nesting season, following prey south as far as southern South America. Faithful to nesting sites and aeries, some of which have been used by generations of peregrines for centuries. Lives on buildings in large cities.
- **BREEDING** Monogamous. Solitary nester.
- **NESTING** Incubation 28–32 days mostly by female. Semialtricial young stay in nest 35–42 days. Fed by both sexes. 1 brood per year.
- **POPULATION** Common to fairly common on tundra; fairly common in migration; uncommon to rare as breeding bird in US. Increasing since continental lows suffered in 1960s and 1970s.
- **CONSERVATION** Federally listed as threatened. Regulation of DDT along with captive breeding and release program have sparked comeback.

black head from crown to below eye with "sideburns" gives helmeted look

fleshy yellow eye ring

slate-blue upperparts

slate-blue bill with dark tip

white to buff chin

patch behind ear

JUVENILE

white underparts with dark brown to black barring (except throat and chin)

yellow feet and legs

long slate-blue tail with dusky barring and white terminal tip

Similar Birds

MERLIN ♂
Smaller; heavily streaked underparts; pale face with narrow mustache mark.

GYRFALCON
Much larger; more uniform and paler coloration; pale head with thin mustache mark.

PRAIRIE FALCON
Paler overall; light brown upperparts; whitish underparts streaked with heavy brown spots; whitish face and supercilium; dark brown postocular stripe; thin mustache; brown barred tail; black axillars and inner wing linings.

Flight Pattern
Direct flight with rapid wing beats like a pigeon.

Nest Identification	
Shape 〜 ♋ Abandoned nests	Made of debris on ledge • lined with grass • mostly on cliffs in southern US; also in hollows of old trees or open tops of cypress, sycamore, or cottonwood, 50–90 feet above ground • rarely uses old tree nest or cavity • built by female • 2–6 cream or buff eggs, heavily marked with brown and red, 2.1 inches long.
Location 🐦 🌲 🏙 〰	

Plumage Sexes similar	Habitat 〜 ♒	Migration Some migrate	Weight 1.3 pounds

DATE _____ TIME_____ LOCATION _____

Family PHASIANIDAE	Species *Meleagris gallopavo*	Length 37–46 inches	Wingspan 4–5 feet

WILD TURKEY

The largest game bird in North America, the Wild Turkey once was so widespread it was considered for the US national emblem. Male turkeys gobble year round, but in spring they are easily startled and will gobble at any abrupt noise. Today this unmistakable symbol of a US national holiday is becoming common again due to conservation efforts and its own adjustments to changes in its original woodland habitat.

bare blue and pink head

large iridescent dark body glistens with greens and bronzes

red wattles

MALE

white-barred flight feathers

blackish breast tuft or "beard"

proportionally smaller head

spurred pinkish legs

lacks breast tuft (small "beard" present in some older females)

duller in color and less iridescent than male

smaller than male

FEMALE

medium-length broad tail

- **SONG** Gobbling may be heard up to a mile away and is easily imitated, with bird often responding to it. Several different clucking calls given by both sexes: *cluk, cluck, cut, putt,* and others.
- **BEHAVIOR** Powerful muscular gizzard can grind hardest foods. Eats nuts, seeds, large insects, frogs, lizards, wild fruits, and grapes. Flies to tree roosts for the night. Male displays by strutting with tail spread, wings drooped to ground, bare skin of head intensified in color, and frequent gobbling.
- **BREEDING** Polygamous.
- **NESTING** Incubation 27–28 days by female. First flight in about 14 days. Tended by female. 1 brood per year.
- **POPULATION** Rare to fairly common. Wild birds unlikely in areas of human habitation, though widely domesticated. Increasing.
- **CONSERVATION** Trap and transfer programs have helped reestablish some populations. Increased comeback of blocks of forest interspersed with agricultural areas, as well as wildlife management programs, have helped increase populations.

Flight Pattern
Swift powerful flight for short distances with rapid wing beats and deep strokes; often glides after several series of wing beats.

Nest Identification	
Shape ⚬ Location ▬	Lined with a few dead leaves and grass • on ground concealed under shrub or in grass • built by female • 8–20 white to cream or buff eggs, sometimes blotched or spotted with brown or red, 2.5 inches long.

Plumage Sexes differ	Habitat 🐾 🌿 ⛰ ✈	Migration Nonmigratory	Weight 16.3 pounds

DATE 7/04   TIME_____   LOCATION _____

Family ODONTOPHORIDAE	Species *Colinus virginianus*	Length 9–10 inches	Wingspan 14–16 inches

NORTHERN BOBWHITE

This familiar eastern quail, named for the male's loud call, inhabits farmlands, fields, lightly grazed pastures, and grasslands. The "Masked Bobwhite," a southwestern race with a black face and cinnamon-rufous underparts, formerly of Mexico and southeast Arizona, has been reintroduced into Arizona grasslands.

- **SONG** Rising clear whistle, *bob-WHITE!* or *bob-bob-WHITE!*, given most often by males in spring and summer. Also whistles *hoy*.
- **BEHAVIOR** Solitary or in pairs in spring; family groups in summer; coveys of 8–15 in fall and winter. Roosts on ground in groups of up to 30, tails pushed together and heads facing out of a tight wagon wheel–shaped circle. Eats seeds, insects, worms, and spiders.
- **BREEDING** Monogamous; some evidence of polygamy.
- **NESTING** Incubation 23–24 days by both sexes. Young leave nest soon after hatching; tended by both sexes. First flight at 12–14 days. 1 brood per year.
- **POPULATION** Uncommon to common in brushlands and open woodland. Introduced into northwestern US. Significantly declining over much of range.
- **FEEDERS** Scattered grains on ground or man-made permanent sources of water.

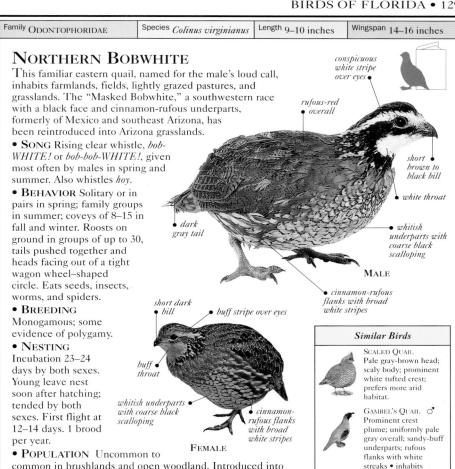

conspicuous white stripe over eyes

rufous-red overall

short brown to black bill

white throat

whitish underparts with coarse black scalloping

dark gray tail

MALE

cinnamon-rufous flanks with broad white stripes

short dark bill

buff stripe over eyes

buff throat

whitish underparts with coarse black scalloping

cinnamon-rufous flanks with broad white stripes

FEMALE

Similar Birds

SCALED QUAIL Pale gray-brown head; scaly body; prominent white tufted crest; prefers more arid habitat.

GAMBEL'S QUAIL ♂ Prominent crest plume; uniformly pale gray overall; sandy-buff underparts; rufous flanks with white streaks • inhabits desert scrublands of the Southwest.

- **CONSERVATION** Hunted as a game bird; highly managed in some states. Decline may be due to habitat loss and changes in farming practices. Sensitive to cold winter weather; entire populations may be wiped out by hard freezes.

Flight Pattern
Rises swiftly with whirring rapid wing beats then sails away, wings curved downward. Alternates series of stiff wing beats with short glides on drooping wing tips.

Nest Identification	
Shape ⌣ Location ⁂ ▬	Lined with grasses • leaves small openings in sides • on ground • built by both sexes • 14–16 white or cream-white eggs; subpyriform and sometimes quite pointed, 1.2 inches long.

Plumage Sexes differ	Habitat ⌐ ♟♦ ♦	Migration Nonmigratory	Weight 6.3 ounces

DATE _____ TIME_____ LOCATION _____

Family RALLIDAE	Species *Coturnicops noveboracensis*	Length 6–7.25 inches	Wingspan 10–13 inches

YELLOW RAIL

The sparrow-sized Yellow Rail is one of the least-known rails. It is so reluctant to fly that trained dogs can catch it. If flushed it flies weakly with its feet dangling, showing a white patch on the trailing edge of the inner wing before dropping back into cover. Its narrow body, strong toes, and flexible wings help it survive in dense marsh grasses. Adults have olive-gray legs, a buff chest, dark brown flanks with white bars, white-spotted wing coverts, and cinnamon undertail coverts. Juveniles are darker gray-black above with slight buffy striping; more white spotting on head, neck, breast, and sides; and more black barring on the flanks.

dark brown upperparts with broad buff stripes and narrow white crossbars

dark brown crown

broad dark smudge through eye

short yellowish to greenish gray bill

- **SONG** Like pebbles tapping, *tick-tick, tick-tick-tick.* Usually at night.
- **BEHAVIOR** Secretive; difficult to see in the open; sticks to thick grasses and marsh vegetation. Prefers to walk or run if disturbed. Flutters in air when flushed, then quickly drops and runs on the ground to escape. Averse to flying yet able to migrate great distances. Eats insects, small snails, seeds, tender leaves of clover, and grasses.
- **BREEDING** Monogamous. Solitary nester.
- **NESTING** Incubation 16–18 days by female. Precocial young leave nest shortly after hatching. Probably tended by female. May be independent of parents at 35 days. 1 brood per year.
- **POPULATION** Uncommon to rare and poorly known. Declining due to loss of habitat.
- **CONSERVATION** Draining and development of wetlands negatively impacting populations. Considered a game bird in some states.

Similar Birds
SORA Juveniles are twice as large; bright yellow bill; lack buff stripes on upperparts; lacks white wing patch in flight.

Flight Pattern	
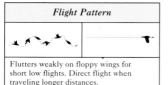	
Flutters weakly on floppy wings for short low flights. Direct flight when traveling longer distances.	

Nest Identification	Canopy of vegetation pulled to cover mat of fine dead grass • above damp soil on bare ground or flattened vegetation • a little above water of marsh or meadow and screened by small blades of grass • built by both sexes • 7–10 creamy buff eggs occasionally spotted with reddish brown and capped; ovate but often markedly elongated, 1.1 inches long.
Shape ⬤ ⬤ Location ▬ ▬▬	

Plumage Sexes similar	Habitat 〰 ▬▬ 〰〰 〰	Migration Migratory	Weight 1.8 ounces

DATE _____ TIME_____ LOCATION _____

Family RALLIDAE	Species *Laterallus jamaicensis*	Length 6 inches	Wingspan 10.5–11.5 inches

BLACK RAIL

The smallest and perhaps most secretive member of the rail family, this bird was first recorded on the island of Jamaica and is extremely difficult to find. Its range is not well known, and small populations and individual records scattered widely across the United States provide our only information. If glimpsed, it appears like a rodent scampering. Its flight is faint and shaky with legs dangling,

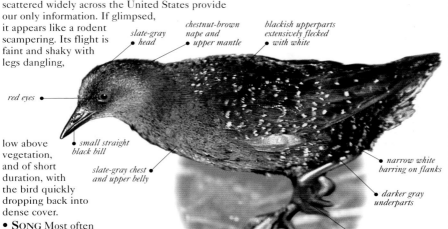

chestnut-brown nape and upper mantle

slate-gray head

blackish upperparts extensively flecked with white

red eyes

small straight black bill

low above vegetation, and of short duration, with the bird quickly dropping back into dense cover.

slate-gray chest and upper belly

narrow white barring on flanks

darker gray underparts

dusky greenish gray legs

• **SONG** Most often given at night beginning a couple of hours after sunset. Repeated *kik-kee-do* or *kik-kee-derr*, sometimes gives 4 notes, *kik-kik-kee-do*.

• **BEHAVIOR** Remains in cover of vegetation; rarely stays exposed for long. Rarely flies. Lives in freshwater marshes and wet meadows or in shallow margins of saltwater marshes above the beach line. Sometimes found in grain fields and dry hay fields. Eats seeds of aquatic plants, grasses and grains, insects, and isopods (small marine crustaceans).

• **BREEDING** Monogamous. Solitary nester.

• **NESTING** Incubation 16–20 days by both sexes. Precocial young leave nest soon after hatching. Tended by both parents. Possibly 2 broods per year.

• **POPULATION** Generally uncommon to rare; although locally common in some places. Declining in most parts of North American range due to loss of habitat, especially coastal marshes. Population stable in protected habitat.

• **CONSERVATION** Wetland conservation important.

Similar Birds
 YELLOW RAIL Larger; buff; white wing patches visible in flight.

Flight Pattern
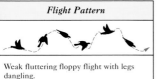
Weak fluttering floppy flight with legs dangling.

Nest Identification	Woven coil of soft grass blades, sedge, or other vegetation • in grass 18–24 inches tall on edge of marsh • built by both sexes • 4–13 white, pinkish white, or creamy white eggs dotted with brown; short subelliptical or elliptical, 1 inch long.
Shape ⬗ Location •••	

Plumage Sexes similar	Habitat 〰 ⚲	Migration Most migrate	Weight 1.2 ounces

DATE _____ TIME_____ LOCATION _____

Family RALLIDAE	Species *Rallus longirostris*	Length 14–16 inches	Wingspan 19–21 inches

CLAPPER RAIL

gray-brown overall

gray or gray-brown cheeks

long thin slightly down-curved bill

whitish or buff underparts

very short tail with white undertail coverts

gray to brown flanks with white barring

As with most rails the Clapper Rail is more often heard than seen. It is named for its noisy rattling call which is said to sound like old-time clappers. Abrupt noises cause these birds to cry in unison; noisiest at night. This large rail is locally known as "marsh hen" and often leaves the cover of the salt marshes it inhabits to work the muddy flats at low tide. As it walks it bobs its head and flips its short tail exposing white undertail coverts.

JUVENILE

• **SONG** A series of grating *kek-kek-kek* notes, accelerating then dropping off. Given most often at dusk on moonlit nights or when suddenly disturbed by loud noise. One call stimulates another; the calls travel like a wave through the marsh.

• **BEHAVIOR** Feeds mostly in the open at low tide on mudflats. At other times forages concealed in salt marsh vegetation. Eats crabs and other crustaceans, worms, amphibians, reptiles, mollusks, small fish, and aquatic insects.

• **BREEDING** Monogamous. Solitary nester.

• **NESTING** Incubation 20–23 days by both sexes. Precocial young abandon nest soon after hatching. Tended by both sexes. Independent after 35–42 days. First flight at 63–70 days. Possibly 2 broods per year.

• **POPULATION** Common in coastal salt marshes but declining on West Coast and in some places in the East. Casual on Atlantic Coast to the Maritimes.

• **CONSERVATION** The inland freshwater race on the lower Colorado River is considered endangered. Also endangered on the West Coast due to habitat loss and perhaps introduced predators.

Similar Birds

KING RAIL
Favors freshwater marshes; bolder black-and-white bars on flanks; bright rufous-brown neck and chest; tawny-buff cheeks; buff-edged back feathers; brown wing coverts; voice differs.

VIRGINIA RAIL
One-third the size; darker overall; blue-gray auriculars; bright rufous upperwing coverts.

Flight Pattern

Low fluttering flight over short distances with legs dangling.

Nest Identification

Shape ⊷ Location 🏚🪺🌾

Basket of aquatic vegetation and tide-deposited materials • elevated on firm bank or under small bush • built by both sexes, but male does more • 5–12 buff or olive-buff eggs marked with brown; subelliptical to long subelliptical to ovate, 1.7 inches long.

Plumage Sexes similar	Habitat	Migration Migratory	Weight 11.4 ounces

DATE _____ TIME _____ LOCATION _____

Family RALLIDAE	Species *Rallus elegans*	Length 15–19 inches	Wingspan 21–25 inches

KING RAIL

This large freshwater rail migrates through the Mississippi Valley and along the Atlantic Coast. Oddly, this bird's population seems tied to that of the muskrat, which creates open spaces in the marsh providing feeding and drinking areas for the rail. Widely

olive-brown upperparts with buff-edged back feathers

olive-brown head and hindneck

long slender, slightly down-curved bill

cinnamon-rufous foreneck and chest

blackish upper bill, orange to red lower bill, and dusky tip

dark blackish brown and white barring on flanks

JUVENILE

distributed in the East in summer, it is found in both freshwater and brackish marshes. Some consider it an inland freshwater race of the smaller Clapper Rail, but the King Rail is more rufous and has buff edging on the back feathers and brown to rufous wing coverts.

- **SONG** Series of less than 10 notes of *kek-kek-kek* or *jupe-jupe-jupe* deeper than those of Clapper Rail and not descending. Various other clucking and grunting notes.
- **BEHAVIOR** Sometimes feeds in open, mostly in shallow water or mudflats exposed at low tide. Variable diet of aquatic and semiaquatic foods includes plant parts, invertebrates, and vertebrates. Terrestrial, yet migrates long distances.
- **BREEDING** Monogamous. Solitary nester.
- **NESTING** Incubation 21–24 days by both sexes. Precocial young abandon nest soon after hatching; stay with parents about 63 days. Possibly 2 broods per year.
- **POPULATION** Fairly common to common in freshwater and brackish habitat near the Gulf Coast. Declined or disappeared in some areas due to loss of and/or contamination of habitat.
- **CONSERVATION** Considered a game bird in some states. Wetland management crucial inland and on coast.

Similar Birds

VIRGINIA RAIL
Much smaller; darker overall; blue-gray auriculars; bright rufous upperwing coverts.

CLAPPER RAIL
Slightly smaller; duller coloring; less barring on flanks; variable plumage, but grayish edge on brown-centered back feathers and olive-brown wing coverts; frequents salt marshes.

Flight Pattern

Slow floppy flight, often low above vegetation with feet dangling.

Nest Identification	
Shape ⌒ Location ⁂ Ɱ	Dry aquatic vegetation • 6–8 inches above water amid aquatic vegetation • built by both sexes, but male does more • 6–15 buff eggs spotted with brown; ovate, 1.6 inches long.

Plumage Sexes similar	Habitat 〰 ⌐	Migration Migratory	Weight 14.6 ounces

DATE _____ TIME_____ LOCATION _____

Family RALLIDAE	Species *Rallus limicola*	Length 9–10 inches	Wingspan 13–14.5 inches

VIRGINIA RAIL

Like all rails, the Virginia Rail generally does not fly when it is being pursued but will run swiftly through the marsh grasses. Note its gray cheeks and the reddish bill and legs. Flanks, lower belly, and undertail coverts are barred with black and white. In flight the wings show chestnut in the leading edge. Although this bird prefers freshwater and brackish marshes, it often inhabits salt marshes in winter. Juveniles have dark blackish brown upperparts and black, gray, and white mottling and barring on underparts.

blue-gray face

blackish crown

whitish to pale chin

cinnamon-rufous throat and breast

reddish legs and feet

slightly down-curved, long, slender reddish bill

JUVENILE

• **SONG** Resembles the clicking of keys on an old typewriter, *kid-ick, kid-ick, kid-ick* or *tic-tic-tic*. Also makes *kik, kik, kik, ki-queea* "kicker" call and descending series of piglike grunts and other odd calls.

• **BEHAVIOR** Somewhat secretive and terrestrial. Feeds primarily on insects but also takes aquatic animals, including worms, spiders, crustaceans, and small fish. Diet is varied, especially in winter, with duckweed and seeds of marsh grasses, rushes, and sedges.

• **BREEDING** Monogamous.

• **NESTING** Incubation 18–20 days by both sexes. Precocial young leave nest soon after hatching. Tended by both parents. First flight at about 25 days. Possibly 2 broods per year.

• **POPULATION** Fairly common to uncommon. Declining but still widespread despite loss of wetland habitat.

• **CONSERVATION** Still hunted as a game bird in some states. Wetland protection and management is crucial.

Similar Birds

KING RAIL
About twice the size • olive-brown head; brown to gray cheeks; cinnamon-rufous underparts; black-and-white barring on flanks.

CLAPPER RAIL
Larger; grayish body; cinnamon to gray underparts; black-and-white barring on flanks; prefers salt marshes.

Flight Pattern

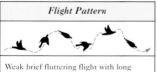

Weak brief fluttering flight with long legs dangling.

Nest Identification

Shape ⌐   Location ••• ⩊

Pile of matted reeds and layers of coarse aquatic vegetation and grass • in tussock or clumped vegetation • built by both sexes • 5–13 off-white or buff eggs spotted with brown and often wreathed; oval to short oval, 1.3 inches long.

Plumage Sexes similar	Habitat ⪥ ⟺	Migration Migratory	Weight 3.1 ounces

DATE _____ TIME_____ LOCATION _____

Family RALLIDAE	Species *Porzana carolina*	Length 8–10 inches	Wingspan 12–14.5 inches

SORA

In late summer large numbers of these birds gather in marshes to feed and build up fat reserves before migrating; they seem especially fond of smartweed seeds and wild rice. Like all rails, the Sora migrates at night, and for a group that hardly distinguishes itself in the air, this species may cover almost 3,000 miles between wintering and breeding grounds. It is identifiable by its short yellow bill framed with black feathers around its base, black throat, and black center in the upper breast. Small and plump, it is one of the most common North American rails. Juveniles lack the black on the face and underparts and, with their buff coloration, sometimes are confused with the much smaller Yellow Rail.

black-and-buff spots on wings and back
black patch on face and throat
irregular barring of thin white lines on gray underparts
short chickenlike yellow bill
yellow-green legs
very long toes
JUVENILE
WINTER PLUMAGE

• **SONG** Descending melodious whinny and abrasive high-pitched *keek*. Makes froglike whistle of *ker-wheer* on breeding ground.

• **BEHAVIOR** Small bill prevents it from probing into marsh mud for animals like the long-billed rails. Eats mainly plant life such as seeds, wild rice, and algae. Also feeds on insects, spiders, small crustaceans, and snails. Often found in the open where it walks slowly with head down and short tail cocked and flicked above white undertail coverts. Can show up in almost any moist habitat, especially in migration.

• **BREEDING** Monogamous.

• **NESTING** Incubation 19–20 days. Precocial young abandon nest soon after hatching. 2 broods per year.

• **POPULATION** Common and widespread despite loss of wetland habitat.

• **CONSERVATION** Recent loss of habitat due to draining and development of marshes; also due to loss of wintering coastal habitat.

Similar Birds

VIRGINIA RAIL
Long, slender, slightly down-curved reddish bill; gray face; rusty-red throat and breast.

YELLOW RAIL
Much smaller; checkered pattern of buff stripes and white bars on a blackish back on upperparts; lacks black on chin and throat; shows white wing patch in flight.

Flight Pattern

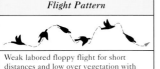

Weak labored floppy flight for short distances and low over vegetation with legs dangling.

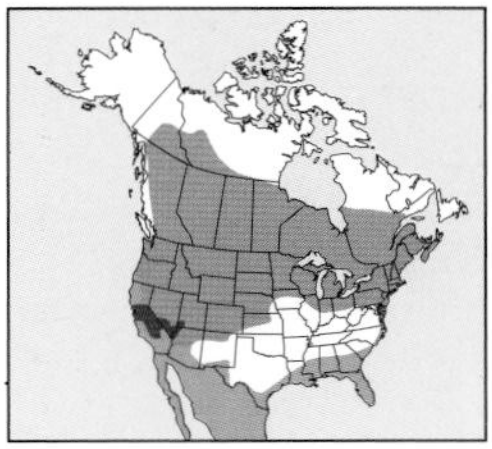

Nest Identification	
Shape / Location	A bowl of cattails, dry leaves, grasses, and reeds • about 6 inches in diameter • connected to stems of marsh vegetation a few inches above water • in reeds, cattails, or grasses over deeper water • 10–12 rich buff eggs irregularly spotted with browns and grays; ovate, 1.2 inches long.

Plumage Sexes similar	Habitat	Migration Migratory	Weight 2.6 ounces

DATE ______________ TIME ______________ LOCATION ______________

| Family RALLIDAE | Species *Porphyrula martinica* | Length 13–14 inches | Wingspan 22 inches |

PURPLE GALLINULE

This beautiful brightly colored member of the rail family can be seen walking gracefully on lily pads on extremely long yellow feet or swimming in open water with its head pumping back and forth. Most often seen in protected areas in the south, such as the Everglades National Park, individuals have wandered as far north as New England. Gaudy in color, the hues blend with the greens of marsh vegetation and the reflections of blue sky on water, sometimes making the bird difficult to see if not for the flicking tail revealing white undertail coverts. Juveniles have chocolate-brown to bluish olive upperparts and paler underparts.

glossy brownish green back

pale blue frontal shield

red bill with yellow tip

bright purplish head and neck

bright purplish underparts

snow-white undertail coverts

yellow legs and feet

JUVENILE

• **SONG** Various abrasive shrieking calls and hoarse chatters: sharp *kr'lik'* or *kee-k'*, gruff *kruk kruk-kruk-kruk*, screaming *whiehrrr* or *w'heehrr*, series of rapid clucking *kahw cohw-cohw-cohw* or *keh-keh-keh*.

• **BEHAVIOR** Feeds on seeds, fruits, and other parts of wild rice; grasses; fruit of water lily; grains; insects; crustaceans; snails; eggs and sometimes nestlings of marsh birds; amphibians; and small fish. Pumps and bobs head. Flicks short cocked tail when walking. Climbs well in vegetation.

• **BREEDING** Cooperative.

• **NESTING** Incubation 22–25 days by both sexes. Precocial young abandon nest soon after hatching and drying off. Tended and fed by both sexes, often with help from other birds. First flight at about 63 days. Possibly 2 broods per year.

Similar Birds

COMMON MOORHEN
White line separates flanks from upperparts in juveniles and adults • adults have red frontal shield; gray underparts; brownish upperparts.

AMERICAN COOT
Gray body; blackish head and neck; white bill and reddish brown frontal shield.

• **POPULATION** Fairly common in southern and coastal freshwater marshes, vegetated lakes, overgrown swamps, and lagoons. Decline due to loss of wetlands habitat.

• **CONSERVATION** Wetland conservation critical.

Flight Pattern

Labored slow flight with legs dangling just above water.

Nest Identification

Shape 🔾   Location 🔾 🔾

Green and dry stems with leaves • floating island of vegetation • built by both sexes • 5–10 cinnamon-pink or buff eggs marked with brown, 1.5 inches long.

| Plumage Sexes similar | Habitat 〰 〰 | Migration Migratory | Weight 9.1 ounces |

DATE 7/17/04   TIME_____   LOCATION _____

Family RALLIDAE	Species *Gallinula chloropus*	Length 14 inches	Wingspan 20–23 inches

COMMON MOORHEN

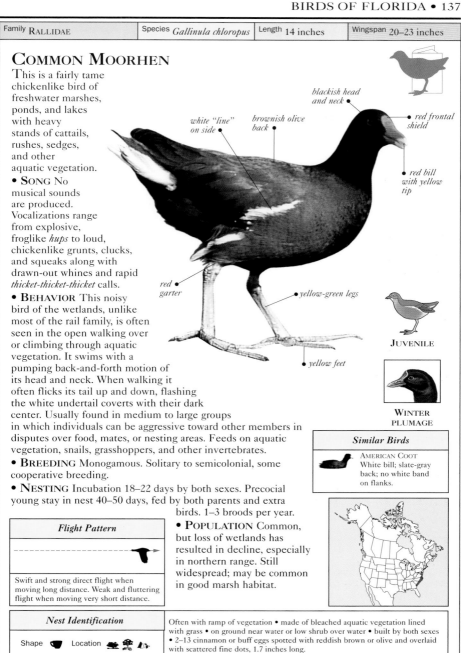

This is a fairly tame chickenlike bird of freshwater marshes, ponds, and lakes with heavy stands of cattails, rushes, sedges, and other aquatic vegetation.

- **SONG** No musical sounds are produced. Vocalizations range from explosive, froglike *hups* to loud, chickenlike grunts, clucks, and squeaks along with drawn-out whines and rapid *thicket-thicket-thicket* calls.
- **BEHAVIOR** This noisy bird of the wetlands, unlike most of the rail family, is often seen in the open walking over or climbing through aquatic vegetation. It swims with a pumping back-and-forth motion of its head and neck. When walking it often flicks its tail up and down, flashing the white undertail coverts with their dark center. Usually found in medium to large groups in which individuals can be aggressive toward other members in disputes over food, mates, or nesting areas. Feeds on aquatic vegetation, snails, grasshoppers, and other invertebrates.
- **BREEDING** Monogamous. Solitary to semicolonial, some cooperative breeding.
- **NESTING** Incubation 18–22 days by both sexes. Precocial young stay in nest 40–50 days, fed by both parents and extra birds. 1–3 broods per year.
- **POPULATION** Common, but loss of wetlands has resulted in decline, especially in northern range. Still widespread; may be common in good marsh habitat.

Labels on image: blackish head and neck • red frontal shield • white "line" on side • brownish olive back • red bill with yellow tip • red garter • yellow-green legs • yellow feet

JUVENILE

WINTER PLUMAGE

Similar Birds

AMERICAN COOT
White bill; slate-gray back; no white band on flanks.

Flight Pattern

Swift and strong direct flight when moving long distance. Weak and fluttering flight when moving very short distance.

Nest Identification

Shape ⬛ Location 🌿🌿🌿

Often with ramp of vegetation • made of bleached aquatic vegetation lined with grass • on ground near water or low shrub over water • built by both sexes • 2–13 cinnamon or buff eggs spotted with reddish brown or olive and overlaid with scattered fine dots, 1.7 inches long.

Plumage Sexes similar	Habitat 〰〰	Migration Some migrate	Weight 12.0 ounces

DATE 7/17/04   TIME_____   LOCATION _____

Family RALLIDAE	Species *Fulica americana*	Length 15 inches	Wingspan 23–28 inches

AMERICAN COOT

This close relative of the gallinules and moorhens lives on open water and is often mistaken for a duck. It pumps its small head back and forth like a chicken when walking or swimming and usually travels and feeds in flocks. A common and widely distributed species over much of North America, the American Coot is easily distinguished by its overall slate-gray plumage, which is

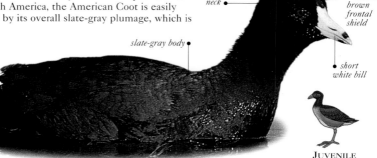

gray-black head and neck

reddish brown frontal shield

slate-gray body

short white bill

JUVENILE

blacker on the head and neck, its white bill, and small reddish brown frontal shield. Juveniles are similar to adults but paler, particularly on the underparts, with a darker bill.

• **SONG** Grunts, grating quacks, and hoarse chatters of *ke-yik* and *k-rrk!* or *krek!* Drawling *k-yew-r* and laughing *wah wahk* or *kuk-kuk-kuk-kuk-kuk.*

• **BEHAVIOR** Feeds by immersing head and neck in shallows with body and tail tipped up. May also pick food off surface. Dives 10–25 feet deep for fronds, leaves, seeds, and roots of aquatic plants, which make up most of diet. Also eats insects, amphibians, mollusks, and small fish. Runs with wings flapping rapidly to gain flight from water. Often aggressive toward other waterbirds, chasing them nosily from its vicinity.

• **BREEDING** Monogamous. Pairs display in front of each other on water in courtship. The male also chases the female across surface of water.

• **NESTING** Incubation 21–25 days by both sexes. Precocial young abandon nest shortly after hatching and drying off. Tended by both sexes. First flight at 49–56 days. 1–2 broods per year.

• **POPULATION** Common to abundant. Has decreased in the East in recent years.

Similar Birds

COMMON MOORHEN Red shield; yellow-tipped red bill; brown back; white-tipped flank feathers form line between flank and back • juvenile paler with white flank stripe.

PURPLE GALLINULE Dark bluish purple head, neck, and underparts; greenish brown back; yellow-tipped red bill; pale blue shield • juvenile has olive-brown upperparts; pale brown underparts; dull yellowish bill.

Flight Pattern
Fairly swift direct flight with rapid wing beats and feet protruding beyond tail.

Nest Identification	
Shape 🐾 Location 🐾 |||	Made of dead stems • lined with finer material • floating and anchored to vegetation • built by both sexes • 2–12 pinkish buff eggs marked with blackish brown, 1.9 inches long.

Plumage Sexes similar	Habitat 〜〜 ↘≈	Migration Migratory	Weight 1.6 pounds

DATE _____ TIME_____ LOCATION _____

Family ARAMIDAE	Species *Aramus guarauna*	Length 26–28 inches	Wingspan 42 inches

LIMPKIN

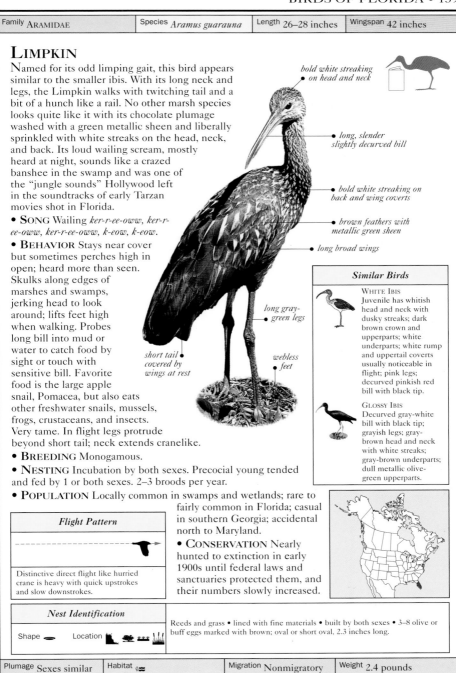

Named for its odd limping gait, this bird appears similar to the smaller ibis. With its long neck and legs, the Limpkin walks with twitching tail and a bit of a hunch like a rail. No other marsh species looks quite like it with its chocolate plumage washed with a green metallic sheen and liberally sprinkled with white streaks on the head, neck, and back. Its loud wailing scream, mostly heard at night, sounds like a crazed banshee in the swamp and was one of the "jungle sounds" Hollywood left in the soundtracks of early Tarzan movies shot in Florida.

bold white streaking on head and neck

long, slender slightly decurved bill

bold white streaking on back and wing coverts

brown feathers with metallic green sheen

long broad wings

- **SONG** Wailing *ker-r-ee-oww, ker-r-ee-oww, ker-r-ee-oww, k-eow, k-eow.*
- **BEHAVIOR** Stays near cover but sometimes perches high in open; heard more than seen. Skulks along edges of marshes and swamps, jerking head to look around; lifts feet high when walking. Probes long bill into mud or water to catch food by sight or touch with sensitive bill. Favorite food is the large apple snail, Pomacea, but also eats other freshwater snails, mussels, frogs, crustaceans, and insects. Very tame. In flight legs protrude beyond short tail; neck extends cranelike.

long gray-green legs

short tail covered by wings at rest

webless feet

Similar Birds

WHITE IBIS Juvenile has whitish head and neck with dusky streaks; dark brown crown and upperparts; white underparts; white rump and uppertail coverts usually noticeable in flight; pink legs; decurved pinkish red bill with black tip.

GLOSSY IBIS Decurved gray-white bill with black tip; grayish legs; gray-brown head and neck with white streaks; gray-brown underparts; dull metallic olive-green upperparts.

- **BREEDING** Monogamous.
- **NESTING** Incubation by both sexes. Precocial young tended and fed by 1 or both sexes. 2–3 broods per year.
- **POPULATION** Locally common in swamps and wetlands; rare to fairly common in Florida; casual in southern Georgia; accidental north to Maryland.
- **CONSERVATION** Nearly hunted to extinction in early 1900s until federal laws and sanctuaries protected them, and their numbers slowly increased.

Flight Pattern

Distinctive direct flight like hurried crane is heavy with quick upstrokes and slow downstrokes.

Nest Identification

Shape ➡   Location 🪶 🦆 🌾 🌱

Reeds and grass • lined with fine materials • built by both sexes • 3–8 olive or buff eggs marked with brown; oval or short oval, 2.3 inches long.

Plumage Sexes similar	Habitat 〰	Migration Nonmigratory	Weight 2.4 pounds

DATE 7/04   TIME_____   LOCATION _____

Family GRUIDAE	Species *Grus canadensis*	Length 34–48 inches	Wingspan 73–90 inches

SANDHILL CRANE

The five North American subspecies of this crane (plus one in Cuba) differ in size and intensity of coloration. The small southern sedentary populations are the most threatened. On the ground cranes look stately with long necks, heavy straight bills, long legs, "bustle" of tertials drooping over the tail, and upright stance. In flight they are distinguished from herons because the neck and head are extended and the slow downward wing beat is jerked quickly upward. This bird may probe for food in mud that contains iron, which deposits on the bill and stains the feathers rusty-brown when the bird preens.

- **SONG** Noisy trumpetlike *garoo-oo-a-a-a-a*; can carry more than a mile.
- **BEHAVIOR** Roosts communally at night in winter, standing on damp low land or in shallow water. Courtship dances in late winter and spring involve bounding 6–8 feet into air with wings half spread and calling loudly. Eats variety of plants and animals. In summer feeds in breeding marshes or nearby meadows. Walks great distances for food. May soar on thermals and migrate so high it is invisible from the ground.
- **BREEDING** Monogamous. Thought to mate for life.
- **NESTING** Incubation 28–32 days by both sexes. Precocial young leave nest soon after hatching. First flight at 65 days. 1 brood per year.
- **POPULATION** Common to fairly common and local. Stable or increasing, though vulnerable to habitat loss.
- **CONSERVATION** Killing and habitat loss to agriculture depleted southern numbers in the last two centuries. Degradation of habitat at major migration stopping points seriously impacting species. Mississippi Sandhill Crane National Wildlife Refuge houses most remaining Mississippi Sandhill Cranes, and there is an active propagation program.

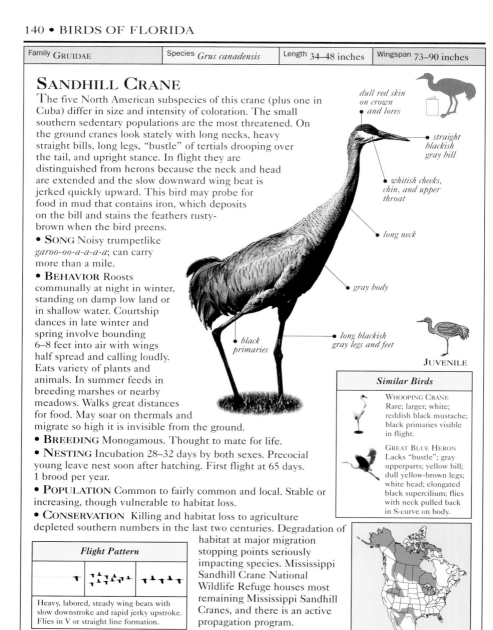

dull red skin on crown and lores

straight blackish gray bill

whitish cheeks, chin, and upper throat

long neck

gray body

black primaries

long blackish gray legs and feet

JUVENILE

Similar Birds

WHOOPING CRANE Rare; larger; white; reddish black mustache; black primaries visible in flight.

GREAT BLUE HERON Lacks "bustle"; gray upperparts; yellow bill; dull yellow-brown legs; white head; elongated black supercilium; flies with neck pulled back in S-curve on body.

Flight Pattern
Heavy, labored, steady wing beats with slow downstroke and rapid jerky upstroke. Flies in V or straight line formation.

Nest Identification	
Shape ⬡ Location ⬱ ▬ 〰	Dead sticks, moss, reeds, and grass • built by both sexes • 2 buff eggs marked with olive or 2 olive eggs marked with brown; subelliptical to long oval, 3.7–3.8 x 2.3 inches.

Plumage Sexes similar	Habitat 〰 〰	Migration Some migrate	Weight 7.4 pounds

DATE _____ TIME_____ LOCATION _____

Family GRUIDAE	Species *Grus americana*	Length 52 inches	Wingspan 87 inches

WHOOPING CRANE

The stately Whooping Crane is the tallest bird in North America and one of the most endangered. By 1941 only fifteen individuals wintering on the Texas coast were left in the wild. The breeding grounds of these birds were unknown until 1954 when they were discovered in Wood Buffalo National Park in Alberta in central Canada. Intensive conservation and management programs have slowly increased this flock to more than one hundred fifty individuals. Juveniles are white with a rusty red head and neck and have rusty red feathers scattered over the rest of the body.

bright red bare skin on crown

long heavy dull yellow bill

white eyes

long neck

blackish red mustache-like wedge extends from bill below eye to back of face

white overall

black wing tips

long black legs and feet

• **SONG** Piercing trumpetlike *ker-loo ker-lee-loo* that can be heard for more than 2 miles. This volume is achieved by the 5-foot-long trachea coiled within the keel of the breast bone.

• **BEHAVIOR** Eats fish, frogs, small mammals, mollusks, crustaceans, corn, other grains, and roots of water plants.

• **BREEDING** Monogamous; mates for life. In courtship dance, one of pair begins by lowering head and flapping wings. Bird leaps 3 feet in air with head back, bill pointed skyward, neck arched over back, legs stiff, and wings flapping. Mate runs forward a few steps, pumping head up and down and flapping wings. Then both leap into air and bounce up and down. The silent dance ends as suddenly as it begins. On wintering grounds do not form flocks but maintain family groups of 3–4 birds and hold winter territory.

• **NESTING** Incubation 29–35 days by both sexes. Precocial young abandon nest soon after hatching; tended by both parents. First flight at approximately 80–90 days. 1 brood per year.

• **POPULATION** Increasing. Populations introduced in Idaho and Florida.

• **CONSERVATION** Endangered, but public education as well as intensive management and protection programs, slowly succeeding.

Similar Birds

SANDHILL CRANE
Smaller; lacks mustache; bare red skin also on forehead and lores; pale gray overall; black bill and legs; shows black primaries in flight.

AMERICAN WHITE PELICAN
Larger; white with black outer secondaries, primaries, and upper primary coverts; short legs; flies with neck folded and long yellow-orange bill resting on breast.

Flight Pattern

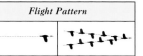

Typical crane flight of slow downward wing beat with powerful flick or jerk on upbeat. Flies in V formation in migration.

Nest Identification

Shape ⬛   Location ▬ ▬ 🌿

Soft or coarse grass, reeds, or sod • built on a mound by both sexes • 1–3 cream-olive buff eggs marked with brown; ovate or elliptical ovate, 3.9 x 2.5 inches.

Plumage Sexes similar	Habitat 〰	Migration Migratory	Weight 12.8 pounds

DATE _____ TIME_____ LOCATION _____

Family CHARADRIIDAE	Species *Pluvialis squatarola*	Length 11.5–13 inches	Wingspan 22–25 inches

BLACK-BELLIED PLOVER

The largest of the North American plovers, this stocky bird has a cautious nature and tends to travel in flocks, which helped it survive during a period when many plovers were destroyed by market hunters. This is the grayest of all the New World plovers in both breeding and winter plumages. In flight it shows a bold white wing stripe, white uppertail coverts, and black axillars. Seen on

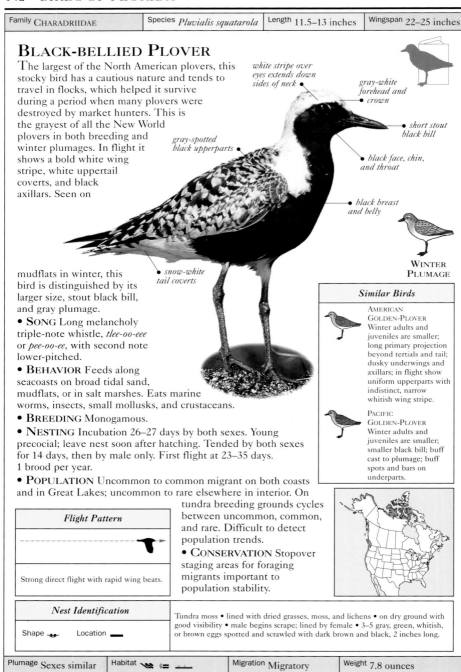

white stripe over eyes extends down sides of neck

gray-white forehead and crown

gray-spotted black upperparts

short stout black bill

black face, chin, and throat

black breast and belly

snow-white tail coverts

WINTER PLUMAGE

mudflats in winter, this bird is distinguished by its larger size, stout black bill, and gray plumage.

• **SONG** Long melancholy triple-note whistle, *tlee-oo-eee* or *pee-oo-ee*, with second note lower-pitched.

• **BEHAVIOR** Feeds along seacoasts on broad tidal sand, mudflats, or in salt marshes. Eats marine worms, insects, small mollusks, and crustaceans.

• **BREEDING** Monogamous.

• **NESTING** Incubation 26–27 days by both sexes. Young precocial; leave nest soon after hatching. Tended by both sexes for 14 days, then by male only. First flight at 23–35 days. 1 brood per year.

• **POPULATION** Uncommon to common migrant on both coasts and in Great Lakes; uncommon to rare elsewhere in interior. On tundra breeding grounds cycles between uncommon, common, and rare. Difficult to detect population trends.

• **CONSERVATION** Stopover staging areas for foraging migrants important to population stability.

Similar Birds

AMERICAN GOLDEN-PLOVER
Winter adults and juveniles are smaller; long primary projection beyond tertials and tail; dusky underwings and axillars; in flight show uniform upperparts with indistinct, narrow whitish wing stripe.

PACIFIC GOLDEN-PLOVER
Winter adults and juveniles are smaller; smaller black bill; buff cast to plumage; buff spots and bars on underparts.

Flight Pattern
Strong direct flight with rapid wing beats.

Nest Identification	
Shape	Location

Tundra moss • lined with dried grasses, moss, and lichens • on dry ground with good visibility • male begins scrape; lined by female • 3–5 gray, green, whitish, or brown eggs spotted and scrawled with dark brown and black, 2 inches long.

Plumage Sexes similar	Habitat	Migration Migratory	Weight 7.8 ounces

DATE _____ TIME_____ LOCATION _____

Family CHARADRIIDAE	Species *Pluvialis dominica*	Length 10–11 inches	Wingspan 18–22.5 inches

AMERICAN GOLDEN-PLOVER

This expert long-distance migrant flies at a rate of sixty miles per hour and covers thousands of miles per year between Arctic tundra nesting grounds and winter quarters as far away as Argentina. Once an abundant bird, the American Golden-Plover was almost eradicted by market hunters during the late 1800s. Winter adults and juveniles are

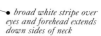

short thin black bill

dark brown upperparts dappled profusely with golden spots

broad white stripe over eyes and forehead extends down sides of neck

black face and foreneck

black breast

WINTER PLUMAGE

brown overall with darker upperparts than underparts and lack the distinctive black-and-white markings. In flight in all plumages the uppertail coverts and back are the same color, the underwings are gray throughout, and there is an indistinct pale wing stripe. Primaries of standing birds extend well past the tail.

black underparts, including undertail coverts

- **SONG** Shrieking *ku-wheep* or *quee-dle*.
- **BEHAVIOR** Often flies in small swiftly moving flocks. Holds wings back after alighting; often bobs head. Feeds on insects (mostly grasshoppers, crickets, and larvae), small mollusks, and crustaceans. On tundra often gorges on crowberry in preparation for autumn migration.
- **BREEDING** Monogamous.
- **NESTING** Incubation 26–27 days by both sexes in turn; male by day, female at night. Precocial young abandon nest soon after hatching. Tended by both sexes. First flight at 21–24 days. 1 brood per year.
- **POPULATION** Uncommon. May be limited because of habitat loss on South American winter range; perhaps never fully recovered from 19th-century market hunting.

Similar Birds

PACIFIC GOLDEN-PLOVER ♂ Longer tertials; shorter primary projection • juveniles and winter birds appear golden yellow overall with spangling and spotting on upperparts; less contrasting crown.

MOUNTAIN PLOVER Plainer overall without markings on lower breast or belly; pale legs.

BLACK-BELLIED PLOVER In winter plumage has black axillaries; white rump.

Flight Pattern

Swift strong direct flight on steady rapid wing beats. Flies in tight flocks that constantly change shape.

Nest Identification

Shape ⚭   Location ⁂

Lined with lichens, moss, grass, and leaves • on ground in tundra • built by male • 3–4 cinnamon to light buff or cream eggs marked with black and brown spots and blotches, 1.9 inches long.

Plumage Sexes similar	Habitat 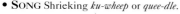	Migration Migratory	Weight 5.1 ounces

DATE _____ TIME_____ LOCATION _____

Family CHARADRIIDAE	Species *Charadrius alexandrinus*	Length 6–7 inches	Wingspan 13.5 inches

SNOWY PLOVER

The smallest and whitest of the North American plovers inhabits barren sandy beaches. Unlike all other "ringed" plovers in North America, breast band is never complete. Females and juveniles resemble males except for

smaller lighter breast band

black forehead

sand-colored upperparts

long thin black bill

sand-colored upperparts

black patch

black forehead

long thin black bill

FEMALE

dark legs

large dark breast band

their smaller lighter breast bands. Adults have a blackish forehead with a patch behind the eye.

dark legs

MALE

JUVENILE

• **SONG** Soft *krut* and a mellow *kuwheet* or *pee-e-et*.

• **BEHAVIOR** Feeds like Sanderlings, chasing waves in and out to glean small crustaceans and soft invertebrates from the wet sand. Inland foraging birds add small insects to their diets. Gathers in flocks in nonbreeding season. Tends to run away rapidly when approached on open flats.

• **BREEDING** Monogamous; some individuals polygamous.

• **NESTING** Incubation 24–32 days by both sexes. Precocial young fed by both sexes. 1–2 broods per year.

• **POPULATION** Rare. Declining in some areas, especially Gulf Coast and parts of Pacific Coast.

Similar Birds

PIPING PLOVER
Breeding plumage has complete breast band, yellow bill with black tip; yellow legs and feet; no dark ear patch • in winter has dark bill, but larger; legs and feet dark but not black; lacks dark ear patch.

• **CONSERVATION** Human disturbance on beaches often causes failed nesting attempts. Considered threatened in parts of range. Declining populations have prompted management by state and federal agencies.

Flight Pattern
Direct flight with rapid wing beats.

Nest Identification	
Shape ⚬ Location ▬	Lined with bits of shell, grass, and pebbles by female • marked with twigs and debris • built by male • very often on edge of Least Tern colonies, whose eggs look remarkably similar • 2–3 pale, buff eggs dotted, spotted, and scrawled with black or gray; conical to elliptical, 1.2 inches long.

Plumage Sexes differ	Habitat 〜 ≈	Migration Some migrate	Weight 1.4 ounces

DATE _____ TIME_____ LOCATION _____

| Family CHARADRIIDAE | Species *Charadrius wilsonia* | Length 7–8 inches | Wingspan 14–16 inches |

WILSON'S PLOVER

Like other plovers, if a human intrudes upon its nest, the female will dash around, pretending to scrape various nests, to distract the trespasser. Both sexes perform the "crippled bird" act to lure predators away from the nest. This coastal species flies effortlessly, yet if presented with danger on land it usually runs down the beach instead of flying. The duller-colored female is similar to the male but has a brown neck band, forecrown, and lores. Juveniles resemble females, but have scalier upperparts.

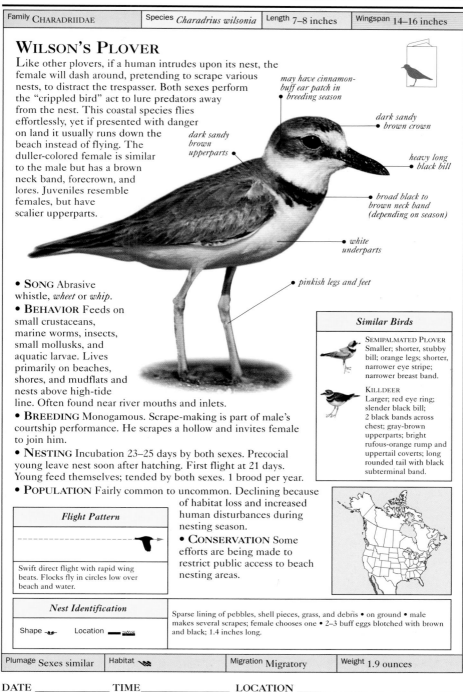

may have cinnamon-buff ear patch in breeding season

dark sandy brown crown

dark sandy brown upperparts

heavy long black bill

broad black to brown neck band (depending on season)

white underparts

pinkish legs and feet

- **SONG** Abrasive whistle, *wheet* or *whip.*
- **BEHAVIOR** Feeds on small crustaceans, marine worms, insects, small mollusks, and aquatic larvae. Lives primarily on beaches, shores, and mudflats and nests above high-tide line. Often found near river mouths and inlets.
- **BREEDING** Monogamous. Scrape-making is part of male's courtship performance. He scrapes a hollow and invites female to join him.
- **NESTING** Incubation 23–25 days by both sexes. Precocial young leave nest soon after hatching. First flight at 21 days. Young feed themselves; tended by both sexes. 1 brood per year.
- **POPULATION** Fairly common to uncommon. Declining because of habitat loss and increased human disturbances during nesting season.
- **CONSERVATION** Some efforts are being made to restrict public access to beach nesting areas.

Similar Birds

SEMIPALMATED PLOVER Smaller; shorter, stubby bill; orange legs; shorter, narrower eye stripe; narrower breast band.

KILLDEER Larger; red eye ring; slender black bill; 2 black bands across chest; gray-brown upperparts; bright rufous-orange rump and uppertail coverts; long rounded tail with black subterminal band.

Flight Pattern

Swift direct flight with rapid wing beats. Flocks fly in circles low over beach and water.

Nest Identification

Shape ⚬ Location ▬

Sparse lining of pebbles, shell pieces, grass, and debris • on ground • male makes several scrapes; female chooses one • 2–3 buff eggs blotched with brown and black; 1.4 inches long.

| Plumage Sexes similar | Habitat ⚬ | Migration Migratory | Weight 1.9 ounces |

DATE _____ TIME_____ LOCATION _____

Family CHARADRIIDAE	Species *Charadrius semipalmatus*	Length 7 inches	Wingspan 14–15.25 inches

SEMIPALMATED PLOVER

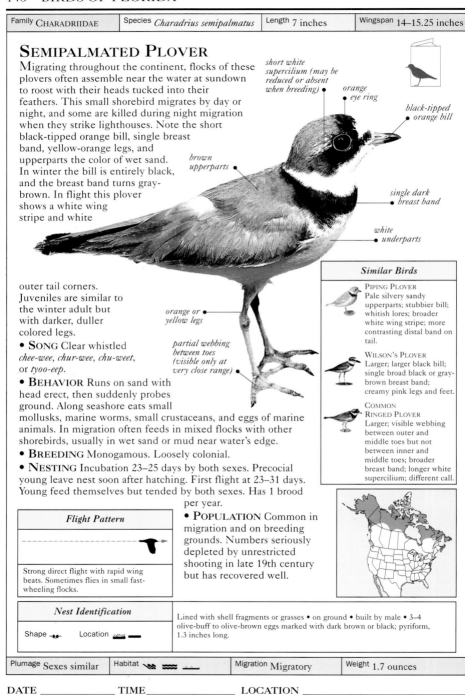

Migrating throughout the continent, flocks of these plovers often assemble near the water at sundown to roost with their heads tucked into their feathers. This small shorebird migrates by day or night, and some are killed during night migration when they strike lighthouses. Note the short black-tipped orange bill, single breast band, yellow-orange legs, and upperparts the color of wet sand. In winter the bill is entirely black, and the breast band turns gray-brown. In flight this plover shows a white wing stripe and white

short white supercilium (may be reduced or absent when breeding)

orange eye ring

black-tipped orange bill

brown upperparts

single dark breast band

white underparts

outer tail corners. Juveniles are similar to the winter adult but with darker, duller colored legs.

orange or yellow legs

partial webbing between toes (visible only at very close range)

- **SONG** Clear whistled *chee-wee, chur-wee, chu-weet,* or *tyoo-eep.*
- **BEHAVIOR** Runs on sand with head erect, then suddenly probes ground. Along seashore eats small mollusks, marine worms, small crustaceans, and eggs of marine animals. In migration often feeds in mixed flocks with other shorebirds, usually in wet sand or mud near water's edge.
- **BREEDING** Monogamous. Loosely colonial.
- **NESTING** Incubation 23–25 days by both sexes. Precocial young leave nest soon after hatching. First flight at 23–31 days. Young feed themselves but tended by both sexes. Has 1 brood per year.

Similar Birds

PIPING PLOVER
Pale silvery sandy upperparts; stubbier bill; whitish lores; broader white wing stripe; more contrasting distal band on tail.

WILSON'S PLOVER
Larger; larger black bill; single broad black or gray-brown breast band; creamy pink legs and feet.

COMMON RINGED PLOVER
Larger; visible webbing between outer and middle toes but not between inner and middle toes; broader breast band; longer white supercilium; different call.

- **POPULATION** Common in migration and on breeding grounds. Numbers seriously depleted by unrestricted shooting in late 19th century but has recovered well.

Flight Pattern
Strong direct flight with rapid wing beats. Sometimes flies in small fast-wheeling flocks.

Nest Identification	
Shape · Location	Lined with shell fragments or grasses • on ground • built by male • 3–4 olive-buff to olive-brown eggs marked with dark brown or black; pyriform, 1.3 inches long.

Plumage Sexes similar	Habitat	Migration Migratory	Weight 1.7 ounces

DATE _____ TIME_____ LOCATION _____

Family CHARADRIIDAE	Species *Charadrius melodus*	Length 7.25 inches	Wingspan 14–15.5 inches

PIPING PLOVER

This plover is difficult to spot until it moves, as its plumage blends in with the dry summer sand along the Atlantic Coast and south shores of the Great Lakes region. Endemic to central and eastern North America, and once common on beaches, this bird is now endangered because of human activity and disturbance during nesting season. Note the dry sand color of the upperparts, the yellow legs, and in flight the white wing stripe and white rump with contrasting black tail tip. Winter plumaged birds have a blackish orange bill, darker duller orange legs, and the sandy breast band may be broken. Juveniles are similar to winter adults.

white forehead and lores

sandy buff overall

orange bill with black tip

narrow blackish breast band (may be incomplete in females and East Coast birds)

white underparts

yellow-orange legs and feet

WINTER PLUMAGE

- **SONG** Clear *peep-lo*.
- **BEHAVIOR** Gregarious in post-breeding seasons, but territorial when nesting. Sprints, then stops to inspect sand with head cocked to one side; picks food off ground. Eats fly larvae, beetles, crustaceans, and marine worms. Often feeds higher on the beach (where upperparts more closely match sand) than other small plovers. In migration feeds in mixed flocks with other shorebirds.
- **BREEDING** Monogamous. Loosely colonial. Territorial during breeding season.
- **NESTING** Incubation 26–28 days by both sexes. Precocial young stay in nest 20–35 days. Fed by both sexes. Has 1 brood per year.
- **POPULATION** Uncommon to rare and declining in many parts of range, especially in Midwest and Great Lakes. Uncommon migrant inland.
- **CONSERVATION** Endangered; almost eliminated as a breeder in Great Lakes region due to human activity on beaches. Irregular pattern of water release from dams affects nesting on interior rivers.

Similar Birds

SEMIPALMATED PLOVER
Dark brown upperparts the color of wet sand; dark rump in flight.

SNOWY PLOVER
Smaller; long dark legs; slim dark bill; lateral dark breast patches; lacks white rump patch in flight.

Flight Pattern

Wild direct flight with twists and turns and rapid steady wing beats; often in small flocks.

Nest Identification	
Shape 🐾 Location 🏖 ▬	Lined with broken shells, small stones, or driftwood • on sandy shore of lake or ocean well above high-water mark • built by both sexes • 3–4 pale buff eggs blotched with black and dark brown; short oval to short pyriform, 1.2 inches long.

Plumage Sexes similar	Habitat 〜 ⌐	Migration Migratory	Weight 1.9 ounces

DATE _____ TIME_____ LOCATION _____

Family CHARADRIIDAE	Species *Charadrius vociferus*	Length 9–10.5 inches	Wingspan 19–21 inches

KILLDEER

Named for its distinctive call, this bird is the largest of the ringed plovers and the only double-banded plover within its range. Perhaps the most familiar shorebird in North America, in summer it is found across almost the entire continent south of the tundra. In flight note the long pointed wings with long white stripe and the rufous-gold rump and long tail with subterminal black tail band. Juveniles are similar in appearance but have only one black band across the chest.

red eye ring

slim black bill

gray-brown upperparts

long rounded tail with black subterminal band and white tip

bright rufous-orange rump and uppertail coverts

white underparts with 2 black bands across chest

creamy pink legs and feet

• **SONG** Loud cry, *kill-dee* or *kill-deear* or *kill-deeah-dee-dee*. And ascending *dee-ee*. Also long trilled *trrrrrrrr* during display or when young are threatened.

• **BEHAVIOR** Alternately runs, then stands still as though to look or listen, then dabs suddenly with bill at ground. More than 98 percent of food consists of insects from riverbanks, golf courses, fields, and even lawns. Runs well. Leads intruders away from nest and young with "broken wing" act, rapid calls, one or both wings dragging, tail spread, and often limping or listing to one side. Once lured far enough from the nest/young, the "crippled" bird suddenly "heals" and flies away, calling all the while.

• **BREEDING** Monogamous. Solitary nester. Often returns to same mate and breeding site.

• **NESTING** Incubation 24–28 days by both sexes. Precocial young leave nest soon after hatching and feed themselves, but are tended by parents. First flight at 25 days. 2 broods per year.

• **POPULATION** Abundant to common in the northernmost regions of the range.

Similar Birds

SEMIPALMATED PLOVER Smaller; single breast band; rump and tail same color as back; yellow-orange legs.

WILSON'S PLOVER Smaller; single breast band; brown back, rump, and tail; large black bill.

Flight Pattern

Flies in wavering erratic manner on territory. Capable of swift direct flight.

Nest Identification

Shape ～ꞏ Location ～～ ꞏꞏꞏ ▬ ▷

Unlined or lined with pebbles, grass, and twigs • on ground with good visibility • built by male • 3–5 buff eggs with black and brown blotches; oval to pyriform, typically quite pointed; 1.4 inches long.

Plumage Sexes similar	Habitat ～ ꞏ● ～ ～ ～	Migration Migratory	Weight 3.2 ounces

DATE _____ TIME _____ LOCATION _____

Family HAEMATOPODIDAE	Species *Haematopus palliatus*	Length 18–20 inches	Wingspan 30–36 inches

AMERICAN OYSTERCATCHER

Like all oystercatchers, this bird uses its three- to four-inch, laterally compressed, sharp chisel-tipped bill to pry open shells for food, but it sometimes hammers and chips them open as well. The largest oystercatcher is coastal in all seasons; only vagrants are seen inland.

• black head
• yellow eyes
• long red-orange bill
• brownish back
• dark brown tail end
• black neck
• white underparts
• white wing patches
• long white wing stripe shows in flight
• pink legs and feet

In flight it shows large white patches on the wings and base of the upper tail. Juveniles have a black-tipped dark red bill, brown head and neck, and scaly brown underparts.

JUVENILE

• **SONG** *Kleep*, *wheep*, or *peep*. Makes loud *crik*, *crik*, *crik* when it takes flight.

• **BEHAVIOR** Wary; usually does not allow close approach. Eats oysters, clams, and other bivalves; also small sea urchins, marine worms, and starfish. Usually solitary or in pairs or family groups; never in large flocks. Often feeds with other birds.

• **BREEDING** Monogamous. Solitary nester.

• **NESTING** Incubation 24–29 days by both sexes. Precocial young leave nest shortly after hatching. First flight at about 5 weeks. Tended by both sexes. 1 brood per year.

• **POPULATION** Uncommon or rare resident in most of coastal North America from southern California to Pacific Coast of Mexico and from Gulf Coast of Mexico to Maryland. In summer expanding breeding range in the Northeast to Cape Cod.

• **CONSERVATION** Declined in late 19th century principally because of overshooting; however, protection by law helped population recover and species currently is expanding back into some of its former range in the Northeast.

Similar Birds

EURASIAN OYSTERCATCHER Longer white wing patches; black upperparts; white back, rump, and tail; black tail band;
• juvenile has white patch on foreneck.

BLACK OYSTERCATCHER Smaller; entirely dark body; no white on wings.

Flight Pattern

Rapid strong swift direct flight.

Nest Identification	
Shape ⟍ Location ▬ ⟍	Rimmed with shells • usually unlined • small hills of sand on dry flat beaches • above high-water line • built by both sexes • 1–4 buff-gray eggs often with dark brown speckles; ovoid, 2.2 inches long.

Plumage Sexes similar	Habitat ⟍	Migration Most do not migrate	Weight 1.4 pounds

DATE _____ TIME_____ LOCATION _____

Family RECURVIROSTRIDAE	Species *Himantopus mexicanus*	Length 14–15.5 inches	Wingspan 25–27 inches

BLACK-NECKED STILT

Extremely protective of its nest, this stilt will try to attack an intruder or will splash water with its breast as a distraction. This bird's reddish legs, which are eight to ten inches long, may be the longest, in proportion to its body size, among all birds. The female is duller and has more brown on its back. In flight the black upperparts and wings contrast strongly with the white underparts, rump, and tail, and the long legs trail far behind.

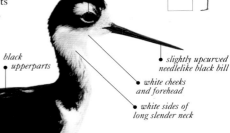

• crimson eye

black • upperparts

• slightly upcurved needlelike black bill

• white cheeks and forehead

• white sides of long slender neck

• white underparts

• **SONG** Loud *kek-kek-kek* or *yip-yip-yip*, sometimes with barking yelps.
• **BEHAVIOR** Actively feeds by walking, often rapidly, and picking up insects in shallow water along shores. Sometimes wades up to its belly. Prefers freshwater. Also eats small crustaceans, worms, small fish, and some seeds. Solitary, in pairs, or in small flocks.
• **BREEDING** Monogamous. Loosely colonial.
• **NESTING** Incubation 22–25 days by both sexes; done by female at night, by male during day. Precocial young leave nest after hatching and feed themselves, but are tended by both sexes. First flight at 4–5 weeks. 1 brood per year.
• **POPULATION** Fairly common to uncommon. Casual north of breeding range. May be increasing as range expands.

• long pink or red legs

Similar Birds

AMERICAN AVOCET
Black-and-white pattern on back and wings; white underparts and upper back; long, slender upturned bill • rusty cinnamon head and neck in breeding plumage • grayish buff head and neck in winter.

BLACK-WINGED STILT
Face entirely white; base of hind neck and shoulders white • male has black crown and hind neck in breeding plumage • female head and neck entirely white • male like female in winter • juveniles have brown upperparts • accidental on Aleutian Islands.

Flight Pattern
Strong swift direct flight with somewhat shallow wing beats.

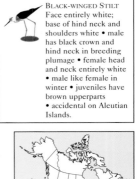

Nest Identification	
Shape 〜 Location ▬	Lined with stems, weeds, sticks, grasses, fragments of shells, small rocks, fish bones, and rubbish • on ground • sometimes hidden by grasses • built by both sexes • 3–5 yellow or buff eggs heavily blotched with black or brown; pyriform, 1.7 inches long.

Plumage Sexes similar	Habitat 〜 ▬ ≋	Migration Most migrate	Weight 5.9 ounces

DATE _____ TIME_____ LOCATION _____

| Family RECURVIROSTRIDAE | Species *Recurvirostra americana* | Length 18–20 inches | Wingspan 27–38 inches |

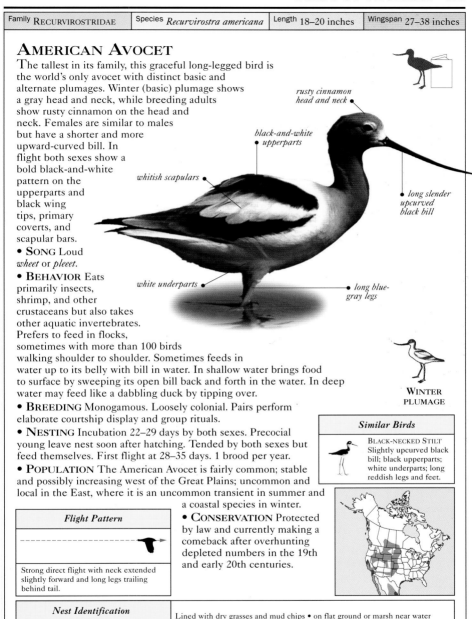

AMERICAN AVOCET

The tallest in its family, this graceful long-legged bird is the world's only avocet with distinct basic and alternate plumages. Winter (basic) plumage shows a gray head and neck, while breeding adults show rusty cinnamon on the head and neck. Females are similar to males but have a shorter and more upward-curved bill. In flight both sexes show a bold black-and-white pattern on the upperparts and black wing tips, primary coverts, and scapular bars.

rusty cinnamon head and neck

black-and-white upperparts

whitish scapulars

long slender upcurved black bill

white underparts

long blue-gray legs

- **SONG** Loud *wheet* or *pleeet*.
- **BEHAVIOR** Eats primarily insects, shrimp, and other crustaceans but also takes other aquatic invertebrates. Prefers to feed in flocks, sometimes with more than 100 birds walking shoulder to shoulder. Sometimes feeds in water up to its belly with bill in water. In shallow water brings food to surface by sweeping its open bill back and forth in the water. In deep water may feed like a dabbling duck by tipping over.
- **BREEDING** Monogamous. Loosely colonial. Pairs perform elaborate courtship display and group rituals.
- **NESTING** Incubation 22–29 days by both sexes. Precocial young leave nest soon after hatching. Tended by both sexes but feed themselves. First flight at 28–35 days. 1 brood per year.
- **POPULATION** The American Avocet is fairly common; stable and possibly increasing west of the Great Plains; uncommon and local in the East, where it is an uncommon transient in summer and a coastal species in winter.

WINTER PLUMAGE

Similar Birds
BLACK-NECKED STILT Slightly upcurved black bill; black upperparts; white underparts; long reddish legs and feet.

- **CONSERVATION** Protected by law and currently making a comeback after overhunting depleted numbers in the 19th and early 20th centuries.

Flight Pattern
Strong direct flight with neck extended slightly forward and long legs trailing behind tail.

Nest Identification	
Shape ⚬ Location ▬ ✱✱	Lined with dry grasses and mud chips • on flat ground or marsh near water • built by both sexes • 3–4 olive-buff eggs blotched with brown and black; pyriform to long pyriform, 2 inches long.

| Plumage Sexes similar | Habitat ≈≈ ⚫ ⟿ ⟿ | Migration Migratory | Weight 11.1 ounces |

DATE _____ TIME_____ LOCATION _____

Family SCOLOPACIDAE	Species *Tringa melanoleuca*	Length 14 inches	Wingspan 23–26 inches

GREATER YELLOWLEGS

The largest of the North American *Tringa*, this common sandpiper is almost a third larger than the very similar Lesser Yellowlegs. It is closely related to the Old World "shanks," but differs from them by having a squarish white rump patch and a dark back. Its large size and long bright yellow legs distinguish this gray shorebird from most others. Paler winter plumage shows fainter streaking, spotting, and barring on the

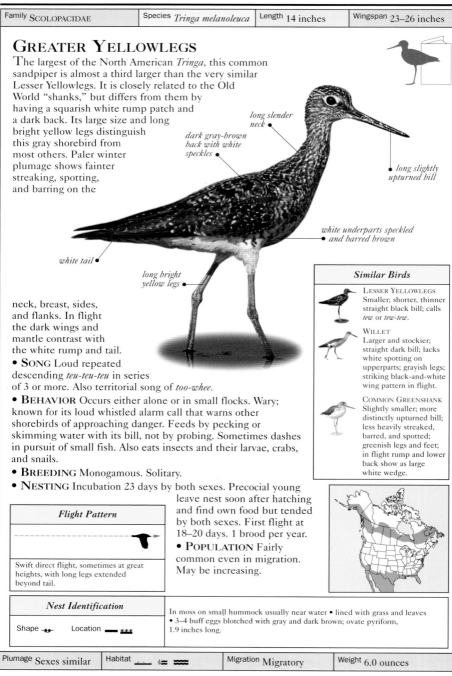

long slender neck

dark gray-brown back with white speckles

long slightly upturned bill

white underparts speckled and barred brown

white tail

long bright yellow legs

neck, breast, sides, and flanks. In flight the dark wings and mantle contrast with the white rump and tail.

• **SONG** Loud repeated descending *teu-teu-teu* in series of 3 or more. Also territorial song of *too-whee*.

• **BEHAVIOR** Occurs either alone or in small flocks. Wary; known for its loud whistled alarm call that warns other shorebirds of approaching danger. Feeds by pecking or skimming water with its bill, not by probing. Sometimes dashes in pursuit of small fish. Also eats insects and their larvae, crabs, and snails.

• **BREEDING** Monogamous. Solitary.

• **NESTING** Incubation 23 days by both sexes. Precocial young leave nest soon after hatching and find own food but tended by both sexes. First flight at 18–20 days. 1 brood per year.

• **POPULATION** Fairly common even in migration. May be increasing.

Similar Birds

LESSER YELLOWLEGS
Smaller; shorter, thinner straight black bill; calls *tew* or *tew-tew*.

WILLET
Larger and stockier; straight dark bill; lacks white spotting on upperparts; grayish legs; striking black-and-white wing pattern in flight.

COMMON GREENSHANK
Slightly smaller; more distinctly upturned bill; less heavily streaked, barred, and spotted; greenish legs and feet; in flight rump and lower back show as large white wedge.

Flight Pattern

Swift direct flight, sometimes at great heights, with long legs extended beyond tail.

Nest Identification

Shape ⌣ Location ▬ ✸✸✸

In moss on small hummock usually near water • lined with grass and leaves • 3–4 buff eggs blotched with gray and dark brown; ovate pyriform, 1.9 inches long.

Plumage Sexes similar	Habitat	Migration Migratory	Weight 6.0 ounces

DATE _____ TIME_____ LOCATION _____

Family SCOLOPACIDAE	Species *Tringa flavipes*	Length 10.5 inches	Wingspan 19–22 inches

LESSER YELLOWLEGS

Often seen walking gracefully on mudflats or shores, this sandpiper is tame and approachable. It is best distinguished from the Greater Yellowlegs by its smaller size and its bill, which is completely straight and only one-third the length of its cousin's bill, as well as by its different voice. Winter plumage is grayer and paler overall with little or no streaking. In flight the dark wings and back contrast sharply with the white tail and rump.

heavy brown streaks on head and neck

blackish grayish scapulars and mantle with white spots

long straight thin bill

blackish grayish tertials with white spots

heavy brown streaks on breast

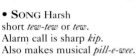

sparse brown streaks on flanks

long orange-yellow legs

• **SONG** Harsh short *tew-tew* or *tew*. Alarm call is sharp *kip*. Also makes musical *pill-e-wee*.
• **BEHAVIOR** Gregarious; occurs in flocks, sometimes large, in winter and migration. Slowly picks food from surface of water. Feeds with a delicate high-stepping gait. Eats insects, small crustaceans, bloodworms, and small fish.
• **BREEDING** Monogamous. Loosely colonial. Noisy on nesting grounds.
• **NESTING** Incubation 22–23 days by both sexes. Precocial young leave nest soon after hatching and feed themselves, but are tended by both sexes for 18–20 days. 1 brood per year.
• **POPULATION** Common on breeding grounds. In migration, common in the East and the Midwest; uncommon in the far West. Fairly common in winter in Baja and on the Gulf Coast. Stable or slightly increasing.

Similar Birds

GREATER YELLOWLEGS Larger; longer, often slightly upturned bill; more heavily barred breast and flanks; makes descending whistled series of 3 or more, *teu-teu-teu*.

SOLITARY SANDPIPER Slightly smaller; darker brown upperparts; heavier brownish streaking on neck and breast; white eye ring; dull greenish yellow legs; dark rump; in flight shows barred dark tail edged with white.

Flight Pattern
Swift direct flight with rapid wing beats.

Nest Identification	
Shape	Location	In grass marshes and bogs surrounded by black spruce trees • on raised pile of leaves or vegetation near water • lined with small amount of grass and leaves • built by female • 3–4 buff to yellow or gray eggs with brown blotches; ovate pyriform, 1.7 x 1.2 inches.

Plumage Sexes similar	Habitat	Migration Migratory	Weight 2.9 ounces

DATE _____ TIME_____ LOCATION _____

Family SCOLOPACIDAE	Species *Tringa solitaria*	Length 8–9 inches	Wingspan 15–17 inches

SOLITARY SANDPIPER

As its name suggests, this sandpiper is often seen alone or in small loose groups in its habitat of freshwater lakes, ponds, marshes, and rivers. This shorebird is not wary around humans and often exhibits an up-and-down bobbing or jerking motion with its head and body similar to a Spotted Sandpiper's bobbing. In flight the dark

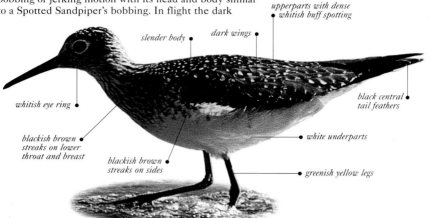

dark brown upperparts with dense whitish buff spotting

dark wings

slender body

whitish eye ring

black central tail feathers

blackish brown streaks on lower throat and breast

blackish brown streaks on sides

white underparts

greenish yellow legs

rump patch and central tail feathers contrast with the white outer tail feathers, which have black bars. Also note the dark wings without a wing stripe, dark underwings.

- **SONG** High shrill *pit-peet-wheet* or *peet*.
- **BEHAVIOR** Searches for food by stirring up water, especially in stagnant pools, with bill and feet. Picks food from surface or probes with bill. Eats insects and insect larvae, small fish, small crustaceans, and other invertebrates. Somewhat aggressive toward other birds when feeding. Migrates singly or in small groups. Upon landing holds wings above back before folding.
- **BREEDING** Monogamous.
- **NESTING** Incubation 23–24 days by female. Precocial young leave nest soon after hatching and are tended by female. First flight at 17–20 days. 1 brood per year.
- **POPULATION** Fairly common on breeding grounds; fairly common and widespread in migration. Seems stable.

Similar Birds

SPOTTED SANDPIPER Smaller; less upright stance; teeters body; yellowish or creamy pink legs; pink bill with dark tip; white supercilium; white wing stripe; shallow stiff wing beats • spotted underparts in summer.

Flight Pattern

Often zigzags on takeoff; light buoyant swallowlike direct flight.

Nest Identification

Shape   Location

Female strengthens abandoned nest with other material • most often in conifers, 4–40 feet above ground • 4–5 olive eggs marked with brown, usually in wreath shape; pyriform to oval, 1.5 x 1.1 inches.

Plumage Sexes similar	Habitat	Migration Migratory	Weight 1.7 ounces

DATE _____ TIME_____ LOCATION _____

| Family SCOLOPACIDAE | Species *Catoptrophorus semipalmatus* | Length 13–16 inches | Wingspan 24–31 inches |

WILLET

This large gray sandpiper is named for its song of *pill-will-willet* given loudly and frequently on the breeding grounds. A rather nondescript shorebird, the Willet may initially thwart your efforts at identification as it sleeps standing on one leg with its head tucked in on its back or probes in mud with its long gray-black bill. But the moment it takes flight it is readily identified by the mostly white tail, white rump, bold black-and-white wing pattern, and loud call of its name. In winter the light upperparts lack the variegated/barred pattern.

white spectacles

variegated light brownish gray to light gray overall

light underparts

bold black-and-white wing pattern

blue-gray legs

WINTER PLUMAGE

• **SONG** Alarm or scolding call of *kip* or *wiek*. In flight makes *wee-wee-wee*. Well-known call of *pill-will-will*, *pill-o-will-o-willet*, or *pill-will-willet*.

• **BEHAVIOR** Generalist. Wades, probing for food with bill. In water eats aquatic insects, marine worms, crabs, mollusks, and small fish. On land eats seeds, fresh shoots, and rice. On breeding grounds often perches high on rocks, posts, shrubs, or other tall objects, from which it may scold intruders in its territory. Becomes noisy when alarmed. Mobs will attack interlopers, especially at nesting time.

• **BREEDING** Monogamous. Semicolonial. Nests are 200 or more feet apart.

• **NESTING** Incubation 22–29 days by both sexes (male at night; female at other times). Precocial young leave nest soon after hatching but tended by both sexes. Parents sometimes abandon unhatched eggs after first young leaves nest even though they have well-developed embryos. First flight at about 28 days. 1 brood per year.

Similar Birds

GREATER YELLOWLEGS Slimmer; grayer; thinner, more needlelike, often slightly upturned bill; yellow legs; in flight has white rump and tail with distal tail bands; no wing pattern.

• **POPULATION** Common. Has recovered from hunting in late 19th century and expanded into new or parts of ranges where it had been extirpated.

• **CONSERVATION** Habitat disturbance is beginning to negatively affect population.

Flight Pattern	
Short low flight; series of rapid wing beats alternates with glides. Over long distances direct flight with steady rapid wing beats.	

Nest Identification	
Shape ⚬ Location ⚬⚬⚬	Lined with dry grass • on sand away from shrubbery, tucked in cups of vegetation or tall grasses • 4–5 grayish to olive-buff eggs blotched with brown; 2.1 inches long.

| Plumage Sexes similar | Habitat 〰 〰 | Migration Migratory | Weight 7.6 ounces |

DATE _____ TIME _____ LOCATION _____

Family SCOLOPACIDAE	Species *Actitis macularia*	Length 7.5 inches	Wingspan 13–14 inches

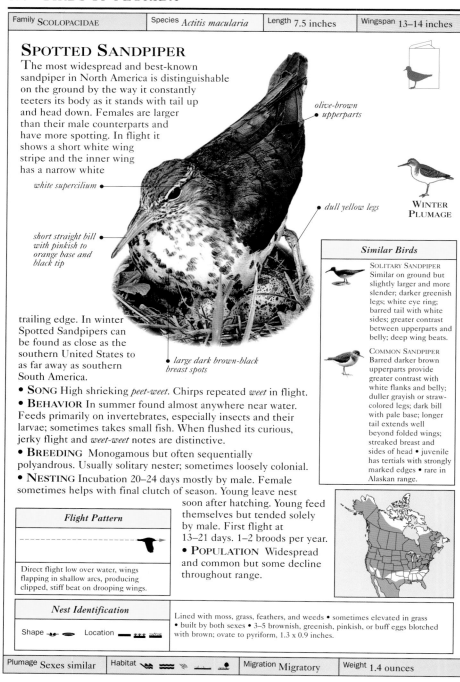

SPOTTED SANDPIPER

The most widespread and best-known sandpiper in North America is distinguishable on the ground by the way it constantly teeters its body as it stands with tail up and head down. Females are larger than their male counterparts and have more spotting. In flight it shows a short white wing stripe and the inner wing has a narrow white

olive-brown upperparts

white supercilium

dull yellow legs

WINTER PLUMAGE

short straight bill with pinkish to orange base and black tip

trailing edge. In winter Spotted Sandpipers can be found as close as the southern United States to as far away as southern South America.

large dark brown-black breast spots

Similar Birds

SOLITARY SANDPIPER Similar on ground but slightly larger and more slender; darker greenish legs; white eye ring; barred tail with white sides; greater contrast between upperparts and belly; deep wing beats.

COMMON SANDPIPER Barred darker brown upperparts provide greater contrast with white flanks and belly; duller grayish or straw-colored legs; dark bill with pale base; longer tail extends well beyond folded wings; streaked breast and sides of head • juvenile has tertials with strongly marked edges • rare in Alaskan range.

• **SONG** High shrieking *peet-weet*. Chirps repeated *weet* in flight.
• **BEHAVIOR** In summer found almost anywhere near water. Feeds primarily on invertebrates, especially insects and their larvae; sometimes takes small fish. When flushed its curious, jerky flight and *weet-weet* notes are distinctive.
• **BREEDING** Monogamous but often sequentially polyandrous. Usually solitary nester; sometimes loosely colonial.
• **NESTING** Incubation 20–24 days mostly by male. Female sometimes helps with final clutch of season. Young leave nest soon after hatching. Young feed themselves but tended solely by male. First flight at 13–21 days. 1–2 broods per year.
• **POPULATION** Widespread and common but some decline throughout range.

Flight Pattern

Direct flight low over water, wings flapping in shallow arcs, producing clipped, stiff beat on drooping wings.

Nest Identification

Shape ⌒ ⬭   Location ▬ ⋆⋆⋆ ⬱

Lined with moss, grass, feathers, and weeds • sometimes elevated in grass • built by both sexes • 3–5 brownish, greenish, pinkish, or buff eggs blotched with brown; ovate to pyriform, 1.3 x 0.9 inches.

Plumage Sexes similar	Habitat	Migration Migratory	Weight 1.4 ounces

DATE _____ TIME_____ LOCATION _____

Family SCOLOPACIDAE	Species *Bartramia longicauda*	Length 12 inches	Wingspan 17–20 inches

UPLAND SANDPIPER

The distinctive silhouette of the Upland Sandpiper is often seen perched on fences, utility poles, rocks, and stumps watching for intruders and predators in the grasslands and prairies it inhabits in summer. This large pale sandpiper has a long slender neck, small dovelike head, large dark eyes, and long tail. In winter the Upland Sandpiper migrates long distances to eastern South America.

- **SONG** Trilling *pulip pulip*. In low circling stiff-winged flight on breeding grounds, emits wolflike whistle *wheelooooooooo*. Usual flight call is piping *quip-ip-ip-ip*.
- **BEHAVIOR** Has ploverlike feeding patterns: runs, stops, then runs again. Not a bird of shores and wetlands like most sandpipers, it frequents hay fields, pastures, and prairies and often perches on poles. Feeds on insects, other invertebrates, and seeds of weeds, grasses, and grains. Upon landing often holds wings above body for 1–2 seconds before folding them.
- **BREEDING** Monogamous. Loose colonies. During courtship flight spreads wings and circles high in sky, singing a melodious song that can be heard up to a mile away.
- **NESTING** Incubation 21–27 days. Precocial young leave nest soon after hatching. First flight at about 30–31 days. Young feed themselves but are tended and protected by both sexes. 1 brood per year.
- **POPULATION** Mostly recovered since large decline in late 1800s. Common in parts of the Great Plains; some decline has been recorded in local populations throughout much of the East and the Northeast.
- **CONSERVATION** Eastern decline due to habitat loss and increased human disturbance.

small dovelike head

large dark brown eye

long slender neck

brown-streaked buff-edged upperparts

short thin yellow-brown bill slightly decurved toward tip

buff neck and breast with streaks, bars, and chevrons

whitish belly and undertail coverts

dark rump

wedge-shaped tail with white border and thin black bars

yellow-green legs and feet

Similar Birds

BUFF-BREASTED SANDPIPER Smaller; black bill; short yellow legs; buff face and underparts; wings project beyond tail.

Flight Pattern

Swift direct flight when traveling some distance. In breeding display flies slowly with flickering wing beats.

Nest Identification

Shape ⸱⸱ Location ▬ ⸱⸱⸱

Lined with dry grass • built by both sexes • 4 creamy pale buff to pinkish buff eggs speckled red-brown; pyriform, 1.8 inches long.

Plumage Sexes similar	Habitat	Migration Migratory	Weight 4.8 ounces

DATE _____ TIME_____ LOCATION _____

Family SCOLOPACIDAE	Species *Numenius phaeopus*	Length 17–18 inches	Wingspan 31–33 inches

WHIMBREL

Easily identified by its large size, distinctive head stripes, and decurved bill, this bird is the most widespread of the curlews in North America. During migration it makes frequent stops at salt marshes, coastal shores, and inland lakes and rivers. In flight this bird can easily be distinguished from European and Asian races that occur on the East and West Coasts, respectively, by its dark rump and underwings.

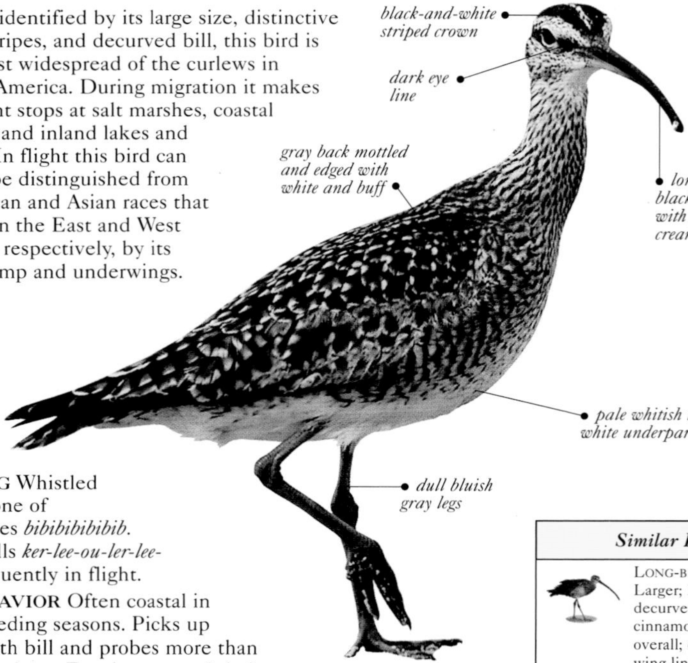
black-and-white striped crown
dark eye line
gray back mottled and edged with white and buff
long decurved blackish brown bill with pale brown or creamy pink base
pale whitish to buff-white underparts
dull bluish gray legs

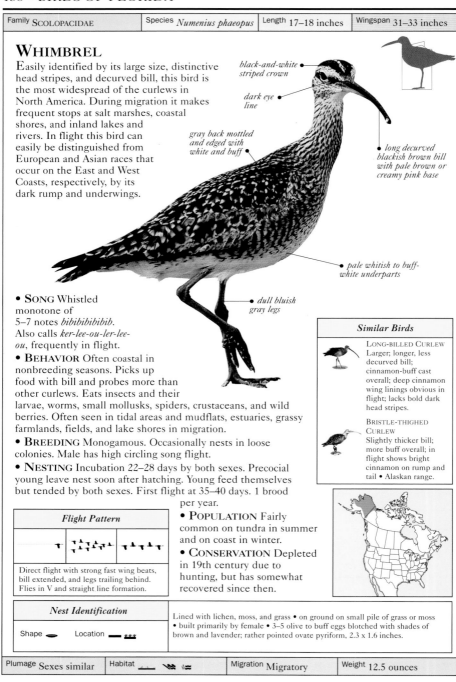

• **SONG** Whistled monotone of 5–7 notes *bibibibibibib*. Also calls *ker-lee-ou-ler-lee-ou*, frequently in flight.

• **BEHAVIOR** Often coastal in nonbreeding seasons. Picks up food with bill and probes more than other curlews. Eats insects and their larvae, worms, small mollusks, spiders, crustaceans, and wild berries. Often seen in tidal areas and mudflats, estuaries, grassy farmlands, fields, and lake shores in migration.

• **BREEDING** Monogamous. Occasionally nests in loose colonies. Male has high circling song flight.

• **NESTING** Incubation 22–28 days by both sexes. Precocial young leave nest soon after hatching. Young feed themselves but tended by both sexes. First flight at 35–40 days. 1 brood per year.

• **POPULATION** Fairly common on tundra in summer and on coast in winter.

• **CONSERVATION** Depleted in 19th century due to hunting, but has somewhat recovered since then.

Similar Birds

LONG-BILLED CURLEW
Larger; longer, less decurved bill; cinnamon-buff cast overall; deep cinnamon wing linings obvious in flight; lacks bold dark head stripes.

BRISTLE-THIGHED CURLEW
Slightly thicker bill; more buff overall; in flight shows bright cinnamon on rump and tail • Alaskan range.

Flight Pattern

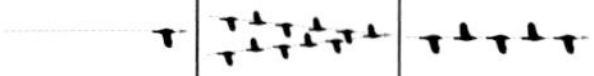

Direct flight with strong fast wing beats, bill extended, and legs trailing behind. Flies in V and straight line formation.

Nest Identification

Shape — Location

Lined with lichen, moss, and grass • on ground on small pile of grass or moss • built primarily by female • 3–5 olive to buff eggs blotched with shades of brown and lavender; rather pointed ovate pyriform, 2.3 x 1.6 inches.

Plumage Sexes similar	Habitat	Migration Migratory	Weight 12.5 ounces

DATE _______________ TIME _______________ LOCATION _______________

Family SCOLOPACIDAE	Species *Numenius americanus*	Length 23 inches	Wingspan 36–40 inches

LONG-BILLED CURLEW

The largest North American member of the sandpiper family has a very long, slender decurved bill. The male claims and defends large territories with a flapping gliding flight. After courtship and mating, these birds usually nest in dry uplands often near rivers but sometimes nest in rangelands or farmlands. As with other curlews the female is larger than the male. It is distinguished in flight by the long decurved bill and cinnamon underwing linings.

indistinct eye line

cinnamon-brown upperparts

long decurved bill

pinkish or grayish brown base on lower mandible

buff-brown underparts

dull blue-gray legs

- **SONG** Solid melodic ascending *cur-lee*. On breeding grounds gives bubbling warbled *curleeeeeeeeeeuuu*.
- **BEHAVIOR** Feeds by probing mud with bill or dunking head under water. Eats adult insects, fly larvae, aquatic insects, mollusks, crustaceans, and small amphibians. Often flies in wedge-shaped flocks, especially in migration.
- **BREEDING** Monogamous. Colonial or semicolonial.
- **NESTING** Incubation 27–30 days by both sexes. Incubating bird sits motionless on nest even if approached. Precocial young leave nest soon after hatching. Tended by both sexes. First flight at 32–45 days. 1 brood per year.
- **POPULATION** Common and widespread in nesting area. Casual to rare on southeastern Atlantic Coast in winter.
- **CONSERVATION** Overgrazing in nesting areas has caused some decline.

Similar Birds

WHIMBREL
Smaller; grayer overall; gray-brown head with distinctive stripes; pale whitish gray underparts.

MARBLED GODWIT
Smaller; straight or slightly upturned bill; cinnamon secondaries; brighter inner primaries with fewer brown markings.

Flight Pattern

Steady strong wing beats in direct flight. Gliding flight in display on breeding grounds.

Nest Identification

Shape ⬥ ⬥   Location ▬

Lined with a few bits of grass, weeds, and chips • on ground in open prairie • 3–5 pale to olive-buff eggs with brown and olive spotting, 2.6 inches long.

Plumage Sexes similar	Habitat	Migration Migratory	Weight 1.2 pounds

DATE _____ TIME_____ LOCATION _____

Family SCOLOPACIDAE	Species *Limosa fedoa*	Length 18–20 inches	Wingspan 32 inches

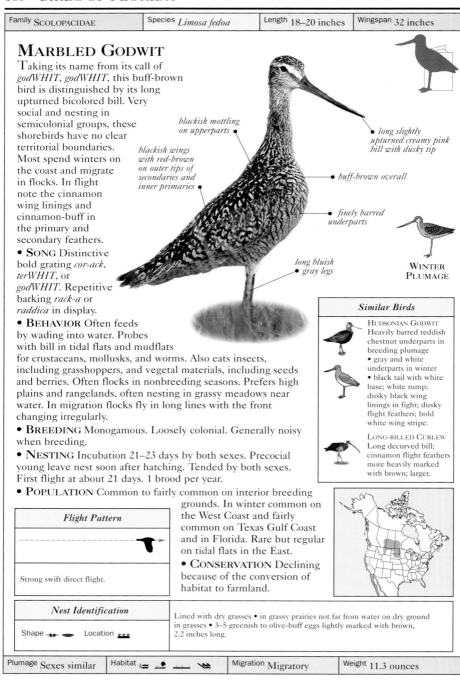

MARBLED GODWIT

Taking its name from its call of *godWHIT, godWHIT*, this buff-brown bird is distinguished by its long upturned bicolored bill. Very social and nesting in semicolonial groups, these shorebirds have no clear territorial boundaries. Most spend winters on the coast and migrate in flocks. In flight note the cinnamon wing linings and cinnamon-buff in the primary and secondary feathers.

blackish mottling on upperparts

blackish wings with red-brown on outer tips of secondaries and inner primaries

long slightly upturned creamy pink bill with dusky tip

buff-brown overall

finely barred underparts

long bluish gray legs

WINTER PLUMAGE

- **SONG** Distinctive bold grating *cor-ack*, *terWHIT*, or *godWHIT*. Repetitive barking *rack-a* or *raddica* in display.
- **BEHAVIOR** Often feeds by wading into water. Probes with bill in tidal flats and mudflats for crustaceans, mollusks, and worms. Also eats insects, including grasshoppers, and vegetal materials, including seeds and berries. Often flocks in nonbreeding seasons. Prefers high plains and rangelands, often nesting in grassy meadows near water. In migration flocks fly in long lines with the front changing irregularly.
- **BREEDING** Monogamous. Loosely colonial. Generally noisy when breeding.
- **NESTING** Incubation 21–23 days by both sexes. Precocial young leave nest soon after hatching. Tended by both sexes. First flight at about 21 days. 1 brood per year.
- **POPULATION** Common to fairly common on interior breeding grounds. In winter common on the West Coast and fairly common on Texas Gulf Coast and in Florida. Rare but regular on tidal flats in the East.
- **CONSERVATION** Declining because of the conversion of habitat to farmland.

Similar Birds

HUDSONIAN GODWIT
Heavily barred reddish chestnut underparts in breeding plumage
- gray and white underparts in winter
- black tail with white base; white rump; dusky black wing linings in fight; dusky flight feathers; bold white wing stripe.

LONG-BILLED CURLEW
Long decurved bill; cinnamon flight feathers more heavily marked with brown; larger.

Flight Pattern
Strong swift direct flight.

Nest Identification	
Shape ⚬⚬ ⬤ Location ▲▲▲	Lined with dry grasses • in grassy prairies not far from water on dry ground in grasses • 3–5 greenish to olive-buff eggs lightly marked with brown, 2.2 inches long.

Plumage Sexes similar	Habitat 〰 ⬤ 〰 ⬗	Migration Migratory	Weight 11.3 ounces

DATE _____ TIME_____ LOCATION _____

Family SCOLOPACIDAE	Species *Arenaria interpres*	Length 9–10 inches	Wingspan 17–18 inches

RUDDY TURNSTONE

The alarm cry of this stout little ploverlike shorebird alerts other birds to possible danger. It often is seen probing the drift line on beaches, even cleaning up leftovers from beach picnics. Some will take bread from a human hand. In flight the vividly patterned body and wings are unmistakable in bold rusty reds, blacks, and white. Winter plumage shows a brown-and-white face, dull brown wings and back, and a brown bib but retains the striking white stripes on the wings, back, and tail.

black-and-white face

short pointed dark bill tilts up at tip

black, white, and rusty red harlequin-patterned back and wings

white chin

black bib on breast

white underparts

short orange-red legs (duller in winter)

WINTER PLUMAGE

- **SONG** Low guttural rattle. Alarm call is *chick-ik* or *kewk*. Flight call is *ket-ah-kek* or *kit-it-it*. While feeding gives contact call of *tut*.
- **BEHAVIOR** Roots through seaweed and tips over stones, shells, and other things washed up onto shore. Feeds on insects, mollusks, crustaceans and their eggs, worms, and bird eggs. Sometimes eats discards of birds such as oystercatchers, including carrion. May eat coconut meat as well. Forages alone or in small flocks often mixed with other shorebirds. Other shorebirds may nest near Turnstones to gain protection from predators.
- **BREEDING** Monogamous.
- **NESTING** Incubation 21–24 days by both sexes, but female does more. Precocial young leave nest soon after hatching but feed themselves. Tended by both sexes, but female leaves before first flight at 19–21 days. 1 brood per year.
- **POPULATION** Common and widespread on tundra breeding grounds and on coasts in winter. Casual to rare inland in migration, except around the Great Lakes where the species is more common.

Similar Birds

BLACK TURNSTONE Dark chin; lacks chestnut or rust coloring; dark reddish brown legs • Alaskan and West Coast range.

Flight Pattern

Swift direct flight with rapid wing beats.

Nest Identification

Shape — Location —

Lined with bits of dry plants, withered leaves, moss, grass, or seaweed • in open tundra • built by female • 2–4 olive-green to olive-buff eggs marked with browns and blacks, 1.6 inches long.

Plumage Sexes similar	Habitat	Migration Migratory	Weight 3.9 ounces

DATE _____ TIME_____ LOCATION _____

Family SCOLOPACIDAE	Species *Calidris canutus*	Length 10–11 inches	Wingspan 20 inches

RED KNOT

At one time the Red Knot was one of the most abundant shorebirds in North America, but 19th-century market hunters diminished its population by slaughtering it in both spring and autumn migrations. It can be distinguished by its chunky body, short bill, and short greenish legs. Known as classic high-arctic breeders and long-distance migrants, Red Knots winter mostly in the lower half of South America and may travel 19,000 miles per year. Dappled brown-black upperparts and chestnut underparts turn to pale gray upperparts and white underparts in winter.

buff-chestnut face

dappled brown-black upperparts

WINTER PLUMAGE

short, slightly curved black bill

buff-chestnut breast

finely barred pale grayish white tail and rump

short greenish legs

• **SONG** Generally silent. Feeding birds and flocks in flight emit harsh monosyllabic *knut*. Males on breeding grounds whistle a melodious *poor-me*.

• **BEHAVIOR** Generally feeds on beaches, tidal flats, and lagoons. Eats mollusks, crabs, and insects and their larvae. When feeding in mud probes for food with bill. Often migrates and winters in large flocks that wheel, bank, and roll together in tight, dashing formations. Breeding display flight involves high, circling flight on still or quivering wings, ending with a rapid, tumbling fall, and landing with wings upraised.

• **BREEDING** Monogamous. Gregarious.

• **NESTING** Incubation 21–23 days by both sexes. Precocial young leave nest soon after hatching. Tended by both sexes. First flight at 18–20 days. Female leaves before first flight. 1 brood per year.

• **POPULATION** Uncommon to fairly common on breeding grounds and in migration on Atlantic Coast. Uncommon transient on Pacific Coast. A rare transient inland.

• **CONSERVATION** Federal protection has helped increase populations of this bird.

Similar Birds

CURLEW SANDPIPER
Slim and small; longer curved bill; pale rump • red underparts in breeding plumage.

GREAT KNOT
Longer bill; large body; lacks robin-red face, neck, and underparts; heavily spotted white underparts; heavy black spotting on breast; black streaking on neck and head; more heavily barred pale rump and tail • spring migrant in western Alaska.

Flight Pattern

Swift direct flight with rapid wing beats. Flies in V or straight line formation.

Nest Identification

Shape ⚬ᵥ   Location ▬ ⁙ ▨

Lined with leaves, lichen, and moss • hollow in clumps of lichens among rocks and scant plant life near water • built by both sexes, but male does most • 3–4 olive-buff eggs marked with brown-black spot; pyriform, 1.6 inches long.

Plumage Sexes similar	Habitat ⤳ ⬗	Migration Migratory	Weight 4.4 ounces

DATE _____ TIME_____ LOCATION _____

Family SCOLOPACIDAE	Species *Calidris alba*	Length 8 inches	Wingspan 15 inches

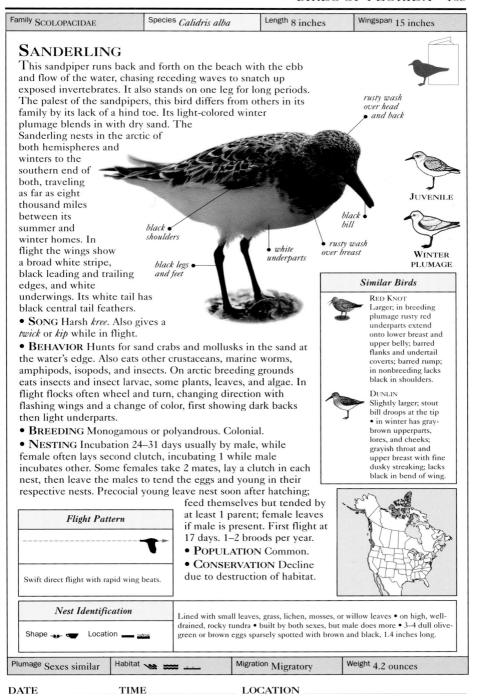

SANDERLING

This sandpiper runs back and forth on the beach with the ebb and flow of the water, chasing receding waves to snatch up exposed invertebrates. It also stands on one leg for long periods. The palest of the sandpipers, this bird differs from others in its family by its lack of a hind toe. Its light-colored winter plumage blends in with dry sand. The Sanderling nests in the arctic of both hemispheres and winters to the southern end of both, traveling as far as eight thousand miles between its summer and winter homes. In flight the wings show a broad white stripe, black leading and trailing edges, and white underwings. Its white tail has black central tail feathers.

rusty wash over head and back

JUVENILE

black bill

black shoulders

white underparts

rusty wash over breast

black legs and feet

WINTER PLUMAGE

• **SONG** Harsh *kree*. Also gives a *twick* or *kip* while in flight.

• **BEHAVIOR** Hunts for sand crabs and mollusks in the sand at the water's edge. Also eats other crustaceans, marine worms, amphipods, isopods, and insects. On arctic breeding grounds eats insects and insect larvae, some plants, leaves, and algae. In flight flocks often wheel and turn, changing direction with flashing wings and a change of color, first showing dark backs then light underparts.

• **BREEDING** Monogamous or polyandrous. Colonial.

• **NESTING** Incubation 24–31 days usually by male, while female often lays second clutch, incubating 1 while male incubates other. Some females take 2 mates, lay a clutch in each nest, then leave the males to tend the eggs and young in their respective nests. Precocial young leave nest soon after hatching, feed themselves but tended by at least 1 parent; female leaves if male is present. First flight at 17 days. 1–2 broods per year.

• **POPULATION** Common.

• **CONSERVATION** Decline due to destruction of habitat.

Similar Birds

RED KNOT
Larger; in breeding plumage rusty red underparts extend onto lower breast and upper belly; barred flanks and undertail coverts; barred rump; in nonbreeding lacks black in shoulders.

DUNLIN
Slightly larger; stout bill droops at the tip • in winter has gray-brown upperparts, lores, and cheeks; grayish throat and upper breast with fine dusky streaking; lacks black in bend of wing.

Flight Pattern

Swift direct flight with rapid wing beats.

Nest Identification

Shape ⌣ ▬ Location ▬ ▨

Lined with small leaves, grass, lichen, mosses, or willow leaves • on high, well-drained, rocky tundra • built by both sexes, but male does more • 3–4 dull olive-green or brown eggs sparsely spotted with brown and black, 1.4 inches long.

Plumage Sexes similar	Habitat	Migration Migratory	Weight 4.2 ounces

DATE _____ TIME_____ LOCATION _____

Family SCOLOPACIDAE	Species *Calidris pusilla*	Length 6.5 inches	Wingspan 11–13 inches

SEMIPALMATED SANDPIPER

This coastal inhabitant gets its name from the partial webbing it has between its front toes. This bird often mingles with other shorebirds such as sanderlings and Semipalmated Plovers around the time of high tide. Like most shorebirds, Semipalmated Sandpipers will frequently sleep standing on one or both legs, with their bill tucked into their back feathers. Sometimes they will travel along the beach hopping on one leg. Grayer in all plumages than most peeps and have less streaking on the breast and no spotting on the flanks.

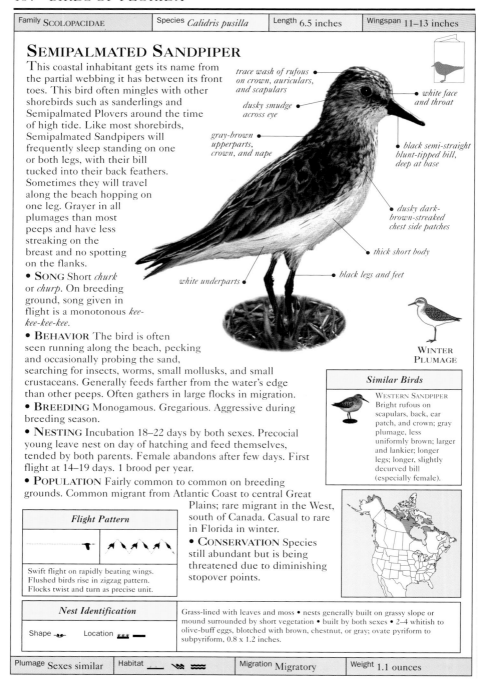

trace wash of rufous on crown, auriculars, and scapulars

dusky smudge across eye

gray-brown upperparts, crown, and nape

white face and throat

black semi-straight blunt-tipped bill, deep at base

dusky dark-brown-streaked chest side patches

thick short body

black legs and feet

white underparts

WINTER PLUMAGE

- **SONG** Short *churk* or *churp*. On breeding ground, song given in flight is a monotonous *kee-kee-kee-kee*.

- **BEHAVIOR** The bird is often seen running along the beach, pecking and occasionally probing the sand, searching for insects, worms, small mollusks, and small crustaceans. Generally feeds farther from the water's edge than other peeps. Often gathers in large flocks in migration.

- **BREEDING** Monogamous. Gregarious. Aggressive during breeding season.

- **NESTING** Incubation 18–22 days by both sexes. Precocial young leave nest on day of hatching and feed themselves, tended by both parents. Female abandons after few days. First flight at 14–19 days. 1 brood per year.

- **POPULATION** Fairly common to common on breeding grounds. Common migrant from Atlantic Coast to central Great Plains; rare migrant in the West, south of Canada. Casual to rare in Florida in winter.

- **CONSERVATION** Species still abundant but is being threatened due to diminishing stopover points.

Similar Birds

WESTERN SANDPIPER Bright rufous on scapulars, back, ear patch, and crown; gray plumage, less uniformly brown; larger and lankier; longer legs; longer, slightly decurved bill (especially female).

Flight Pattern

Swift flight on rapidly beating wings. Flushed birds rise in zigzag pattern. Flocks twist and turn as precise unit.

Nest Identification

Shape ⌣   Location ⚬⚬⚬ ▬

Grass-lined with leaves and moss • nests generally built on grassy slope or mound surrounded by short vegetation • built by both sexes • 2–4 whitish to olive-buff eggs, blotched with brown, chestnut, or gray; ovate pyriform to subpyriform, 0.8 x 1.2 inches.

Plumage Sexes similar	Habitat	Migration Migratory	Weight 1.1 ounces

DATE _____ TIME_____ LOCATION _____

Family SCOLOPACIDAE	Species *Calidris mauri*	Length 6–7 inches	Wingspan 12–14 inches

WESTERN SANDPIPER

A long-distance migrant, the Western Sandpiper flies southeast and remains on North and South American coasts during the winter months. It is the western relative of the Semipalmated Sandpiper, which it closely resembles

bright rufous crown

rufous base of scapulars

long tapered black bill slightly drooped at the tip

bright rufous ear patches

except for a longer bill that usually appears slightly drooped at the tip. In breeding plumage it has arrow-shaped spots on the sides and breast and rufous on the crown, ear patches, and scapulars. In winter plumage it is one of the palest "peeps," with almost no contrast in the faintly mottled upperparts.

arrow-shaped spots on sides

black legs and feet

partially webbed toes

WINTER PLUMAGE

- **SONG** High raspy *jeet* or *cheet*.
- **BEHAVIOR** Often can be identified by a distinctive feeding pattern: while snatching invertebrates it occasionally eats with its head immersed in the water. Feeds primarily on insects but also takes small crustaceans, mollusks, and worms. In migration and on wintering grounds, often occurs in large flocks. Coastal outside breeding season, but fairly common inland in migration.
- **BREEDING** Monogamous. Colonial. Highly gregarious.
- **NESTING** Incubation 18–21 days by both sexes. Precocial young leave nest a few hours after hatching. Female departs, but male tends young. Young feed themselves. First flight at 17–21 days. 1 brood per year.
- **POPULATION** Common to abundant on breeding grounds; common in migration and on US coastal wintering grounds.
- **CONSERVATION** Abundant but still vulnerable to habitat loss at stopover points.

Similar Birds

SEMIPALMATED SANDPIPER Shorter bill without drooped tip; duller in color; less rufous; faint or nonexistent mantle and scapular lines; dark brown upperparts edged with buff; makes harsh *churk*.

LEAST SANDPIPER Smaller; brown wash on head, head, neck, and breast with dark brown streaking; yellow-green legs and feet.

Flight Pattern
Swift direct flight with rapid wing beats. Large tight flocks twist and turn in coordinated movements.

Nest Identification	
Shape ⚲ Location ▬ 🪹	Lined with leaves, grass, and lichens • slightly elevated on moist or dry tundra near water • male hollows out several sites; female chooses one and lines nest • 3–5 whitish brown eggs marked with red-brown spots; pyriform, 0.87 x 1.2 inches.

Plumage Sexes similar	Habitat ▬ ▲ 🦆	Migration Migratory	Weight 0.8 ounce

DATE _____ TIME_____ LOCATION _____

Family SCOLOPACIDAE	Species *Calidris minutilla*	Length 6 inches	Wingspan 11–12 inches

LEAST SANDPIPER

During migration a small sandpiper on the edge of an inland pool or wet area is likely to be this species. The Least Sandpiper is the smallest of the native North American sandpipers and among the smallest waders

streaked dark neck

brown-gray upperparts

slender slightly decurved dark bill

streaked dark breast

white belly

white undertail coverts

pale green-yellow legs

WINTER PLUMAGE

in the world. These tame birds will walk close to humans along the shore. With a buff-brown wash on its streaked breast, it is one of the brownest and darkest of the "peeps." The legs and feet are dull yellowish or greenish yellow rather than black like those of most small North American sandpipers.

• **SONG** High *kneet* or *knee-eet*.

• **BEHAVIOR** Usually found in wet habitats where it obtains food by picking small animals from surface of mud and by probing mud for insects, insect larvae, and small crustaceans. Gregarious, occurring in small to large flocks. Often mixes and forages with other species of shorebirds, especially in migration and on wintering grounds. Relatively tame. Migrates at night. When flushed often rises quickly in zigzag fashion.

• **BREEDING** Monogamous. Colonial. Male announces territory by singing continuously, often for several minutes, while performing display flight.

• **NESTING** Incubation 19–23 days by both sexes (female at night; male during day; male does more). Precocial young leave nest day of hatching and feed themselves. Tended by both sexes. First flight at 14–16 days. 1 brood per year.

• **POPULATION** Common.

Similar Birds

SEMIPALMATED SANDPIPER
Slightly larger; straighter bill; whiter face, throat, and chest; black legs.

WESTERN SANDPIPER
Larger; long bill is heavier at base and slightly downcurved at tip; rustier back, ear patch, and crown; black legs • in breeding plumage has more heavily streaked breast.

Flight Pattern

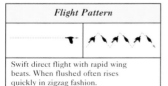

Swift direct flight with rapid wing beats. When flushed often rises quickly in zigzag fashion.

Nest Identification

Shape   Location

Lined with grass and dry leaves • on small pile of grass or moss near water • male begins building; female finishes • 3–4 olive, pinkish, or buff eggs with dark brown spots; ovate pyriform, 1.2 x 0.85 inches.

Plumage Sexes similar	Habitat	Migration Migratory	Weight 0.8 ounce

DATE _____ TIME_____ LOCATION _____

Family SCOLOPACIDAE	Species *Calidris fuscicollis*	Length 7–8 inches	Wingspan 14–16.5 inches

WHITE-RUMPED SANDPIPER

The white rump, best seen in flight, can sometimes be glimpsed on a standing bird when it spreads its wings slightly. At rest the wing tips extend well beyond the tail. In flight the rump is a distinctive field mark shared by only one other small sandpiper, the Curlew Sandpiper (a casual to rare Eurasian species). A long-distance champion flier, this bird migrates from the Canadian Arctic to southern South America, a distance of more than eight thousand miles. It appears larger in flight than it does on the ground. Crown and back are rusty.

whitish face and throat

gray to gray-brown head

small streaks on head and neck

gray to gray-brown upperparts

straight slightly tapered bill

wingtips extend beyond tail

yellow or greenish brown spot often at base of lower mandible

small streaks on breast, sides, and flanks

blackish legs

whitish underparts

WINTER PLUMAGE

- **SONG** High-pitched *jeet* described as insectlike, mouselike, or batlike.
- **BEHAVIOR** Gregarious. Often wades when foraging and may immerse entire head in water. Also probes with bill in mud for food. Feeds on marine worms, insects, weed seeds, snails, and crustaceans. Often forms single-species flocks or mixes with other shorebirds.
- **BREEDING** Polygamous. Male leaves breeding ground once eggs are laid.
- **NESTING** Incubation 21–22 days by female. Precocial young leave nest soon after hatching and feed themselves. Tended by female. First flight at 16–17 days. 1 brood per year.
- **POPULATION** Fairly common. Casual in the West.
- **CONSERVATION** Vulnerable to habitat destruction in staging areas.

Similar Birds

BAIRD'S SANDPIPER More brown overall; less-contrasting supercilium; buff edging on upperparts; buff wash on face and across streaked breast; lacks white uppertail patch.

WESTERN SANDPIPER Smaller; shorter wings do not extend past tail; dark-centered uppertail.

Flight Pattern
Strong direct flight with rapid wing beats.

Nest Identification	
Shape	Location	Lichens, moss, and leaves, especially dry willow • on pile of grass or moss near water • built by female • 3–4 olive-buff to light green eggs marked with brown; pyriform to ovate, 0.9 x 1.4 inches.

Plumage Sexes similar	Habitat	Migration Migratory	Weight 1.2 ounces

DATE _____ TIME_____ LOCATION _____

Family SCOLOPACIDAE	Species *Calidris melanotos*	Length 8–9 inches	Wingspan 15–16 inches

PECTORAL SANDPIPER

This bird is named for the two saclike structures under the neck and breast of the male. During courtship the male inflates these sacs, thus enhancing the appearance of the heavy streaking on its breast. The streaking ends abruptly in a sharp line, separating it from the snow-white belly. During flight the sacs pump up and down in rhythm with the bird's hooting calls. In flight this bird shows a blackish brown rump and tail. Males and females are similar but the male has darker brown streaking on the throat and breast with white mottling. Winter plumage is pale brown overall.

dark brown crown with black, chestnut, and pale olive-brown stripes

white stripe over each eye

thin white stripes on back and scapulars

slender black bill with greenish yellow base to lower mandible

streaked brown breast

scapular, tertial, and mantle feathers have blackish brown centers with chestnut to buff fringes

whitish underparts

greenish yellow legs

• **SONG** Low reedy *churk* or *churrrt*. Male has hooting courtship call; murmuring foghornlike *khoor, khoor*; or loud coarse *gr, gr, gr* repeated several times per second.

• **BEHAVIOR** Forages in vegetation. Feeds by pecking and shallow probing. Eats insects and larvae, small crustaceans, spiders, seeds, and amphipods. In migration prefers meadows, marshes, pond edges, tidal flats, and mudflats. Usually in small flocks of 20–40 birds. Relatively tame. May fly short distance, then pitch back into grass.

• **BREEDING** Promiscuous. Males mate several times. Females visit territories of other males. Males leave territories prior to hatching of eggs.

• **NESTING** Incubation 19–23 days by female. Precocial young leave nest soon after hatching and feed themselves, tended by female. First flight at 18–21 days. 1 brood per year.

• **POPULATION** Fairly common to common on breeding grounds and in migration on East Coast and in Midwest; uncommon from Great Plains to West Coast.

Similar Birds

SHARP-TAILED SANDPIPER
Lacks sharply defined streaked breast; buff wash across breast • in breeding plumage has streaking on crissum, sides, and flanks • juvenile has buff-orange breast and rusty crown.

RUFF ♀
Larger; longer neck; gray-brown breast with heavy spotting and blotches; in flight shows large white ovals on uppertail and stronger wing bars.

Flight Pattern

Swift direct flight with rapid wing beats. When flushed climbs with zigzag flight.

Nest Identification

Shape ● Location ▪▪▪ ▬

Grass and leaves • on dry ground near water • built by female • whitish to olive-buff eggs splotched with dark browns; pyriform to oval, 1.5 x 1.0 inches.

Plumage Sexes similar	Habitat ～～ ～	Migration Migratory	Weight 3.5 ounces

DATE _____ TIME_____ LOCATION _____

| Family SCOLOPACIDAE | Species *Calidris alpina* | Length 7.5–8.5 inches | Wingspan 14.5–15.75 inches |

DUNLIN

Impressive fliers, these small brown sandpipers are able to migrate at speeds of more than a hundred miles per hour and travel in flocks that can be so large they look like a swarm of insects. Once known as the Red-backed Sandpiper, the breeding bird is unmistakable with its long sturdy droop-tipped bill, rusty red upperparts, and black belly patch. Females are similar to males but have brown napes. When feeding it often gives the appearance of being hunchbacked.

variegated chestnut cap

whitish or light gray nape with brown streaks

patterned reddish brown back and wings

long stout black bill decurved toward tip

white throat with brown streaking that increases toward breast

tail with dark brown center, gray distal sides, and white basal sides

black legs and feet

black belly patch surrounded by white

WINTER PLUMAGE

• **SONG** Nasal slurred reedy call of *cheezp, kreeep,* or *treezp.* Flocks make soft twittering noises at roost and on feeding grounds. Alarm call on breeding grounds is *quoi.*

• **BEHAVIOR** Eats insects and larvae, marine worms, small crustaceans, snails, and small fish. Wades in shallows and uses bill to probe and pick up food. Probes with rapid up-and-down stitching motion several times per second. Gregarious, often in large flocks in migration and winter. On tundra breeding grounds male makes territorial display of lifting one wing over its back when another male enters the breeding ground. Fly rapidly while performing synchronized maneuvers as a flock.

• **BREEDING** Monogamous.

• **NESTING** Incubation 20–23 days by both sexes. Precocial young leave nest day of hatching. Tended by both sexes, but primarily by male, for several days. First flight at 19–23 days. 1 brood per year.

• **POPULATION** Common on breeding grounds, both coasts, and inland to the Great Plains in migration. Rare on the Great Plains. Common on coastal wintering grounds. Has been declining since the 1970s for undetermined reasons.

• **CONSERVATION** Vulnerable to habitat loss in staging and wintering areas.

Similar Birds

ROCK SANDPIPER Yellow-green base of bill, legs, and feet; • in breeding plumage has black chest patch • western range.

CURLEW SANDPIPER Long decurved bill • in breeding plumage has bright rusty red underparts, neck, and head; white belly, undertail coverts, and rump patch • in winter plumage has white rump without black center line.

Flight Pattern
Swift direct flight with rapid wing beats.

Nest Identification	Leaves and grasses • hummock or raised dry area on wet, grass, or sedge tundra • both sexes make scrapes, but female chooses one and completes nest • 4 olive, bluish green, or buff eggs blotched with browns or gray; pyriform, 1.4 inches long.
Shape ⬗ Location ▴▴▴	

| Plumage Sexes similar | Habitat | Migration Migratory | Weight 1.9 ounces |

DATE _____ TIME_____ LOCATION _____

Family SCOLOPACIDAE	Species *Calidris himantopus*	Length 7.5–8.5 inches	Wingspan 15.5–17 inches

STILT SANDPIPER

This long-legged sandpiper can be seen during migration feeding in dense flocks in shallow waters along the Atlantic coast. It is unwary and approachable, attributes that were exploited by early nineteenth-century market hunters to the point that it became rare and irregular in New England, where it was once common. Today this slender, long-necked, long-legged shorebird seems to be increasing in numbers and is once again common. In flight it shows a white rump. In winter, the Stilt Sandpiper displays gray upperparts and white underparts.

rufous patch on cheeks

long, slender, slightly decurved black bill

- **SONG** Low hoarse whistled *whu* or rattling trill *querrp*. Also brays, whines, and utters guttural trills on breeding ground.

horizontal barlike marking on chest and belly

- **BEHAVIOR** Eats mostly insects and their larvae, but also takes small crustaceans and mollusks and some plant materials, including seeds. May wade belly-deep in water and feed by thrusting head underwater while probing mud with beak in a stitching motion. Usually tame around humans; however, this bird has been known to attack when an intruder approaches the nest.

dark-patterned wings show narrow white bar in flight

long greenish yellow legs

WINTER PLUMAGE

- **BREEDING** Monogamous. Male chases female in flight until he flies ahead, then male dives downward singing and raising wings over back.

- **NESTING** Incubation 19–21 days by both parents; male by day, female at night. Precocial young leave nest shortly after hatching, tended by parents for about 14 days. First flight at 17–18 days. 1 brood per year.

- **POPULATION** Common on breeding grounds and in the interior east of the Rockies during migration. Rare on West Coast, primarily in fall. Uncommon on East Coast in spring; common in fall. Rare in winter in coastal southern US.

- **CONSERVATION** Populations seem to be slowly on the increase.

Similar Birds

CURLEW SANDPIPER
Winter plumage • black legs; beak more curved.

LESSER YELLOWLEGS
Winter plumage • larger; darker gray upperparts with extensive white speckling; dusky lores; white supralorals; white eye ring; bright yellow legs and feet; long straight black bill.

Flight Pattern
Strong powerful direct flight on long, rapidly beating wings.

Nest Identification	
Shape 〰 Location 〰〰 ▬	On small piles of sedge or low well-drained rocky ledges • pair may return to former nest site from year to year • male scrapes, but female decides which nest to use • 4 pale green to olive-green or cream eggs with brown spots; pyriform, 1.4 inches long.

Plumage Sexes similar	Habitat 〰 〰	Migration Migratory	Weight 2.1 ounces

DATE _____ TIME_____ LOCATION _____

Family SCOLOPACIDAE	Species *Limnodromus griseus*	Length 10.5–12 inches	Wingspan 18–22 inches

SHORT-BILLED DOWITCHER

This snipelike sandpiper is commonly seen in open marshes and mudflats during migration. Dowitchers are known by the long bill, a white wedge from the barred tail to the back that is only visible in flight, and a light belly. Although its call differs from that of the Long-billed Dowitcher, they are difficult to distinguish in the field because of the variety of breeding plumages in its three races and the overlap in bill length between the two species. Juveniles are the easiest to separate by plumage from August to October. Winter plumage is gray overall. The female is similar to the male but larger.

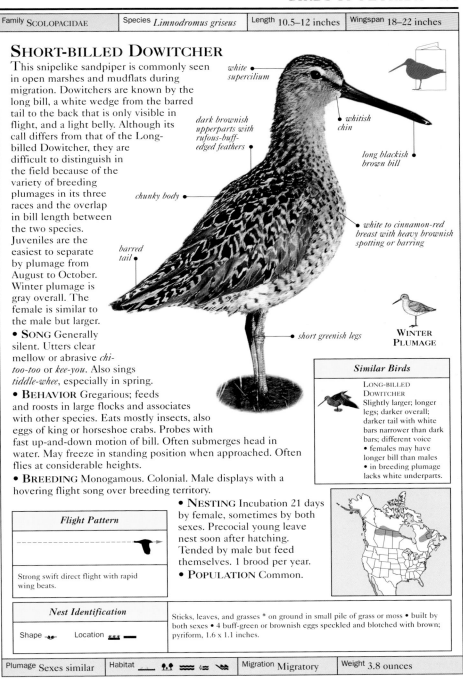

white supercilium

dark brownish upperparts with rufous-buff-edged feathers

whitish chin

long blackish brown bill

chunky body

white to cinnamon-red breast with heavy brownish spotting or barring

barred tail

short greenish legs

WINTER PLUMAGE

• **SONG** Generally silent. Utters clear mellow or abrasive *chi-too-too* or *kee-you*. Also sings *tiddle-whee*, especially in spring.

• **BEHAVIOR** Gregarious; feeds and roosts in large flocks and associates with other species. Eats mostly insects, also eggs of king or horseshoe crabs. Probes with fast up-and-down motion of bill. Often submerges head in water. May freeze in standing position when approached. Often flies at considerable heights.

• **BREEDING** Monogamous. Colonial. Male displays with a hovering flight song over breeding territory.

• **NESTING** Incubation 21 days by female, sometimes by both sexes. Precocial young leave nest soon after hatching. Tended by male but feed themselves. 1 brood per year.

• **POPULATION** Common.

Similar Birds

LONG-BILLED DOWITCHER
Slightly larger; longer legs; darker overall; darker tail with white bars narrower than dark bars; different voice
• females may have longer bill than males
• in breeding plumage lacks white underparts.

Flight Pattern

Strong swift direct flight with rapid wing beats.

Nest Identification

Shape 🐦 Location 🌿 ▬

Sticks, leaves, and grasses * on ground in small pile of grass or moss • built by both sexes • 4 buff-green or brownish eggs speckled and blotched with brown; pyriform, 1.6 x 1.1 inches.

Plumage Sexes similar	Habitat ⬚ 🌿 ≈≈ ⬚ 🌾	Migration Migratory	Weight 3.8 ounces

DATE _____ TIME_____ LOCATION _____

Family SCOLOPACIDAE	Species *Limnodromus scolopaceus*	Length 11–12.5 inches	Wingspan 18–20 inches

LONG-BILLED DOWITCHER

Despite its name, only the female has a slightly longer bill than its cousin, the Short-billed Dowitcher. The Long-billed prefers freshwater habitats and migrates south later in the season than the Short-billed. Winter plumage shows gray overall. In breeding plumage birds show no white on the underparts, and the tail is darker than that of the Short-billed,

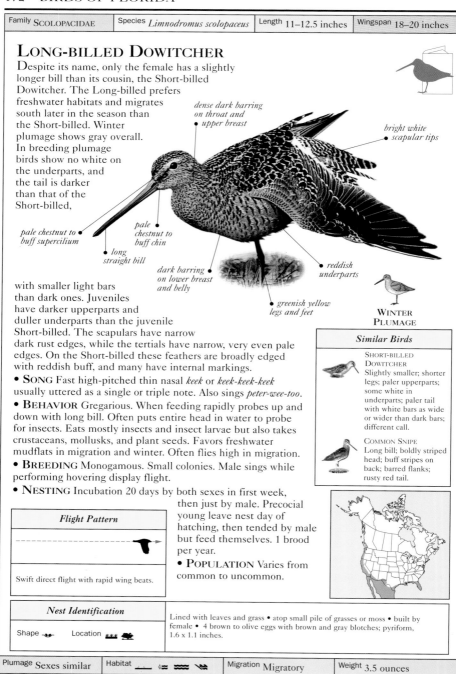

dense dark barring on throat and upper breast

bright white scapular tips

pale chestnut to buff superciliumum

pale chestnut to buff chin

long straight bill

dark barring on lower breast and belly

reddish underparts

greenish yellow legs and feet

WINTER PLUMAGE

with smaller light bars than dark ones. Juveniles have darker upperparts and duller underparts than the juvenile Short-billed. The scapulars have narrow dark rust edges, while the tertials have narrow, very even pale edges. On the Short-billed these feathers are broadly edged with reddish buff, and many have internal markings.

• **SONG** Fast high-pitched thin nasal *keek* or *keek-keek-keek* usually uttered as a single or triple note. Also sings *peter-wee-too*.
• **BEHAVIOR** Gregarious. When feeding rapidly probes up and down with long bill. Often puts entire head in water to probe for insects. Eats mostly insects and insect larvae but also takes crustaceans, mollusks, and plant seeds. Favors freshwater mudflats in migration and winter. Often flies high in migration.
• **BREEDING** Monogamous. Small colonies. Male sings while performing hovering display flight.
• **NESTING** Incubation 20 days by both sexes in first week, then just by male. Precocial young leave nest day of hatching, then tended by male but feed themselves. 1 brood per year.
• **POPULATION** Varies from common to uncommon.

Similar Birds

SHORT-BILLED DOWITCHER
Slightly smaller; shorter legs; paler upperparts; some white in underparts; paler tail with white bars as wide or wider than dark bars; different call.

COMMON SNIPE
Long bill; boldly striped head; buff stripes on back; barred flanks; rusty red tail.

Flight Pattern

Swift direct flight with rapid wing beats.

Nest Identification

Shape ⤙   Location ⁙ ⬗

Lined with leaves and grass • atop small pile of grasses or moss • built by female • 4 brown to olive eggs with brown and gray blotches; pyriform, 1.6 x 1.1 inches.

Plumage Sexes similar	Habitat ⏚ ⥱ ≋ ⬲	Migration Migratory	Weight 3.5 ounces

DATE _____ TIME_____ LOCATION _____

Family SCOLOPACIDAE	Species *Gallinago gallinago*	Length 10–11 inches	Wingspan 17–20 inches

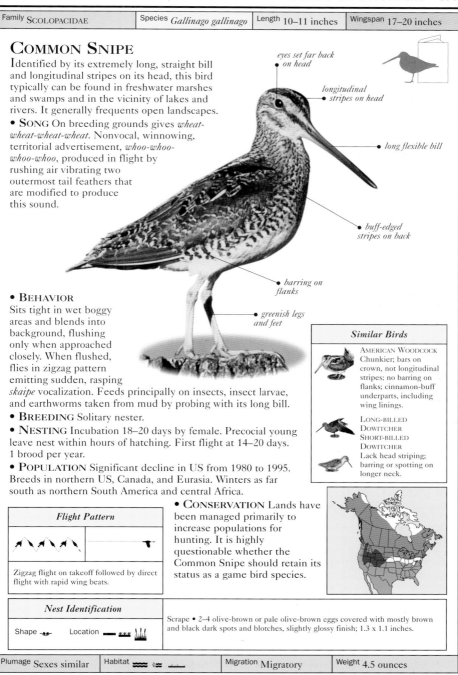

COMMON SNIPE

Identified by its extremely long, straight bill and longitudinal stripes on its head, this bird typically can be found in freshwater marshes and swamps and in the vicinity of lakes and rivers. It generally frequents open landscapes.

• **SONG** On breeding grounds gives *wheat-wheat-wheat-wheat*. Nonvocal, winnowing, territorial advertisement, *whoo-whoo-whoo-whoo*, produced in flight by rushing air vibrating two outermost tail feathers that are modified to produce this sound.

eyes set far back on head

longitudinal stripes on head

long flexible bill

buff-edged stripes on back

barring on flanks

greenish legs and feet

• **BEHAVIOR**
Sits tight in wet boggy areas and blends into background, flushing only when approached closely. When flushed, flies in zigzag pattern emitting sudden, rasping *skaipe* vocalization. Feeds principally on insects, insect larvae, and earthworms taken from mud by probing with its long bill.

• **BREEDING** Solitary nester.

• **NESTING** Incubation 18–20 days by female. Precocial young leave nest within hours of hatching. First flight at 14–20 days. 1 brood per year.

• **POPULATION** Significant decline in US from 1980 to 1995. Breeds in northern US, Canada, and Eurasia. Winters as far south as northern South America and central Africa.

• **CONSERVATION** Lands have been managed primarily to increase populations for hunting. It is highly questionable whether the Common Snipe should retain its status as a game bird species.

Similar Birds

AMERICAN WOODCOCK Chunkier; bars on crown, not longitudinal stripes; no barring on flanks; cinnamon-buff underparts, including wing linings.

LONG-BILLED DOWITCHER SHORT-BILLED DOWITCHER Lack head striping; barring or spotting on longer neck.

Flight Pattern	
Zigzag flight on takeoff followed by direct flight with rapid wing beats.	

Nest Identification	
Shape · Location	Scrape • 2–4 olive-brown or pale olive-brown eggs covered with mostly brown and black dark spots and blotches, slightly glossy finish; 1.3 x 1.1 inches.

Plumage Sexes similar	Habitat	Migration Migratory	Weight 4.5 ounces

DATE _____ TIME_____ LOCATION _____

Family SCOLOPACIDAE	Species *Scolopax minor*	Length 10.5–11 inches	Wingspan 18 inches

AMERICAN WOODCOCK

The long bill of this upland shorebird is sensitive and flexible, allowing it to feel for worms in deep soil. Woodcocks are rarely seen during the day unless flushed and escaping straightaway in flight on twittering rounded wings. Chunky, short-necked, and short-legged, its plumage matches the dead leaves of the forest floor and old fields where it roosts by day.

• **SONG** Generally silent. In spring, male on display ground has nasal call of *peeant*, similar to that of the Common Nighthawk. During display flights male produces a musical twittering with wings and a liquid, bubbling song from high overhead.

• **BEHAVIOR** Crepuscular and nocturnal.

short black tail with silvery white terminal band

gray-striped upperparts

black and brown barring on crown

big eyes set high on head

long, thin creamy pinkish brown bill

rusty underparts and underwing linings

overall black and brown barring and markings

Solitary. Eats mostly earthworms, but also takes slugs, insects, and some seeds and berries. Before probing into soil with bill, often stamps foot on ground, causing earthworms to move. During feeding, walks slowly with a back and forth rocking motion.

• **BREEDING** Polygamous; loose colonies. Male has complex courtship flight: he flies from ground, circling as high as 300 feet, hovers, chirps, and glides earthward in a series of zigzags.

• **NESTING** Incubation 20–21 days by female. Precocial young leave nest 1–2 days after hatching to feed themselves, tended by female. First flight at 14 days; independent at 42–56 days. 1 brood per year.

• **POPULATION** Fairly common. Casual to eastern Colorado and eastern New Mexico; accidental to southeastern California.

• **CONSERVATION** Hunted and managed as a game bird.

Similar Birds

COMMON SNIPE
More slender overall; longer bill; striped head pattern; pointed wings; barred sides, flanks, and undertail coverts; streaked neck and upper breast; buffy white stripes on back; reddish tail with white terminal band; longer greenish legs and feet.

EURASIAN WOODCOCK
Accidental — no recent records • much larger; brown- and pale buff-barred underparts; pointier, longer wings.

Flight Pattern
Most often has swift direct flight; when flushed, flies low for short distance before dropping back into cover.

Nest Identification	
Shape 🐦 Location 🌿 🌾 🌳	Lined with twigs and dried leaves • on ground, hidden in tall grasses, weeds, or near stump of tree • built by female • 4 buff or cinnamon eggs, with gray, purple, and brown spots; oval, 1.5 x 1.1 inches.

Plumage Sexes similar	Habitat 🐾 🪨 🌱	Migration Migratory	Weight 6.2 ounces

DATE _____ TIME_____ LOCATION _____

Family SCOLOPACIDAE	Species *Phalaropus lobatus*	Length 7.75–8 inches	Wingspan 14–15 inches

RED-NECKED PHALAROPE

Formerly called the Northern Phalarope, this bird is the smallest of the phalaropes, as well as the most abundant and widely distributed. Like all birds in its genus, the male is the only gender with brood patches with which to incubate the clutch. Male and female have similar plumage, but male looks more washed-out. White wing bars show in flight. In winter plumage both sexes have heavily streaked gray upperparts, whitish underparts, a black line through the eyes, and dark legs and feet.

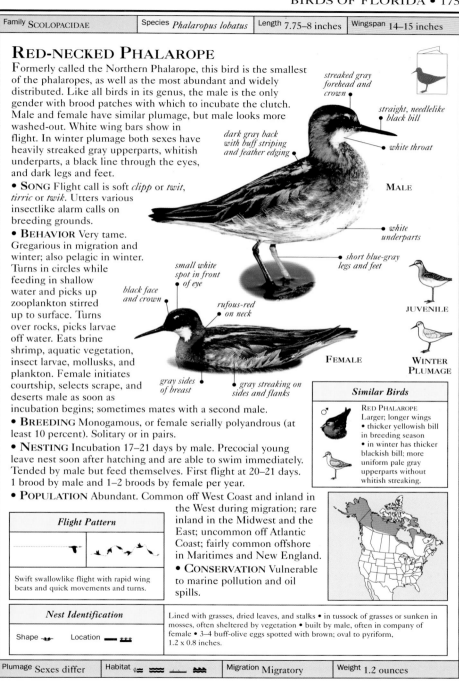

streaked gray forehead and crown

straight, needlelike black bill

dark gray back with buff striping and feather edging

white throat

MALE

• **SONG** Flight call is soft *clipp* or *twit*, *tirric* or *twik*. Utters various insectlike alarm calls on breeding grounds.

• **BEHAVIOR** Very tame. Gregarious in migration and winter; also pelagic in winter. Turns in circles while feeding in shallow water and picks up zooplankton stirred up to surface. Turns over rocks, picks larvae off water. Eats brine shrimp, aquatic vegetation, insect larvae, mollusks, and plankton. Female initiates courtship, selects scrape, and deserts male as soon as incubation begins; sometimes mates with a second male.

white underparts

short blue-gray legs and feet

small white spot in front of eye

black face and crown

rufous-red on neck

JUVENILE

gray sides of breast

gray streaking on sides and flanks

FEMALE

WINTER PLUMAGE

• **BREEDING** Monogamous, or female serially polyandrous (at least 10 percent). Solitary or in pairs.

• **NESTING** Incubation 17–21 days by male. Precocial young leave nest soon after hatching and are able to swim immediately. Tended by male but feed themselves. First flight at 20–21 days. 1 brood by male and 1–2 broods by female per year.

• **POPULATION** Abundant. Common off West Coast and inland in the West during migration; rare inland in the Midwest and the East; uncommon off Atlantic Coast; fairly common offshore in Maritimes and New England.

• **CONSERVATION** Vulnerable to marine pollution and oil spills.

Similar Birds

RED PHALAROPE
Larger; longer wings
• thicker yellowish bill in breeding season
• in winter has thicker blackish bill; more uniform pale gray upperparts without whitish streaking.

Flight Pattern

Swift swallowlike flight with rapid wing beats and quick movements and turns.

Nest Identification

Shape   Location

Lined with grasses, dried leaves, and stalks • in tussock of grasses or sunken in mosses, often sheltered by vegetation • built by male, often in company of female • 3–4 buff-olive eggs spotted with brown; oval to pyriform, 1.2 x 0.8 inches.

Plumage Sexes differ	Habitat	Migration Migratory	Weight 1.2 ounces

DATE _____ TIME_____ LOCATION _____

Family LARIDAE	Species *Stercorarius maccormicki*	Length 21 inches	Wingspan 52 inches

SOUTH POLAR SKUA

Rarely seen from shore, this skua spends much of its time at sea, scavenging around fishing boats and chasing gulls and shearwaters. It nests along the coast of Antarctica but winters (our summer) in northern oceans; vagrants have been spotted in the Aleutians and once in North Dakota. They may be seen well off the Atlantic and Pacific coasts from May to November. In flight, the South Polar Skua looks stout-bodied and chunky, with a "hunched shoulder" appearance. The smallest of the skuas, this bird has a smaller head than the Great Skua; both a light and dark morph with gradations in between may range from almost white-bodied to blackish. The intermediate morph has a medium-brown nape and underparts.

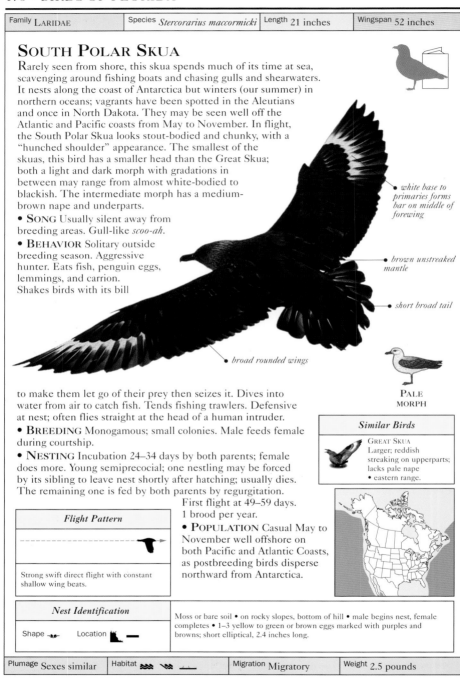

white base to primaries forms bar on middle of forewing

brown unstreaked mantle

short broad tail

broad rounded wings

PALE MORPH

• **SONG** Usually silent away from breeding areas. Gull-like *scoo-ah*.

• **BEHAVIOR** Solitary outside breeding season. Aggressive hunter. Eats fish, penguin eggs, lemmings, and carrion. Shakes birds with its bill to make them let go of their prey then seizes it. Dives into water from air to catch fish. Tends fishing trawlers. Defensive at nest; often flies straight at the head of a human intruder.

• **BREEDING** Monogamous; small colonies. Male feeds female during courtship.

• **NESTING** Incubation 24–34 days by both parents; female does more. Young semiprecocial; one nestling may be forced by its sibling to leave nest shortly after hatching; usually dies. The remaining one is fed by both parents by regurgitation. First flight at 49–59 days. 1 brood per year.

• **POPULATION** Casual May to November well offshore on both Pacific and Atlantic Coasts, as postbreeding birds disperse northward from Antarctica.

Similar Birds

GREAT SKUA
Larger; reddish streaking on upperparts; lacks pale nape
• eastern range.

Flight Pattern

Strong swift direct flight with constant shallow wing beats.

Nest Identification

Shape ⌣ Location 🏔 ▬

Moss or bare soil • on rocky slopes, bottom of hill • male begins nest, female completes • 1–3 yellow to green or brown eggs marked with purples and browns; short elliptical, 2.4 inches long.

Plumage Sexes similar	Habitat 〰〰 〰 ⌐	Migration Migratory	Weight 2.5 pounds

| Family LARIDAE | Species *Stercorarius pomarinus* | Length 20–23 inches | Wingspan 48 inches |

POMARINE JAEGER

The largest and strongest jaeger is about the size of a Ring-billed or Heermann's Gull, with a bulky body, thick neck, and wide-based wings. Like many of the skuas, its nesting is related to lemming populations on the Arctic tundra. When the brown lemming is numerous these seabirds nest, and when the rodent is not abundant they may not breed at all. It has a light color morph and a more rare dark morph. Adults

yellowish wash over nape and cheeks

chocolate-brown back, upperwing coverts, secondary flight feathers, and tail feathers

dark helmeted appearance

heavy hooked bill

2 long central tail feathers twisted 90 degrees

LIGHT MORPH

have 2 blunt central tail feathers with vanes twisted vertically. In flight this bird appears bulkier, with a slower wing beat, than other jaegers, and displays a larger white patch at the base of the primaries, often with a second smaller and fainter patch nearby.

dark band mottled across chest

chocolate-brown underwing coverts

white to pale base of primary flight feathers, darker toward tips

• **SONG** Often silent, except on breeding grounds. Sharp *which-yew* or *yeew*; high-pitched *week-week* or *yeew-eee*.

• **BEHAVIOR** Solitary or in pairs. Predatory. Eats small mammals, fish, birds, carrion, and refuse. Often steals from other seabirds. Picks up prey with bill, never talons. Found at sea outside breeding season.

DARK MORPH

• **BREEDING** Monogamous; small colonies. During courtship, male and female face one another and vibrate wings while singing.

• **NESTING** Incubation 25–27 days by both sexes. Semiprecocial young leave nest after a few days, but tended 42 days or more. First flight at 21–27 days after fledging nest. Average less than 1 brood per year.

JUVENILE

Similar Birds

PARASITIC JAEGER Smaller; more slender; two central tail feathers extended and pointed but not twisted; smaller bill; less white at base of primaries.

SOUTH POLAR SKUA Bulky, heavy body; golden streaking on nape; hunchback appearance; short wedge-shaped tail with central tail feathers not extended.

• **POPULATION** Uncommon to fairly common on tundra breeding grounds. Common to uncommon far offshore on both coasts outside breeding season.

Flight Pattern
Strong steady flight with slow deep wing beats like a large gull; may alternate several wing beats with long glide.

Nest Identification	
Shape 〰 Location ▬	Lined with plant material • on ground • built by both parents • 2 olive to brown eggs, with dark brown blotches; short elliptical, 2.6 inches long.

| Plumage Sexes similar | Habitat 〰 | Migration Migratory | Weight 1.4 pounds |

DATE _____ TIME _____ LOCATION _____

Family LARIDAE	Species *Stercorarius parasiticus*	Length 15–21 inches	Wingspan 36 inches

PARASITIC JAEGER

This skua can sometimes be seen from shore, intruding upon migrating flocks of terns and stealing food from other seabirds. It has two distinct color morphs, light and dark, and many intermediates. Falconlike in pursuit, it is about the size of a Laughing or Mew Gull and normally flies with quick wing beats broken by short glides. It is not known to breed until three to five years of age.

• **SONG** Usually silent when not on breeding grounds. Yelping notes and rising *skooo-a* or *ka-aaow*.

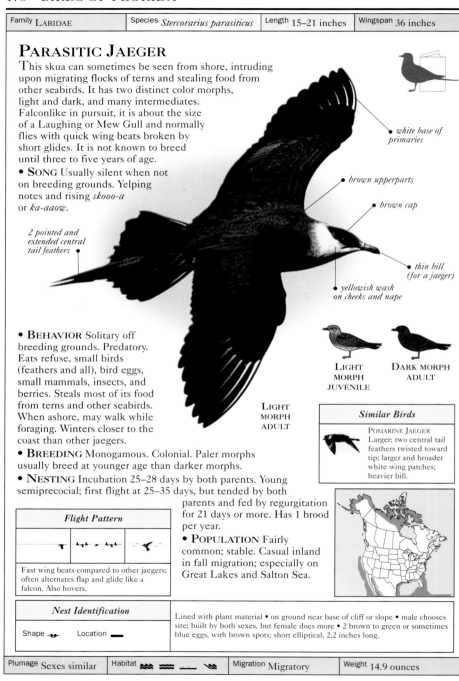

• white base of primaries

• brown upperparts

• brown cap

• thin bill (for a jaeger)

• yellowish wash on cheeks and nape

2 pointed and extended central tail feathers •

LIGHT MORPH JUVENILE

DARK MORPH ADULT

LIGHT MORPH ADULT

• **BEHAVIOR** Solitary off breeding grounds. Predatory. Eats refuse, small birds (feathers and all), bird eggs, small mammals, insects, and berries. Steals most of its food from terns and other seabirds. When ashore, may walk while foraging. Winters closer to the coast than other jaegers.

• **BREEDING** Monogamous. Colonial. Paler morphs usually breed at younger age than darker morphs.

• **NESTING** Incubation 25–28 days by both parents. Young semiprecocial; first flight at 25–35 days, but tended by both parents and fed by regurgitation for 21 days or more. Has 1 brood per year.

• **POPULATION** Fairly common; stable. Casual inland in fall migration; especially on Great Lakes and Salton Sea.

Similar Birds
POMARINE JAEGER Larger; two central tail feathers twisted toward tip; larger and broader white wing patches; heavier bill.

Flight Pattern
Fast wing beats compared to other jaegers; often alternates flap and glide like a falcon. Also hovers.

Nest Identification	
Shape ⤙ Location ▬	Lined with plant material • on ground near base of cliff or slope • male chooses site; built by both sexes, but female does more • 2 brown to green or sometimes blue eggs, with brown spots; short elliptical, 2.2 inches long.

Plumage Sexes similar	Habitat ≈≈ ≈≈ ⌁ ⩘	Migration Migratory	Weight 14.9 ounces

DATE _____ TIME_____ LOCATION _____

Family LARIDAE	Species *Stercorarius longicaudus*	Length 20–23 inches	Wingspan 30–33 inches

LONG-TAILED JAEGER

Distinguished by its eight- to ten-inch central tail feathers, this jaeger is rarely seen from land outside breeding season in the Arctic. These birds migrate in family groups to the central Pacific and south Atlantic in winter, but their route is unknown. The smallest of the jaegers, it is the least likely to steal food from other seabirds and is highly dependent on the tundra's small rodent populations in summer. In flight adults do not show a breast band, as do other jaegers. They have light grayish brown upperparts and long slender wings without a white patch at the base of the primaries (shafts of three outer primaries are white) and a slender body. Juveniles have a short tail and a white patch at the base of the primaries under the wing.

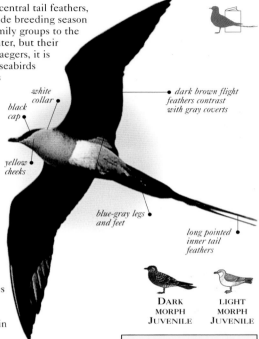

white collar

black cap

yellow cheeks

dark brown flight feathers contrast with gray coverts

blue-gray legs and feet

long pointed inner tail feathers

DARK MORPH JUVENILE

LIGHT MORPH JUVENILE

- **SONG** While flying, *pheu-pheu-pheu*. When irritated utters *kr-r-r-r, kr-r-r-r, kir-kri-kri*.
- **BEHAVIOR** In summer eats mostly lemmings and other small rodents, but also takes birds, eggs, insects, carrion, and berries. In winter eats fish, squid, carrion, and refuse. Uses beak to pick up food. Catches insects and other prey in flight. Often flies low over land or water. Most pelagic jaeger in postbreeding season.
- **BREEDING** Monogamous. Colonial. Does not breed until 3–4 years old. Courtship display features zigzag chasing flight. During courtship, male feeds female from the ground.
- **NESTING** Incubation 23–25 days by both sexes. Young semiprecocial; first flight at 22–27 days, but both sexes tend and feed by regurgitation for 7–21 days. 1 brood per year unless lemmings are scarce, then birds will not breed at all.

Similar Birds
PARASITIC JAEGER Larger; black legs; larger white patch on outer wings; grayish breast band; short, pointed central tail feathers.

- **POPULATION** Common on tundra breeding grounds. Trends stable. Disperses widely at sea outside breeding season. Fairly common to uncommon off West Coast; casual in Gulf of Mexico and on East Coast. Rare to accidental inland.

Flight Pattern
Light floating buoyant ternlike flight is graceful compared with other jaegers. Hovers before dipping to pick up prey.

Nest Identification	
Shape	Location	Lined with grasses, moss, and leaves • on ground near edge of slope • built mostly by female • 2 brown to olive eggs with dark brown and gray blotches; short elliptical, 2.2 inches long.

Plumage Sexes similar	Habitat	Migration Migratory	Weight 9.9 ounces

DATE _____ TIME_____ LOCATION _____

Family LARIDAE	Species *Larus atricilla*	Length 15–17 inches	Wingspan 40–42 inches

LAUGHING GULL

Named for its laughterlike call, this gull was threatened by the feather trade in the early 20th century. Now this coastal inhabitant forms colonies with thousands of nests. A distinguishing habit is its tendency to steal food from the Brown Pelican by snatching it out of the pelican's pouch after it surfaces with a catch. This three-year gull passes through two different winter plumages prior to attaining adult plumage. Adults have a white tail year round. In winter adults the black head is replaced by a gray smudge on the nape, and the bill, legs, and feet are dull blackish.

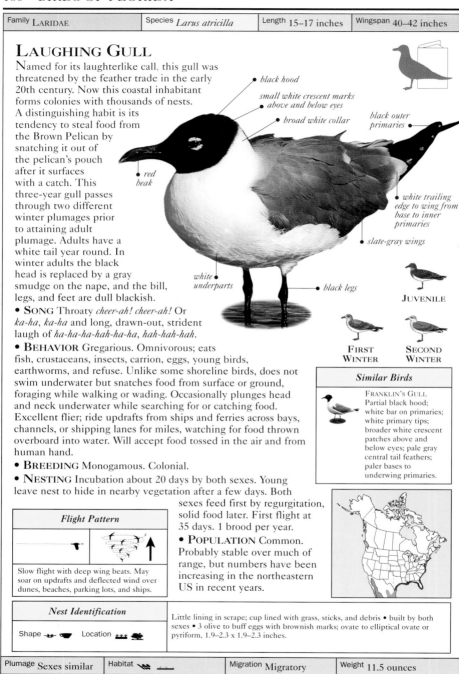

black hood

small white crescent marks above and below eyes

broad white collar

black outer primaries

red beak

white trailing edge to wing from base to inner primaries

slate-gray wings

white underparts

black legs

JUVENILE

FIRST WINTER

SECOND WINTER

• **SONG** Throaty *cheer-ah! cheer-ah!* Or *ka-ha, ka-ha* and long, drawn-out, strident laugh of *ha-ha-ha-hah-ha-ha, hah-hah-hah.*

• **BEHAVIOR** Gregarious. Omnivorous; eats fish, crustaceans, insects, carrion, eggs, young birds, earthworms, and refuse. Unlike some shoreline birds, does not swim underwater but snatches food from surface or ground, foraging while walking or wading. Occasionally plunges head and neck underwater while searching for or catching food. Excellent flier; ride updrafts from ships and ferries across bays, channels, or shipping lanes for miles, watching for food thrown overboard into water. Will accept food tossed in the air and from human hand.

• **BREEDING** Monogamous. Colonial.

• **NESTING** Incubation about 20 days by both sexes. Young leave nest to hide in nearby vegetation after a few days. Both sexes feed first by regurgitation, solid food later. First flight at 35 days. 1 brood per year.

• **POPULATION** Common. Probably stable over much of range, but numbers have been increasing in the northeastern US in recent years.

Similar Birds

FRANKLIN'S GULL Partial black hood; white bar on primaries; white primary tips; broader white crescent patches above and below eyes; pale gray central tail feathers; paler bases to underwing primaries.

Flight Pattern

Slow flight with deep wing beats. May soar on updrafts and deflected wind over dunes, beaches, parking lots, and ships.

Nest Identification

Shape ⚬ Location

Little lining in scrape; cup lined with grass, sticks, and debris • built by both sexes • 3 olive to buff eggs with brownish marks; ovate to elliptical ovate or pyriform, 1.9–2.3 x 1.9–2.3 inches.

Plumage Sexes similar	Habitat	Migration Migratory	Weight 11.5 ounces

DATE ___7/04___ TIME_____ LOCATION _____

| Family LARIDAE | Species *Larus philadelphia* | Length 12–14 inches | Wingspan 33–36 inches |

BONAPARTE'S GULL

This is one of the smallest gulls in North America and the smallest native species. It is named for French zoologist Charles Lucien Bonaparte, a nephew of Napoleon. In winter plumage it shows a plain white head without the black hood, leaving only a distinctive black spot between the eye and ear. In flight, note a white wedge on the leading edge of the outer wing, black tips on the primaries, and pale underwings. This is a two-year gull.

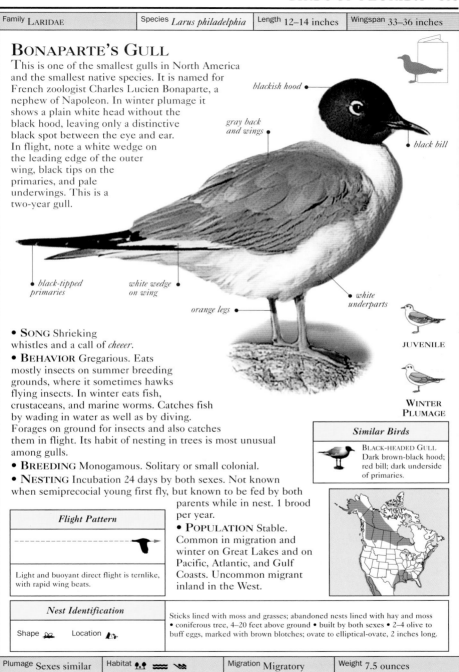

blackish hood

gray back and wings

black bill

black-tipped primaries

white wedge on wing

orange legs

white underparts

JUVENILE

WINTER PLUMAGE

• **SONG** Shrieking whistles and a call of *cheeer.*
• **BEHAVIOR** Gregarious. Eats mostly insects on summer breeding grounds, where it sometimes hawks flying insects. In winter eats fish, crustaceans, and marine worms. Catches fish by wading in water as well as by diving. Forages on ground for insects and also catches them in flight. Its habit of nesting in trees is most unusual among gulls.
• **BREEDING** Monogamous. Solitary or small colonial.
• **NESTING** Incubation 24 days by both sexes. Not known when semiprecocial young first fly, but known to be fed by both parents while in nest. 1 brood per year.
• **POPULATION** Stable. Common in migration and winter on Great Lakes and on Pacific, Atlantic, and Gulf Coasts. Uncommon migrant inland in the West.

Similar Birds

BLACK-HEADED GULL Dark brown-black hood; red bill; dark underside of primaries.

Flight Pattern
Light and buoyant direct flight is ternlike, with rapid wing beats.

Nest Identification	
Shape 🐚 Location 🌲	Sticks lined with moss and grasses; abandoned nests lined with hay and moss • coniferous tree, 4–20 feet above ground • built by both sexes • 2–4 olive to buff eggs, marked with brown blotches; ovate to elliptical-ovate, 2 inches long.

| Plumage Sexes similar | Habitat 🏖️ 〰️ 🦆 | Migration Migratory | Weight 7.5 ounces |

DATE _____ TIME_____ LOCATION _____

| Family LARIDAE | Species *Larus delawarensis* | Length 18–19 inches | Wingspan 48 inches |

RING-BILLED GULL

One of the most widespread and familiar gulls in North America, the Ring-billed Gull can be distinguished by the black subterminal band on its yellow bill.

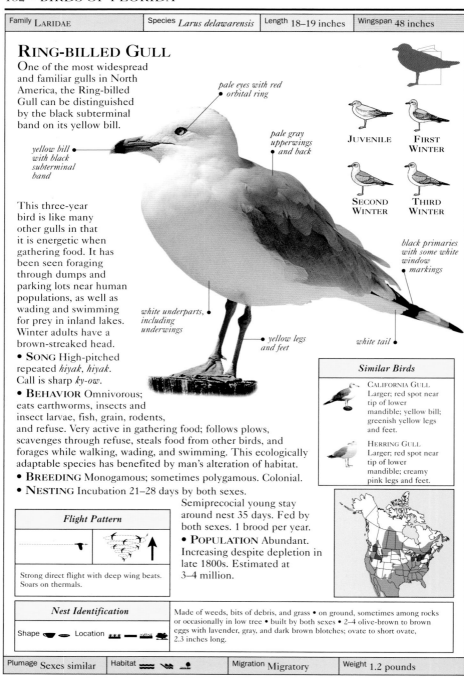

pale eyes with red orbital ring

pale gray upperwings and back

JUVENILE   FIRST WINTER

yellow bill with black subterminal band

SECOND WINTER   THIRD WINTER

black primaries with some white window markings

This three-year bird is like many other gulls in that it is energetic when gathering food. It has been seen foraging through dumps and parking lots near human populations, as well as wading and swimming for prey in inland lakes. Winter adults have a brown-streaked head.

white underparts, including underwings

yellow legs and feet

white tail

• **SONG** High-pitched repeated *hiyak, hiyak*. Call is sharp *ky-ow*.

• **BEHAVIOR** Omnivorous; eats earthworms, insects and insect larvae, fish, grain, rodents, and refuse. Very active in gathering food; follows plows, scavenges through refuse, steals food from other birds, and forages while walking, wading, and swimming. This ecologically adaptable species has benefited by man's alteration of habitat.

• **BREEDING** Monogamous; sometimes polygamous. Colonial.

• **NESTING** Incubation 21–28 days by both sexes. Semiprecocial young stay around nest 35 days. Fed by both sexes. 1 brood per year.

• **POPULATION** Abundant. Increasing despite depletion in late 1800s. Estimated at 3–4 million.

Similar Birds

CALIFORNIA GULL
Larger; red spot near tip of lower mandible; yellow bill; greenish yellow legs and feet.

HERRING GULL
Larger; red spot near tip of lower mandible; creamy pink legs and feet.

Flight Pattern

Strong direct flight with deep wing beats. Soars on thermals.

Nest Identification

Shape ⬎ ⬒   Location ⋯ ▬ ▦

Made of weeds, bits of debris, and grass • on ground, sometimes among rocks or occasionally in low tree • built by both sexes • 2–4 olive-brown to brown eggs with lavender, gray, and dark brown blotches; ovate to short ovate, 2.3 inches long.

| Plumage Sexes similar | Habitat 〰 🦅 ⚓ | Migration Migratory | Weight 1.2 pounds |

DATE _____ TIME_____ LOCATION _____

Family LARIDAE	Species *Larus argentatus*	Length 22–26 inches	Wingspan 54–58 inches

HERRING GULL

After facing a serious decrease in population in the 19th century, the Herring Gull has recovered and is once again numerous along the Atlantic Coast. Its range continues to expand, making it the most widespread and best-known gull in North America. This four-year gull usually nests on the ground, but when humans intrude, it will

heavy yellow bill

light yellow eyes

red spot on lower mandible

light gray upperwings and back

white head and neck

DARK JUVENILE

black wing tips with white spots

white breast

SECOND WINTER

white tail

creamy pinkish legs and feet

white underparts

THIRD WINTER

FOURTH WINTER

choose trees or even rooftops. Winter adults have a white head, neck, and upper breast streaked with pale brown. Plumage is highly variable.

• **SONG** Noisy with various calls, including loud *cleew cleew*, strident *kyow*, or trumpetlike *kee-ou, kee-ou*. Also has alarm call of *kek-kek-kek* or *hyiah–hyak*.

• **BEHAVIOR** Opportunistic. Often follows ships in sea lanes to feed on refuse thrown overboard. Along seacoasts eats fish, wide variety of marine invertebrates, refuse, carrion, and algae. On land eats worms, insects and insect larvae, berries, rodents, and eggs and young of other birds. Active forager. Like other gulls, carries hard-shelled mollusks into the air, then drops them on hard surface to break open shells. Sometimes steals food from other birds. Frequents garbage dumps.

• **BREEDING** Monogamous. Colonial.

Similar Birds

CALIFORNIA GULL
Smaller; dark eye; red spot edged with black on lower mandible; darker gray mantle and wings; dusky trailing edge on underwing; yellow-green legs and feet.

RING-BILLED GULL
Smaller yellow bill has black subterminal ring; greenish yellow legs.

• **NESTING** Incubation 23–27 days by both sexes. Semiprecocial young stay around nest 24–49 days. Fed by both sexes. 1 brood per year.

• **POPULATION** Abundant. Today all gulls are protected by federal law.

Flight Pattern

Strong steady flight with deep wing beats. Soars on thermals and deflected updrafts.

Nest Identification

Shape

Location

Lined with weeds, grass, and seaweed • on ground sheltered by shrubs or rock, in tree, or on roof • 2–3 gray, green, bluish, or brown eggs with brown, lavender, and black streaks; ovoid, 2.6–3 x 1.8–2.2 inches.

Plumage Sexes similar	Habitat	Migration Migratory	Weight 2.7 pounds

DATE _____ TIME_____ LOCATION _____

Family LARIDAE	Species *Larus fuscus*	Length 21–22 inches	Wingspan 54 inches

LESSER BLACK-BACKED GULL

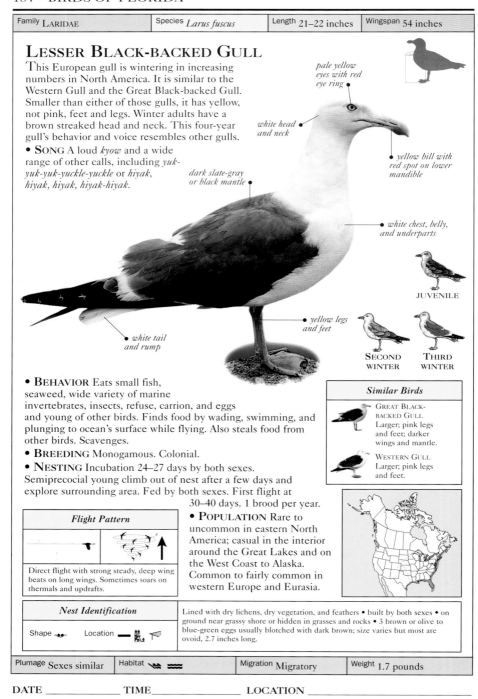

This European gull is wintering in increasing numbers in North America. It is similar to the Western Gull and the Great Black-backed Gull. Smaller than either of those gulls, it has yellow, not pink, feet and legs. Winter adults have a brown streaked head and neck. This four-year gull's behavior and voice resembles other gulls.

• **SONG** A loud *kyow* and a wide range of other calls, including *yuk-yuk-yuk-yuckle-yuckle* or *hiyak, hiyak, hiyak, hiyak-hiyak.*

pale yellow eyes with red eye ring

white head and neck

yellow bill with red spot on lower mandible

dark slate-gray or black mantle

white chest, belly, and underparts

JUVENILE

yellow legs and feet

white tail and rump

SECOND WINTER

THIRD WINTER

• **BEHAVIOR** Eats small fish, seaweed, wide variety of marine invertebrates, insects, refuse, carrion, and eggs and young of other birds. Finds food by wading, swimming, and plunging to ocean's surface while flying. Also steals food from other birds. Scavenges.

• **BREEDING** Monogamous. Colonial.

• **NESTING** Incubation 24–27 days by both sexes. Semiprecocial young climb out of nest after a few days and explore surrounding area. Fed by both sexes. First flight at 30–40 days. 1 brood per year.

• **POPULATION** Rare to uncommon in eastern North America; casual in the interior around the Great Lakes and on the West Coast to Alaska. Common to fairly common in western Europe and Eurasia.

Similar Birds

GREAT BLACK-BACKED GULL Larger; pink legs and feet; darker wings and mantle.

WESTERN GULL Larger; pink legs and feet.

Flight Pattern

Direct flight with strong steady, deep wing beats on long wings. Sometimes soars on thermals and updrafts.

Nest Identification

Shape •─•   Location ▬ 🐦 🌿

Lined with dry lichens, dry vegetation, and feathers • built by both sexes • on ground near grassy shore or hidden in grasses and rocks • 3 brown or olive to blue-green eggs usually blotched with dark brown; size varies but most are ovoid, 2.7 inches long.

Plumage Sexes similar	Habitat ⌇⌇ ⌇⌇	Migration Migratory	Weight 1.7 pounds

DATE _____ TIME_____ LOCATION _____

Family LARIDAE	Species *Larus marinus*	Length 28–31 inches	Wingspan 60–66 inches

GREAT BLACK-BACKED GULL

This predatory and domineering bird is the largest gull in North America. It is highly aggressive toward other birds but will nest harmoniously in colonies with other gulls. A four-year gull, it frequents the northern Atlantic Coast of North America. The adult is snow-white below with a white tail and black mantle and upperwings. Winter adults have very little streaking on the white head and nape. In all plumages it has pink legs and feet. The prevalence of garbage dumps in coastal areas has led to an increase in population of this species.

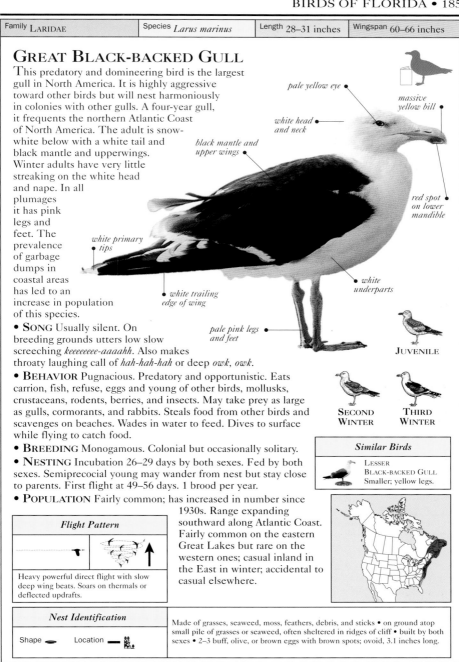

pale yellow eye

massive yellow bill

white head and neck

black mantle and upper wings

red spot on lower mandible

white primary tips

white underparts

white trailing edge of wing

pale pink legs and feet

JUVENILE

SECOND WINTER

THIRD WINTER

• **SONG** Usually silent. On breeding grounds utters low slow screeching *keeeeeeee-aaaahh*. Also makes throaty laughing call of *hah-hah-hah* or deep *owk, owk.*

• **BEHAVIOR** Pugnacious. Predatory and opportunistic. Eats carrion, fish, refuse, eggs and young of other birds, mollusks, crustaceans, rodents, berries, and insects. May take prey as large as gulls, cormorants, and rabbits. Steals food from other birds and scavenges on beaches. Wades in water to feed. Dives to surface while flying to catch food.

• **BREEDING** Monogamous. Colonial but occasionally solitary.

• **NESTING** Incubation 26–29 days by both sexes. Fed by both sexes. Semiprecocial young may wander from nest but stay close to parents. First flight at 49–56 days. 1 brood per year.

• **POPULATION** Fairly common; has increased in number since 1930s. Range expanding southward along Atlantic Coast. Fairly common on the eastern Great Lakes but rare on the western ones; casual inland in the East in winter; accidental to casual elsewhere.

Similar Birds

LESSER BLACK-BACKED GULL
Smaller; yellow legs.

Flight Pattern

Heavy powerful direct flight with slow deep wing beats. Soars on thermals or deflected updrafts.

Nest Identification

Shape ⬛   Location ▬

Made of grasses, seaweed, moss, feathers, debris, and sticks • on ground atop small pile of grasses or seaweed, often sheltered in ridges of cliff • built by both sexes • 2–3 buff, olive, or brown eggs with brown spots; ovoid, 3.1 inches long.

Plumage Sexes similar	Habitat	Migration Most do not migrate	Weight 4.0 pounds

DATE _____ TIME_____ LOCATION _____

Family LARIDAE	Species *Sterna nilotica*	Length 13–14 inches	Wingspan 33–34 inches

GULL-BILLED TERN

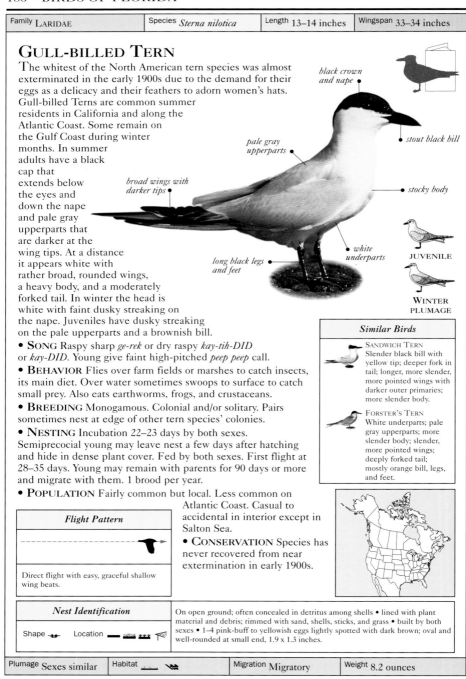

The whitest of the North American tern species was almost exterminated in the early 1900s due to the demand for their eggs as a delicacy and their feathers to adorn women's hats. Gull-billed Terns are common summer residents in California and along the Atlantic Coast. Some remain on the Gulf Coast during winter months. In summer adults have a black cap that extends below the eyes and down the nape and pale gray upperparts that are darker at the wing tips. At a distance it appears white with rather broad, rounded wings, a heavy body, and a moderately forked tail. In winter the head is white with faint dusky streaking on the nape. Juveniles have dusky streaking on the pale upperparts and a brownish bill.

black crown and nape

pale gray upperparts

stout black bill

broad wings with darker tips

stocky body

long black legs and feet

white underparts

JUVENILE

WINTER PLUMAGE

- **SONG** Raspy sharp *ge-rek* or dry raspy *kay-tih-DID* or *kay-DID*. Young give faint high-pitched *peep peep* call.
- **BEHAVIOR** Flies over farm fields or marshes to catch insects, its main diet. Over water sometimes swoops to surface to catch small prey. Also eats earthworms, frogs, and crustaceans.
- **BREEDING** Monogamous. Colonial and/or solitary. Pairs sometimes nest at edge of other tern species' colonies.
- **NESTING** Incubation 22–23 days by both sexes. Semiprecocial young may leave nest a few days after hatching and hide in dense plant cover. Fed by both sexes. First flight at 28–35 days. Young may remain with parents for 90 days or more and migrate with them. 1 brood per year.
- **POPULATION** Fairly common but local. Less common on Atlantic Coast. Casual to accidental in interior except in Salton Sea.
- **CONSERVATION** Species has never recovered from near extermination in early 1900s.

Similar Birds

SANDWICH TERN
Slender black bill with yellow tip; deeper fork in tail; longer, more slender, more pointed wings with darker outer primaries; more slender body.

FORSTER'S TERN
White underparts; pale gray upperparts; more slender body; slender, more pointed wings; deeply forked tail; mostly orange bill, legs, and feet.

Flight Pattern

Direct flight with easy, graceful shallow wing beats.

Nest Identification

Shape ⚬⚬   Location ▬▬ ⟋⟍ ♦♦♦ ⚑

On open ground; often concealed in detritus among shells • lined with plant material and debris; rimmed with sand, shells, sticks, and grass • built by both sexes • 1–4 pink-buff to yellowish eggs lightly spotted with dark brown; oval and well-rounded at small end, 1.9 x 1.3 inches.

Plumage Sexes similar	Habitat ⟋⟍ ⟋⟍	Migration Migratory	Weight 8.2 ounces

DATE _____ TIME_____ LOCATION _____

Family LARIDAE	Species *Sterna caspia*	Length 19–23 inches	Wingspan 50–55 inches

CASPIAN TERN

The largest and least sociable tern is easily distinguished by its large size, stout red-orange bill, and tail forked to a quarter of its length. In flight the underside of the outer primaries are dark. Caspian Terns are known for their predatory feeding habits, sometimes stealing catches from other seabirds and eating eggs and young of other terns and gulls. Many Caspian Terns migrate to coastal regions during winter months, moving as far south as the West Indies and the northern regions of South America. Some remain in coastal locales year-round. Juveniles and winter adults have a streaked dusky-and-white cap that extends below the eye.

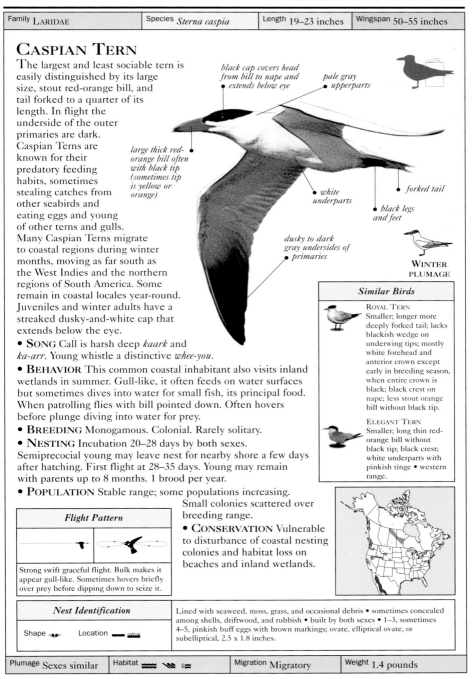

black cap covers head from bill to nape and extends below eye

pale gray upperparts

large thick red-orange bill often with black tip (sometimes tip is yellow or orange)

white underparts

forked tail

black legs and feet

dusky to dark gray undersides of primaries

WINTER PLUMAGE

Similar Birds

ROYAL TERN
Smaller; longer more deeply forked tail; lacks blackish wedge on underwing tips; mostly white forehead and anterior crown except early in breeding season, when entire crown is black; black crest on nape; less stout orange bill without black tip.

ELEGANT TERN
Smaller; long thin red-orange bill without black tip; black crest; white underparts with pinkish tinge • western range.

• **SONG** Call is harsh deep *kaark* and *ka-arr*. Young whistle a distinctive *whee-you*.

• **BEHAVIOR** This common coastal inhabitant also visits inland wetlands in summer. Gull-like, it often feeds on water surfaces but sometimes dives into water for small fish, its principal food. When patrolling flies with bill pointed down. Often hovers before plunge diving into water for prey.

• **BREEDING** Monogamous. Colonial. Rarely solitary.

• **NESTING** Incubation 20–28 days by both sexes. Semiprecocial young may leave nest for nearby shore a few days after hatching. First flight at 28–35 days. Young may remain with parents up to 8 months. 1 brood per year.

• **POPULATION** Stable range; some populations increasing. Small colonies scattered over breeding range.

• **CONSERVATION** Vulnerable to disturbance of coastal nesting colonies and habitat loss on beaches and inland wetlands.

Flight Pattern
Strong swift graceful flight. Bulk makes it appear gull-like. Sometimes hovers briefly over prey before dipping down to seize it.

Nest Identification	
Shape ⚬ Location ▬ ▬	Lined with seaweed, moss, grass, and occasional debris • sometimes concealed among shells, driftwood, and rubbish • built by both sexes • 1–3, sometimes 4–5, pinkish buff eggs with brown markings; ovate, elliptical ovate, or subelliptical, 2.5 x 1.8 inches.

Plumage Sexes similar	Habitat ~~~	Migration Migratory	Weight 1.4 pounds

DATE _____ TIME_____ LOCATION _____

Family LARIDAE	Species *Sterna maxima*	Length 18–21 inches	Wingspan 42–44 inches

ROYAL TERN

pumpkin-orange to yellow-orange bill

black crest and head

pale gray mantle

white body

black legs and feet

The second-largest tern in North America sometimes is seen snatching food from the Brown Pelican's pouch. Briefly in spring and early summer adults have a shaggy black crown from bill to nape; the rest of the year the forehead and forecrown are white. In flight birds show a tail forked to about half its length, pale underwings to the tips of dusky outermost primaries, and an orange bill. Juveniles look like winter adults but have more faint streaking on the upperparts and yellowish or orange feet and legs.

WINTER PLUMAGE

• **SONG** Large repertoire of calls includes bleating *ee-ah* and melodic trilled whistle, *tourreee*. In nesting areas often squawks *quak*, *kak*, or *kowk*.

• **BEHAVIOR** Plunge dives, from a hover 40–60 feet above ocean or inlets, and goes below surface for a catch. Eats mostly fish but also takes marine invertebrates, including shrimp and squid. When not feeding often loafs on sandbars, beaches, or mudflats with other species of terns and gulls.

• **BREEDING** Monogamous. Colonial. Often nests in mixed colonies with other species of terns.

• **NESTING** Incubation 20–31 days by both sexes. Young semiprecocial; upon leaving nest a few days after hatching, young often gather in creche, where they recognize parents by voice and beg for food. First flight at 28–35 days. May remain with parents up to 8 months or longer and migrate with them.

• **POPULATION** Declining. Has declined in California since 1950. Fairly common in breeding range; uncommon to rare north of it in late summer on Atlantic Coast. Fairly common in winter in southern California; rare to accidental inland from coasts.

• **CONSERVATION** Vulnerable to disturbance on nesting beaches by humans and wild and domestic predators.

Similar Birds

ELEGANT TERN
Smaller body; more slender reddish orange bill that appears slightly drooped at tip; longer shaggy crest extends down nape; • western range.

CASPIAN TERN
Larger body; black cap extends below eyes; lacks white forehead; thicker bright red bill; tail not as deeply forked; dark underside and pale upperside on primaries.

Flight Pattern

Direct flight with deep, more rangy, continual slow wing beats. Hovers briefly before plunge diving for prey.

Nest Identification

Shape ⌣   Location 〰

Sometimes sparsely lined with debris • built by both sexes • 1–2, sometimes 3–4, whitish buff to brown eggs with reddish brown markings, occasionally wreathed; ovate to elliptical ovate, 2.5 inches long.

Plumage Sexes similar	Habitat 〰 〰	Migration Migratory	Weight 1.0 pound

DATE _____ TIME_____ LOCATION _____

Family LARIDAE	Species *Sterna sandvicensis*	Length 14–16 inches	Wingspan 34 inches

SANDWICH TERN

This medium-sized tern is the only one that has a long slender black bill tipped with yellow. A coastal bird, it migrates short to medium distances from the Atlantic Coast above Florida in winter, and many disperse widely along the Gulf Coast. Generally seen inland only after storms, it rarely visits freshwater locales. In flight it is slender and shows dark above on the three to four outer primaries, a mostly white underwing, and a deeply forked, short tail. Winter adults (after July) have a white forehead and forecrown, and the tail is more gray. Juveniles are similar to winter adults but have mottled dark markings on the back and upperwings and may lack the yellow tip on the bill.

black crown
short black crest
white face and neck
pale gray upperparts
long slender black bill with yellow tip
deeply forked white tail and white rump
white underparts
black legs and feet

WINTER

- **SONG** Whistles abruptly; makes grating *gwit gwit* and *kir-rick* notes.
- **BEHAVIOR** More than other terns, it prefers to feed at sea and dives from great heights to catch prey under water. Usually hovers before diving for fish. Eats variety of small fish, squid, and shrimp. Often rests/roosts on beaches and bars with other terns, especially in the company of Royal Terns.
- **BREEDING** Monogamous. Colonial. Often in mixed colonies with other terns. Colony disturbance causes young to leave nest and gather in group. Young recognize parents by voice.
- **NESTING** Incubation 21–29 days by both sexes. Semiprecocial young fed by both sexes. First flight at 28–32 days. Remains with parents for 4 months after first flight. 1 brood per year.
- **POPULATION** Increasing but still uncommon. Casual spring and summer visitor to coastal southern California.
- **CONSERVATION** Vulnerable to disturbance and predation at nesting colonies.

Similar Birds
GULL-BILLED TERN Silver-gray upperparts, tail, and rump; paler wing tips above and below; heavy black bill; short forked tail • black cap until early autumn.

Flight Pattern
Powerful direct flight heavier and less graceful than that of similar-sized terns. Usually hovers before diving for fish.

Nest Identification	
Shape ⌣ Location ▬ ▬	Lined with debris or unlined • on ground in open above tidemark • built by both sexes • 1–3 pale cream to pinkish buff eggs with brown, black, and gray markings; subelliptical, 2 x 1.4 inches.

Plumage Sexes similar	Habitat ⌁	Migration Migratory	Weight 7.3 ounces

DATE _____ TIME_____ LOCATION _____

Family LARIDAE	Species *Sterna dougallii*	Length 14–17 inches	Wingspan 30 inches

ROSEATE TERN

The Roseate Tern's pale pearl-gray plumage helps distinguish it from Common and Arctic Terns. Its wing tips and tail are also paler than in those species, and the tail is more deeply forked. The pinkish tinge on the underparts, which gives the bird its name, is rarely seen except under favorable conditions. When it is perched, the long white outer tail feathers extend well beyond the tips of its folded wings. It has a mostly black bill, even in summer when the base may be red. In fall it leaves North America for South America where it winters along the coast of eastern Brazil. Winter adults have a black bill and white forehead and crown that extend past the eye.

glossy black cap and nape

pale gray upperparts

white rump

deeply forked white tail

mostly black bill

white underparts with a pinkish tinge

dark red legs and feet

JUVENILE

FIRST SUMMER

• **SONG** Sings a gentle *chi-weep*. When alarmed issues a drawling *zra-ap*, low rasping *aaak*, and a quiet *chivy*.

• **BEHAVIOR** Highly marine and coastal, coming ashore only to breed. Often forms noisy active flocks when large predatory fish drive large schools of small fish to the water's surface. Plunge dives for prey and often resumes hovering before making its next catch. Eats mainly small fish. Never seen in large numbers except over waters surrounding nesting colonies.

• **BREEDING** Monogamous. Colonial.

• **NESTING** Incubation 21–26 days by both sexes. Semiprecocial young may leave nest a few days after hatching. First flight at 27–30 days, but fed by both sexes for additional 2 months. 1 brood per year.

• **POPULATION** Uncommon to rare off the Atlantic Coast, coming ashore only to breed.

Similar Birds

COMMON TERN
Slightly smaller; black-tipped red bill; dark wing tips; shorter, less deeply notched tail with dark outer border; different voice.

ARCTIC TERN
Grayer; gray mantle, wings, and underparts; white cheeks; dusky gray wing tips; long, deeply forked tail with gray on outer margins; red bill; different voice.

• **CONSERVATION** Endangered in the Northeast where Herring Gulls have overrun island colonies. Vulnerable to human disturbance as well as domesticated and feral predators on nesting grounds.

Flight Pattern
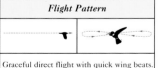
Graceful direct flight with quick wing beats. Hovers prior to plunge diving for prey.

Nest Identification	
Shape Location	Lined with bits of debris, dry grass, seaweed, and rubbish • on ground under cover • built by both sexes • 1–3 cream to buff to pale eggs speckled with reddish brown and gray, occasionally wreathed; subelliptical, 1.6–1.7 x 1.1–1.2 inches.

Plumage Sexes similar	Habitat	Migration Migratory	Weight 3.8 ounces

DATE _____ TIME_____ LOCATION _____

Family LARIDAE	Species *Sterna hirundo*	Length 13–16 inches	Wingspan 30–31 inches

COMMON TERN

black cap
and nape

red bill, usually
black-tipped

pale gray
underparts

JUVENILE

red legs and feet

dusky-tipped
wings

forked white tail with
dark outer margins
and white rump

FIRST
SUMMER

Often called the Mackerel Gull, the Common Tern is seen tending areas where large fish, such as mackerel and tuna, drive schools of smaller fish to the surface. By following the Common Tern, fishermen often find the best place to cast their nets. Although common throughout their range, today's northeastern populations of this tern are lower than previously recorded. Inland populations are suspected to be on the decline as well. The upperwings and mantle are a darker gray than most other similar-sized terns; the wing tips are dark; and the short tail is not as deeply forked. Winter adults have white foreheads and crowns past the eye, and also have dark bills.

• **SONG** Low piercing drawn-out *kee-ar-r-r-r.* Also rolling *tee-ar-r-r-r*, and high slightly grating *kik-kik-kik.*

• **BEHAVIOR** Coastal and widespread inland in breeding season. Hovering, it spots fish and plunges, knifing into water, earning the name "striker" on the mid-Atlantic shore. Principally eats small fish, generally between 3–4 inches, and some crustaceans.

• **BREEDING** Monogamous. Colonial. Often nests in mixed colonies with other terns.

• **NESTING** Incubation 21–27 days by both sexes. Young leave nest after a few days, but remain nearby. First flight at 22–28 days, but may remain with parents at least another 2 months. Fed by both sexes. 1–2 broods per year.

• **POPULATION** Common on breeding grounds and in migration on both coasts; rare in winter on southern California coast and Gulf Coast.

• **CONSERVATION** Almost completely extirpated in early 1900s by plume hunters for fashion markets. Has largely recovered since full protection established in 1913.

Similar Birds

FORSTER'S TERN
Similar in size; paler underparts and upperparts; heavier black-tipped orange bill; primaries often silver-white above, producing frosty wing tips; long forked tail, gray-edged on inner side.

ARCTIC TERN
Similar in size; shorter neck; darker gray underparts and upperparts; white cheeks; red bill without black tip; paler wing tips.

Flight Pattern

Direct flight is light and buoyant. Hovers when feeding prior to plunge-diving into water for prey.

Nest Identification

Shape Location

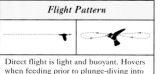

Lined with vegetation and debris, including grass, shells, and seaweed • built by both sexes • 1–3 buff to cinnamon-brown eggs, generally heavily spotted and overlaid with shades of dark brown and black; generally wreathed; oval to subelliptical, 1.6 inches long.

Plumage Sexes similar	Habitat	Migration Migratory	Weight 4.2 ounces

DATE _____ TIME_____ LOCATION _____

Family LARIDAE	Species *Sterna paradisaea*	Length 14–17 inches	Wingspan 29–33 inches

ARCTIC TERN

Distinguishable from similar terns by its short red bill, neck and legs, the Arctic Tern sometimes appears to huddle on the ground. It is perhaps the champion long-distance migrant of the world, nesting in the Arctic and wintering in Antarctica during their summer, traveling an annual distance of more than 25,000 miles. In flight, note the translucent flight feathers with a narrow trailing black border on the primaries; gray underparts; and deeply forked tail. Winter adults have white foreheads and crowns to the back of the eye, and dark bills and feet. Juveniles have white foreheads, and silvery white secondaries and outer coverts.

medium gray wings and mantle

black cap and nape

white cheeks

white rump and deeply forked tail with gray outer margins

JUVENILE

FIRST SUMMER

somewhat short, deep red bill

pale gray underparts

short red legs and small feet

- **SONG** Calls include a throaty *tr-tee-ar* and a shrieking *kee-kee*, similar to Common Tern, but higher and harsher, with emphasis on second or third note. Alarm call sounds like a brief *kee-kahr*.
- **BEHAVIOR** Often observed hovering 30–40 feet above water while searching for prey. Plunge dives to catch fish. Eats small fish and marine invertebrates, including small crustaceans. Very defensive at nest, often flying out and striking intruder while continuously vocalizing. Often follows fishing vessels.
- **BREEDING** Monogamous. Pairs or colonial.
- **NESTING** Incubation 20–24 days by both sexes. Semiprecocial young leave nest 1–3 days after hatching to hide nearby. First flight at 21–28 days. Young remain with parents additional 30 to 60 days, fed by both sexes. 1 brood per year.
- **POPULATION** Common to fairly common on breeding grounds. Casual to uncommon well offshore during migration. Steadily declining on southern end of breeding range along Atlantic Coast.

Similar Birds

FORSTER'S TERN
Similar in size; longer, orange, black-tipped bill and orange legs and feet; white underparts; frosty wing-tips; forked white tail with dusky inner margins; rarely seen well offshore.

COMMON TERN
Slightly stockier; flatter crown; longer neck and long red, black-tipped bill; shorter notched tail; dusky gray wing-tips above and below.

Flight Pattern

Buoyant graceful flight with nearly constant wing beats. Hovers above prey before plunge diving or dipping to surface.

Nest Identification

Shape ⌣⌣   Location ▬ ▨▨ ♦♦♦

Vegetation lined with debris, occasionally grass and shells • built by both sexes • 1–3 buff to pale olive eggs, blotched with black and brown markings; oval to subelliptical, 1.6 inches long.

Plumage Sexes similar	Habitat ⌣⌣ ﹏ ≈≈ ≋≋	Migration Migratory	Weight 3.8 ounces

DATE _____ TIME_____ LOCATION _____

Family LARIDAE	Species *Sterna forsteri*	Length 14–15 inches	Wingspan 30–31 inches

FORSTER'S TERN

Frequenting inland marshes as well as the coast, this widespread tern feeds and flocks with other terns. It can be distingushed by its long tail and orange-red bill. In flight note the pale frosty wing tips, white rump, and deeply forked

black cap and nape

pale gray upperparts

orange-red bill with dark tip

snowy white underparts

orange-red legs and feet

long deeply forked gray tail with white-trimmed outer margins

gray tail with white outer margins. Winter plumage shows dull yellow feet, a dark bill, and a white head with a black patch through the eye and ear. Juveniles are like winter adults but have a shorter tail, a ginger crown, and darker upperwings.

- **SONG** Throaty nasal *ki-arr*, *za-a-ap*, or *zrurrr*, with nighthawklike quality. Also gives piercing *kit, kit, kit* cry.
- **BEHAVIOR** Catches insects in flight. Eats dragonflies and other insects. Hovers above water, then plunge dives for small fish. Dips to water's surface to catch floating insects, keeping its feathers dry.
- **BREEDING** Monogamous. Loose colonies.
- **NESTING** Incubation 23–25 days by both sexes. Semiprecocial young leave nest after a few days but tended by both sexes until able to fly. 1 brood per year.
- **POPULATION** Common. Declining in some areas because of loss of marshlands.
- **CONSERVATION** Vulnerable to habitat loss to agriculture and development in draining of wetlands.

JUVENILE

WINTER PLUMAGE

Similar Birds

COMMON TERN
Shorter legs and bill; dark wing tips; white tail with dark outer margins • winter adults and juveniles have white forehead and forecrown; dark shoulder; dark eye patch joins at nape; higher-pitched call.

ARCTIC TERN
Shorter red bill without dark tip; shorter legs; gray underparts; gray throat and chin contrast with white face; white tail with dark outer margins; pale underwing with black trailing margins.

Flight Pattern

Shallow slow graceful strong flight with body moving up and down. Hovers over water prior to diving for prey.

Nest Identification	
Shape  Location	Atop floating dried reeds and lined with grass and reeds; in mud or sand and lined with bits of shells and grass; sometimes uses old grebe nests or muskrat houses • built by both sexes • 1–4 olive or buff eggs with brown or olive splotches and sometimes marked with dark brown lines; oval to short elliptical, 1.7 inches long.

Plumage Sexes similar	Habitat	Migration Migratory	Weight 5.6 ounces

DATE _____ TIME _____ LOCATION _____

Family LARIDAE	Species *Sterna antillarum*	Length 8–9 inches	Wingspan 20 inches

LEAST TERN

The smallest North American tern has a graceful airy flight. Like other terns, it is very protective of its nest and will divebomb intruders, screeching and releasing droppings. The female is similar to the male but smaller. The small size; yellow-orange bill, legs, and feet; black lores, crown, and nape; and white forehead distinguish this species. In flight it shows a deeply forked tail. Winter adults show a dark bill and dusky-streaked whitish crown. Juveniles are similar to winter adults but have darker outer wings and a dusky carpal bar on the leading edge of the inner wings.

black cap and nape

white forehead

gray upperparts

black lores

orange-yellow bill with dark tip

white underparts

orange-yellow legs

black wedge on outer primaries

- **SONG** Piercing *kip, kip, kip* or rapid repeated *kid-ik, kid-ik*. Also makes a grating *zr-e-e-ep*.
- **BEHAVIOR** Catches food in bill in flight by swooping down to surface or by diving. After catching prey often swallows it while flying or brings it to nest. Eats small fish, crustaceans, and sand eels. Hovers prior to plunge diving.
- **BREEDING** Monogamous. Colonial. Occasionally solitary.
- **NESTING** Incubation 20–25 days by both sexes (female begins incubation; male finishes it). Semiprecocial young leave nest a few days after hatching, hide nearby, and are fed and tended by both sexes for 60–90 days after first flight. First flight at 19–20 days. 1–2 broods per year.
- **POPULATION** Fairly common but local in the East and on the Gulf Coast. Some decline in interior, Mississippi Valley, and on southern California coast.
- **CONSERVATION** Some populations considered endangered due to human disturbance of nesting areas.

JUVENILE   FIRST SUMMER

Similar Birds
BLACK TERN Winter adults and juveniles have dark bill; dusky crown and ear patch; darker mantle; darker legs and feet; larger; tail not deeply forked.

Flight Pattern
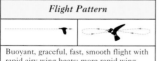
Buoyant, graceful, fast, smooth flight with rapid airy wing beats; more rapid wing beats than any other tern in range. Hovers briefly before dipping down to seize prey.

Nest Identification	
Shape 〜 Location ▬ 〜 	Sometimes lined with pebbles, grass, and debris • on ground in sand or sometimes on roof • built by female • 1–3 buff to pale green eggs with black, gray, or brown markings; oval or subelliptical, 1 x 1.4 inches.

Plumage Sexes similar	Habitat 〜 〜	Migration Migratory	Weight 1.5 ounces

DATE _____ TIME_____ LOCATION _____

| Family LARIDAE | Species *Sterna anaethetus* | Length 14–15 inches | Wingspan 30 inches |

BRIDLED TERN

This shy tern is rarely seen from shore except after storms when it is blown off course. In North America it spends most of its time in the warm waters of the Gulf of Mexico and the Gulf Stream as far north as North Carolina. It often nests in colonies with Sooty Terns and other seabirds. In flight, note the white collar separating the black crown from the grayish brown back, the grayish band on the trailing edge of the underwing, and the extensive white in the tail and underwing.

black cap

white patch
from forehead
to behind eye

white collar on
back of neck

grayish brown
back and
upperwings

slim pointed
wings

black bill

forked gray tail with
much white on outside
margins and tips

white
underparts

black legs and feet

Juveniles have smoky gray upperparts with white mottling.

• **SONG** High-pitched harsh yapping crowlike call of *wep-wep-wep* or *wup-wup*.

• **BEHAVIOR** Oceanic. Eats small fish, squid, crustaceans, and insects. Hovers over water, then dips to grip food with bill. Feeds day or night. Sometimes swims. Frequents inshore waters but usually returns to land to roost.

• **BREEDING** Monogamous. Colonial.

• **NESTING** Incubation 28–30 days by both sexes. Semiprecocial young stay in nest a couple of days after hatching, then move to nearby sheltered area. First flight at 55–63 days. Young are fed by both sexes. 1 brood per year.

• **POPULATION** Common Caribbean species; nests locally off the Florida Keys (Pelican Shoals). Uncommon to fairly common well offshore in the Gulf of Mexico and in the Gulf Stream to North Carolina. Rare farther north to New England and inland when it is blown in by the occasional hurricane.

• **CONSERVATION** Vulnerable to introduced domestic predators and human disturbance on nesting islands; some humans collect this bird's eggs for food.

JUVENILE

Similar Birds

SOOTY TERN
Lacks white collar between cap and back; white patch extends from forehead to eye but not beyond it; darker upperparts; deeply forked tail with narrow white edging.

Flight Pattern

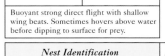

Buoyant strong direct flight with shallow wing beats. Sometimes hovers above water before dipping to surface for prey.

Nest Identification	
Shape ⬮ 🥚 🥚	Unlined • hides egg under matted plant material • built by both sexes • 1 whitish to pale buff egg marked with various shades of brown; oval, 2 x 1.4 inches.
Location 🏠 🌿 ▬	

| Plumage Sexes similar | Habitat 〜〜 〜 | Migration Migratory | Weight 3.4 ounces |

DATE _____ TIME_____ LOCATION _____

Family LARIDAE	Species *Sterna fuscata*	Length 16–17 inches	Wingspan 32–34 inches

SOOTY TERN

For years, tuna fishermen have followed feeding flocks of Sooty Terns to locate schools of tuna. Sailors sometimes call this bird "wide-awake," because of its loud night call from the nesting colony, which sounds like *wide-a-wake.* These birds do not breed until they are at least four to eight years of age. Adults have clean-cut black upperparts and white underparts, wing linings, forehead, and short eye stripe. Juvenile is sooty brown overall with white speckling on mantle and upperwings, white lower belly and undertail coverts, white underwing lining, and forked tail.

blackish brown cap

white forehead patch

blackish brown upperparts

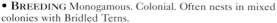

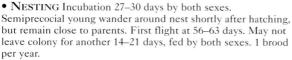

black bill

- **SONG** A high nasal *ker-wacky-wack* or *wide-a-wake.*

- **BEHAVIOR** Highly gregarious. Eats small fish and small squid. It is believed these birds sleep "on the wing," because they do not land on water and return to shore only when nesting. Banding in Dry Tortugas indicates adults are not highly migratory but that juveniles migrate as far as west Africa and may be gone 2–6 years before returning to the Florida Keys.

white underparts

black legs and feet

dark forked tail with white edges

- **BREEDING** Monogamous. Colonial. Often nests in mixed colonies with Bridled Terns.

- **NESTING** Incubation 27–30 days by both sexes. Semiprecocial young wander around nest shortly after hatching, but remain close to parents. First flight at 56–63 days. May not leave colony for another 14–21 days, fed by both sexes. 1 brood per year.

- **POPULATION** Abundant. Widespread throughout tropical oceans. Large nesting colony on the Dry Tortugas; also nests on islands off Texas and Louisiana and on barrier islands of North Carolina. Regular in summer in Gulf Stream to North Carolina; casual to southern coastal California. Storm-blown birds to Maritimes and Great Lakes.

JUVENILE

Similar Birds

BRIDLED TERN
White patch on forehead extends beyond eye; more pointed wings; paler lead-gray upperparts; white collar separates crown from back; forked tail paler with more white edging on tip.

- **CONSERVATION** Strict protection laws on the Tortugas and some Hawaiian colonies. Vulnerable to human disturbance and introduced predators on breeding islands.

Flight Pattern

Buoyant direct flight with strong, steady, shallow wing beats. Hovers above water before dipping to surface to pick up food.

Nest Identification

Shape ⬗   Location ▬ ▰▰▰ ▰▰

Lined with leaves • built by both sexes • 1 white to buff egg, with brown, gray, lavender, or black markings; oval, 2.0 x 1.4 inches.

Plumage Sexes similar	Habitat ≈≈≈ ⟿	Migration Migratory	Weight 6.3 ounces

DATE _____ TIME_____ LOCATION _____

Family LARIDAE	Species *Chlidonias niger*	Length 9–10 inches	Wingspan 20–24 inches

BLACK TERN

A black-bodied tern that prefers to breed and nest in the inland marshes of the North American prairie country but winters at sea. It is distinguishable by its overall black breeding plumage, gray upperparts, and dark red legs and feet. Its head and underparts turn white in winter and produce a strange-looking pied bird in late summer as winter molt begins. Winter adults have a black crown with an attached ear patch, a white collar, and a dusky black side bar. Juveniles are similar to winter adults with brownish mottling on the back and a dark carpal bar.

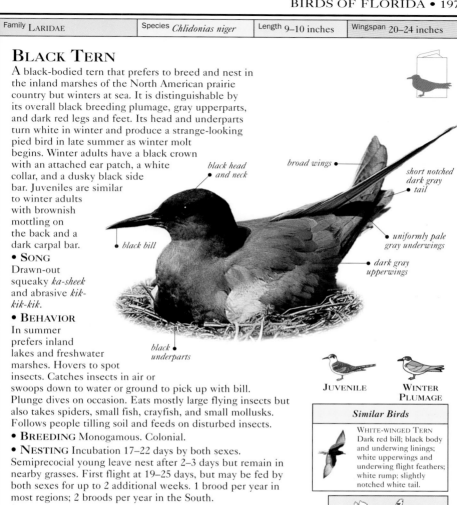

black head and neck
broad wings
short notched dark gray tail
black bill
uniformly pale gray underwings
dark gray upperwings
black underparts

- **SONG**
Drawn-out squeaky *ka-sheek* and abrasive *kik-kik-kik*.

- **BEHAVIOR**
In summer prefers inland lakes and freshwater marshes. Hovers to spot insects. Catches insects in air or swoops down to water or ground to pick up with bill. Plunge dives on occasion. Eats mostly large flying insects but also spiders, small fish, crayfish, and small mollusks. Follows people tilling soil and feeds on disturbed insects.

- **BREEDING** Monogamous. Colonial.

- **NESTING** Incubation 17–22 days by both sexes. Semiprecocial young leave nest after 2–3 days but remain in nearby grasses. First flight at 19–25 days, but may be fed by both sexes for up to 2 additional weeks. 1 brood per year in most regions; 2 broods per year in the South.

- **POPULATION** Common to fairly common in the East; common in middle and western parts of range; uncommon to rare on the West Coast.

- **CONSERVATION** Has declined inland and on the East Coast from wetlands drainage.

JUVENILE

WINTER PLUMAGE

Similar Birds

WHITE-WINGED TERN
Dark red bill; black body and underwing linings; white upperwings and underwing flight feathers; white rump; slightly notched white tail.

Flight Pattern

Buoyant direct flight with deep rapid wing beats. Hovers for insects. Uneven foraging flight with much stopping and starting.

Nest Identification

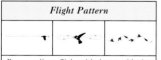

Shape ⬛ 🐦   Location 🌾 🐦 🌊

Dried reeds, stalks, and grasses • on floating dried vegetation • built by both sexes • 2–4 light buff to olive eggs with black, brown, and greenish buff blotches, usually wreathed; oval to long oval, 1.7 x 1.2 inches.

Plumage Sexes similar	Habitat ⎯ ≈ ⊭ 🌾 ≋	Migration Migratory	Weight 2.3 ounces

DATE _____ TIME_____ LOCATION _____

Family LARIDAE	Species *Anous stolidus*	Length 16 inches	Wingspan 33 inches

BROWN NODDY

The Brown Noddy is the only noddy that nests in North America. Like other gulls and terns, it usually is tame but will become aggressive and attack any intruder that threatens its young. Nests are reused each year and become large as materials are added each breeding season. Long-winged, with a long, wedge-shaped tail, this tern appears dark overall from a distance. Adults have a grayish white cap that blends into a brown nape. Juveniles are similar to adults but have only a white line on the forehead.

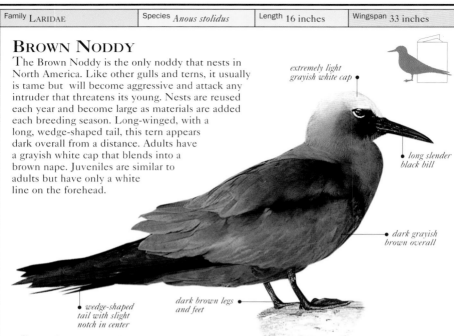

extremely light grayish white cap

long slender black bill

dark grayish brown overall

wedge-shaped tail with slight notch in center

dark brown legs and feet

- **SONG** Crowlike *karrk* or *arrowk* or harsh *eye-ak*.
- **BEHAVIOR** Pelagic in warm oceans. Sometimes forages in small flocks. Uses beak to scoop up small prey that is flushed to surface or escaping bigger fish. Eats small fish and squid that it picks from the surface or dives from the surface to catch. Does not plunge dive like other terns. Swims. Flies low over water somewhat like a shearwater.
- **BREEDING** Monogamous. Colonial. Noisy on nesting grounds, especially at night.
- **NESTING** Incubation 35–38 days by both sexes. Incubating bird fed by its mate. Young stay in nest 20 days; both sexes feed by regurgitation. First flight at about 30 days. 1 brood per year.
- **POPULATION** Common on and around Dry Tortugas. Casual in Gulf to Texas and Gulf Stream to Outer Banks of North Carolina. Accidental elsewhere when blown by storm.
- **CONSERVATION** Breeding colony on Dry Tortugas off Florida coast is protected.

Similar Birds

SOOTY TERN
Juvenile has forked tail; lacks distinct cap; white underwing linings, lower belly, and undertail coverts.

BLACK NODDY
Smaller; darker; white cap; longer bill.

Flight Pattern
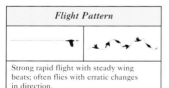
Strong rapid flight with steady wing beats; often flies with erratic changes in direction.

Nest Identification	
Shape ⌒ 🐦 Location 🪹 🌿 ▬ 🌳	Old tree branches and seaweed • lined with shells and bits of coral • in cacti and bay cedar bushes about 12 feet above ground • built by both sexes • 1 pinkish buff egg marked with dark reddish brown; oval to short subelliptical, 2.1 x 1.4 inches.

Plumage Sexes similar	Habitat 〰 🐚 〰	Migration Migratory	Weight 7.0 ounces

DATE _____ TIME_____ LOCATION _____

Family LARIDAE	Species *Anous minutus*	Length 12–13.5 inches	Wingspan 28–30 inches

BLACK NODDY

Sometimes called the White-capped Noddy, this tropical tern is similar to the Brown Noddy but smaller and darker, with a whiter cap and a longer thinner bill. It often feeds farther out on the open sea. Known to be very tame, this bird sometimes will allow physical human contact. Juveniles are similar to adults, but the white on their heads is more sharply defined and does not blend gradually into the surrounding dark plumage of the head.

white cap and forehead

black body and wings

long slender black bill

short blackish brown legs and feet

wedge-shaped tail slightly notched in center

- **SONG** A chattering *crick-crick-crick* and a sustained *kehrrrrrr.*
- **BEHAVIOR** Feeds far out at sea, using its bill to scoop prey from the water. Often feeds in flocks. Eats small fish and squid that it picks from the surface of the water; also swims in shallow water and dives beneath the surface to catch food. Flies close to water. More sedentary than Brown Noddy, with most populations roosting at breeding sites throughout the year, departing at dawn and returning at dusk.
- **BREEDING** Monogamous. Colonial.
- **NESTING** Incubation 34–39 days by both sexes. Young stay in nest 39–52 days, fed by both parents. 1 brood per year.
- **POPULATION** Nonbreeding individuals are uncommon to rare on the Dry Tortugas off the Florida coast with colony of Brown Noddies. Casual to Texas coast.

Similar Birds

BROWN NODDY
Lighter and more brown; larger; longer legs; shorter, thicker bill.

Flight Pattern

Strong, swift, and erratic, but more fluttering than Brown Noddy. Typically flies close to the surface of the ocean.

Nest Identification

Shape ➝ Location

No nesting material if crevice is used; otherwise, dead tree branches and seaweed, lined with shells, rock, and bits of coral • cactus and bay cedar bushes, about 12 feet above ground • built by both sexes • 1 white to light red egg, tinted with buff; oval or short subelliptical, 1.7 x 1.2 inches.

Plumage Sexes similar	Habitat	Migration Migratory	Weight 4.2 ounces

DATE _____ TIME_____ LOCATION _____

Family LARIDAE	Species *Rynchops niger*	Length 18–19 inches	Wingspan 42–50 inches

BLACK SKIMMER

This crow-sized bird's Spanish name, *rayador*, is derived from the word *rayar*, for its habit of making lines in the ground by skimming sand around the nest with its long bill. The Black Skimmer is the largest of the world's three species and, like them, has unique compressed, knifelike mandibles, with the lower one one-third longer than the upper one. This long-winged bird has black upperparts, white underparts, a black rump and a slightly notched tail. Winter adults have a white collar. Juveniles are similar to winter adults but they have mottled brown upperparts. Nestlings are camouflaged by their buff coloring, which blends with the seashore. The lower and upper mandibles are similar in length until young are almost fully grown.

long pointed wings with white trailing edge

black crown

white forehead

short forked white tail with black central tail feathers

bright red bill with black tip

white underparts

short red legs and feet

long lower mandible

JUVENILE

- **SONG** Low throaty bark of *kak-kak-kak*, *kuk-kuk-kuk*, or *yap-yap-yap*. Pairs sometimes sing together, *kow-kow* or *keow-keow*.
- **BEHAVIOR** Crepuscular and partially nocturnal. Often begins foraging in late evening when waters are calmer and prey rises to surface. Flies low and skims water with lower mandible to locate prey by touch, then snaps the bill shut. Grasps small fish and crustaceans with upper mandible, tilts head, and swallows while still flying. Spends much of day loafing on beaches.
- **BREEDING** Monogamous. Small colonies.
- **NESTING** Incubation 21–23 days by both sexes. Semiprecocial young remain in nest area 23–25 days. Fed by both sexes. 1 brood per year.
- **POPULATION** Common in coastal areas. Casual to accidental inland; birds are often driven there by storms.
- **CONSERVATION** Vulnerable to disturbance of nesting colonies. Eggs and young often trampled by dogs or humans, especially runners on beach.

Flight Pattern	
Graceful buoyant direct flight with measured wing beats. In perfect synchrony flocks wheel, twist, and glide.	

Nest Identification	
Shape ⬚ Location ▬▬ 🦅	No materials added • on upper beach above high tidemark • built by both sexes • 4–5 bluish white or pinkish white eggs with brown, lilac, and gray blotches; round ovate to elongated ovate, 1.3 inches long.

Plumage Sexes similar	Habitat 🌊 〰	Migration Some migrate	Weight 12.3 ounces

DATE _____ TIME _____ LOCATION _____

| Family COLUMBIDAE | Species *Columba livia* | Length 13–14 inches | Wingspan 24–25 inches |

ROCK DOVE

Introduced into North America by Europeans in the early 1600s, the Rock Dove is often called homing pigeon or carrier pigeon. Early Romans are said to have used the Rock Dove to carry the report of Caesar's conquest of Gaul back to Rome, and legend says the Rock Dove brought news of Napoleon's defeat at Waterloo to England days before messages sent via horses and ships. Although native to wild rocky habitats, today these birds are most common in urban and rural settings, and they are still raised in coops or pigeon lofts.

blue-gray overall

iridescent feathers on head and neck reflect green, bronze, and purple

2 thick broad bars across each wing

WILDTYPE

They can vary in color from wildtype to browns, grays, white-gray, mosaics, or pure white, but they always show a white rump pattern.

COLOR VARIATIONS

• **SONG** Sings a repetitive cooing *coo-a-roo, coo-roo-cooo* or *cock-a-war* or *coo-cuk-cuk*.

• **BEHAVIOR** In wild eats grass, weed seeds, grains, clover, and berries. In cities eats bread crumbs and garbage. Will take food from the hand, but when frightened claps wings over the back while flying up. Able to fly faster than 85 miles per hour.

• **BREEDING** Male displays by turning in circles while cooing. Monogamous.

• **NESTING** Incubation 16–19 days by both sexes. Altricial young remain in nest about 27–35 days. Fed by both parents. Young thrust bills into parents' mouths to eat regurgitated food. 5 or more broods per year.

• **POPULATION** Common, especially in urban settings.

Similar Birds

BAND-TAILED PIGEON
West • white bar on nape; broad gray tail band; lacks white rump.

MOURNING DOVE
Much smaller; long pointed tail; lacks white rump patch.

Flight Pattern

Swift direct flight with rapid wing beats.

Nest Identification

Shape   Location

Unlined platform of sticks, twigs, leaves, grasses • building ledges, barn rafters, gutters, sheltered cliff edges, or rocks • built by female with materials gathered by male • 2 white eggs, about 1.6 inches long.

| Plumage Sexes similar | Habitat | Migration Nonmigratory | Weight 13.0 ounces |

DATE 7/04   TIME _____   LOCATION _____

Family COLUMBIDAE	Species *Columba leucocephala*	Length 14–15 inches	Wingspan 25 inches

WHITE-CROWNED PIGEON

Widespread in the West Indies this species reaches the northern limit of its range in South Florida. Travelers to Key West often see these dark birds perched at close range along the highway or may spot large flocks flying overhead from one feeding area to another. The male has a shining white crown. Females and juveniles are similar in appearance, but the female's crown is dull white, while young birds have a gray or brownish gray crown.

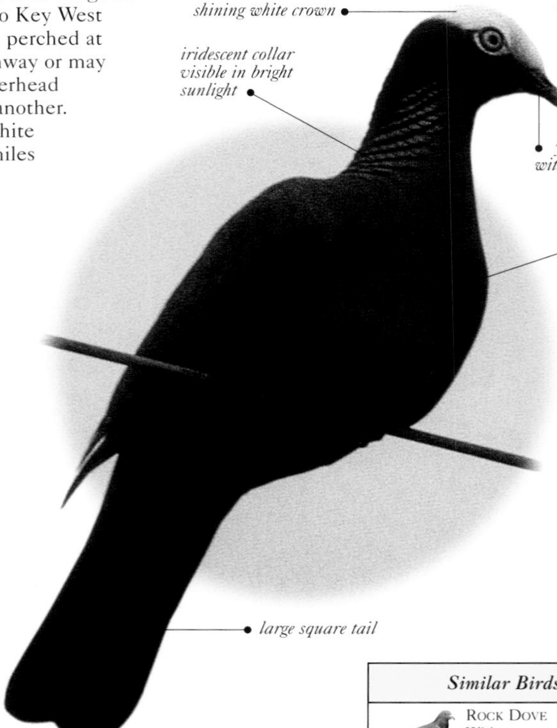
shining white crown
iridescent collar visible in bright sunlight
yellow bill with red base
slate gray overall
large square tail

• **SONG** Owl-like, tremulous *wof, wof, woo, cowoo* or a loud, deep *coo-cura-cooo* or *coo-croo*.

• **BEHAVIOR** Usually lives in trees and shrubs. Eats berries, seeds, and some insects. Seldom visits ground. Often seen in flight above trees, especially in early morning and when returning to roosts at evening.

• **BREEDING** Monogamous. Colonial.

• **NESTING** Incubation 18–20 days by both sexes. Altricial young fed by both sexes; leave nest after 30–35 days. Up to 3 broods per year.

• **POPULATION** Fairly common. Stable in Florida; decreasing in the Caribbean.

Similar Birds

ROCK DOVE
White rump patch in all plumages; generally not uniformly dark; lacks white crown.

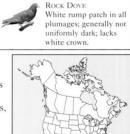

Flight Pattern

Swift direct flight with strong rapid wing beats.

• **CONSERVATION** Not a concern in US, where species is protected. Population declines in Caribbean due to habitat loss, encroachment by growing human populations, and hunting (even in protected areas and out of season).

Nest Identification	
Shape · Location	Twigs, grass, and roots • lined with grasses and fine material • in low fork of tree • built by both sexes • 1–2 unmarked white eggs, 1.4 x 1 inches.

Plumage Sexes similar	Habitat	Migration Migratory	Weight 9.2 ounces

DATE _______________ TIME_________________ LOCATION _________________________

Family COLUMBIDAE	Species *Streptopelia decaocto*	Length 12.5 inches	Wingspan 18–19 inches

EURASIAN COLLARED-DOVE

This large dove, a native of Eurasia, was introduced into the Bahama Islands in 1974. By the end of the 1970s, it had found its way to Florida, where it could be seen feeding in backyard gardens, towns, and parks. By the beginning of the new millennium this now established exotic had spread up the Atlantic Coast to North Carolina, across the Gulf Coast to Texas, and up the Mississippi River to Tennessee, with records in Oklahoma and Pennsylvania. Although similar to other doves

pale gray-pink head, neck, and breast

black bill

very pale buff upperparts

black "half-moon" trimmed with white on nape

pink legs and feet

in its habits, this dove is less shy around people and prefers life in and around human habitation. In flight, it shows a two-toned tail, gray base, and white-tipped blackish primaries.

- **SONG** Soft, continual cooing *hoo-hoooo-hoo* with emphasis on the second syllable; also a complaining *mair*.
- **BEHAVIOR** Solitary; pairs and family groups, but not in large flocks. Feeds close to houses; trusting of human contact. Eats mostly grain and seeds. Feeds on lawns, roadsides, feed mills, farms, and agricultural areas.
- **BREEDING** Monogamous. Male gives displays and coos while perched in tree or roof.
- **NESTING** Incubation 14–18 days by both sexes. Young stay in nest 15–20 days, fed and tended by both parents for an additional week. Up to 6 broods per year in Europe, possibly same in Florida.
- **POPULATION** Fairly common to common. Spreading quickly in southeastern US cities, villages, and gardens.
- **FEEDERS** Attracted to feeding stations, bird feeders, birdbaths, and garden pools.

Similar Birds

MOURNING DOVE Smaller; pinkish fawn head and underparts; pinkish iridescence on neck; black spot on auriculars; brownish gray upperparts and unmarked nape; long, pointed tail with white tips and black subteminal band on all but two central feathers; black spots on upper inner wing • wings make whistling sound in flight.

Flight Pattern

Swift strong direct flight on rapidly beating wings.

Nest Identification

Shape   Location   Twigs and dry stalks • in tree, shrub, and balconies or eves of houses, 6–7 feet above ground • male collects materials, female builds • 2 pure white eggs; oval to elliptical, 1.2 inches.

Plumage Sexes similar	Habitat	Migration Nonmigratory	Weight 5.4 ounces

DATE ___7/04___ TIME_____ LOCATION _____

Family COLUMBIDAE	Species *Zenaida asiatica*	Length 11–12 inches	Wingspan 17–18 inches

WHITE-WINGED DOVE

Its distinctive white wing patches set this dove apart from other doves and pigeons; when the bird perches the patch shows only as a narrow white line outlining the bottom of the folded wing. Often making its home in the desert, it will fly more than twenty miles for drinking water, using both natural and man-made sources. The female is smaller than the male and duller in color.

• SONG A low-pitched cooing *who-cooks-for-you; who koo-koo-koo.*

• BEHAVIOR Gregarious. Sometimes seen in flocks of thousands in the West. Eats seeds, grains, and fruits from trees, shrubs, and cacti. Feeds in flocks. Obtains drinking water

orange-red eyes surrounded by bare blue skin

reddish purple crown and nape

iridescent greenish gold on sides of neck

brownish upperparts

dark blue bill

black mark below ear coverts

rounded gray tail with white corners, black-trimmed inside

large white wing patches and dark gray flight feathers

red legs and feet

from streams and cacti, as well as from various man-made sources, such as reservoirs, irrigation canals, windmill troughs, and cattle tanks.

• BREEDING Monogamous. Small colonies. In display flight, male climbs with clapping wing beats, then glides down on stiff, slightly downward-bowed wings.

• NESTING Incubation 13–14 days by both sexes. Young stay in nest 13–16 days, tended by both sexes. 2–3 broods per year.

• POPULATION Common in the Southwest; locally fairly common in southern Florida; Casual elsewhere.

• FEEDERS Attracted to birdbaths, garden pools, and bird feeders and feeding stations providing small seeds.

• CONSERVATION Harvested and managed as a game species in the western United States.

Similar Birds

MOURNING DOVE
Lacks white wing patch; longer, more pointed tail; gray-brown flight feathers.

Flight Pattern

Fairly fast direct flight, but slower and usually higher and without the zigzagging of the Mourning Dove.

Nest Identification	
Shape	Location	Sticks, grasses, and stems of weeds • cactus, shrub, or low in tree, 4–30 feet above ground • built by both sexes; male gathers material, female builds • 2 creamy buff eggs; oval to elliptical, 1.2 inches.

Plumage Sexes similar	Habitat	Migration Migratory	Weight 5.4 ounces

DATE _____ TIME_____ LOCATION _____

Family COLUMBIDAE	Species *Zenaida macroura*	Length 12 inches	Wingspan 17–19 inches

MOURNING DOVE

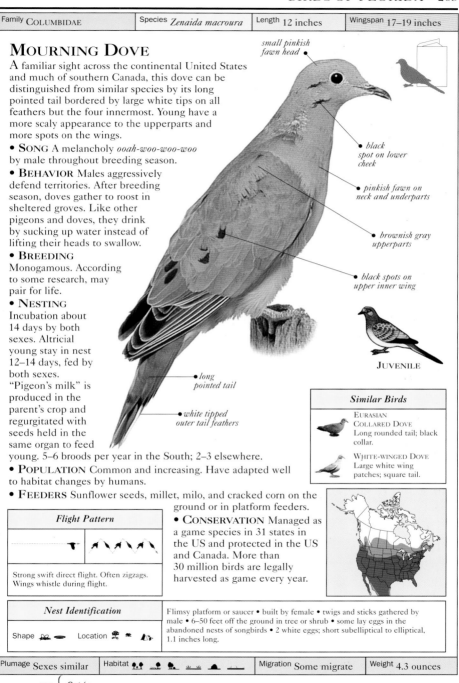

small pinkish fawn head

black spot on lower cheek

pinkish fawn on neck and underparts

brownish gray upperparts

black spots on upper inner wing

long pointed tail

white tipped outer tail feathers

JUVENILE

A familiar sight across the continental United States and much of southern Canada, this dove can be distinguished from similar species by its long pointed tail bordered by large white tips on all feathers but the four innermost. Young have a more scaly appearance to the upperparts and more spots on the wings.

• **SONG** A melancholy *ooah-woo-woo-woo* by male throughout breeding season.

• **BEHAVIOR** Males aggressively defend territories. After breeding season, doves gather to roost in sheltered groves. Like other pigeons and doves, they drink by sucking up water instead of lifting their heads to swallow.

• **BREEDING** Monogamous. According to some research, may pair for life.

• **NESTING** Incubation about 14 days by both sexes. Altricial young stay in nest 12–14 days, fed by both sexes. "Pigeon's milk" is produced in the parent's crop and regurgitated with seeds held in the same organ to feed young. 5–6 broods per year in the South; 2–3 elsewhere.

• **POPULATION** Common and increasing. Have adapted well to habitat changes by humans.

• **FEEDERS** Sunflower seeds, millet, milo, and cracked corn on the ground or in platform feeders.

• **CONSERVATION** Managed as a game species in 31 states in the US and protected in the US and Canada. More than 30 million birds are legally harvested as game every year.

Similar Birds

EURASIAN COLLARED DOVE
Long rounded tail; black collar.

WHITE-WINGED DOVE
Large white wing patches; square tail.

Flight Pattern

Strong swift direct flight. Often zigzags. Wings whistle during flight.

Nest Identification

Shape   Location

Flimsy platform or saucer • built by female • twigs and sticks gathered by male • 6–50 feet off the ground in tree or shrub • some lay eggs in the abandoned nests of songbirds • 2 white eggs; short subelliptical to elliptical, 1.1 inches long.

Plumage Sexes similar	Habitat	Migration Some migrate	Weight 4.3 ounces

DATE __7 / 04__   TIME _____   LOCATION _____

Family COLUMBIDAE	Species *Columbina passerina*	Length 6–7 inches	Wingspan 8.75–10 inches

COMMON GROUND-DOVE

The Common Ground-Dove is about the size of a sparrow and often can be seen perched on fences, roofs of buildings, and trees. Known as tame, this bird sometimes will not fly away until almost stepped upon. The female is grayer than the male and more uniformly colored. In flight this small dove has flashing rufous-red primaries and wing linings and a black tail with white corners.

scaly head

brown back

brown wings with brown-black spots

rounded wings show red-brown primaries and wing linings in flight

dusky black bill with pink base

scaly breast

pinkish brown underparts

stubby black tail

pink or yellow feet and legs

• **SONG** Continual soft melancholy *coo-oo* or *woo-oo*, rising on second syllable and often for hours at a time. Also soft *wah-up*.
• **BEHAVIOR** Terrestrial, walking on rapidly moving short legs with head bobbing. Eats seeds of grasses and weeds, waste grain in fields, insects, and small berries off ground. Often frequents quiet roadsides in early morning and late afternoon, where it may feed and pick up grit. Usually stays in pairs or small flocks.
• **BREEDING** Monogamous. Thought to mate for life.
• **NESTING** Incubation 12–14 days by both sexes. Altricial young fed by both sexes. Young leave nest as soon as they can fly, at about 11–12 days. 2–4 broods per year.
• **POPULATION** Declining in recent decades, especially in the southeastern states and along the Gulf Coast.
• **FEEDERS** Will feed on seeds scattered on ground or on platform feeders.

Similar Birds

INCA DOVE
Much larger; longer white-edged tail; scaly upperparts and underparts.

RUDDY GROUND-DOVE ♂
Rufous on upperparts; lacks scaling; dark bill.

Flight Pattern

Rapid direct flight with swift wing beats.

Nest Identification	Sometimes flimsy platform of twigs and plant fibers or slight depression on ground with little or no materials • on beach or floor of woods or fields; in low bush, stump, or vine; or on top of fence post or tree branch, 1–21 feet above ground • sometimes uses abandoned nest of songbird or other dove species • built by both sexes • 2–3 white eggs, 0.8 inches long.
Shape	
Location	

Plumage Sexes similar	Habitat	Migration Nonmigratory	Weight 1.1 ounces

DATE _____ TIME_____ LOCATION _____

Family PSITTACIDAE	Species *Melopsittacus undulatus*	Length 6–7 inches	Wingspan 10 inches

BUDGERIGAR

Originally from Australia, the Budgerigar is perhaps the best-known parrot in the world. The name originates from the native Australian word *betcherrygah*, which means "good parrot." It has gained popularity as a caged bird in the United States and many other parts of the world. A breeding population of escaped and released birds exists in Florida. Wild-type birds have a yellow face and upperparts, barring and scalloping on the back, and greenish underparts. Its overall color can be blue, yellow, or white due to breeding of captive birds for plumage. In flight look for the long, pointed tail and yellow wing stripe. Juveniles are similar to adults but have less-distinct spotting on the throat. Breeding females are similar to males but have a brown cere.

yellow head

blue cere

black bars on auriculars, crown, and nape

small, deeply hooked olive-gray bill

yellow back and upperwing coverts with black scalloping

yellow throat with row of large black dots

long graduated blue tail

bluish feet and legs

COLOR VARIATIONS

- **SONG** Garrulous. Musical, mellow *chirrup* is continuous when flocks gather. Also gives sharp, rasping scolds. When alarmed makes *zizzing* chatter.

- **BEHAVIOR** Gregarious. Eats mainly small seeds, especially of grass and weed, and some plant materials such as new leaves, buds, and blossoms. Walks on ground searching for food. Often gathers in flocks in early morning and late afternoon to drink at waterholes, ponds, streams, garden pools, etc. Prefers suburbs with adjacent open, grassy areas.

- **BREEDING** Monogamous. Solitary.

- **NESTING** Incubation 18 days by female. Male feeds female in nest hole. Altricial young stay in nest 30–36 days. Fed by both sexes. 1–2 broods per year.

- **POPULATION** Exotic. Introduced in southwestern Florida in 1960s; established populations of thousands by 1980s. Serious decline since then; may be due to competition for nesting cavities. Accidental anywhere as escapees from captivity.

- **BIRDHOUSES** Will nest in man-made nest boxes.

- **CONSERVATION** Introduced by accidental escape or release of caged birds.

Flight Pattern
Swift direct and slightly undulating flight with rapid wing beats.

Nest Identification	
Shape ▨² ▮ Location ❀ ▲ 🛈	No nest materials • in tree cavity or nest box • 4–8 white eggs; round, 0.75 inches long.

Plumage Sexes similar	Habitat ▃● 〰	Migration Nonmigratory	Weight 1.0 ounce

DATE _____ TIME_____ LOCATION _____

Family PSITTACIDAE	Species *Myiopsitta monachus*	Length 11.5 inches	Wingspan 17–18 inches

MONK PARAKEET

Introduced as an escaped or intentionally released bird in North America, this parakeet has established itself primarily in and around cities from New England to the Midwest, southeast Texas, and Florida. The most widespread breeding populations are found in south Florida. Using sticks and twigs, Monk Parakeets build large condominium nests in trees and on man-made structures. The nests contain separate compartments for as many as twenty pairs. It is the only parrot in the world to build large communal nests. In its native South American temperate habitat, flocks of Monk Parakeet destroy crops, particularly corn and sunflowers, and the species is considered the foremost avian threat to agriculture.

gray face and forehead

green overall

dark eyes set in white eye ring

hooked creamy pink bill

gray chest

yellow-green belly

deep blue flight feathers

long pointed green-and-blue tail

bluish legs and feet

• **SONG** Garrulous. Wide range of high staccato shrieks and screams. Makes high-pitched chattering when feeding.

• **BEHAVIOR** Gregarious. Searches for food in flocks, often tearing apart crops. Eats legumes, grains, seeds, fruits, and insects. Frequents areas near human habitation. Builds large conspicuous domed nests of sticks with entrance on side. Pairs roost throughout the year in their chambers within.

• **BREEDING** Monogamous. Loosely colonial, often communal in a single large multichambered nest.

• **NESTING** Incubation 25–31 days by both sexes. Fed by both sexes. Altricial young stay in nest 38–42 days. 2 broods per year.

• **POPULATION** Exotic. Very popular and common caged bird. Found in Florida, Texas, southeastern cities, the Northeast, and the Midwest.

• **FEEDERS** Groups attend feeders, especially in the winter, and eat seeds, cracked corn, pine seeds, suet, acorns, grass seeds, apples, cherries, grapes, raisins, and currants.

• **CONSERVATION** Attempts to control and/or eliminate this exotic species in many areas of the US are destroying both birds and nests.

Similar Birds

WHITE-WINGED PARAKEET
In south Florida only
• also similar to Yellow-chevroned Parakeet
• smaller; yellow-green overall; yellow edge on folded wing shows as yellow patch at bend of wing in flight; dark green flight feathers; lacks gray on face, crown, and breast.

Flight Pattern

Swift direct flight with rapid wing beats, often in flocks. Sometimes slight undulating flight.

Nest Identification

Shape   Location

Sticks and twigs • in highest branches of tree or leaning against tree or any tall structure • built by both sexes, often with other birds in colony • 5–9 white eggs; short subelliptical ovate, 1.1 x 0.8 inches.

Plumage Sexes similar	Habitat	Migration Nonmigratory	Weight Undetermined

DATE _____ TIME_____ LOCATION _____

Family CUCULIDAE	Species *Coccyzus erythropthalmus*	Length 11–12 inches	Wingspan 15–17 inches

BLACK-BILLED CUCKOO

This shy bird spends most of its time skulking in deep wooded forests. In rare instances, instead of incubating its own eggs it will lay its eggs in the nests of Yellow-billed Cuckoos, Gray Catbirds, Wood Thrushes, Yellow Warblers, or Chipping Sparrows. In flight note the long tail, which has small crescent-shaped white spots on the tips of all but the two central tail feathers, and the uniformly grayish brown wings and back. Juveniles are similar to adults but have a buff eye ring, paler undertail, and buff wash on the underparts, especially the undertail coverts.

narrow red eye ring

decurved black bill

grayish brown upperparts

white underparts

gray legs and feet

long graduated brown tail

- **SONG** Generally silent. Repeated monotone *cu-cu-cu* or *cu-cu-cu-cu* in series of 3–4 notes. Also gives series of rapid *kowk-kowk-kowk* notes all on a single pitch. Sometimes sings at night.
- **BEHAVIOR** Skulks through thick vegetation in shrubs and trees. Often sits quietly on branch scanning in all directions before changing perches. Eats primarily caterpillars, especially hairy tent caterpillars, and other insects; occasionally eats small mollusks, fish, and some wild fruits. Often found in damp thickets and wet places. Engages in courtship feeding.
- **BREEDING** Monogamous.
- **NESTING** Incubation 10–14 days by both sexes. Altricial young stay in nest 7–9 days; fed by both sexes. Young leave nest before they can fly and climb around on nest tree or shrub for about 14 days. 1 brood per year.
- **POPULATION** Uncommon to fairly common. Somewhat dependant on caterpillar populations; larger clutches laid when food is plentiful.

Similar Birds

YELLOW-BILLED CUCKOO
Yellow bill with dark tip; rufous primaries contrast with wing coverts and upperparts; larger white spots on undertail.

Flight Pattern
Often flies low and makes short flights from one tree to the next.

Nest Identification	
Shape	Location

Dried twigs • lined with fresh grass, leaves, pine needles, catkins, and vegetation • in tree or shrub 2–20 feet above ground • 2–5 blue-green eggs with dark blotches, 1.1 x 0.8 inches.

Plumage Sexes similar	Habitat	Migration Migratory	Weight 3.6 ounces

DATE _____ TIME_____ LOCATION _____

Family CUCULIDAE	Species *Coccyzus americanus*	Length 11–13 inches	Wingspan 15–17 inches

YELLOW-BILLED CUCKOO

Like most of the cuckoos, this bird prefers to perch unobtrusively in thick forests or shrubs. Many rural people know this bird as the "Rain Crow." Sometimes it lays its eggs in nests of the Black-billed Cuckoo but rarely in nests of other birds. It is often a casualty at "tower kills" while migrating at night. In flight, note the long tail and the contrast of rufous primaries against gray-brown wing coverts and upperparts. The juvenile shows a paler undertail pattern, and the lower mandible may not be yellow.

decurved bill with dark upper mandible and tip

grayish brown upperparts

rufous primaries

yellow lower mandible

white underparts

gray feet and legs

• **SONG** Often silent; song heard more often in summer. A monotonous throaty *ka-ka-ka-ka-kow-kow-kow-kow-kowlp—kowlp——kowl*, pruning down and slowing at the end.

• **BEHAVIOR** Slips quietly and somewhat stealthily through tangles; flies easily from tree to tree. Often sits motionless on an interior branch and slowly surveys the surrounding vegetation. Eats mostly hairy caterpillars; also insects, larvae, and small fruits and berries. Sometimes eats small frogs and lizards and the eggs of other birds. Engages in courtship feeding in which the male lands by perched female, climbs on her shoulder, and places food in her bill.

large white spots on black undertail

• **BREEDING** Monogamous. Solitary nester.

• **NESTING** Incubation 9–11 days by both sexes. Altricial young stay in nest 7–9 days, fed by both sexes. Young leave nest before able to fly but remain in vicinity, climbing in branches; fed by parent for about 14 more days. 1 brood per year.

• **POPULATION** Uncommon to common. Somewhat dependent on caterpillar population; species produces greater number of eggs when plentiful.

• **CONSERVATION** Neotropical migrant that has declined significantly over much of its range.

Similar Birds

BLACK-BILLED CUCKOO Entirely black bill; red eye ring; no rufous in wing; gray underside of tail with smaller crescent-shaped white spots; voice differs.

MANGROVE CUCKOO Gray-brown wings and coverts; black mask extends past eye; tawny-buff lower breast, sides, belly, flanks, and undertail coverts; decurved black bill, yellow at base of lower mandible • limited range in Florida; accidental on Gulf Coast.

Flight Pattern
Direct flight with slow light steady wing beats; often flies low from tree to tree with flash of rufous in wings.

Nest Identification	Small sticks, with lining of leaves, grasses, mosses, bits of fabric, and catkins from oaks and willow trees • so flimsy eggs can sometimes be seen from beneath • in tree or shrub, 2–12 feet above ground • built by both sexes • 1–5 pale bluish green eggs that fade to light greenish yellow, unmarked; elliptical to cylindrical, 1.2 x 0.9 inches.
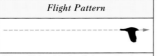 Shape 🐛 ⟶ Location 🌳 🌿	

Plumage Sexes similar	Habitat 🌾 ▲ 🏔 🌱	Migration Migratory	Weight 3.6 ounces

DATE _____ TIME_____ LOCATION _____

Family CUCULIDAE	Species *Coccyzus minor*	Length 12.5 inches	Wingspan 16 inches

MANGROVE CUCKOO

A shy resident of the West Indies, this bird also inhabits the black and red mangroves of the central and southern Gulf Coast, southern Florida Gulf Coast, Biscayne Bay, and the Florida Keys. Birdwatchers may spot this timid bird as it flies quickly from tree to tree, but most often it prefers to hide in thick vegetation. Like other cuckoos it is heard more often than seen. Note the combination of black ear patch, buff underparts, lack of rufous in the wing, and long tail with large white spots underneath.

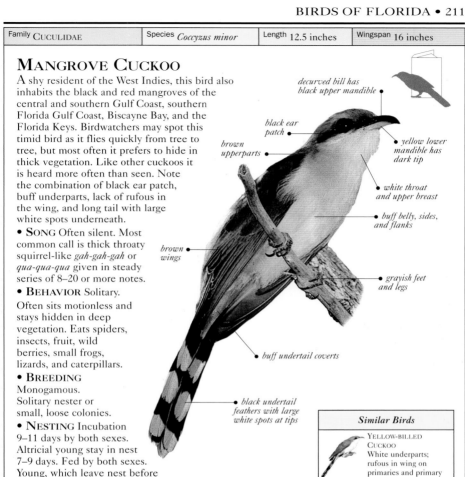

decurved bill has black upper mandible

black ear patch

brown upperparts

yellow lower mandible has dark tip

white throat and upper breast

buff belly, sides, and flanks

brown wings

grayish feet and legs

buff undertail coverts

black undertail feathers with large white spots at tips

• **SONG** Often silent. Most common call is thick throaty squirrel-like *gah-gah-gah* or *qua-qua-qua* given in steady series of 8–20 or more notes.

• **BEHAVIOR** Solitary. Often sits motionless and stays hidden in deep vegetation. Eats spiders, insects, fruit, wild berries, small frogs, lizards, and caterpillars.

• **BREEDING** Monogamous. Solitary nester or small, loose colonies.

• **NESTING** Incubation 9–11 days by both sexes. Altricial young stay in nest 7–9 days. Fed by both sexes. Young, which leave nest before flight capable, skillfully climb about near nest; continue to be fed by parents for 10–12 days. 1–2 broods per year.

• **POPULATION** Rare to uncommon in Florida, where it may be slowly expanding range. Declining in Florida Keys.

• **CONSERVATION** Decline in Florida Keys may be caused by development in mangrove swamps and subtropical hardwood forests, resulting in habitat loss and fragmentation.

Similar Birds

YELLOW-BILLED CUCKOO
White underparts; rufous in wing on primaries and primary coverts; lacks black ear patch.

Flight Pattern

Rapid direct flight with quick wing beats. Flies low across roads and from tree to tree.

Nest Identification

Shape

Location

Flimsy structure made with a few twigs and leaves • in mangrove tree or shrub 8–10 feet above water level • built by both sexes • 2–3 light bluish eggs; elliptical to cylindrical, 1.2 x 0.9 inches.

Plumage Sexes similar	Habitat	Migration Nonmigratory	Weight 3.6 ounces

Family CUCULIDAE	Species *Crotophaga ani*	Length 12–14.5 inches	Wingspan 17–18 inches

SMOOTH-BILLED ANI

These West Indian natives are now established in Florida apparently after storm winds blew some of them there in 1937. The breeding females lay their eggs in a large, communal nest, holding up to twenty eggs. All members in the colony tend the nestlings. The Smooth-billed Ani is a gracklelike bird with a large flattened puffinlike bill and a long tail that looks loosely attached to the body.

high curved ridge of ungrooved deep-based black bill extends higher than crown

black overall with shimmering bronze overtones

• **SONG** A whining high-pitched *quee-lick* or *weu-ick; weu-ick* somewhat reminiscent of the call of a female Wood Duck.

• **BEHAVIOR** Gregarious. Feeds in scrublands and fields; often accompanies livestock to feed on insects stirred up by them. Eats mainly insects, but also

long tail

takes lizards, cattle parasites, snails, seeds, fruit, and berries. Often spreads wings and tail to bask in morning sun. Individuals in the communal group sit side by side on perch and mutually groom each other. Tail often dipped and wagged side to side.

• **BREEDING** Communal; cooperative. Each breeding female contributes 2–4 (sometimes 6) eggs to clutch.

• **NESTING** Incubation 14 days by both sexes and extra birds. Altricial young are fed by all adults in group. Fledge the nest in 7–10 days after hatching. 1–2 broods per year.

• **POPULATION** Uncommon and local. Declining in Florida since the 1970s, but increasing in the tropics. Rare to accidental outside southern Florida.

• **CONSERVATION** Apparently declining as southern Florida continues to develop, and the brushland shrub/scrub habitat is lost.

Similar Birds

GROOVE-BILLED ANI Distinctive grooves on high ridge of upper mandible; smaller bill with culmen not extending above crown; different call.

Flight Pattern

Slow weak flight, alternating a series of rapid shallow stiff wing beats with short glides. Often flies low to the ground from one patch of vegetation to the next.

Nest Identification

Shape 🍵   Location 🌿🌳🐦

Twigs and weeds lined with grasses • in dense shrub or tree, 5–30 feet above ground • built by all adults in colony • nest holds up to 20 eggs • 3–6 pale blue eggs per female; oval to long oval, 1.4 x 1.0 inches.

Plumage Sexes similar	Habitat 🪶 🌱🌳 🐦	Migration Nonmigratory	Weight 4.2 ounces

DATE _____ TIME_____ LOCATION _____

Family TYTONIDAE	Species *Tyto alba*	Length 14–20 inches	Wingspan 43–47 inches

BARN OWL

no ear tufts

dark eyes

heart-shaped face

golden tawny upperparts

white to cinnamon underparts with spots instead of streaks

barring in wings

long legs

barred tail

Associating more closely with man than any other owl, the nearly cosmopolitan Barn Owl often roosts and nests in buildings and hunts in areas cleared for agriculture, particularly meadows and pastures. It is perhaps the most distinctive looking owl with its long legs and heart-shaped "monkey" face. The unexpected gasping screech of this owl nearby in the darkness can raise the hair on the back of one's head. Like other species of owls it can locate and capture its prey in total darkness using its hearing alone. This is accomplished with asymetrically positioned ear openings, and the aid of the facial disks.

• **SONG** Harsh hissing screaming grating whistling gasp, *eeeeeeSEEek*.
• **BEHAVIOR** Nocturnal. Feeds primarily on small mammals such as rodents and shrews, but occasionally takes small birds. May nest during any month of the year, and pairs are believed to mate for life. Many farmers encourage the presence of this excellent mouser in their barns.
• **BREEDING** Monogamous.
• **NESTING** Incubation 29–34 days by female. Semialtricial young stay in nest 55–65 days. Fed by both sexes. 1–3 broods per year.
• **POPULATION** Rare to uncommon. Stable in most areas, but some declines noted in the East.
• **BIRDHOUSES** Nest boxes.
• **CONSERVATION** Listed as threatened in some states.

Similar Birds

SHORT-EARED OWL
Yellow to orange eyes; short ear tufts; heavily streaked underparts; often diurnal.

Flight Pattern

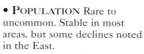

Slow light silent mothlike flight.

Nest Identification	
Shape	Debris arranged into crude depression • in tree cavity, barn loft, building, nest box, crevice, mine shaft, or cave • 2–12 whitish eggs, sometimes nest-stained; short subelliptical, 1.7 inches long.
Location	

Plumage Sexes similar	Habitat	Migration Some migrate	Weight 1.1 pounds

DATE _____ TIME_____ LOCATION _____

| Family STRIGIDAE | Species *Otus asio* | Length 8–10 inches | Wingspan 18–24 inches |

EASTERN SCREECH-OWL

Perhaps the best-known owl in eastern North America, this small tufted bird is found in a great variety of habitats, from wooded lots to urban gardens. It is able to flatten its ear tufts, which gives the head a rounded appearance. There are two distinct color phases, reddish brown and gray, plus there are brown intermediates. Its voice is not a screech but rather a mournful whinny familiar to many.

RED MORPH

tufted head

yellow eyes

pale bill

bright rusty brown to gray body

streaked underparts

• **SONG** Series of melancholy tremulous whistles descending in pitch; drawn-out trilling note. Simple to imitate.

• **BEHAVIOR** Nocturnal; becomes active at dusk. Feeds on wide variety of small vertebrates and invertebrates, including insects, arachnids, crayfish, mammals, amphibians, reptiles, birds, and fish. When using a cavity for a day roost, often will sit in the entrance. When approached on its roost, will flatten its body, erect its ear tufts, and close its eyes in an attempt to hide by blending into the background.

BROWN INTERMEDIATE

GRAY MORPH

white spots on scapulars

Similar Birds

NORTHERN SAW-WHET OWL
Smaller; lacks ear tufts; blackish bill; large white spots on upperparts; small white streaking on forehead, crown, and nape.

WESTERN SCREECH-OWL
Gray to brown; dark bill; different voice
• western range.

• **BREEDING** Monogamous.

• **NESTING** Incubation about 26 days mostly by female. Semialtricial young stay in nest about 28 days. Fed by both sexes. 1 brood per year.

• **POPULATION** Widespread and fairly common, but with gradual decline.

• **BIRDHOUSES** Will roost and nest in nesting boxes sized for wood ducks or flickers.

| **Flight Pattern** |
| |
| Buoyant flight with silent wing beats. |

| **Nest Identification** | |
| Shape  Location | Lined with feathers and debris from food • 10–30 feet above ground in tree • 2–8 white eggs; round oval, 1.4 inches long. |

| Plumage Sexes similar | Habitat  | Migration Nonmigratory | Weight 5.9 ounces |

| Family STRIGIDAE | Species *Bubo virginianus* | Length 18–25 inches | Wingspan 36–60 inches |

GREAT HORNED OWL

The most widespread owl in North America and perhaps the most powerful, this owl often attacks animals much larger and heavier than itself, including domestic cats, skunks, and porcupines. Its color varies regionally from pale arctic birds to dark northwestern ones.

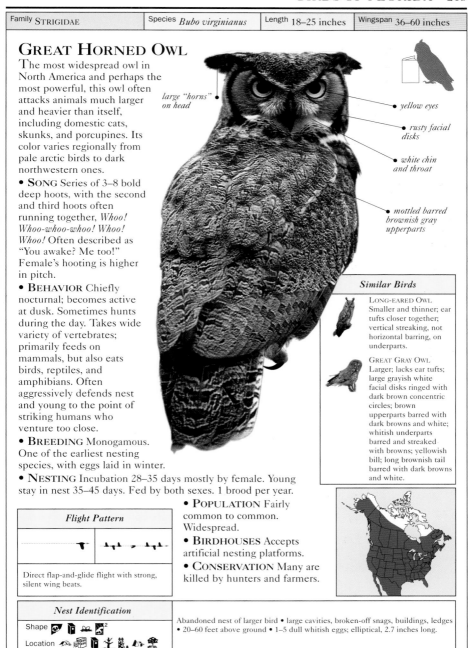

large "horns" on head

yellow eyes

rusty facial disks

white chin and throat

mottled barred brownish gray upperparts

- **SONG** Series of 3–8 bold deep hoots, with the second and third hoots often running together, *Whoo! Whoo-whoo-whoo! Whoo! Whoo!* Often described as "You awake? Me too!" Female's hooting is higher in pitch.

- **BEHAVIOR** Chiefly nocturnal; becomes active at dusk. Sometimes hunts during the day. Takes wide variety of vertebrates; primarily feeds on mammals, but also eats birds, reptiles, and amphibians. Often aggressively defends nest and young to the point of striking humans who venture too close.

- **BREEDING** Monogamous. One of the earliest nesting species, with eggs laid in winter.

- **NESTING** Incubation 28–35 days mostly by female. Young stay in nest 35–45 days. Fed by both sexes. 1 brood per year.

Similar Birds

LONG-EARED OWL Smaller and thinner; ear tufts closer together; vertical streaking, not horizontal barring, on underparts.

GREAT GRAY OWL Larger; lacks ear tufts; large grayish white facial disks ringed with dark brown concentric circles; brown upperparts barred with dark browns and white; whitish underparts barred and streaked with browns; yellowish bill; long brownish tail barred with dark browns and white.

- **POPULATION** Fairly common to common. Widespread.

- **BIRDHOUSES** Accepts artificial nesting platforms.

- **CONSERVATION** Many are killed by hunters and farmers.

Flight Pattern

Direct flap-and-glide flight with strong, silent wing beats.

Nest Identification

Shape

Location

Abandoned nest of larger bird • large cavities, broken-off snags, buildings, ledges • 20–60 feet above ground • 1–5 dull whitish eggs; elliptical, 2.7 inches long.

| Plumage Sexes similar | Habitat | Migration Nonmigratory | Weight 3.0 pounds |

DATE _____ TIME_____ LOCATION _____

Family STRIGIDAE	Species *Athene cunicularia*	Length 9–11 inches	Wingspan 20–24 inches

BURROWING OWL

This long-legged, short-tailed little owl inhabits grassland and prairies, but in its range it also can be found in similar habitats near humans such as golf courses and airports. In the West the Burrowing Owl often is associated with prairie dog towns, and the historical poisoning of the prairie dogs also brought declines in the owl's populations. The owls use an abandoned burrow for their nest and daytime roost, usually after some additional digging to enlarge and reshape it.

• **SONG** High melancholy cry, *coo-coo-roo* or *co-hoo;* twittering series of *chack* notes. If disturbed in nest, young give alarm that mimics the buzzing of a rattlesnake.

• **BEHAVIOR** Terrestrial. Primarily nocturnal and crepuscular. Perches on ground, fence posts, utility wires, rocks, or mounds near burrow during day. Inhabits open country where it feeds primarily on large insects, some of which it catches in flight, and small mammals.

white streaking on head

brown upperparts with white spotting

yellow eyes

white chin and throat

spotted white chest

white to buff underparts with brown barring

long legs

short tail

• **BREEDING** Monogamous. Often colonial.

• **NESTING** Incubation 21–30 days by female. Semialtricial young remain in nest 28 days, fed by both sexes. Typically 1–2 broods per year.

• **POPULATION** Fairly common to common but local.

• **BIRDHOUSES** Will nest in artificial man-made burrows.

• **CONSERVATION** Endangered or threatened over much of its range. Declining because of prairie dog and ground squirrel poison-control programs and habitat loss. Many killed by automobiles. Some attempts at management being made due to declining local populations.

Similar Birds

SHORT-EARED OWL
Larger; long tail; short legs; buff-brown; heavily streaked upperparts and underparts.

Flight Pattern

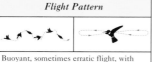

Buoyant, sometimes erratic flight, with show silent wing beats; may hover briefly above prey.

Nest Identification

Shape ▨ ▯   Location ▬

Lined with cow manure, horse dung, food debris, dry grass, weeds, pellets, and feathers • built by both sexes, but male does more • 7–10 white nest-stained eggs (4–6 in Florida); round to ovate, 1.2 inches long.

Plumage Sexes similar	Habitat	Migration Some migrate	Weight 5.3 ounces

DATE _____ TIME_____ LOCATION _____

Family STRIGIDAE	Species *Strix varia*	Length 17–24 inches	Wingspan 50–60 inches

BARRED OWL

The "hoot owl" of southern swamps, this puffy-headed owl can also be found in woodlands. It lacks ear tufts, is stoutly built, and is heavily streaked, spotted, and variegated brown, buff, and white. This is one of only three large owls with dark eyes in North America.

large, round head

brown upperparts with heavy white spotting

dark eyes

horizontal barring on upper breast

heavily streaked paler underparts

long barred tail

- **SONG** Usually 8 or more drawn-out notes, *"Who cooks for you; who cooks for you-all?"* Call is drawn-out, descending *hoooAwllll*. Group of 2 or more owls make a loud, excited caterwauling. Often heard in daytime. Responds readily to imitations of its call by coming closer and often calling back.

- **BEHAVIOR** Mostly nocturnal and crepuscular but often active in daylight. Prefers deep woods; inhabits conifer, riparian, and swampy habitats. Feeds on wide variety of animals, including small mammals, birds, frogs, salamanders, lizards, snakes, fish, large insects, crabs, and crayfish.

- **BREEDING** Monogamous. Thought to pair for life.

- **NESTING.** Incubation 28–33 days by female. Young stay in nest 42 days. Fed by both sexes. 1 brood per year.

- **POPULATION** Very common to common and widespread. Swamp habitat population in the South has diminished. Range increasing now in the Northwest, where hybridizes with Spotted Owl.

Similar Birds

GREAT GRAY OWL Much larger and grayer; yellow eyes.

SPOTTED OWL White spotting on underparts, not barring or streaking • western range.

Flight Pattern

Short flights with steady, shallow wing beats, longer flights on silent rapid wing strokes followed by short glide.

Nest Identification

Shape   Location

In the East uses abandoned nests • 15–80 feet above ground in tree • 2–3 white eggs, 2 inches long.

Plumage Sexes similar	Habitat	Migration Nonmigratory	Weight 1.4 pounds

DATE _____ TIME_____ LOCATION _____

Family CAPRIMULGIDAE	Species *Chordeiles minor*	Length 8–10 inches	Wingspan 21–24 inches

COMMON NIGHTHAWK

Like all members of the nightjar family, the adult bird flutters its gular pouch during intense heat to cool itself. The eggs and nestlings are sometimes carried to another location if temperatures become extreme. The female is similar to the male, but has a buffy, rather than white, throat and lacks the white tail band. Juveniles also lack this tail band. Note the long pointed wings with the white bar through the primaries, and the mothlike flight of the "bullbat," which is the colloquial name used for this nighthawk in the South. Although predominantly grayish brown overall, there is much color variation over the large North American range.

grayish brown overall

long dark pointed wings

white throat

notched tail with thick white band

distinctive white bar across primaries

• **SONG** Has raspy nasal somewhat froglike call of *peeant* or *beant*.

• **BEHAVIOR** Solitary or in small groups. Sometimes migrates in large flocks in fall. Crepuscular and nocturnal, but often feeds day or night, catching insects in flight. Eats a wide range of flying insects. Attracted to street lights and other outdoor lights at night to scoop up swarming insects. Bird species seen by many because of its habit of feeding over towns and cities. Skims over lakes and streams to drink water from surface.

• **BREEDING** Monogamous. Solitary. Male displays with a courtship power-dive, at the end of which the air rushes through his wings, making a loud *sw-r-r-r-oonk* sound like a rubber band or banjo string being plucked.

• **NESTING** Incubation 19–20 days, mostly by female. Young semiprecocial; first flight at 21 days, fed by both sexes. 1–2 broods per year.

• **POPULATION** Common but declining in parts of continent.

• **CONSERVATION** Neotropical migrant. Became common in towns and cities with the introduction of flat graveled roofs in mid-1800s as well as increased use of outside lighting, which attracts insects.

Similar Birds

LESSER NIGHTHAWK
Shorter, more rounded wings; whitish bar across primaries slightly closer to tip; paler upperparts with more uniform mottling; generally flies closer to ground; does not power-dive; voice differs.

ANTILLEAN NIGHTHAWK
Smaller; shorter wings; more fluttery flight; much more buffy overall; voice differs.
• rare in eastern range.

Flight Pattern

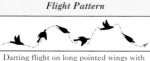

Darting flight on long pointed wings with erratic twists and turns and changes of direction. Wing beats slow and steady.

Nest Identification	
Shape 	Lays eggs on rocks, small pebbles, abandoned fields, stumps, fence rails, and even on tarred or graveled roofs; 0–8 feet above ground • female chooses site • 2 creamy white to pale olive-buff eggs, with brown and gray speckles; oval to elliptical oval, 1.2 x 0.9 inches.
Location	

Plumage Sexes similar	Habitat	Migration Migratory	Weight 2.2 ounces

DATE 7 / 01   TIME _____   LOCATION _____

| Family CAPRIMULGIDAE | Species *Chordeiles gundlachii* | Length 8 inches | Wingspan 20–22 inches |

ANTILLEAN NIGHTHAWK

This rather rare and local nighthawk of the West Indies visits and nests in southern Florida and the Florida Keys every summer. The Antillean Nighthawk was formerly considered a subspecies of the Common Nighthawk and is extremely similar to that species. It is best distinguished from Common Nighthawk by voice. Females of the two species are probably not distinguishable. Its biology is not well known.

buff to pale cinnamon overall with dark brown barring

FEMALE

long, pointed wings with white primary bar

slightly forked tail

- **SONG** Has call of *pity-pit-pit* or *kady-dit, kady-dit, kady-dit.*
- **BEHAVIOR** Crepuscular and nocturnal. Like other nightjars, perches parallel to branch, rail, wire, or perch, not perpendicular like other perching species. Catches insects while in flight. Similar to the Common Nighthawk, males perform a power-dive as part of their aerial courtship display, but the booming sound produced at the bottom of the dive is higher pitched and does not travel as far.
- **BREEDING** Monogamous. Solitary.
- **NESTING** Breeding biology poorly known, but incubation estimated at 19–20 days, mostly by female. Young semiprecocial; first flight takes place around 21 days. Fed by both sexes. 1–2 broods per year.
- **POPULATION** Rare to uncommon on Florida Keys and the southeast Florida mainland. Accidental to Louisiana and the Outer Banks of North Carolina.
- **CONSERVATION** Has increased on the Florida Keys and in the southern part of the state since the 1960s, possibly due to changes in habitat. Human development has opened up larger patches in the woody vegetation, creating favorable habitat for this species.

Similar Birds
 COMMON NIGHTHAWK Larger; longer wings; voice differs.

Flight Pattern
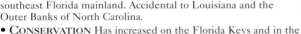
Fluttery and darting mothlike flight with erratic changes of direction; buoyant; slow measured wing beats.

Nest Identification	
Shape 🐾 Location 	No nest • 1–2 white to olive eggs, blotched with olive, heavily marked with large dark spots; oval to elliptical oval, 1.2 inches long.

| Plumage Sexes similar | Habitat 🌿 ⛰ 〰 | Migration Migratory | Weight Undetermined |

DATE _____ TIME_____ LOCATION _____

Family CAPRIMULGIDAE	Species *Caprimulgus carolinensis*	Length 11–13 inches	Wingspan 24.5–25.5 inches

CHUCK-WILL'S-WIDOW

True to its name, this bird can be heard singing *chuck-will's-widow* continuously in the early evening on a summer's night in the rural South. The largest North American nightjar is shy and will often flush at the slightest disturbance, fluttering away on silent wings like a huge brown moth. The female is similar to the male but has tan feathers on her throat and in her tail corners.

• **SONG** A bold *chuck-will's-WID-ow* in 4 parts, with the *chuck* low-pitched (sometimes inaudible at a distance) and the other 3 notes clearly whistled, with emphasis on the *wid*. While hunting, may give low growl or croak in flight.

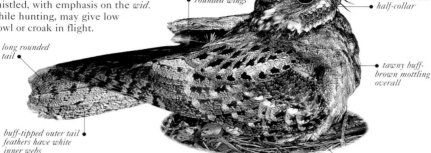

long grayish supercilium

brownish red throat with white half-collar

rounded wings

tawny buff-brown mottling overall

long rounded tail

buff-tipped outer tail feathers have white inner webs

some whitish feathers form bar on tips of lesser wing coverts

• **BEHAVIOR** Solitary. Nocturnal feeder. While in flight, catches numerous insects at a time with its cavernous mouth, which has a 2-inch gap and rictal bristles in its corners to aid in trapping prey. Eats mainly insects and an occasional small bird, which it swallows whole. Roosts like other nightjars, perched parallel to the limb or on the ground, where its cryptic plumage makes it all but impossible to see unless it moves. Roosts on the same perch daily.

• **BREEDING** Monogamous. Solitary nester.

• **NESTING** Incubation 20–24 days by female, who will move eggs if nest is disturbed. Semiprecocial young brooded by female; remain in nest approximately 17 days, fed by female. Female tends young until independent. 1 brood per year.

• **POPULATION** Fairly common in pine-oak and live-oak woodlands, as well as in deciduous forests.

• **CONSERVATION** Neotropical migrant. May be declining due to habitat loss from lack of proper forest management.

Similar Birds

WHIP-POOR-WILL
Smaller; grayer; rufous bar on shoulder; voice differs • male has more white in tail and white crescent at lower edge of black throat • female has dark brown throat, buffy necklace, and pale buff tips to outer tail feathers.

Flight Pattern

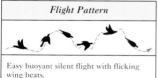

Easy buoyant silent flight with flicking wing beats.

Nest Identification

Shape ♣   Location ▬

No nest materials • on ground atop dried leaves, shaded by dense trees or ground cover • 2 shiny pinkish cream or buff eggs, with brown, lavender, or gray markings; oval to elliptical, 1.4 x 1.0 inches.

Plumage Sexes similar	Habitat ♠♦ ♣♣	Migration Migratory	Weight 4.2 ounces

DATE _____ TIME_____ LOCATION _____

Family CAPRIMULGIDAE	Species *Caprimulgus vociferus*	Length 9–10 inches	Wingspan 16–19.5 inches

WHIP-POOR-WILL

The Whip-poor-will is best located and identified by its distinctive calls. It is nearly impossible to see because it tends to sit on the ground or lengthwise on a branch, and its pattern closely matches the leaf litter of the wood lots it frequents. "Whips" have rounded wings that when folded do not reach to the tip of the tail. Males are similar to females but the throat is bordered with white and the tail has large white patches.

white necklace

large eyes

• **SONG** A loud, clear *whip-poor-will* often repeated at night in eastern birds; call is more coarse among southwestern birds.

dark throat with a buff border

long tail with buff tips

FEMALE

• **BEHAVIOR** Incubating or perched birds often allow a close approach. They fly close to the ground at night and catch large flying insects, especially medium to large moths. Their large eyes, like those of other creatures active at night, reflect light with a red eye-shine. In rural areas, birds often sit along dirt or gravel roads in the open at night.

• **BREEDING** Monogamous.

• **NESTING** Incubation 19–20 days by female. Semiprecocial young stay in nest 20 days. Fed by both sexes. 1–2 broods per year.

Similar Birds

CHUCK–WILL'S WIDOW
Lacks wing bars and black wing and tail
• breeds throughout much of North, Southwest.

COMMON NIGHTHAWK
Yellow undertail coverts
• ranges in Northwest, Rockies, and much of the Southwest.

• **POPULATION** Uncommon. Has declined in the East in recent decades because of habitat loss caused by forest fragmentation and development.

• **CONSERVATION** Species federally protected.

Flight Pattern

Erratic mothlike flight. Male hovers during display, with slow smooth flight.

Nest Identification

Shape ♣   Location ▬

Eggs laid on flat ground on leaf litter • 2 whitish eggs marked with brown and gray overlaid with brown, olive, and lavender; 1.2 inches long.

Plumage Sexes similar	Habitat 🌾 🌱 ⛰ 🌳	Migration Most migrate	Weight 2.0 ounces

DATE _____ TIME_____ LOCATION _____

Family APODIDAE	Species *Chaetura pelagica*	Length 5.5 inches	Wingspan 12–12.75 inches

CHIMNEY SWIFT

Often referred to as "a cigar with wings" because of its flight silhouette, this is the only swift normally found in eastern North America. Named for its habit of building nests inside chimneys or air shafts, it uses its gluelike saliva to attach its nest to the brick or concrete and to bind together the individual sticks. Adult birds feed their young until they are old enough to fly out of the chimney. In fall migration, hundreds may swirl above a large chimney at dusk before dropping into it to roost for the night. This bird has become so adapted to life in man-made structures that it now is a common summer species sweeping the skies over our towns, cities, and suburbs.

sooty gray overall

blackish gray bill

short cigar-shaped body

blackish gray legs and feet

long narrow curved wings

• **SONG** Bold chattering; rapid twittering calls cascade down from above.

• **BEHAVIOR** Gregarious. Eats flying insects and ballooning spiders in the air column. Catches food while flying. Roosted and nested in hollow trees before Europeans settled North America; now uses chimneys and air shafts. Almost always seen on the wing. Aerial courtship and mating with courtship V-ing display – pairs flying with wings held in extreme dihedral V above their backs.

• **BREEDING** Monogamous. Solitary or colonial. Sometimes with helpers at the nest.

• **NESTING** Incubation 19–21 days by both sexes, sometimes with the aid of helpers. Young altricial; stay in nest 30 days, fed by both sexes, but female feeds more. 1 brood per year.

• **POPULATION** Fairly common to common in range. Has increased dramatically with the abundance of artificial nesting sites created by European settlement of North America. Rare in southern California.

• **CONSERVATION** Neotropical migrant that winters in South America's Amazon Basin.

Similar Birds

VAUX'S SWIFT Smaller; shorter wings; paler underparts and rump; voice differs; soars less frequently.

Flight Pattern

Rapid batlike flight on stiff swept-back wings alternates with long sweeping glides. Darts erratically. Soars on thermal drafts.

Nest Identification	
Shape ⬌ Location	Half saucer of sticks and saliva • hollow interior of tree, chimney, air shaft, vertical pipe, silo, barn, open well or cistern, fruit cellar, or side of building • nest built by both sexes • 2–7 white eggs, may be nest stained; long oval to cylindrical, 0.8 x 0.5 inches.

Plumage Sexes similar	Habitat	Migration Migratory	Weight 0.8 ounce

DATE _____ TIME_____ LOCATION _____

Family TROCHILIDAE	Species *Archilochus colubris*	Length 3–3.75 inches	Wingspan 4.25–4.5 inches

RUBY-THROATED HUMMINGBIRD

The only hummer known by most Easterners has a range that covers most of eastern North America. This is the hummingbird that frequents Eastern gardens and feeders. Both sexes have glittering green crown and upperparts, and the underparts are grayish to white. Males have black faces and a deep red to orange-red throat, or gorget. The humming of its wings is clearly discernible from some distance.

• **SONG** Series of rapid squeaky *chipping* notes.

• **BEHAVIOR** Feeds primarily on nectar but takes some insects and spiders, also sap from sapsucker drill wells. In courtship flight male makes huge a 180-degree arc back and forth, emitting a buzzing sound at its lowest point. Males often arrive on breeding grounds well ahead of females. These birds are strongly attracted to the color red, as are many other hummers.

• **BREEDING** Solitary.

• **NESTING** Incubation 11–16 days by female. Altricial young stay in nest 20–22 days. Fed by female. 1–3 broods per year.

• **POPULATION** Common to fairly common in breeding range. A few winter regularly in south Florida. Rare elsewhere.

• **FEEDERS** Red columbine in spring; saliva, trumpet or coral honeysuckle, and bee balm later in year. Also jewelweed, phlox, petunias, lilies, trumpet creeper, Siberian peatree, nasturtium, cone-shaped red flowers (wild and domesticated), and sugar water.

• **CONSERVATION** Red food dyes added to sugar water may harm birds. Sometimes attracted to red supporting insulators on electrical fences, then killed.

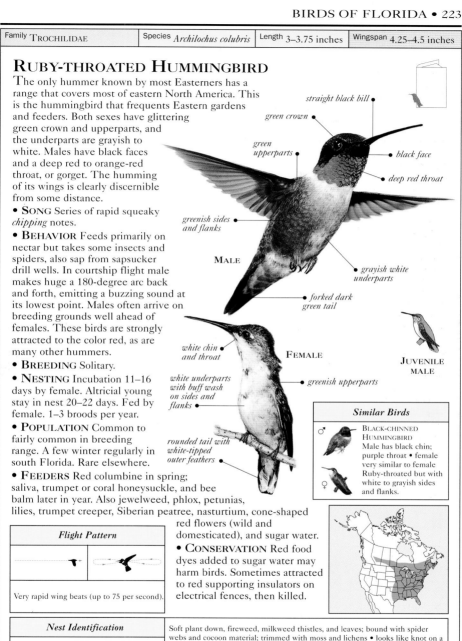

straight black bill

green crown

green upperparts

black face

deep red throat

greenish sides and flanks

MALE

grayish white underparts

forked dark green tail

white chin and throat

FEMALE

greenish upperparts

JUVENILE MALE

white underparts with buff wash on sides and flanks

rounded tail with white-tipped outer feathers

Similar Birds

♂ BLACK-CHINNED HUMMINGBIRD Male has black chin; purple throat • female very similar to female Ruby-throated but with white to grayish sides and flanks. ♀

Flight Pattern
Very rapid wing beats (up to 75 per second).

Nest Identification

Shape   Location

Soft plant down, fireweed, milkweed thistles, and leaves; bound with spider webs and cocoon material; trimmed with moss and lichens • looks like knot on a branch • 5–20 feet above ground, often on downsloping branch over brook and sheltered by leaves • built by female • 2 white eggs; elliptical, 0.5 x 0.3 inches.

Plumage Sexes differ	Habitat	Migration Migratory	Weight 0.1 ounce

DATE _____ TIME_____ LOCATION _____

Family TROCHILIDAE	Species *Selasphorus rufus*	Length 3.75 inches	Wingspan 4.75 inches

RUFOUS HUMMINGBIRD

This tenacious hummingbird aggressively defends its territory and will attack not only larger birds such as blackbirds and thrushes, but also chipmunks. At feeders it is intolerant of all other would-be visitors and spends much of its time driving them away from the nectar. Like most hummingbirds, highly attracted to the color red, it has been known to examine human clothing, magazine covers, and other items showing this color. This is the only hummingbird in North America with a rufous back, and the one most likely to be seen in the East in the fall and winter after the Ruby-throated Hummingbirds have migrated south. The male has green markings on his rufous back, a rufous tail, and his gorget sparkles copper-red in good light; the female also has small spots on her throat that appear red in certain light.

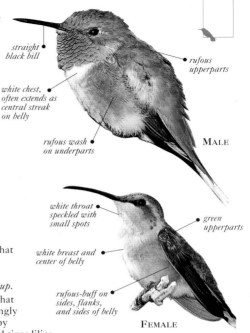

straight
black bill

rufous
upperparts

white chest,
often extends as
central streak
on belly

rufous wash
on underparts

MALE

white throat
speckled with
small spots

green
upperparts

white breast and
center of belly

rufous-buff on
sides, flanks,
and sides of belly

FEMALE

• **SONG** Call is sibilant *chewp chewp*; in defense chases, proclaims *zeee-chupppity-chup*.

• **BEHAVIOR** Solitary. A hardy hummer that nests as far north as southern Alaska. Strongly prefers red to any other color and hovers by red tubular flowers, such as columbine and tiger lilies, to gather nectar. Feeds and perches at low to middle levels. Catches insects in midair and eats sap from holes drilled by sapsuckers. Plucks spiders and insects from webs. Wings make buzzy whistle in flight. Male displays for female in U-shaped or oval pattern; ascends with back to female, then dives, turning toward her on whistling wings with orange-red gorget flashing.

• **BREEDING** Polygamous. Solitary in small loose semicolonies.

• **NESTING** Incubation 12–14 days by female. Altricial young stay in nest 20 days, fed by female. 1–2 broods per year.

Similar Birds
ALLEN'S HUMMINGBIRD ♂ Male has green back • females cannot be distinguished in the field ♀ • in the hand, tail feathers more slender.

• **POPULATION** Abundant to common. Rare in the East in fall and winter.

• **FEEDERS** Sugar water.

• **CONSERVATION** Neotropical migrant. Possible decline in recent years; no noted cause.

Flight Pattern	

Hovers while feeding; darts up and down, in and out, and backwards; swift and dashing flight on a blur of whirring wings.

Nest Identification	
Shape 🥄 Location 🌿	Plant down, covered with lichen, moss, bud scales, leaves, shredded bark, and plant fibers; bound with spider silk and lined with plant down • most often on drooping limb; occasionally in fork of tree or shrub, 5–50 feet above ground • built by female • 2 white eggs; elliptical oval or subelliptical, 0.5 x 0.33 inches.

Plumage Sexes differ	Habitat 🌱 🌿 🔺	Migration Migratory	Weight 0.1 ounce

DATE _____ TIME_____ LOCATION _____

| Family ALCEDINIDAE | Species *Ceryle alcyon* | Length 11–14.5 inches | Wingspan 22–26 inches |

BELTED KINGFISHER

Widely distributed and common along freshwater bodies of water as well as the coast, this is the only kingfisher across most of its range, except along the Mexican border. It is one of the few North American birds in which the female is more colorful than the male. The male has blue-gray upperparts with a blue-gray band across the breast and appears big-headed with its large bill and ragged crest. In flight it shows a white patch on the upperwing at the base of the primaries.

• **SONG** Bold raspy rattle sounds like a heavy fishing reel.

• **BEHAVIOR** Generally solitary. Plunges headfirst into water from perch or a hover up to 20 feet or more above water to catch fish. Feeds primarily on fish but also takes amphibians, reptiles, insects, crustaceans, and mollusks. Frequents favorite perches along waterways for hunting. Pair digs burrow in bank 3–7 feet deep (can be up to 15 feet).

• **BREEDING** Monogamous; solitary nester.

• **NESTING** Incubation 23–24 days by both sexes. Altricial young stay in nest 27–29 days. Fed by both sexes. 1–2 broods per year.

• **POPULATION** Slight decline in North America.

• **CONSERVATION** Often viewed as problem at fish hatcheries; before regulation they were shot and killed at hatcheries and along trout streams. This may still occur at some hatcheries.

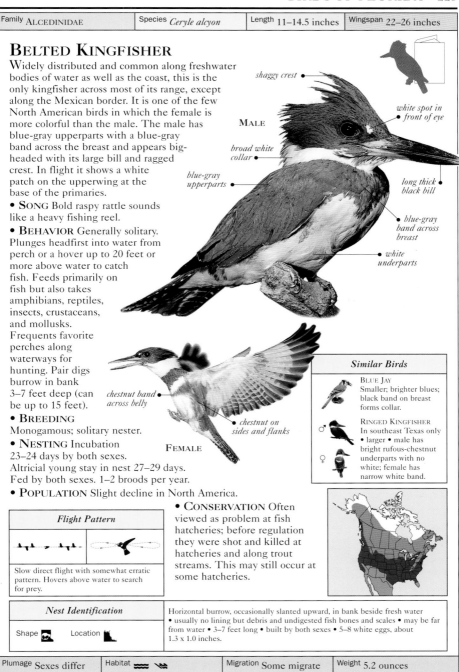

shaggy crest

MALE

white spot in front of eye

broad white collar

blue-gray upperparts

long thick black bill

blue-gray band across breast

white underparts

chestnut band across belly

chestnut on sides and flanks

FEMALE

Similar Birds

BLUE JAY
Smaller; brighter blues; black band on breast forms collar.

RINGED KINGFISHER
In southeast Texas only • larger • male has bright rufous-chestnut underparts with no white; female has narrow white band.

Flight Pattern

Slow direct flight with somewhat erratic pattern. Hovers above water to search for prey.

Nest Identification

Shape ___ Location ___

Horizontal burrow, occasionally slanted upward, in bank beside fresh water • usually no lining but debris and undigested fish bones and scales • may be far from water • 3–7 feet long • built by both sexes • 5–8 white eggs, about 1.3 x 1.0 inches.

| Plumage Sexes differ | Habitat ～～ ～ | Migration Some migrate | Weight 5.2 ounces |

DATE _____ TIME_____ LOCATION _____

| Family PICIDAE | Species *Melanerpes erythrocephalus* | Length 8.5–9.25 inches | Wingspan 16–18 inches |

RED-HEADED WOODPECKER

red head, neck, and throat

black bill

red upper breast

black back

black wing coverts and primaries

black legs and feet

white underparts

The ecological eastern counterpart of Lewis's Woodpecker, this is the only woodpecker in the East with an entirely red head. Unlike many other woodpeckers, the Red-headed Woodpecker catches most of its food in flight, from the ground, or by gleaning it from tree trunks and limbs; it rarely bores holes in trees to probe for insects. The male does, however, vigorously drill its nest cavity with the aid of its mate. In flight the white underparts, white rump, and large white secondary patches contrast sharply with the black tail, wings, and back. Juveniles have brownish black upperparts and brown heads.

- **SONG** Fairly noisy. In breeding season has bold grating *queark* or *queer, queer, queer.* Also sounds like a chicken clucking, *kerr-uck, kerr-uck.*

- **BEHAVIOR** Solitary or in pairs. Eats various insects, spiders, millipedes, and centipedes; sometimes takes eggs and young of other birds, mice, corn, grains, various nuts, and berries. Often hunts from low perches, flying to ground to pick up prey or nut. Caches acorns and nuts, removing shells and storing the meat for winter.

- **BREEDING** Monogamous. Solitary nester.

- **NESTING** Incubation 12–14 days by both sexes. Altricial young stay in nest 27–31 days. Fed by both sexes. 1–2 broods per year.

- **POPULATION** Uncommon and declining. Casual to accidental west of the Rocky Mountains.

- **FEEDERS AND BIRDHOUSES** Suet, sunflower seeds, cracked corn, raisins, nuts, and bread. Some will nest in birdhouse built for woodpeckers.

- **CONSERVATION** Listed as species of special concern by National Audubon Society. Decline in past century due to habitat loss, collisions with automobiles, and competition for nesting cavities with European Starling. Creosote-coated utility poles are lethal to eggs and young.

black tail

JUVENILE

Similar Birds

RED-BELLIED WOODPECKER ♂
Red crown and nape only; barred black-and-white upperparts; white patches at bases of primaries; grayish face and underparts.

Flight Pattern

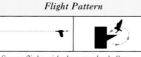

Strong flight with slow steady shallow wing beats. Sallies for flying insects, then returns to same or nearby perch.

Nest Identification

Shape ▓ Location 🌿 🌳 🦅 🏚 🏢

In snag, limb of living tree, stump, or dead tree • 1.75-inch entrance; 8–24 inches deep; 8–80 feet above ground • drilled mostly by male • 4–7 white eggs; oval to elliptical, 1 inch in diameter.

| Plumage Sexes similar | Habitat  | Migration Some migrate | Weight 2.5 ounces |

DATE _____ TIME_____ LOCATION _____

Family PICIDAE	Species *Melanerpes carolinus*	Length 9–10.5 inches	Wingspan 15–18 inches

RED-BELLIED WOODPECKER

This noisy common woodpecker of eastern US forests and forest edges has adapted to different habitats, from southern pine forests to northern hardwoods, scattered trees, and urban parks. The bird's upperparts have black-and-white barring in a zebra pattern. The "red belly" that gives the bird its name is a reddish wash low on the belly and between the legs that is actually difficult to see in the field. In flight it shows a white rump, white patches at the base of the primaries, and white-barred central tail feathers. Juvenile birds are similar to adults but have a gray-brown head.

pale grayish tan face and chin

red crown and nape

MALE

black-and-white barring on upperparts

pale grayish tan underparts

gray crown

red nape

FEMALE

• **SONG** Quavering *churr-churr* or *querrr-querrr* and abrupt *chuck, chuck, chuck*, softer than Golden-fronted Woodpecker.

• **BEHAVIOR** Conspicuous, with noisy vocalizations and drumming in breeding season. Nests and roosts nightly in tree cavities. Eats wide variety of fare, including insects, fruits, vegetables, seeds, and sap from sapsucker drill wells.

• **BREEDING** Monogamous. Solitary nester.

• **NESTING** Incubation 11–14 days by both sexes; male at night, female during day. Young stay in nest 22–27 days. Fed by both sexes. 1 brood per year in the North; 2–3 broods per year in the South.

Similar Birds

GOLDEN-FRONTED WOODPECKER Black tail without white barring; golden-orange nape; yellow patch at base of upper mandible; indistinct yellowish wash on belly • male has red cap.

• **POPULATION** Common to fairly common. Expanding northward in recent decades to southern border of Canada. Seems stable overall; may be increasing slightly.

• **FEEDERS** Nuts, sunflower seeds, peanut butter, and suet.

Flight Pattern

Undulating flight with fairly rapid wing beats interspersed with periods of roller-coaster flight with wings folded.

Nest Identification

Shape 🪶 Location 🌳 ⚘

In tree 5–70 feet above ground • built by both sexes • sometimes uses abandoned holes of other woodpeckers • 3–8 white eggs, 1 inch in diameter.

Plumage Sexes differ	Habitat 🌲🌳🌿	Migration Nonmigratory	Weight 2.4 ounces

DATE _____ TIME_____ LOCATION _____

Family PICIDAE	Species *Sphyrapicus varius*	Length 8–9 inches	Wingspan 16–18 inches

YELLOW-BELLIED SAPSUCKER

Eastern counterpart to the Red-naped Sapsucker, this is the most widespread of the four North American sapsuckers. In breeding season male and female perform continual loud drumming duets, including ritual tapping at the nest entrance. The female is similar to the male but has a white throat. In flight birds show a white rump and white shoulder patches. Juveniles have brown mottling on the chest, head, and upperparts, and a white shoulder patch but lack the bright head and throat colors.

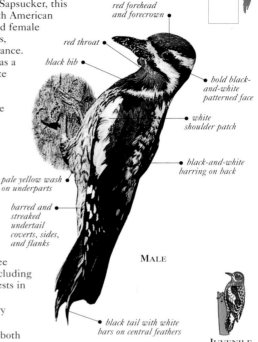

red forehead and forecrown

red throat

black bib

bold black-and-white patterned face

white shoulder patch

black-and-white barring on back

pale yellow wash on underparts

barred and streaked undertail coverts, sides, and flanks

MALE

• **SONG** Often silent. Low, growling nasal *mew* sounds somewhat catlike. Alarm call of *cheee-er, cheeee-er*. During courtship display cries *hoih-hoih*. Males make staccato drumming sounds.

• **BEHAVIOR** Solitary or in pairs. Bores series of small holes, often in horizontal rows, in trees to drink the sap that collects. Eats insects attracted to drill wells, plus fruits, berries, and tree buds. Guards wells from other birds, including hummingbirds, and small mammals. Nests in soft deciduous trees, often near water.

• **BREEDING** Monogamous. Small, very loose colonies.

• **NESTING** Incubation 12–13 days by both sexes (male at night, female during day). Altricial young stay in nest 25–29 days; fed mixture of sap and insects by both sexes. Taught sapsucking by both sexes. 1 brood per year.

• **POPULATION** Common to fairly common in deciduous and mixed forests. Accidental to rare in West during migration and winter.

• **FEEDERS** In winter, mixture of suet and sugar. Will eat sweets, like jelly or doughnuts. Drinks sugar water from hummingbird feeders.

black tail with white bars on central feathers

JUVENILE

Similar Birds

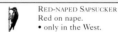

RED-NAPED SAPSUCKER
Red on nape.
• only in the West.

• **CONSERVATION** People dislike the drill wells created in their shade and fruit trees; fearing the tree will be injured or diseased, they often kill sapsuckers, although the birds are protected by law.

Flight Pattern

Alternates several rapid shallow wing beats with short glides, producing undulating flight as the bird progresses.

Nest Identification

Shape — Location —

Usually no materials except bark chips • in dead or live tree (prefers live tree); 6–60 feet above ground • built by both sexes in 7–10 days • 1.25 x 1.6-inch entrance hole; 5 x 14-inch gourd-shaped cavity • 4–7 white eggs; oval to elliptical, 0.9 x 0.7 inches.

Plumage Sexes similar	Habitat	Migration Migratory	Weight 1.8 ounces

DATE _____ TIME_____ LOCATION _____

Family PICIDAE	Species *Picoides pubescens*	Length 6.75–7 inches	Wingspan 11–12 inches

DOWNY WOODPECKER

The smallest woodpecker in North America is found across most of the continent, ranging from coast to coast and from the northern tree line south to the Gulf and the deserts and dry grasslands just north of the Mexican border. The combination of small size, white back, and small stubby bill distinguishes this common woodpecker. The female differs from the male only in that it lacks the red occipital patch. In the Pacific Northwest these birds show pale brownish gray underparts and back.

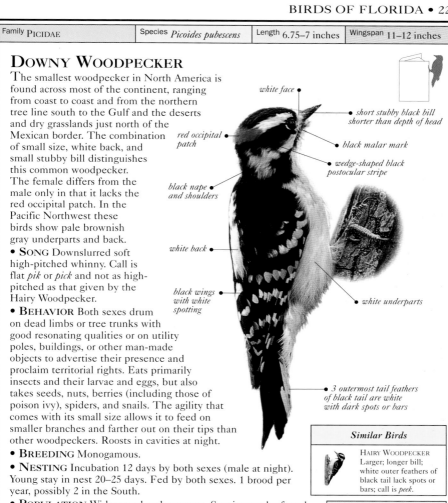

white face

short stubby black bill shorter than depth of head

red occipital patch

black malar mark

wedge-shaped black postocular stripe

black nape and shoulders

white back

black wings with white spotting

white underparts

3 outermost tail feathers of black tail are white with dark spots or bars

• **SONG** Downslurred soft high-pitched whinny. Call is flat *pik* or *pick* and not as high-pitched as that given by the Hairy Woodpecker.
• **BEHAVIOR** Both sexes drum on dead limbs or tree trunks with good resonating qualities or on utility poles, buildings, or other man-made objects to advertise their presence and proclaim territorial rights. Eats primarily insects and their larvae and eggs, but also takes seeds, nuts, berries (including those of poison ivy), spiders, and snails. The agility that comes with its small size allows it to feed on smaller branches and farther out on their tips than other woodpeckers. Roosts in cavities at night.
• **BREEDING** Monogamous.
• **NESTING** Incubation 12 days by both sexes (male at night). Young stay in nest 20–25 days. Fed by both sexes. 1 brood per year, possibly 2 in the South.
• **POPULATION** Widespread and common. Species can be found almost anywhere there are trees.
• **FEEDERS AND BIRDHOUSES** Will come to feeders for suet, peanut butter, sunflower seeds, and bread. Will nest in bird box designed for it.

Similar Birds

HAIRY WOODPECKER Larger; longer bill; white outer feathers of black tail lack spots or bars; call is *peek*.

Flight Pattern

Undulating flight with rapid wing beats alternating with pauses on folded wings, which produces bouncing flight.

Nest Identification

Shape Location

Excavated in dead tree trunk or branch; pair usually leaves chips in bottom • usually 12–30 feet above ground, sometimes 5–60 feet • built by both sexes • 3–7 white eggs, 0.8 inch in diameter.

Plumage Sexes similar	Habitat	Migration Nonmigratory	Weight 1.0 ounce

DATE _____ TIME_____ LOCATION _____

Family PICIDAE	Species *Picoides villosus*	Length 8.5–10.5 inches	Wingspan 15–17.5 inches

HAIRY WOODPECKER

The Hairy Woodpecker and the Northern Flicker are the two most widely distributed woodpeckers in North America. This woodpecker is found almost anywhere forests exist. Similar in appearance to the smaller Downy Woodpecker, it is noisier but less confiding in humans and does not often allow a close approach before it flies away. Learning its high-pitched *peek* call note will make this shy bird easier to locate. Look for a white back when bird is in flight. The only difference between male and female birds is that the female lacks the red occipital patch. Birds in the Pacific Northwest show pale brownish gray underparts.

long black bill is nearly as long as head is deep

red occipital patch

black nape

white face with black malar mark and wedge-shaped postocular stripe

black shoulders

white underparts

black wings with white spotting/barring

black tail with 3 entirely white outermost feathers on each side

• **SONG** Loud downslurred whinny reminiscent of Belted Kingfisher's rattle. Call is bold, grating, sharp *peek*.

• **BEHAVIOR** Roosts in cavities at night. Feeds primarily on wood-boring insects and their larvae, other insects, nuts, seeds, and from the drill wells of sapsuckers. Both sexes drum to advertise presence and maintain territory.

• **BREEDING** Monogamous. Some individuals known to remain with same mate for at least 4 years.

• **NESTING** Incubation 11–15 days by both sexes (male at night). Altricial young remain in nest 28–30 days. Fed by both sexes. 1 brood per year unless nest is robbed or disturbed.

• **POPULATION** Fairly common, but sometimes local, over most of range. Sometimes more common in northern hardwood and boreal forests; rare in the Deep South and in Florida.

• **FEEDERS** Sometimes comes for sunflower seeds, nuts, fruits, peanut butter, and suet.

Similar Birds

DOWNY WOODPECKER Smaller; shorter, stubby bill (length much less than depth of head); white outer tailfeathers with dark spots/bars.

THREE-TOED WOODPECKER Black-and-white barring on back; dark barred sides • male has yellow crown.

Flight Pattern

Undulating flight with rapid wing beats alternating with pauses on folded wings, which produces bouncing flight.

Nest Identification

Shape 🪵¹   Location 🌱 🌳 🌿

4–60 feet above ground • built by both sexes • 3–6 white eggs, 1 inch in diameter.

Plumage Sexes differ	Habitat 🌿 🌳	Migration Most do not migrate	Weight 2.5 ounces

DATE _____ TIME_____ LOCATION _____

Family PICIDAE	Species *Picoides borealis*	Length 8.5 inches	Wingspan 16 inches

RED-COCKADED WOODPECKER

The white cheeks of this woodpecker are a more accurate field mark than the male's red cockade, which is indistinct in the field. In summer, the male begins drilling a large roosting and nesting cavity, which takes more than a year to complete. These cavities may be used for forty to fifty years. The Red-cockaded is unique among North American woodpeckers because it requires a living pine tree for its nesting cavity. When the cavity is drilled, sap and resins flow around the entrance, serving as a predator guard. Females lack the small red cockade.

- **SONG** Noisy. Call is *yank, yank,* somewhat like White-breasted Nuthatch. Also has hoarse *sripp* and high-pitched *tsick.*
- **BEHAVIOR** Gregarious. In clans of 3–7, consisting of mated pair, current young, and unmated adult helper(s). Forages and drills for insects on trunks of pine trees, sometimes circling tree as it climbs. In summer may feed on earworms in corn. Also eats berries and nuts. Nesting and roosting holes are marked by long strands of sap and resin oozing from inch-wide drill holes in rows above and below them; drill holes are maintained by clan who may remove bark from around hole.
- **BREEDING** Monogamous. Cooperative breeding in small colonies or clans. Mates for life.
- **NESTING** Incubation 10–15 days by both sexes. Young altricial; stay in nest 22–29 days, fed by both sexes and helpers. 1 brood per year.
- **POPULATION** Uncommon. Declined in 20th century.
- **FEEDERS AND BIRDHOUSES** Comes to mixture of suet and water. Will accept artificial nest cavities inserted into pine trees.
- **CONSERVATION** Has been designated an endangered species as a result of the over-cutting of mature pine forests as well as by fire suppression in the fire-maintained ecosystem of the Southeast.

black forehead, cap, and nape

black postocular stripe

black malar mark

red cockade

white cheeks

black-and-white cross-barred back

whitish underparts

black-spotted sides, flanks, and crissum

black wings and wing coverts with white spots and bars

black tail with black-spotted white outer tail feathers

Similar Birds

HAIRY WOODPECKER
Black ear patch; white back; unmarked white underparts; unmarked white outer tail feathers; voice differs
- male has red occipital patch.

DOWNY WOODPECKER
Smaller in size; black ear patch; white back; unmarked white underparts; voice differs
- male has red occipital patch.

Flight Pattern

Alternates several rapid wing beats with short glide with wings partially folded to sides, producing up-and-down flight.

Nest Identification

Shape   Location

Dried wood chips • in live mature pine tree, often infected with heart fungus, 12–70 feet above ground • built by male and extra birds with some help from female • 2–5 white eggs; oval to elliptical, 1.0 x 0.75 inches.

Plumage Sexes similar	Habitat	Migration Nonmigratory	Weight 1.6 ounces

DATE _____ TIME_____ LOCATION _____

Family PICIDAE	Species *Colaptes auratus*	Length 12.75–14 inches	Wingspan 19–21 inches

NORTHERN FLICKER

This large woodpecker is often found in open spaces where it spends considerable time on the ground foraging for ants. Two distinct geographical groups, which were considered separate species until the early 1980s, occur: in the East and Northwest, Yellow-shafted Flicker has yellow underwings and undertail, and a black mustache; and, in the West, Red-shafted Flicker has bright salmon-red to red-orange underwings and undertail, and a red mustache. Although the two forms have similar bodies, the Red-shafted form shows a different pattern on its head with colors that are basically reversed from those of the Yellow-shafted form: a gray face and brown forehead, crown, and nape with no red crescent. Females are similar to males, lacking only the mustache. All birds have brown backs and wings with dark barring, a black crescent bib, buff to grayish underparts with heavy spotting, and a white rump patch.

red crescent on back of crown

gray nape

brown back and upperwings with black barring

gray crown and forehead

tan face

black mustache

YELLOW-SHAFTED MALE

buff-white underparts with heavy black spotting

RED-SHAFTED MALE

• **SONG** In breeding season, long bold repeated *wick-er, wick-er, wick-er* notes. Year-round, makes single loud *klee-yer* or *clearrrr*.

• **BEHAVIOR** Most terrestrial North American woodpecker. An analysis of the contents of a single flicker stomach revealed 3,000 ants. Spring courtship displays are noisy and animated, as pair bonds are established and rivals are driven away.

• **BREEDING** Monogamous. Solitary nester.

• **NESTING** Incubation 11–16 days by both sexes. Altricial young stay in nest 4 weeks, fed by both sexes. Usually 1 brood per year, sometimes 2 in the South.

• **POPULATION** Yellow-shafted form common. Red-shafted form is fairly common to common. Both thought to be declining.

• **BIRDHOUSES** Nests in houses and boxes.

• **CONSERVATION** Declining. Introduced European Starlings successfully compete for nest sites.

Similar Birds

GILDED FLICKER Limited range but overlaps with Red-shafted form; like a smaller, more washed out Red-shafted Flicker; yellow wash under wings and tail • only in the West.

Flight Pattern

Several rapid wing beats followed by a pause with wings folded at sides produces up-and-down flight pattern.

Nest Identification	
Shape	Location	In snag, poles, posts, buildings, nest boxes, and banks (sometimes driving out the kingfisher or Bank Swallow tenants) • 6–20 feet above ground, sometimes higher • built by both sexes • sometimes uses same nest hole for second season • 3–12 white eggs; oval to short-oval; 1.1 x 0.8 inches.

Plumage Sexes differ	Habitat	Migration Most do not migrate	Weight 4.8 ounces

DATE _____ TIME_____ LOCATION _____

| Family PICIDAE | Species *Dryocopus pileatus* | Length 16.5–19.5 inches | Wingspan 27–30 inches |

PILEATED WOODPECKER

These crow-sized woodpeckers drum on trees to claim territory and attract a mate; the loud heavy sound is as if the tree is being hit with a wooden mallet. Each member of a mated pair excavates several roosting cavities and may retire for the evening in one of them. The male roosts in the current nesting cavity before the eggs are laid and afterward incubates them there at night. In flight both sexes show a large white patch at the base of the primaries as well as white underwing linings.

red crest extending from forehead to nape

large black bill

white chin
scarlet mustache

white line from base of bill crosses face to back of neck and extends down neck to side

solid black back

MALE

- **SONG** Location call to mate is a deliberate loud *cuck, cuck, cuck.* Both sexes have a call of *yucca, yucca, yucca,* similar to a flicker, that changes in pitch, loudness, and in its cadence.

- **BEHAVIOR** Solitary or in pairs. Loud and often conspicuous. Bores deep into trees and peels off large strips of bark for food. Also digs on ground and on fallen logs. Eats ants, beetles, and a variety of other insects, especially tree-boring ones, acorns, beechnuts, seeds of tree cones, nuts, and various fruits.

black forehead

black mustache

- **BREEDING** Monogamous.

- **NESTING** Incubation 15–18 days by both sexes, mostly male. Young altricial; brooded by female; stay in nest 26–28 days, fed by both sexes. 1 brood per year.

- **POPULATION** Common to fairly common in the Southeast; uncommon and local elsewhere.

FEMALE

Similar Birds

♂ IVORY- BILLED WOODPECKER
Probably extinct
- larger; 2 white stripes on back extending from sides of neck; white secondaries make white patch on back when wings fold; black chin; ivory-white bill; in flight, shows white secondaries and tips of inner primaries; white lining onedge of underwing • female has black crest.

- **FEEDERS** Mixture of melted suet, pecans, and walnut meats.

- **CONSERVATION** Vulnerable to habitat loss and forest fragmentation. Sharp decline in early 20th century, but has adapted to habitat changes. Competes for excavated nesting cavities with European Starlings.

Flight Pattern

Strong powerful wing beats when traveling distances; alternates rapid wing strokes with brief periods of wings folded to sides on short flights beneath the canopy.

Nest Identification

Shape ◥ Location 🌳🌲🌴

Few wood chips • dead or live tree in shaded area, 15–85 feet above ground • excavated by both sexes; female sometimes does more • 3–8 white eggs; oval to elliptical, 1.3 x 1.0 inches.

| Plumage Sexes differ | Habitat 🌲 🌿 🌳 | Migration Nonmigratory | Weight 10.9 ounces |

DATE ___7 / 04___ TIME _____ LOCATION _____

Family TYRANNIDAE	Species *Contopus virens*	Length 6.25 inches	Wingspan 10.5 inches

EASTERN WOOD-PEWEE

Although this bird is very difficult to distinguish visually from its western counterpart, the Western Wood-Pewee, their ranges barely overlap and their voices differ. Like most flycatchers, it tends to perch on an open lookout among thick trees or shrubs, sailing into the open only to feed. It is often first detected by its voice, because it often calls its distinctive *pee-a-wee* while perched, awaiting its next chance at a flying insect. Juveniles are similar to adults but both upper and lower mandibles showing dark coloration.

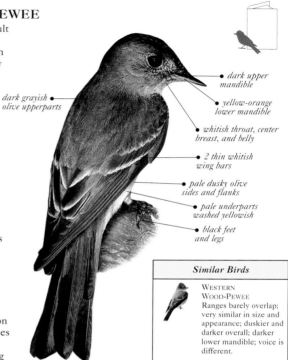

dark upper mandible

dark grayish olive upperparts

yellow-orange lower mandible

whitish throat, center breast, and belly

2 thin whitish wing bars

pale dusky olive sides and flanks

pale underparts washed yellowish

black feet and legs

- **SONG** During the day whistles distinctive, slow plaintive *pee-a-wee*, with second note lower; on second or third repeat, often followed by *pee-yeer*; second note lower. At dusk and early dawn, sings *ah-de-deee*.

- **BEHAVIOR** Solitary. Perches on open and/or dead branches in trees to spot prey; flies out to catch food. Eats a wide variety of flying insects, including beetles, flies, moths, wasps, and bees. Takes some spiders and a few berries. Like other flycatchers, it often defends its territory even from larger birds by flying at them and pecking at their backs.

- **BREEDING** Monogamous.

- **NESTING** Incubation 12–13 days by female. Young altricial; stay in nest 14–18 days, fed by both sexes. 1 brood per year.

Similar Birds

WESTERN WOOD-PEWEE Ranges barely overlap; very similar in size and appearance; duskier and darker overall; darker lower mandible; voice is different.

EASTERN PHOEBE Slightly larger; paler whitish to yellow underparts; lacks wing bars; both mandibles dark; pumps tail up and down while perched, especially upon landing; voice differs.

- **POPULATION** Fairly common and widespread. Casual in the West in migration.

- **CONSERVATION** Neotropical migrant. Infrequent host to cowbird's eggs. Decline due to possible loss of South American wintering habitat.

Flight Pattern

Rather slow fluttering direct flight on shallowly beating wings. Sallies forth to catch insects in midair, returning to perch.

Nest Identification	
Shape ☕ Location 🌲 🐦	Grass, plant fibers, and spider web, covered with thick layer of lichens • fork of tree or saddled on horizontal branch, 15–50 feet above ground • built by female • 2–4 whitish eggs, with brown blotches and purple, often wreathed at large end; oval to short ovate, 0.7 x 0.5 inches.

Plumage Sexes similar	Habitat	Migration Migratory	Weight 0.5 ounce

DATE _____ TIME_____ LOCATION _____

Family TYRANNIDAE	Species *Empidonax virescens*	Length 5.75 inches	Wingspan 8.75 inches

ACADIAN FLYCATCHER

Its scientific genus name, which means "mosquito king," widely misses the mark in describing this bird's feeding habits, but it is an apt description of the small size of a flycatcher that lords over a realm of small insects. It is the only Empidonax flycatcher to breed in the deep southern states of North America, where it rules in heavily wooded deciduous bottomlands, swamps, and riparian thickets, and in the wooded ravines of drier uplands. Like other empids it is best known by its voice.

• **SONG** Soft call of *peace* or *peeet*. Its explosive *PIZ-zza!!* sounds like a bird sneezing. On territory, males utter a mechanical *ti, ti, ti, ti* as they move from one perch to the next beneath the canopy.

• **BEHAVIOR** Solitary. Easily overlooked except for its occasional vocalizations. Perches in shade on lower to mid-level branches in thick trees to search for food, then dashes out to snatch insect. Eats wide variety of flying insects. Frequents wet areas in open woodlands where it aggressively drives away larger birds and other intruders from the breeding territory.

• **BREEDING** Monogamous.

• **NESTING** Incubation 13–15 days by female. Young altricial; fed by both sexes, but more by female. First flight at 13–15 days; male may feed fledglings while female starts second clutch. 2 broods per year.

• **POPULATION** Common; range expanding in Northeast.

• **CONSERVATION** Neotropical migrant. Frequently nest parasitized by Brown-headed Cowbird.

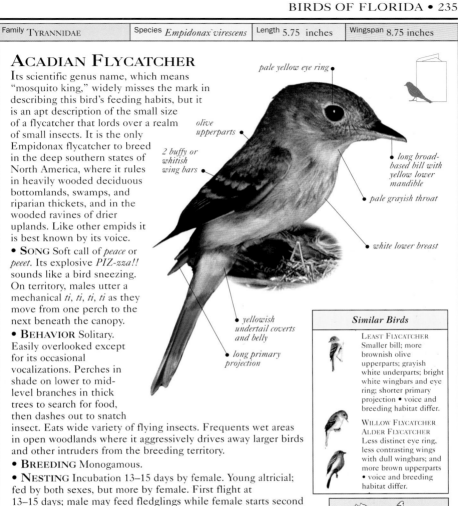

pale yellow eye ring

olive upperparts

2 buffy or whitish wing bars

long broad-based bill with yellow lower mandible

pale grayish throat

white lower breast

yellowish undertail coverts and belly

long primary projection

Similar Birds

LEAST FLYCATCHER Smaller bill; more brownish olive upperparts; grayish white underparts; bright white wingbars and eye ring; shorter primary projection • voice and breeding habitat differ.

WILLOW FLYCATCHER ALDER FLYCATCHER Less distinct eye ring, less contrasting wings with dull wingbars; and more brown upperparts • voice and breeding habitat differ.

Flight Pattern

Weak fluttering flight with shallow wing beats on rapidly beating wings. Sallies out from perch and takes insects in flight, then returns to same or nearby perch.

Nest Identification

Shape — Location

Sticks, grass, dried stems, and bits of bark and cobweb; lined with grass, hair, and plant down • sloppy/messy-looking with long streamers of grasses hanging beneath cup • in fork of horizontal limb well out from trunk • 3–25 feet up • built by female • 2–4 creamy white eggs, with sparse brown spots; oval to short oval; 0.7 x 0.6 inches.

Plumage Sexes similar	Habitat	Migration Migratory	Weight 0.5 ounce

DATE _____ TIME_____ LOCATION _____

| Family TYRANNIDAE | Species *Empidonax minimus* | Length 5.25 inches | Wingspan 7.5–8.5 inches |

LEAST FLYCATCHER

A common summer breeding resident in North America and the smallest of the eastern empids, the Least Flycatcher is perhaps the most often-encountered small flycatcher in the East. During breeding season the male makes a noisy territorial display, calling *chee-BECK* more than sixty times per minute while chasing other flycatchers in its territory. Note its small size, small bill, brown to olive wash on the upperparts, and conspicuous eye ring and wing bars.

large head

short triangular bill

white eye ring

whitish throat

pale lower mandible with dusky tip

gray wash on breast

olive-green to brown upperparts

paler underparts

white wing bars

short primary projection

pale yellow belly

pale yellow undertail coverts

- **SONG** Sings raspy repetitive *chee-BECK*. Call is piercing *whitt-whitt-whitt*.

- **BEHAVIOR** Active, often changing perches. Flicks tail and wings a lot; jerks tail strongly upward. Chases female in courtship; chases ecologically similar American Redstart out of nesting territory. Perches to spot prey, then catches it in the air while flying. Also gleans insects from branches and foliage. Eats wide variety of insects, some spiders, and a few berries and seeds.

- **BREEDING** Monogamous. Sometimes in loose colonies.

- **NESTING** Incubation 13–15 days by female. Altricial young stay in nest 12–17 days. Fed by both sexes. 1–2 broods per year.

- **POPULATION** Common and widespread but declining in parts of range.

- **CONSERVATION** Neotropical migrant. Uncommon host to cowbird. Declining population noted by National Audubon Society.

Similar Birds

WILLOW, ALDER, AND ACADIAN FLYCATCHERS Larger; larger bills; greener upperparts; longer primary extensions; different voices • Willow Flycatcher has less prominent eye ring but similar *whit* call note.

DUSKY FLYCATCHER Slightly longer, narrower bill; longer tail; grayer throat; less contrast in wings; more narrow eye ring; different song.

HAMMOND'S FLYCATCHER Small narrow bill; part of lower mandible is orangish; gray throat; darker olive-gray breast; more distinct teardrop-shaped eye ring; long primary projection; different voice.

Flight Pattern

Weak fluttering direct flight with shallow wing beats. Sallies to take insects in flight and returns to same or nearby perch.

Nest Identification	
Shape 　Location	Grass, bark strips, twigs, lichens, and plant fibers; bound by spider or caterpillar webs • in fork of tree or shrub 2–60 feet above ground • built by female • 3–6 creamy white eggs; ovate, 0.6 x 0.5 inches.

| Plumage Sexes similar | Habitat | Migration Migratory | Weight 0.4 ounce |

DATE _____ TIME_____ LOCATION _____

Family TYRANNIDAE	Species *Sayornis phoebe*	Length 7 inches	Wingspan 11.5 inches

EASTERN PHOEBE

An early migration makes the Eastern Phoebe a common harbinger of spring north of the Mason-Dixon Line. It is easily identified by its wagging tail and distinctive, harsh *fee-be* calls. The subject of the first bird-banding experiment in North America, by John James Audubon in 1840, the Eastern Phoebe has provided researchers with much information about longevity, site fidelity, dispersal, and migratory movements. Phoebes are hardy birds that often winter near water as far north as the Ohio River. This is the only species of flycatcher to winter in the eastern United States. In the bird's nesting range it seems almost every concrete bridge and culvert over small to medium streams has a phoebe nest beneath it.

dark brownish gray head

black bill

brownish gray upperparts

hint of olive on sides and breast

white underparts (washed with yellow in fall)

black feet and legs

dark brownish wings

dark brownish tail

- **SONG** Sharp *chip* is one of most common calls. Also issues brusque pointed *FEE-be* accented on first syllable. Song often repeated, especially when male establishes territory and attempts to attract mate; may repeat many times per minute from high, exposed perch.
- **BEHAVIOR** Solitary or in pairs. Often bobs tail when perched, especially after landing with the tail swept downward, then raised upward, and sometimes pushed sideways in an arc. While sitting atop tree branches and other perches, watches for insects and sallies to catch them in midair. Also catches food in foliage and on ground. In addition to insects, also eats small fish, berries, and fruit.
- **BREEDING** Monogamous. Solitary nester.
- **NESTING** Incubation about 16 days by female. Altricial young stay in nest 15–16 days. Fed by both sexes. 2 broods per year, sometimes 3 in the South.
- **POPULATION** Common and increasing.
- **BIRDHOUSES** Accepts nesting ledges glued to vertical walls under concrete bridges.
- **CONSERVATION** Neotropical migrant. Parasitized by cowbirds. Buildings, dams, bridges, and culverts have provided more nesting areas.

Similar Birds

EASTERN WOOD-PEWEE Darker underparts; yellowish lower mandible; 2 whitish wing bars; does not pump tail; different voice.

Flight Pattern

Weak buoyant fluttering flight with shallow wing beats. Hawks insects by flying from perch and taking insect in flight with audible pop of the mandibles.

Nest Identification	
Shape ▟ Location	Mud pellets covered with moss • lined with grass, weeds, leaves, hair, and feathers • often built on top of remains of old nest • attached to a vertical wall or on a shelf or beam • built by female • 2–8 white eggs with occasional reddish brown spots; oval, 0.8 x 0.6 inches.

Plumage Sexes similar	Habitat	Migration Most migrate	Weight 0.7 ounce

DATE _____ TIME_____ LOCATION _____

Family TYRANNIDAE	Species *Myiarchus crinitus*	Length 8.5 inches	Wingspan 12–14 inches

GREAT CRESTED FLYCATCHER

This big eastern flycatcher with a rusty tail and shaggy crest stays hidden in tall trees, but its coarse song is heard throughout the forest. Although similar in size to the Eastern Kingbird, the Great Crested Flycatcher prefers thickly wooded areas. Males defend their large territories by battling in the air with other males, clawing one another and sometimes pulling out feathers. Like some other members of its genus, it often tops off the nest with a discarded snakeskin, but in today's throwaway society it more readily finds cellophane and plastic. Upperparts are olive-green, and the bird shows two white wing bars.

darker gray crown

heavy black bill

gray throat and upper breast

lemon-yellow belly and undertail coverts

- **SONG** Bold melodic whistle of *wheeep!* and rolling *prrrrrrrrrreeeet. Wheeep* notes often given in rapid succession in series of 3 or more.

primaries show cinnamon-rufous edges

- **BEHAVIOR** Solitary or in pairs. Often ranges high in the canopy, sitting on exposed limbs in the crown of a tall tree or on top of a dead snag. Catches prey higher above ground than most flycatchers. Sallies from perch to snatch insects from foliage and catch them in midair, often returning to same or nearby perch. Eats variety of larger insects, including beetles, crickets, katydids, caterpillars, moths, and butterflies. Also eats some fruits and berries. Male chases female in courtship flight close to possible nesting cavity.

rufous inner webs on tail feathers

- **BREEDING** Monogamous. Solitary nester.
- **NESTING** Incubation 13–15 days by female. Altricial young remain in nest 12–21 days. Fed by both sexes. 1 brood per year.
- **POPULATION** Common in open wooded lots and on forest edge. Rare on California coast in autumn migration.
- **BIRDHOUSES** Sometimes uses nest boxes placed on trees or buildings 6–50 feet high.
- **CONSERVATION** Neotropical migrant. Vulnerable to habitat loss.

Similar Birds

ASH-THROATED FLYCATCHER
Smaller bill; paler underparts with whitish throat and pale gray breast; pale yellow belly and crissum; brown-tipped outer tail feathers; different voice.

BROWN-CRESTED FLYCATCHER
Bigger heavier bill; paler gray throat and breast; paler yellow belly; different voice.

Flight Pattern		

Fairly swift buoyant direct flight. Hawks insects in flight, returning to perch. Hovers over foliage or ground then dips for food.

Nest Identification	
Shape Location	Filled and lined with grass, weeds, bark strips, rootlets, feathers, fur, snakeskin, onion skin, cellophane, and clear plastic • in cavity, abandoned holes of other birds, or bird boxes • built by both sexes • 4–8 creamy white to pale buff eggs marked with brown, olive, and lavender; ovate to short ovate, sometimes elliptical ovate or elongate ovate, 0.9 x 0.67 inches.

Plumage Sexes similar	Habitat	Migration Migratory	Weight 1.2 ounces

DATE _____ TIME _____ LOCATION _____

Family TYRANNIDAE	Species *Tyrannus verticalis*	Length 8.75 inches	Wingspan 15–16 inches

WESTERN KINGBIRD

The most common and well-known kingbird in the West has easily adapted to the ongoing development of its habitat. It even takes advantage of it by using telephone poles and other artificial structures as nesting areas and fences and utility wires as hunting perches. Often found in urban areas, it is more gregarious than any other kingbird, with two or more pairs occasionally nesting in the same tree. Aggressive, it also is known for its tenacity for chasing hawks, crows, ravens, and other large birds away from its nesting territory. It can be distinguished from other large flycatchers and kingbirds by the black tail with white edging on each side. A red-orange crown patch usually is concealed.

pale ashy gray head, neck, and breast

dark thin gray eye patch

olive-green tinted back

small black bill

bright lemon-yellow underparts

black legs and feet

dark brownish black wings contrast with paler back

black squared tail with white edges

- **SONG** Call is a rather quiet clipped *bek*. Has an abrasive and bickering chatter of *ker-er-ip, ker-er-ip, pree pree pr-prrr.*
- **BEHAVIOR** Solitary or in pairs or small groups. Gregarious in winter. Conspicuous. Hunts from open perches at low, middle, and high levels. Sits on perch to spot prey, flies out to catch in midair, and returns to perch to eat. Often hovers above foliage or ground and dips down to pick up food. Feeds on various insects, fruits, and berries. Male performs hectic courtship flight, darting upward into air, fluttering, vibrating feathers, and delivering trilling song.
- **BREEDING** Monogamous. Solitary. Sometimes can be found in loose semicolonies.
- **NESTING** Incubation 18–19 days by female. Young stay in nest 16–17 days, fed by both sexes. 1–2 broods per year.
- **POPULATION** Common in semiarid open country. Range has expanded during the 20th century as expansion of agriculture has created more suitable nesting and foraging areas. Some winter in southern Florida. Accidental in fall migration to New England and the Atlantic Coast.
- **CONSERVATION** Neotropical migrant.

Similar Birds

CASSIN'S KINGBIRD
Darker gray head, breast, and neck; darker olive-brown back; pale buffy white tips on dusky brown tail feathers; whiter throat; voice differs.

TROPICAL AND COUCH'S KINGBIRDS
Larger, longer bills; darker ear patches; darker upperparts; yellow of underparts extends upward to throats; slightly notched tails; voices differ.

Flight Pattern

Buoyant fluttering flight on shallow wing beats. Sallies for insects in flight, returns to perch. Hovers over prey and dips down.

Nest Identification	
Shape Location 	Grass, weeds, twigs, and plant fibers, lined with finer materials, including hair, plant down, and cotton • near trunk on horizontal limb or fork of tree, 8–40 feet above ground • sometimes on brace or cross-arm of utility pole, church steeple, or other man-made structure • built by both sexes • 3–7 whitish eggs, heavily blotched with brown, lavender, and black; oval to short oval, 1.0 x 0.6 inches.

Plumage Sexes similar	Habitat	Migration Migratory	Weight 1.4 ounces

DATE _____ TIME_____ LOCATION _____

Family TYRANNIDAE	Species *Tyrannus tyrannus*	Length 8.5 inches	Wingspan 14–15 inches

EASTERN KINGBIRD

True to its name, this kingbird is the only one nesting in the East north of southern Florida. It has an extensive breeding range that covers most of North America: from the Atlantic Coast north almost to the treeline in the southern Yukon. Its Latin name means "king of the tyrants," and when defending its nest this aggressive bird sometimes will land on the backs of hawks, crows, and vultures, pecking and pulling their feathers. In winter flocks fly to South America and survive on a diet of mostly berries. This species is fashionably decked with blackish upperparts, white underparts, and a distinctive white terminal tail band. A red stripe on its crown, usually concealed, is seen only when the bird is displaying.

black cap, forehead, and sides of face

black bill

charcoal-gray back and rump

white throat

grayish wash on breast

charcoal-gray wings

white underparts

black feet and legs

black tail with white terminal band

• **SONG** Utters grating buzzing high-pitched *dzeet* note combined with a rapid *tzi, tzeet, tzi, tzeet, tzi, tzeet.*

• **BEHAVIOR** Solitary or in pairs. Gregarious in migration and winter. Often sits on exposed, low- to mid-level perches and high on trees, shrubs, weed stalks, fences, utility wires, etc. Sits on perch to spot prey, hawks insects in air, and returns to perch to eat them. Also hovers to pick food off leaves or ground. Eats various insects, fruits, and berries. Male performs erratic courtship flights, hovering, circling, and tumbling with tail spread and crown patch revealed.

• **BREEDING** Monogamous. Solitary nester.

• **NESTING** Incubation 16–18 days mostly by female. Altricial young stay in nest approximately 16–18 days. Fed by both sexes. 1 brood per year.

• **POPULATION** Common, widespread, and conspicuous. Has expanded its range and increased its numbers along with agricultural expansion.

• **CONSERVATION** Neotropical migrant. Common cowbird host, but often damages cowbird eggs.

Similar Birds

GRAY KINGBIRD
Pale gray upperparts; white underparts; black mask through eyes; forked tail lacks white terminal band • limited US range.

Flight Pattern

Fluttering stiff-winged direct flight with shallow wing beats. Sallies to snatch insects in flight, then returns to perch.

Nest Identification	
Shape 🥄 Location 🌳 🌿 🏠	Weed stalks, twigs, and grass • lined with fine grass, sometimes animal hair • far to midway out on horizontal tree branch or shrub; sometimes on post or stump; 7–60 feet above ground, usually near water • built by female with help from male • 3–5 white to pinkish white eggs with heavy brown, lavender, and gray blotches; long and pointed to very round, but most ovate, 0.9 x 0.7 inches.

Plumage Sexes similar	Habitat 🌿 🌱 🌾	Migration Migratory	Weight 1.5 ounces

DATE _____ TIME_____ LOCATION _____

Family TYRANNIDAE	Species *Tyrannus dominicensis*	Length 9 inches	Wingspan 14.5–16 inches

GRAY KINGBIRD

A common inhabitant of the Caribbean islands, the Gray Kingbird usually nests in the United States along the coastlines of Georgia, Florida, and eastern Alabama. It is common in the Florida Keys. In Florida this bird generally nests in mangrove swamps, eating fruit from tropical trees, insects, and an occasional lizard. Superficially similar to the Eastern Kingbird, this bird has paler gray upperparts, a noticeable black mask, a very large bill, and a forked tail without any white on the tips of the tail feathers. A red patch on the crown is seldom visible.

pale gray upperparts

dark blackish brown wings with whitish edges

blackish mask

long, thick bill

mostly white underparts

pale yellowish wash on belly and undertail coverts

black feet and legs

forked blackish brown tail

- **SONG** Call is insectlike *peCHEER-ry*, with accent on the second syllable. Also gives harsh, trill calls of *trii-ill-ill-it*.
- **BEHAVIOR** Solitary or in pairs; forms small flocks in winter. Conspicuous; often seen perched on utility wires. Perches at mid to high levels and sallies to catch flying insects. Often catches insects low over water's surface. Sometimes eats various worms or caterpillars from ground or nearby foliage. May hover briefly to pick up insects, fruits, berries, or lizards. Often found in towns. Aggressively defensive around nest and nesting territory, chasing and attacking larger birds, cats, dogs, and sometimes humans.
- **BREEDING** Monogamous. Solitary nester.
- **NESTING** Breeding biology poorly known. Incubation estimated at 16–18 days by female. Altricial young stay in nest an estimated 16–20 days. Fed by both sexes. 1–2 broods per year.
- **POPULATION** Increasing in interior of Florida. Locally common in that state and Caribbean. Casually to rarely wanders to Maritimes in fall and west along Gulf Coast to Texas. Accidental elsewhere inland.
- **CONSERVATION** Neotropical migrant. Vulnerable to loss of coastal habitat, particularly mangroves. Formerly known to breed in South Carolina, but breeding range may be declining.

Similar Birds

EASTERN KINGBIRD
Smaller bill; rounded blackish tail with white terminal band; blackish head without mask; white underparts with grayish wash across breast; shallow, stiff-winged flight
• different voice.

Flight Pattern

Buoyant fluttering direct flight with shallow wing beats. Sallies to hawk insects, returning to perch. Sometimes hovers over food, then dips to pick it up.

Nest Identification

Shape ⬐　Location 🐦 🌲 🌳

Lined with fine grass, twigs, and roots • flimsy, often showing eggs and young through bottom • among coastal mangrove branches or other trees on horizontal branch 4–50 feet above ground • built by both sexes • 3–5 pale pink to buff eggs with brown, lavender, and gray blotches; oval to long oval, 1 x 0.7 inches.

Plumage Sexes similar	Habitat 🪵 🏔 🌾	Migration Migratory	Weight 1.5 ounces

DATE _____ TIME_____ LOCATION _____

Family TYRANNIDAE	Species *Tyrannus forficatus*	Length 11.5–15 inches	Wingspan 14.25–15.5 inches

SCISSOR-TAILED FLYCATCHER

Unmistakable, graceful, and beautiful, the Scissor-tailed Flycatcher, often seen darting above grasslands, is named for the way it opens and closes its tail like a pair of scissors. During courtship the male performs a spectacular sky dance. From about a hundred feet above the ground, the male suddenly plunges, flies in a zigzag pattern with a trilling cackle, then flies straight up and falls over backward in two or three backward somersaults, displaying his long streaming tail. He repeats this courtship flight, sometimes until the eggs are hatched. In flight the salmon-pink and red axillaries can be seen. Juveniles are paler overall with a yellow to salmon wash on the underparts and a short tail.

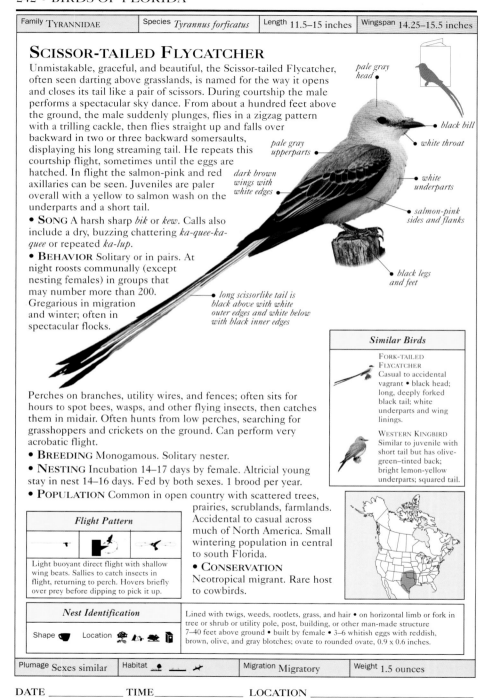

pale gray head

black bill

white throat

pale gray upperparts

dark brown wings with white edges

white underparts

salmon-pink sides and flanks

black legs and feet

long scissorlike tail is black above with white outer edges and white below with black inner edges

- **SONG** A harsh sharp *bik* or *kew*. Calls also include a dry, buzzing chattering *ka-quee-ka-quee* or repeated *ka-lup*.
- **BEHAVIOR** Solitary or in pairs. At night roosts communally (except nesting females) in groups that may number more than 200. Gregarious in migration and winter; often in spectacular flocks.

Perches on branches, utility wires, and fences; often sits for hours to spot bees, wasps, and other flying insects, then catches them in midair. Often hunts from low perches, searching for grasshoppers and crickets on the ground. Can perform very acrobatic flight.

- **BREEDING** Monogamous. Solitary nester.
- **NESTING** Incubation 14–17 days by female. Altricial young stay in nest 14–16 days. Fed by both sexes. 1 brood per year.
- **POPULATION** Common in open country with scattered trees, prairies, scrublands, farmlands. Accidental to casual across much of North America. Small wintering population in central to south Florida.
- **CONSERVATION** Neotropical migrant. Rare host to cowbirds.

Similar Birds

FORK-TAILED FLYCATCHER Casual to accidental vagrant • black head; long, deeply forked black tail; white underparts and wing linings.

WESTERN KINGBIRD Similar to juvenile with short tail but has olive-green–tinted back; bright lemon-yellow underparts; squared tail.

Flight Pattern

Light buoyant direct flight with shallow wing beats. Sallies to catch insects in flight, returning to perch. Hovers briefly over prey before dipping to pick it up.

Nest Identification

Shape 🪹   Location 🌳 🌿 🪵 🏠

Lined with twigs, weeds, rootlets, grass, and hair • on horizontal limb or fork in tree or shrub or utility pole, post, building, or other man-made structure 7–40 feet above ground • built by female • 3–6 whitish eggs with reddish, brown, olive, and gray blotches; ovate to rounded ovate, 0.9 x 0.6 inches.

Plumage Sexes similar	Habitat	Migration Migratory	Weight 1.5 ounces

DATE _____ TIME_____ LOCATION _____

Family LANIIDAE	Species *Lanius ludovicianus*	Length 9 inches	Wingspan 12.5–13 inches

LOGGERHEAD SHRIKE

This large-headed bird with whitish underparts is one of two shrike species that nest and breed in North America. Known as the "Butcher Bird" across its range, this adept hunter usually perches in the open to watch for prey. It has the unusual behavior of caching the bodies of its prey by suspending them impaled on a plant spine or the barbed wire of a fence. The caches may serve as larder for future use, to soften the food for easier rendering, or to passively advertise the presence of the territory and its owner. Juveniles have brownish upperparts and more distinct barring on their underparts.

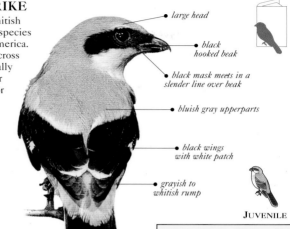

- large head
- black hooked beak
- black mask meets in a slender line over beak
- bluish gray upperparts
- black wings with white patch
- grayish to whitish rump

JUVENILE

- slender black tail with white outer feathers

- **SONG** Variety of squeaking notes and low warbles, delivered in slow deliberate phrases, often repeated, *queedle, queedle*. Call is a grating *shak-shak*.
- **BEHAVIOR** Solitary. Pairs in breeding season. Often sits immobile, hawklike, watching for prey for long periods. Flies down to catch prey with bill or sharp claws; also catches insects in flight. Eats small rodents, birds, reptiles, amphibians, and insects. Pair defends territory in breeding season but defend separate territories in winter.
- **BREEDING** Monogamous. Solitary nester.
- **NESTING** Incubation 16–17 days by female. Young altricial; brooded by female; stay in nest 17–21 days, fed by both sexes. 2 broods per year (occasionally 3 in the South).
- **POPULATION** Fairly common in habitats with open fields and scattered trees. Now rare over much of central part of range.
- **CONSERVATION** Some are neotropical migrants. Declining seriously in coastal California, the Northeast, and the eastern Midwest due to habitat loss and insecticide/pesticide use.

Similar Birds

NORTHERN SHRIKE
Larger; paler head and back; narrower mask does not meet above bill; larger, more deeply hooked bill, often pale at base of lower mandible; barred underparts; bobs tail • juvenile much browner in color.

NORTHERN MOCKINGBIRD
Longer thinner straighter bill; lighter wings with larger white patches; paler tail with more extensive white in outer feathers; head proportionally smaller.

Flight Pattern

Rapid flight on rapidly beating wings with brief periods of wings pulled to sides. Often flies low across the ground.

Nest Identification

Shape   Location

Twigs lined with grasses, string, feathers, and hair • in bush or tree, 8–15 feet above ground (but as high as 50 feet) • built by female or sometimes both sexes • 4–7 white to grayish buff eggs, marked with grays, browns, or blacks, often concentrated near large end; oval to long oval, 1.0 x 0.74 inches.

Plumage Sexes similar	Habitat	Migration Migratory	Weight 1.7 ounces

DATE __07 / 01__ TIME _____ LOCATION _____

| Family VIREONIDAE | Species *Vireo griseus* | Length 5 inches | Wingspan 8 inches |

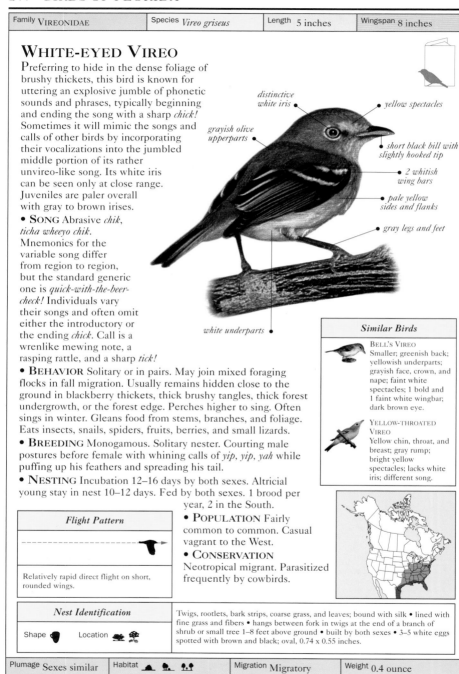

WHITE-EYED VIREO

Preferring to hide in the dense foliage of brushy thickets, this bird is known for uttering an explosive jumble of phonetic sounds and phrases, typically beginning and ending the song with a sharp *chick!* Sometimes it will mimic the songs and calls of other birds by incorporating their vocalizations into the jumbled middle portion of its rather unvireo-like song. Its white iris can be seen only at close range. Juveniles are paler overall with gray to brown irises.

- **SONG** Abrasive *chik, ticha wheeyo chik*. Mnemonics for the variable song differ from region to region, but the standard generic one is *quick-with-the-beer-check!* Individuals vary their songs and often omit either the introductory or the ending *chick*. Call is a wrenlike mewing note, a rasping rattle, and a sharp *tick!*

distinctive white iris

grayish olive upperparts

white underparts

yellow spectacles

short black bill with slightly hooked tip

2 whitish wing bars

pale yellow sides and flanks

gray legs and feet

- **BEHAVIOR** Solitary or in pairs. May join mixed foraging flocks in fall migration. Usually remains hidden close to the ground in blackberry thickets, thick brushy tangles, thick forest undergrowth, or the forest edge. Perches higher to sing. Often sings in winter. Gleans food from stems, branches, and foliage. Eats insects, snails, spiders, fruits, berries, and small lizards.

- **BREEDING** Monogamous. Solitary nester. Courting male postures before female with whining calls of *yip, yip, yah* while puffing up his feathers and spreading his tail.

- **NESTING** Incubation 12–16 days by both sexes. Altricial young stay in nest 10–12 days. Fed by both sexes. 1 brood per year, 2 in the South.

- **POPULATION** Fairly common to common. Casual vagrant to the West.

- **CONSERVATION** Neotropical migrant. Parasitized frequently by cowbirds.

Similar Birds

BELL'S VIREO
Smaller; greenish back; yellowish underparts; grayish face, crown, and nape; faint white spectacles; 1 bold and 1 faint white wingbar; dark brown eye.

YELLOW-THROATED VIREO
Yellow chin, throat, and breast; gray rump; bright yellow spectacles; lacks white iris; different song.

Flight Pattern

Relatively rapid direct flight on short, rounded wings.

Nest Identification

Shape

Location

Twigs, rootlets, bark strips, coarse grass, and leaves; bound with silk • lined with fine grass and fibers • hangs between fork in twigs at the end of a branch of shrub or small tree 1–8 feet above ground • built by both sexes • 3–5 white eggs spotted with brown and black; oval, 0.74 x 0.55 inches.

| Plumage Sexes similar | Habitat | Migration Migratory | Weight 0.4 ounce |

DATE _____ TIME _____ LOCATION _____

Family VIREONIDAE	Species *Vireo flavifrons*	Length 5.5 inches	Wingspan 9.5 inches

YELLOW-THROATED VIREO

Considered the most brilliantly colored vireo, this bird is most often observed in deciduous forests. Its characteristic song is a series of short phrases similar in pattern to several other vireos in its range but with long pauses between phrases and a coarse quality.

• **SONG** Burry series of 2-note or sometimes 3-note phrases with hesitantly long pauses between them sounding like *three-EIGHT, three-EIGHT . . . three-EIGHT*, repeated with the pattern and quality of a Blue-headed Vireo with a sore throat. Calls harsh, nasal, accelerating, rapid series of *cheh, cheh, cheh* notes.

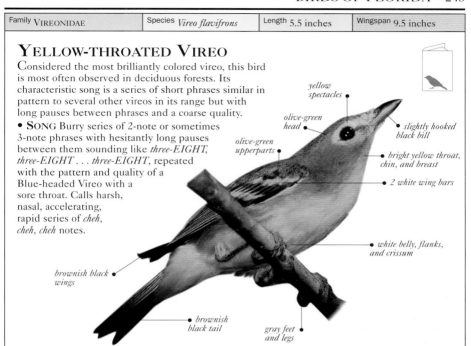

yellow spectacles

olive-green head

olive-green upperparts

slightly hooked black bill

bright yellow throat, chin, and breast

2 white wing bars

white belly, flanks, and crissum

brownish black wings

brownish black tail

gray feet and legs

• **BEHAVIOR** Solitary or in pairs. In autumn migration may form mixed foraging flocks. Generally forages in treetops, eating mostly insects. Also eats some small fruits and berries. In courtship male performs nest-building display, singing and crouching before female. He often begins several nests in his territory before pairing.

• **BREEDING** Monogamous. Solitary nester.

• **NESTING** Incubation 14 days by both sexes. Altricial young stay in nest 14 days. Fed by both sexes. 1 brood per year.

• **POPULATION** Fairly common and stable overall but declining in the Northeast (particularly in areas with insecticide spraying of shade trees) and increasing in the upper Midwest. Rare vagrant in the West; casual in winter in south Florida.

• **CONSERVATION** Neotropical migrant. Common brood parasite host for Brown-headed Cowbird; sometimes builds second floor to cover its own eggs as well as cowbird's.

Similar Birds

PINE WARBLER Slender, pointed bill; slightly notched tail; yellow chin and throat; yellow breast and sides with dusky streaking; thin, broken yellow eye ring; narrow yellow superciliary mark; thin, straight black bill; white tail spots.

Flight Pattern

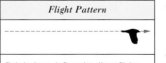

Relatively weak fluttering direct flight with rapid wing beats.

Nest Identification

Shape ● Location ✿

Grass covered with lichens • lined with grass, shredded bark, spider webs, and cocoons • in deciduous trees 3–60 feet above ground • built by both sexes • 3–5 white to pinkish white eggs with brown spots, especially near large end; oval, 0.7 x 0.5 inches.

Plumage Sexes similar	Habitat 🐾🐦 🌿	Migration Migratory	Weight 0.6 ounce

DATE _____ TIME_____ LOCATION _____

Family VIREONIDAE	Species *Vireo solitarius*	Length 5.25 inches	Wingspan 8.5 inches

BLUE-HEADED VIREO

This bird makes its home in the thick coniferous and mixed coniferous-deciduous forests of Canada and the eastern United States, where it breeds southward through the southern Appalachians. The Appalachian race is larger, with a bluish gray back and the

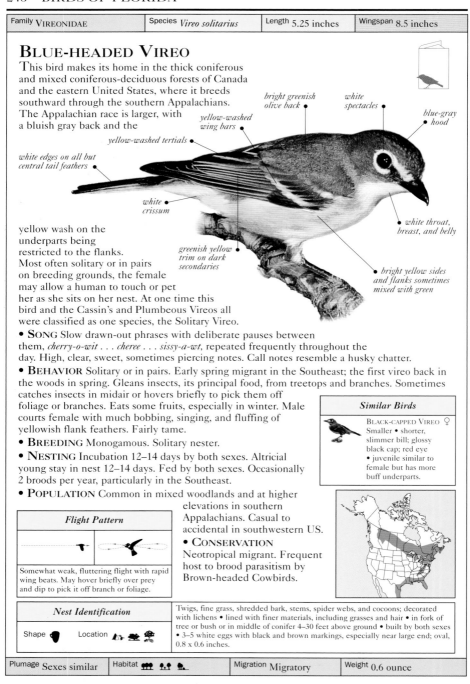

bright greenish olive back

white spectacles

blue-gray hood

yellow-washed wing bars

yellow-washed tertials

white edges on all but central tail feathers

white crissum

greenish yellow trim on dark secondaries

white throat, breast, and belly

bright yellow sides and flanks sometimes mixed with green

yellow wash on the underparts being restricted to the flanks. Most often solitary or in pairs on breeding grounds, the female may allow a human to touch or pet her as she sits on her nest. At one time this bird and the Cassin's and Plumbeous Vireos all were classified as one species, the Solitary Vireo.

• **SONG** Slow drawn-out phrases with deliberate pauses between them, *cherry-o-wit . . . cheree . . . sissy-a-wt*, repeated frequently throughout the day. High, clear, sweet, sometimes piercing notes. Call notes resemble a husky chatter.

• **BEHAVIOR** Solitary or in pairs. Early spring migrant in the Southeast; the first vireo back in the woods in spring. Gleans insects, its principal food, from treetops and branches. Sometimes catches insects in midair or hovers briefly to pick them off foliage or branches. Eats some fruits, especially in winter. Male courts female with much bobbing, singing, and fluffing of yellowish flank feathers. Fairly tame.

• **BREEDING** Monogamous. Solitary nester.

• **NESTING** Incubation 12–14 days by both sexes. Altricial young stay in nest 12–14 days. Fed by both sexes. Occasionally 2 broods per year, particularly in the Southeast.

• **POPULATION** Common in mixed woodlands and at higher elevations in southern Appalachians. Casual to accidental in southwestern US.

• **CONSERVATION** Neotropical migrant. Frequent host to brood parasitism by Brown-headed Cowbirds.

Similar Birds

BLACK-CAPPED VIREO ♀ Smaller • shorter, slimmer bill; glossy black cap; red eye • juvenile similar to female but has more buff underparts.

Flight Pattern

Somewhat weak, fluttering flight with rapid wing beats. May hover briefly over prey and dip to pick it off branch or foliage.

Nest Identification

Shape ● Location 🌳 🌿 🌲

Twigs, fine grass, shredded bark, stems, spider webs, and cocoons; decorated with lichens • lined with finer materials, including grasses and hair • in fork of tree or bush or in middle of conifer 4–30 feet above ground • built by both sexes • 3–5 white eggs with black and brown markings, especially near large end; oval, 0.8 x 0.6 inches.

Plumage Sexes similar	Habitat 🌾 🌳 🪨	Migration Migratory	Weight 0.6 ounce

DATE _____ TIME_____ LOCATION _____

Family VIREONIDAE	Species *Vireo olivaceus*	Length 6 inches	Wingspan 10 inches

RED-EYED VIREO

One of the most abundant in North American deciduous forests, this bird sings almost nonstop from dawn to dusk and often all night. It delivers its brief trilled phrases as it sits on the nest, forages for food, even as it swallows insects. A researcher once totaled the number of song repetitions uttered by an individual in one summer day as a remarkable 22,197 songs. These "sermons" have lent it the handle of "preacher bird." The black-bordered white eyebrow stripe distinguishes this bird from other vireos. The red iris is not visible at a distance; juveniles have a brown iris. Juveniles and autumn birds may have a yellowish wash on the flanks.

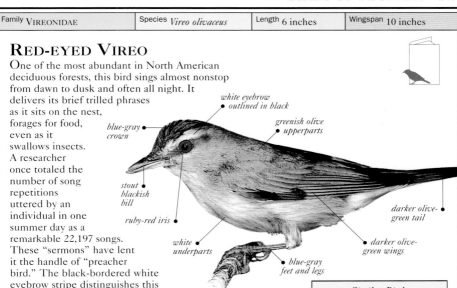

white eyebrow outlined in black
blue-gray crown
greenish olive upperparts
stout blackish bill
ruby-red iris
white underparts
blue-gray feet and legs
darker olive-green tail
darker olive-green wings

• **SONG** Repeated phrases and pauses, *look up! . . . see me? . . . over here . . . this way! . . . higher still!* Individuals sing many different repertoires. Call is whining nasal *chewy!*

• **BEHAVIOR** Solitary or in pairs. Picks food off leaves and twigs. Sometimes hovers to snatch food off foliage, bark, or branch. Eats mostly insects; in fall migration lots of fruits and berries. Defensive at nest. Responds readily to pishing and squeaking noises. In migration often joins mixed feeding flocks.

• **BREEDING** Monogamous. Solitary nester.

• **NESTING** Incubation 11–14 days by female. Altricial young stay in nest 10–12 days. Fed by both sexes. 1–2 broods per year.

• **POPULATION** Common in eastern woodlands. Some decline due to clearing of forests in the East. Rare vagrant in migration in the Southwest and on the Pacific Coast.

• **CONSERVATION** Neotropical migrant. Frequent cowbird brood parasitism. Vulnerable to poisoning by ingesting insects sprayed with pesticides and Gypsy Moth control programs.

Similar Birds

BLACK-WHISKERED VIREO
Larger bill; lacks dark border on upper side of eyebrow; dull green upperparts; black mustache mark; different song • only in the Southeast.

YELLOW-GREEN VIREO
Olive-green upperparts; whitish throat and underparts; bright yellow sides, flanks, and undertail coverts; pale gray or whitish supercilium; gray crown; pale olive auriculars; dusky lores; red eyes.

Flight Pattern	

Alternates series of rapid wing beats with short glides within forest. Also hovers briefly to pick insects or berries off foliage.

Nest Identification	
Shape 🐦 Location 🌳 🌲 🌿	Grapevine bark, fine grasses, rootlets, paper from wasp nests, lichens, spider webs, and cocoons • hanging on fork of tree branch or shrub 2–60 feet above ground • built by both sexes, but mostly by female • 3–5 white eggs, most often with fine brown and black dots, especially toward large end; oval, 0.8 x 0.55 inches.

Plumage Sexes similar	Habitat 🌾 🌳 🌊 🏞️	Migration Migratory	Weight 0.6 ounce

DATE _____ TIME_____ LOCATION _____

Family VIREONIDAE	Species *Vireo altiloquus*	Length 6.25 inches	Wingspan 10.5 inches

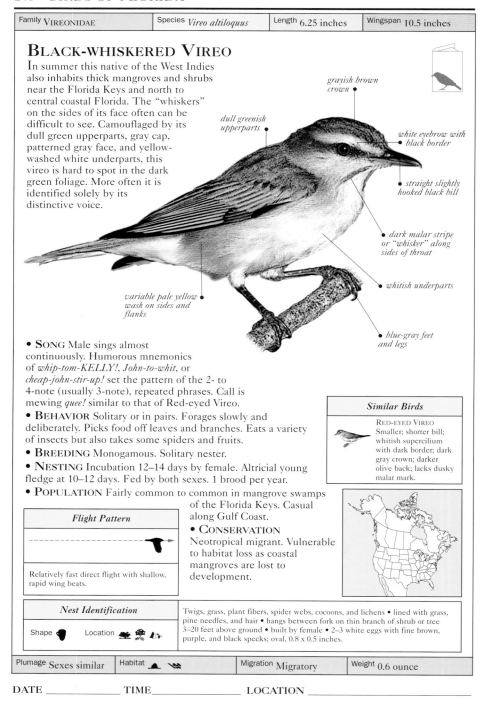

BLACK-WHISKERED VIREO

In summer this native of the West Indies also inhabits thick mangroves and shrubs near the Florida Keys and north to central coastal Florida. The "whiskers" on the sides of its face often can be difficult to see. Camouflaged by its dull green upperparts, gray cap, patterned gray face, and yellow-washed white underparts, this vireo is hard to spot in the dark green foliage. More often it is identified solely by its distinctive voice.

grayish brown crown

dull greenish upperparts

white eyebrow with black border

straight slightly hooked black bill

dark malar stripe or "whisker" along sides of throat

whitish underparts

variable pale yellow wash on sides and flanks

blue-gray feet and legs

- **SONG** Male sings almost continuously. Humorous mnemonics of *whip-tom-KELLY!*, *John-to-whit*, or *cheap-john-stir-up!* set the pattern of the 2- to 4-note (usually 3-note), repeated phrases. Call is mewing *quee!* similar to that of Red-eyed Vireo.
- **BEHAVIOR** Solitary or in pairs. Forages slowly and deliberately. Picks food off leaves and branches. Eats a variety of insects but also takes some spiders and fruits.
- **BREEDING** Monogamous. Solitary nester.
- **NESTING** Incubation 12–14 days by female. Altricial young fledge at 10–12 days. Fed by both sexes. 1 brood per year.
- **POPULATION** Fairly common to common in mangrove swamps of the Florida Keys. Casual along Gulf Coast.
- **CONSERVATION** Neotropical migrant. Vulnerable to habitat loss as coastal mangroves are lost to development.

Similar Birds

RED-EYED VIREO Smaller; shorter bill; whitish supercilium with dark border; dark gray crown; darker olive back; lacks dusky malar mark.

Flight Pattern

Relatively fast direct flight with shallow, rapid wing beats.

Nest Identification

Shape ● Location 🌳🌲🌿

Twigs, grass, plant fibers, spider webs, cocoons, and lichens • lined with grass, pine needles, and hair • hangs between fork on thin branch of shrub or tree 3–20 feet above ground • built by female • 2–3 white eggs with fine brown, purple, and black specks; oval, 0.8 x 0.5 inches.

Plumage Sexes similar	Habitat 🏔️ 🌿	Migration Migratory	Weight 0.6 ounce

DATE _____ TIME_____ LOCATION _____

Family CORVIDAE	Species *Cyanocitta cristata*	Length 11 inches	Wingspan 16 inches

BLUE JAY

Once considered primarily a forest dweller, the Blue Jay has adapted to cities, parks, gardens, and forest fragmentation. Some populations remain in locales year-round, while more northern ones migrate south in flocks of 50–100. Common despite clear-cutting in eastern forests, its range is expanding northwest. It is easily recognized by its large size; blue-purple upperparts, wings, and tail; and jaunty bluish purple crest.

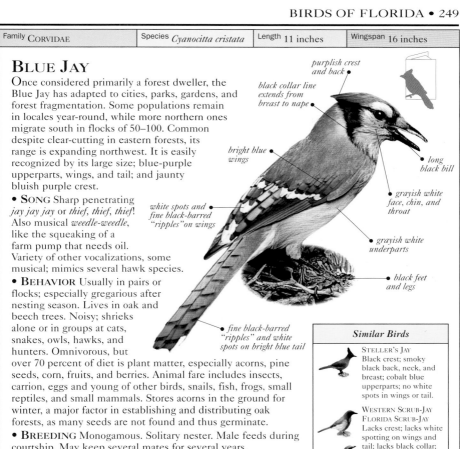

purplish crest and back

black collar line extends from breast to nape

bright blue wings

long black bill

grayish white face, chin, and throat

white spots and fine black-barred "ripples" on wings

grayish white underparts

black feet and legs

fine black-barred "ripples" and white spots on bright blue tail

• **SONG** Sharp penetrating *jay jay jay* or *thief, thief, thief*! Also musical *weedle-weedle*, like the squeaking of a farm pump that needs oil. Variety of other vocalizations, some musical; mimics several hawk species.

• **BEHAVIOR** Usually in pairs or flocks; especially gregarious after nesting season. Lives in oak and beech trees. Noisy; shrieks alone or in groups at cats, snakes, owls, hawks, and hunters. Omnivorous, but over 70 percent of diet is plant matter, especially acorns, pine seeds, corn, fruits, and berries. Animal fare includes insects, carrion, eggs and young of other birds, snails, fish, frogs, small reptiles, and small mammals. Stores acorns in the ground for winter, a major factor in establishing and distributing oak forests, as many seeds are not found and thus germinate.

• **BREEDING** Monogamous. Solitary nester. Male feeds during courtship. May keep several mates for several years.

• **NESTING** Incubation 16–18 days by both sexes but most often by female. Altricial young stay in nest 17–21 days; brooded by female; fed by both sexes. 1 brood per year in the North, 2–3 in the South.

• **POPULATION** Common and widespread in woodlands and residential areas with big shade trees. Casual in the Northwest in autumn and winter.

• **FEEDERS** Suet, sunflower seeds, peanuts, cracked nuts; birdbaths.

Similar Birds

STELLER'S JAY
Black crest; smoky black back, neck, and breast; cobalt blue upperparts; no white spots in wings or tail.

WESTERN SCRUB-JAY
FLORIDA SCRUB-JAY
Lacks crest; lacks white spotting on wings and tail; lacks black collar; grayish underparts contrast with gray-streaked white throat • Florida Scrub-Jay restricted to Florida.

Flight Pattern
Direct flight with steady, buoyant wing beats. Often glides between perches within or between trees, or to ground.

Nest Identification	
Shape ⬤ Location 🌳 🪴 🌲	Twigs, bark, moss, lichens, grass, and sometimes paper and string • built by both sexes • on horizontal branch near trunk or in crotch or vines 5–20 feet above ground; sometimes up to 50 feet • 3–7 pale greenish blue or bluish green eggs with dark brown markings; subelliptical, 1.1 x 0.85 inches.

Plumage Sexes similar	Habitat 🌲 🌿 🪵	Migration Migratory	Weight 3.0 ounces

DATE _____ TIME_____ LOCATION _____

Family CORVIDAE	Species *Aphelocoma coerulescens*	Length 11 inches	Wingspan 16 inches

FLORIDA SCRUB-JAY

This threatened species is restricted to scrublands across central Florida and dense growths of low oaks, myrtles, sand pines, palmettos, and thickets along the East and West Coasts. Inquisitive and intelligent, the Florida Scrub-Jay steals and stashes bright items such as forks, bits of glassware, and jewelry, much like the American Crow. It also caches acorns and nuts, storing them in shallow pits or sand and covering them with leaves and stones.

white supercilium

blue head

black bill

grayish tan back

blackish eye patch

long slender body

white breast and throat with dusky bluish streaks

blue tail

pale gray to tannish gray underparts

blue wings

black legs and feet

While searching for buried food, this bird swings its bill from side to side. It is quiet for a jay and is rather easily overlooked by the casual observer.

• **SONG** Harsh throaty *quay-quay-quay* or *cheek-cheek-cheek*.

• **BEHAVIOR** Gregarious. Sometimes solitary but usually in small family groups. Hops on ground as it forages for food at low to middle levels in vegetation. Omnivorous; eats wide variety of mice, eggs and young of smaller birds, scorpions, turtles, mollusks, insects, spiders, ticks, and mites; also eats plant matter, including acorns, nuts, corn, and fruit. Tame in picnic areas and campgrounds; will pilfer food and take peanuts from human fingers or lips. Major disperser for oaks and pines.

• **BREEDING** Monogamous. Cooperative. Fledglings often remain in territory for several years to help care for nestlings.

• **NESTING** Incubation 15–17 days by female. Altricial young stay in nest 18–19 days. Fed by both sexes and other helper birds. 1 brood per year (rarely 2).

• **POPULATION** Uncommon. Declining and threatened; reduced by an estimated 90 percent during 20th century.

• **FEEDERS** Sunflower seeds, scratch feed, suet, and bread.

• **CONSERVATION** Decline due to habitat destruction. Often hit and killed by automobiles.

Similar Birds
 BLUE JAY Slightly larger, chunkier body; blue crest; black collar from breast to nape; blue back; bold white spots on wings and tail.

Flight Pattern
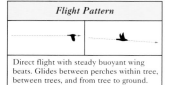
Direct flight with steady buoyant wing beats. Glides between perches within tree, between trees, and from tree to ground.

Nest Identification	
Shape 🥣 Location 🌳 🕊 🌲	Bulky sticks • lined with roots, twigs, moss, grass, and hair • on horizontal branch or in crotch of low tree or bush 2–12 feet above ground • built by both sexes • 2–5 pale green eggs irregularly spotted with reddish brown; ovate to elongate ovate, 1.1 x 0.8 inches.

Plumage Sexes similar	Habitat ⤴ ▲	Migration Nonmigratory	Weight 2.8 ounces

DATE _____ TIME_____ LOCATION _____

Family CORVIDAE	Species *Corvus brachyrhynchos*	Length 17.5 inches	Wingspan 33–40 inches

AMERICAN CROW

One of the most widely distributed and recognized birds in North America, the American Crow is entirely black from beak to toe to tail with a glossy violet sheen. Studies of these intelligent birds have shown that they can count, solve puzzles, learn symbols, and retain information. They often are seen chasing and mobbing owls and hawks. Huge flocks from a few hundred to as many as 200,000 birds may assemble in winter to roost, travel, and feed together. Often persecuted, shot, poisoned, and even bombed on its roost in the past, this crow still lives among us by its intelligence and adaptability and is common throughout its range.

brown eyes

black bill

black overall with iridescent violet gloss on body

iridescent blue-violet and green-blue gloss on wings

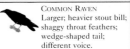

black feet and legs

fan-shaped tail

• **SONG** Familiar loud call of *caw-caw* with many variations. Nasal begging call like *uh-uah* of the Fish Crow.

• **BEHAVIOR** Gregarious. Omnivorous; eats insects, many other small invertebrates from millipedes to snails, small amphibians, small reptiles, small mammals, eggs and young of other birds, waste corn and other grains, fruits, field crops, garbage, and carrion. Mobs avian predators, calling gangs of crows together to harass a large hawk or owl on a perch or drive it out of the area. Catches up to a soaring hawk and repeatedly dives on it from above, often forcing it down into the shelter of trees below. Breaks mollusk shells by dropping them on rocks from above.

• **BREEDING** Monogamous. Solitary nester. Sometimes known to be cooperative.

• **NESTING** Incubation 18 days by both sexes. Altricial young stay in nest 28–35 days. Brooded by female. Fed by both sexes and extra birds. 1 brood per year, 2 in the South.

• **POPULATION** Abundant. Adapting as habitat developed by humans.

• **CONSERVATION** Widely persecuted in the past by farmers and hunters. Still legally hunted for sport in many states.

Similar Birds

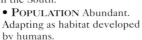

COMMON RAVEN
Larger; heavier stout bill; shaggy throat feathers; wedge-shaped tail; different voice.

FISH CROW
Smaller; more pointed wings; proportionally smaller more slender bill and longer tail; nasal, higher-pitched call • eastern range.

Flight Pattern

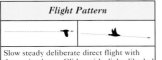

Slow steady deliberate direct flight with deep wing beats. Glides with slight dihedral from altitude to perch or ground, between perches, and from perch to ground.

Nest Identification	
Shape Location	Made of twigs and branches • lined with tree material, grass, feathers, moss, leaves, and hair • in fork of tree or shrub or cross arms of utility pole 0–100 feet above ground; sometimes on ground in prairie • built by both sexes and sometimes extra birds • 3–7 bluish green to olive-green eggs marked with brown and gray; oval, 1.6 x 1.1 inches.

Plumage Sexes similar	Habitat	Migration Some migrate	Weight 1.0 pound

DATE ___7\04___ TIME_____ LOCATION _____

Family CORVIDAE	Species *Corvus ossifragus*	Length 15 inches	Wingspan 30–40 inches

FISH CROW

An active scavenger, the Fish Crow frequently harasses gulls and terns in attempts to force them to surrender their prey. It also raids the unguarded nests of other birds, particularly shorebirds, egrets and herons, or turtles, flying away with their eggs in its bill. In the winter, sometimes thousands of these crows can be seen roosting together. Smaller than the similar American Crow, the Fish Crow is never far away from water, living along the coast and penetrating inland mainly along major rivers. Although primarily nonmigratory, birds in the northwestern part of the range are migratory inland.

slender black bill

pointed wings

slender black body

fan-shaped tail

black feet and legs

• **SONG** Call is a high-pitched nasal *ca-hah* or *aw-uk*.
• **BEHAVIOR** Gregarious and sociable. Will feed inland but usually feeds in shallow waters along coastline and salt marshes. Omnivorous. Sometimes a major nest predator at heronries. Eats a wide variety of crustaceans, carrion, eggs of other birds, insects and insect larvae, fish, ticks from livestock, various berries, and some fruits. Drops mollusks from the air to break them on rocks, highways, or wharves. Often hovers over water or land, searching for prey before dropping down to grab it.
• **BREEDING** Monogamous. Small colonies.
• **NESTING** Incubation 16–18 days by both sexes. Young altricial; brooded by female; stay in nest at least 21 days, fed by both sexes. 1 brood per year.
• **POPULATION** Common especially along the coast. This bird's range is increasing and expanding to the north as well as inland.

Similar Birds

AMERICAN CROW
Slightly larger; larger bill; proportionally larger head; shorter tail; call is a lower clearer *caw*.

Flight Pattern

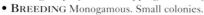

Flies with somewhat stiff wing beats, alternating several quick wing strokes with long glides. Hovers when foraging.

Nest Identification

Shape 　Location

Dried twigs with lining of bark chips, pine needles, feathers, horse and cattle hair, and soft grasses • set fairly high in fork of shrub or topmost crotch of deciduous tree or conifer, 6–90 feet above ground • built by both sexes • 4–5 bluish or grayish green eggs marked with brown and gray spots; oval, 1.5 inches long.

Plumage Sexes similar	Habitat	Migration Nonmigratory	Weight 10.6 ounces

DATE _____ TIME_____ LOCATION _____

| Family ALAUDIDAE | Species *Eremophila alpestris* | Length 7–8 inches | Wingspan 12.5–14 inches |

HORNED LARK

The Horned Lark is one of the most widespread songbirds in North America. The spectacular display flight of the male bird begins with an ascending flight as high as 800 feet. Singing, he then circles, closes his wings, and drops headfirst almost to the ground, where he opens his wings at the last second. He then struts around the female with his wings drooped and horns erect. The female appears similar to the male but is duller in color and lacks the black crown. In flight note the white underparts, including the wings and wing linings, the black tail with white outer tail feathers, and black legs and feet.

hornlike black tufts on head connected by black-bordered forecrown

yellowish to white face and forehead

black "sideburns" and lores

black bill

brown back and rump

pale yellow to white throat

brown wings

black bib

whitish underparts with sandy buff wash on sides and flanks

black tail with white outer feathers

• **SONG** Given from ground or in high, circling flight. Sings series of bell-like, tinkling notes *pit-wit, wee-pit, pit-wee*. Call is *tsee-tete* or *zeet*.

• **BEHAVIOR** Pairs; gregarious in winter, forming large flocks sometimes mixed with Snow Buntings and longspurs. Walks and runs rather than hops. Forages on ground, often in open fields with bare soil, pebbles, or short, sparse vegetation. Eats mostly seeds, grains, insects, and small mollusks. Often found in agricultural areas, to which it has adapted for nesting and foraging, on country roadways and farm roads standing and walking on pavement or gravel. This bird nests as early as February in the South. In courtship males perform display flights and skylark.

• **BREEDING** Monogamous. Solitary to gregarious.

• **NESTING** Incubation 11–12 days by female. Altricial young stay in nest 9–12 days. Brooded by female. Fed by both sexes. 1 brood per year in the North, 2 in the South.

• **POPULATION** Common. Has expanded eastern range since early 1800s because of agricultural development.

Similar Birds

AMERICAN PIPIT
Gray upperparts; brown-streaked whitish underparts; dark grayish brown tail with white outer tail feathers; bobs tail continuously; lacks horns, face pattern, and black bib • cinnamon-buff underparts in summer.

Flight Pattern

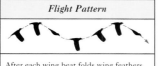

After each wing beat folds wing feathers close to body.

Nest Identification

Shape ⚬⚬ 🥄 Location ▬ ⁂

Grass • lined with feathers and soft materials • in shallow depression, natural or dug by female, often near clumps of dirt or animal manure • built by female • 2–5 gray or greenish eggs dotted with browns; subelliptical, 0.8 x 0.6 inches.

| Plumage Sexes differ | Habitat | Migration Migratory | Weight 1.1 ounces |

DATE _____ TIME_____ LOCATION _____

Family HIRUNDINIDAE	Species *Progne subis*	Length 7.25–8.5 inches	Wingspan 15.5–16.75 inches

PURPLE MARTIN

Colonies once nested in holes in tall dead trees and saguaro cacti. Today the largest North American swallow usually nests in man-made multidwelling martin houses, sometimes with hundreds of pairs nesting together. Martin houses were inspired by the Native American custom of placing empty gourds on tall poles to attract the Purple Martin for aesthetic reasons and to reduce the insect population around villages and crops. Juvenile males have browner upperparts with whitish bellies and some purple sheen to their bodies. Juvenile females are brown overall with whitish bellies. A long-distant migrant, it winters from Venezuela to southeastern Brazil.

MALE

• *dark iridescent purplish blue overall*

FIRST SPRING MALE

• **SONG** A variety of rich low-pitched liquid gurgling notes and chirruping, mixed with cackling and varying in pitch. Songs often given predawn and in flight.

• **BEHAVIOR** In pairs or colonies. In fall, communal migratory and roosting flocks may number in the tens of thousands. Mostly catches and eats insects in flight, but also forages on ground. Nesting birds will eat broken eggshells placed for them. Frequents open country, rural agricultural areas, especially near water, and urban/suburban areas.

bluish gray upperparts •

grayish to whitish lower breast and belly •

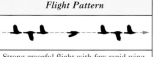

• **BREEDING** Monogamous. Colonial.

• **NESTING** Incubation 15–18 days by female. Young altricial; brooded by female; stay in nest 26–31 days, fed by both sexes. 1–3 broods per year.

• *forked tail*

forked tail •

• **POPULATION** Common; declining, especially in the West.

FEMALE

• **BIRDHOUSES** Man-made martin houses and gourds.

• **CONSERVATION** Neotropical migrant. National Audubon Society Blue List. Practice of removing dead cavity-filled trees, especially in riparian areas, has reduced nesting sites. Introduced European Starling and House Sparrow compete for nesting cavities.

Similar Birds

TREE SWALLOW
Smaller; entire underparts are bright white with no grayish tone; dark glossy blue-green upperparts • juveniles and first spring adults have browner upperparts.

GRAY-BREASTED MARTIN ♂
Smaller; gray-brown face, throat, and flanks; dusky gray-brown underparts; dark bluish upperparts; cleft tail • eastern range.

Flight Pattern

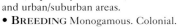

Strong graceful flight with few rapid wing beats followed by long glides. Often flies in circles while gliding.

Nest Identification

Shape

Location

Grasses, leaves, mud, feathers, and bits of debris • in martin houses, old woodpecker holes in trees and cacti, or in ridges in cliffs or large rocks • 5–20 feet above ground • built by both sexes • 3–8 plain white eggs; oval to long oval, 0.96 x 0.68 inches.

Plumage Sexes differ	Habitat	Migration Migratory	Weight 1.7 ounces

DATE _____ TIME _____ LOCATION _____

Family HIRUNDINIDAE	Species *Tachycineta bicolor*	Length 5.75 inches	Wingspan 12.5 inches

TREE SWALLOW

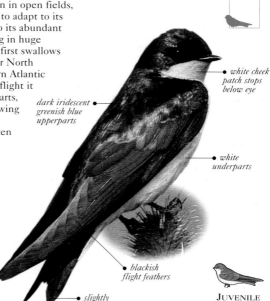

The Tree Swallow is equally common in open fields, marshes, or towns. This bird's ability to adapt to its ever-changing environment has led to its abundant and widespread population. Migrating in huge flocks during the day, it is one of the first swallows to travel to its summer home in upper North America. Many winter on the southern Atlantic Coast, Gulf Coast, and in Florida. In flight it shows dark upperparts, white underparts, triangular wings with greenish underwing linings, and a notched tail. Juveniles have dusky brown upperparts and often a dusky wash on the breast.

dark iridescent greenish blue upperparts

white cheek patch stops below eye

white underparts

blackish flight feathers

slightly notched tail

JUVENILE

- **SONG** Utters quick repetitious *silip* or *chi-veet*. In flight makes pleasant liquid gurgling chatter.
- **BEHAVIOR** Gregarious in migration and winter; often occurs in huge flocks. Feeds in mixed flocks with other swallow species. Catches insects in flight; sometimes forages on ground. Eats mainly flying insects but also may take small crustaceans and spiders. Often eats berries and seeds during cold snaps on wintering grounds or in spring migration. Inhabits open country and woodland edges near water. Male displays for female with series of aerial gymnastics.
- **BREEDING** Most often polygamous. Loose social colonies. Males may have 2 mates simultaneously and different mates each year.
- **NESTING** Incubation 13–16 days by female. Altricial young remain in nest 16–24 days. Fed by both sexes. 1 brood per year (rarely 2).
- **POPULATION** Abundant and increasing.

Similar Birds

VIOLET-GREEN SWALLOW
White rump patches extend onto sides of rump; white on cheek extends up to, behind, and above eye; purple-green gloss on upperparts • sympatric only in the West.

- **BIRDHOUSES** Uses man-made bird boxes and gourds.
- **CONSERVATION** Some are neotropical migrants. Forestry practice of removing dead trees eliminates many potential nesting sites.

Flight Pattern

Swift graceful flight with slow deep wing beats alternated with long to short glides. Turns back sharply on insects it passes.

Nest Identification

Shape [icons] Location [icons]
Abandoned Nests [icons]

Dried stems and grass • lined with down and feathers • in tree cavity, abandoned nest, bird box, or other man-made structure • built by both sexes, but female does more • 4–6 white eggs; oval to long oval, 0.8 x 0.5 inches.

Plumage Sexes similar	Habitat [icons]	Migration Migratory	Weight 0.7 ounce

DATE _____ TIME_____ LOCATION _____

Family HIRUNDINIDAE	Species *Stelgidopteryx serripennis*	Length 5.5 inches	Wingspan 11–12 inches

NORTHERN ROUGH-WINGED SWALLOW

This bird is named for the tiny hooks found on its outer primary feathers. Their function is unknown, but they may produce a sound during courtship display. The male and female use their feet to dig nesting burrows, some as long as six feet, depending on the nature of the soil, but most are nine to twenty-eight inches deep. Since it is highly adaptable this bird has a wide breeding range. Juveniles are similar to adults but show more cinnamon tones in their upperparts and have cinnamon wing bars.

medium brown upperparts

short black bill

light gray-brown wash on chin, throat, and upper breast

- **SONG** Usually remains silent, but sometimes utters harsh, buzzing *quiz-z-zeeitp* or *zzrrit*.

- **BEHAVIOR** Solitary or in pairs or small flocks. Gregarious during migration. Catches and consumes a variety of flying insects while in flight. Also occasionally takes insects from ground. Often feeds low over open landscapes or water and sometimes feeds along with other species of swallows. Quickly adapted nesting to utilize crevices in rock cuts along interstate highways. During courtship male chases female, flying with white undertail coverts spread along sides of tail.

dark brownish black wings and wing linings

dull white underparts

slightly forked dark brownish black tail

- **BREEDING** Monogamous. Solitary or in small colonies.

- **NESTING** Incubation 12 days by female. Altricial young remain in nest 19–21 days. Fed by both sexes. 1 brood per year.

- **POPULATION** Common and increasing.

Similar Birds

BANK SWALLOW
Smaller; darker brown upperparts; dark brown breast band; snow-white underparts; faster wing beats with quick changes of direction.

- **BIRDHOUSES** Will nest in some types of man-made structures but has not been recorded to use nest boxes.

- **CONSERVATION** Neotropical migrant.

Flight Pattern

Swift graceful flight with several deep slow wing beats, pulling back wings after each stroke, then a short to long glide.

Nest Identification

Shape ▪ ▪ ▪ Location ▪ ▪ ▪ ▪ ▪

No nest materials except a few bark chips, grass, and leaves • on bank, sides of rough cliff, highway/railroad rock cuts, or building or in abandoned burrows, drain pipes, or sewer pipes • dug by both sexes • 4–8 plain white eggs; long oval, 0.7 x 0.5 inches.

Plumage Sexes similar	Habitat ▪ ▰▰ ▪ ▪ ▪ ▪ ▪	Migration Migratory	Weight 0.6 ounce

DATE ___7/04___   TIME_____   LOCATION _____

Family HIRUNDINIDAE	Species *Riparia riparia*	Length 4.75 inches	Wingspan 10–11 inches

BANK SWALLOW

The smallest member of the North American swallow family is an aerial gymnast that twists and turns in the air over its breeding territory. Males and females take turns digging burrows into vertical banks with their bills. Once a hole is made, they use their feet to finish the tunnel, which sometimes is as long as five to six feet. The scientific name refers to their association with rivers during migration and their predilection for nesting along sandy gravelly river banks. The dark narrow breast band is difficult to see when the bird is in flight, but the combination of an erratic flight pattern, chocolate-brown upperparts, paler brown rump, dark brown wing linings, and snowy white underparts serve to identify this bird. Juvenile wing coverts and tertials are edged cinnamon and the throat and upper breast are washed pale cinnamon.

chocolate-brown upperparts

snowy white chin

blackish brown flight feathers

brownish gray breast band, sometimes extending down midline of upper breast

snowy white underparts

slightly forked tail

- **SONG** Dry chattering, *zzzrt orzzzrt, zzzrtt.*
- **BEHAVIOR** Gregarious. Often migrates and feeds with other swallows. Gathers in large premigratory and communal roosts. Catches insects while flying. Occasionally takes insects from ground or water's surface. Courtship includes dropping and catching feathers in the air, as if playing, by each member of pair; copulation in the nest burrow often follows such "play" and many feathers are used in the nest lining.
- **BREEDING** Monogamous. Colonial.
- **NESTING** Incubation 14–16 days by both sexes. Altricial young stay in nest 18–24 days, fed by both sexes. 1–2 broods per year.
- **POPULATION** Common and widespread; often near water. Numbers are stable overall, but species is declining in California due to river bank alteration for flood control.
- **CONSERVATION** Neotropical migrant.

Similar Birds

NORTHERN ROUGH-WINGED SWALLOW
Larger; paler brown upperparts; lacks brown chest band; dusky white underparts; light gray-brown wash on chin, throat, and upper breast; slower deeper wing beats.

TREE SWALLOW
Juvenile is larger; white underparts from chin to undertail coverts; often with dusky breast band; greenish blue upperparts.

Flight Pattern

Swift erratic fluttering flight on shallow wing beats; often alternates several rapid wing beats with short to long glides.

Nest Identification

Shape ◼ ◼   Location ◼ ◼

Lined with grass, rootlets, weed stems, horsehair, and feathers • in sandy or rocky bank, gravel pit, or man-made embankment, such as a highway road cut • dug by both sexes • 3–7 plain white eggs; oval to short oval, 0.7 x 0.5 inches.

Plumage Sexes similar	Habitat ≈ ▲	Migration Migratory	Weight 0.5 ounce

DATE _____ TIME_____ LOCATION _____

Family HIRUNDINIDAE	Species *Petrochelidon pyrrhonota*	Length 5.5 inches	Wingspan 12 inches

CLIFF SWALLOW

Hundreds of gourd-shaped "mud jugs" plastered to the side of a barn or under a bridge or highway overpass are a typical nesting territory for these highly adaptable birds. Farmers heartily welcome this resident because it eats numerous flying insects that are harmful to crops. Nesting colonies may number from eight hundred to more than one thousand birds. Note the dark rusty brown throat, and in flight the brown underwing linings, cinnamon buff rump, square tail, dusky cinnamon undertail coverts with dark centers, and whitish buff edged feathers of back and tertials. Juveniles have dusky brown upperparts and paler underparts. This swallow has successfully expanded its range in the Southeast and the West. The southwestern race displays a cinnamon forehead similar to the Cave Swallow.

squared blackish tail with slight cleft

chestnut sides of face extend to sides of nape

blue-black crown

whitish forehead

short black bill

black center patch on chestnut throat

blue-black wings and back

whitish underparts with dusky gray-brown sides and flanks

JUVENILE

• **SONG** Utters a dry guttural *churr* or *zarp*. Alarm call is burry *keeer*. During breeding, a chattering, squeaking, sputtering warble.

• **BEHAVIOR** Gregarious. Catches food in flight; sometimes forages on ground. Eats variety of flying insects and some berries and fruit. Constructs one of the most complex swallow nests: a sphere of mud pellets with a tubular entrance on one side. Colonies are source of foraging information for other birds; birds follow members who are successfully feeding young back to food sources.

• **BREEDING** Monogamous. Large colonies.

• **NESTING** Incubation 14–16 days by both sexes. Altricial young in nest 21–24 days, fed by both sexes. 1–3 broods a year.

• **POPULATION** Common in open country, especially near water. Range is expanding and numbers are increasing.

> **Similar Birds**
>
>
> CAVE SWALLOW
> Pale cinnamon-buff throat; cinnamon forehead; richer cinnamon-rust rump.

• **CONSERVATION** Neotropical migrant. Previously listed as being of special concern, but successful adaptation to nesting on man-made structures such as buildings, highway bridges and overpasses, railroad bridges, dams, and other vertical walls has greatly expanded populations and range.

Flight Pattern	
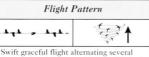	
Swift graceful flight alternating several deep rapid wing beats with long elliptical glides with sharp sweeping upturns at the end. Soars on thermals and updrafts.	

Nest Identification	
Shape ◗ Location 🏢 〰 🐾 🏠	Pellets of clay or mud, with lining of grasses, down, and feathers • usually under eaves of buildings or under dams or bridges; sometimes on ridges of canyons; rarely on trunk of conifer tree under overhanging branch • built by both sexes • 3–6 white, cream, or pinkish eggs, marked with browns; oval to long oval, 0.8 x 0.5 inches.

Plumage Sexes similar	Habitat 🌱 ⚓ 〰	Migration Migratory	Weight 0.8 ounce

DATE _____ TIME_____ LOCATION _____

Family HIRUNDINIDAE	Species *Petrochelidon fulva*	Length 5.5 inches	Wingspan 12 inches

CAVE SWALLOW

This bird plasters its cuplike nests to the sides of caves, but it has adapted to man-made structures and now also uses buildings, bridges, culverts, and even drainage pipes. A native of Mexico and the West Indies, in North America two races nest, one in the Southwest and one in Florida. One of the most visited colonies is established in the entrance to Carlsbad Caverns. Similar in appearance to the Cliff Swallow, it

cinnamon forehead

blue-black upperparts with whitish buff streaks on back

whitish buff edging to tertials

chestnut rump

blackish flight feathers

squared tail

cinnamon-buff throat extends around neck as a collar

whitish underparts with rufous wash on breast and sides

dusky cinnamon undertail coverts with dark centers

often nests with them, and with Barn Swallows. In flight it shows brownish underwing linings. The southwestern race of the Cliff Swallow has the cinnamon forehead but has a dark throat.

JUVENILE

- **SONG** Series of dry warbling buzzy chatters; sometimes calls *chu-chu* or *zweih*.
- **BEHAVIOR** Gregarious. Eats insects caught in flight. Builds a complex nest: a sphere constructed of mud pellets with a tubular entrance on one side. Colonies often active on same site year after year and may repair and reuse old nests.
- **BREEDING** Monogamous. Colonial.
- **NESTING** Incubation 15–18 days by both sexes. Young altricial; remain in nest 21–33 days, fed by both sexes. Has 2 broods per year.
- **POPULATION** Fairly common but somewhat local. Expanding range and increasing in number. Casual in Northeast.
- **CONSERVATION** Neotropical migrant.

Similar Birds

CLIFF SWALLOW
Pale whitish to buff forehead; dark rusty brown throat with black center patch; pale cinnamon-buff rump
• southwestern race has cinnamon forehead.

Flight Pattern

Swift graceful flight, alternating several rapid deep wing beats with long elliptical glides ending on sharp sweeping upturns. Soars on winds and thermals.

Nest Identification

Shape

Location

Pellets of clay and mud with lining of grasses and a few feathers • plastered to sides of caves, sinkholes, bridges, culverts, buildings, or even drainage pipes • built by both sexes • 3–5 white eggs, marked with browns; oval to long oval, 0.8 x 0.5 inches.

Plumage Sexes similar	Habitat	Migration Migratory	Weight 0.7 ounce

DATE _____ TIME_____ LOCATION _____

Family HIRUNDINIDAE	Species *Hirundo rustica*	Length 6.75–7.5 inches	Wingspan 12.5–13.5 inches

BARN SWALLOW

Since early colonial times this bird has been a welcome presence on farms because it eats many crop-destroying insects. Usually nesting inside of barns or other buildings, it is the only North American swallow with buffy to cinnamon underparts and underwing linings and a white-spotted deeply forked tail. The female is similar to the male but most often is duller in color. Juveniles have shorter forked tails and creamy white underparts. The most wide-ranging swallow in the world, it is cosmopolitan, found breeding or wintering on almost all continents.

rusty forehead

dark bluish black breast band

FEMALE

dark rusty brown throat

blackish flight feathers

dark iridescent blue-black upperparts

deeply forked blackish tail with white spots

JUVENILE

• **SONG** Utters a repetitive clipped *chi-dit, chi-dit* or *wit-wit*. Song is a prolonged twittering warble with liquid guttural notes interspersed.

• **BEHAVIOR** Gregarious. Often feeds close to ground or water. Eats a wide variety of flying insects, and follows farm machinery, even riding lawnmowers, to feed on stirred-up insects. Courtship flights may include pairs dropping and catching feathers in midair; upon landing pairs may engage in mutual preening. Individuals show strong site fidelity, and colonies may exist over long periods on the same site, with the same individuals sometimes building nests on the same site used the previous year. Has adapted to nesting in and on man-made structures.

• **BREEDING** Monogamous. Small colonies. During courtship, male chases female, flying over acres of land.

• **NESTING** Incubation 13–17 days by both sexes, but female does more. Young altricial; stay in nest 18–23 days, fed by both sexes. 2 broods per year.

Similar Birds

CLIFF SWALLOW
Blue-black upperparts; rusty cinnamon to buffy cinnamon rump; pale forehead; short squared tail without white spots.

CAVE SWALLOW
Blue-black upperparts; chestnut rump; short, squared tail without white spots.

• **POPULATION** Abundant and widespread in open country, agricultural lands, and savanna, especially near water. Increasing. Eurasian races are accidental to casual in Alaska.

• **CONSERVATION** Neotropical migrant.

Flight Pattern
Swift and graceful with deep wing beats and wing-tips pulled back at the end of each stroke; glides are short and infrequent.

Nest Identification	
Shape Location	Clay or mud, dried stems, grasses, and straw, with thick lining of horsehair, down, and feathers • inside barn or other building, in ridges of cliff, under bridge, under culvert, or attached to bank • built by both sexes • 4–7 white eggs, marked with browns; oval to long oval, 0.8 x 0.5 inches.

Plumage Sexes similar	Habitat	Migration Migratory	Weight 0.6 ounce

DATE _____ TIME_____ LOCATION _____

Family PARIDAE	Species *Poecile carolinensis*	Length 4.75 inches	Wingspan 7.5 inches

CAROLINA CHICKADEE

Readily attracted to feeders supplying sunflower seeds, this little chickadee is a familiar bird to many who operate feeding stations in its range, where it is the only songbird with a black bib and black cap. This energetic bird, a common inhabitant of the southeastern United States primarily south of the zone of glaciation, ranges north to New Jersey and west into Ohio, Indiana, Illinois, and to the 100th meridian in eastern Texas. When disturbed in the nest cavity during incubation, it will hiss and strike intruders, behaving similarly to copperheads and other snakes.

white cheeks
gray upperparts
black cap
short black bill
black bib
narrow grayish white edging on wings
white underparts with buff-gray wash on lower belly, crissum sides, and flanks
short slightly notched tail
blackish gray feet and legs

- **SONG** Calls include a higher-pitched rapid *chick-a-dee-dee-dee* and a 4-note whistled *fee-bee-fee-bay*, an octave higher than that of the Black-capped Chickadee, with lower-pitched 2nd and 4th notes. Also makes variety of high-pitched thin squeaky notes when foraging with others. Call notes are more complex than song.
- **BEHAVIOR** Pairs or small groups. After breeding often joins mixed feeding flocks with titmice, nuthatches, kinglets, warblers, Downy Woodpeckers, and others. Eats moths, caterpillars, and a wide variety of other insects when available; in winter and spring eats mostly seeds and some berries. May excavate own nest or enlarge cavity if wood is soft enough.
- **BREEDING** Monogamous. Very early nester.
- **NESTING** Incubation 11–12 days by both sexes. Altricial young stay in nest 13–17 days. Brooded by female. Fed by both sexes, mostly larval insects. 1–2 broods per year.
- **POPULATION** Common in open deciduous forests, woodland clearings, forest edges, and suburban areas.
- **FEEDERS AND BIRDHOUSES** Suet, doughnuts, and sunflower seeds. Nests in birdhouses.
- **CONSERVATION** Sometimes competes for nest sites with House Wren, especially in suburban areas.

Similar Birds

BLACK-CAPPED CHICKADEE
Larger body; white-edged greater wing coverts; broad white markings on edge of secondaries; more boldly edged tertials with darker centers; black bib extends farther down chest; olive flanks; lower, slower *chick-a-dee-dee-dee* call; typically gives 2- to 3-note *fee-bee* or *fee-bee-be* song.

Flight Pattern

Short weak fluttering flight with rapid beats; sometimes in longer flights folds wings to sides after several quick strokes.

Nest Identification

Shape ⬥¹ ⬥² Location 🌳 🪶 🦅

Lined with plant material, including grass and moss, as well as feathers and hair • in tree or snag 1–23 feet above ground or in man-made nest box • built by both sexes • 5–8 white eggs with reddish brown markings; oval to short oval, 0.6 x 0.45 inches.

Plumage Sexes similar	Habitat 🌳 🌾 ⛰	Migration Nonmigratory	Weight 0.4 ounce

DATE _____ TIME_____ LOCATION _____

| Family PARIDAE | Species *Baeolophus bicolor* | Length 6.5 inches | Wingspan 10.75 inches |

TUFTED TITMOUSE

Undaunted by the presence of people, this lively bird sometimes will swoop down and pluck out a human hair to use for its nest. The largest titmouse, it will fly toward people making squeaking or pishing sounds to attract birds. It is intelligent and may learn to eat food out of a human hand. Often it can be seen digging in the ground, where it stores surplus sunflower seeds. Adapted to wooded residential areas with large shade trees and to bird feeders and nesting boxes, it has become a familiar yard bird with its jaunty crest and large black eyes set against gray plumage. The black-crested form in southern and western Texas was formerly considered a separate species, the Black-crested Titmouse.

medium gray upperparts
tufted dark gray head
straight black bill
gray tail
rusty sides and flanks
whitish gray underparts
gray-black feet and legs

BLACK-CRESTED FORM

- **SONG** Bold, high-pitched, whistled *peter, peter, peter* or *peto, peto, peto*. Sometimes females sing but not as much as males. Calls vary from high-pitched, thin squeaky notes to low, harsh, fussy scolding notes.

- **BEHAVIOR** Relatively tame; social. Pairs or small family groups; joins mixed foraging flocks after nesting season. Inspects and forages in trees and shrubs for food, sometimes clinging upside down on trunk or branch tips. Uses bill to pound open nut, while anchoring it with feet. Eats insects and their larvae, spiders, snails, various berries, acorns and other nuts, and seeds. Male feeds female during courtship.

- **BREEDING** Monogamous. Solitary nester. Mates for life.

- **NESTING** Incubation 13–14 days by female. Altricial young stay in nest 15–18 days. Brooded by female. Fed by both sexes. 1 brood per year, 2 in the South.

Similar Birds

PHAINOPEPLA ♀
Small range overlap in Big Bend area of Texas with black-crested form • larger; medium sooty gray overall; crested; darker gray wing edges; white on wing coverts and tertials; whitish gray patch at base of primaries flashes in flight; long, rounded tail.

- **POPULATION** Abundant to common in forests, parks, and shaded suburbs.

- **FEEDERS AND BIRDHOUSES** Feeders with sunflower seeds, suet, cornmeal, and peanut butter. Will nest in man-made birdhouses.

Flight Pattern	
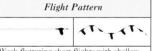	
Weak fluttering short flights with shallow rapid wing beats. Flitting flight with several quick wing beats alternating with wings drawn to sides, then repeated.	

Nest Identification	
Shape 〼2 〼1 Location 🐦 ⚘ 🏠 ⚘ 🏠	Lined with bark, leaves, soft grass and moss, snakeskin, and bits of animal fur and hair • in natural cavity, bird box, or woodpecker hole 3–90 feet above ground • built by female • 4–8 white to creamy white eggs speckled with browns, occasionally wreathed; short subelliptical, 0.7 x 0.55 inches.

| Plumage Sexes similar | Habitat 🌳 🌲 | Migration Nonmigratory | Weight 0.8 ounce |

DATE _____ TIME _____ LOCATION _____

Family SITTIDAE	Species *Sitta canadensis*	Length 4.5 inches	Wingspan 8 inches

RED-BREASTED NUTHATCH

This bird often will eat from the human hand. To protect young from predators, male and female smear pine pitch around the nest entrance. Females differ from males by the dark gray cap and nape and lighter underparts. The blue-gray tail spread in display or flight shows a white subterminal band. Winter range varies yearly, particularly in the East; this sedentary species remains in its breeding range as long as winter food supplies can support it.

• **SONG** Calls are nasal and high pitched, resembling the sound of a tiny tin horn, *ank, ink,* or *enk,* often repeated in a rapid series.

• **BEHAVIOR** Solitary or in pairs. May join mixed-species feeding flocks after breeding season. Climbs up and down tree trunks, often headfirst, and walks on the underside of limbs. Forages for conifer seeds, nuts, and some insects by gleaning them from bark or foliage; wedges food in tree bark crevices and pounds with bill to break shell or exoskeleton. Male courts female by feeding her, also by turning his back to her and lifting his head and tail, raising his back feathers and drooping his wings, swaying from side to side. Irruptive migrant.

• **BREEDING** Monogamous. Solitary.

• **NESTING** Incubation 12 days by female. Young altricial; brooded by female; stay in nest 14–21 days, fed by both sexes. 1 brood per year.

• **POPULATION** Fairly common to common in boreal and subalpine conifer forests and mixed conifer-deciduous northern montane forests. Stable. Eastern breeding range currently expanding southward.

• **FEEDERS** Sunflower seeds, peanut butter, and suet.

• **CONSERVATION** Vulnerable to habitat loss due to logging operations.

black eye line from beak to back of head • black cap and nape • blue-gray back, shoulders, wings, and rump • white eyebrow • white cheeks • rust-colored underparts • short blue-gray tail

MALE

blue-gray upperparts • dark gray crown and nape • **FEMALE** lighter buff underparts are rustier on flank and crissum

Similar Birds

WHITE-BREASTED NUTHATCH Larger; white face lacks black eye line; white underparts with rusty wash on flanks and crissum; blue-gray tail with black outer tail feathers edged and tipped white; voice differs.

Flight Pattern

Somewhat weak fluttering flight of short duration, with rapid wing strokes followed by brief folding of wings to sides; repeated.

Nest Identification

Shape 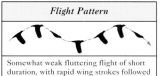 Location

Lined with shredded bark, grass, and roots • usually 5–40 feet above ground (but up to 120 feet) in conifer • built by both sexes, but female does most of work • 4–7 white to pinkish white eggs, marked with reddish browns; oval to short oval, 0.6 x 0.46 inches.

Plumage Sexes differ	Habitat 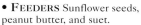	Migration Some migrate	Weight 0.4 ounce

DATE _____ TIME _____ LOCATION _____

Family SITTIDAE	Species *Sitta carolinensis*	Length 5–6 inches	Wingspan 9–11 inches

WHITE-BREASTED NUTHATCH

The largest and most widespread of the North American nuthatches, this nimble bird can balance upside down on tree trunks, catch a falling nut in midair, and rapidly hop down skinny branches. In winter it joins mixed-species flocks and often feeds together in the same tree with chickadees, Downy Woodpeckers, and Brown Creepers. It is quick to accept bird feeders, and will often attempt to intimidate other avian visitors by spreading its wings and tail and swaying back and forth. Females in the Northeast have dark blue-gray crowns.

black cap and nape extend onto hindneck as partial collar

long black bill with slightly upturned tip

blackish blue tertials, secondaries, primaries, and wing coverts with white edging

blue-gray upperparts

white face and breast

white patches in blue-black tail

white underparts with rusty wash on flanks, lower belly, and crissum

black feet and legs

- **SONG** Sings an ascending *wee-wee-wee-wee-wee-wee-wee*. Call is a hoarse *yank-yank-yank*.
- **BEHAVIOR** Solitary or in pairs; sociable in nonbreeding season. Eats various nuts, seeds, spiders, and insects. Inspects trees with head pointed downward and circles around and underneath limb in search of food. Spends most of its time in trees. Roosts in tree cavities in the winter; often roosts in crevices of bark in summer, some sleeping in the head down, tail up position.
- **BREEDING** Monogamous. Solitary. Sometimes known to form small colonies.
- **NESTING** Incubation 12 days by female. Young altricial; brooded by female; stay in nest 14 days, fed by both sexes. 1 brood per year.
- **POPULATION** Common in deciduous woodlots and in mixed coniferous-deciduous woods in the North and West.

<table>
<tr><th colspan="2">Similar Birds</th></tr>
<tr><td></td><td>RED-BREASTED NUTHATCH Smaller; white face broken by long, black eye stripe; uniform rusty chestnut underparts; smaller bill; voice differs.</td></tr>
</table>

- **FEEDERS AND BIRDHOUSES** Comes to feeders for suet and/or seeds; will nest in nest boxes.
- **CONSERVATION** Vulnerable to habitat loss due to logging operations.

Flight Pattern

Weak fluttering flight of short duration; several rapid wing beats alternated with wings drawn to sides; repeated.

Nest Identification	
Shape 🪺² 🪶 Location 🌲🏠 🦅🕊️	Lined with bark shreds, hair, and feathers • natural cavity, knothole, woodpecker's hole, or bird box, 10–60 feet above ground • built by both sexes; female does more • 3–10 white to pinkish eggs, with brown, gray, purple, and red blotches; oval to short oval, 0.8 x 0.56 inches.

Plumage Sexes similar	Habitat 🌱 🌳 🏔	Migration Nonmigratory	Weight 0.7 ounce

DATE _____ TIME_____ LOCATION _____

Family SITTIDAE	Species *Sitta pusilla*	Length 4.5 inches	Wingspan 8.5 inches

BROWN-HEADED NUTHATCH

The only North American songbird to use a tool while foraging, this nuthatch lives in the southern woodlands, especially in open stands of pine. It sometimes holds a piece of bark in its bill and uses it to pry up another bark chip, uncovering insects. This bird travels in small flocks of family groups. Often foraging high in the trees and well out toward the tips of the branches, it would be easily overlooked but for its constant peeping calls and twittering.

buffy brown cap and nape with white spot on nape

blue-gray upperparts

thin dark eye line borders cap

straight black bill

white chin, cheeks, and throat

buffy whitish underparts

black legs and feet

• **SONG** Has various squeaky *bit-bit-bit* calls and a *dee-dee-dee*. During courtship, sings *pri-u, de-u, de-u*, like a squeaky toy.

• **BEHAVIOR** In pairs or small family groups, often including an unmated male helper that helps excavate the nesting cavity and feed female and young. Forages over, around, and up and down branches, small twigs, and trunks, even hanging upside down. Picks seeds from pinecones. Eats insects and their larvae and spiders. Caches pine seeds. Forms mixed-species foraging flocks with chickadees, titmice, kinglets, warblers, woodpeckers, and others.

• **BREEDING** Monogamous. Cooperative.

• **NESTING** Incubation 14 days by female. Young altricial; brooded by female; stay in nest 18–19 days, fed by both sexes and extra birds. 1 brood per year.

• **POPULATION** Fairly common in mature open pine forests and mixed pine-deciduous woodlands along the coastal plain.

• **FEEDERS AND BIRDHOUSES** Will come to eat at bird feeders and will nest in birdhouses built for them.

• **CONSERVATION** Vulnerable to habitat loss due to the cutting of pine forests and the replacement with pine plantations that are on short harvest rotations.

Similar Birds

♂ ♀ **RED-BREASTED NUTHATCH**
Larger; black cap; white face with long black eye stripe; rusty chestnut underparts; black nape; voice differs.

WHITE-BREASTED NUTHATCH
Larger; black cap; completely white face, breast, and underparts; rusty-washed flanks and crissum.

Flight Pattern

Weak fluttering flight of short duration, with series of rapid wing beats followed by wings pulled in to sides; repeated.

Nest Identification

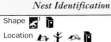

Shape

Location

Soft bark shreds, wood chips, grasses, wool, hair, and feathers • in dead or live tree, bird box, stump, or old post, usually 2–12 feet above ground (but up to 90 feet) • built by both sexes and extra birds • 3–9 white or off-white eggs, with reddish brown speckles; short subelliptical to short oval, 0.6 x 0.45 inches.

Plumage Sexes similar	Habitat	Migration Nonmigratory	Weight 0.4 ounce

DATE _____ TIME_____ LOCATION _____

Family CERTHIIDAE	Species *Certhia americana*	Length 5.25 inches	Wingspan 7–8 inches

BROWN CREEPER

This tree-dwelling bird roosts by hanging onto a tree trunk or the side of a house with its sharp claws. Unlike the nuthatches, it does not move sideways or upside down when foraging for insects. Rather, it circles the tree in an upward direction, as if it were ascending a spiral staircase, or it takes a straighter path up, then drops to the base of a nearby tree and starts working its way up again. The long decurved bill is an efficient tool for picking insects out of bark crevices, and the stiff tail feathers prop the bird upright just as a woodpecker's tail does.

- **SONG** Call is a soft musical *see-see-titi-see*, similar to that of the Golden-crowned Kinglet, but thinner. Call note is a soft thin *seee*.
- **BEHAVIOR** Solitary or in pairs. Tame. Often joins mixed-species foraging flocks in winter. Forages for food by spiraling up tree, but does not move down or sideways. Hops back occasionally, but then moves on up. Eats various insects, larvae, seeds, and some nuts. Well camouflaged and difficult to spot; often escapes predators by pressing its body tightly against tree, spreading wings and tail, and remaining motionless. Fledglings roost in tight circle with heads in center of ring.
- **BREEDING** Monogamous. Solitary nester.
- **NESTING** Incubation 13–17 days by female. Young altricial; brooded by female; stay in nest 13–16 days. Fed by both sexes. 1 brood per year.
- **POPULATION** Fairly common in pine, spruce-fir, mixed coniferous-deciduous, swampy forests; declining in some areas.

slender decurved pointed bill

white line over eyes

buff-streaked brown upperparts

sharp claws

white underparts

wings and coverts edged and tipped with buff and white

long rufous tail with stiff pointed tail feathers at end

- **FEEDERS** Will come to feeders for mixture of nuts, peanut butter, suet, and cornmeal. Mixture can be put directly on tree trunk.
- **CONSERVATION** Nesting area threatened due to cutting of forest habitat.

Flight Pattern
Strong direct flights of short duration with rapid shallow wing beats.

Nest Identification	Twigs, moss, conifer needles, pieces of bark, and silk, lined with shredded bark and feathers • in cavity of dead tree, or beneath piece of bark against tree, 5–50 feet above ground • built by both sexes; female does more • 4–8 white eggs, sparsely flecked with reddish brown and often wreathed; oval to short oval, 0.6 x 0.46 inches.
Shape	
Location	

Plumage Sexes similar	Habitat	Migration Migratory	Weight 0.3 ounce

DATE _____ TIME_____ LOCATION _____

Family TROGLODYTIDAE	Species *Thryothorus ludovicianus*	Length 5.5 inches	Wingspan 7.75 inches

CAROLINA WREN

South Carolina's state bird is sensitive to cold weather. Mild winters allow Carolina Wrens to expand their range northwards but most will not survive the next hard winter. Energetic, loud, and conspicuous, the largest wren in eastern North America is equally at home in moist deciduous woodlots, on the farm, or in shaded suburbs. Pairs stay together on their territories all year, and the male may sing at any time of day, any day of the year. The female often responds with a quick "growl" of *t-shihrrr*.

bold white stripe above eye

rusty brown upperparts with dark brown bars on wings and tail

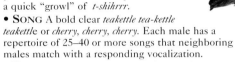

long slightly decurved bill

white chin, throat, and upper breast

rich buffy underparts

• **SONG** A bold clear *teakettle tea-kettle teakettle* or *cherry, cherry, cherry*. Each male has a repertoire of 25–40 or more songs that neighboring males match with a responding vocalization.

• **BEHAVIOR** Most often in pairs. Sings from exposed perch. Usually stays hidden in undergrowth, but will emerge if it hears squeaking noises. Pokes into every nook and cranny, hopping with tail cocked over back. Eats mostly insects, larvae, and insect eggs, but will take small vertebrates, snails, berries, and some fruits. Common around human habitation; enters open buildings to inspect dark recesses for insects or spiders. Builds its bulky nest in any container large enough to hold it, from coat pockets and boots to buckets, flower baskets, and mailboxes.

• **BREEDING** Monogamous. Solitary nester.

• **NESTING** Incubation 12–14 days by female. Altricial young brooded by female; stay in nest 12–14 days, fed by both sexes but often tended by the male while female begins another clutch. 2 broods per year, often 3 in the South.

• **POPULATION** Common. Numbers decrease in northern range after harsh winters, but overall population stable except in the Northeast and Midwest where it is recorded as declining.

• **FEEDERS AND BIRDHOUSES** Suet and peanut butter. Will use nest boxes, often filling several with dummy nests.

• **CONSERVATION** Declines are of some concern.

Similar Birds

BEWICK'S WREN Whitish underparts; long rounded tail edged with white spots; reddish brown to gray-brown upperparts; long white eye stripe; frequently flips long tail; voice differs.

MARSH WREN White-striped back; long white eye stripe; white underparts washed rufous-buff on sides and flanks; habitat and voice differ.

Flight Pattern

Direct flight somewhat weak and fluttering with shallow rapid wing beats.

Nest Identification

Shape   Location

Stems, leaves, grasses, bark pieces, mosses, feathers, and snakeskin • cavity of tree, stump, or bank; sometimes old woodpecker hole, rafter, mailbox, bird box, or almost any cavity • built by both sexes • 4–8 white or light pink eggs, marked with brown; oval, 0.8 x 0.6 inches.

Plumage Sexes similar	Habitat	Migration Nonmigratory	Weight 0.7 ounce

DATE _____ TIME_____ LOCATION _____

| Family TROGLODYTIDAE | Species *Troglodytes aedon* | Length 4.75 inches | Wingspan 6–7 inches |

HOUSE WREN

This plain bird has a wide range, breeding from southern Canada to Mexico. However, even though its range spread southward in the East throughout most of the 20th century, it is not currently found nesting in southeastern states. Despite its size, the House Wren is highly competitive when searching for nesting territory. It often invades nests of other wrens and songbirds, puncturing their eggs and killing their young. When it comes to selecting a nesting site, the male begins building dummy nests in almost any available cavity in his territory, from natural cavities and nesting boxes to boots, cans, buckets, toolboxes, coat pockets, and mailboxes. Birds in southeastern Arizona mountains have a buff supercilium, throat, and breast.

pale streak above eyes

grayish brown upperparts

narrow pale eye ring

narrow black barring on tail

narrow black barring on wings

thin slightly decurved bill

pale gray underparts

narrow black barring on sides, lower belly, and crissum

• **SONG** Sings beautiful, trilling, energetic flutelike melody delivered in a gurgling outburst and repeated at short intervals. Call is rough scolding *cheh-cheh*, often run into a scolding chatter.

• **BEHAVIOR** Solitary or in pairs. Loud and conspicuous. Relatively tame and bold. Often cocks tail upward. Eats various insects, spiders, millipedes, and some snails. Male starts several dummy nests in territory as part of courtship, then female joins him to inspect them and selects one to complete for nest. Highly migratory except in extreme southwestern US.

• **BREEDING** Usually monogamous but sometimes polygamous. Males occasionally have 2 mates at same time.

• **NESTING** Incubation 13–15 days by female. Altricial young stay in nest 12–18 days. Brooded by female. Fed by both sexes or female only. 2–3 broods per year.

• **POPULATION** Common in open woodlands, shrubs, farmlands, suburbs, gardens, and parks.

• **FEEDERS** Will nest in man-made bird boxes.

• **CONSERVATION** Neotropical migrant. Nestlings sometimes are affected by bluebottle fly larvae and may die in nest.

Similar Birds

WINTER WREN Smaller; darker; heavier black barring on tail, flanks, and underparts; shorter tail; different voice.

Flight Pattern

Weak fluttering direct flight with rapid shallow wing beats.

Nest Identification

Shape ___ Location ___

Base made of sticks • lined with hair, feathers, cocoons, and fine material • almost anywhere in cavity of tree, bird box, abandoned hole or nest, cow skull, pipes, watering cans, etc. • male builds platform; female lines • 5–9 white eggs with brown flecks, occasionally wreathed; short rounded ovate to oval, 0.6 x 0.5 inches.

| Plumage Sexes similar | Habitat | Migration Most migrate | Weight 0.4 ounce |

DATE _____ TIME_____ LOCATION _____

Family TROGLODYTIDAE	Species *Troglodytes troglodytes*	Length 4 inches	Wingspan 6 inches

WINTER WREN

One of the smallest songbirds in North America, this short-tailed wren nests primarily in the coniferous forests of Canada and the northern US, but it also resides along the Pacific Coast from central California to the Aleutians, and in the Appalachians south to northern Georgia. It usually hides in thick undergrowth, but when excited it will fly up, perch, bob its head up and down, and deliver an alarm call or a rapid, cascading song that may last six to seven seconds and contain more than a hundred notes. This is the only member of the wren family found in Europe.

gray to brown superciliary stripe

stubby tail

dark brown upperparts with faint barring

- **SONG** Male sings warbling melody of varied up-and-down notes with rapid trills; some notes high, thin, and silvery. Also has whisper song. Call is abrasive *chirrr* or *tik-tik-tik*.
- **BEHAVIOR** Often solitary; pairs in breeding season. Scampers on ground and in low trees while foraging, ducking in and out of root wads, in and around logs, into brush piles, and any opening or cranny large enough. Gleans food from surfaces, mostly insects, caterpillars, and berries. Sometimes will approach humans for bread crumbs. Bobs head and body and flicks tail, which is often cocked over back. Frequents habitats near water.

dark brown underparts

heavy, dark brownish black barring on flanks, underparts, and tail

- **BREEDING** Polygamous.
- **NESTING** Incubation 12–16 days by female. Altricial young stay in nest 16–19 days, fed by female or both sexes. 1–2 broods per year.
- **POPULATION** Abundant. West Coast, northwest montane, and southern Appalachian populations permanent; others highly migratory.
- **BIRDHOUSES** Will roost in bird box.
- **CONSERVATION** Vulnerable to habitat loss caused by logging operations.

Similar Birds

HOUSE WREN
Larger; longer tail; less prominent barring on belly, sides, and flanks; faint eye stripe; voice differs.

Flight Pattern

Weak fluttering flights of short duration on rapidly beating wings.

Nest Identification

Shape

Location

Cavity filled with platform of sticks, covered with moss and grass, lined with hair and feathers • in cavity of log or stump, under tree roots, and sometimes in building • 0–6 feet above ground • male builds 1–5 nests; female chooses • 4–7 white eggs with brown flecks concentrated at large end; oval, 0.65 x 0.5 inches.

Plumage Sexes similar	Habitat	Migration Most migrate	Weight 0.3 ounce

DATE _____ TIME_____ LOCATION _____

Family TROGLODYTIDAE	Species *Cistothorus platensis*	Length 4.5 inches	Wingspan 5.5–6 inches

SEDGE WREN

Camouflaged by its plumage, this wren stays hidden in dense marsh grasses, except when it perches to sing, which it sometimes does at night. The female chooses one of several rather well-concealed nests built by the male, then lines it with materials of her choice. This wren ranges over much of the grasslands and marshlands of the central and north-central United States and south-central Canada, often going where the habitat is most suitable and often changing nesting areas from year to year.

brownish black streaking on crown

brown upperparts

short slender bill

whitish eyebrow

brownish black and white streaking on back and scapulars

buff to whitish underparts

short barred tail

• **SONG** Sings a bold melody of single disconnected notes, followed by a rapid chatter of dry notes. Has call of *chip-chip*.

• **BEHAVIOR** Solitary on wintering grounds; often in pairs in small habitats; in small colonies in larger more favorable habitats. Secretive, staying down in the foliage except while singing, when it often ascends to a more exposed perch. Scampers on ground in wet meadows and in low brush, foraging for food. Eats mostly insects and spiders. Male builds several dummy nests and female chooses one; males will often destroy other bird's eggs when they discover them, including those of other Sedge Wrens.

• **BREEDING** Polygamous.

• **NESTING** Incubation 12–16 days by female. Young altricial; stay in nest 12–14 days. Fed by both sexes, but female does more. 2 broods per year.

• **POPULATION** Common in range but often very local; numbers may change from year to year. Rare in winter in New Mexico and casual to California in fall migration.

• **CONSERVATION** Neotropical migrant with some birds wintering in northeast Mexico. Vulnerable to habitat loss caused by agriculture.

Similar Birds

MARSH WREN
Larger; longer bill; dark crown; darker and more brown overall; unbarred rufous rump • western birds have duller, paler plumage with less distinct white streaking on back • eastern birds have richer browns and distinct back streaking.

Flight Pattern

Weak fluttering flight with shallow, rapid wing beats; alternating several wing strokes with wings being drawn to sides; repeated.

Nest Identification

Shape ⬤   Location

Stems, grasses, and sedges • lined with plant down, feathers, and fur • on grasses or reeds, usually near water or marshy area • 0–2 feet above ground in grass • male builds several nests; female selects one and lines • 4–8 white eggs; oval to pyriform, 0.6 x 0.47 inches.

Plumage Sexes similar	Habitat	Migration Migratory	Weight 0.3 ounce

DATE _____ TIME_____ LOCATION _____

Family TROGLODYTIDAE	Species *Cistothorus palustris*	Length 4.5–5 inches	Wingspan 5.5–7 inches

MARSH WREN

This bird usually stays hidden, but its song can be heard over the reeds and cattails of the marshlands. The male builds several intricate globular-shaped nests, which have side doors; the female chooses one and adds the lining of shredded plants and feathers. The male often roosts in one of the dummy nests. Some males have more than one mate, with each one occupying a small section of his territory. The black-and-white streaking on the back of the Marsh Wren is less distinct in western birds.

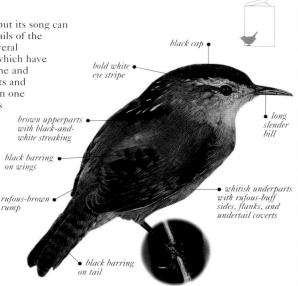

black cap

bold white
eye stripe

brown upperparts
with black-and-
white streaking

black barring
on wings

rufous-brown
rump

long
slender
bill

whitish underparts
with rufous-buff
sides, flanks, and
undertail coverts

black barring
on tail

- **SONG** Sings a gurgling trilling melody, with western birds singing a harsher song than eastern birds. Call is an abrasive *te-suk-te-suk*. Western birds may have more than 200 songs in their varied repertoire, while eastern males may have only around 70.

- **BEHAVIOR** Solitary; in pairs or small colonies, depending on the size and quality of the habitat. Often secretive, foraging for food in tall marsh grasses and reeds, where it gleans aquatic insects, larvae, caterpillars, snails, and sometimes other bird's eggs. Males often sing from exposed perches or even skylark before dropping back into the cover of the thick vegetation; sometimes sing at night. Often enters the nests of other birds and destroys their eggs, sometimes having its own eggs destroyed in turn.

- **BREEDING** Polygamous. Colonial.

- **NESTING** Incubation 12–16 days by female. Young altricial; stay in nest 11–16 days, fed by both sexes, but female does more. 2 broods per year.

- **POPULATION** Common despite loss of freshwater wetlands. Most populations are migratory, but some in the West and on the coasts, are nonmigratory year round residents.

- **CONSERVATION** Neotropical migrant; vulnerable to habitat lost to development, agriculture, wetland drainage.

Similar Birds

SEDGE WREN
Smaller; shorter bill; buffy brown head and upperparts; dark streaking on cinnamon rump; less distinct eye stripe; voice differs.

Flight Pattern

Weak fluttering flights, often of short duration; alternates several quick wing beats with brief pause and wings at sides.

Nest Identification		Reeds, grass, sedge, bulrushes for outer layer; grasses, reeds, and cattails for central cavity, lined with shredded soft materials • about 1–3 feet above water (but up to 15 feet) • male builds several nests, female selects and completes • 3–10 brown eggs, flecked with darker brown and sometimes wreathed; usually ovate, 0.7 x 0.55 inches.
Shape	Location	

Plumage Sexes similar	Habitat	Migration Migratory	Weight 0.4 ounce

DATE _____ TIME_____ LOCATION _____

Family PYCNONOTIDAE	Species *Pycnonotus jocosus*	Length 7 inches	Wingspan 11.1 inches

RED-WHISKERED BULBUL

A popular caged bird in its native homelands of India and Asia because of its cheerful chattering and active manners, the Red-whiskered Bulbul has become established in south Florida with the escape of caged birds from the Miami area. Birds have been able to establish themselves in the southern suburbs of the city because of all the ornamental, berry-bearing shrubs and trees that provide them with their principal foods. The red "whisker" for which it is named is an ear patch behind the eye of adults. Juveniles lack the deep red ear patch and their plumage is duller overall.

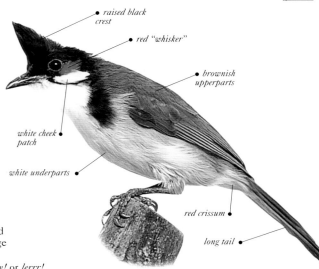

raised black crest

red "whisker"

brownish upperparts

white cheek patch

white underparts

red crissum

long tail

• **SONG** A whistled *queekey!* or *lerrr!* Also mimics lively cheerful phrases such as "the rice must be finished off" and "pleased to MEET you."

• **BEHAVIOR** Sometimes secretive and difficult to locate; other times lively and noisy. Singing birds often sit on exposed perches such as wires, poles, antennas, and bare branches. Often stays in small "family" groups. More gregarious in nonbreeding season, often roosts in flocks in winter.

• **BREEDING** Monogamous.

• **NESTING** Incubation time 12–14 days. Young stay in nest 10–12 days. Broods per year unknown in U.S.

JUVENILE

• **POPULATION** The small established US population has expanded its range little since its escape and is still within the urban area of Miami. Small population exists in Los Angeles area, also due to the escape of caged birds.

Flight Pattern

Direct flight with rapid wing beats.

Nest Identification	
Shape 🥄 Location 🌳🌳	Shallow to deep • in crotch of tree • dead leaves, grass, paper, bark, and plastic • sometimes topped off with a snake skin • lined with fine roots and hair • 3–9 feet above ground • built by both sexes • 2–4 pinkish white eggs; oval-shaped and spotted with reddish brown and purple.

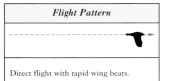

Plumage Sexes similar	Habitat 🔺	Migration Nonmigratory	Weight 1.0 ounce

DATE _____ TIME_____ LOCATION _____

Family REGULIDAE	Species *Regulus satrapa*	Length 4 inches	Wingspan 6.5–7 inches

GOLDEN-CROWNED KINGLET

Living in dense coniferous forests, this tiny bird's baseball-sized sphere-shaped nest is so small that its clutch of half-inch eggs must be laid in two layers. A tame bird, it will sometimes enter human habitations and not try to escape if held. It often feeds in mixed-species foraging flocks with woodpeckers, creepers, chickadees, nuthatches, and others. Females and juveniles have a yellow crown bordered by black.

- **SONG** Sings a song beginning with 3–4 high-pitched *tsee, tsee, tsee* notes, followed by a rapid trill. Call is a series of 3–4 high-pitched *tsee* notes.
- **BEHAVIOR** Solitary or in pairs. Tame. Flits wings as it hops along branches. Forages through dense foliage of trees to pick off food. Eats mainly insects, their eggs, and larvae; takes some seeds. Drinks tree sap, sometimes taking it from sapsucker drill wells. May hawk insects or hover briefly to glean them from trunk, branch, or foliage.
- **BREEDING** Monogamous. Solitary nester.
- **NESTING** Incubation 14–15 days by female. Young altricial; stay in nest 14–19 days, fed by both sexes. 1–2 broods per year.
- **POPULATION** Common in coniferous woodlands. Populations may drop after harsh cold seasons on winter range; long-term stable, with range expanding to northeast. Many populations nonmigratory.
- **CONSERVATION** Neotropical migrant. Vulnerable to habitat loss caused by logging, especially of mature coniferous forests.

orange patch on crown bordered by yellow

broad whitish stripe above eye

olive-green upperparts

black yellowish-edged tertials and secondaries

short straight black bill

2 whitish wing bars

pale buff to whitish underparts

MALE

yellow crown patch bordered by black

FEMALE

Similar Birds

RUBY-CROWNED KINGLET
White eye ring instead of white stripe over eye; underparts are darker, dusky greenish yellow; olive-green crown and upperparts; different call • only male has concealed red crown patch.

Flight Pattern
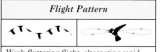
Weak fluttering flight, alternating rapid shallow wing strokes with a brief pull of wings to sides. Hovers over food before dipping down to pick it up with beak.

Nest Identification	
Shape ● ☙ Location 🌿	Lichen and moss, with lining of bark chips, rootlets, and feathers • in branch of conifer, 30–60 feet above ground • built by female • 5–11 creamy white to muddy cream eggs splotched brown or gray, usually wreathed; elliptical ovate, 0.5 inch long.

Plumage Sexes differ	Habitat 🌲🌲 🌱🌱	Migration Migratory	Weight 0.2 ounce

DATE _____ TIME_____ LOCATION _____

Family REGULIDAE	Species *Regulus calendula*	Length 4.25 inches	Wingspan 6.75–7.5 inches

RUBY-CROWNED KINGLET

This small bird often is seen in mixed-species foraging flocks with creepers, nuthatches, titmice, warblers, and other kinglets. The red patch on the male's crown usually is not visible, unless he becomes excited, at which time he flashes it open and the whole crown seems to be gushing blood. The female and juvenile are similar to the male but lack the red patch. This species is widely distributed in the boreal zone across northern and western North America as a breeding bird, it is highly migratory.

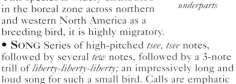

small, often concealed, red patch on crown

white eye ring

short black bill

dusky buff to whitish underparts

olive-green upperparts

MALE

• **SONG** Series of high-pitched *tsee, tsee* notes, followed by several *tew* notes, followed by a 3-note trill of *liberty-liberty-liberty;* an impressively long and loud song for such a small bird. Calls are emphatic *je-ditt* and *cack-cack.*

• **BEHAVIOR** Solitary or in pairs. Tame and active. Picks food off tree trunks, branches, and dense foliage; may hawk or hover to take food. Eats mainly insects, their eggs, and larvae. Also eats some fruits and seeds. Drinks tree sap, especially from the drill wells of sapsuckers. Has "nervous" habit of flicking wings when foraging, perhaps to startle insects into flinching and revealing themselves.

2 white wing bars

yellowish edged secondaries and tertials

FEMALE

Similar Birds

GOLDEN-CROWNED KINGLET
White stripe above eye; paler underparts; song differs • male has orange crown patch with yellow and black border • females and juveniles have yellow crown patch with black border.

HUTTON'S VIREO
Stockier; larger head; stout bill; pale lores; olive-gray upperparts; secondaries and tertials lack yellow edging; does not flick wings; white eye ring broken above eyes; voice differs • western range.

• **BREEDING** Monogamous. Solitary nester.

• **NESTING** Incubation 12–14 days by female. Altricial young leave nest at 10–16 days, fed by both sexes. 1 brood per year.

• **POPULATION** Common and widespread in coniferous and mixed conifer-deciduous forests. Studies indicate that populations may be regulated by conditions on the wintering grounds.

• **CONSERVATION** Neotropical migrant. Vulnerable to habitat lost to logging operations. Rare cowbird host.

Flight Pattern
Weak fluttering flight with shallow wing beats, alternating several quick strokes with brief periods of wings folded to sides. Hovers over branches to pick off food.

Nest Identification	
Shape 🐦 ● Location 🪹	Moss, lichen, down, twigs, and dead leaves, lined with finer materials, including feathers • hanging from tree branch, 2–100 feet above ground • built by female • 5–11 creamy white to muddy cream eggs, splotched with brown or gray, usually wreathed; elliptical ovate to oval, 0.5 inch long.

Plumage Sexes differ	Habitat 🌱🌱	Migration Migratory	Weight 0.2 ounce

DATE _____ TIME_____ LOCATION _____

Family SYLVIIDAE	Species *Polioptila caerulea*	Length 4.25 inches	Wingspan 5.75–6.5 inches

BLUE-GRAY GNATCATCHER

This slender bird can be seen in the East foraging in the foliage of tall trees; in the West it can be seen in thickets or chaparral. Females are similar to males but have less blue in their plumage and, like the juvenile male, lack the black line on the sides of the crown. The high thin *speee, speee, speee* notes, sounding like the calls of a baby bird, may attract attention before the tiny bird is seen.

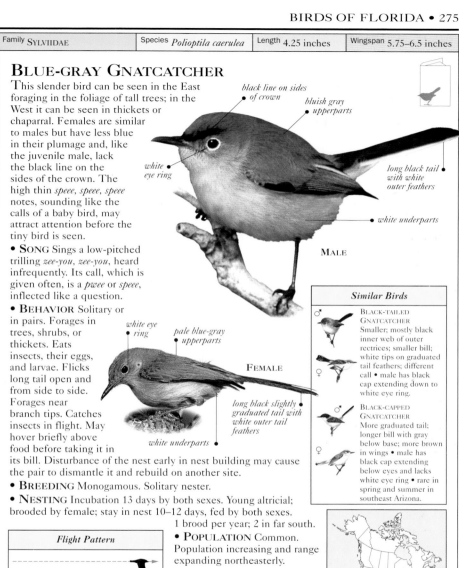

black line on sides of crown

bluish gray upperparts

white eye ring

long black tail with white outer feathers

white underparts

MALE

- **SONG** Sings a low-pitched trilling *zee-you, zee-you,* heard infrequently. Its call, which is given often, is a *pwee* or *speee,* inflected like a question.

- **BEHAVIOR** Solitary or in pairs. Forages in trees, shrubs, or thickets. Eats insects, their eggs, and larvae. Flicks long tail open and from side to side. Forages near branch tips. Catches insects in flight. May hover briefly above food before taking it in its bill. Disturbance of the nest early in nest building may cause the pair to dismantle it and rebuild on another site.

white eye ring

pale blue-gray upperparts

FEMALE

long black slightly graduated tail with white outer tail feathers

white underparts

- **BREEDING** Monogamous. Solitary nester.

- **NESTING** Incubation 13 days by both sexes. Young altricial; brooded by female; stay in nest 10–12 days, fed by both sexes. 1 brood per year; 2 in far south.

- **POPULATION** Common. Population increasing and range expanding northeasterly.

- **CONSERVATION** Neotropical migrant. Common victim of cowbird parasitism.

Similar Birds

BLACK-TAILED GNATCATCHER Smaller; mostly black inner web of outer rectrices; smaller bill; white tips on graduated tail feathers; different call • male has black cap extending down to white eye ring.

BLACK-CAPPED GNATCATCHER More graduated tail; longer bill with gray below base; more brown in wings • male has black cap extending below eyes and lacks white eye ring • rare in spring and summer in southeast Arizona.

Flight Pattern
Weak fluttering direct flight with shallow wing beats, often of short duration.

Nest Identification		Fine plant fibers, with lining of bark pieces and finer materials; covered with lichen bound by spider silk • saddled on branch or in fork of tree, usually 3–25 feet above ground • built by both sexes • 4–5 pale blue to bluish white eggs, usually flecked with browns, occasionally wreathed; oval to short oval, 0.6 x 0.44 inches.
Shape	Location	

Plumage Sexes differ	Habitat	Migration Migratory	Weight 0.2 ounce

DATE _____ TIME_____ LOCATION _____

Family TURDIDAE	Species *Sialia sialis*	Length 7–7.75 inches	Wingspan 11.5–13 inches

EASTERN BLUEBIRD

This brightly colored bird inhabits open woodlands, meadows, and fields. Its population has been in serious decline due to competition from other birds for its nesting holes, as well as occasional severe snowstorms in the South that kill them in great numbers. Juveniles show gray-brown upperparts with white spotting on the back, a brownish chest with white scalloping, a white belly and crissum, a white eye ring, and a bluish tail and wings.

MALE

bright blue upperparts

reddish brown chin, throat, and sides of neck

reddish brown breast, sides, and flanks

white belly and undertail coverts

- **SONG** Sings melodic *chur chur-lee chur-lee*. Male gives call of *true-a-ly, true-a-ly*.
- **BEHAVIOR** Pairs, family groups, or small flocks. Gregarious in winter, often forming large flocks and roosting communally in natural cavities or nest boxes at night. Forages in open from low perches. Flies from perch to ground and forages for food. Eats mostly insects, earthworms, and spiders but also takes snails, lizards, and frogs. In winter eats mostly berries and seeds.
- **BREEDING** Monogamous. In pairs and small groups.
- **NESTING** Incubation 12–14 days by female. Altricial young stay in nest 15–20 days; brooded by female, fed by both sexes. 2–3 broods per year.
- **POPULATION** Fairly common, but declined by more than 90 percent in 20th century. Adversely affected by severe winters.
- **FEEDERS AND BIRDHOUSES** Peanut butter–cornmeal mixture and commercial bluebird food. Nests in man-made bird boxes.

gray upperparts

white eye ring

pale chestnut throat, breast, sides, and flanks

white belly and undertail coverts

FEMALE

blue wings, rump, and tail

JUVENILE

Similar Birds

WESTERN BLUEBIRD Blue throat and sides of neck; chestnut-red breast, sides, and flanks; pale grayish belly and crissum; rusty brown back • female has gray-rusty brown tinge on nape and back • western range.

- **CONSERVATION** European Starling, House Sparrow, and other's intrude on nesting sites. Many nesting sites lost to cutting cavity trees. Bird boxes have helped recovery, especially those with proper hole sizes and predator guards.

Flight Pattern

Relatively slow direct flight with shallow, somewhat jerky wing beats. Sallies from perch to catch insect in air.

Nest Identification

Shape

Location

Grass, weed stems, pine needles, twigs, and occasionally hair or feather • in abandoned woodpecker hole, natural hollow in tree or stump, or bird box 2–50 feet above ground • built by female • 2–7 light blue or white eggs; subelliptical to short subelliptical, 0.8 x 0.64 inches.

Plumage Sexes differ	Habitat	Migration Some migrate	Weight 1.1 ounces

DATE _____ TIME _____ LOCATION _____

Family TURDIDAE	Species *Catharus fuscescens*	Length 7–7.5 inches	Wingspan 11–11.5 inches

VEERY

This bird is named for the lovely ethereal downward-slurring song of the male, which is heard at sunset, a repeated *veer-u*. It is one of the most splendid songs of any bird in North America. Its tawny and buff plumage serves as camouflage in the forest it calls home. The Veery is the least spotted of North America's brown-backed thrushes, with the western populations slightly more spotted than the eastern ones. This bird haunts shaded moist woodlands with dense to scattered understory.

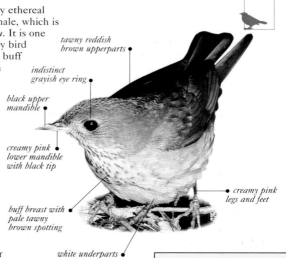

tawny reddish brown upperparts

indistinct grayish eye ring

black upper mandible

creamy pink lower mandible with black tip

buff breast with pale tawny brown spotting

white underparts

creamy pink legs and feet

- **SONG** Sings pleasant liquid descending *veer-u, veer-u, veer-u*, with each note sung lower, repeated frequently with variation in phrasing. Call is harsh down-slurred *veer*. Summer evenings, woodlots and forests fill with the song of one singer cascading into that of another; the chorus at twilight is one of the truly beautiful sounds of nature in the Northwoods.
- **BEHAVIOR** Solitary or in pairs. Somewhat shy and retiring. Forages on ground and in trees; swoops from low perch to take prey on ground, or gleans food from branches, foliage, or ground. Eats various insects, caterpillars, spiders, berries, and fruit. Agitated birds flick wings and raise small crest. Both sexes guard and defend young.
- **BREEDING** Monogamous. Solitary nester.
- **NESTING** Incubation 10–12 days by female. Young altricial; brooded by female; remain in nest 10 days, fed by both sexes. 1 brood per year (sometimes 2 in the South).
- **POPULATION** Fairly common but numbers declining due to habitat loss on breeding and wintering grounds.
- **CONSERVATION** Neotropical migrant. Common nest host to Brown-headed Cowbird. Vulnerable to habitat loss due to deforestation.

Similar Birds

WOOD THRUSH
Larger; dark spotting on breast, sides, and upper belly; rufous on upperparts, brightest on nape and crown; black streaking on face; white eye ring.

HERMIT THRUSH
Olive- to russet-brown upperparts; pale grayish white underparts with blackish brown spots and speckles; reddish brown tail and rump; white eye ring.

Flight Pattern
Relatively swift direct flight with somewhat hesitant motion on rapidly beating wings.

Nest Identification	
Shape ⌣ ♥ Location ▬ 🌿 🌳	Grass, bark strips, weed stems, twigs, and moss, with lining of soft bark and dry leaves • atop platform on dry ground, sheltered by shrubs, grasses, or weeds; sometimes in low tree or shrub, 0–6 feet above ground • built by female • 3–5 pale blue eggs, usually unmarked; subelliptical to short subelliptical, 0.9 x 0.65 inches.

Plumage Sexes similar	Habitat 🐾 🌾	Migration Migratory	Weight 1.1 ounces

DATE _____ TIME_____ LOCATION _____

Family TURDIDAE	Species *Catharus minimus*	Length 7–7.75 inches	Wingspan 11.5–13.5 inches

GRAY-CHEEKED THRUSH

This bird is a truly long-distance migrant. Each spring some of its population fly from southern Brazil to Alaska, across the Bering Strait, and on to their nesting grounds in eastern Siberia. Others spread across the arctic tundra and northern taiga from Alaska to Newfoundland. It has the most northern nesting range of any spotted thrush. In migration it can be found in almost any habitat from woodlots to city parks. The Newfoundland race has warmer-toned upperparts with a sepia back.

inconspicuous gray eye ring

black upper mandible

olive-gray brown upperparts

black lower mandible with yellowish pink base

gray cheeks

pale buff wash on breast and throat, with black-brown spots

• **SONG** Male sings thin oboelike phrases, somewhat

grayish white underparts

pink legs and feet

like the Veery, but middle phrases rise and first and last ones drop, *wheeoo-titi-wheeoo*. Call is a thin high abrasive *phreu*. Vocal at dawn and especially at dusk.

• **BEHAVIOR** Solitary or in pairs. Shy and retiring, often staying in the dense understory and thickets. More heard than seen. Feeds on spiders, caterpillars, earthworms, various insects, and even small crayfish. In fall migration, feeds more on berries and some fruits.

• **BREEDING** Monogamous. Solitary nester.

• **NESTING** Incubation 13–14 days by female. Young altricial; brooded by female; stay in nest 11–13 days. Fed by female. 1–2 broods per year.

• **POPULATION** Common; southern breeding populations declining due to loss of habitat.

Similar Birds

SWAINSON'S THRUSH
Conspicuous eye ring; browner upperparts; buffy lores, cheeks, throat, and upper breast; buffy underwing linings; different voice.

BICKNELL'S THRUSH
Formerly considered subspecies of Gray-cheeked Thrush
• smaller; warmer brown tones on upperparts, especially on tail and rump; more extensive yellow on lower mandible
• limited range in extreme northeast US
• best separated by voice.

• **CONSERVATION** Neotropical migrant. Vulnerable on both breeding grounds and wintering areas to habitat loss from logging operations and forest fragmentation.

Flight Pattern

Relatively swift direct flight with somewhat jerky wing strokes.

Nest Identification	
Shape 🐚 Location 🌿🌳🌲	Grass, sedge, bark, weed stems, twigs, and moss, with lining of grass, leaves, and fine rootlets • on low branch of tree or shrub, usually 0–10 feet above ground (but as high as 20 feet) • built by female • 3–6 greenish blue to pale blue eggs, most often speckled brown; oval to short oval, 0.9 x 0.65 inches.

Plumage Sexes similar	Habitat 🐦 🌾 🌿	Migration Migratory	Weight 1.2 ounces

DATE _____ TIME_____ LOCATION _____

| Family TURDIDAE | Species *Catharus bicknelli* | Length 6.25 inches | Wingspan 10–11 inches |

BICKNELL'S THRUSH

Except when the male perches at the top of a tree to sing, this shy bird remains hidden in trees and bushes. It is a long-distance migrant that until recently was considered a subspecies of the Gray-cheeked Thrush, from which it is difficult to separate in the field. Its eastern breeding range in the northeastern US, southeastern Canada, and the Maritimes helps to isolate it for identification purposes from the more northern and widespread Gray-cheeked Thrush.

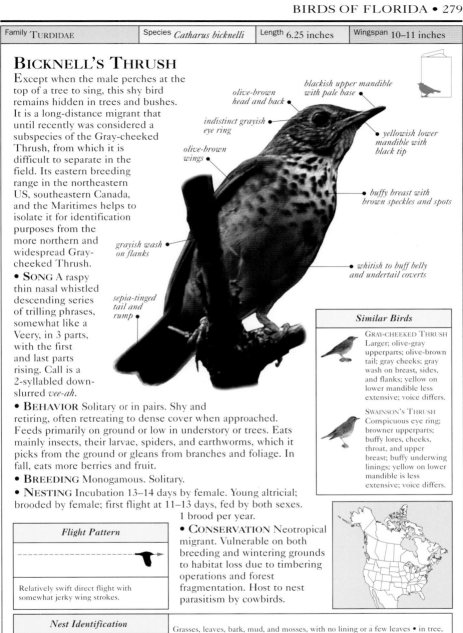

olive-brown head and back
indistinct grayish eye ring
olive-brown wings
blackish upper mandible with pale base
yellowish lower mandible with black tip
buffy breast with brown speckles and spots
grayish wash on flanks
whitish to buff belly and undertail coverts
sepia-tinged tail and rump

• **SONG** A raspy thin nasal whistled descending series of trilling phrases, somewhat like a Veery, in 3 parts, with the first and last parts rising. Call is a 2-syllabled down-slurred *vee-ah*.

• **BEHAVIOR** Solitary or in pairs. Shy and retiring, often retreating to dense cover when approached. Feeds primarily on ground or low in understory or trees. Eats mainly insects, their larvae, spiders, and earthworms, which it picks from the ground or gleans from branches and foliage. In fall, eats more berries and fruit.

• **BREEDING** Monogamous. Solitary.

• **NESTING** Incubation 13–14 days by female. Young altricial; brooded by female; first flight at 11–13 days, fed by both sexes. 1 brood per year.

• **CONSERVATION** Neotropical migrant. Vulnerable on both breeding and wintering grounds to habitat loss due to timbering operations and forest fragmentation. Host to nest parasitism by cowbirds.

Similar Birds

GRAY-CHEEKED THRUSH Larger; olive-gray upperparts; olive-brown tail; gray cheeks; gray wash on breast, sides, and flanks; yellow on lower mandible less extensive; voice differs.

SWAINSON'S THRUSH Conspicuous eye ring; browner upperparts; buffy lores, cheeks, throat, and upper breast; buffy underwing linings; yellow on lower mandible is less extensive; voice differs.

Flight Pattern

Relatively swift direct flight with somewhat jerky wing strokes.

Nest Identification

Shape ● Location

Grasses, leaves, bark, mud, and mosses, with no lining or a few leaves • in tree, about 3–20 feet above ground • built by female • 3–6 greenish blue to pale blue eggs, with faint blotches of brown; oval to short oval, 0.8 x 0.6 inches.

| Plumage Sexes similar | Habitat | Migration Migratory | Weight Undetermined |

DATE _____ TIME_____ LOCATION _____

Family TURDIDAE	Species *Catharus ustulatus*	Length 7 inches	Wingspan 11.5 inches

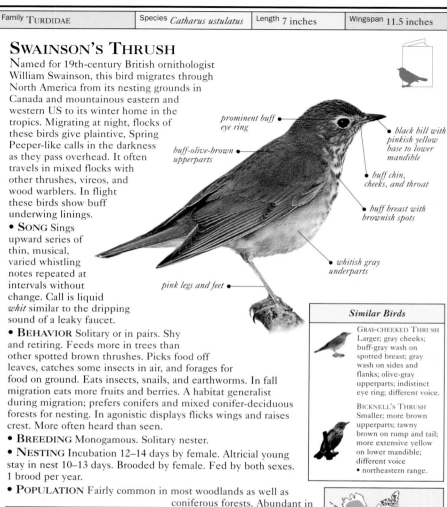

SWAINSON'S THRUSH

Named for 19th-century British ornithologist William Swainson, this bird migrates through North America from its nesting grounds in Canada and mountainous eastern and western US to its winter home in the tropics. Migrating at night, flocks of these birds give plaintive, Spring Peeper-like calls in the darkness as they pass overhead. It often travels in mixed flocks with other thrushes, vireos, and wood warblers. In flight these birds show buff underwing linings.

prominent buff eye ring

buff-olive-brown upperparts

black bill with pinkish yellow base to lower mandible

buff chin, cheeks, and throat

buff breast with brownish spots

whitish gray underparts

pink legs and feet

- **SONG** Sings upward series of thin, musical, varied whistling notes repeated at intervals without change. Call is liquid *whit* similar to the dripping sound of a leaky faucet.
- **BEHAVIOR** Solitary or in pairs. Shy and retiring. Feeds more in trees than other spotted brown thrushes. Picks food off leaves, catches some insects in air, and forages for food on ground. Eats insects, snails, and earthworms. In fall migration eats more fruits and berries. A habitat generalist during migration; prefers conifers and mixed conifer-deciduous forests for nesting. In agonistic displays flicks wings and raises crest. More often heard than seen.
- **BREEDING** Monogamous. Solitary nester.
- **NESTING** Incubation 12–14 days by female. Altricial young stay in nest 10–13 days. Brooded by female. Fed by both sexes. 1 brood per year.
- **POPULATION** Fairly common in most woodlands as well as coniferous forests. Abundant in boreal forests.
- **CONSERVATION** Neotropical migrant. Vulnerable to habitat loss from logging and deforestation on breeding and wintering grounds.

Similar Birds

GRAY-CHEEKED THRUSH Larger; gray cheeks; buff-gray wash on spotted breast; gray wash on sides and flanks; olive-gray upperparts; indistinct eye ring; different voice.

BICKNELL'S THRUSH Smaller; more brown upperparts; tawny brown on rump and tail; more extensive yellow on lower mandible; different voice
• northeastern range.

Flight Pattern

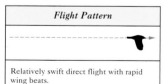

Relatively swift direct flight with rapid wing beats.

Nest Identification	
Shape	Location

Sticks, moss, leaves, plant fibers, and bark with occasional middle layer of mud • lined with lichens, dried leaves, and rootlets • on branch close to trunk of conifer, or occasionally in other trees or shrubs, 0–40 feet (usually 4–20 feet) above ground • built by female • 3–5 pale blue eggs usually flecked with browns; oval to short oval, 0.8 x 0.6 inches.

Plumage Sexes similar	Habitat	Migration Migratory	Weight 1.1 ounces

DATE _____ TIME_____ LOCATION _____

| Family TURDIDAE | Species *Catharus guttatus* | Length 6.75 inches | Wingspan 11.5 inches |

HERMIT THRUSH

Often considered to have one of the most beautiful songs of all North American birds, the Hermit Thrush lives in habitats with coniferous and deciduous trees and along forest edges. It is Vermont's state bird and the only brown-backed spotted thrush to winter in the US. Color variations exist across its broad breeding range: northern Pacific Coast races are smaller and darker with gray flanks; western mountain races are larger and paler also with gray flanks; and eastern races are brownish gray with buff-brown flanks.

distinct white eye ring

blackish upper mandible

olive-brown to russet-brown upperparts

black-tipped lower mandible with pinkish yellow at base

buff wash on breast and throat

reddish brown tail and rump

pale grayish white underparts with blackish brown spots and speckles

pinkish legs and feet

• **SONG** Song begins with long clear low flutelike note and then rises with delicate ringing tones ending in thin, silvery notes; each phrase is repeated, and the pitch differs from that of the previous song. Call note is *chuck*, often doubled; also gives upslurred *whee*.

• **BEHAVIOR** Solitary or in pairs. Often curious and approachable. Responds to pishing sound or imitations of Eastern Screech-Owl by coming close, flicking wings, raising crest, and raising and lowering tail. Often slightly raises and lowers tail upon landing. Sometimes hovers above food on branch or foliage and picks it off with beak. Forages on ground for various insects, insect larvae, and other small invertebrates, including earthworms and snails. Also eats berries and some fruit, especially in autumn migration and winter.

• **BREEDING** Monogamous. Solitary nester.

• **NESTING** Incubation 12–13 days by female. Altricial young remain in nest 12 days; brooded by female, fed by both sexes. 2–3 broods per year.

Similar Birds

VEERY
Reddish brown upperparts; lacks dark spotting on breast; inconspicuous eye ring; different voice.

WOOD THRUSH
Reddish brown upperparts; brightest on crown and nape; heavy black spotting on underparts; different voice.

Flight Pattern
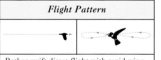
Rather swift direct flight with rapid wing beats. Sometimes hovers briefly over prey before dipping to pick it up.

• **POPULATION** Fairly common. Breeding range is extending southward in southern Appalachians.

• **CONSERVATION** Neotropical migrant. Uncommon host to cowbirds.

Nest Identification	Weeds, rotted wood, twigs, mud, and other fine materials • lined with moss and grass • on ground or low on branch of tree 0–8 feet above ground • occasionally nests in rafters of mountain buildings • built by female • 3–6 greenish blue eggs usually unmarked but sometimes with black flecks; oval to short oval, 0.8 x 0.6 inches.
Shape 🐦 Location	

| Plumage Sexes similar | Habitat 🌳 🌿 🏔 | Migration Most migrate | Weight 1.1 ounces |

DATE _____ TIME_____ LOCATION _____

Family TURDIDAE	Species *Hylocichla mustelina*	Length 7.75–8 inches	Wingspan 13–14 inches

WOOD THRUSH

In early spring, the peaceful flutelike songs of the males are heard throughout the nesting territory, announcing their arrival. It frequents moist forests or large woodlots, but also can be seen in parks, towns, and country gardens. When this heavy-bodied big-eyed short-tailed thrush is agitated, it lifts the feathers on its head like a crest. The song, one of the most beautiful thrush songs, is given before daybreak, but is most prolonged at dusk, when the singer perches high above ground and delivers it in leisurely fashion, rising and falling, until darkness silences him.

bright russet nape and crown

reddish brown upperparts

white eye ring surrounds large dark eye

black bill with creamy pink base to lower mandible

black streaking on white face

large black spots on breast, sides, and flanks

creamy pink legs and feet

• **SONG** A serene flutelike series of triple phrases, the middle note lower than the first, the last note highest and trilled, *ee-o-lee, ee-o-lay*. Call is an abrasive *quirt* or rapid *pit, pit, pit*.

• **BEHAVIOR** Solitary or in pairs. Somewhat shy and retiring but may feed in the open on wooded lawns. Feeds on ground or in trees close to ground, gleaning food from ground or from branches and foliage. Eats various insects, spiders, and fruits; feeds largely on fruits and berries in fall migration. In courtship, male chases female in series of fast twisting circling flights within the male's territory. Territorial in winter.

• **BREEDING** Monogamous. Solitary.

• **NESTING** Incubation 13–14 days by female. Young altricial; brooded by female; remain in nest 12 days, fed by both sexes. 1–2 broods per year.

• **POPULATION** Common in moist deciduous or mixed deciduous-conifer woodlands, often near water. Casual in the West during migration.

• **CONSERVATION** Neotropical migrant. Population declining in recent decades due to nest parasitism by cowbirds, forest fragmentation on breeding grounds, and habitat loss on wintering grounds in Central America.

Similar Birds

VEERY
Smaller; uniform reddish brown upperparts; lacks black spotting of underparts; longer tail; voice differs.

HERMIT THRUSH
Smaller; rich brown to gray-brown upperparts; buff wash on breast; dark spotting confined to throat and upper breast; rufous rump and tail; voice differs.

Flight Pattern
Relatively swift direct flight on rapidly beating wings. Flights in woodlots often of short duration.

Nest Identification	
Shape  Location	Moss, mud, and dried leaves, with lining of fine rootlets • in fork of tree or shrub, usually 6–50 feet above ground (but generally 6–12 feet) • built by female • 2–5 unmarked pale blue or bluish green eggs; short oval to short subelliptical, slightly pointed at end, 1.0 x 0.75 inches.

Plumage Sexes similar	Habitat	Migration Migratory	Weight 1.7 ounces

DATE _____ TIME_____ LOCATION _____

Family TURDIDAE	Species *Turdus migratorius*	Length 10 inches	Wingspan 14–16 inches

AMERICAN ROBIN

In many areas this bird is considered a sign of spring, though it is a year-round resident in most of its US range. It is among the most common, widely distributed, and most well-known birds in North America. Juveniles are similar to adults but have heavily spotted underparts and white spotting and edging on the back and shoulders.

• **SONG** A bold gurgling leisurely *sing-song cheerily cheer-up cheerio*, with phrases often repeated. Has rapid call of *tut-tut-tut* or *hip-hip-hip*.

• **BEHAVIOR** Solitary or in pairs. Gregarious after breeding season; in winter often in flocks and roosts communally with other species. Eats earthworms, insects, and berries. Berries and fruits are principal diet in winter. Defensive of nest site and young. Adapted to human disturbance, especially agricultural areas and the combination of shade trees and lawns. Running-stopping foraging style in fields and lawns.

• **BREEDING** Monogamous. Solitary. Sometimes observed in loose colonies.

• **NESTING** Incubation 12–14 days by female. Altricial young brooded by female; stay in nest 14–16 days; female does more feeding. Male often tends first brood while female begins to incubate second clutch. 2–3 broods per year in south; fewer in north.

• **POPULATION** Abundant and widespread in variety of habitats, including forests, woodlands, gardens, and parks.

• **FEEDERS AND BIRDHOUSES** Will come to feeders for breadcrumbs. Attracted to birdbaths. Uses nesting shelves.

• **CONSERVATION** Neotropical migrant. Becoming more common in the Midwest and onto the Great Plains with planting of shelter belt trees and irrigation. Vulnerable to pesticide poisoning in the food chain.

blackish head

broken white eye ring

dark brownish gray upperparts

yellow bill

white throat with black striping

brick red breast

MALE

white lower belly and undertail coverts

blackish tail has white outer corners

dark brownish gray head

dark brownish gray upperparts

yellow bill

chestnut-orange breast

JUVENILE

FEMALE

Similar Birds

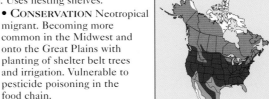

RUFOUS-BACKED ROBIN Rufous chest, back, and wing coverts; gray head and tail; heavy streaking on throat; yellow bill; yellow eye ring • southwestern range.

Flight Pattern

Swift rapid direct flight on strongly beating wings.

Nest Identification

Shape ● Location

Grasses and mud, with lining of fine grass • in all areas of tree, but with shelter from rain, or in building or nest shelf * female does more building • 3–7 pale blue eggs, occasionally white, usually unmarked, but occasionally flecked with brown; oval to short oval, 1.1 x 0.8 inches.

Plumage Sexes differ	Habitat 	Migration Migratory	Weight 2.7 ounces

DATE _____ TIME_____ LOCATION _____

Family MIMIDAE	Species *Dumetella carolinensis*	Length 8.5–9 inches	Wingspan 11–12 inches

GRAY CATBIRD

Its black cap, long tail, and gentle mewing calls are helpful in identifying this tame gray bird. Frequenting thick undergrowth and bushes, it will reside in summer in the ornamental shrubs, thickets, and hedges in farmyards and towns. An accomplished songster with the quality of the other members of the mimic thrush family, it patterns its song with phrases, some squeaky, some melodious, but none repeated. The song is often interrupted with catlike mewing notes. This bird migrates at night. Although primarily migratory, birds on the coastal plain are nonmigratory.

slate-gray upperparts

black tail

black cap

reddish chestnut undertail coverts

short dark bill

pale gray underparts

• **SONG** A mixture of sweet to melodious, thin to squeaky, and sometimes abrasive pharases mixed with pauses. Does not repeat phrases like other eastern mimic thrushes. Some individuals mimic sounds of other birds, amphibians, and machinery, and incorporate them into their song. Distinctive *mew* notes often included in the phrases. Has call of quiet *mew*. Also a harsh *quit* or *chack*.

• **BEHAVIOR** Solitary or in pairs. Often stays low in thick bush and is easily overlooked. Relatively tame, frequently allowing a close approach. Sings from an exposed perch; sometimes sings at night. Often cocks tail upward and flicks from side to side. Gleans food from branches and foliage and picks it from ground. Eats mostly insects, spiders, berries, and fruits. Strongly defends nest and nestlings from predators and intruders. Uncommon cowbird host; recognizes their eggs and ejects them from nest. Often in loose flocks with other species in winter.

• **BREEDING** Monogamous. Solitary nester.

• **NESTING** Incubation 12–13 days by female. Young altricial; brooded by female; stay in nest 10–11 days, fed by both sexes but more by male. 2 broods per year.

• **POPULATION** Common.

Similar Birds
No other bird in its range is slate gray above and below with a long tail.

• **FEEDERS** Cheese, bread, raisins, cornflakes, milk, cream, currants, peanuts, and crackers.

• **CONSERVATION** Neotropical migrant. Uncommon cowbird host.

Flight Pattern
Swift direct flight on rapid wing beats over some distance; short flights often with several rapid wing beats and a short period with wings pulled to sides.

Nest Identification	
Shape 🥄 Location 🪹 🌿	Grass, stems, twigs, and leaves, lined with fine materials • in shrub or tree, 3–10 feet above ground (as high as 50 feet) • built by both sexes but female does more • 2–6 dark blue-green eggs; subelliptical, 0.9 x 0.7 inches.

Plumage Sexes similar	Habitat 🌿 🌲 🏞️	Migration Most migrate	Weight 1.3 ounces

DATE _____ TIME_____ LOCATION _____

Family MIMIDAE	Species *Mimus polyglottos*	Length 10 inches	Wingspan 13–15 inches

NORTHERN MOCKINGBIRD

True to its scientific name, *polyglottos*, meaning "many tongued," this bird imitates dozens of other birds, as well as other animals, insects, machinery, and even musical instruments. Traditionally considered a southern bird, it has adapted to a wide range of habitats, from lush southern plantation gardens to dry cactus land. Although nonmigratory over most of its range, northernmost populations do migrate. When sparring with a rival or when in flight, the large white wing patches and the white outer tail feathers flash conspicuously. Juveniles have underparts spotted with gray-browns.

medium gray upperparts

2 white wing bars

short blackish bill

long blackish gray tail with white outer feathers

large white wing patches on blackish wings

gray-white underparts

• **SONG** Perches to sing a variety of original and imitative sounds, each repeated 3–5 (or more) times. Also has an evening "whisper song." Call is a bold abrasive *check*. Often flutters skyward while singing and tumbles back to perch. May sing well into the night or, on moonlit nights or under the glow of a security light, may sing all night.

JUVENILE

• **BEHAVIOR** Solitary or in pairs. Conspicuous. Forages on ground and in bushes and trees. Lifts wings straight up with a jerky snap to bring insects out of hiding. Eats various insects and fruit. Very defensive during breeding season, especially close to the nest or young. Will attack larger birds and mammals that come too near. Sexes defend separate winter feeding territory. Has adapted well to disturbed habitats created by man and thrives in suburbs, towns, villages, and farmlands.

• **BREEDING** Monogamous. Solitary nester. Long-term pair bonds. Males perform display where they face one another and hop sideways, trying to keep other birds out of territory.

• **NESTING** Incubation 12–13 days by female. Young altricial; brooded by female; stay in nest 11–13 days, fed by both sexes. 2–3 broods per year.

Similar Birds

BAHAMA MOCKINGBIRD
Larger; lacks white wing patches; browner upperparts; streaking on neck and flanks; white-tipped tail
• eastern range.

TOWNSEND'S SOLITAIRE
Darker gray; white eye ring; buff wing patches; shorter bill; white outer tail feathers.

• **POPULATION** Common. Range is expanding north, particularly to the Northeast. Casual north of the mapped distribution range, sometimes as far north as Alaska.

• **FEEDERS** Will come for bread, suet, and raisins.

Flight Pattern

Long flight is swift and strong on steadily beating wings. Shorter flights with several quick wing strokes alternated with wings pulled to sides; repeated.

Nest Identification

Shape 🦅 Location 🌳 🌿 🌱

Sticks, stems, bits of fabric, dead leaves, and string, lined with finer materials • set in fork on branch of tree or shrub, usually 3–10 feet above ground • built by both sexes • 2–6 blue-green eggs, with splotches of brown; oval to short oval, occasionally short subelliptical, 1.0 x 0.8 inches.

Plumage Sexes similar	Habitat 🌲 🏞️ 🌊 🌾	Migration Nonmigratory	Weight 1.7 ounces

DATE ___7|ᵗᵒ|___ TIME_____ LOCATION _____

7|04

Family MIMIDAE	Species *Mimus gundlachii*	Length 11 inches	Wingspan 15.5 inches

BAHAMA MOCKINGBIRD

This native of the West Indies is a rare visitor to the Florida Keys and southern Florida. It is similar to but larger than the Northern Mockingbird. In flight it lacks the large white wing patches of the Northern Mockingbird and the larger, more fan-shaped tail is white only on the tip. It mostly frequents thick scrubby areas but has also made itself at home in the towns, villages, parks, and gardens within its Caribbean range.

- **SONG** Sings a variety of musical melodies, which are loud and varied, but does not imitate other birds or animals. Certain characteristic notes recur with enough frequency to identify the singer, *cheewee, chipwee, chipwoo, cheewoo*. Call is a grating *check* or *chup*.

- **BEHAVIOR** Solitary or in pairs. Somewhat retiring, but male sings from a conspicuous perch, often fluttering straight up for several feet while singing, only to fall back to the perch. Eats various insects, spiders, berries, fruits, and occasionally small reptiles. Snaps wings up with a jerking movement to bring insects out of their hiding places.

- **BREEDING** Monogamous. Solitary nester. Males face one another on the edge of territory, hop sideways, and try to prevent the other male bird from entering its territory.

- **NESTING** Incubation 12–13 days by female. Young altricial; brooded by female; stay in nest 10–12 days, fed by both sexes. 2–3 broods per year.

- **POPULATION** Rare in North America on Dry Tortugas, the Florida Keys (may have nested at Key West), and the mainland of southern Florida.

- **FEEDERS** Will come for raisins, suet, and bread.

- **CONSERVATION** Vulnerable to habitat loss on the Caribbean islands; perhaps some displacement on islands where Northern Mockingbird has been introduced.

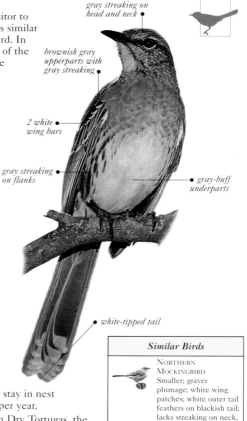

gray streaking on head and neck

brownish gray upperparts with gray streaking

2 white wing bars

gray streaking on flanks

gray-buff underparts

white-tipped tail

Similar Birds

NORTHERN MOCKINGBIRD Smaller; grayer plumage; white wing patches; white outer tail feathers on blackish tail; lacks streaking on neck, back, and flanks.

Flight Pattern

Rather swift direct flight with purposeful wing strokes.

Nest Identification	
Shape ☕ Location 🌳 🌳	Sticks, stems, dried leaves, fiber, paper, bits of fabric, and string, with lining of finer materials • in fork of shrub or low in tree • built by both sexes • 2–6 creamy white or pinkish white eggs, with brown markings; oval to short oval, 1.0 x 0.8 inches.

Plumage Sexes similar	Habitat 🪨 ✈ 🌿 🌲	Migration Nonmigratory	Weight 2.4 ounces

DATE _____ TIME_____ LOCATION _____

Family MIMIDAE	Species *Toxostoma rufum*	Length 11.5 inches	Wingspan 12.5–14 inches

BROWN THRASHER

This shy bird becomes highly aggressive when defending its young, often charging toward the head of any intruder. The male bird sings from an exposed perch, sometimes quite high. It is able to imitate other birds but most often sings its own song, which is a curious mixture of musical phrases. Its bright rufous upperparts and heavily streaked underparts distinguish this species from all other thrashers in its range. Although primarily migratory, birds in the South do not migrate.

long decurved brownish black bill with paler base to lower mandible

deep yellow eyes

reddish brown upperparts

pale buff to white underparts with heavy streaking

2 white wing bars

- **SONG** Male sings conversation-like phrases of *hello, hello, yes, yes, who is this? Who is this? I should say, I should say*, with the varied phrases being given in two's and three's. Reported to have the largest song repertoire of all North American birds with more than 1,100 song types recorded. Call is a bold *smack* or *churr*.
- **BEHAVIOR** Solitary or in pairs. Highly terrestrial; forages on or near ground for food. Finds insects by digging with bill. Eats mainly insects, small amphibians, fruit, and some grains. Runs quickly on ground; turns over leaves and moves debris with bill. Frequents dense brush, early successional stage woodlots, and forest edges. Has adapted to living in shrubby ornamental vegetation of suburbs and gardens.
- **BREEDING** Monogamous. Solitary nester.
- **NESTING** Incubation 11–14 days by both sexes. Young altricial; brooded by female; stay in nest 9–13 days, fed by both sexes. 2–3 broods per year.

long reddish brown tail

Similar Birds

LONG-BILLED THRASHER More brownish gray upperparts; darker streaking on creamy white underparts; 2 white wing bars; longer, more decurved bill; reddish orange eye; long gray-brown tail.

- **POPULATION** Common to fairly common. Rare in the Maritimes and in the West.
- **FEEDERS** Will sometimes tend feeders for raisins, suet, and bread.

Flight Pattern
Rather fast flight on shallow wing beats. Short flights are made with several rapid wing beats alternated with brief periods with wings pulled to sides; repeated.

Nest Identification	
Shape ◗ Location 🐦 ▬ 🌿🌳	Sticks, grasses, and dried leaves, lined with fine grasses • in bush, on ground, or in low tree, usually 1–10 feet above ground • built by both sexes • 2–6 pale bluish white or white eggs, with pale brown specks, occasionally wreathed; oval to short oval, 0.1 x 0.8 inches.

Plumage Sexes similar	Habitat 🏞 🐦 ⛰	Migration Migratory	Weight 2.4 ounces

DATE _____ TIME_____ LOCATION _____

Family STURNIDAE	Species *Sturnus vulgaris*	Length 8.5 inches	Wingspan 15.5 inches

EUROPEAN STARLING

This chunky Eurasian species was introduced to North America in 1890 in New York City's Central Park and has become so well established that large flocks have in some cases become a nuisance, roosting in cities and towns from coast to coast and north into Canada to the tree line. Tenacious in nature, this bird competes with native species such as woodpeckers, flycatchers, and bluebirds for nesting holes. This bird's winter plumage shows white specks and its yellow bill becomes a dull gray. Juveniles are sooty gray-brown overall with pale streaking on the underparts and a dull brown bill.

buffy tips and edging to mantle feathers

short tail

long pointed yellow bill

black overall with iridescent sheen of green and purple

- **SONG** Sings various trilling melodies, clear whistles, clatters, and twitters in groups. Imitates songs of other birds, including Eastern Wood-Pewee and Northern Bobwhite, as well as mechanical sounds. Also has a flutelike *pheeEW*. Singing male often stands erect and flaps wings vigorously in display.

- **BEHAVIOR** Solitary or in pairs in breeding season. Juveniles form foraging flocks. Gregarious after breeding season, forming flocks with juveniles for foraging and roosting. Joins other species in winter roosts, which may number more than a million birds. Most often feeds in open areas, primarily on the ground. Eats various insects, fruits, and grains. The muscles that open its bill are stronger than those that close it, a unique trait that allows this bird to insert its bill in vegetation or into the ground and then pry it open to reveal food.

JUVENILE

- **BREEDING** Monogamous. Often forms loose colonies. Some individual males polygynous. Aggressive in claiming nesting chambers.

- **NESTING** Incubation 12–14 days by both sexes, but female does more. Young altricial; brooded by female; stay in nest 18–21 days, fed by both sexes. First flight at about 26 days. 2–3 broods per year.

- **POPULATION** Common. Stable over most of continent; perhaps still expanding range north and south.

- **FEEDERS AND BIRDHOUSES** Bread, peanut butter, suet, and small seeds. Uses bluebird-sized or larger nest boxes.

- **CONSERVATION** US laws do not protect nongame, nonnative species.

Similar Birds

No native species of blackbird has yellow bill; short tail; chunky body; buffy streaking on back and wing coverts; and a notched tail.

Flight Pattern

Strong swift direct flight on rapidly beating wings.

Nest Identification

Shape

Location

Grass, twigs, forbs, rootlets, and straw • in natural hollow of tree, bird box, crevice in man-made structure, or abandoned woodpecker hole, 10–25 feet above ground (but up to 60 feet) • built by both sexes • 4–8 pale bluish or greenish white eggs, usually unmarked, but sometimes marked with browns; short oval to long oval, 1.2 x 0.8 inches.

Plumage Sexes similar	Habitat	Migration Northern birds migrate	Weight 3.0 ounces

DATE 7/04 TIME _____ LOCATION _____

Family MOTACILLIDAE	Species *Anthus rubescens*	Length 6.5 inches	Wingspan 10–11 inches

AMERICAN PIPIT

This sparrow-sized bird spends most of its time on the open ground, where it runs and walks, rather than hops. Like many of the pipits, the male has a dramatic song flight in which he flies to a height of fifty to two hundred feet then floats down with feet dangling below and tail cocked upward, all the while continuing to sing. The American Pipit's breeding ranges extend from alpine tundra in the high mountains of the western US to arctic tundra across the top of the continent. Winter birds have browner upperparts and they have more heavily streaked underparts.

slim blackish bill

grayish brown upperparts

buffy wing bars on dark gray wings

buff underparts with faint brown streaking

• **SONG** A repetitive rapid series of notes, *chee-chee-chee* or *cheedal-cheedal-cheedal*. Call sounds like *wit, wit* or *pip-pit* and is most often given in flight.

• **BEHAVIOR** Solitary or in pairs; gregarious after breeding season, forming flocks that may be very large and mixed with other species, including Horned Larks and longspurs.

white outer tail feathers

black legs and feet

Walks on ground, often bobbing its head while pumping tail up and down or wagging it. Forages in foliage, grass, and soil. Also wades into shallow waters to pick food from surface. Eats insects and their larvae, seeds, small mollusks, and crustaceans. Alpine species may escape severe weather by moving down mountain slopes to warmer valleys.

• **BREEDING** Monogamous. Solitary nester. Male has courtship song flight.

• **NESTING** Incubation 13–15 days by female. Young altricial; brooded by female; stay in nest 13–15 days, when they can make short flight. Fed by both sexes. 1 brood per year.

• **POPULATION** Common and widespread in tundra and alpine tundra; in winter, in fields and on beaches.

• **CONSERVATION** Neotropical migrant. Vulnerable to habitat loss on wintering grounds as well as foraging areas used during migration.

Similar Birds

SPRAGUE'S PIPIT
Buff- and blackish-streaked upperparts; dark eye on pale buff face with pale eye ring; pinkish to yellow legs and feet; slender yellowish bill; white underparts with deeper buff on lightly streaked breast; does not pump tail.

Flight Pattern

Swift flight on series of rapidly beating wings, alternated with wings pulled to sides; repeated.

Nest Identification	
Shape ᵕ 🥄 Location ▬ ✳✳	Often no nest materials; sometimes sticks and grass, occasionally with lining of small amount of mammal hair • sheltered by bank, rocks, or hillock • built by female • 3–7 grayish white eggs, with brown splotches; subelliptical, 0.8 x 0.6 inches.

Plumage Sexes similar	Habitat ▬ ▲ ▬ 🐾	Migration Migratory	Weight 0.8 ounce

DATE _____ TIME_____ LOCATION _____

Family BOMBYCILLIDAE	Species *Bombycilla cedrorum*	Length 7 inches	Wingspan 11–12.25 inches

CEDAR WAXWING

Named for the red waxlike tips on its secondaries, this social bird travels in large flocks in the nonbreeding season and may even nest in loose colonies. The purpose of the "red wax" is long-debated, but younger birds do not have it and the older birds that do often choose each other as mates and produce more young than the younger pairs. At times this bird may become so intoxicated on overripe fruit that it cannot fly. Females are similar to males but show a brownish rather than a blackish throat (a difficult field mark that can be observed only at close range). Juveniles have streaked upperparts and underparts.

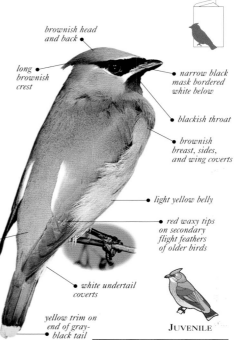

brownish head and back
long brownish crest
narrow black mask bordered white below
blackish throat
brownish breast, sides, and wing coverts
light yellow belly
red waxy tips on secondary flight feathers of older birds
gray rump and uppertail coverts
white undertail coverts
yellow trim on end of gray-black tail

JUVENILE

- **SONG** Call is thin, high-pitched warbled *zeeee* or *zeeeet*, more protracted just before leaving perch; may call constantly in flight.
- **BEHAVIOR** In pairs or in small to large flocks. Gregarious, especially in migration and winter. Tame and sociable. Feeds close to other birds in trees or on ground. Eats fruit, flower petals, and insects; drinks sap. Several may sit on a wire or branch and pass a piece of fruit back and forth, beak to beak. Hawks insects, particularly mayfly hatches and those of similar species, especially along streams.
- **BREEDING** Monogamous. Solitary to colonial. During courtship, male and female will sit together and pass flower petals back and forth, share food, and rub bills.
- **NESTING** Incubation 12–16 days by both sexes. Young altricial; brooded by female; stay in nest 14–18 days, fed by both sexes. 1–2 broods per year.
- **POPULATION** Fairly common to uncommon in woodland, forest edge, farmlands with fruit trees, towns, and suburbs.
- **FEEDERS** Raisins and berries; attracted to birdbaths.
- **CONSERVATION** Neotropical migrant. Not a common cowbird host; often rejects or damages its eggs.

Similar Birds

BOHEMIAN WAXWING
Larger; grayer; cinnamon undertail coverts; white and yellow spots and bars on wings; white bar at base of primaries on folded wing shows as white patch in flight.

Flight Pattern

Strong rapid flight with several quick wing strokes alternating with brief periods of wings pulled to sides.

Nest Identification

Shape ⟶ 🐦 Location 🌲 🌳

Sticks, mosses, and grass, lined with fine grass, moss, rootlets, hair, and pine needles • on limb or in fork of conifer or deciduous tree, 6–60 feet above ground • built by both sexes • 2–6 pale bluish gray eggs, dotted with black and brown; oval, 0.8 x 0.6 inches.

Plumage Sexes similar	Habitat 🐦 🐦	Migration Migratory	Weight 1.1 ounces

DATE _____ TIME_____ LOCATION _____

Family PARULIDAE	Species *Vermivora pinus*	Length 4.75 inches	Wingspan 6.75–7.5 inches

BLUE-WINGED WARBLER

Except when the male perches high to sing, this unobtrusive, deliberate bird usually forages low, amid brushy overgrown fields and thickets. It often interbreeds with the Golden-winged Warbler, producing the fertile hybrids known as Lawrence's Warbler and Brewster's Warbler. The female is similar to the male but duller in color and has less yellow on her crown. When its range overlaps that of the Golden-winged Warbler, it tends to displace it.

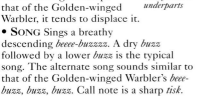

black eye line
olive-green upperparts
bold yellow crown
blue-gray wings with 2 white wing bars
yellowish to white undertail coverts and white underside of tail
long slim bill
bold yellow underparts

- **SONG** Sings a breathy descending *beeee-buzzzz*. A dry *buzz* followed by a lower *buzz* is the typical song. The alternate song sounds similar to that of the Golden-winged Warbler's *beee-buzz, buzz, buzz*. Call note is a sharp *tisk*.
- **BEHAVIOR** Solitary or in pairs. Somewhat tame, but also somewhat inconspicuous. Feeds low in trees and close to ground, often hanging upside down in the manner of a chickadee. Often probes into curled dead leaves with long bill. Eats insects and spiders. Sometimes hover gleans. More generalized in habitat requirements than Golden-winged Warbler, it lives in a wide variety of early successional stages from old fields to young clear-cuts to power line right-of-ways.
- **BREEDING** Monogamous. Solitary or small loose colonies.
- **NESTING** Incubation 10–12 days by female. Young altricial; brooded by female; stay in nest 8–11 days, fed by both sexes. 1–2 broods per year.
- **POPULATION** Uncommon to fairly common in second growth and early successional habitat. Expanding in northern and northeastern portions of range. Casual in West on migration.
- **CONSERVATION** Neotropical migrant. Host to cowbird parasitism. Decreasing in the Midwest due to habitat lost to agriculture.

Similar Birds

YELLOW WARBLER
♀ Female and juvenile • yellow wing bars, tail spots, and undertail coverts; lacks bluish wings, black eye stripe.

PROTHONOTARY WARBLER
♂ Golden yellow head, neck, and underparts; white undertail coverts; blue-gray wings and tail; large white tail patches; olive green back; long black bill; no wing bars or eyeline.

BREWSTER'S WARBLER
Blue-winged/Golden-winged hybrid • yellow or whitish underparts tinged with yellow; whitish to yellowish wing bars.

Flight Pattern

Weak fluttering flight with wings briefly pulled to sides; repeated. Sometimes hovers to glean insects from foliage or branches.

Nest Identification

Shape ●   Location ▬ ⁂

Grasses, dried leaves, and bits of bark, with lining of fine grasses, vines, and hair • on ground, usually in vines or grasses and sheltered by shrub • built by female, perhaps aided by male • 4–7 white eggs; with flecks of brown and gray; oval to short oval, 0.6 x 0.49 inches.

Plumage Sexes similar	Habitat 🌲 〰 🌱	Migration Migratory	Weight 0.3 ounce

DATE _____ TIME_____ LOCATION _____

Family PARULIDAE	Species *Vermivora peregrina*	Length 4.75 inches	Wingspan 7.5–8 inches

TENNESSEE WARBLER

Despite its name, this short-tailed plump-bodied warbler nests almost entirely in Canada and is found in Tennessee only during migration. Fall adults and juveniles are similar to females but have a yellowish wash on the underparts, except for the undertail coverts, which are almost always white.

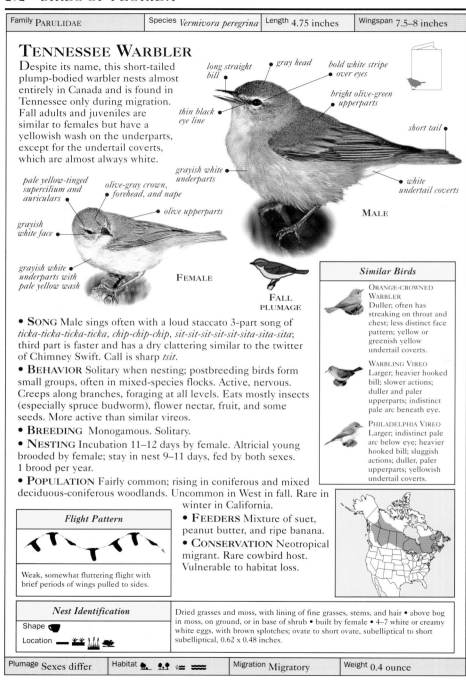

long straight bill

gray head

bold white stripe over eyes

bright olive-green upperparts

thin black eye line

short tail

grayish white underparts

pale yellow-tinged supercilium and auriculars

olive-gray crown, forehead, and nape

white undertail coverts

grayish white face

olive upperparts

MALE

grayish white underparts with pale yellow wash

FEMALE

FALL PLUMAGE

Similar Birds

ORANGE-CROWNED WARBLER
Duller; often has streaking on throat and chest; less distinct face pattern; yellow or greenish yellow undertail coverts.

WARBLING VIREO
Larger; heavier hooked bill; slower actions; duller and paler upperparts; indistinct pale arc beneath eye.

PHILADELPHIA VIREO
Larger; indistinct pale arc below eye; heavier hooked bill; sluggish actions; duller, paler upperparts; yellowish undertail coverts.

• **SONG** Male sings often with a loud staccato 3-part song of *ticka-ticka-ticka-ticka, chip-chip-chip, sit-sit-sit-sit-sit-sita-sita-sita*; third part is faster and has a dry clattering similar to the twitter of Chimney Swift. Call is sharp *tsit*.

• **BEHAVIOR** Solitary when nesting; postbreeding birds form small groups, often in mixed-species flocks. Active, nervous. Creeps along branches, foraging at all levels. Eats mostly insects (especially spruce budworm), flower nectar, fruit, and some seeds. More active than similar vireos.

• **BREEDING** Monogamous. Solitary.

• **NESTING** Incubation 11–12 days by female. Altricial young brooded by female; stay in nest 9–11 days, fed by both sexes. 1 brood per year.

• **POPULATION** Fairly common; rising in coniferous and mixed deciduous-coniferous woodlands. Uncommon in West in fall. Rare in winter in California.

• **FEEDERS** Mixture of suet, peanut butter, and ripe banana.

• **CONSERVATION** Neotropical migrant. Rare cowbird host. Vulnerable to habitat loss.

Flight Pattern
Weak, somewhat fluttering flight with brief periods of wings pulled to sides.

Nest Identification	Dried grasses and moss, with lining of fine grasses, stems, and hair • above bog in moss, on ground, or in base of shrub • built by female • 4–7 white or creamy white eggs, with brown splotches; ovate to short ovate, subelliptical to short subelliptical, 0.62 x 0.48 inches.
Shape ◗	
Location ▬ ✹ ⸜⸝⸜ ⸙	

Plumage Sexes differ	Habitat 🐾 🌿 ⸗ 〰	Migration Migratory	Weight 0.4 ounce

DATE _____ TIME_____ LOCATION _____

Family PARULIDAE	Species *Vermivora celata*	Length 4.75–5 inches	Wingspan 7–8 inches

ORANGE-CROWNED WARBLER

The brownish orange head patch for which this warbler is named is rarely noticeable unless the bird is frightened or agitated. It most often lives and nests in thick foliage close to the ground, but the male perches at the tops of tall trees to sing. Considerable color variation in this widely distributed species ranges from dull greenish birds in the East to brighter yellow birds in the West. The female

pale yellowish supercilium

indistinct dark eye line

thin slightly decurved bill

olive-green upperparts

faint streaking on sides of breast

small yellowish patch on marginal wing coverts

paler yellowish green underparts

yellow undertail coverts

sometimes lacks the crown patch. Juveniles are similar to adults but may show indistinct wing bars.

• **SONG** Male sings a high-pitched abrupt trill, which changes pitch toward the end, often slowing and dropping, *chip-ee, chip-ee, chip-ee*. Call note is a rough *stic*.

• **BEHAVIOR** Solitary. Vocal. Slow deliberate actions. Forages for food along branches and in foliage low in trees, shrubs, and grasses. Probes curled dead leaves. Eats mainly insects, flower nectar, and some fruits. Feeds from sapsucker drill wells. Hardy species, wintering farther north than most other warblers. Inquisitive; will respond to pishing and squeaking by birders.

• **BREEDING** Monogamous. Solitary.

• **NESTING** Incubation 12–14 days by female. Young altricial; brooded by female; stay in nest 8–10 days, fed by both sexes. 1 brood per year.

Similar Birds

YELLOW WARBLER ♀
Female and juvenile
• pale edging to tertials, flight feathers, and wing coverts; yellow tail spots; dark eye on pale face.

NASHVILLE WARBLER
Clear yellow underparts with no streaking; clear white eye ring; shorter tail.

TENNESSEE WARBLER
Fall plumage • greener upperparts; shorter tail; unstreaked underparts; white undertail coverts.

• **POPULATION** Common in the West; rarer in the East.

• **FEEDERS** Mixture of peanut butter and suet. Also eats doughnuts.

• **CONSERVATION** Neotropical migrant. Rare cowbird host.

Flight Pattern

Somewhat weak flight with series of wing beats followed by brief period of wings pulled to sides.

Nest Identification

Shape 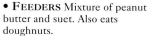 Location

Bark pieces, grass, leaves, and plant fibers, with lining of hair, feathers, and grass • on ground, usually sheltered by shrub or grasses • built by female • 3–6 white eggs, with dark red and brown blotches; short ovate, 0.65 x 0.5 inches.

Plumage Sexes similar	Habitat	Migration Migratory	Weight 0.3 ounce

DATE _____ TIME_____ LOCATION _____

Family PARULIDAE	Species *Vermivora ruficapilla*	Length 4.75 inches	Wingspan 7.25–7.75 inches

NASHVILLE WARBLER

First collected while migrating near Nashville, Tennessee, this is the only North American warbler with a yellow throat, no wing bars, a white eye ring, and a blue-gray head. It also has a chestnut crown that is rarely noticeable. It has two breeding populations: one in the Pacific Coast states that often wags its tail, and another in northeastern and midwestern North America that does not wag its tail. The female is similar to the male but is duller in color and often lacks the chestnut crown.

white eye ring

blue-gray head

olive-green upperparts

bright yellow throat

yellowish underparts

white area between yellow belly and yellow undertail

- **SONG** High-pitched and loud, in 2 parts, *see-bit, see-bit, see-bit, titititititit* in the eastern birds, similar to that of the Tennessee Warbler. Western bird's songs begin the same way, but the second part is more musical, richer, and generally without the trill at the end. Call note is a sharp *pink*.
- **BEHAVIOR** Solitary. Frequent singer on territory. Sometimes gives song in flight. Sings from high exposed perch. Forages low in trees and in undergrowth for food, but often at the tips of branches or stems. Eats mostly insects.
- **BREEDING** Monogamous. Solitary.
- **NESTING** Incubation 11–12 days by both sexes; female does more. Young altricial; brooded by female; stay in nest 11 days, fed by both sexes but mostly by female. 1 brood per year.
- **POPULATION** Common to fairly common in riparian woodlands and bogs, deciduous or coniferous woodlands, and thickets.
- **CONSERVATION** Neotropical migrant. Rare cowbird host. Vulnerable to habitat loss.

Similar Birds

VIRGINIA'S WARBLER Grayer overall; yellow underparts restricted to chest and undertail coverts; white eye ring; shorter tail • ranges do not overlap.

CONNECTICUT WARBLER Larger; gray head; grayish throat; white eye ring; pink legs and feet; yellow underparts, including belly; sluggish behavior walking on limbs and on ground.

Flight Pattern

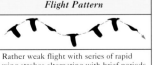

Rather weak flight with series of rapid wing strokes alternating with brief periods of wings pulled to sides.

Nest Identification

Shape   Location

Plant stems, pine needles, mosses, and rabbit fur, with lining of finer materials • on ground, sheltered by shrub or small tree, or sometimes placed on grassy or mossy tussock • built by female • 4–5 white or cream-white eggs, with fine dots of brown; ovate to short ovate, 0.6 x 0.47 inches.

Plumage Sexes similar	Habitat	Migration Migratory	Weight 0.3 ounce

DATE _____ TIME_____ LOCATION _____

Family PARULIDAE	Species *Parula americana*	Length 4.25 inches	Wingspan 7 inches

NORTHERN PARULA

The male often can be heard singing its buzzy song during migration and from the tops of tall trees on its nesting ground. Nesting in the Deep South, it most often is associated with Spanish moss-covered trees, while more northern nests are in trees laced with the lichen *Usnea*. Both are important for construction of the nest. Females lack the chestnut/slate breast bands.

broken white eye ring

bluish gray upperparts

2 bold white wing bars

bold yellow chin, throat, and breast

chestnut and slate to blackish bands across upper breast

white belly and undertail coverts

short blue-gray tail with white spots in outer tail feathers

• **SONG** Ascending insectlike buzzy trill of *zeeeeeeee-yip*, which rises and trips over the top; the equivalent of the bird filling a cup with its song and running it over the rim. Secondary song is series of slow rising buzzy notes ending in a trill, reminiscent of the Cerulean Warbler. Regional variation; western birds often lack the abrupt downward ending note. Call note is a sharp *chip*.
• **BEHAVIOR** Solitary or in pairs. Allows close approach. Active, acrobatic forager; sometimes upside down to hunt for insects on trunk, cluster of leaves, or branch tip; hover gleans and hawks flying insects. Eats insects, caterpillars and larvae, and spiders. One of the smallest warblers, often dominated by other birds, including other warbler species.
• **BREEDING** Monogamous. Solitary.
• **NESTING** Incubation 12–14 days by both sexes; more by female. Altricial young brooded by and fed mostly by female. 1–2 broods per year.
• **POPULATION** Common in boreal forest, mixed hardwoods, bottomland forests, riparian corridors, and swamps. Rare in the West in migration.
• **CONSERVATION** Neotropical migrant. Rare cowbird host. Vulnerable to habitat loss due to logging, clearing of bottomland hardwoods for agriculture. Declining in Great Lakes region and on Atlantic Coast due to loss of *Usnea* lichen as a result of air pollutants.

Similar Birds
 TROPICAL PARULA More extensive yellow on underparts; orange wash on breast; lacks chestnut and gray-black chest bands; lacks white eye ring; often has dark mask.

Flight Pattern
Relatively swift flight of short duration on rapidly beating wings. Sallies forth to take insects in midair, returning to perch.

Nest Identification	
Shape Location	Lined with fine grasses, moss, and plant down • in Spanish moss, *Usnea* lichen, or tangled vine, hanging from tree, 0–55 feet above ground • built by female • 3–7 white to creamy white eggs, splotched and flecked with browns; subelliptical to short subelliptical, 0.64 x 0.47 inches.

Plumage Sexes differ	Habitat	Migration Migratory	Weight 0.3 ounce

DATE _____ TIME_____ LOCATION _____

Family PARULIDAE	Species *Dendroica petechia*	Length 5 inches	Wingspan 7.75 inches

YELLOW WARBLER

This plump-bodied bird has a wider range than any other North American warbler, nesting from Canada to Mexico and from the Pacific to the Atlantic Coasts. A habitat generalist, like many warblers, it feeds harmful leaf-eating caterpillars to its nestlings. When a cowbird invades and lays eggs in this warbler's nest, the female builds a roof over all of the eggs, both hers and the brood parasite's, and often lays a new set on the "new" nest floor. As many as six stories have been found in a single nest, each floor containing entombed cowbird eggs. Bright red streaking on the male's underparts distinguishes him from the female and all other North American warblers. Females may have faint reddish streaking on their underparts. Juveniles resemble adult females.

bright yellow head

dark eye contrasts with yellow face

short tail with yellow edging on feathers

yellowish overall

MALE

bright yellow underparts with reddish streaking

- **SONG** Sings a swift warbling *sweet-sweet, I'm-so-sweet* or *tseet-tseet-tseet-titi-deet*, bouncy and variable. Similar to some songs of Chestnut-sided Warbler and American Redstart.
- **BEHAVIOR** Solitary or in pairs. Tame and conspicuous. Active. Forages in bushes, shrubs, or trees. Gleans food from branches and foliage; sometimes hawks insects. Eats mostly insects, larvae, and some fruit.
- **BREEDING** Monogamous. Solitary.
- **NESTING** Incubation 11–12 days by female. Altricial young brooded by female; stay in nest 9–12 days, fed by both sexes. 1–2 broods per year.
- **POPULATION** Common and widespread in riparian thickets, second-growth woodlands, gardens, orchards, and wetlands.
- **CONSERVATION** Neotropical migrant. Common host to cowbird parasitism. Vulnerable to habitat loss, especially in riparian areas, and to herbicide spraying of willow thickets for grazing.

yellowish olive back, wings, and tail

yellow wing bars and edging

FEMALE

Similar Birds

WILSON'S WARBLER ♀
Female and juvenile
• longer darker tail; lacks yellow tail spots; more uniform olive-green coloring on upperparts; no wing bars; female may show trace of dark cap.

ORANGE-CROWNED WARBLER
Olive-green overall; paler underparts with dusky streaking; uniform dark tail without pale edging or spots; lacks wing bars.

Flight Pattern

Weak, fluttering flight with brief periods of wings drawn to sides. Sallies out to snatch insects in air and returns to perch.

Nest Identification

Shape ◗ Location 🌿 🌳

Strongly built from plant material, grasses, moss, lichen, and fur, bound with spider's silk and cocoon material; lined with fine materials • in fork of tree or bush, 6–14 feet high (but up to 60 feet) • built mostly by female; male watches • 3–6 grayish, green, or bluish white eggs, splotched with grays, olives, and browns, wreathed at large end; oval to short oval, 0.7 x 0.5 inches.

Plumage Sexes differ	Habitat	Migration Migratory	Weight 0.3 ounce

DATE _____ TIME_____ LOCATION _____

Family PARULIDAE	Species *Dendroica pensylvanica*	Length 5–5.25 inches	Wingspan 7.5–8.25 inches

CHESTNUT-SIDED WARBLER

The only North American warbler with pure white underparts in all seasons, this bird most often lives in second-growth deciduous woodlands. An active feeder, it often cocks its tail high above its back, exposing a white crissum. Birds in fall plumage have a white eye ring on a gray face, a green crown, and creamy yellow wing bars; males have chestnut on the sides and black streaking on a green back.

light olive-green upperparts with black streaking

yellow crown

black lores and eye stripe

2 pale yellow wing bars

black malar mark

MALE

rich chestnut sides

slate-blue legs and feet

white underparts

- **SONG** High-pitched *please-please-pleased-to-meetcha.* Alternate or "second" song lacks strong up-and-down slurred notes at the end and is similar to that of the Yellow Warbler, *deet-deet-deet-titi-deet.* Call is a husky slurred *chip.*
- **BEHAVIOR** Solitary or in pairs. Tame and active. Singing male is conspicuous on territory. Eats insects, caterpillars, seeds, and berries. Picks food off leaves of trees and forages on ground. Catches insects in flight.
- **BREEDING** Monogamous. Solitary.
- **NESTING** Incubation 11–13 days by female. Altricial young brooded by female; remain in nest 10–12 days, fed by both sexes. 1–2 broods per year.
- **POPULATION** Fairly common to common in brushy thickets, second-growth deciduous woodlands, brushy old fields, and young clear-cuts. Rare migrant in West.
- **CONSERVATION** Neotropical migrant. Vulnerable to habitat loss through natural succession processes. Rare in the early 1800s, but became increasingly common as eastern forests were cut, and brushy, early succession-stage woody habitats emerged. Declining in some areas as current forests mature.

2 yellowish white wing bars

greenish upperparts with black streaking

yellow-green crown and forehead

FALL PLUMAGE

FEMALE

blackish gray lores, malar, and postocular stripe

less chestnut on sides

Similar Birds

All plumages are distinctive and if seen well are not likely to be confused with any other warbler.

Flight Pattern

Weak fluttering flight with brief periods of wings drawn to sides. Sallies forth to snatch insects in air, returning to perch.

Nest Identification

Shape ☕   Location 🪹 🌿

Bark chips, vines, and plant material, with lining of animal hair and grasses • in fork of small tree or shrub, or in blackberry thicket, 1–4 feet above ground • built by female • 3–5 white to greenish white or creamy white eggs, with purple and brown blotches; oval to short oval, 0.66 x 0.5 inches.

Plumage Sexes differ	Habitat 🪶 🔺	Migration Migratory	Weight 0.4 ounce

DATE _____ TIME_____ LOCATION _____

Family PARULIDAE	Species *Dendroica magnolia*	Length 5 inches	Wingspan 7.75 inches

MAGNOLIA WARBLER

Often fanning its tail to show its broad white subterminal band and yellow rump, this bird nests in damp coniferous forests. The tail from below is white at the base with a black terminal band. From above, the white band is interrupted in the middle. Females are similar but show two white wing bars and sometimes a white eye ring during their first spring; a black loral mask may extend onto auriculars. Juveniles and fall-plumaged birds have gray heads with white eye rings, greenish gray upperparts with black streaking on the males, black streaking on the sides and flanks of males, and faint streaking on the flanks of females.

- **SONG** Brief high-pitched *wee-o, wee-o, wee-chew* or *weety-weety-weeteeo*, 2 or 3 slurred phrases with an ending note higher in pitch, emphatic and down-slurred. Call is distinctive nasal dry chip *tzek.*
- **BEHAVIOR** Solitary or in pairs. Tame and active. Males sing from conspicuous perches or while foraging. Often spreading tail, busily gleans insects from branches and foliage; occasionally hawks them in flight. Eats insects, larvae, caterpillars, and spiders.
- **BREEDING** Monogamous. Solitary.
- **NESTING** Incubation 11–13 days by female. Altricial young brooded by female; stay in nest 8–10 days, fed by both sexes. 1 brood per year.
- **POPULATION** Fairly common to common; slight decline in parts of Appalachians, increase in southern Appalachians and in New England. Casual in winter in Florida. Rare migrant in West.
- **CONSERVATION** Neotropical migrant. Vulnerable to habitat loss. The loss of eastern spruce-fir forests to adelgids and air pollution is causing a decline in numbers.

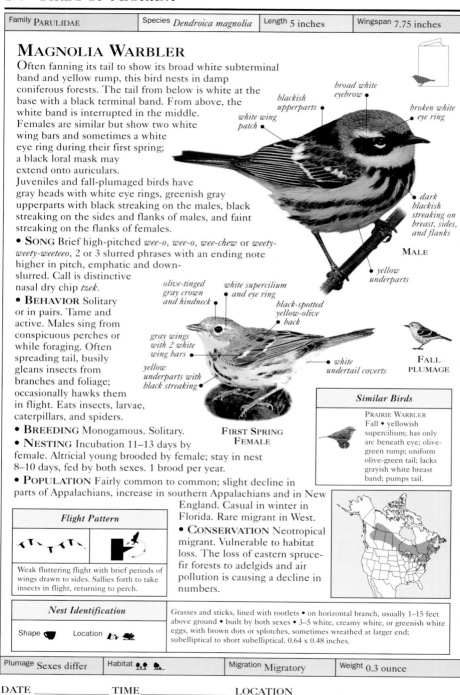

broad white eyebrow

blackish upperparts

broken white eye ring

white wing patch

dark blackish streaking on breast, sides, and flanks

MALE

yellow underparts

olive-tinged gray crown and hindneck

white supercilium and eye ring

black-spotted yellow-olive back

gray wings with 2 white wing bars

yellow underparts with black streaking

white undertail coverts

FALL PLUMAGE

FIRST SPRING FEMALE

Similar Birds

PRAIRIE WARBLER
Fall • yellowish supercilium; has only arc beneath eye; olive-green rump; uniform olive-green tail; lacks grayish white breast band; pumps tail.

Flight Pattern

Weak fluttering flight with brief periods of wings drawn to sides. Sallies forth to take insects in flight, returning to perch.

Nest Identification

Shape 🥣 Location 🌿 🌳

Grasses and sticks, lined with rootlets • on horizontal branch, usually 1–15 feet above ground • built by both sexes • 3–5 white, creamy white, or greenish white eggs, with brown dots or splotches, sometimes wreathed at larger end; subelliptical to short subelliptical, 0.64 x 0.48 inches.

Plumage Sexes differ	Habitat 🌿 🌳	Migration Migratory	Weight 0.3 ounce

DATE _____ TIME_____ LOCATION _____

Family PARULIDAE	Species *Dendroica tigrina*	Length 4.75 inches	Wingspan 7 inches

CAPE MAY WARBLER

Identifiable by its chestnut cheek patches, this bird is named after Cape May, New Jersey, where it was discovered in 1811. This fairly common inhabitant of northern spruce forests is known for its aggressive behavior of chasing other birds from treetop foraging areas. Females are duller but are easily identified by the yellow rump and patches on the side of the neck. Juveniles and fall-plumaged birds are similar to females, but many have faint gray streaking on pale yellow to whitish underparts.

• **SONG** Sounds like *seet seet seet seet*, high-pitched, wiry, and upslurred, usually in series of 5–6 notes. Call is high thin *seet*.

• **BEHAVIOR** Solitary or in pairs. Forages in thickets or high in trees, particularly in conifers on breeding grounds. Hawks insects and spruce budworms. Sometimes drinks tree sap, juice from grapes, and flower nectar.

• **BREEDING** Monogamous. Solitary.

• **NESTING** Breeding biology poorly known. Incubation about 11–13 days by female. Altricial young brooded by female; fed by both sexes; stay in nest estimated 10–12 days. 1 brood per year.

• **POPULATION** Uncommon in spruce fir forests; may become locally common during spruce budworm outbreaks. Declining short-term populations. Very rare to casual in West during migration.

• **CONSERVATION** Neotropical migrant. Vulnerable to loss of breeding and wintering grounds due to deforestation and forest fragmentation.

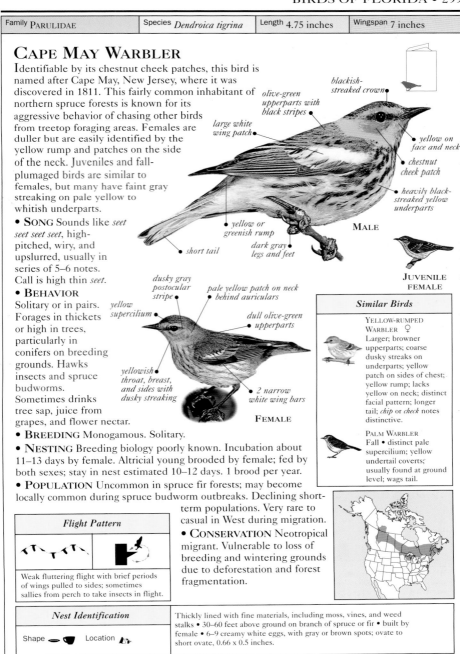

blackish-streaked crown

olive-green upperparts with black stripes

large white wing patch

yellow on face and neck

chestnut cheek patch

heavily black-streaked yellow underparts

yellow or greenish rump

short tail

dark gray legs and feet

MALE

JUVENILE FEMALE

dusky gray postocular stripe

pale yellow patch on neck behind auriculars

yellow supercilium

dull olive-green upperparts

yellowish throat, breast, and sides with dusky streaking

2 narrow white wing bars

FEMALE

Similar Birds

YELLOW-RUMPED WARBLER ♀
Larger; browner upperparts; coarse dusky streaks on underparts; yellow patch on sides of chest; yellow rump; lacks yellow on neck; distinct facial pattern; longer tail; *chip* or *check* notes distinctive.

PALM WARBLER
Fall • distinct pale supercilium; yellow undertail coverts; usually found at ground level; wags tail.

Flight Pattern	

Weak fluttering flight with brief periods of wings pulled to sides; sometimes sallies from perch to take insects in flight.

Nest Identification	
Shape Location	Thickly lined with fine materials, including moss, vines, and weed stalks • 30–60 feet above ground on branch of spruce or fir • built by female • 6–9 creamy white eggs, with gray or brown spots; ovate to short ovate, 0.66 x 0.5 inches.

Plumage Sexes differ	Habitat	Migration Migratory	Weight 0.4 ounce

DATE _____ TIME_____ LOCATION _____

Family PARULIDAE	Species *Dendroica caerulescens*	Length 5.25 inches	Wingspan 7–7.5 inches

BLACK-THROATED BLUE WARBLER

Easily identified by its deep blue-gray back, white underparts, and white wing patch, this common migratory bird can be seen across eastern North America every spring and fall. Its nesting ranges from southern Canada through the Appalachians to northern Georgia. Females differ from their mates more than any of the wood warblers, with brownish olive to gray upperparts, whitish supercilium, and small white patch at the base of the primaries. Juvenile females sometimes lack the white patch.

dark blue-gray upperparts

black lores, cheeks, chin, and throat

small white tail patches

bold white patch at base of primaries

black sides

white underparts

pale eyebrow contrasts with dark face

brownish olive to bluish gray upperparts

blackish legs and feet

dark b

MALE

- **SONG** A breathy buzzy *zwee-zwee-zwee-zweeeee,* "*I am lazy,*" or *zur-zurr-zree.* Call is abrasive *dit.*

- **BEHAVIOR** Solitary or in pairs. Tame and trusting. Forages in low and middle level trees and underbrush. Sometimes hawks insects in flight. Eats insects and their larvae. In migration and winter, also takes fruit and seeds and may feed from sapsucker drill wells.

buff underparts

smaller white wing patch

FEMALE

- **BREEDING** Monogamous. Solitary nester.
- **NESTING** Incubation 12–13 days by female. Young altricial; brooded by female; stay in nest 1–12 days, fed by both sexes. 1 brood per year.
- **POPULATION** Common in deciduous and mixed coniferous forests with dense undergrowth, rhododendron thickets, and bogs, often on mountain slopes. Western vagrant in migration. Uncommon in winter in Florida.

- **FEEDERS** Suet and peanut butter in migration and winter.
- **CONSERVATION** Neotropical migrant. Uncommon host to cowbird parasitism. Vulnerable to habitat loss due to deforestation.

Similar Birds

TENNESSEE WARBLER Unbroken whitish supercilium; lacks white wing patch; bright greenish olive back; grayish white underparts with white crissum; short tail.

ORANGE-CROWNED WARBLER Yellow to greenish olive upperparts; yellow-green underparts; yellowish crissum; indistinct supercilium.

Flight Pattern

Relatively weak flight with series of rapid wing beats alternating with brief periods of wings pulled to sides. Sallies from perch to snatch insect in air; returns to perch.

Nest Identification

Shape 🐦   Location 🪹 🌳

Bark pieces, dried grasses, stems, and leaves, with lining of fur, hair, mosses, and rootlets • built by both sexes • 0.5–3 feet above ground • 3–5 white to creamy white eggs, flecked or marked with grays and browns; ovate to short ovate, rarely tending to elongate ovate, 0.66 x 0.5 inches.

Plumage Sexes differ	Habitat 🌿 🐦 🌲 🔺	Migration Migratory	Weight 0.4 ounce

DATE _____ TIME_____ LOCATION _____

| Family PARULIDAE | Species *Dendroica coronata* | Length 5.5 inches | Wingspan 8.5 inches |

YELLOW-RUMPED WARBLER

In the East this is the most prevalent migrating warbler, and in winter it is the most abundant in North America. Plumage varies with geography. In the West the group known as Audubon's Warbler has a yellow throat and broken white eye ring. The northern and eastern group known as the Myrtle Warbler has white eyebrows, a white arc beneath the eye, and white on the throat and both sides of the neck. Until recently these groups were considered two species, but they interbreed where their ranges overlap and have been classified as geographic races of one species. Juveniles are similar to winter adults.

black auricular patch
yellow crown patch
gray upperparts
2 white wing bars
yellow rump
black streaking on breast, sides, and flanks

MALE MYRTLE WARBLER

white underparts

- **SONG** Variable slow warble that often slows in the middle then speeds up and ends on rising or falling notes. Some have musical trill. Call is loud *check*, *chup*, or *chip*.

black-streaked gray-brown upperparts
gray-brown wings
white arc below eye

FEMALE MYRTLE WARBLER

yellow side patches

AUDUBON'S BREEDING MALE

white underparts with gray streaks on breast and sides

WINTER PLUMAGE   **FALL MYRTLE**

- **BEHAVIOR** Solitary or in pairs. Gregarious in winter, often joins mixed feeding flocks. Gleans or hover-gleans on ground and in bushes and trees; also hawks. Able to live for long periods on berries and seeds. Also eats insects and spiders, and drinks tree sap and juice from fallen oranges.
- **BREEDING** Monogamous. Solitary.
- **NESTING** Incubation 12–13 days by female. Altricial young brooded by female; stay in nest 10–12 days, fed by both sexes. 2 broods per year.
- **POPULATION** Abundant in coniferous or mixed forests; wooded and brushy habitats in winter. In winter Myrtle form common in East, fairly common on West Coast; Audubon's form casual in East in winter.
- **FEEDERS** Suet, doughnuts, and peanut butter.
- **CONSERVATION** Neotropical migrant. Myrtles are common cowbird hosts.

Similar Birds

PALM WARBLER Juvenile • yellow undertail coverts; white spots in tail corners; pumps tail.

CAPE MAY WARBLER Juvenile • smaller; yellow on sides of neck; shorter tail; dull green rump; pale yellow wash on center of breast.

Flight Pattern

Fairly rapid flight with quick wing strokes, alternating with brief periods of wings pulled to sides. Sallies forth and takes insects in flight, returning to perch.

Nest Identification

Shape / Location

Shredded bark, weed stalks, twigs, and roots, lined with feathers • 4–50 feet above ground in conifer • built by female • 3–5 white to creamy eggs, with brown and gray markings, occasionally wreathed; oval to short oval, 0.7 x 0.53 inches.

| Plumage Sexes differ | Habitat | Migration Migratory | Weight 0.5 ounce |

DATE _____ TIME _____ LOCATION _____

Family PARULIDAE	Species *Dendroica virens*	Length 4.75–5 inches	Wingspan 7.5–8 inches

BLACK-THROATED GREEN WARBLER

Like many in its family, the individual Black-throated Green Warbler sings two different songs, but in two different contexts: one in the vicinity of the female or nest and the other near the territorial boundaries or when stimulated by another male. It is the only warbler in eastern North America with bold yellow cheeks. The female is similar to the male but shows fewer black streaks on the sides of her body, less black on her throat, and has a yellowish chin and upper throat. The juvenile is similar to the female but has a white throat and lacks the black on its breast.

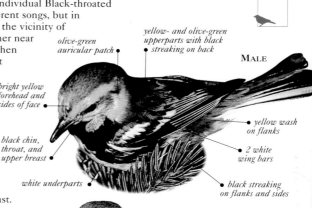

olive-green auricular patch

yellow- and olive-green upperparts with black streaking on back

MALE

bright yellow forehead and sides of face

black chin, throat, and upper breast

white underparts

yellow wash on flanks

2 white wing bars

black streaking on flanks and sides

yellowish chin

black throat veiled with whitish feather tips

FEMALE

- **SONG** A throaty *trees-trees-whispering-trees* (the territorial/male interaction song) and a hoarse *zay-zay-zay-zoo-zeee* (the pair bonding/nest vicinity song). Call is a flat soft *tsip*.
- **BEHAVIOR** Solitary or in pairs. Forages at mid-level in vegetation and in the interior of branches, usually not at the tips. Gleans from twigs and foliage; hover-gleans and may hawk flying prey. Eats adult insects, caterpillars, larvae, and some berries, particularly in migration.
- **BREEDING** Monogamous. Solitary.
- **NESTING** Incubation 12 days by female. Young altricial; brooded by female; remain in nest 8–10 days, fed by both sexes, but female does more. 1–2 broods per year.
- **POPULATION** Fairly common in a variety of habitats of conifer, mixed deciduous-conifer, and deciduous woodlands. Some winter regularly in southern Florida; casual to accidental in the West. Numbers decreasing in the Great Lakes areas and in parts of New England.
- **CONSERVATION** Neotropical migrant. Vulnerable to habitat loss. Rare host to cowbird parasitism.

Similar Birds

♂ ♀ **GOLDEN-CHEEKED WARBLER** Gray to black upperparts with black streaking; black or black-streaked crown; yellow face; black eye line connected to the dark color of nape; black ear patch; white crissum • restricted range in Texas.

Flight Pattern	

Somewhat weak flight with rapid wing strokes, alternating with brief periods of wings pulled to sides. Sallies from perch, takes insect in air, and returns to perch.

Nest Identification	
Shape 🍵 Location	Dead grasses, plant fibers, and stems, with lining of animal hair, flower stems, and feathers • usually in crotch of small or large evergreen in hardwood tree on horizontal branch, 3–80 feet above ground • built by both sexes • 3–5 gray-white or creamy white eggs, with brown and purple dots and blotches, often wreathed; oval to short oval, 0.65 x 0.5 inches.

Plumage Sexes differ	Habitat	Migration Migratory	Weight 0.3 ounce

DATE _____ TIME_____ LOCATION _____

Family PARULIDAE	Species *Dendroica fusca*	Length 5 inches	Wingspan 8 inches

BLACKBURNIAN WARBLER

Head and throat glowing like embers, the males are unmistakable. Juveniles and fall males are similar. It frequents coniferous or mixed deciduous-conifer forests in most of its breeding range; in the Appalachians, it is also found in lower drier forests of pine-oak-hickory.

- **SONG** Thin high-pitched ascending trill in 2–3 parts, ending with upslurred note that some people cannot hear: *seep seep seep seep titi zeeeeee*. Call is rich *tsip*.
- **BEHAVIOR** Solitary or in pairs. May join mixed foraging flocks after breeding. Gleans prey from branches, twigs, and foliage in treetops. Sometimes catches insects in flight. Eats insects, caterpillars, and some berries.

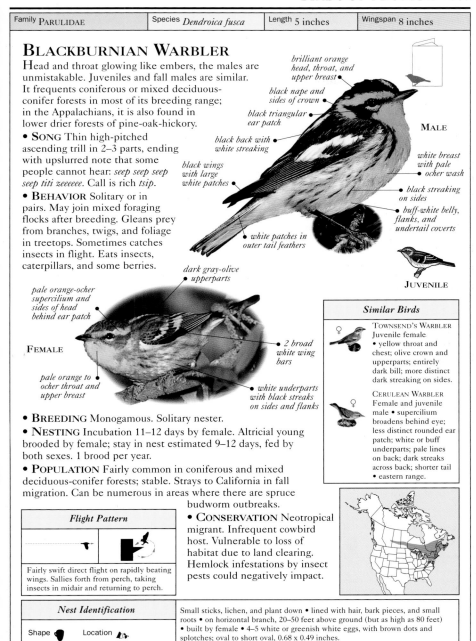

brilliant orange head, throat, and upper breast

black nape and sides of crown

black triangular ear patch

black back with white streaking

black wings with large white patches

MALE

white breast with pale ocher wash

black streaking on sides

buff-white belly, flanks, and undertail coverts

white patches in outer tail feathers

dark gray-olive upperparts

JUVENILE

pale orange-ocher supercilium and sides of head behind ear patch

FEMALE

pale orange to ocher throat and upper breast

2 broad white wing bars

white underparts with black streaks on sides and flanks

- **BREEDING** Monogamous. Solitary nester.
- **NESTING** Incubation 11–12 days by female. Altricial young brooded by female; stay in nest estimated 9–12 days, fed by both sexes. 1 brood per year.
- **POPULATION** Fairly common in coniferous and mixed deciduous-conifer forests; stable. Strays to California in fall migration. Can be numerous in areas where there are spruce budworm outbreaks.
- **CONSERVATION** Neotropical migrant. Infrequent cowbird host. Vulnerable to loss of habitat due to land clearing. Hemlock infestations by insect pests could negatively impact.

Similar Birds

♀ **TOWNSEND'S WARBLER** Juvenile female • yellow throat and chest; olive crown and upperparts; entirely dark bill; more distinct dark streaking on sides.

♀ **CERULEAN WARBLER** Female and juvenile male • supercilium broadens behind eye; less distinct rounded ear patch; white or buff underparts; pale lines on back; dark streaks across back; shorter tail • eastern range.

Flight Pattern

Fairly swift direct flight on rapidly beating wings. Sallies forth from perch, taking insects in midair and returning to perch.

Nest Identification

Shape ◖   Location 🪹

Small sticks, lichen, and plant down • lined with hair, bark pieces, and small roots • on horizontal branch, 20–50 feet above ground (but as high as 80 feet) • built by female • 4–5 white or greenish white eggs, with brown dots and splotches; oval to short oval, 0.68 x 0.49 inches.

Plumage Sexes differ	Habitat 🌲 🌿	Migration Migratory	Weight 0.4 ounce

DATE _____ TIME_____ LOCATION _____

Family PARULIDAE	Species *Dendroica dominica*	Length 5.25 inches	Wingspan 8.5 inches

YELLOW-THROATED WARBLER

Some of these birds frequent the old oak trees of the Southeast and Mississippi Valley, where Spanish moss is abundant. Their habitat varies regionally from tall swampy bottomland hardwoods, to oak-pine woods on ridges, to lowland pine forests, to sycamores in riparian corridors. In all habitats, this long-billed warbler sings loudly from the tops of trees, and can be identified by the black face set off by a bold white supercilium and bright yellow chin and throat. The female is similar to the male but duller and has fewer black markings. Most migrate but southern populations are sedentary.

Labels on illustration:
black-and-white head with white patch on sides of neck
white arc under eye, white stripe over eye
white or yellow supraloral
long black bill
blue-gray upperparts
bright yellow chin, throat, and breast
2 white wing bars
white underparts
black stripes on flanks, sides, and sides of breast
large white tail spots

• **SONG** Loud descending series of 3–4 measured whistles, followed by 2–3 weaker notes and more rapid notes, ending with sharper ascending note, *tweede-tweede-tweede-tweede-dee-da-m-deet.* Call note is high soft *tsip.*

• **BEHAVIOR** Solitary or in pairs. Somewhat sluggish and deliberate. Joins mixed-species feeding flocks after breeding season. Creeps along inner branches, twigs, and in foliage, foraging generally in the upper parts of trees; however, sometimes lower and even on the ground. Uses long bill and behavior similar to that of Brown Creeper to extract insects from bark crevices and pick them from the surface. Also catches insects in flight. Eats insects, caterpillars, and spiders.

• **BREEDING** Monogamous. Solitary nester.

• **NESTING** Breeding biology poorly known. Incubation by female estimated at 12–13 days. Altricial young brooded by female; stay in nest estimated 10 days, fed by female (possibly some by male). 1–2 broods per year.

• **POPULATION** Fairly common in habitat. Numbers stable overall; some expansion in the Northeast and noted decline in the Florida Panhandle and southern Alabama. Casual in the West during fall migration; rare to casual in southeastern Canada during spring migration.

• **FEEDERS** Will eat bread crumbs and suet.

• **CONSERVATION** Neotropical migrant. Infrequent cowbird host. Vulnerable to habitat loss due to logging, land clearing, and development.

Similar Birds

BLACKBURNIAN WARBLER
Juvenile fall male
• shorter bill; yellow-orange throat and supercilium; yellow patch on side of head; blackish back with white stripes; 2 white wing bars; dusky streaks on sides and flanks.

Flight Pattern

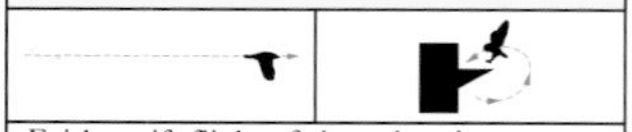

Fairly swift flight of short duration on rapidly beating wings. Sallies forth from perch, taking insects in air, and returns to perch.

Nest Identification

Shape ☙   Location 🌿 🌱

Plant down, stems, grasses, and cocoon material, with lining of feathers and fine plant material • tucked into Spanish moss or on or near end of branch, 10–100 feet above ground • built mostly by female • 4–5 grayish white or greenish white eggs, with lavender, reddish, and grayish flecks and splotches; subelliptical to short subelliptical, 0.68 x 0.51 inches.

Plumage Sexes similar	Habitat 🌿 🌳	Migration Migratory	Weight 0.3 ounce

DATE _____ TIME_____ LOCATION _____

Family PARULIDAE	Species *Dendroica pinus*	Length 5.25 inches	Wingspan 8.5 inches

PINE WARBLER

True to its name, the long-tailed somewhat heavy-billed Pine Warbler inhabits open pine tree groves, where it conceals its nest among needles near the branch tips. It is distinguished from other warblers by its tendency to winter throughout much of its breeding range. Males and females are similar, both showing a white belly and undertail coverts, although females are duller in color with less yellow on their breasts. Juveniles have brownish to brownish olive upperparts with white wing bars, and underparts varying from white to yellowish with a brownish wash on the flanks.

blackish eye line

yellow line over eyes

large bill

greenish olive upperparts with no streaking

yellow chin and throat

yellow breast has dark streaks on sides

2 white wing bars

white belly and undertail coverts

long tail projects beyond undertail coverts

white patches at ends of 2 outer tail feathers

JUVENILE
FEMALE

- **SONG** Twittering musical trill similar to Chipping Sparrow but varying in speed, loudness, and pitch. Call is slurred *tsup*.
- **BEHAVIOR** Solitary or in pairs. Very vocal. Gregarious in winter; often joins mixed feeding flocks. Gleans food by creeping slowly and deliberately along branches, usually high in trees, but sometimes lower, even on ground. Often flies from tree to tree, diving for passing insects. Eats insects, caterpillars, and spiders. Also eats seeds, wild grapes, and some berries. Aggressive toward other species sharing same pine habitat.
- **BREEDING** Monogamous. Solitary.
- **NESTING** Incubation 10 days by both sexes. Young altricial; brooded by female; leave nest within 10 days, fed by both sexes. 2–3 broods per year in the South, 1 brood per year in the North.
- **POPULATION** Fairly common to common. Stable or increasing slightly, but some decline in coastal New England and Great Lakes region due to clearing of pines. Subject to loss in severe winters. Increases occur as pines mature. Casual in West.
- **FEEDERS** Peanut butter and cornmeal mixture.
- **CONSERVATION** Neotropical migrant. Infrequent host to cowbird parasitism. Vulnerable to fragmentation and clearing of pine forests.

Similar Birds

YELLOW-THROATED VIREO
Heavier hooked bill; yellow spectacles; white belly and flanks; no streaking on sides or breast; gray rump and crissum; no white in tail corners; sluggish.

♂ BAY-BREASTED WARBLER
♀ BLACKPOLL WARBLER
Basic plumage • black streaking on back; much less white in tail corners; shorter tails with less extension from undertail coverts; paler cheeks contrast less with throat color.

Flight Pattern
Weak flight, rapid wing beats alternated with brief period of wings pulled to sides. Sallies out to take flying insects, returns.

Nest Identification	Lined with feathers, weeds, grass, bark, pine needles, twigs, and spider webs • built on or near end of limb, 10–135 feet above ground • built by female • 3–5 off-white eggs, with brown specks near larger end; oval to short oval, 0.7 x 0.5 inches.
Shape Location	

Plumage Sexes similar	Habitat	Migration Northern birds migrate	Weight 0.4 ounce

DATE _____ TIME_____ LOCATION _____

Family PARULIDAE	Species *Dendroica discolor*	Length 4.75 inches	Wingspan 7.5 inches

PRAIRIE WARBLER

Rather than the prairies as its name might imply, this bird can be found in brushy old fields, open pine stands, and sometimes in coastal mangroves in eastern and southern North America. Like many warblers, the male sings from an exposed perch at the tops of tall trees. Females are similar to males but duller in color. Juvenile females are duller still, with grayish olive upperparts, pale supercilium, and broken eye rings.

yellow sides of face with black streak through eyes, outlining ear patch

bright yellow eyebrow

olive-green upperparts with chestnut markings on back

2 light yellow wing bars

black streaking on sides

white patches on outer tail feathers

bright yellow underparts

• **SONG** An ascending trilling *zzee-zzee-zzee-zzee-zzee-zzee-zzee,* starting at one pitch and rising sharply over the last half of song. Call note is a rich smacking *tchick*.

• **BEHAVIOR** Solitary or in pairs. Joins mixed feeding flocks after breeding season. Tame. Active and restless. Constantly pumps or wags tail while feeding. Forages in low branches of trees and bushes and sometimes on ground. Catches some insects in flight but primarily gleans from foliage; sometimes hover-gleans. Eats mostly insects and spiders.

• **BREEDING** Monogamous; some males polygynous in midnesting season. Solitary nester.

• **NESTING** Incubation 11–14 days by female. Young altricial; brooded by female; stay in nest 8–11 days, fed by both sexes. Both sexes tend for additional 40–50 days. 2 broods per year.

Similar Birds
PINE WARBLER Yellow-green face; indistinct yellowish eye ring and supercilium; olive-green back without streaking; yellowish underparts with indistinct dusky streaking; extensive white tail spots; bobs tail but not as strongly.

• **POPULATION** Common but is declining.

• **CONSERVATION** Neotropical migrant. Frequently host to cowbird parasitism. Vulnerable to habitat loss that occurs with maturation of forests.

Flight Pattern	
Fairly fast flight with rapidly beating wings, alternating with brief periods of wings pulled to sides. May sally forth and take insects in flight.	

Nest Identification	Grasses, stems, bark pieces, plant down, and leaves, bound with spider's silk and lined with feathers and mammal hair • hidden in tree or bush, usually 10–15 feet above ground (but ranges from 1–45 feet) • built by female • 4–5 white, creamy white, or greenish white eggs, with fine and large dots of brown, concentrated on larger end; oval to short oval, 0.6 x 0.48 inches.
Shape	
Location	

Plumage Sexes differ	Habitat	Migration Migratory	Weight 0.3 ounce

DATE _____ TIME _____ LOCATION _____

| Family PARULIDAE | Species *Dendroica palmarum* | Length 5.25 inches | Wingspan 8.5 inches |

PALM WARBLER

This inhabitant of northern bogs pumps its tail up and down more than any other warbler. Two subspecies occur: the eastern form with strongly washed yellow underparts and the western form with whitish underparts with stronger streaking. Both nest on knolls of moss at the foot of small spruce or pine trees. A medium-distance migrant, the Palm Warbler winters in the South and frequents open habitats such as cultivated fields, marshes, pastures, parks, and gardens. Some winter in open pine woods or along their edges. The species is associated with palms only on some of its wintering areas and shows no inclination to seek them out. Fall adults and juveniles are drab, washed out, and lack the chestnut cap.

grayish to olive-brown upperparts

chestnut cap

white to yellowish wing bars

white spots on tail corners

yellow to whitish supercilium

chestnut to brownish streaks on sides of breast

greenish yellow undertail coverts and rump

streaked whitish underparts

WESTERN RACE

WINTER PLUMAGE

- **SONG** Monotone buzzlike fast trill, often stronger in middle, *zwee-zwee-zwee-zwee-zwee-zwee*. Call is forceful slurred *tsik*.

- **BEHAVIOR** Solitary or in pairs. Gregarious after breeding season, forming flocks and often mixing in foraging flocks with other species. Terrestrial; searches for food on ground or along beaches during migration, particularly among twigs and cones from conifers. Also foliage-gleans and hover-gleans in shrubs and trees; sometimes hawks prey in flight. Eats insects and caterpillars, also bayberries and raspberries.

- **BREEDING** Monogamous. Solitary.

- **NESTING** Incubation 12 days by both sexes. Young altricial; brooded by female; stay in nest 12 days, fed by both sexes. 2 broods per year.

- **POPULATION** Fairly common to common. Stable with some decline noted in wintering numbers in Florida.

- **CONSERVATION** Neotropical migrant. Rare cowbird host; buries eggs of parasite in floor of nest. Vulnerable to loss of habitat due to forest fragmentation.

Similar Birds
CAPE MAY WARBLER ♀ Pale lemon supercilium; white undertail coverts; does not wag short tail.
YELLOW-RUMPED WARBLER Myrtle form, basic plumage • brown to gray upperparts with black streaking on back; white supercilium; bright yellow rump; streaked underparts; does not pump tail.

Flight Pattern

Weak flight; rapid wing beats alternate with brief periods of wings pulled to sides. Sallies from perch to take insects in air.

Nest Identification

Shape   Location

Grass and shredded bark, lined with feathers • built on or near ground or up to 4 feet above ground in coniferous tree • built by female • 4–5 white to creamy eggs, with brown markings; ovate, short ovate, or elongated ovate, 0.7 x 0.5 inches.

| Plumage Sexes similar | Habitat | Migration Migratory | Weight 0.4 ounce |

DATE _____ TIME_____ LOCATION _____

Family PARULIDAE	Species *Dendroica castanea*	Length 5.5 inches	Wingspan 8.5 inches

BAY-BREASTED WARBLER

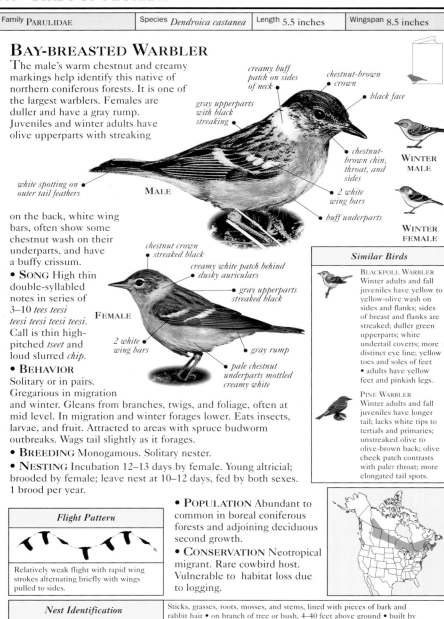

The male's warm chestnut and creamy markings help identify this native of northern coniferous forests. It is one of the largest warblers. Females are duller and have a gray rump. Juveniles and winter adults have olive upperparts with streaking

creamy buff patch on sides of neck

chestnut-brown crown

black face

gray upperparts with black streaking

chestnut-brown chin, throat, and sides

WINTER MALE

white spotting on outer tail feathers

MALE

2 white wing bars

buff underparts

WINTER FEMALE

on the back, white wing bars, often show some chestnut wash on their underparts, and have a buffy crissum.

chestnut crown streaked black

creamy white patch behind dusky auriculars

gray upperparts streaked black

FEMALE

2 white wing bars

gray rump

pale chestnut underparts mottled creamy white

- **SONG** High thin double-syllabled notes in series of 3–10 *tees teesi teesi teesi teesi teesi*. Call is thin high-pitched *tseet* and loud slurred *chip*.
- **BEHAVIOR** Solitary or in pairs. Gregarious in migration and winter. Gleans from branches, twigs, and foliage, often at mid level. In migration and winter forages lower. Eats insects, larvae, and fruit. Attracted to areas with spruce budworm outbreaks. Wags tail slightly as it forages.
- **BREEDING** Monogamous. Solitary nester.
- **NESTING** Incubation 12–13 days by female. Young altricial; brooded by female; leave nest at 10–12 days, fed by both sexes. 1 brood per year.

Similar Birds

BLACKPOLL WARBLER
Winter adults and fall juveniles have yellow to yellow-olive wash on sides and flanks; sides of breast and flanks are streaked; duller green upperparts; white undertail coverts; more distinct eye line; yellow toes and soles of feet • adults have yellow feet and pinkish legs.

PINE WARBLER
Winter adults and fall juveniles have longer tail; lacks white tips to tertials and primaries; unstreaked olive to olive-brown back; olive cheek patch contrasts with paler throat; more elongated tail spots.

Flight Pattern
Relatively weak flight with rapid wing strokes alternating briefly with wings pulled to sides.

- **POPULATION** Abundant to common in boreal coniferous forests and adjoining deciduous second growth.
- **CONSERVATION** Neotropical migrant. Rare cowbird host. Vulnerable to habitat loss due to logging.

Nest Identification	
Shape 🐦 Location 🌿🌳🌲	Sticks, grasses, roots, mosses, and stems, lined with pieces of bark and rabbit hair • on branch of tree or bush, 4–40 feet above ground • built by female • 4–6 white, greenish white, or bluish white eggs, with lavender or brown splotches at larger end; varying from ovate to elongate ovate, 0.7 x 0.5 inches.

Plumage Sexes differ	Habitat 🌿🌾	Migration Migratory	Weight 0.5 ounce

DATE _____ TIME _____ LOCATION _____

Family PARULIDAE	Species *Dendroica striata*	Length 5.25 inches	Wingspan 8.5 inches

BLACKPOLL WARBLER

This summer resident of Canadian boreal forests migrates more than twenty-five hundred miles in the fall, flying nonstop over water to winter in northern South America. Juveniles and fall adults have streaked greenish upperparts; a pale greenish yellow wash on the face, throat, and breast; a white belly and crissum; legs that are pale pinkish on the front and back but dark on the sides; and yellow soles.

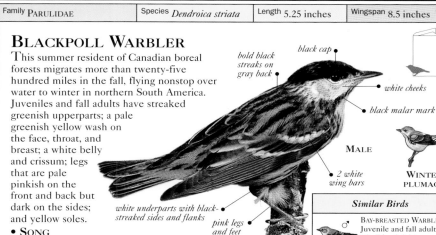

bold black streaks on gray back

black cap

white cheeks

black malar mark

MALE

2 white wing bars

WINTER PLUMAGE

white underparts with black-streaked sides and flanks

pink legs and feet

dusky eye line and gray-buff supercilium

grayish head and neck

olive-gray crown

FEMALE

white underparts

blackish streaked throat, sides, and flanks

- **SONG** Mechanical series of high thin *tseet* notes that begin softly and get louder and more intense; may contain 10–20 notes. Much variation between individuals. Call is sharp loud *chip*.

- **BEHAVIOR** Solitary or in pairs. Sluggish and deliberate. Forages low to high in migration, but stays in middle to upper levels on breeding grounds. Catches insects in air or combs leaves and twigs for food. Eats insects, caterpillars, cankerworms, spiders and their eggs, and pokeberries.

- **BREEDING** Monogamous. Polygynous. Females breed with the territory-holding male on the previous year's nesting site.

- **NESTING** Incubation 12 days by female. Altricial young brooded by female; stay in nest 11–12 days, fed by both sexes. 1–2 broods per year.

Similar Birds

BAY-BREASTED WARBLER
Juvenile and fall adults
- bulkier; brighter green upperparts; thicker wing bars; little or no streaking on underparts; many show buff sides and/or flanks; creamy undertail coverts; gray legs and feet.

PINE WARBLER
Larger bill; unstreaked olive upperparts; shorter undertail coverts make tail look longer; more white in tail corners; brown legs and feet.

BLACK-AND-WHITE WARBLER
Black-and-white-striped crown; black back with white stripes; black spotting and streaking on undertail coverts; black legs and feet
- male has black throat and cheeks.

- **POPULATION** Abundant in northern boreal coniferous forests. May be declining in southern part of breeding range.
- **CONSERVATION** Neotropical migrant. Vulnerable to habitat loss from logging and forest fragmentation.

Flight Pattern

Fairly swift direct flight on rapidly beating wings.

Nest Identification	
Shape 🥣 Location 🪺	Lined with spruce sprigs, twigs, bark, dried grass, feathers, weeds, moss, and lichen • on branch near trunk, 2–33 feet above ground • built by female • 3–5 white to off-white eggs, with brown or lavender markings, occasionally wreathed; oval to long oval, 0.72 x 0.53 inches.

Plumage Sexes differ	Habitat 🌳 🌿	Migration Migratory	Weight 0.5 ounce

DATE _____ TIME_____ LOCATION _____

Family PARULIDAE	Species *Dendroica cerulea*	Length 4.5 inches	Wingspan 7.25 inches

CERULEAN WARBLER

Although its buzzy song can be heard from dawn until dusk, this bird, one of the smallest warblers, is difficult to spot, as it stays hidden in dense foliage in the crowns of tall deciduous trees. This habit of remaining high in mature trees has made studies of its natural history difficult, and its breeding biology and feeding habits are poorly known. Juveniles are similar to females.

• **SONG** A series of accelerating buzzy notes on the same or slightly ascending pitch, ending in a drawn-out buzz, *zray, zray, zray, zray, zeeeeeee,* reminiscent of the slower second song of the Northern Parula. Call is a slurred *chip.*

• **BEHAVIOR** Solitary or in pairs. Vigorous and persistent singer on breeding grounds. Eats mainly insects, larvae, and spiders. Very active and acrobatic forager but sometimes moves sluggishly, gleaning food off leaves and branches while staying hidden in trees. Also catches insects in flight.

• **BREEDING** Monogamous. Solitary nester.

• **NESTING** Incubation about 12–13 days by female. Altricial young brooded by female; stay in nest estimated 8–10 days, fed by both sexes. 1–2 broods per year.

• **POPULATION** Fairly common to uncommon in mature deciduous forest. Declining dramatically, particularly in the heart of range, but range is expanding north and northeast, on the Atlantic coastal plain, and the Piedmont.

• **CONSERVATION** Neotropical migrant. Moderate host to cowbird parasitism. Vulnerable to habitat loss and forest fragmentation.

white tail spots

bluish to blue-gray upperparts with black streaking on back

2 white wing bars

black streaking on flanks and sides

bluish black chest band

white underparts

MALE

blue-gray to greenish mantle

bluish green crown

whitish supercilium widens behind eye

white tail spots

FEMALE

pale yellowish buff breast and throat

Similar Birds

The small and short-tailed male is the only warbler with a blue back, black necklace, and white throat.

♀ **BLACKBURNIAN WARBLER** Female and juvenile • pale orange supercilium broadens behind eye; white or buff underparts; longer tail; triangular cheek patch; pale lines and dark streaking on back.

Flight Pattern

Relatively weak flight with quick wing strokes alternating with brief periods of wings pull to sides; repeated.

Nest Identification

Shape 🥄   Location 🪹

Stems, grasses, mosses, bark pieces, and spider's silk, with lining of mammal hair and mosses • far out on branch of tree, usually 30–60 feet above ground • built by female • 3–5 grayish or creamy white eggs, with fine dots or splotches of brown, usually loosely wreathed; oval to short oval, 0.7 x 0.5 inches.

Plumage Sexes differ	Habitat 🌳 🐦 🌿	Migration Migratory	Weight 0.3 ounce

DATE _____ TIME_____ LOCATION _____

Family PARULIDAE	Species *Mniotilta varia*	Length 5 inches	Wingspan 8.5–9 inches

BLACK-AND-WHITE WARBLER

This mostly black-and-white striped bird feeds nuthatch-style, moving up and down the trunks of trees and crawling over and under branches, a foraging behavior unlike any other warbler. It is one of the earliest warblers to return to the breeding grounds in early spring, because its bark-gleaning foraging habit does not require it to linger on wintering grounds until the leaves begin to develop. Females are similar to males but have cream-colored flanks and creamy whitish rather than black cheeks. Juveniles are similar to females.

bold black-and-white stripes on head and most of body

distinctive white stripe over and under each eye

slightly curved slim bill

black cheeks and throat

2 white wing bars

white belly

JUVENILE

- **SONG** Repetitive thin high-pitched series of 6–10 *wee-sea*, *wee-sea* notes like the sound of a turning squeaky wheel. Sometimes a trill is added as an ending to the cadence. Has call of an abrasive *chip* or *tink*, and a *seap*.

- **BEHAVIOR** Solitary or in pairs. Probes into bark crevices with long bill; does not prop body on tree with tail as do woodpeckers and creepers. Eats adult insects, caterpillars, and spiders. Occasionally hawks and hover-gleans. If flushed from ground nest, female performs distraction display, dragging wings with tail spread.

- **BREEDING** Monogamous. Solitary.

- **NESTING** Incubation 10–12 days by female. Young altricial; brooded by female; remain in nest 8–12 days but still not able to fly well; fed by both sexes. 1–2 broods per year.

- **POPULATION** Widespread in mature and second-growth deciduous or mixed deciduous-conifer woodlands with large trees. Declining in the Midwest and Great Lakes region because of habitat loss and cowbird parasitism. Vagrant in the West during migration as far north as Alaska.

- **CONSERVATION** Neotropical migrant. Common host to cowbird eggs. Vulnerable to forest fragmentation and habitat loss due to logging operations in mature forests.

Similar Birds

BLACK-THROATED GRAY WARBLER ♂
Small yellow spot between eye and bill; blackish crown; gray back with black streaking; white undertail coverts; lacks central crown stripe.

BLACKPOLL WARBLER ♂
Black crown; white cheeks; gray back with black streaking; white throat; white undertail coverts.

Flight Pattern

Relatively weak flight with rapid wing strokes alternating with brief periods of wings pulled to sides; repeated.

Nest Identification

Shape 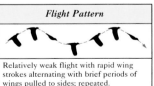 Location

Grasses, bark pieces, dead leaves, rootlets, and pine needles, lined with moss and mammal hair • on ground, near base of tree or bush, or in small hollow of rock, stump, or log • built by female • 4–6 creamy white or white eggs, flecked with brown; short subelliptical to subelliptical, 0.67 x 0.52 inches.

Plumage Sexes similar	Habitat	Migration Migratory	Weight 0.4 ounce

DATE _____ TIME_____ LOCATION _____

Family PARULIDAE	Species *Setophaga ruticilla*	Length 5 inches	Wingspan 8 inches

AMERICAN REDSTART

Birders enjoy watching this vivacious bird as it flits to catch insects or sits on a perch, partially spreading and drooping its wings and spreading its tail. Other warblers pump or flick their tails, but this bird fans its tail and holds it there for a second. The male's tail can be either orange and black or yellow and dusky olive-gray. This woodland inhabitant is one of the most common warblers nesting in North America. Juvenile males look like females but with an orange wash on the sides.

glossy black overall

orange patches on wings, sides, and tail

white belly and undertail coverts

MALE

- **SONG** Variable. Sings often and through the heat of midday. Basic song is 4–8 high-pitched, somewhat coarse notes, with explosive accented lower-ending *zeet-zeet-zeet-zeet-zeeeah*. Other songs have unaccented ending. Some are reminiscent of the Yellow, Chestnut-sided, and Black-and-white Warblers. Territorial males have repertoire of several songs. Call is slurred thin *chip*.

FEMALE

thin white supercilium and eye ring

grayish olive upperparts

- **BEHAVIOR** Solitary or in pairs. Tame. Conspicuous. Sings often. Responds to squeaking or pishing by birders. Sallies into air to catch insects, perching between hawking events like a small flycatcher. Gleans food from branches and foliage; hover-gleans. Eats insects, caterpillars, spiders, berries, fruit, and seeds.

whitish underparts from chin to tip of undertail coverts

yellow patches on sides, wings, and tail

- **BREEDING** Monogamous. Solitary nester.
- **NESTING** Incubation 11–12 days by female. Altricial young brooded by female; stay in nest 9 days, fed by both sexes. 1–2 broods per year.

FIRST SPRING
MALE

- **POPULATION** Common to fairly common in wet deciduous and mixed conifer-deciduous woodlands with understory, woodland edges, riparian woodlands, and second growth. Widespread but declining in the Midwest, Great Lakes, the Northeast, and the Maritime Provinces. Rare to uncommon migrant in the West to California.

Similar Birds
None in range.

- **CONSERVATION** Neotropical migrant. Common cowbird host. Vulnerable to habitat loss caused by deforestation or maturation of second-growth forests.

Flight Pattern
Somewhat weak flight on rapidly beating wings, alternating with brief periods of wings pulled to sides. Flies into air from perch to take flying insects, and returns.

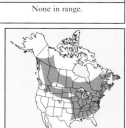

Nest Identification	Grasses, pieces of bark, rootlets, and plant down, decorated with lichens, birch bark, and spider's silk, and lined with feathers • in fork of tree or bush, usually 10–20 feet above ground (but ranges from 4–70 feet) • built by female • 2–5 off-white, greenish white, or white eggs, flecked and dotted with browns or grays; ovate, occasionally short ovate, 0.63 x 0.48 inches.
Shape ⬤ Location 🌲 🌿	

Plumage Sexes differ	Habitat 🐦 〰️ 🐦	Migration Migratory	Weight 0.3 ounce

DATE _____ TIME_____ LOCATION _____

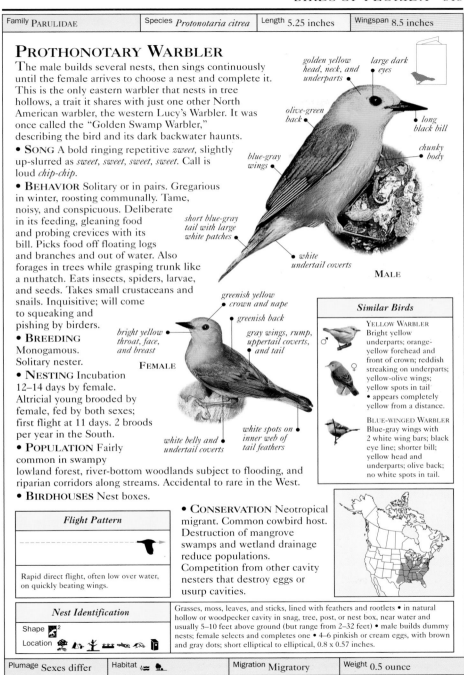

Family PARULIDAE	Species *Protonotaria citrea*	Length 5.25 inches	Wingspan 8.5 inches

PROTHONOTARY WARBLER

The male builds several nests, then sings continuously until the female arrives to choose a nest and complete it. This is the only eastern warbler that nests in tree hollows, a trait it shares with just one other North American warbler, the western Lucy's Warbler. It was once called the "Golden Swamp Warbler," describing the bird and its dark backwater haunts.

golden yellow head, neck, and underparts

large dark eyes

olive-green back

long black bill

chunky body

blue-gray wings

• **SONG** A bold ringing repetitive *zweet*, slightly up-slurred as *sweet, sweet, sweet, sweet*. Call is loud *chip-chip*.

• **BEHAVIOR** Solitary or in pairs. Gregarious in winter, roosting communally. Tame, noisy, and conspicuous. Deliberate in its feeding, gleaning food and probing crevices with its bill. Picks food off floating logs and branches and out of water. Also forages in trees while grasping trunk like a nuthatch. Eats insects, spiders, larvae, and seeds. Takes small crustaceans and snails. Inquisitive; will come to squeaking and pishing by birders.

short blue-gray tail with large white patches

white undertail coverts

MALE

greenish yellow crown and nape

greenish back

gray wings, rump, uppertail coverts, and tail

bright yellow throat, face, and breast

FEMALE

• **BREEDING** Monogamous. Solitary nester.

• **NESTING** Incubation 12–14 days by female. Altricial young brooded by female, fed by both sexes; first flight at 11 days. 2 broods per year in the South.

• **POPULATION** Fairly common in swampy lowland forest, river-bottom woodlands subject to flooding, and riparian corridors along streams. Accidental to rare in the West.

white belly and undertail coverts

white spots on inner web of tail feathers

Similar Birds

YELLOW WARBLER
Bright yellow underparts; orange-yellow forehead and front of crown; reddish streaking on underparts; yellow-olive wings; yellow spots in tail • appears completely yellow from a distance.

BLUE-WINGED WARBLER
Blue-gray wings with 2 white wing bars; black eye line; shorter bill; yellow head and underparts; olive back; no white spots in tail.

• **BIRDHOUSES** Nest boxes.

Flight Pattern	
Rapid direct flight, often low over water, on quickly beating wings.	

• **CONSERVATION** Neotropical migrant. Common cowbird host. Destruction of mangrove swamps and wetland drainage reduce populations. Competition from other cavity nesters that destroy eggs or usurp cavities.

Nest Identification	Grasses, moss, leaves, and sticks, lined with feathers and rootlets • in natural hollow or woodpecker cavity in snag, tree, post, or nest box, near water and usually 5–10 feet above ground (but range from 2–32 feet) • male builds dummy nests; female selects and completes one • 4–6 pinkish or cream eggs, with brown and gray dots; short elliptical to elliptical, 0.8 x 0.57 inches.
Shape 2	
Location	

Plumage Sexes differ	Habitat	Migration Migratory	Weight 0.5 ounce

DATE _____ TIME_____ LOCATION _____

Family PARULIDAE	Species *Helmitheros vermivorus*	Length 5.25 inches	Wingspan 8.5 inches

WORM-EATING WARBLER

Similar to a sparrow in color, size, and habits, the Worm-eating Warbler's steady diet of moth caterpillars and worms has earned this bird its name. An inhabitant of deciduous forests, it seldom is observed combing the forest floor for food; rather, it usually forages in the understory vegetation, where it often probes for food in clusters of dead leaves. While primarily a solitary bird, the Worm-eating Warbler sometimes is known to associate loosely with foraging flocks of mixed bird species.

buff-colored head with 2 pairs of bold dark stripes

brownish olive upperparts

long spikelike bill

buff-colored underparts

• **SONG** A buzzy insectlike fricative trill, often beginning softly and fading away at the end with a series of *chip* notes. Song is similar to the Chipping Sparrow's but more rapid and given in a thick shaded wooded habitat. Call is a *zit-zit*.

• **BEHAVIOR** Solitary or in pairs. More often heard than seen in the breeding season. Most often observed foraging alone for insects, spiders, and some worms. Gleans food by moving along branches like a Black-and-white Warbler, but specializes in probing clusters of dead leaves for food. Usually forages in low to middle levels, but sometimes in treetops; rarely in leaf litter on ground. Frequents deciduous woodlots on slopes, along ravines, or mountain sides. When flushed from nest, female drags wings and spreads tail, running on ground in distraction display. Mixed flocks postbreeding season.

• **BREEDING** Monogamous. Solitary.

• **NESTING** Incubation 13 days by female. Young altricial; brooded by female; stay in nest 10 days, fed by both sexes. 1–2 broods per year.

• **POPULATION** Fairly common to common in ravines, hillsides, and mountainsides in thick deciduous woodlands. Stable in most of its range but regional declines noted. Casual to rare vagrant in migration in the West to California.

• **CONSERVATION** Neotropical migrant. Frequent host to cowbird parasitism. Vulnerable to habitat loss due to forest fragmentation.

Similar Birds
SWAINSON'S WARBLER Larger; longer bill; browner upperparts; grayish buff underparts; brown cap without stripes; pale supercilium; thin dark eye line.

Flight Pattern
Fairly fast direct flight on rapidly beating wings.

Nest Identification	
Shape ⬤ Location ▬	Lined with dead leaves, animal hair, fungus, moss, and tree stems • often built on sloping ground near base of deciduous shrubs or saplings or on ridges of leaves on forest floor • built by female • 4–6 white eggs, with brown spots or blotches, often wreathed; short ovate, 0.7 x 0.55 inches.

Plumage Sexes similar	Habitat 🐾	Migration Migratory	Weight 0.7 ounce

DATE _____ TIME _____ LOCATION _____

Family PARULIDAE	Species *Limnothlypis swainsonii*	Length 5.25 inches	Wingspan 8.5 inches

SWAINSON'S WARBLER

This recluse hides in dense thickets, except when the male perches to sing, which he does with his head thrown back and his bill lifted in the air. It is found in two habitats: in the low coastal and river-bottom country of the Southeast it inhabits canebrakes and thickets in swamps and among hardwoods; in

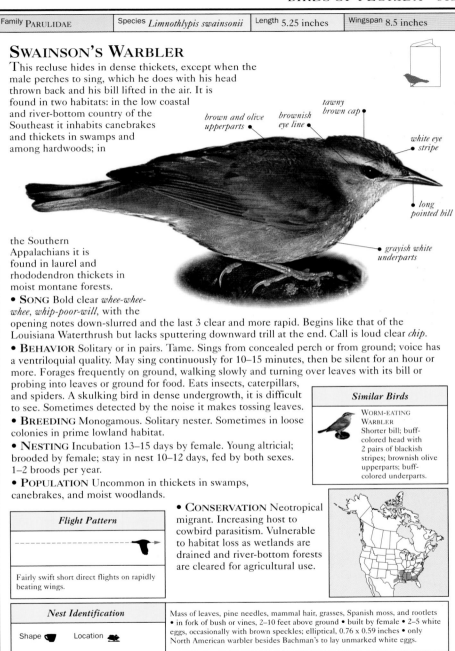

brown and olive upperparts

brownish eye line

tawny brown cap

white eye stripe

long pointed bill

grayish white underparts

the Southern Appalachians it is found in laurel and rhododendron thickets in moist montane forests.

• **SONG** Bold clear *whee-whee-whee, whip-poor-will*, with the opening notes down-slurred and the last 3 clear and more rapid. Begins like that of the Louisiana Waterthrush but lacks sputtering downward trill at the end. Call is loud clear *chip*.

• **BEHAVIOR** Solitary or in pairs. Tame. Sings from concealed perch or from ground; voice has a ventriloquial quality. May sing continuously for 10–15 minutes, then be silent for an hour or more. Forages frequently on ground, walking slowly and turning over leaves with its bill or probing into leaves or ground for food. Eats insects, caterpillars, and spiders. A skulking bird in dense undergrowth, it is difficult to see. Sometimes detected by the noise it makes tossing leaves.

• **BREEDING** Monogamous. Solitary nester. Sometimes in loose colonies in prime lowland habitat.

• **NESTING** Incubation 13–15 days by female. Young altricial; brooded by female; stay in nest 10–12 days, fed by both sexes. 1–2 broods per year.

• **POPULATION** Uncommon in thickets in swamps, canebrakes, and moist woodlands.

• **CONSERVATION** Neotropical migrant. Increasing host to cowbird parasitism. Vulnerable to habitat loss as wetlands are drained and river-bottom forests are cleared for agricultural use.

Similar Birds

WORM-EATING WARBLER
Shorter bill; buff-colored head with 2 pairs of blackish stripes; brownish olive upperparts; buff-colored underparts.

Flight Pattern

Fairly swift short direct flights on rapidly beating wings.

Nest Identification

Shape ╼ Location ╾

Mass of leaves, pine needles, mammal hair, grasses, Spanish moss, and rootlets • in fork of bush or vines, 2–10 feet above ground • built by female • 2–5 white eggs, occasionally with brown speckles; elliptical, 0.76 x 0.59 inches • only North American warbler besides Bachman's to lay unmarked white eggs.

Plumage Sexes similar	Habitat ▲ 🌲 ♣♣ ▲ 🍂 〰	Migration Migratory	Weight 0.7 ounce

DATE _____ TIME_____ LOCATION _____

Family PARULIDAE	Species *Seiurus aurocapillus*	Length 6 inches	Wingspan 9 inches

OVENBIRD

In the leaf litter under tall deciduous trees, the female bird builds a small oven-shaped nest with a side entrance. Unlike many warblers, it does not often forage in live vegetation; instead it walks on the ground, foraging among the leaf litter and twigs, its wings partially drooped and its tail cocked upward and sometimes quickly raised and slowly lowered. It is sometimes called the Wood Wagtail because it moves its tail up and down. Most singing is done from an elevated perch, and the song of one territorial male initiates a response song from each neighbor, which in turn stimulates another to do so, until a wave of Ovenbird songs sweeps across the woodlot.

brownish orange stripe, edged in black, over head from bill to nape

white eye ring

olive-brown upperparts

pale pink legs and feet

white underparts with dark brown splotching

• **SONG** More often heard than seen. Sings a loud and repetitive *TEAcher-TEAcher-TEAcher*, rising and becoming more emphatic. There is regional variation, with some birds singing *teach-teach-teach-teACH!* From a distance the song sounds like two stones being tapped together harder and harder. Call note is a loud sharp *tsick.*

• **BEHAVIOR** Solitary or in pairs. Tame. Eats adult insects, caterpillars, snails, slugs, earthworms, small amphibians, seeds, berries, and fruit. When flushed, usually flies up to perch. Walks on limbs in interior of trees.

• **BREEDING** Monogamous. Solitary nester.

• **NESTING** Incubation 11–14 days by female. Young altricial; brooded by female; remain in nest 8–11 days, fed by both sexes. 1–2 broods per year (occasionally 3 in regions with spruce budworm outbreaks).

• **POPULATION** Common to fairly common in mature deciduous forests; rarely in pine forests. Rare in the west of the Rockies in migration; rare to casual on southern Atlantic Coast and Gulf Coast in winter.

• **CONSERVATION** Neotropical migrant. Host to cowbird parasitism. Significant declines documented in the northeast beginning in the 1970s but now increasing in much of its range.

Similar Birds

LOUISIANA WATERTHRUSH
NORTHERN WATERTHRUSH
White to yellowish supercilium; lack eye ring and black border to crown; brownish upperparts; usually near water; habitual tail bobbing.

Flight Pattern
Relatively swift, short direct flight on rapidly beating wings.

Nest Identification	
Shape ⬡ Location ▬	Leaves, grasses, stems, rootlets, mosses, and hair • in slight hollow on ground of forest, concealed by leaves on top of nest, creating a dome • built by female • 3–6 white eggs, with gray or brown flecks; subelliptical to short subelliptical, 0.79 x 0.6 inches.

Plumage Sexes similar	Habitat	Migration Migratory	Weight 0.7 ounce

DATE _____ TIME_____ LOCATION _____

Family PARULIDAE	Species *Seiurus noveboracensis*	Length 5.75 inches	Wingspan 8.75 inches

NORTHERN WATERTHRUSH

Northern lakeshores, slow-running streams, and bogs are the most common habitats of the Northern Waterthrush. Walking, rather than hopping, along the ground, the Northern Waterthrush often is observed repeatedly bobbing the rear part of its body and its tail while searching for food. An early migrant, the Northern Waterthrush generally begins traveling southward by mid-July.

pale yellow to whitish supercilium

olive-brown to gray-brown upperparts

heavily streaked throat, upper breast, and sides

- **SONG** Begins with loud insistent notes, tapering to rapidly whistled lower tones, *twit twit twit twit sweet sweet sweet chew chew chew*, with the individual notes grouped in series of 3's and 4's. Call is a very loud ringing metallic *chink.*

pale yellow to whitish underparts

- **BEHAVIOR** Solitary or in pairs. Terrestrial but often sings from elevated perches and walks, bobbing, on branches. Forages on ground by picking up leaves with its bill and tossing them aside or turning them over. Eats aquatic and terrestrial adult insects, caterpillars, and case worms; also sometimes slugs, mollusks, crustaceans, and small fish. Frequents areas with dense shrub and slowly moving or still water.
- **BREEDING** Monogamous. Solitary.
- **NESTING** Breeding biology poorly known. Estimated incubation 13 days by female. Young altricial; brooded by female; stay in nest estimated 10 days, fed by both sexes. 1 brood per year.
- **POPULATION** Generally common in wooded swamps, forests with standing water, bogs, and thickets with slowly running or standing water. Rare to uncommon in migration in the Southwest to California. Rare to casual in winter in the US, except for southern Florida where it is uncommon.
- **CONSERVATION** Neotropical migrant. Uncommon host to cowbird parasitism. Some declines in southern portions of breeding range and increases in New England portions. Vulnerable to habitat loss due to deforestation and drainage.

Similar Birds

LOUISIANA WATERTHRUSH Longer stouter bill; white supercilium broadens behind eye; fewer and less-contrasting streaks on underparts; unmarked white throat; contrasting pinkish buff wash on flanks; bright pink legs and feet; more deliberate and exaggerated tail bobbing with a circular body motion; song differs.

Flight Pattern

Fairly swift direct flight for short distances on rapidly beating wings.

Nest Identification	
Shape ◥ Location ▬◣ ✿	Lined with grass, animal hair, moss, twigs, pine needles, bark strips, and roots • often built in moss-covered stumps near water • 0–2 feet above ground • built by female • 3–6 cream or buff-white eggs, with brown or gray spots or speckles; ovate to short ovate, 0.8 x 0.57 inches.

Plumage Sexes similar	Habitat 	Migration Migratory	Weight 0.8 ounce

DATE _____ TIME_____ LOCATION _____

Family PARULIDAE	Species *Seiurus motacilla*	Length 6 inches	Wingspan 9 inches

LOUISIANA WATERTHRUSH

The less common of the two waterthrush species frequents fast-running streams and floodplain river swamps, where it hides its nests on streamside banks, under tree roots, or in rock crevices. This bird has a nesting range from Minnesota to New England and as far south as Texas and Georgia. In spring it is one of the earliest warblers to arrive on the nesting grounds and one of the first to depart in late summer and early fall.

darker crown
broad gray-buff stripe broadens behind eye and becomes white
long stout bill
olive-gray to olive-brown upperparts
unstreaked white throat and chin
olive-striped breast, sides, and flanks
white or buff-white underparts
pinkish buff flanks contrast with white underparts
bright pink legs and feet

- **SONG** Loud and clear, beginning with 3–4 high-pitched downslurred notes, followed by a brief rapid medley of jumbled notes that cascade up and down prior to fading away, *SWEER SWEER SWEER chee chi-wit-it chit swee-yuu*. The combination of slurred opening notes and ending twittering is diagnostic. Call is a loud bright *chik*.
- **BEHAVIOR** Solitary or in pairs. Sings on ground or from elevated perch in trees. Bobs rear and tail while walking. Terrestrial, primarily foraging on ground, along stream banks, on rocks and logs in water, and in the stream shallows. Bobs up and down while foraging, much like a sandpiper, with a slow circular exaggerated motion. Dines on adult aquatic and terrestrial insects, caterpillars, mollusks, snails, and small fish. Territories are linear along stream.
- **BREEDING** Monogamous. Solitary.
- **NESTING** Incubation 12–14 days by female. Young altricial; brooded by female; remain in nest 9–10 days, fed by both sexes. 1 brood per year.
- **POPULATION** Uncommon to fairly common. Restricted habitat specialist along fast-flowing streams within woodlands, often in mountains or hilly terrain, or in floodplain forests and swamps in lower country. Casual in the West during migration.
- **CONSERVATION** Neotropical migrant. Frequent host to cowbird parasitism. Deforestation and stream siltation negatively impact both breeding and wintering areas.

Similar Birds

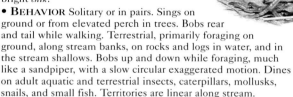

NORTHERN WATERTHRUSH Narrow buff to white eye stripes of uniform color and width; smaller bill; streaked and spotted throat; pale yellow to white underparts with darker, more uniform streaking; olive-brown to gray-brown upperparts; dull pink legs and feet; different voice.

Flight Pattern

Swift short direct flights on rapidly beating wings.

Nest Identification	
Shape ☕ Location 🔨	Lined with roots, fern stems, grass, animal fur, dead leaves, moss, and twigs • 0–2 feet above ground, on bank, rock crevice, or roots of tree, no further than 3–6 feet from water • built by both sexes, but female does more • 4–6 white or cream-colored eggs, with brown and gray specks or blotches; oval to short oval, 0.78 x 0.6 inches.

Plumage Sexes similar	Habitat	Migration Migratory	Weight 0.7 ounce

DATE _____ TIME_____ LOCATION _____

Family PARULIDAE	Species *Oporornis formosus*	Length 5.25 inches	Wingspan 8.25 inches

KENTUCKY WARBLER

This retiring, short-tailed chunky bird is named for the state where it was first encountered, but it is common throughout most of the damp shaded woodlands in southeastern North America. The female is especially wary and will sometimes abandon her nest if she is threatened. She appears similar to the male, but her black areas are duller. Juvenile females have dark olive plumage in place of black.

short tail

bright olive upperparts

long pink legs and feet

black crown

bold yellow spectacles

black on face and sides of neck

yellow underparts

• **SONG** Loud and rich. A rolling melody of 5–8 notes with 2 syllables, *churry-churry-churry-churry-churry*, but sometimes 3 syllables, with an upward inflection at the end of each phrase. Reminiscent of the Carolina Wren, but drier sounding, and although the wren may give 2-syllabled notes, more often has 3-syllabled notes in its song series. Has call of low abrasive *chuck chuck*.

• **BEHAVIOR** Solitary or in pairs. Rather secretive; more often heard than seen. Terrestrial, but also forages and sings in low to middle levels of vegetation. Hops or runs on ground while flicking its tail, which is usually partially cocked upward. Forages for food by picking over foliage and branches and overturning leaves. Jumps up to pick insects off bottom side of leaves. Eats adult insects, spiders, and caterpillars.

• **BREEDING** Monogamous. Solitary nester.

• **NESTING** Incubation 12–13 days by female. Altricial young brooded by female; stay in nest 8–10 days, fed by both sexes, but female does more. 1 brood per year.

• **POPULATION** Common in moist woodlands with dense understory; large tracts are optimum. In migration, casual to rare in the Southwest to California.

• **CONSERVATION** Neotropical migrant. Frequent cowbird host. Vulnerable to deforestation; sensitive to forest fragmentation and overbrowsing by deer.

Similar Birds

COMMON YELLOWTHROAT First fall male • some black on sides of face; olive-gray to olive-brown upperparts; paler yellow underparts; whitish belly; brownish flanks; longer tail.

Flight Pattern

Swift short direct flights with rapidly beating wings.

Nest Identification

Shape ◣   Location ▬

Grasses, stems, vines, and leaves • lined with mammal hair and rootlets • on ground, near base of tree or bush, or clump of vegetation, sometimes in fork of low shrub • build by both sexes • 3–6 white or creamy white eggs, with brown flecks and splotches; short oval to long oval, 0.75 x 0.58 inches.

Plumage Sexes similar	Habitat ♠♦ ♣♣	Migration Migratory	Weight 0.5 ounce

DATE _____ TIME_____ LOCATION _____

Family PARULIDAE	Species *Oporornis agilis*	Length 5.5 inches	Wingspan 8.75 inches

CONNECTICUT WARBLER

Although this large chunky short-tailed shy bird does not nest in Connecticut, it was first seen in that state and is a regular autumn visitor. Its secretive habits make this a poorly known species. Its wintering grounds in South America are not clearly defined, and as one of the year's latest migrants, taking vastly different spring and fall routes, it often is not seen. Males and females have long yellowish undertail coverts.

• **SONG** Bold rocking jerky *whipity-whipity-whipity* or *beacher, beacher, beacher*. Call is *plink* or *chimp*.

• **BEHAVIOR** Solitary or in pairs. Secretive. Terrestrial; also forages low in vegetation. Singing males may move higher in trees. Female lands 30–60 feet from nest and walks to conceal location. Walks with slight bobbing of tail instead of hopping. Walks on logs and branches. Gleans insects and spiders; also snails, berries, and seeds. When flushed, flies up to perch and may sit still for several minutes, thrushlike.

• **BREEDING** Monogamous. Solitary nester.

• **NESTING** Breeding biology poorly known. Estimated incubation 11–12 days by female. Young altricial; brooded by female; stay in nest estimated 8–9 days, fed by both sexes. 1 brood per year.

• **POPULATION** Uncommon in most woodlands. Fall migrants uncommon in East.

• **CONSERVATION** Neotropical migrant. Infrequent host to cowbirds. Species may be declining; reasons unknown.

white or buffy eye ring

gray hood over head and throat

olive-green upperparts

long bicolored bill

gray upper breast

MALE

dull yellow underparts

pinkish legs and feet

brownish olive hood

olive-green upperparts

white or buffy eye ring

FEMALE

grayish chest and face

dull pale yellow underparts

JUVENILE

Similar Birds

MOURNING WARBLER
Smaller; thinner; thin broken grayish white eye ring; shorter undertail coverts; richer yellow underparts; hops rather than walks
• juvenile has paler throat.

NASHVILLE WARBLER
Smaller; thinner; white eye ring with pale lores; short undertail coverts; yellow throat; dark legs; short bill.

Flight Pattern

Rather swift direct flight for short distances on rapidly beating wings.

Nest Identification

Shape — Location —

Bark pieces and grass, with lining of fine plant materials and mammal hair • on small hillock of moss or sheltered by reeds and grasses • may be built by both sexes • 3–5 creamy white eggs, splotched and flecked with lavender, browns, and black; short ovate, 0.74 x 0.57 inches.

Plumage Sexes differ	Habitat	Migration Migratory	Weight 0.5 ounce

DATE _____ TIME_____ LOCATION _____

Family PARULIDAE	Species *Geothlypis trichas*	Length 5 inches	Wingspan 8 inches

COMMON YELLOWTHROAT

One of the most numerous and widespread warblers usually stays close to the ground, concealed in vegetation. The amount of yellow on the underparts, the shade of olive on the upperparts, and the color of the pale border between the mask and crown all vary with geography.

- **SONG** Bold rhythmic *wichity wichity wich;* varies with range. Sharp raspy call of *chuck* or *djip;* sometimes flat *pit* note.

- **BEHAVIOR** Solitary or in pairs. Wrenlike; skulks in vegetation, climbs vertically on stems, cocks and flicks tail, and

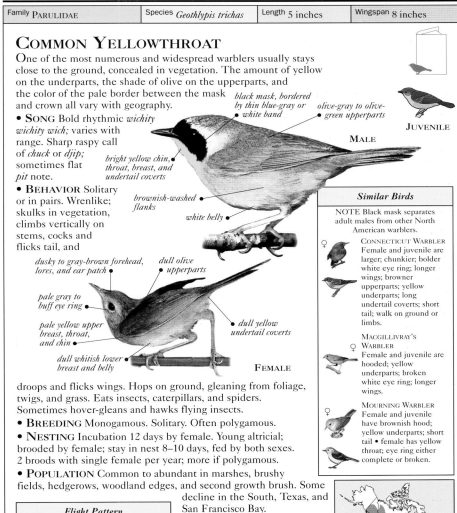

black mask, bordered by thin blue-gray or white band

olive-gray to olive-green upperparts

JUVENILE

MALE

bright yellow chin, throat, breast, and undertail coverts

brownish-washed flanks

white belly

dusky to gray-brown forehead, lores, and ear patch

dull olive upperparts

pale gray to buff eye ring

pale yellow upper breast, throat, and chin

dull yellow undertail coverts

dull whitish lower breast and belly

FEMALE

droops and flicks wings. Hops on ground, gleaning from foliage, twigs, and grass. Eats insects, caterpillars, and spiders. Sometimes hover-gleans and hawks flying insects.

- **BREEDING** Monogamous. Solitary. Often polygamous.

- **NESTING** Incubation 12 days by female. Young altricial; brooded by female; stay in nest 8–10 days, fed by both sexes. 2 broods with single female per year; more if polygamous.

- **POPULATION** Common to abundant in marshes, brushy fields, hedgerows, woodland edges, and second growth brush. Some decline in the South, Texas, and San Francisco Bay.

- **CONSERVATION** Neotropical migrant. Frequent cowbird host. Vulnerable to habitat loss caused by wetland drainage and stream channelization.

Similar Birds

NOTE Black mask separates adult males from other North American warblers.

♀ CONNECTICUT WARBLER Female and juvenile are larger; chunkier; bolder white eye ring; longer wings; browner upperparts; yellow underparts; long undertail coverts; short tail; walk on ground or limbs.

MACGILLIVRAY'S WARBLER ♀ Female and juvenile are hooded; yellow underparts; broken white eye ring; longer wings.

MOURNING WARBLER ♀ Female and juvenile have brownish hood; yellow underparts; short tail • female has yellow throat; eye ring either complete or broken.

Flight Pattern

Slow weak jerky flight with rapid wing beats, alternating with brief periods of wings pulled to sides. Sallies from perch to take insects in midair, returning to perch.

Nest Identification

Shape ⬤   Location ⚬⚬⚬ ▬ ⸾⸾

Dried grasses, dried leaves, stems, bark chips, and sedges • lined with fine grasses, hair, and bark fibers • atop small pile of weeds or grass or atop cattails, sometimes in small shrub, less than 3 feet above ground • built by female • 3–6 creamy white or white eggs, flecked with black, grays, and browns, mostly at larger end; oval to short oval, 0.7 x 0.5 inches.

Plumage Sexes differ	Habitat 〰 ▬ ▲ ♠	Migration Migratory	Weight 0.4 ounce

DATE _____ TIME_____ LOCATION _____

Family PARULIDAE	Species *Wilsonia citrina*	Length 5.25 inches	Wingspan 8 inches

HOODED WARBLER

This bird resides in the thick foliage of the understory beneath tall deciduous trees. When the male sings from his high perch, often concealed, he may sit almost motionless as he delivers his ringing song. The juvenile female lacks the black on her crown but has dusky lores and white tail spots.

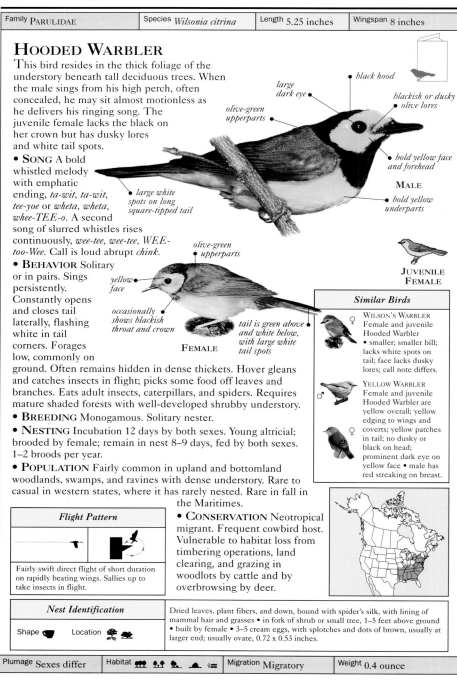

large dark eye

black hood

blackish or dusky olive lores

olive-green upperparts

bold yellow face and forehead

MALE

bold yellow underparts

large white spots on long square-tipped tail

olive-green upperparts

yellow face

occasionally shows blackish throat and crown

FEMALE

tail is green above and white below, with large white tail spots

JUVENILE FEMALE

- **SONG** A bold whistled melody with emphatic ending, *ta-wit, ta-wit, tee-yoe* or *wheta, wheta, whee-TEE-o*. A second song of slurred whistles rises continuously, *wee-tee, wee-tee, WEE-too-Wee*. Call is loud abrupt *chink*.
- **BEHAVIOR** Solitary or in pairs. Sings persistently. Constantly opens and closes tail laterally, flashing white in tail corners. Forages low, commonly on ground. Often remains hidden in dense thickets. Hover gleans and catches insects in flight; picks some food off leaves and branches. Eats adult insects, caterpillars, and spiders. Requires mature shaded forests with well-developed shrubby understory.
- **BREEDING** Monogamous. Solitary nester.
- **NESTING** Incubation 12 days by both sexes. Young altricial; brooded by female; remain in nest 8–9 days, fed by both sexes. 1–2 broods per year.
- **POPULATION** Fairly common in upland and bottomland woodlands, swamps, and ravines with dense understory. Rare to casual in western states, where it has rarely nested. Rare in fall in the Maritimes.
- **CONSERVATION** Neotropical migrant. Frequent cowbird host. Vulnerable to habitat loss from timbering operations, land clearing, and grazing in woodlots by cattle and by overbrowsing by deer.

Similar Birds

WILSON'S WARBLER Female and juvenile Hooded Warbler • smaller; smaller bill; lacks white spots on tail; face lacks dusky lores; call note differs.

YELLOW WARBLER Female and juvenile Hooded Warbler are yellow overall; yellow edging to wings and coverts; yellow patches in tail; no dusky or black on head; prominent dark eye on yellow face • male has red streaking on breast.

Flight Pattern

Fairly swift direct flight of short duration on rapidly beating wings. Sallies up to take insects in flight.

Nest Identification

Shape — Location —

Dried leaves, plant fibers, and down, bound with spider's silk, with lining of mammal hair and grasses • in fork of shrub or small tree, 1–5 feet above ground • built by female • 3–5 cream eggs, with splotches and dots of brown, usually at larger end; usually ovate, 0.72 x 0.53 inches.

Plumage Sexes differ	Habitat	Migration Migratory	Weight 0.4 ounce

DATE _____ TIME_____ LOCATION _____

Family PARULIDAE	Species *Wilsonia pusilla*	Length 4.75 inches	Wingspan 7.5 inches

WILSON'S WARBLER

Making its home in the thick damp woodlands and bogs of western North America, this active warbler has a wide nesting range, from Alaska to New Mexico, in the boreal forest from the Pacific to the Atlantic coast in Canada, and south into the New England states. The female is similar to the male but lacks the black cap or has only a light gray-black wash on her crown. Juvenile females lack the black crown altogether.

black cap • olive-green upperparts • **MALE**

bright yellow face and lores •

long brownish olive tail •

bold yellow to greenish yellow underparts •

- **SONG** Quick series of slurred *chee-chee-chee* notes, dropping in pitch at the end. Subject to much individual and regional variation. Call is abrasive nasal *chimp*.
- **BEHAVIOR** Solitary or in pairs. Tame and inquisitive; responds to pishing by birders. Energetic. Moves tail up and down or in a circular fashion, similar to a gnatcatcher, as it picks food off foliage by gleaning and hover-gleaning. Also catches insects in flight. Eats spiders, insects, and berries.
- **BREEDING** Monogamous. Solitary in coastal areas. Forms loose colonies and is polygynous at high elevations.
- **NESTING** Incubation 10–13 days by female. Young altricial; brooded by female; stay in nest 8–11 days, fed by both sexes. 1 brood per year.
- **POPULATION** Common to fairly common in dense moist woodlands, willow and alder bogs, riparian corridors, and dense brushy ground cover in moist situations. Much more numerous in the West than in the East.

olive to grayish crown •

dusky yellow ear patch •

FEMALE

Similar Birds

HOODED WARBLER
White spots on tail, which it constantly flicks open and closed; longer bill; dark dusky lores; black hood in males, with suggestion of hood in many females.

YELLOW WARBLER ♀
Female and juvenile
• yellow edging to wings and wing coverts; yellow spots in tail; short tail with undertail coverts reaching closer to tip; more subdued tail wag.

- **CONSERVATION** Neotropical migrant. Uncommon cowbird host, except in the coastal lowlands of California. Vulnerable to habitat loss from destruction of lowland riparian thickets.

Flight Pattern	

Swift flight of short duration on rapidly beating wings. Sallies forth from perch to take insects in midair before returning.

Nest Identification	
Shape 🥣 Location ▬ ᏪᏪᏪ 🌳	Dried leaves, stalks, moss, and grass, with lining of fine grasses • atop grassy tussock, pile of moss, or sedges, or set at base of tree or bush, or in low shrub • 0–3 feet above ground • built by female • 4–7 creamy white or white eggs, with flecks of brown, sometimes wreathed; oval to short oval, 0.6 inch long.

Plumage Sexes differ	Habitat 🌿🌱 🪵 〰️ ⛰️	Migration Migratory	Weight 0.3 ounce

DATE _____ TIME_____ LOCATION _____

Family PARULIDAE	Species *Wilsonia canadensis*	Length 5–6 inches	Wingspan 7.5–8.75 inches

CANADA WARBLER

This bird sings frequently from the dense forest undergrowth it favors, or from an exposed perch just above it, with a jumbled warbling song that defies a fitting mnemonic. It actively forages for insects by flushing them from the foliage and chasing them. Males have been observed in "anticipatory feeding," offering insects to the unhatched eggs in the well-concealed nest on the ground. Canada Warblers are more often seen than heard on the breeding grounds, but a bird often will reveal itself, coming close to squeaking and pishing sounds made by birders. This early fall migrant heads southward before many other warblers begin their migrations. During migration they are often seen in pairs, and may be traveling with their mate of the season.

yellow supraloreal stripe

whitish eye ring forms spectacles

black necklace on breast

lacks wing bars

MALE

• **SONG** *Chip* followed by explosive staccato series of short notes ending with 3-note phrase, the last note rising in pitch. Song carries well and is given often on breeding grounds.

• **BEHAVIOR** Skulks in the undergrowth; often concealed when perched. Frequently found in low, dense, luxuriant undergrowth under mixed hardwoods. Gleans insects from foliage, stems, and ground; sometimes flycatches.

• **BREEDING** Solitary nester.

• **NESTING** Incubation 12 days by female. Altricial young fledge at 10–12 days. Probably 1 brood per year.

• **POPULATION** Common to fairly common in breeding range and in migration in the East; casual to accidental elsewhere. Declining.

pinkish legs and feet

black lores

spectacles

gray upperparts, wings, and tail

yellow underparts with faint gray streaking on breast

white undertail coverts

pinkish legs and feet

FEMALE

Similar Birds

MAGNOLIA WARBLER ♂ Black streaking extends onto sides; yellow rump; white wing patch or bars; white patches in tail; white supercilium; ♀ black lores and cheeks.

• **CONSERVATION** Neotropical migrant. Host to Brown-headed Cowbirds. Vulnerable to disturbance of mature forest on wintering ground. Habitat loss and forest fragmentation negatively affecting populations.

Flight Pattern

Direct flight with rapid somewhat fluttering wing beats.

Nest Identification

Shape ◥   Location ▬▐ ⬅

Generally on the ground • bulky cup of dead leaves, grasses, dried plants, and ferns • lined with finer grasses and rootlets • on a bank, upturned tree roots, or mossy hummocks • built by female • 3–5 brown, buff, or creamy white eggs with speckled dots and small blotches of various shades of brown, gray, and purple; oval to short oval, 0.68 x 0.5 inches.

Plumage Sexes differ	Habitat 🐦 🌿 🔺	Migration Migratory	Weight 0.4 ounce

DATE _____ TIME_____ LOCATION _____

Family PARULIDAE	Species *Basileuterus culicivorus*	Length 5 inches	Wingspan 7.5 inches

GOLDEN-CROWNED WARBLER

This bird, which nests in and is a resident of northern Mexico, Central America, and ranges well into South America, is an occasional visitor to the lower Rio Grande Valley of southern Texas, usually recorded in winter. There it often flocks with other warblers outside its breeding season but often remains hidden in dense moist forests. When visiting the southern United States, the bird is often found in the company of mixed-species foraging flocks of

greenish yellow supercilium

dusky olive auriculars

olive-gray upperparts

grayish olive face

yellow-orange stripe with black borders on midcrown

yellowish white arc under eye

bold yellow breast, belly, and underparts

titmice, gnatcatchers, warblers, and other songbirds. Juveniles resemble adults.

• **SONG** A rich whistled warble of *wee-wee-wee-seee'* or *chew-chew-chew-weee'*, ending with an up-slurred note. Call is a series of *tick* or *chip*.

• **BEHAVIOR** Solitary or in pairs. A shy skulking species. Active and restless; often flicks open or jerks tail and wings. Forages on ground and low in trees by picking food off foliage; occasionally hawks prey. Eats mainly insects and spiders.

• **BREEDING** Monogamous. Solitary nester.

• **NESTING** The breeding biology of the Golden-crowned Warbler is poorly known. The time of incubation and the time nestlings stay in the nest is also unknown. The role of the sexes in nesting and in the number of broods per year is unknown or has not been published.

• **POPULATION** This bird is casual in the lower Rio Grande Valley of southern Texas.

• **CONSERVATION** Not of special concern. There are no published records of any degree of cowbird parasitism.

Similar Birds

ORANGE-CROWNED WARBLER
Olive-green upperparts; olive-yellow underparts with faint dusky streaking; dusky eye stripe; greenish yellow supercilium; yellow crissum; lacks yellow-orange crown stripe with black border; sometimes shows rusty orange patch on crown.

Flight Pattern	
Weak fluttering direct flight of short duration on rapidly beating wings.	

Nest Identification	
Shape ⬡ Location ▬ 🪨	Grasses and plant fibers, oven or dome-shaped with lining of fine materials • sheltered by bank, clump of grass, or large boulder • built by female • 2–4 white eggs, with reddish brown markings, concentrated at larger end; oval to short oval, 0.68 x 0.53 inches.

Plumage Sexes similar	Habitat 🌿 ▲ 🌾 〰	Migration Nonmigratory	Weight 0.4 ounce

DATE _____ TIME_____ LOCATION _____

Family PARULIDAE	Species *Icteria virens*	Length 7.25 inches	Wingspan 9–10 inches

YELLOW-BREASTED CHAT

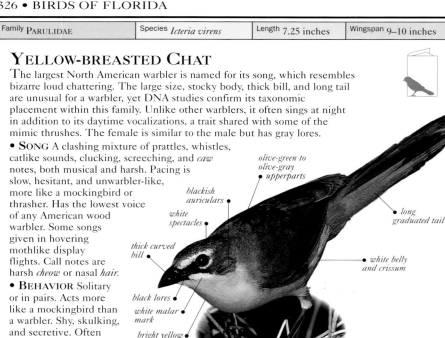

The largest North American warbler is named for its song, which resembles bizarre loud chattering. The large size, stocky body, thick bill, and long tail are unusual for a warbler, yet DNA studies confirm its taxonomic placement within this family. Unlike other warblers, it often sings at night in addition to its daytime vocalizations, a trait shared with some of the mimic thrushes. The female is similar to the male but has gray lores.

olive-green to olive-gray upperparts

blackish auriculars

white spectacles

thick curved bill

long graduated tail

white belly and crissum

black lores

white malar mark

bright yellow throat and breast

- **SONG** A clashing mixture of prattles, whistles, catlike sounds, clucking, screeching, and *caw* notes, both musical and harsh. Pacing is slow, hesitant, and unwarbler-like, more like a mockingbird or thrasher. Has the lowest voice of any American wood warbler. Some songs given in hovering mothlike display flights. Call notes are harsh *cheow* or nasal *hair.*
- **BEHAVIOR** Solitary or in pairs. Acts more like a mockingbird than a warbler. Shy, skulking, and secretive. Often remains hidden in thick foliage. Best seen when male sings from an exposed perch or is displaying. Display flight lasts several seconds, head held high, tail pumping, legs dangling, and singing all the while. Forages low in dense brushy shrubbery and sometimes on the ground, gleaning insects, larvae, berries, and fruits. The only warbler known to hold food in its feet.
- **BREEDING** Monogamous. Solitary nester or small colonies.
- **NESTING** Incubation 11–12 days by female. Altricial young brooded by female; stay in nest 8–11 days, fed by both sexes. 2 broods per year.
- **POPULATION** Common in dense thickets, brush, or scrub, especially along swamp margins and streams. Significant decline over much of its eastern range.
- **CONSERVATION** Neotropical migrant. Common host to Brown-headed Cowbird. Vulnerable to habitat loss due to land development and clearing, urbanization, and natural succession from old fields to maturation of forests.

Similar Birds
No similar species in North America.

Flight Pattern

Weak direct flights of short duration. In singing display, flies with legs dangling and wings flapping limply.

Nest Identification	
Shape ◗ Location 🐝	Dried stems, leaves, grasses, and bark pieces, lined with soft grasses, stems, and leaves • in bush, vines, or thorny shrub, 2–8 feet above ground • built by female • 3–6 white or creamy white eggs, with flecks of rust or violet, concentrated at larger end; oval, 0.86 x 0.67 inches.

Plumage Sexes similar	Habitat 🗶 ▲ 〰	Migration Migratory	Weight 0.9 ounce

DATE _____ TIME_____ LOCATION _____

| Family THRAUPIDAE | Species *Piranga rubra* | Length 7.75 inches | Wingspan 11–12 inches |

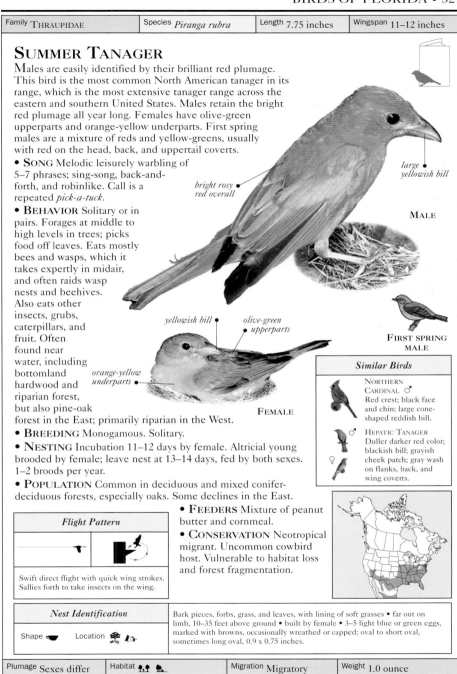

SUMMER TANAGER

Males are easily identified by their brilliant red plumage. This bird is the most common North American tanager in its range, which is the most extensive tanager range across the eastern and southern United States. Males retain the bright red plumage all year long. Females have olive-green upperparts and orange-yellow underparts. First spring males are a mixture of reds and yellow-greens, usually with red on the head, back, and uppertail coverts.

• **SONG** Melodic leisurely warbling of 5–7 phrases; sing-song, back-and-forth, and robinlike. Call is a repeated *pick-a-tuck*.

bright rosy red overall

large yellowish bill

MALE

• **BEHAVIOR** Solitary or in pairs. Forages at middle to high levels in trees; picks food off leaves. Eats mostly bees and wasps, which it takes expertly in midair, and often raids wasp nests and beehives. Also eats other insects, grubs, caterpillars, and fruit. Often found near water, including bottomland hardwood and riparian forest, but also pine-oak forest in the East; primarily riparian in the West.

yellowish bill

olive-green upperparts

FIRST SPRING MALE

orange-yellow underparts

FEMALE

• **BREEDING** Monogamous. Solitary.

• **NESTING** Incubation 11–12 days by female. Altricial young brooded by female; leave nest at 13–14 days, fed by both sexes. 1–2 broods per year.

• **POPULATION** Common in deciduous and mixed conifer-deciduous forests, especially oaks. Some declines in the East.

Similar Birds

NORTHERN CARDINAL ♂
Red crest; black face and chin; large cone-shaped reddish bill.

HEPATIC TANAGER ♂
Duller darker red color; blackish bill; grayish ♀ cheek patch; gray wash on flanks, back, and wing coverts.

• **FEEDERS** Mixture of peanut butter and cornmeal.

• **CONSERVATION** Neotropical migrant. Uncommon cowbird host. Vulnerable to habitat loss and forest fragmentation.

Flight Pattern

Swift direct flight with quick wing strokes. Sallies forth to take insects on the wing.

Nest Identification

Shape ⌒   Location 🌸 🐦

Bark pieces, forbs, grass, and leaves, with lining of soft grasses • far out on limb, 10–35 feet above ground • built by female • 3–5 light blue or green eggs, marked with browns, occasionally wreathed or capped; oval to short oval, sometimes long oval, 0.9 x 0.75 inches.

| Plumage Sexes differ | Habitat 🌿 🌾 | Migration Migratory | Weight 1.0 ounce |

DATE __7 | 04__ TIME _____ LOCATION _____

Family THRAUPIDAE	Species *Piranga olivacea*	Length 7 inches	Wingspan 11–12 inches

SCARLET TANAGER

No other bird in North America has the breeding male's unique plumage of a rich scarlet body with black wings and tail. When the male arrives on the breeding grounds, he perches at the tops of tall trees and sings to defend his territory and attract a mate. In the molt following the breeding season, the male retains his black wings and tail, but his plumage becomes a mixture of green, yellow, and red patches, later becoming dull green and yellow, appearing similar to the female bird. Juveniles and first fall males are similar in appearance to the adult female.

bright scarlet overall

black wings and tail

tan to creamy pink bill with blackish culmen

MALE

pale broken eye ring

dull green upperparts

blackish wings and tail

FALL MALE

lemon-yellow underparts

FEMALE

- **SONG** A breathy, coarse series of 4–5 notes, somewhat rapidly delivered, *querit-queer-query-querit-queer*. Pattern is sing-song and back-and-forth, somewhat like a robin with a sore throat. Has call of *chip-burrr*.
- **BEHAVIOR** Solitary or in pairs. May forage for food on ground but more often high in tops of trees. Eats insects, including wasps, bees, and caterpillars. Also takes berries and fruit. Gleans food from branches and foliage and frequently hawks insects. Frequents drier forests, often pine and pine-oak.
- **BREEDING** Monogamous; solitary or in pairs. Male displays by perching below female, opening his wings and showing off his scarlet back.
- **NESTING** Incubation 13–14 days by female. Young altricial; brooded by female; stay in nest 9–11 days, fed by both sexes. 1 brood per year.
- **POPULATION** Fairly common in deciduous and mixed conifer-hardwood forests. Some recent declines. Casual in West.
- **FEEDERS** Will come to feeders for mixture of bread crumbs, cornmeal, and peanut butter.
- **CONSERVATION** Neotropical migrant. Vulnerable to loss of habitat and forest fragmentation, as it requires large areas of forest for breeding. Fairly common host to cowbird parasitism.

Similar Birds

♂ WESTERN TANAGER
Male has additional yellow upper wing bar • females and winter males are similar to their counterparts but have white wing bars.

Flight Pattern

Swift rapid flight with quick wing strokes. Sallies forth to take insects in flight.

Nest Identification

Shape ▭   Location ✿ ⚶

Forbs, grasses, sticks, rootlets, and twigs, with lining of soft grasses and conifer needles • far out on limb, 5–70 feet above ground • built by female • 2–5 bluish greenish eggs, marked with brown, often wreathed; oval to short oval, 0.9 x 0.7 inches.

Plumage Sexes differ	Habitat 🌿 🌲	Migration Migratory	Weight 1.0 ounce

DATE _____ TIME_____ LOCATION _____

Family EMBERIZIDAE	Species *Pipilo erythrophthalmus*	Length 7–7.5 inches	Wingspan 10–11 inches

EASTERN TOWHEE

Sometimes called a Ground Robin in the South, this is the eastern counterpart of the Spotted Towhee. Until recently these birds were classified as one species, the Rufous-sided Towhee. The two species hybridize where their ranges overlap along rivers in the Great Plains. The smaller Florida race has whitish eyes instead of red like most other races. In flight the white undertail corners flash conspicuously. Juveniles are brown overall with pale chins and dark streaking on underparts and upperparts.

black upperparts and hood

red eyes

MALE

white outer tail feathers

tawny buff undertail coverts

rufous sides

white underparts

distinct white patch at base of primaries and distinct white tertial edges

• **SONG** A clear whistled *drink-your-teeeaaa*, with the "tea" trilled. Much individual variation, with some birds leaving off the introductory note and some omitting the ending trill. Has calls of *toe-WHEEE* and *che-wink* or *wank*.

• **BEHAVIOR** Solitary or in pairs. Secretive; stays low in underbrush and on ground. Frequents brushy thickets, woodland edges, and riparian areas. Males are conspicuous when singing, often choosing an exposed perch. Usually detected by the rustle of dry leaves on ground; forages by double-scratching, pulling both legs sharply backward at once. Eats insects, caterpillars, small salamanders, fruits, and seeds.

brown upperparts and hood

white outer tail feathers

tawny buff undertail coverts

rufous sides

white patch at base of primaries and white tertial edges

white underparts

FEMALE

JUVENILE

• **BREEDING** Monogamous. Solitary. Courting male chases female and fans tail to show off white spots on outer feathers.

• **NESTING** Incubation 12–13 days by female. Young altricial; brooded by female; stay in nest 10–12 days, fed by both sexes, more by male. 2–3 broods per year.

• **POPULATION** Common to fairly common. Major decline in Northeast in last half of 20th century.

• **FEEDERS** Mixture of oats, suet, and seeds.

• **CONSERVATION** Declines in Northeast poorly understood; vulnerable to loss of habitat, clearing of land, development, and pesticides in food chain. Frequent cowbird host.

Similar Birds

SPOTTED TOWHEE
Extensive white spotting on back and scapulars • female shows darker browns on head, breast, and upperparts.

Flight Pattern

Short bouncy flights with tail spread; series of rapid wing beats alternating with wings pulled to sides; repeated.

Nest Identification

Shape 	Location	Sticks, rootlets, grass, bark, and leaves, with lining of soft grasses • on ground, sheltered by grassy tussock or bush, occasionally in low bush or tree, 1–5 feet above ground (but up to 20 feet) • built by female • 2–6 creamy white or grayish eggs; oval, 0.9 x 0.66 inches.

Plumage Sexes differ	Habitat	Migration Northern birds migrate	Weight 1.5 ounces

DATE _____ TIME _____ LOCATION _____

Family EMBERIZIDAE	Species *Aimophila aestivalis*	Length 6 inches	Wingspan 8 inches

BACHMAN'S SPARROW

In the early spring, the male bird's lovely territorial flight song contrasts with its drab coloring. This large-bodied sparrow skulks and forages on the ground, hidden in the brushy understory of the dry wooded areas of the South. Easiest to locate by the male's song, birds often drop down into the underbrush and remain out of sight when approached, not responding to pishing sound by birders. Juveniles have buffy washes on the face, chest, and underparts, are streaked on the throat, breast, and sides, and show a distinct pale eye ring.

thin dark line extending back from eye

buffy gray sides of head

gray upperparts with heavy chestnut-brown streaking

large dark bill

buff or gray breast, sides, and flanks

whitish belly

long dark rounded tail

JUVENILE

• **SONG** A pure fluted introductory note followed by a warbling or trilled melody, varied in pitch. Successive songs by the same male are pitched in different keys, and the song's musical quality has been favorably compared to that of the Hermit Thrush or the pattern of a Bewick's Wren. This sparrow's call is a snakelike hiss.

• **BEHAVIOR** Solitary or in pairs. Secretive. Often difficult to see, because birds flushed from groundcover tend to fly only a very short distance before dropping back into cover. Male sings from a low exposed perch. Forages for food on ground. Eats mostly insects. Also eats seeds, snails, and spiders.

• **BREEDING** Monogamous. Solitary.

• **NESTING** Incubation 12–14 days by female. Young altricial; brooded by female; stay in nest 10–11 days, fed by both sexes. 2–3 broods per year.

• **POPULATION** Uncommon. Declining in most of northern range due to loss of habitat. Frequents open dry woodlands, especially pines with grassy or scrub palmetto undergrowth.

• **CONSERVATION** Uncommon cowbird host. Vulnerable to habitat loss due to logging, development, land clearing, and ecological succession. National Audubon Society Blue List. Listed as threatened in many states.

Similar Birds

FIELD SPARROW
Smaller; smaller pinkish bill; gray head; brown crown; brownish ear patch; white eye ring; 2 white wing bars; gray underparts with buffy wash; notched tail.

GRASSHOPPER SPARROW
Chunkier; light buff crown stripe; much shorter, notched tail; buffy underparts; buffy lores; buffy streaking and feather edging on back; white eye ring
• different habitat, lives in meadows.

Flight Pattern

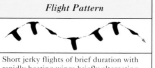

Short jerky flights of brief duration with rapidly beating wings briefly alternating with wings pulled to body.

Nest Identification

Shape 🐚 ⬤   Location ▬ 🔺🔺🔺

Grass and forbs, with lining of plant down, grasses, and hair • on ground or grassy tussock, sheltered by tall grasses, vines, or shrub • built by female • 3–5 plain white eggs; ovate, 0.8 x 0.6 inches.

Plumage Sexes similar	Habitat 🌿 🌱 🌿🌿	Migration Nonmigratory	Weight 0.7 ounce

DATE _____ TIME _____ LOCATION _____

Family EMBERIZIDAE	Species *Spizella passerina*	Length 5.5 inches	Wingspan 8–9 inches

CHIPPING SPARROW

Its bold chestnut cap, bordered by a long white superciliary stripe during breeding season, helps identify this tiny sparrow. Named for its song and call, it sings from its high perch during the day, and sometimes even at night, or calls as it forages for food in trees, gardens, and backyards. One of the tamest sparrows, it will take food from human hands. Juveniles lack the white eyebrow and

chestnut cap

gray nape and cheeks

white supercilium

black bill

light brown upperparts with black or brown streaking

black line extends from bill through eye to ear

long slightly notched tail

2 white wing bars

gray underparts

JUVENILE

WINTER PLUMAGE

chestnut cap but have a streaked crown and nape, streaked underparts, and buffy wing bars. Winter birds have brown-streaked crowns, brown faces, and dark lores.

- **SONG** A repetitive series of trilled chip notes, *chip-chip-chip-chip-chip-chip-chip*, all the same pitch. Has a call of *seek*.
- **BEHAVIOR** Solitary or in pairs. In small family groups after breeding season. May join mixed-species foraging flocks in winter. Forages on ground and picks off foliage. Eats seeds, insects, their caterpillars, and spiders.
- **BREEDING** Monogamous. Solitary. A few males polygynous.
- **NESTING** Incubation 11–14 days by female. Young altricial; brooded by female; stay in nest 8–12 days, fed by both sexes. 2 broods per year.
- **POPULATION** Common and widespread in open mixed coniferous-deciduous forests, forest edges, gardens, lawns, and short-grass fields.
- **FEEDERS** Comes to feeders for breadcrumbs and seeds.
- **CONSERVATION** Neotropical migrant. Common host to cowbird parasitism.

Similar Birds

CLAY-COLORED SPARROW
Black-streaked brown crown with gray center stripe; buffy brown cheek patch bordered by dark postocular stripe and dark mustache mark; pale grayish eyebrow; whitish chin and submustachial stripe separated by buffy malar mark; whitish underparts with buffy wash on breast.

Flight Pattern

Typically, short flights with rapidly beating wings alternating with brief periods of wings pulled to sides; repeated.

Nest Identification

Shape    Location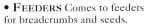

Grass, forbs, weed stalks, and rootlets, with lining of mammal hair and grass • on branch or vine tangle, rarely on ground • most often 3–11 feet above ground (but up to 60 feet) • built by female • 2–5 bluish green eggs, marked with dark browns, blues, and blacks, often wreathed; subelliptical to short subelliptical, 0.7 x 0.5 inches.

Plumage Sexes similar	Habitat	Migration Migratory	Weight 0.4 ounce

DATE _____ TIME_____ LOCATION _____

Family EMBERIZIDAE	Species *Spizella pallida*	Length 5.5 inches	Wingspan 8 inches

CLAY-COLORED SPARROW

The male bird perches to claim its territory while singing its buzzy insectlike song across the grasslands. Wintering primarily in the highlands of central Mexico, this tiny bird flies north to summer in the prairies of Canada and the northern United States. In flight this frequent visitor to backyard feeders shows a dark buff rump. Juveniles have a gray nape, buffy brown cheek patch, and streaked underparts.

white supercilium

white malar stripe

dark mustache stripe

brown ear patches

pale gray-white underparts with buffy wash on breast

brown crown with black streaks

whitish stripe in middle of crown

dark stripe from behind eye

JUVENILE

light brown back with dark streaks

2 white wing bars

- **SONG** Insectlike repetitive *bzzz-bzzzz-zeee-zeee*. Has a call of *chip* or *sip*.
- **BEHAVIOR** In pairs during breeding season. Small family groups prior to fall migration. Males vigorously defend small territory. Sings often and well into the heat of July. Forages on ground or low in trees. Eats seeds and insects. May join mixed-species feeding flocks with other sparrows in winter.
- **BREEDING** Monogamous. Solitary.
- **NESTING** Incubation 10–12 days by both sexes, but female does more. Young altricial; brooded by female; stay in nest 8–9 days, fed by both sexes. 1–2 broods per year.
- **POPULATION** Fairly common in brushy weedy fields, riparian thickets, and forest edges. Slight decline over recent decades due to loss of habitat after human populations increased in the North and East. Rare to casual visitor in migration and winter on both coasts, the Southwest, and southern Florida.
- **FEEDERS** Will come to feeding stations for breadcrumbs, cracked corn, sunflower seeds, and millet.
- **CONSERVATION** Neotropical migrant. Common host to cowbird parasitism. Vulnerable to habitat loss due to development and land clearing for agriculture.

Similar Birds

CHIPPING SPARROW
Winter adults have gray rump; brown crown with black streaking and whitish central crown stripe; gray underparts • first winter birds have buffy underparts.

BREWER'S SPARROW
Lacks whitish crown stripe; blacker streaking on upperparts; paler brown ear patch lacks black outline; whitish eye ring.

Flight Pattern

Typically, short flight on rapidly beating wings alternating with brief periods of wings pulled to sides.

Nest Identification

Shape ☙   Location ▬ 🐦 🌿

Sticks, grass, forbs, and rootlets, with lining of mammal hair and rootlets • atop grassy tussock, on ground sheltered by bush, or low in branch of shrub or tree • less than 5 feet above ground • built by female • 3–5 bluish green eggs, marked with dark browns and blacks, often wreathed; ovate, 0.67 x 0.5 inches.

Plumage Sexes similar	Habitat 	Migration Migratory	Weight 0.4 ounce

DATE _____ TIME_____ LOCATION _____

Family EMBERIZIDAE	Species *Spizella pusilla*	Length 5.75 inches	Wingspan 8.5 inches

FIELD SPARROW

This sparrow stays near the ground in fields and open woodlands. When defending its nest, the male flies from tree to tree singing a melody that accelerates like the bouncing of a dropped rubber ball. The clearing of the primeval eastern forest provided thousands of acres of habitat ideally suited for this

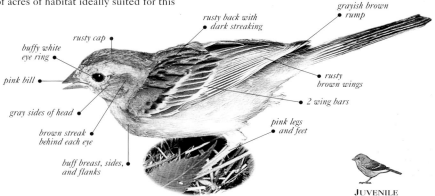

grayish brown rump

rusty back with dark streaking

rusty cap

buffy white eye ring

pink bill

rusty brown wings

gray sides of head

2 wing bars

brown streak behind each eye

pink legs and feet

buff breast, sides, and flanks

JUVENILE

small sparrow. Now, as the old farms become suburbs or succumb to the woodlots brought on by ecological succession, this bird is declining in this range.

• **SONG** A pleasant *seea-seea-seea-wee-wee-wee*, which begins with separate clear whistled notes and accelerates, either ascending, descending, or staying on the same pitch. Call is abrasive *chip*.

• **BEHAVIOR** Solitary or in pairs in breeding season. In small family flocks after nesting. In winter, forms flocks that may join mixed-species foraging flocks. Forages on ground or low in shrubbery for insects, caterpillars, seeds, and spiders. Tame and curious; responds to squeaking and pishing by birders.

• **BREEDING** Monogamous. Solitary.

• **NESTING** Incubation 10–17 days by female. Young altricial; brooded by female; stay in nest 7–8 days, fed by both sexes. Male tends and feeds fledglings while female incubates second clutch. 2–3 broods per year.

• **POPULATION** Fairly common in old fields, open brushy woodlands, thorn scrub, and forest edge. Casual in West. Uncommon in the Maritimes.

• **FEEDERS** Small grain.

• **CONSERVATION** Common host to cowbird parasitism.

Similar Birds

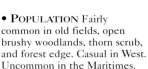

CLAY-COLORED SPARROW
Brown crown with central stripe; buffy cheek patch; buffy brown malar mark; gray nape; buffy edges and streaks on upperparts; whitish underparts with buffy wash on chest and flanks; 2 buffy wing bars.

Flight Pattern

Short flights with rapid wing beats alternating with brief periods of wings pulled to sides; repeated.

Nest Identification

Shape 🥣   Location ▬ ✦✦✦ 🌲

Fine grasses, leaves, and dried grass, with lining of mammal hair and rootlets • atop grassy tussock or clump of vegetation, sometimes in vine or bush • less than 3 feet above ground • built by female • 2–6 creamy pale greenish bluish white eggs, marked with browns, occasionally wreathed; short subelliptical, 0.7 x 0.53 inches.

Plumage Sexes similar	Habitat 🏚 ▬ ▲	Migration Northern birds migrate	Weight 0.4 ounce

DATE _____ TIME_____ LOCATION _____

Family EMBERIZIDAE	Species *Pooecetes gramineus*	Length 5.5–6.75 inches	Wingspan 10–11.25 inches

VESPER SPARROW

This bird is named for the time of day it usually sings its best and most continuous choruses, which is at twilight when many other songbirds have become silent. Its song is not limited to the vespers hour, however, for during nesting season, it sings throughout the day from the highest perch available in its territory. This sparrow, with chestnut lesser coverts on its shoulder and white outer tail feathers, has a vast geographical distribution, its home habitats ranging from dry grasslands and farmlands to sagebrush flats. Juveniles resemble adults but have more extensive streaking on the underparts.

brown ear patch bordered behind and below with white

upperparts streaked gray-brown

chestnut patch at bend of wing, with row of black spots beneath

white eye ring

grayish brown streaking on breast, throat, and sides

white underparts

• **SONG** Two drawled clear notes followed by two higher notes, then a short descending trill. Call is a high thin *tssit*.

• **BEHAVIOR** Solitary or in pairs. May form small family groups after breeding season. May join loose flocks in winter. Walks on ground. Runs from danger instead of flying. Forages on ground, in grasses, and in low shrubbery for insects and seeds. Very fond of dust baths. Neither bathes in nor drinks water, meeting all internal water needs through diet.

white outer tail feathers

long notched tail

• **BREEDING** Monogamous. Solitary or loose colonies.

• **NESTING** Incubation 11–13 days by both sexes, but female does more. Young altricial; brooded by female; stay in nest 7–14 days, fed by both sexes. Fledglings tended and fed by male while female starts another nest. 1–3 broods per year.

• **POPULATION** Uncommon to fairly common. Numbers declining in the East as habitat is lost to development and because logged areas become older and less suitable for nesting.

• **CONSERVATION** Neotropical migrant. Common host to cowbird parasitism. Nesting sites are being lost due to agricultural mowing and other operations.

Similar Birds

SAVANNAH SPARROW
Shorter tail; yellow supercilium; pale central crown stripe; central "stickpin" spot on chest; lacks chestnut lesser coverts; lacks white eye ring and outer tail feathers.

Flight Pattern
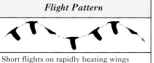
Short flights on rapidly beating wings alternating with brief periods of wings pulled to sides; repeated.

Nest Identification	
Shape 〜 Location ▬ ♦♦♦	Dry grasses, weed stalks, and rootlets, lined with finer grasses and animal hair • in scraped-out depression on ground • hidden under vegetation, in field, near tall grass clump, on sand or dirt • built by female • 2–6 creamy white or pale greenish white eggs with brown markings; oval, 0.8 x 0.6 inches.

Plumage Sexes similar	Habitat ♦ ▬ ⟿	Migration Migratory	Weight 1.0 ounce

DATE _____ TIME_____ LOCATION _____

Family EMBERIZIDAE	Species *Passerculus sandwichensis*	Length 5.25–6.25 inches	Wingspan 8–9.5 inches

SAVANNAH SPARROW

Named for the city in Georgia where it was first spotted, this bird has a wide range, living in grassy marshes and wet meadows to grasslands and cultivated grass to tundra. It also has considerable variation between the many races that make up the species. Like many sparrows, it spends most of its time on the ground; when disturbed, it scurries through the grasses, running mouselike rather than flying away. But if hard-pressed it flies up a short distance then drops back into the grasses.

whitish or pale median crown stripe

yellow or whitish supercilium

dark brown-streaked upperparts

central "stickpin" on chest

pinkish legs and feet

buff to white underparts with brown streaking

IPSWICH FORM

• **SONG** Begins with 2–3 *chip* notes followed by 2 buzzy insectlike trills, *tip-tip-seeeee-saaaay*. Call note is *seeep*.

• **BEHAVIOR** Solitary or in pairs. May form small family groups after breeding season. Gregarious; forms flocks in migration and winter. Forages for food on ground, sometimes scratching in dirt and foliage. Eats seeds, insects, spiders, and sometimes snails. Roosts in small tight groups on the ground.

• **BREEDING** Monogamous. Solitary. Some marsh-dwelling populations tend to be polygynous. Sometimes loose colonies.

• **NESTING** Incubation 10–13 days by both sexes, but female does most. Young altricial; brooded by female; stay in nest 7–14 days; fed by both sexes. 1–2 broods per year.

short notched tail

Similar Birds

SONG SPARROW
Longer rounded tail without notch; heavier streaking on the underparts; large central "stickpin" on chest in most races; lacks yellow in lores and supercilium.

VESPER SPARROW
Gray-brown streaking on upperparts, throat, breast, and sides; wing has chestnut patch at bend; white outer tail feathers; white eye ring; brown ear patch.

• **POPULATION** Abundant and widespread in open grassy landscapes and tundra. May be extending range farther south in the southern Appalachians.

• **CONSERVATION** Neotropical migrant. Uncommon cowbird host.

Flight Pattern

Short flights with rapidly beating wings alternating with brief periods of wings pulled to sides.

Nest Identification

Shape   Location

Moss and dried grasses • lined with fine hair, fine grasses, and roots • in depression or scrape, sheltered by vines, grasses, or dune • built by female • 2–6 pale greenish blue or whitish eggs, marked with brown, sometimes wreathed; ovate to short ovate, 0.8 x 0.57 inches.

Plumage Sexes similar	Habitat	Migration Migratory	Weight 0.8 ounce

DATE _____ TIME_____ LOCATION _____

Family EMBERIZIDAE	Species *Ammodramus savannarum*	Length 4.75–5.5 inches	Wingspan 8–8.5 inches

GRASSHOPPER SPARROW

These birds are named for their insectlike song. The male claims his territory by singing from a low exposed perch during the day. Hidden in tall grasses, this bird runs rather than flies from danger. Because it nests on the ground in cultivated grasslands, lives are lost when the crop is mowed; after mowing, predators take eggs, young, and adults.

dark crown with pale stripe through center

yellow lore

white eye ring

gray-brown streaking on upperparts

buff breast, sides, flanks, and undertail coverts

yellow at bend of wings

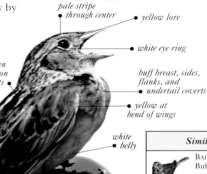

JUVENILE

- **SONG** High thin insectlike buzzing with 2 notes then a trill, *pit-tuck, zeeeeeeeeeeee*. At dusk may sing with more squeaky buzzy notes and trills. Call is soft insectlike *tisk*.

white belly

- **BEHAVIOR** Solitary or in pairs. May form small family groups after breeding season. Forages on ground and from low vegetation. Eats insects, worms, snails, seeds, and grains. Males sing from any exposed perch. When disturbed on nest, female flutters away in distraction display.

short notched tail

- **BREEDING** Monogamous Loose colonies.

- **NESTING** Incubation 11–12 days by female. Young altricial; brooded by female; stay in nest 9 days, fed by both sexes. 2–3 broods per year.

- **POPULATION** Common in cultivated fields, grasslands, prairies, savanna, and palmetto scrub. Declining in eastern part of its range.

- **CONSERVATION** Neotropical migrant. Uncommon host to cowbird parasitism. Declining due to changes in grasses grown and losses to agricultural operations. Threatened or endangered in Florida and parts of the Appalachian Mountains.

Similar Birds

BAIRD'S SPARROW
Buffy orange crown and supercilium; dark spot in each rear corner of ear patch; blackish malar mark; necklace of dark brown streaks on breast; chestnut scapulars with pale edging forming scaly appearance on upperparts.

HENSLOW'S SPARROW
Greenish buff head and nape; blackish crown stripes; black-bordered ear patch; rusty brown upperparts edged whitish and streaked black; dark brown streaking on breast, sides, and flanks • juvenile is paler and more washed with buffy head, nape, upperparts, and underparts; faint dusky streaking on sides • eastern range.

Flight Pattern

Flies close to the ground with a fluttering rapid undulating flight, similar to a wren.

Nest Identification

Shape 🥄 Location ▬

Dried grass with lining of rootlets, hair, and grass, partially domed on one side • in slight hollow on ground, sheltered by tall grasses • built by female • 3–6 creamy white eggs with flecks and dots of reddish brown, occasionally wreathed; ovate, 0.8 x 0.56 inches.

Plumage Sexes similar	Habitat	Migration Migratory	Weight 0.8 ounce

DATE _____ TIME_____ LOCATION _____

| Family EMBERIZIDAE | Species *Ammodramus henslowii* | Length 4.75–5.25 inches | Wingspan 7–7.5 inches |

HENSLOW'S SPARROW

Upon arrival at the nesting grounds, the male begins singing day or night, rain or shine, perched or concealed. He cocks his tail down, elevates his head, and expels with a bodily shudder one of the shortest songs of any songbird. Occasionally, these sparrows battle one another in defense of territory. Their plumage serves as camouflage in the marshes and meadows. Juveniles resemble adults but are buffier and paler and have only faint streaking on their underparts.

flat greenish ocherous head with black stripes

green wash on neck and nape

large grayish bill

reddish back and wings with black streaking and white to buff edging

buff-green mustache, bordered black on both sides

conspicuous streaking on breast and sides

whitish underparts with buff wash on chest, sides, and flanks

- **SONG** Sings *flee-LICK*, like an explosive bird hiccup, with emphasis on the second note. Call is a thin high *tsip*.

short notched tail

JUVENILE

- **BEHAVIOR** Solitary or in pairs. Unobtrusive, secretive, and easily overlooked, except for the persistent song of the male, from low concealed or higher exposed perches. Singing males allow reasonably close approach. Forages and skulks on ground among vegetation. Eats insects, caterpillars, and seeds.
- **BREEDING** Monogamous. Loose colonies.
- **NESTING** Incubation 11 days by female. Young altricial; brooded by female; stay in nest 9–10 days, fed by both sexes. 2 broods per year.
- **POPULATION** Uncommon in weedy meadows, grassy fields (especially wet), and reclaimed strip mine benches in pine-grass savannas in the West. Declining, particularly in the Northeast.
- **CONSERVATION** Some concern has been recorded. Uncommon host to cowbird parasitism. Vulnerable to habitat loss due to grazing, agricultural mowing operations, land clearing, and development.

Similar Birds

GRASSHOPPER SPARROW
Brown to buffy head; pale central crown stripe; dark postocular stripe; buffy wash on white underparts, particularly on chest, sides, flanks, and crissum; lacks streaking on underparts.

Flight Pattern

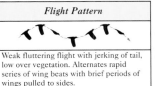

Weak fluttering flight with jerking of tail, low over vegetation. Alternates rapid series of wing beats with brief periods of wings pulled to sides.

Nest Identification

Shape ● Location ▬ ✻✻✻

Grass and forbs, with lining of fine grass and hair • on ground in slight hollow or sheltered by grassy clump or weeds • built by female • 3–5 creamy or pale greenish white eggs, marked with reddish browns, often wreathed; oval, 0.7 x 0.55 inches.

| Plumage Sexes similar | Habitat ▬ ◢ | Migration Migratory | Weight 0.5 ounce |

DATE _____ TIME_____ LOCATION _____

Family EMBERIZIDAE	Species *Ammodramus leconteii*	Length 4.5–5.25 inches	Wingspan 6.5–7.25 inches

LE CONTE'S SPARROW

One of the smallest sparrows, this bird is most often found in prairie wetlands. A secretive bird, Le Conte's Sparrow often scurries mouselike in thick cover when flushed, rarely flying, and only a few feet at a time when it does. The species has declined in some parts of its range with the disappearance of damp fields and other similar habitats. This sparrow is a casual migrant in the Northeast and West, traveling only short distances off the main migration pathways. Juveniles are buffier overall and are heavily streaked on their underparts.

white central crown stripe
bright broad buff-orange eyebrows
thin bill
grayish ear patches
dark brown-streaked orange-buff sides and breast
chestnut streaks on nape
straw-colored streaks on back
bristly tail

- **SONG** Call resembles a short shrill grasshopper-like *buzz*. High-pitched and thin, it has a short squeaky introductory note followed by a buzzy trill and ending with a final *chip* note. Call note is a thin *tsip*.
- **BEHAVIOR** Solitary or in pairs. Secretive. Skulking. Walks and runs on ground to forage within matted vegetation, often in wet grasslands and bogs. In winter months, combs ground for seeds from grass and weeds. During summer, eats wide variety of insects, seeds, and spiders. Territorial male sings from exposed perch, with head pulled back and bill pointed skyward.
- **BREEDING** Monogamous. Solitary.
- **NESTING** Incubation 12–13 days by female. Young altricial; brooded by female; stay in nest estimated 8–10 days, fed by both sexes. 1–2 broods per year.
- **POPULATION** Fairly common and somewhat local in wet meadows, bog, and marsh edges. Declining in parts of range.
- **CONSERVATION** Uncommon host to cowbird parasitism. Vulnerable to loss of habitat due to draining of wetlands and development of habitat for agriculture.

Similar Birds

NELSON'S SHARP-TAILED SPARROW
Broad blue-gray crown stripe; unstreaked blue-gray nape; less color contrast on upperparts; olive-brown body with whitish streaks; frequents marsh habitat.

GRASSHOPPER SPARROW
Whitish to buff eyebrows; brown, black, and buff nape; brown auricular patch with dark borders; whitish underparts with buffy wash on chest and sides; lacks streaks on breast and sides.

Flight Pattern
Alternates of rapid wing beats with brief periods of wings pulled to sides; flies short distances before dropping back into grass.

Nest Identification	
Shape ⬤ Location ▬ ✦✦	Grass, rushes, and stems, lined with fine materials • usually on or near ground • built by female • 3–5 grayish white eggs with brown spots; ovate, 0.7 x 0.53 inches.

Plumage Sexes similar	Habitat	Migration Migratory	Weight 0.5 ounce

DATE _____ TIME_____ LOCATION _____

Family EMBERIZIDAE	Species *Ammodramus nelsoni*	Length 4.75 inches	Wingspan 7.25 inches

NELSON'S SHARP-TAILED SPARROW

Its streaked plumage serves as camouflage in the dense freshwater marsh grasses it inhabits in Canada, the northern prairie marshes of the US, and parts of Maine. When frightened, it scampers mouselike, with its head held low, and does not fly. It recently was determined to be a separate species from the Saltmarsh Sharp-tailed Sparrow; both were formerly lumped together under the name Sharp-tailed Sparrow. Adults show whitish or gray streaking on scapulars. Juveniles have buffier underparts and buffy heads without the gray auriculars and nape and lack streaking on the breast and flanks.

gray median crown stripe

plain gray nape and ear patch

buff to light brownish upperparts with blackish streaking

ocherous orange on face

gray to dark-brown streaked ocherous buff breast, sides, and flanks

white belly

JUVENILE

- **SONG** An explosive wheezy descending *p-tsssshh-uk*, like the sound of cold water tossed on hot metal.
- **BEHAVIOR** In pairs or small groups. Secretive. Difficult to observe unless male is singing, which it does from conspicuous perches. Curious, and will come up in vegetation and draw closer to pishing and squeaking by birders. Walks around on ground and picks up food or gleans from vegetation. Eats insects, their caterpillars, various seeds, and small snails. Males loosely territorial or nonterritorial. Flushed birds usually fly short distance before dropping back down into dense cover.
- **BREEDING** Polygamous. Loose colonies.
- **NESTING** Incubation 11 days by female. Young altricial; brooded by female; stay in nest 10 days, fed mostly by female. 1 brood per year.
- **POPULATION** Fairly common in wet meadows, freshwater marshes, and tule beds. Numbers decline with habitat drainage.
- **CONSERVATION** Rare host to cowbird parasitism. Vulnerable to loss of habitat due to marsh draining and agricultural practices, including cattle grazing.

Similar Birds

LE CONTE'S SPARROW Bold dark brown stripes on sides; white median crown stripe; gray nape with chestnut streaking; straw-colored streaking on back and scapulars; lives in prairies
- juveniles have heavily streaked underparts.

SALTMARSH SHARP-TAILED SPARROW Larger orange-buff facial triangle contrasts sharply with body; larger bill; black-streaked supercilium behind eye
- juveniles have heavily streaked underparts
- eastern range.

Flight Pattern

Short flights low over vegetation, with rapid wing beats alternating with brief periods of wings pulled to sides; repeated.

Nest Identification

Shape   Location ⸻ 🌱 ***

Dried grasses and stems • atop grassy tussock or on pile of reeds • built by female • 3–7 light green eggs, with heavy brown spotting; oval, 0.76 x 0.57 inches.

Plumage Sexes similar	Habitat 〰	Migration Migratory	Weight Undetermined

Family EMBERIZIDAE	Species *Ammodramus caudacutus*	Length 5 inches	Wingspan 7.5 inches

SALTMARSH SHARP-TAILED SPARROW

This bird was formerly lumped in one species, the Sharp-tailed Sparrow, with the Nelson's Sharp-tailed Sparrow. Its recent taxonomic split gives it the distinction of tying for the longest English name of any bird species in North America. Making its home in the Atlantic coastal marshes, it walks on the ground in search of food and scurries through the grasses, head down and mouselike, when frightened. If flushed into flight, it flutters weakly, with its tail jerking, for a short distance before dropping back down into dense cover.

unstreaked blackish cap

ocher-orange eyebrow, streaked black behind eye

large bill

gray-brown back with light streaks

gray ear patches

rich buff triangle on side of face

sharply streaked pale buff breast, sides, and flanks

JUVENILE

• **SONG** A soft insectlike *ts-ts-ssssss-tsik*. Call is a sharp *chuck*.

• **BEHAVIOR** In pairs or small groups. Males are weakly territorial and sometimes do not defend territory at all. Skulking and somewhat secretive. Males sing from exposed perches. Curious, this bird will investigate squeaking or pishing by birders. Forages on ground and in dense vegetation to glean food from surfaces. Eats insects, caterpillars, seeds, small crustaceans, and snails.

• **BREEDING** Polygamous. Colonial.

• **NESTING** Incubation 11 days by female. Altricial young brooded by female; stay in nest 10 days, fed by female. 2 broods per year.

• **POPULATION** Uncommon to fairly common and somewhat local primarily in saltwater marshes. Declining.

• **CONSERVATION** Rare host to cowbird parasitism. Destruction of coastal salt marshes by draining and because of development has significantly reduced populations of this species.

Similar Birds

NELSON'S SHARP-TAILED SPARROW Shorter bill; head is less flat; less defined markings on head and around eye; more intense ocherous buff on breast, sides, and flanks • juveniles are buffy overall, with the much reduced streaking on underparts restricted to sides.

SEASIDE SPARROW Larger; darker grayer upperparts; longer heavier bill; yellow supraloral patch; dark malar stripe separates white mustache from white throat; broadly streaked underparts.

Flight Pattern

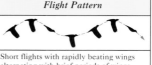

Short flights with rapidly beating wings alternating with brief periods of wings pulled to sides; repeated.

Nest Identification

Shape ◖ Location 🌾 ✳✳✳ ▬

Reeds, grasses, and seaweed, with lining of finer materials • on ground, set in grasses or reeds • built by female • 3–7 pale greenish eggs, marked with reddish browns; short ovate to ovate, 0.8 x 0.6 inches.

Plumage Sexes similar	Habitat ﹍﹍	Migration Migratory	Weight 0.7 ounce

DATE _____ TIME_____ LOCATION _____

Family EMBERIZIDAE	Species *Ammodramus maritimus*	Length 5.25–6.5 inches	Wingspan 8–8.5 inches

SEASIDE SPARROW

This shy bird makes its home in the salt marshes of the eastern coasts. Like many sparrows, the male perches atop reeds, grasses, or fences to sing his territorial song. Walking or running on the ground, its large feet prevent it from sinking in the soft marsh mud. There is much variation in size and color across the range, but the most widespread race, *A. m. maritimus*, is pictured here. Another race, *A. m. nigrescens,* is darkest, with the heaviest streaking on the underparts, and was formerly recognized as the species Dusky Seaside Sparrow. Found only near Titusville, Florida, it became extinct in 1987. Another species, *A. m. mirabilis*, called Cape Sable Sparrow, also found only in the Florida Everglades, is listed as federally endangered. All races show rufous greater primary coverts. Juveniles are duller with finer streaking on the underparts.

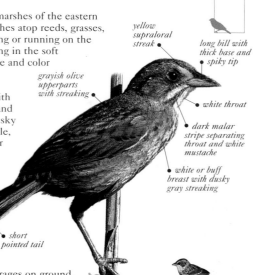

yellow supraloral streak

long bill with thick base and spiky tip

grayish olive upperparts with streaking

white throat

dark malar stripe separating throat and white mustache

white or buff breast with dusky gray streaking

short pointed tail

- **SONG** Harsh buzzy *oka-cheee-weee*, reminiscent of Red-winged Blackbird. Call note is *chip*.
- **BEHAVIOR** In pairs or small groups. Forages on ground, gleaning food as it walks upright, like a small rail; also wades, rail-like, in shallow water. Eats small snails, terrestrial and aquatic insects, crabs and other small crustaceans, and some seeds. Males fly 20–30 feet high in fluttering skylarking display flights and slowly descend back down to a perch — singing all the while.
- **BREEDING** Monogamous. Loose colonies.
- **NESTING** Incubation 12–13 days by female. Young altricial; brooded by female; stay in nest 8–10 days, fed by both sexes. 1–2 broods per year.
- **POPULATION** Fairly common in coastal salt marshes but declining from destruction of this habitat.
- **CONSERVATION** Rare host to cowbird parasitism. Destruction of coastal marshes, application of DDT in the 1970s, and flooding of marshes for mosquito control led to the extinction of one race and contributed to the near extinction of another in Florida, as well as the significant decline of other populations.

JUVENILE

Similar Birds

SALTMARSH SHARP-TAILED SPARROW Smaller; paler; buffier in overall color; ocherous orange triangle frames gray ear patch; whiter underparts with sharper dark streaking on breast, sides, and flanks; black crown patch; gray nape.

Flight Pattern

Short flights low over vegetation on rapidly beating wings alternating with brief periods of wings pulled to sides.

Nest Identification

Shape ◗ Location ▟▟

Dried grass and sedges • lined with soft finer grasses • attached to marsh reeds or set on clump of grass, from 9–11 inches to 5 feet above mud (but up to 14 feet) • built by female • 3–6 white to pale greenish eggs, marked with reddish browns; short ovate to elongated ovate, 0.8 x 0.6 inches.

Plumage Sexes similar	Habitat ▃▃	Migration Northern birds migrate	Weight 0.8 ounce

DATE _____ TIME_____ LOCATION _____

| Family EMBERIZIDAE | Species *Melospiza melodia* | Length 5.75–7.5 inches | Wingspan 8.25–12.5 inches |

SONG SPARROW

Even with its drab plumage, this bold songbird is easy to spot when it perches in the open, trilling its pleasant melody. In flight it pumps its tail up and down. Inhabiting a wide range, this bird is found throughout most of North America and is perhaps the continent's most variable species, with approximately thirty-one subspecies recognized. The Aleutian race, *M. m. maxima*, is so large and dark it looks like a different species. Because of the work of Ohio bird biologist Margaret Morse Nice, the biology of this bird may be the best-known of any songbird on the continent. Juveniles are similar to adults but appear buffier overall with finer streaking.

dark malar stripe borders white throat

broad grayish eyebrow

brownish, grayish, or brownish gray upperparts, usually streaked

streaking on sides and breast meet in center and form "stickpin"

whitish underparts

pinkish legs and feet

long rounded tail

ALEUTIAN RACE

- **SONG** Whistles 2–3 clear introductory notes, followed by a trill. Much variation in each individual's song and between individuals. Call is *chimp* or *what* and a high thin *ssst*.

- **BEHAVIOR** Solitary or in pairs. May be in small loose flocks in winter, often with other species of sparrows. Forages in trees, bushes, and on ground by picking food off foliage, grass, and soil; also scratches on ground. Eats insects, larvae, grains, seeds, berries, and some fruits. Coastal species take small mollusks and crustaceans. Males sing from exposed perches to claim territory.

- **BREEDING** Monogamous. Polygynous in some cases. Male vigorously defends territory and battles with other males. Often chases invading birds from territory.

- **NESTING** Incubation 12–14 days by female. Young altricial; brooded by female; stay in nest 9–16 days, fed by both sexes. 2–3 broods per year (occasionally 4 in southern parts of range).

- **POPULATION** Widespread and abundant to common in brushy areas, thickets, riparian scrub, weedy fields, urban/suburban lawns, and forest edge.

- **FEEDERS** Birdseed.

- **CONSERVATION** Species is one of the most frequent victims of parasitism by the Brown-headed Cowbird.

Similar Birds

SAVANNAH SPARROW
Yellowish above eye; shorter notched tail; pinker legs; finer streaking on upperparts; central "stickpin" on chest.

LINCOLN'S SPARROW
Smaller; buff wash on chest; more distinct markings; finer streaking on throat, breast, sides, and flanks; lacks central "stickpin" on chest.

Flight Pattern

Short flights close to ground, tail pumping up and down. Alternates rapid wing beats with brief periods of wings pulled to sides.

Nest Identification	
Shape 🥄 Location ▬ 🐦🌿 🌾	Grass, forbs, leaves, and bark strips, with lining of fine materials • usually on ground, sheltered by grassy tussock or reeds • sometimes in bush or tree, 2–4 feet above ground (but up to 12 feet) • built by female • 2–6 greenish white eggs, marked with reddish browns; oval to short oval, 0.8 x 0.61 inches.

| Plumage Sexes similar | Habitat 🌲 🌿 🏔 ⬖ ⬩ 〰 | Migration Northern birds migrate | Weight 0.7 ounce |

DATE _____ TIME_____ LOCATION _____

Family EMBERIZIDAE	Species *Melospiza lincolnii*	Length 5.25–6 inches	Wingspan 7.25–8.75 inches

LINCOLN'S SPARROW

This inhabitant of northern bogs and mountain meadowlands is skittish, often raising its slight crest when disturbed. It is sometimes overlooked because of its furtive habits and similarity to the Song Sparrow, with which it may compete when nesting territories overlap. This sparrow can be distinguished by its sweet gurgling melody that sounds similar to that of a House Wren or Purple Finch, and by the buffy band crossing the chest and separating the white chin and throat from the white lower breast and belly. Juveniles are paler and buffier overall with more streaking on their underparts.

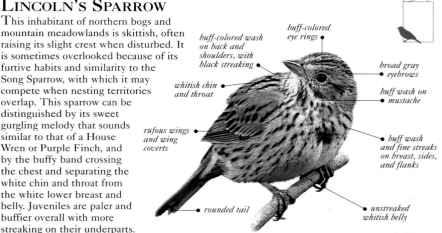

buff-colored eye rings

buff-colored wash on back and shoulders, with black streaking

whitish chin and throat

broad gray eyebrows

buff wash on mustache

rufous wings and wing coverts

buff wash and fine streaks on breast, sides, and flanks

rounded tail

unstreaked whitish belly

• **SONG** Features rapid bubbling trilled notes, with last notes harsher, louder, and lower in pitch, *chur-chur-chur-wee-wee-wee-wee-wah*. Alarm call is a flat-toned repetitious *tschup*. Calls also include a sharp buzzlike *zeee*.

• **BEHAVIOR** Solitary or in pairs. Sometimes joins mixed-species foraging flocks on wintering grounds. Secretive. Skulks low in thickets or on ground. Kicks backward with both feet like a towhee as it scratches among leaves on the ground; feeds on insects and small grains, as well as seeds from weeds and grasses. In migration, often found in brushy tangles near water. Often sings from a concealed perch during spring migration.

• **BREEDING** Monogamous. Solitary.

• **NESTING** Incubation 12–14 days by female. Young altricial; brooded by female; stay in nest 9–12 days, fed by both sexes. 1–2 broods per year.

• **POPULATION** Uncommon to fairly common in bogs, wet meadows, riparian thickets, and mountain meadows. Uncommon to fairly common in thickets and weedy fields in winter.

• **FEEDERS** Attracted by seed, particularly in migration.

• **CONSERVATION** Neotropical migrant. Rare host to cowbird parasitism. Vulnerable to loss of habitat because of logging operations and development.

Similar Birds

SONG SPARROW Longer tail; thicker bill; thicker malar stripe; heavier streaking on underparts; central "stickpin" on chest; white underparts lack buffy wash on chest; brown upperparts with rufous and black streaking.

SWAMP SPARROW Duller breast with thinner blurry streaks; gray head; rufous-brown crown with gray central stripe; unstreaked white throat; rufous wings and primary coverts.

Flight Pattern
Short flights with rapid wing beats alternating with brief periods of wings pulled to sides; repeated.

Nest Identification	
Shape ◢ Location 	Grass or sedge lined, sometimes with hair • often built in grass, hollow depressions, or moss • built by female • 3–6 pale green to greenish white eggs, with reddish brown markings; oval to short oval, 0.8 x 0.6 inches.

Plumage Sexes similar	Habitat ▲ ▲ ⚶ ⩾	Migration Migratory	Weight 0.8 ounce

DATE _____ TIME_____ LOCATION _____

Family EMBERIZIDAE	Species *Melospiza georgiana*	Length 4.75–5.75 inches	Wingspan 7.5–8 inches

SWAMP SPARROW

This small stocky sparrow will nest anywhere within its range where there is sufficient emergent dense vegetation in marshes, bogs, wet meadows, or sluggish streams. As nestlings learn to fly, they must stay above the water, so as not to be eaten by turtles, frogs, or fish. Adult females are similar to males but have brown-striped crowns. Juveniles are buffy with reddish wings and tails and heavily streaked underparts. Immatures resemble winter adults with rich buff sides, gray central crown stripe, and buffy wash overall.

reddish crown

deep rufous upperparts with black streaking

deep rufous wings

gray face

whitish throat

gray breast

whitish belly

JUVENILE   WINTER PLUMAGE

• **SONG** A bold slow melodious musical trill of either sharp single-note or slurred double-note phrases, *peat-peat-peat-peat-peat-peat-peat*. Has a call of *zeee* or *chip*.

• **BEHAVIOR** Solitary or in pairs in breeding season. May form loose flocks in winter. Secretive and skulking in dense vegetation or on ground. Curious, it will come to pishing or squeaking by birders. Forages by wading in water and picking up food with bill or by gleaning prey from vegetation or ground. Eats insects and seeds. Male sings to claim territory.

• **BREEDING** Monogamous. Loose colonies. Male often feeds incubating or brooding female while on nest.

• **NESTING** Incubation 12–15 days by female. Young altricial; brooded by female; stay in nest 11–13 days, fed by both sexes. 2 broods per year.

• **POPULATION** Common in marshes, bogs, and riparian stands of reeds, cattails, and sedges. Rare in the West. Some population declines due to loss of marsh habitat.

• **CONSERVATION** Neotropical migrant. Common host to cowbird parasitism. Vulnerable to habitat loss due to draining of wetlands, livestock overgrazing, and development.

Similar Birds

WHITE-THROATED SPARROW
Stockier; larger; yellow supraloral spot; whitish or buff supercilium; two whitish wing bars; gray underparts; white-and-black- or brown-and-tan-striped crown.

LINCOLN'S SPARROW
Buffy back and shoulders with black streaking; buffy breast band, sides, and flanks; black streaking on throat, breast, sides, and flanks; broad gray supercilium; brown crown with black streaks; buffy eye ring.

Flight Pattern

Short flights low over vegetation on rapidly beating wings alternating with brief periods of wings pulled to sides.

Nest Identification

Shape ◗   Location ⋔⋔ ✿

Dry thick grasses with lining of finer grasses • set in reeds, usually 0–5 feet above water • in some areas, in bush near water, 1–6 feet above ground • built by female • 3–6 greenish white eggs, marked with reddish browns; short subelliptical, 0.8 x 0.57 inches.

Plumage Sexes differ	Habitat 〰 ⌇	Migration Migratory	Weight 0.8 ounce

DATE _____ TIME_____ LOCATION _____

Family EMBERIZIDAE	Species *Zonotrichia albicollis*	Length 6.25–7.5 inches	Wingspan 8.75–10 inches

WHITE-THROATED SPARROW

The song of the White-throated Sparrow is heard in the Canadian wilderness and in the northeastern US where it breeds in woodland undergrowth, clearings, and gardens. Distinguishing marks include a broad yellow eyebrow, or supraloral stripe in the front of the eye, which tapers to either white or tan, and a sharply outlined white throat. Although it is common and widespread, sightings of this bird are rare in the West.

black or brown borders crown stripes and eye line

rusty brown upperparts

yellow supraloral stripe

dark bill

white throat

2 white wing bars

grayish underparts with diffuse streaking

• **SONG** A thin whistle, starting with 2 single notes followed by 3 triple notes: *poor-sam-peabody, peabody, peabody* or *pure-sweet-Canada, Canada, Canada*. Calls include a grating *pink* and a drawled lisping *tseep*. Territorial birds often sing at night. Some black-and-white-striped females sing.

JUVENILE

TAN-STRIPED

Similar Birds

WHITE-CROWNED SPARROW
Black-and-white-striped crown; pink bill; lacks whitish throat contrasting with gray breast; lacks yellow supraloral spot; tertials lack bright rufous coloring.

HARRIS'S SPARROW
Winter adult and juvenile • slightly larger; pink bill; crown varies from tan to black stippling, to black with white spotting, to black; face buffy tan; chin varies from white to blackish; throat white, black-and-white, or black; blackish band crossing upper breast.

• **BEHAVIOR** Solitary or in pairs. In winter joins flocks of other White-throats and mixed species. Hops on ground or forages in shrubs and trees. Scratches among leaves for food. Eats mostly weed seeds, fruit from trees, tree buds, and insects. May hawk insects in midair. Attracted by pishing and squeaking by birders. Two adult color morphs are based on head striping: black-and-white-striped and brown-and-tan-striped. Field studies show that white-striped males tend to mate with tan-striped females, and tan-striped males tend to mate with white-striped females.

• **BREEDING** Monogamous. Solitary.

• **NESTING** Incubation 11–14 days by female. Young altricial; brooded by female; stay in nest 7–12 days, fed by both sexes. 1–2 broods per year.

• **POPULATION** Common and widespread in conifer and mixed-conifer forest, forest edge and clearings, and thickets. Rare in the West.

• **FEEDERS** Seeds and grains.

• **CONSERVATION** Uncommon host to cowbird parasitism. Vulnerable to habitat loss due to logging operations.

Flight Pattern
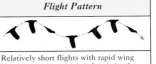
Relatively short flights with rapid wing beats alternating with brief periods of wings pulled to sides; repeated.

Nest Identification	
Shape Location	Lined with coarse grass, wood chips, twigs, pine needles, roots, and other fine materials • often found at edge of clearing • 0–3 feet above ground • built by female • 3–6 greenish, bluish, or cream-white eggs with reddish brown markings; subelliptical or long elliptical, 0.8 x 0.6 inches.

Plumage Sexes similar	Habitat	Migration Migratory	Weight 0.9 ounce

DATE _____ TIME_____ LOCATION _____

Family EMBERIZIDAE	Species *Zonotrichia leucophrys*	Length 6.5–7.5 inches	Wingspan 9.25–10.25 inches

WHITE-CROWNED SPARROW

This bold bird is easy to identify, with conspicuous black stripes on its white crown, a pink to dull yellow bill, and a pale gray throat. Like many sparrows, the male sings to claim its territory and duels to defend its ground. His songs may even continue into the night. As is usual with a wide geographical range, there is morphological and behavioral variation. The most striking subspecies differences include bill color and white versus black supralorals. Juveniles have heavily streaked underparts and a brown-and-buff-streaked head. Immatures have a brown-and-tan-striped head and unstreaked underparts.

white supercilium
black postocular stripe
brownish upperparts with blackish brown streaking
2 white wing bars
brownish wash on sides and flanks

white crown with bold black stripes
pink to dull yellow bill
whitish gray throat
grayish underparts become white on belly

JUVENILE

FIRST WINTER

- **SONG** A melancholy whistled *poor-wet-wetter-chee-zee*. Has call note of *pink* or sharp *tseek*.
- **BEHAVIOR** Solitary or in pairs. In small family groups after breeding season. Forms flocks in winter. Males sing from exposed perches; sometimes in spring on wintering grounds. Gleans food from vegetation; hops on ground and forages by scratching. Eats seeds, insects, caterpillars, and parts of plants.
- **BREEDING** Monogamous. Individuals in some nonmigratory populations may pair for life. Some polygynous.
- **NESTING** Incubation 11–14 days by female. Young altricial; brooded by female; stay in nest 7–12 days, fed by both sexes. Male continues to feed young while female starts another nest. 2–4 broods per year (largest number of broods in southern populations; 1 brood in far north).
- **POPULATION** Common to fairly common in woodlands, thickets, wet meadows, and chaparral.
- **FEEDERS** Baby chick scratch and seeds.
- **CONSERVATION** Neotropical migrant. Uncommon host to cowbird parasitism. Vulnerable in the West to habitat loss because of land development and logging.

Similar Birds

WHITE-THROATED SPARROW More rufous-brown upperparts; mostly dark bill; well-defined white throat patch; yellow spot between eye and bill; gray underparts; two white wing bars; black-and-white- or brown-and-tan-striped cap.

HARRIS'S SPARROW Winter adult and juvenile • slightly larger; pink bill; crown varies from tan with black stippling, to black with white spotting, to black; face buffy tan; chin varies from white to blackish; throat white, black-and-white, or black; blackish band crossing upper breast.

Flight Pattern

Short flights on rapidly beating wings alternating with brief periods of wings pulled to sides; repeated.

Nest Identification

Shape ☕   Location ⚊ ⚊ 🌿 🍃

Grass, sticks, rootlets, and forbs • lined with soft grasses, feathers, and hair • on clump of grass or moss, sheltered by bush, or in small tree • 0–5 feet above ground (but up to 30 feet) • built by female • 2–6 light blue or green eggs marked with reddish browns; ovate to short ovate or long ovate, 0.8 x 0.6 inches.

Plumage Sexes similar	Habitat 🪨 🌿 🌲 🔺	Migration Northern birds migrate	Weight 1.0 ounce

DATE _____ TIME _____ LOCATION _____

Family EMBERIZIDAE	Species *Junco hyemalis*	Length 5.75–6.5 inches	Wingspan 9.25–10 inches

DARK-EYED JUNCO

In 1973 the American Ornithologists' Union grouped under one heading what was once considered five different junco species. Thus, the Dark-eyed Junco is composed of geographic races that differ in color and range but are closely related and have similar habits. All races of the species complex have white outer tail feathers; a black, gray, or brown hood; and white lower breast, belly, and undertail coverts. All have similar songs; all but one have a pink bill. Females tend to be paler and sometimes browner on the back. Juveniles have streaked upperparts and underparts.

dark gray hood
gray upperparts
SLATE-COLORED MALE

white outer tail feathers

SLATE-COLORED JUVENILE

brownish gray hood
brownish gray upperparts

SLATE-COLORED FEMALE

OREGON MALE
PINK-SIDED MALE

WHITE-WINGED MALE
GRAY-HEADED MALE

- **SONG** Melodic trill, varied in pitch and tempo and from dry *chip* notes to tinkling bell-like sounds, similar to Chipping Sparrow. Call is abrasive *dit* produced with sucking smack. Twitters in flight.
- **BEHAVIOR** Solitary or in pairs. In small family groups after breeding season. In spring and fall may join mixed-species foraging flocks; forms flocks in winter. Forages by gleaning from vegetation and scratching on ground. Hops. Eats seeds, grains, berries, insects, caterpillars, and some fruits; occasionally hawks flying insects. The larger males often winter farther north or at higher elevations than juveniles and females.
- **BREEDING** Monogamous. Solitary.
- **NESTING** Incubation 11–13 days by female. Altricial young brooded by female; leave nest at 9–13 days, fed by both sexes. 1–3 broods per year.
- **POPULATION** Common to fairly common in coniferous and mixed conifer-deciduous forests and bogs; winter habitats vary.
- **FEEDERS** Breadcrumbs, nuts, and seeds.
- **CONSERVATION** Uncommon cowbird host. Vulnerable to habitat loss due to logging operations.

Similar Birds

YELLOW-EYED JUNCO
Yellow eyes; black lores; rufous-trimmed greater coverts and tertials; gray head and nape; gray throat and underparts paler than head; white belly
• limited southwest range.

Flight Pattern

Short flights with white outer tail feathers flashing conspicuously. Alternates several rapid wing beats with brief periods of wings pulled to sides.

Nest Identification

Shape ● Location ━ ✿ ♠

Grass, weeds, and leaves, with lining of fine grass, hair, and feathers • on ground, sometimes in cavity, sheltered by bush, tree roots, log, occasionally in shrub or tree, 0–20 feet above ground • male gathers materials and female builds • 3–6 whitish to bluish white eggs, with markings of brown and gray, sometimes concentrated at larger end; oval to short or long oval, 0.8 x 0.56 inches.

Plumage Sexes differ	Habitat ♠♦ ♠ ▲	Migration Northern birds migrate	Weight 0.7 ounce

DATE _____ TIME_____ LOCATION _____

Family CARDINALIDAE	Species *Cardinalis cardinalis*	Length 7.5–9.25 inches	Wingspan 10–12 inches

NORTHERN CARDINAL

The official bird of seven US states sings a variety of cheerful melodies year-round. The male fights other birds to defend his territory and sometimes tries to attack his own reflection in windows, automobile mirrors, chrome, and hubcaps. Having adapted to suburban areas, these birds visit backyard feeders regularly and sometimes take food from the hand. Juveniles resemble the adult female but have a blackish instead of reddish bill.

• SONG Variable. Variety of gurgling and clear whistled melodies. More than 25 different songs. Best-known phrases include *whoit cheer, whoit cheer, cheer-cheer-cheer; cheer, whoit-whoit-whoit-whoit; wheat-wheat-wheat-wheat;* and *bir-dy, bir-dy, bir-dy, bir-dy.* Female in courtship duets with male after territory is established and prior to nesting. Call is abrasive metallic *chip* or *pik.*

• BEHAVIOR Solitary or in pairs during breeding season. Gregarious at other times, forming flocks in winter or joining mixed-species foraging flocks. Forages in trees, bushes, and on ground. Eats insects, seeds, grains, fruits, and snails. Drinks sap from holes drilled by sapsuckers. Hops rather than walks on ground.

• BREEDING Monogamous. Solitary. Male feeds female during courtship and while incubating.

• NESTING Incubation 12–13 days, mostly by female. Young altricial; brooded by female; stay in nest 9–11 days, fed by both sexes. Male may continue to tend fledglings while female begins incubating new set of eggs. 2–4 broods per year.

• POPULATION Abundant and widespread in woodland edges, undergrowth, thickets, and residential areas. Range has expanded north in the last century, partly due to increase of feeding stations. Casual in West.

• FEEDERS Cracked corn, sunflower seeds, birdseed. Will bathe in birdbaths.

• CONSERVATION Common cowbird host, especially in the central portion of its range.

black mask through eyes
accentuated crest
cone-shaped reddish bill
red overall
black patch at base of bill extends onto throat

MALE

red tip
dusky lores and patch at base of bill
buffy golden brown head and underparts
buffy olive upperparts

FEMALE

buff-brown underparts

JUVENILE

red wash on wings and tail

Similar Birds

PYRRHULOXIA ♀
Resembles female and juvenile Northern Cardinal; stubby sharply curved yellowish bill; red eye ring; red tip to long gray crest; grayish upperparts; red edging to primaries; reddish wash on throat and underparts.

Flight Pattern

Short flight just above vegetation or below canopy; rapidly beating wings alternate with brief periods of wings pulled to sides.

Nest Identification

Shape ⬩ Location 🌳 🔝 🌳

Twigs, weeds, grass, bark strips, and leaves • lined with hair and grass • in fork of low tree or bush or set in tangled twigs or vines • usually less than 5 feet above ground (but up to 15 feet) • built by female • 3–4 pale greenish, bluish, or grayish eggs with dots and flecks of gray, purple, and brown; oval, 1.0 x 0.7 inches.

Plumage Sexes differ	Habitat 🌿 ▲ 🌾	Migration Nonmigratory	Weight 1.6 ounces

DATE ⁷/⁰⁴ _____ TIME _____ LOCATION _____

Family CARDINALIDAE	Species *Pheucticus ludovicianus*	Length 7–8.5 inches	Wingspan 12–13 inches

ROSE-BREASTED GROSBEAK

This bird's clear notes are delivered in robinlike phrases, but the song is sweet. Males sing constantly, even while sparring to win a female. In flight the male shows rosy red wing linings, a white rump, and black-tipped white uppertail coverts; females flash yellow wing linings. First fall males have less streaking on underparts than females, buffy wash across the breast, and rose-red wing linings. First spring males are similar to adult males but with brown edges to the black plumage.

• **SONG** Rich warbled melodious phrases interspersed with call notes. Squeaky abrasive call, *eek*.

• **BEHAVIOR** Solitary or in pairs in breeding season. Flocks in migration and winter. Forages in trees, shrubs, and on ground. Eats seeds, insects, caterpillars, tree flowers, fruits, and berries. Hover gleans high in trees at branch tips; females more often than males.

black head and back

white or buff-colored bill

white shoulder patch

white wing patch

black throat

white underparts with rosy red triangular patch on breast

black tail with white inner webs to outer tail feathers

JUVENILE MALE

white eyebrow

brownish upperparts with dark streaking

MALE

2 broad white wing bars

FIRST SPRING MALE

white mustache and throat

FEMALE

whitish to buff underparts with brownish streaking

Similar Birds

BLACK-HEADED GROSBEAK ♀ Buff to white supercilium; pale cinnamon chest with fine streaking on sides and flanks; upperparts have buffy mottling and streaking; lemon-yellow underwing coverts.

• **BREEDING** Monogamous. Solitary. Male and female rub bills to display affection during courtship.

• **NESTING** Incubation 13–14 days by both sexes. Altricial young brooded by both parents, more by female; stay in nest 9–12 days, fed by both sexes. Male may tend while female begins second nesting. 1–2 broods per year.

• **POPULATION** Common to fairly common in deciduous forest, woodland, and second growth. Rare migrant in West. Rare to accidental in winter on southern California coast.

• **FEEDERS** Use increases during migration.

• **CONSERVATION** Neotropical migrant. Common cowbird host. Vulnerable to habitat loss due to logging.

Flight Pattern
Swift flight on rapidly beating wings with brief periods of wings pulled to sides.

Nest Identification	
Shape	Location	Twigs, weeds, and leaves • lined with fine twigs, rootlets, and mammal hair • in vines, low tree, or shrub, 5–15 feet above ground (but up to 50 feet) • built mostly by female, but male helps • 3–5 light greenish or bluish eggs marked with reddish brown; oval, 1.0 x 0.7 inches.

Plumage Sexes differ	Habitat	Migration Migratory	Weight 1.6 ounces

DATE _____ TIME_____ LOCATION _____

Family CARDINALIDAE	Species *Guiraca caerulea*	Length 6.25–7.5 inches	Wingspan 10.5–11.5 inches

BLUE GROSBEAK

MALE

black lores and face around base of bill

deep rich blue overall

blackish wings and tail

thick conical bill with blackish upper mandible and silver-gray lower mandible

2 chestnut wing bars

Often seen flocking in southern fields in spring, this grosbeak, with its deep blue plumage, may appear black from a distance or on a cloudy day. Not shy, it hops on the ground, wagging or spreading its tail, and sings from a conspicuous perch. In nesting season the male attacks other pairs to defend its territory. Females may be mistaken for female Brown-headed Cowbirds, but the large triangular bill and brown wing bars are distinctive, as is their behavior of raising a slight crest and flicking and spreading their tails. Females have a gray-brown rump that can show a bluish cast.

FIRST SPRING MALE

- **SONG** Series of deep rich slightly scratchy warbles that rise and fall in pitch, resembling the Purple Finch. Call is explosive metallic *pink*.

darker brown streaking on back

dull brown overall

2 cinnamon to chestnut wing bars

- **BEHAVIOR** Solitary or in pairs during breeding season. More gregarious in other seasons; forms flocks. Hops on ground to forage; gleans from weeds, bushes, and low in trees. Eats mostly insects in summer; also fruits, seeds, grains, and land snails. May fly considerable distances across fields from one song perch to the next.

paler cinnamon buff on throat

cinnamon buff underparts

FEMALE

Similar Birds

INDIGO BUNTING
♂ Smaller; bright blue overall; smaller bill; lacks chestnut wing bars • female is smaller with smaller bill; brown
♀ overall with faint streaking on breast and narrow brown wing bars.

BLUE BUNTING
♂ Smaller; blue-black overall; smaller bill with rounded culmen; lacks chestnut wing bars
♀ • female has brown plumage overall; lacks wing bars • casual in Texas.

- **BREEDING** Monogamous. Solitary.

- **NESTING** Incubation 11–12 days by female. Young altricial; brooded by female; leave nest at 9–10 days, fed mostly by female. 2 broods per year.

- **POPULATION** Uncommon to fairly common in overgrown fields, riparian thickets, brushy rural roadsides, and woodland edges. Range is expanding in central and northeastern US.

- **FEEDERS** Seeds and grains.

- **CONSERVATION** Neotropical migrant. Fairly common cowbird host.

Flight Pattern

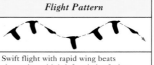

Swift flight with rapid wing beats alternating with brief periods of wings pulled to sides.

Nest Identification

Shape ◗   Location 🏚 🌿 🌳

Twigs, weeds, rootlets, snakeskin, leaves, bark, bits of paper, and string, with lining of finer materials • low in tree, bush, or weed clump • 3–12 feet above ground • built by female • 3–5 light blue eggs occasionally marked with brown; oval, 0.9 x 0.7 inches.

Plumage Sexes differ	Habitat 🌾 🏞 🌊	Migration Migratory	Weight 1.0 ounce

DATE _____ TIME_____ LOCATION _____

Family CARDINALIDAE	Species *Passerina cyanea*	Length 5.25–5.75 inches	Wingspan 8–9 inches

INDIGO BUNTING

The male's distinctive plumage looks blue in sunlight and almost black in shade or backlighting. Populations are expanding with the creation of disturbed habitat after logging, highway and power line construction, and farmland abandonment. Its breeding range now includes much of the Southwest.

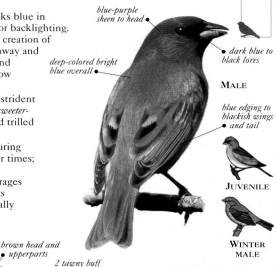

blue-purple sheen to head

dark blue to black lores

deep-colored bright blue overall

MALE

blue edging to blackish wings and tail

JUVENILE

WINTER MALE

- **SONG** Series of varied measured strident phrases, usually paired, *sweet-sweet, sweeter-sweeter, here-here,* often with an added trilled ending. Call is a "wet" *spit* or *plik.*

- **BEHAVIOR** Solitary or in pairs during breeding season. Gregarious at other times; in flocks in winter, often with other buntings, sparrows, and finches. Forages in trees, shrubs, and on ground. Eats variety of insects and larvae, especially in summer; also dandelion seeds, weed seeds, grass seeds, small grains, and wild berries. Males defensive of territory; often engage in colorful chases with other males.

brown head and upperparts

2 tawny buff wing bars

- **BREEDING** Monogamous. Solitary. Some males polygynous when outnumbered by females.

whitish throat and underparts

buffy brown-washed chest and flanks with dusky streaks

FEMALE

tertials edged with contrasting buff

darker brown wings and tail with blue-edged feathers

- **NESTING** Incubation 12–14 days by female. Young altricial; brooded by female; leave nest at 9–12 days, fed mostly by female; some males bring food. 2 broods per year.

- **POPULATION** Fairly common to common. Abundant in some deciduous forest edges, old fields, clearings, and agricultural areas. Expanding.

Similar Birds

BLUE GROSBEAK Larger; large triangular bill; tan wing bars.

VARIED BUNTING ♀ Olive-brown to tawny-brown overall; brown rump; bill with more decurved culmen; narrower tertial edges with less buffy contrast; lacks streaking on underparts; lacks brown wing bars.

- **FEEDERS** Comes for small seeds and grains.

- **CONSERVATION** Neotropical migrant. Common host to cowbird parasitism. Some habitat loss due to maturation of cut-over forests.

Flight Pattern

Short flight low over vegetation with rapid wing beats alternating with brief periods of wings pulled to sides.

Nest Identification	
Shape Location	Weeds, bark, and fine materials, lined with grass and leaves • in weed clump, dense shrub, or low tree • 1–15 feet above ground • built by female • 3–4 pale bluish white to white eggs, sometimes with brown or purple spotting; short oval to short subelliptical, 0.8 x 0.5 inches.

Plumage Sexes differ	Habitat	Migration Migratory	Weight 0.5 ounce

DATE _____ TIME _____ LOCATION _____

Family CARDINALIDAE	Species *Passerina ciris*	Length 5–5.5 inches	Wingspan 8–8.5 inches

PAINTED BUNTING

deep blue-violet head and hindneck

bright lime-green back

red eye ring

scarlet underparts

MALE

dark mouse-gray tail and wings with reddish edges

bright green upperparts

JUVENILE

gray-green tail and wings

FEMALE

yellow-green underparts

olive-washed flanks and chest

Flaunting one of the most brilliant plumages of all North American songbirds, the male is easy to identify by the dark blue head, lime-green back, and red rump and underparts. The green and yellow-green coloring of the female and juvenile serves as camouflage in the dense riparian thickets, woodland edges, and scrubby brushy areas. Males can be highly aggressive and sometimes kill one another in territorial battles. Their striking colors and warbled song have made them a popular cage bird in Mexico, Central America, and the Caribbean. Before laws prevented it, they were sold as cage birds in the United States, sometimes under the name "nonpareil." The first spring male is similar to the female but is brighter overall and has a bluish wash on the head.

• **SONG** High-pitched musical measured warble *pew-eata, pew-eata, I eaty you too.* Call is 2-note *chip* or a "wet" *plik.*

• **BEHAVIOR** Solitary or in pairs during breeding season. Gregarious in other seasons, forming flocks and joining mixed-species foraging flocks. Shy, secretive, and often difficult to see. Male sings from exposed perch. Most often hops on ground. Forages on ground and low in trees and shrubs. Eats seeds, insects, and caterpillars.

• **BREEDING** Mostly monogamous, but some males polygynous.

• **NESTING** Incubation 11–12 days by female. Young altricial; brooded by female; stay in nest 12–14 days, fed by both sexes, but female does more. 2–3 broods per year.

• **POPULATION** Common in riparian thickets and shrubby habitats. Casual north of range.

Flight Pattern
Typically, short flight low over vegetation, with rapid wing beats alternating with brief periods of wings pulled to sides.

• **FEEDERS** Birdseed and sunflower seeds; uses birdbaths.
• **CONSERVATION** Neotropical migrant. Common cowbird host. Declining on the East Coast, where the species is losing habitat to development.

Nest Identification	
Shape 🐦 Location 🌿 🌲	Stalks, leaves, and grasses, with lining of rootlets, snakeskin, and animal hair • in dense part of bush, in low tree, or in vines or moss • 3–6 feet above ground (but up to 25 feet) • built by female • 3–5 pale blue eggs marked with reddish brown, concentrated at larger end; oval to short oval, 0.8 x 0.6 inches.

Plumage Sexes differ	Habitat 🐦 ✈ 🔺 〰	Migration Migratory	Weight 0.8 ounce

DATE _____ TIME_____ LOCATION _____

Family CARDINALIDAE	Species *Spiza americana*	Length 6–7 inches	Wingspan 9–11 inches

DICKCISSEL

This bird is named for its song of *dick-dick-dick-cissel*. Often flying in flocks over grassy prairies, the Dickcissel, with its black bib and yellow breast, looks like a small meadowlark. Females are similar to males but lack the black bib and have duller chestnut wing patches.

• **SONG** Staccato *dick-dick-dick-cissel*. Has an insectlike call of *bzzrrrt*.

• **BEHAVIOR** Solitary or in pairs during breeding season. Gregarious at other times, forming wintering flocks numbering thousands of birds. Joins communal roosts after breeding season. Male sings from exposed perches and in flight. Forages on ground. Eats grains, seeds, and insects.

• **BREEDING** Polygamous, although some birds are monogamous.

• **NESTING** Incubation 12–13 days by female. Altricial young brooded by female; stay in nest 7–10 days, fed by female. 1–2 broods per year.

• **POPULATION** Common to abundant in grasslands, meadows, savannas, and fields. Local and irregular east of Appalachians. Rare in migration on Atlantic and Pacific Coasts. Casual in winter in the East.

• **FEEDERS** Birds in northern part of range come to feeders.

yellowish eyebrow becomes whitish behind eye

thick stout bill with blackish upper mandible

white chin

thin blackish malar stripe

brown auricular patch and crown

brown upperparts

black bib

black streaking on back

bold yellow breast

chestnut wing coverts

dusky white underparts

JUVENILE

WINTER MALE

MALE

yellowish eyebrow becomes whitish behind eye

grayish-brown auricular patch

grayish-brown upperparts

blackish streaking on back

WINTER FEMALE

thin dark brown malar stripe

white throat, chin, and mustache

chestnut wing coverts

FEMALE

dusky white underparts

yellow breast

Similar Birds

HOUSE SPARROW ♀
Similar to female Dickcissel • stubbier yellowish bill; buffy supercilium; brown postocular stripe; single white wing bar; lacks pale throat with dark malar stripe; lacks streaking on flanks.

• **CONSERVATION** Neotropical migrant. Frequent host to cowbird parasitism. Nests and young lost annually to the mowing of fields for hay. Thousands are killed annually on wintering grounds for the protection of rice plantations.

Flight Pattern

Series of rapid wing beats alternating with brief periods of wings pulled to sides. Often flies in large flocks in compact undulating formation.

Nest Identification

Shape   Location

Grasses, stems, and leaves, with lining of soft rootlets, grasses, and hair • low in tree or bush, sometimes atop grassy tussock or on ground in field • 0–6 feet above ground • built by female • 3–5 plain pale blue eggs; oval to long oval, 0.8 x 0.6 inches.

Plumage Sexes differ	Habitat	Migration Migratory	Weight 1.0 ounce

DATE _____ TIME_____ LOCATION _____

Family ICTERIDAE	Species *Dolichonyx oryzivorus*	Length 6.25–8 inches	Wingspan 10.25–12.5 inches

BOBOLINK

In northern meadows and farmland, this bird is known for its cheerful bubbling *bob-o-link* song and handsome plumage. It is said the male wears his breeding plumage upside down, as he has black underparts with a buff nape and hindneck and white scapulars and rump. In all plumages, birds are adorned with sharply pointed tail feathers, unusual for songbirds. All fall-plumaged birds and juveniles are similar to the female but have brighter yellow-buff underparts with less streaking.

• **SONG** Lively bubbling cascade of notes, starting with low reedy notes and rollicking upward, *bob-o-link, bob-o-link, pink, pink, pank, pink.* Call is clear *pink.*

• **BEHAVIOR** Gregarious; in flocks numbering up to thousands. Males sing from perch or in flight display, circling low over fields. In summer eats insects and caterpillars, grass and weed seeds, and grains; eats seeds and grains in migration and winter.

• **BREEDING** Strongly polygynous.

• **NESTING** Incubation 13 days by female. Altricial young brooded by female; stay in nest 10–14 days, fed by both sexes. 1 brood per year.

• **POPULATION** Fairly common to common in tall grass, wet meadows, prairie, hay fields, and grain fields. Decline in the East during 20th century. Rare in the fall on West Coast.

• **CONSERVATION** Neotropical migrant. Rare cowbird host. Vulnerable to destruction of nests and young by mowing of hayfields. Has declined in the Southeast from former 19th-century market hunting for food and from continued destruction to protect rice plantations. Similar killing currently exists on expanding rice plantations on wintering grounds in South America.

buff-colored hindneck

black face and crown

black back

narrow buff stripe in center of back

white scapulars

white rump

black underparts and wings

buff-edged tertials and wing coverts

MALE

black tail

blackish brown crown with buff central crown stripe

pinkish bill

black streaking on back, rump, sides, and flanks

golden buff overall

WINTER MALE

FEMALE

Similar Birds

LARK BUNTING ♂
Entirely black except for large white shoulder patches, white edging to tertials and inner secondaries, and white tips to outer tail feathers.

Flight Pattern

Strong undeviating and slightly undulating flight on rapidly beating wings. Male has display flight with shallow wing strokes on rapidly fluttering wings.

Nest Identification

Shape ⌣   Location ▬ ▬ ₊₊₊

Coarse grasses and weed stalks, lined with finer grasses • in slight depression on ground in tall grass, weeds, or clover, sometimes in rut made by tractors and combines • female digs scrape and then builds nest • 4–7 eggs, irregularly blotched with browns, purple, and lavender; oval to short oval, 0.82 x 0.62 inches.

Plumage Sexes differ	Habitat ▬ ▬ ♣ ⩙	Migration Migratory	Weight 1.7 ounces

DATE _____ TIME_____ LOCATION _____

Family ICTERIDAE	Species *Agelaius phoeniceus*	Length 7.5–9.5 inches	Wingspan 12–14.5 inches

RED-WINGED BLACKBIRD

Believed one of the most numerous land birds in North America, the Red-winged Blackbird is known for aggressively defending its territory from intruders. Many geographical races exist across its extensive range. Females, identifiable by dark brown upperparts and heavily streaked underparts, sometimes show a red tinge on wing coverts, chin, and throat. Males resemble females at a year old but have less streaking and some red on their epaulettes; they develop glossy black plumage after their second year.

red shoulder patches (epaulettes) with broad buff-yellow distal tips

black overall, including wings and tail

MALE

- **SONG** Gurgling reedy *konk-la-ree* or *gurr-ga-leee*. Calls: low *clack*, sharp nasal *deekk*, and metallic *tiink*.
- **BEHAVIOR** Gregarious. Small breeding colonies in summer. Winter flocks often segregated by sex and age. Runs or hops while foraging on ground. Eats mostly seeds, grains, berries, and wild fruit; in summer also eats insects, caterpillars, grubs, spiders, mollusks, and snails. Male's social dominance is proportional to amount of red displayed.
- **BREEDING** Colonial. Some males polygynous.
- **NESTING** Incubation 11–12 days by female. Altricial young brooded by female; stay in nest 10–14 days, fed mostly by female. 2–3 broods per year.
- **POPULATION** Abundant to common in fields, riparian thickets and scrub, freshwater and brackish marshes.

brown crown
dusky tan face
broad dusky tan supercilium
brown upperparts with dark streaks
thin brown malar mark
dark brown postocular stripe
2 thin tan wing bars
dusky white underparts heavily streaked with brown

FIRST YEAR MALE

FEMALE

Similar Birds

♂ TRICOLORED BLACKBIRD Longer, more slender body • male's red epaulettes have whitish borders • females have darker bodies; heavier streaks on underparts; blackish bellies; lack chestnut and buff edges to upperparts; lack pink coloring on throat • West Coast only.

- **FEEDERS** Will attend for breadcrumbs and birdseed.
- **CONSERVATION** Vulnerable to pesticides in food chain and to habitat loss due to the drainage of wetlands. Nests and young are destroyed by mowing operations.

Flight Pattern
Strong flight on rapidly beating wings; displaying males fly with slow stiff shallow wing beats with epaulettes raised.

Nest Identification	
Shape  Location 	Dried cattail leaves and sedges, lined with fine grasses and rushes • fastened to stalks or twigs with plant fibers • in cattails, bushes, trees, dense grass, or on ground, preferably near or over water • built by female • 3–5 (usually 4) pale blue-green eggs spotted or with zigzag lines of black, browns, and purple; oval, 0.97 x 0.75 inches.

Plumage Sexes differ	Habitat	Migration Migratory	Weight 2.3 ounces

DATE 1/7/04   TIME_____   LOCATION _____

Family ICTERIDAE	Species *Sturnella magna*	Length 9–11 inches	Wingspan 13.5–17 inches

EASTERN MEADOWLARK

A common inhabitant of fields and meadows, the Eastern Meadowlark often is observed flicking its tail open and shut while walking through grass and weeds and along roadsides. Clearing of forests in eastern North America has led to the expansion of its breeding range. Fall-plumaged birds show narrow buffy mottling in the black breast band and a buffy wash on the face, supercilium, flanks, and undertail coverts. Juveniles have black spotting on the chest, sides, and flanks.

black-and-white-striped crown

brown upperparts streaked with buff and black

chunky body

white face with black postocular stripe

yellow breast and belly with broad black V on chest

white outer tail feathers

white sides and flanks with black spots and streaks

white undertail coverts with dusky streaking

- **SONG** A plaintive *tee-you, tee-airrr*, or *spring-o'-the-year*. Call given on ground or in flight is high buzzy *zzzzrrt*, and a nasal *sweeink* also is given in flight.

- **BEHAVIOR** Solitary or in pairs during summer. Gregarious during other seasons, forming small flocks in winter. Eats mostly insects, especially in summer. Also eats grains, weed and grass seeds, and tender sprouts of spring plants.

- **BREEDING** Monogamous. Solitary. Some males polygynous.

- **NESTING** Incubation 13–14 days by both sexes. Young altricial; brooded by female; stay in nest 11–12 days, fed by both sexes, but female does more. Male may take over brood while female starts second nest. 2 broods per year.

- **POPULATION** Common in meadows, fields, grasslands, and savanna. Decline reported in the East during last quarter of the 20th century.

- **CONSERVATION** Common host to cowbird parasitism. Nests and young destroyed by mowing operations. Vulnerable to habitat loss due to natural succession of abandoned fields, as well as from overgrazing, development, and grassland habitat fragmentation.

Similar Birds

WESTERN MEADOWLARK
Paler upperparts lack dark centers in most feathers; yellow of throat, especially that of breeding males, extends into submustachial region; sides of crown and postocular stripe usually brownish; most have less white in outer tail feathers.

Flight Pattern

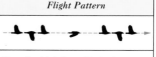

Several rapid shallow stiff wing beats followed by short glides close to landscape.

Nest Identification

Shape 🌀   Location ▬▬▬

Lined with grass, plant stems, and pine needles • domed or partially domed • often next to dense clump of grass or weeds on damp or wet ground • built by female • 3–7 white eggs, suffused with pink, with brown and lavender spots and speckles; oval to short or long oval, 1.1 x 0.8 inches.

Plumage Sexes similar	Habitat 🌄 ▬	Migration Northern birds migrate	Weight 3.6 ounces

DATE _____ TIME_____ LOCATION _____

| Family ICTERIDAE | Species *Euphagus carolinus* | Length 8.25–9.75 inches | Wingspan 13–15 inches |

RUSTY BLACKBIRD

This bird is named for the rusty wash on its fall and winter plumage. Only birds in juvenile plumage have dark eyes; older birds in immature plumage have yellow eyes like adults. Juvenile plumage resembles that of winter adults. Fall males have a blackish loreal mask that contrasts with the rufous wash on the rest of the plumage. The fall female has a gray rump and cinnamon-gray supercilium and underparts. Flying in large flocks from their wintering grounds, these birds will swoop down to forage behind tractors and plows.

faint iridescent green on head

black overall

black wings and tail with bluish sheen

blackish bill

yellow eyes

MALE

• **SONG** A high-pitched creaky *koo-a-lee-m-eek, koo-a-lee—-eek*. Has call notes of *chuck* or *kick*.

• **BEHAVIOR** In pairs during breeding season. Gregarious. After nesting season forms small flocks that forage and roost communally. Forms large flocks in migration and winter and joins mixed flocks with other blackbird species and starlings. Forages on ground of wet woodlands and agricultural lands or wades in marshes and small pools of water. Eats insects, caterpillars, crustaceans, small fish, salamanders, and snails. Also eats grains, seeds, and fruits.

blackish legs

WINTER MALE

WINTER FEMALE

darker gray wings and tail with greenish blue sheen

• **BREEDING** Monogamous. Pairs.

FEMALE

slate-gray overall

• **NESTING** Incubation 14 days by female; male feeds incubating female on nest. Young altricial; brooded by female; stay in nest 11–14 days, fed by both sexes. 1 brood per year.

Similar Birds

♂ **BREWER'S BLACKBIRD** Most males are black throughout year, with purplish gloss on head and neck and blue-green sheen on body, wings, and tail • female ♀ has dark eyes • some variant fall males have buff-brown edging on head and body but ♂ never on wing coverts or tertials.

• **POPULATION** Fairly common in wet coniferous woodlands, bogs, riparian habitats, and swamps. Rare in the West.

• **CONSERVATION** Rare host to cowbird parasitism.

Flight Pattern

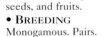

Strong direct flight on rapidly beating wings.

Nest Identification	
Shape 🥄 ⌣ Location 🌿 🌳	Grasses, moss, and twigs, with inner cup of mud lined with soft grasses and rootlets • over water in dense bush or conifer, usually 2–8 feet above ground (but up to 20 feet) • built by female • 4–5 light blue-green eggs, with brown and gray splotches; oval, 1.0 x 0.75 inches.

| Plumage Sexes differ | Habitat 〰️ 🌾 | Migration Migratory | Weight 2.3 ounces |

DATE _____ TIME_____ LOCATION _____

Family ICTERIDAE	Species *Quiscalus quiscula*	Length 11–13.5 inches	Wingspan 17–18.5 inches

COMMON GRACKLE

This gregarious bird has expanded its range by adapting to suburban areas. Outside the nesting season, noisy groups roost together at night, often with other species. Juveniles are sooty brown with dark brown eyes.

• **SONG** Grating squeaky *coguba-leek*, like a creaking rusty hinge. Call is a bold *chuk*.

• **BEHAVIOR** Conspicuous. Nests, forages, and roosts in groups or flocks all year. Large postnesting season flocks can damage crops, and winter flocks may number in the hundreds of thousands. Walks on ground. Forages in trees, shrubs, grass, and croplands; may wade into water. Eats insects, worms, caterpillars, fruits, grains, seeds, small rodents, small fish, salamanders, and eggs and nestlings of other birds. Male displays by fluffing out shoulder feathers to make a ruffled collar, drooping his wings, and singing.

• **BREEDING** Monogamous. Some males polygynous. Colonial.

• **NESTING** Incubation 13–14 days by female. Young altricial; brooded by female; stay in nest 16–20 days, fed by both sexes. 1–2 broods per year.

• **POPULATION** Abundant and widespread in open areas with scattered trees, open woodlands, agricultural areas, parks, and around human habitation. Casual in southern Alaska and in the Pacific states.

• **FEEDERS** Will come for small grains and seeds.

• **CONSERVATION** Rare host to cowbird parasitism. Birds feeding on crops and making a nuisance in large winter roosts sometimes are destroyed.

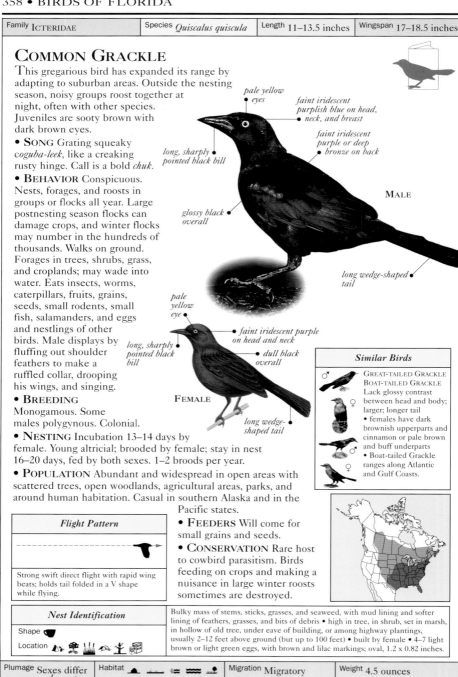

pale yellow eyes

faint iridescent purplish blue on head, neck, and breast

faint iridescent purple or deep bronze on back

long, sharply pointed black bill

MALE

glossy black overall

long wedge-shaped tail

pale yellow eye

long, sharply pointed black bill

faint iridescent purple on head and neck

dull black overall

FEMALE

long wedge-shaped tail

Similar Birds

♂	GREAT-TAILED GRACKLE BOAT-TAILED GRACKLE Lack glossy contrast between head and body; larger; longer tail • females have dark brownish upperparts and cinnamon or pale brown and buff underparts • Boat-tailed Grackle ranges along Atlantic and Gulf Coasts.
♀	
♂	
♀	

Flight Pattern	
Strong swift direct flight with rapid wing beats; holds tail folded in a V shape while flying.	

Nest Identification	
Shape	Bulky mass of stems, sticks, grasses, and seaweed, with mud lining and softer lining of feathers, grasses, and bits of debris • high in tree, in shrub, set in marsh, in hollow of old tree, under eave of building, or among highway plantings, usually 2–12 feet above ground (but up to 100 feet) • built by female • 4–7 light brown or light green eggs, with brown and lilac markings; oval, 1.2 x 0.82 inches.
Location	

Plumage Sexes differ	Habitat	Migration Migratory	Weight 4.5 ounces

DATE 7/17/04 TIME_____ LOCATION _____

Family ICTERIDAE	Species *Quiscalus major*	Length 12–17 inches	Wingspan 18–23.5 inches

BOAT-TAILED GRACKLE

This large noisy grackle travels, eats, sleeps, and nests in groups. It frequents saltwater marshes and, except in Florida, is never found far inland. It walks the beaches, large keel-shaped tail held high above its back, wading into the water for food, examining the wrack line, or gleaning seeds and berries from dune vegetation. Brown eyes occur in western Gulf Coast races east to Mississippi; farther east adults have yellow eyes. Males are larger than females. Juveniles have dark eyes and are similar to respective adults; males lack the iridescent sheen; females have faint spotting and streaking on the breast.

iridescent blue-black overall

brown or yellow eyes

long keel-shaped tail

MALE

tawny cinnamon supercilium

darker brown crown

tawny brown face and throat

dusky brown auricular patch

darker brown upperparts, wings, and tail

tawny brown underparts

FEMALE

- **SONG** Abrasive loud repeated *jeeb, jeeb, jeeb*. Calls a noisy variety of harsh whistles, chucks, guttural rattles, raspy clicks, and wolf whistles.
- **BEHAVIOR** Gregarious. Steals food from other birds. Diet includes small fish, frogs, snails, aquatic and terrestrial insects, shrimp, small birds, eggs and nestlings of other birds, small reptiles, fruit, berries, grain, and seeds. Many in northernmost populations winter in Virginia.
- **BREEDING** Promiscuous. Loose colonies. Displaying male perches, spreads tail and wings, then bows toward female. Does not hybridize with Great-tailed Grackle in overlapping zone.
- **NESTING** Incubation 13–15 days by female. Altricial young brooded by female; stay in nest 12–15 days, fed by female. 2–3 broods per year.
- **POPULATION** Common in coastal salt marshes and adjacent open habitats, agricultural areas, and around human habitations; inland in Florida around lakes, canals, and freshwater marshes. Northeastern range expanding.
- **CONSERVATION** Vulnerable to loss of habitat caused by draining of marshes for agriculture and development.

Similar Birds
♂ GREAT-TAILED GRACKLE Larger; bright yellow eyes; longer bill; flatter crown • inland west of Mississippi River. ♀
SMOOTH-BILLED ANI Dark eyes; thick curved bill; long graduated tail.

Flight Pattern

Strong direct flight on rapidly beating wings with long keeled tail extended behind.

Nest Identification

Shape   Location

In marsh vegetation; bulky and built of dried stalks, grasses, and cattails, usually over or near water in marsh or on ground set in grass • in trees, built of Spanish moss, feathers, mud, cow dung, and bits of debris, 3–50 feet above ground • built by female • 3–5 pale blue to blue-gray eggs with splotches of black, brown, lilac, and gray; oval, 1.3 x 0.88 inches.

Plumage Sexes differ	Habitat	Migration Northern birds migrate	Weight 7.5 ounces

DATE 7/17/04   TIME_____   LOCATION _____

Family ICTERIDAE	Species *Molothrus bonariensis*	Length 7.5 inches	Wingspan 12 inches

SHINY COWBIRD

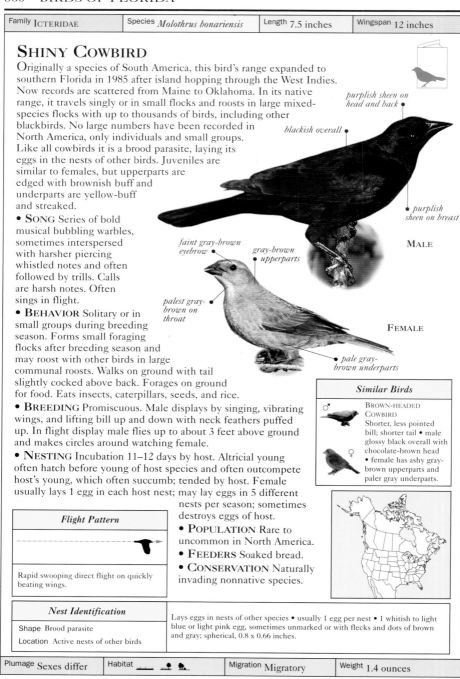

Originally a species of South America, this bird's range expanded to southern Florida in 1985 after island hopping through the West Indies. Now records are scattered from Maine to Oklahoma. In its native range, it travels singly or in small flocks and roosts in large mixed-species flocks with up to thousands of birds, including other blackbirds. No large numbers have been recorded in North America, only individuals and small groups. Like all cowbirds it is a brood parasite, laying its eggs in the nests of other birds. Juveniles are similar to females, but upperparts are edged with brownish buff and underparts are yellow-buff and streaked.

purplish sheen on head and back

blackish overall

purplish sheen on breast

MALE

- **SONG** Series of bold musical bubbling warbles, sometimes interspersed with harsher piercing whistled notes and often followed by trills. Calls are harsh notes. Often sings in flight.

faint gray-brown eyebrow

gray-brown upperparts

palest gray-brown on throat

FEMALE

pale gray-brown underparts

- **BEHAVIOR** Solitary or in small groups during breeding season. Forms small foraging flocks after breeding season and may roost with other birds in large communal roosts. Walks on ground with tail slightly cocked above back. Forages on ground for food. Eats insects, caterpillars, seeds, and rice.
- **BREEDING** Promiscuous. Male displays by singing, vibrating wings, and lifting bill up and down with neck feathers puffed up. In flight display male flies up to about 3 feet above ground and makes circles around watching female.
- **NESTING** Incubation 11–12 days by host. Altricial young often hatch before young of host species and often outcompete host's young, which often succumb; tended by host. Female usually lays 1 egg in each host nest; may lay eggs in 5 different nests per season; sometimes destroys eggs of host.
- **POPULATION** Rare to uncommon in North America.
- **FEEDERS** Soaked bread.
- **CONSERVATION** Naturally invading nonnative species.

Similar Birds

BROWN-HEADED COWBIRD Shorter, less pointed bill; shorter tail • male glossy black overall with chocolate-brown head • female has ashy gray-brown upperparts and paler gray underparts.

Flight Pattern
Rapid swooping direct flight on quickly beating wings.

Nest Identification	
Shape Brood parasite	Lays eggs in nests of other species • usually 1 egg per nest • 1 whitish to light blue or light pink egg, sometimes unmarked or with flecks and dots of brown and gray; spherical, 0.8 x 0.66 inches.
Location Active nests of other birds	

Plumage Sexes differ	Habitat	Migration Migratory	Weight 1.4 ounces

DATE _____ TIME_____ LOCATION _____

Family ICTERIDAE	Species *Molothrus ater*	Length 7–8.25 inches	Wingspan 11.75–13.75 inches

BROWN-HEADED COWBIRD

This common cowbird travels and roosts in large flocks with other blackbirds after breeding season; winter mixed-species flocks can number in the millions. Originally of the Great Plains, where it associated with bison, this species has expanded its range east and west, with the fragmentation of the eastern forest and the increase in range cattle and ranching. Like all cowbirds it is a brood parasite and lays its eggs in the nests of other birds. Juveniles resemble females but are paler overall; upperparts have pale edging, giving a scaly effect; underparts are streaky and throats gray-white.

black overall with faint green sheen

brown head

short conical bill

MALE

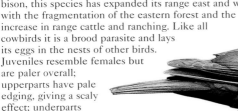

grayish brown upperparts

faint dusky malar mark

FEMALE

JUVENILE

- **SONG** Gurgling liquid *glug-glug-glee*, with tail spread, wings drooped, and a forward bow. Female's call is harsh rattle. Male in flight has high slurred *ts-eeeu!*

pale grayish brown underparts with faint streaking

- **BEHAVIOR** Solitary, in pairs, or small groups during breeding season; otherwise gregarious, foraging and roosting in flocks. Calls and displays from the ground or high exposed perches. Walks on ground to forage. Holds tail cocked over back. Eats insects, caterpillars, spiders, and various grains, seeds, and fruits.
- **BREEDING** Promiscuous.
- **NESTING** Incubation 10–13 days by host. Altricial young usually hatch before host's young and often outcompete them; tended by host. Female usually lays 1 egg in each nest; 10–36 eggs per year.
- **POPULATION** Common in woodlands, forest edge, agricultural areas, and around human habitation.
- **FEEDERS** Attends for small seeds and grains.
- **CONSERVATION** Neotropical migrant. Numbers reduced in Michigan by trapping to protect endangered Kirtland's Warbler in jack pine barrens nesting grounds.

Similar Birds

BRONZED COWBIRD
♂ Slightly larger; much longer, larger bill; red eyes; ruff on nape • male has bronze-green sheen on head and upper body • female is
♀ dull blackish brown overall.

SHINY COWBIRD
♂ Male glossy black overall with purplish sheen on head, back, and breast • female has
♀ gray-brown upperparts; faint gray eyebrow; pale gray-brown underparts; paler gray throat.

Flight Pattern

Swift somewhat swooping direct flight on rapidly beating wings.

Nest Identification	
	Lays eggs in nests of other species • usually 1 egg per nest • up to 36 eggs laid per female per nesting season • light blue eggs, often with brown flecks; oval, 0.84 x 0.64 inches.
Shape Brood parasite	
Location Active nests of other birds	

Plumage Sexes differ	Habitat	Migration Northern birds migrate	Weight 1.7 ounces

DATE _____ TIME_____ LOCATION _____

Family ICTERIDAE	Species *Icterus spurius*	Length 6–7.75 inches	Wingspan 9.25–10.25 inches

ORCHARD ORIOLE

This small oriole with its burnt-orange underparts is found in most of eastern North America in summer. It spends most of its time in trees in suburban and rural open stands and is often unwary when approached. Juveniles resemble females, and first spring males are similar to females but have a black chin and throat. Leaves breeding grounds in early fall.

black hood, back, and wings

single white wing bar

white-edged flight feathers on wings

MALE

- **SONG** Loud rich varied whistled notes, accelerating into a jumbled ending with a slurred *wheer!*, sounding like *look here, what cheer, wee yo, what cheer, whip yo, what wheer!* Calls sharp musical *chuk* and a dry chattering *chuh-huh-huh-huh.*

chestnut rump and shoulders

black tail with narrow white tips

slightly curved bill with black upper mandible and blue-gray lower mandible

chestnut underparts

- **BEHAVIOR** Solitary or in pairs during breeding season. In small family groups after nesting. Vocal and often conspicuous. Relatively approachable. Forages at middle to high levels in trees and shrubs, often at tips of branches; hops from branch to branch. Eats insects; also berries, flower parts, nectar, and fruits.

olive upperparts

dusky wings with 2 white wing bars

yellowish underparts

FIRST SPRING MALE

FEMALE

- **BREEDING** Monogamous. Solitary and loose colonies.
- **NESTING** Incubation 12–14 days by female. Altricial young brooded by female, some by male; stay in nest 11–14 days, fed by both sexes. Mates often divide fledglings and care for them separately, but family group remains intact until fall migration. 1 brood per year.
- **POPULATION** Common to fairly common in open woodland, farmlands, scrub/mesquite, shade trees, and orchards. Species declining in parts of its western range.
  - **FEEDERS** Fruit and nectar.
  - **CONSERVATION** Neotropical migrant. Common host to cowbird parasitism.

Similar Birds

MALE: No other North American songbird is extensively black above and chestnut below.

HOODED ORIOLE ♀ Female and juvenile are larger; longer tail; longer bill; thinner lower wing bar; undertail coverts often washed yellow-orange • juvenile male has more extensive black bib.

Flight Pattern

Swift slightly swooping direct flight on rapidly beating wings.

Nest Identification

Shape ⚇ Location 🌳 🌲

Intricately woven pouch of grasses with lining of plant down • hanging from fork of tree or bush, often hidden in cluster of leaves, 6–20 feet above ground (but up to 50 feet) • 3–7 light blue or gray eggs, splotched with gray, purple, or brown; oval, 0.8 x 0.57 inches.

Plumage Sexes differ	Habitat	Migration Migratory	Weight 0.7 ounce

DATE _____ TIME_____ LOCATION _____

Family ICTERIDAE	Species *Icterus pectoralis*	Length 8.25–9.5 inches	Wingspan 12.5–14.5 inches

SPOT-BREASTED ORIOLE

The black spots on its bold orange breast set this bird apart from other North American orioles. Originally a native of southern coastal Mexico and Central America, it was introduced into southeastern Florida in the late 1940s, where it is now established. It most often makes its home in suburban areas. In flight it shows large white patches in the wings and a yellow-orange to bright orange rump and uppertail coverts. Woven in less than a week, its pendant nest is a pyriform pouch of plant fibers and thin rootlets up to eighteen inches long, with the opening at the top. Immatures are similar to adults but have a dusky olive back and often lack the breast spots. Juveniles resemble immatures but are more yellow overall and lack the breast spotting and black lores and bib.

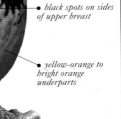

black lores, throat, and center of chest

yellow-orange to bright orange head

black back

orange shoulder patch

long straight black bill with blue base to lower mandible

black spots on sides of upper breast

black wings with extensive white in secondaries and base of primaries

yellow-orange to bright orange underparts

long black tail

JUVENILE

- **SONG** A liquid series of rich clear slow whistles, *whee ch-wee'chu-u.* Male noted for his song. Female also sings. Calls a loud nasal note, *nyeh*, sometimes repeated jerkily.
- **BEHAVIOR** In pairs much of the year. In family groups following nesting. Forages in shrubs and trees, where it gleans insects, prying open rolled leaves. Eats fruit and berries. Uses sharp bill to pull flowers off stems and drink nectar.
- **BREEDING** Monogamous. Solitary.
- **NESTING** Breeding biology poorly known. Estimated incubation 12–14 days by female. Young altricial; brooded by female; stay in nest estimated 12–14 days, fed by both sexes. 2 broods per year.

Similar Birds
There is no bright orange oriole with an orange head, black bib, and breast spots in introduced range during breeding season.
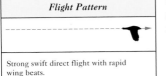 BALTIMORE ORIOLE ♀ Wintering female and juvenile • 2 white wing bars; blue-gray bill; unspotted breast; lacks white patches in secondaries.

- **POPULATION** Uncommon and local in parks, suburbs, and gardens. Numbers declining in Florida since the 1980s.
- **CONSERVATION** Cause of decline in the introduced population is undetermined.

Flight Pattern

Strong swift direct flight with rapid wing beats.

Nest Identification

Shape   Location

Grasses, stems, and fibers, with lining of finer material • hangs across tree branch • 20–60 feet above ground • built by female with some help from male • 3–5 light blue to white eggs, scrawled with black and lilac markings; oval to long oval, 0.9 x 0.7 inches.

Plumage Sexes similar	Habitat	Migration Nonmigratory	Weight 1.6 ounces

DATE _____ TIME_____ LOCATION _____

Family ICTERIDAE	Species *Icterus galbula*	Length 7–8.25 inches	Wingspan 11.25–12.5 inches

BALTIMORE ORIOLE

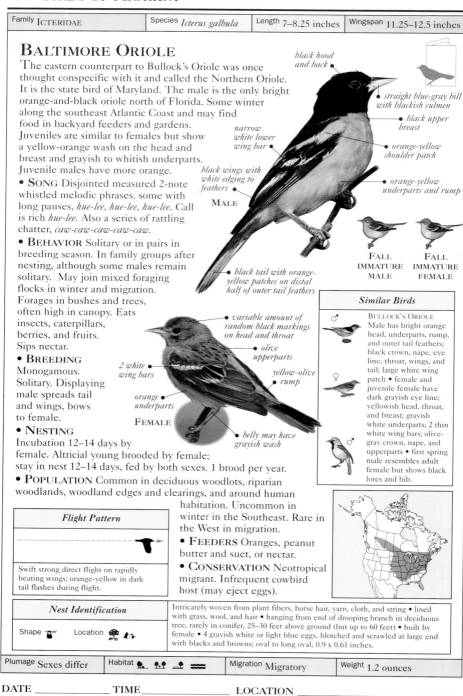

The eastern counterpart to Bullock's Oriole was once thought conspecific with it and called the Northern Oriole. It is the state bird of Maryland. The male is the only bright orange-and-black oriole north of Florida. Some winter along the southeast Atlantic Coast and may find food in backyard feeders and gardens. Juveniles are similar to females but show a yellow-orange wash on the head and breast and grayish to whitish underparts. Juvenile males have more orange.

black hood and back
straight blue-gray bill with blackish culmen
black upper breast
orange-yellow shoulder patch
narrow white lower wing bar
orange-yellow underparts and rump
black wings with white edging to feathers

MALE

• **SONG** Disjointed measured 2-note whistled melodic phrases, some with long pauses, *hue-lee, hue-lee, hue-lee.* Call is rich *hue-lee.* Also a series of rattling chatter, *caw-caw-caw-caw-caw.*

• **BEHAVIOR** Solitary or in pairs in breeding season. In family groups after nesting, although some males remain solitary. May join mixed foraging flocks in winter and migration. Forages in bushes and trees, often high in canopy. Eats insects, caterpillars, berries, and fruits. Sips nectar.

black tail with orange-yellow patches on distal half of outer tail feathers

FALL IMMATURE MALE   **FALL IMMATURE FEMALE**

• **BREEDING** Monogamous. Solitary. Displaying male spreads tail and wings, bows to female.

variable amount of random black markings on head and throat
olive upperparts
2 white wing bars
yellow-olive rump
orange underparts

FEMALE

belly may have grayish wash

Similar Birds

BULLOCK'S ORIOLE
♂ Male has bright orange head, underparts, rump, and outer tail feathers; black crown, nape, eye line, throat, wings, and tail; large white wing patch • female and juvenile female have dark grayish eye line; yellowish head, throat, and breast; grayish white underparts; 2 thin white wing bars; olive-gray crown, nape, and upperparts • first spring male resembles adult female but shows black lores and bib.
♀

• **NESTING** Incubation 12–14 days by female. Altricial young brooded by female; stay in nest 12–14 days, fed by both sexes. 1 brood per year.

• **POPULATION** Common in deciduous woodlots, riparian woodlands, woodland edges and clearings, and around human habitation. Uncommon in winter in the Southeast. Rare in the West in migration.

• **FEEDERS** Oranges, peanut butter and suet, or nectar.

• **CONSERVATION** Neotropical migrant. Infrequent cowbird host (may eject eggs).

Flight Pattern
Swift strong direct flight on rapidly beating wings; orange-yellow in dark tail flashes during flight.

Nest Identification	
Shape ⌇ Location 🌳 🌿	Intricately woven from plant fibers, horse hair, yarn, cloth, and string • lined with grass, wool, and hair • hanging from end of drooping branch in deciduous tree, rarely in conifer, 25–30 feet above ground (but up to 60 feet) • built by female • 4 grayish white or light blue eggs, blotched and scrawled at large end with blacks and browns; oval to long oval, 0.9 x 0.61 inches.

Plumage Sexes differ	Habitat 🪵 🌿 🌱 〰	Migration Migratory	Weight 1.2 ounces

DATE _____ TIME_____ LOCATION _____

Family FRINGILLIDAE	Species *Carpodacus purpureus*	Length 5.5–6.25 inches	Wingspan 9.25–10.5 inches

PURPLE FINCH

The male is easy to identify by its raspberry-colored plumage, brightest on the head, rump, and chest. Foraging in winter flocks, these birds depend on feeders when food supplies are scarce. Juveniles are similar to adult females; both have two white wing bars.

bright rosy red head

MALE

rosy supercilium

rosy red plumage with brown streaking on back and crown

brown loreal mask extending onto auriculars

pinkish edging to wings and 2 pinkish white wing bars

bright rosy red rump

brown loreal mask extending onto auriculars

white belly and undertail coverts

whitish eye line

brown malar mark

brown-gray upperparts with whitish streaks

grayish white underparts with brown streaking

deeply notched tail

FEMALE

• **SONG** Rapid high-pitched rising and falling warble. Late winter/early spring males may sing in chorus. Call is *chur-lee.* Flight notes are sharp *tuck* or *pit.*

• **BEHAVIOR** Solitary or in pairs in nesting season. Male sings from exposed perch. Gregarious, tame. In flocks after breeding; joins mixed-species foraging flocks in winter with siskins and goldfinches. Forages in trees and hopping on ground. Eats seeds; some fruits, insects, and caterpillars in summer.

Similar Birds

CASSIN'S FINCH ♂
Longer bill with straighter culmen; nape often slightly crested; gray-brown back; wings edged with pale pink; long primary projection; streaked undertail coverts; distinct streaks on sides and flanks • western range.

HOUSE FINCH ♂
Slender not chunky; less pointed bill with decurved culmen; indistinct facial pattern; brighter red on crown, rump, throat, and breast; dusky streaked underparts; squared tail.

• **BREEDING** Monogamous. Male displays by dancing around female and vigorously flapping his wings until he ascends to a foot above the ground.

• **NESTING** Incubation about 13 days by female. Altricial young brooded by female; stay in nest 14 days, fed by both sexes. 1–2 broods per year.

• **POPULATION** Fairly common in open coniferous and mixed coniferous-deciduous forests, in forest edge, and in suburbs; in Pacific states, in oak canyons and lower mountain slopes. Declining in the East.

• **FEEDERS** Millet and sunflower seeds.

• **CONSERVATION**
Uncommon cowbird host. Vulnerable to habitat loss due to logging. Decrease in New England due to competition with House Sparrow; recent declines in East suggest same with House Finch.

Flight Pattern

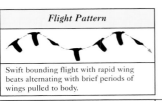

Swift bounding flight with rapid wing beats alternating with brief periods of wings pulled to body.

Nest Identification

Shape ⌣   Location 🐦🌳

Twigs, weeds, rootlets, strips of bark, and string, with lining of moss, soft grasses, moss, and hair • on branch or in fork of tree, 6–40 feet above ground • built by female • 3–5 pale green-blue eggs, marked with black and brown; oval to short oval, 0.8 x 0.57 inches.

Plumage Sexes differ	Habitat 🐦🐦 🌿 ▲ 🔺	Migration Northern birds migrate	Weight 1.2 ounces

DATE _____ TIME_____ LOCATION _____

Family FRINGILLIDAE	Species *Carpodacus mexicanus*	Length 6 inches	Wingspan 9.75 inches

HOUSE FINCH

Originally confined to the West, this finch was called a Linnet and introduced as a cage bird on Long Island, New York, in the 1940s. It became abundant in the East, surpassing the House Sparrow. Today, it is among the most widely distributed songbird species in North America. It often feeds with the Purple Finch, especially in winter. Some male variants are orange or yellow instead of red. Juveniles resemble adult females.

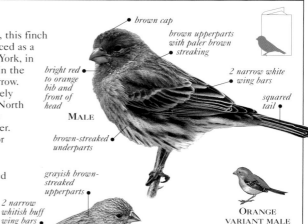

brown cap
brown upperparts with paler brown streaking
bright red to orange bib and front of head
MALE
2 narrow white wing bars
squared tail
brown-streaked underparts

ORANGE VARIANT MALE

grayish brown-streaked upperparts
2 narrow whitish buff wing bars
brown-streaked whitish buff underparts
FEMALE

• **SONG** Varied rich high-pitched scratchy warble composed chiefly of 3-note phrases; many end with rising inflections. Both sexes sing, but male's song is longer, more complex, and more frequent. Call is nasal *chee* or *chee-wheet;* in flight a sharp nasal *nyee-ah.*

• **BEHAVIOR** Solitary or in pairs during nesting season. Gregarious. Forms small family groups when young become independent. Larger foraging flocks in winter may join with other finches. Actively forages on ground, in fields, and in suburban areas. Eats mostly seeds but in summer takes insects and fruits. Drinks maple sap. Males are conspicuous and sing often. Studies indicate that the redder the male's plumage, the more desirable he is to females.

• **BREEDING** Monogamous. Solitary.

• **NESTING** Incubation 12–14 days by female. Altricial young brooded by female; stay in nest 11–19 days, fed by both sexes. 1–3 broods per year.

• **POPULATION** Abundant over much of North America in a wide variety of habitats, from arid scrub, wooded canyons, cultivated fields, and open woodlands to suburban yards and urban areas.

• **FEEDERS** Thistle, millet, sunflower, and other seeds.

• **CONSERVATION** Rare cowbird host in the West; fairly common host in the East.

Similar Birds

PURPLE FINCH ♂
Chunkier; notched tail; distinct rosy eyebrow and submustachial stripe; white crissum lacks streaking; crown does not contrast with face and nape • male shows raspberry-red on head, breast, and rump.

CASSIN'S FINCH ♂
Larger; notched tail; long straight bill; nape often slightly crested; bright red crown; pale pink-edged wings; streaked undertail coverts; distinct streaking on sides and flanks • western range.

Flight Pattern

Swift somewhat bounding flight with rapid wing beats alternating with brief periods of wings pulled to sides.

Nest Identification	
Shape 	Twigs, grass, leaves, rootlets, bits of debris, and feathers • in tree hollow, cactus, on ground, under eaves of building, in bird boxes, abandoned nests, shrub, tree, etc. • built by female • 2–6 light blue eggs, spotted with lilac and black, often concentrated at larger end; oval to long oval, 0.8 x 0.57 inches.
Location	

Plumage Sexes differ	Habitat	Migration Some migrate	Weight 0.7 ounce

DATE _____ TIME_____ LOCATION _____

Family FRINGILLIDAE	Species *Carduelis pinus*	Length 4.5–5.25 inches	Wingspan 8.5–9 inches

PINE SISKIN

In fall and winter this is a common visitor to northern forests, where it forages in flocks that may include several thousand birds. When food is scarce these daytime migrants may travel as far south as Florida and central Mexico, flying in tightly formed flocks. In flight the yellow wing stripe at the base of the flight feathers and the yellow base to the outer tail feathers are conspicuous. Females are similar to males but with more washed-out yellow plumage. Juveniles resemble females but show a yellowish wash overall.

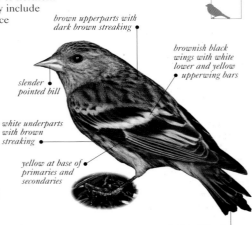

brown upperparts with dark brown streaking

brownish black wings with white lower and yellow upperwing bars

slender pointed bill

white underparts with brown streaking

yellow at base of primaries and secondaries

notched blackish tail with yellow base to outer tail feathers

- **SONG** Husky canary-like twittering warble, rising and falling in pitch and interspersed with a rapid ascending *ZZZzzzzzzzzzzrree!*, sounding like the equivalent of a bird with a chainsaw. Call is rising *tee-ee.* Flight note is hoarse descending *chee.*
- **BEHAVIOR** Tame, may allow close approach. Gregarious. In small groups or flocks year-round. Weakly territorial or not at all, with pairs nesting close to one another, often in the same tree. Forages on ground and in trees for seeds from alders, birches, spruce, and other trees. Also eats thistle seeds and weeds, some insects in summer. Nomadic in fall and winter. Attracted to salt licks and salt-treated winter highways. Feeds on sap at drill wells created by sapsuckers. Mountain populations descent to lower elevations prior to winter onset.
- **BREEDING** Monogamous. Semicolonial.
- **NESTING** Incubation 13 days by female. Young altricial; brooded by female; stay in nest 14–15 days, fed by both sexes. 2 broods per year.
- **POPULATION** Widespread and abundant in coniferous and mixed conifer-deciduous forests, in woodlands, parks, weedy fields, and near human habitation. Erratic irruptions in some winters bring large numbers far south of normal wintering range.
- **FEEDERS** Mixed seed, thistle, and black oil sunflower seed. Also will bathe and drink in birdbaths.
- **CONSERVATION** Fatalities high in winter; birds attracted to salt on roads become reluctant to fly.

Similar Birds

HOUSE FINCH ♀
Stubbier thicker bill; longer tail with squarish tip; 2 narrow white wing bars; lacks yellow at base of tail, primaries, and secondaries.

COMMON REDPOLL ♀
Red cap; black chin; 2 narrow white wing bars; lacks yellow plumage on wings and tail.

Flight Pattern

Flight is high and swift in compact flocks with long undulating sweeps.

Nest Identification	
Shape ⌣ ◖ Location 🪹	Bark, moss, feathers, and animal fur • lined with grass and twigs • usually hidden in conifer, placed far out from trunk • 10–50 feet above ground • built by female • 3–5 pale greenish blue eggs, with brown and black spots concentrated on larger end; short oval to short subelliptical, 0.7 x 0.5 inches.

Plumage Sexes similar	Habitat 🐾 ▲	Migration Migratory	Weight 0.5 ounce

DATE _____ TIME_____ LOCATION _____

Family FRINGILLIDAE	Species *Carduelis tristis*	Length 5 inches	Wingspan 8.75–9 inches

AMERICAN GOLDFINCH

Often called the "wild canary" in the Southeast, the male in breeding plumage is a bright canary yellow. The female is more dull overall, while the young have whitish cinnamon wing bars and rump. Adult males in winter look more like the females and juveniles.

bright yellow

black cap

• SONG A jumbled series of musical warbles and trills often with a drawn-out *baybeee* note. Flight song sounds like *per-chick-oree* or *po-tato-chips*.

black wings with white double wing bars

MALE

• BEHAVIOR Occurs in flocks in nonbreeding season. In spring, feeds on the small seeds from dandelions. In the late summer breeding season, males engage in aerial displays of exaggerated roller coaster–like flights across the sky, singing *po-tato-chip* with each downward glide.

black tail

extensive white edging on wing

JUVENILE

FEMALE
WINTER PLUMAGE

MALE
WINTER PLUMAGE

• BREEDING Monogamous. Among the very latest songbirds to nest each year. Territorial defense and mate selection begins in late summer and continues into early fall.

olive upperparts

pale yellow underparts

FEMALE

Similar Birds

YELLOW WARBLER ♂ Lacks wing bars and black wing and tail • breeds throughout much of the North, Southwest.

LESSER GOLDFINCH ♂ Yellow undertail coverts • ranges in the Northwest, Rockies, and much of the Southwest.

• NESTING Incubation 10–12 days by female. Young stay in nest

Flight Pattern

Undulating, roller coaster–like flight with several rapid wing beats and a pause.

11–17 days, fed by both sexes. 1–2 broods per year.
• POPULATION Common. Declining in eastern North America; stable in the West.
• FEEDERS Black (oil) sunflower seeds, thistle.

Nest Identification

Shape   Location

Pliable vegetation lined with plant down • caterpillar webbing and spider silk often used to bind outer rim • usually along the edge of an open area • built by female • extremely well woven • 4–6 pale blue or bluish white eggs; subelliptical to oval, 0.6 inch long.

Plumage Sexes differ	Habitat	Migration Migratory	Weight 0.5 ounce

DATE _____ TIME_____ LOCATION _____

Family PASSERIDAE	Species *Passer domesticus*	Length 5.5–6.5 inches	Wingspan 9.5–10 inches

HOUSE SPARROW

This bird was introduced in New York City from Europe in the 1850s. By the early 20th century it was established over most of the continent. With the popularity of cars it began to decline; fewer horses meant less undigested grain to be gleaned from horse manure. Sometimes called the English Sparrow, it is the world's most widespread songbird. Juveniles resemble females but have browner upperparts, buffier underparts, and a pinkish bill.

gray crown and cheeks
chestnut nape joins postocular stripe
black bill
buff-brown back and wings with black streaking
black bib and lores
white submustache joins white half-collar
MALE
white wing bar
gray rump and tail
pale gray underparts

dusky postocular stripe below buff eyebrow
blackish-streaked buff-brown upperparts

FEMALE

WINTER MALE

• **SONG** Twittering series of chirps. Call is monotonous repeated *cheep-cheep-cheep.*

• **BEHAVIOR** Aggressive and noisy. In pairs during nesting season; family groups and flocks after breeding. Feeds and roosts in huge flocks. Hops. Forages on ground, in trees and shrubs, in urban and rural areas. Eats insects, caterpillars, seeds, grains, and fruits. Inspects car grilles for insects. Usurps nesting cavities from other species.

dusky bill with yellowish base to lower mandible
white wing bar
brownish gray underparts

• **BREEDING** Monogamous. Some promiscuous. Males form circle around female and aggressively battle with each other.

• **NESTING** Incubation 10–14 days by both sexes, mostly by female. Altricial young brooded by female; stay in nest 14–17 days; both sexes feed by regurgitation. 2–3 broods per year.

• **POPULATION** Abundant and widespread in urban and cultivated areas and around human habitation; gradually declining.

• **FEEDERS AND BIRDHOUSES** Will come to feeders for small seeds and grains; nests in bird boxes.

• **CONSERVATION** Rare cowbird host. Out-competes other secondary-cavity nesters but loses to European Starlings.

Similar Birds

EURASIAN TREE SPARROW
Reddish brown crown; white cheek with black patch; black loral mask and chin; black-streaked brownish upperparts; white wing bar has black upper border; dusky brown underparts • locally common only in and around St. Louis, Missouri, and Illinois.

Flight Pattern
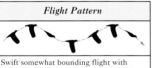
Swift somewhat bounding flight with rapid wing beats alternating with brief periods of wings pulled to sides.

Nest Identification	Grass, straw, weeds, cotton, bits of debris, twigs, and feathers • in tree hollow, under eaves of building or other sheltered areas, or in bird boxes; abandoned nests of other birds • on the backs of highway signs and billboards in the West • built by both sexes • 3–7 light green or blue eggs, dotted with grays and browns, concentrated toward larger end; oval to long oval, 0.9 x 0.7 inches.
Shape 〇 ⬮ ⬯ ²⬮ ⬭	
Location 🪹 ⬮ 🏚 🌿 🌳	

Plumage Sexes differ	Habitat 🌿 🌿🌿 ___ 🌿	Migration Nonmigratory	Weight 1.0 ounce

DATE ⁷ / ٥ ч ___ TIME _____ LOCATION _____

ACCIDENTAL, VAGRANT, & CASUAL SPECIES

The following section (pp. 371–384) contains 139 species for which the American Ornithologists' Union lists accepted records in Florida on an accidental to casual basis. Only those species listed on the current AOU Check-list of North American Birds (7th edition, 1998 and its 42nd Supplement, 2000) and the ABA 1998–99 ABA Check-list Report, Birding 31: 518–524 are included. They appear in taxonomic order.

The species on the following pages fall into one of the following three designations depending on their abundance in this region:

Accidentals: Species that are represented by a single record or several records but have a normal range that is distant from this region. Therefore, these species are not expected to occur in this region.

Vagrants: Species with a natural range that is close to this region, that can be expected to be observed in the region on rare occasions.

Casuals: Species that have either a natural range that borders the region, or an extremely limited range within this region, and that may be expected to be recorded infrequently on an annual basis or over a period of several years.

PACIFIC LOON
Gavia pacifica
Length 26 inches

LEAST GREBE
Tachybaptus dominicus
Length 9–10 inches

EARED GREBE
Podiceps nigricollis
Length 12–13 inches

WESTERN GREBE
Aechmophorus occidentalis
Length 22–29 inches

YELLOW-NOSED ALBATROSS
Thalassarche chlororhynchos
Length 28–32 inches

SCARLET IBIS
Eudocimus ruber
Length 21.5–27.5 inches

WHITE-FACED IBIS
Plegadis chihi
Length 20–26 inches

BLACK-BELLIED WHISTLING-DUCK
Dendrocygna autumnalis
Length 19–22 inches

GREATER WHITE-FRONTED GOOSE
Anser albifrons
Length 26–34 inches

ROSS'S GOOSE
Chen rossii
Length 21–26 inches

BRANT
Branta bernicla
Length 22–26 inches

TUNDRA SWAN
Cygnus columbianus
Length 47–58 inches

MUSCOVY DUCK
Cairina moschata
Length 25–35 inches

EURASIAN WIGEON
Anas penelope
Length 18–20 inches

CINNAMON TEAL
Anas cyanoptera
Length 14–17 inches

WHITE-CHEEKED PINTAIL
Anas bahamensis
Length 18–20 inches

KING EIDER
Somateria spectabilis
Length 18–25 inches

COMMON EIDER
Somateria mollissima
Length 23–27 inches

HARLEQUIN DUCK
Histrionicus histrionicus
Length 15–21 inches

WHITE-WINGED SCOTER
Melanitta fusca
Length 19–24 inches

LONG-TAILED DUCK
Clangula hyemalis
Length 15–22 inches

MASKED DUCK
Nomonyx dominicus
Length 12–14 inches

NORTHERN GOSHAWK
Accipiter gentilis
Length 19–27 inches

SWAINSON'S HAWK
Buteo swainsoni
Length 19–22 inches

NORTHERN LAPWING
Vanellus vanellus
Length 12–13 inches

MOUNTAIN PLOVER
Charadrius montanus
Length 9 inches

BLACK-TAILED GODWIT
Limosa limosa
Length 16 inches

HUDSONIAN GODWIT
Limosa haemastica
Length 15 inches

BAR-TAILED GODWIT
Limosa lapponica
Length 16 inches

SURFBIRD
Aphriza virgata
Length 10 inches

BAIRD'S SANDPIPER
Calidris bairdii
Length 7.5 inches

SHARP-TAILED SANDPIPER
Calidris acuminata
Length 8.5 inches

PURPLE SANDPIPER
Calidris maritima
Length 9 inches

CURLEW SANDPIPER
Calidris ferruginea
Length 7.5–8.5 inches

BUFF-BREASTED SANDPIPER
Tryngites subruficollis
Length 7.5–8.25 inches

RUFF
Philomachus pugnax
Length 9–12.5 inches

WILSON'S PHALAROPE
Phalaropus tricolor
Length 8–9.5 inches

RED PHALAROPE
Phalaropus fulicaria
Length 8–9 inches

FRANKLIN'S GULL
Larus pipixcan
Length 13–15 inches

LITTLE GULL
Larus minutus
Length 10–12 inches

BLACK-HEADED GULL
Larus ridibundus
Length 14–16 inches

BAND-TAILED GULL
Larus belcheri
Length 20 inches

THAYER'S GULL
Larus thayeri
Length 23–25 inches

ICELAND GULL
Larus glaucoides
Length 23–25 inches

GLAUCOUS GULL
Larus hyperboreus
Length 26–30 inches

SABINE'S GULL
Xema sabini
Length 13–14 inches

BLACK-LEGGED KITTIWAKE
Rissa tridactyla
Length 16–17 inches

DOVEKIE
Alle alle
Length 8.5 inches

THICK-BILLED MURRE
Uria lomvia
Length 18 inches

RAZORBILL
Alca torda
Length 16–18 inches

LONG-BILLED MURRELET
Brachyramphus perdix
Length 11.5 inches

ATLANTIC PUFFIN
Fratercula arctica
Length 12 inches

SCALY-NAPED PIGEON
Columba squamosa
Length 15 inches

BAND-TAILED PIGEON
Columba fasciata
Length 14–15 inches

ZENAIDA DOVE
Zenaida aurita
Length 10 inches

KEY WEST QUAIL-DOVE
Geotrygon chrysia
Length 10–11 inches

RUDDY QUAIL-DOVE
Geotrygon montana
Length 8–10 inches

GROOVE-BILLED ANI
Crotophaga sulcirostris
Length 12–14 inches

FLAMMULATED OWL
Otus flammeolus
Length 6–7 inches

LONG-EARED OWL
Asio otus
Length 13–16 inches

SHORT-EARED OWL
Asio flammeus
Length 13–17 inches

NORTHERN SAW-WHET OWL
Aegolius acadicus
Length 7–8 inches

LESSER NIGHTHAWK
Chordeiles acutipennis
Length 8–9 inches

WHITE-COLLARED SWIFT
Streptoprocne zonaris
Length 8.75 inches

VAUX'S SWIFT
Chaetura vauxi
Length 4–4.5 inches

ANTILLEAN PALM-SWIFT
Tachornis phoenicobia
Length 4–4.5 inches

BROAD-BILLED HUMMINGBIRD
Cynanthus latirostris
Length 3–4 inches

BUFF-BELLIED HUMMINGBIRD
Amazilia yucatanensis
Length 4–5 inches

BAHAMA WOODSTAR
Calliphlox evelynae
Length 3–4 inches

BLACK-CHINNED HUMMINGBIRD
Archilochus alexandri
Length 3.5–3.75 inches

ANNA'S HUMMINGBIRD
Calypte anna
Length 3.5–4 inches

CALLIOPE HUMMINGBIRD
Stellula calliope
Length 2.75–3.25 inches

GOLDEN-FRONTED WOODPECKER
Melanerpes aurifrons
Length 8.5–10 inches

CARIBBEAN ELAENIA
Elaenia martinica
Length 5.5–6 inches

OLIVE-SIDED FLYCATCHER
Contopus cooperi
Length 7.5 inches

WESTERN WOOD-PEWEE
Contopus sordidulus
Length 6.25 inches

YELLOW-BELLIED FLYCATCHER
Empidonax flaviventris
Length 5.5 inches

ALDER FLYCATCHER
Empidonax alnorum
Length 5.75 inches

WILLOW FLYCATCHER
Empidonax traillii
Length 5.75 inches

BLACK PHOEBE
Sayornis nigricans
Length 6–7 inches

SAY'S PHOEBE
Sayornis saya
Length 7.5 inches

VERMILION FLYCATCHER
Pyrocephalus rubinus
Length 6 inches

ASH-THROATED FLYCATCHER
Myiarchus cinerascens
Length 8.5 inches

BROWN-CRESTED FLYCATCHER
Myiarchus tyrannulus
Length 8.75 inches

LA SAGRA'S FLYCATCHER
Myiarchus sagrae
Length 8 inches

SULPHUR-BELLIED FLYCATCHER
Myiodynastes luteiventris
Length 8.5 inches

VARIEGATED FLYCATCHER
Empidonomus varius
Length 7.25 inches

TROPICAL KINGBIRD
Tyrannus melancholicus
Length 8–9.25 inches

CASSIN'S KINGBIRD
Tyrannus vociferans
Length 8–9 inches

LOGGERHEAD KINGBIRD
Tyrannus caudifasciatus
Length 9 inches

FORK-TAILED FLYCATCHER
Tyrannus savana
Length 14.5 inches

THICK-BILLED VIREO
Vireo crassirostris
Length 5.5 inches

BELL'S VIREO
Vireo bellii
Length 4.75 inches

PLUMBEOUS VIREO
Vireo plumbeus
Length 5.25 inches

WARBLING VIREO
Vireo gilvus
Length 5–5.5 inches

PHILADELPHIA VIREO
Vireo philadelphicus
Length 4.75–5.25 inches

YELLOW-GREEN VIREO
Vireo flavoviridis
Length 6 inches

CUBAN MARTIN
Progne cryptoleuca
Length 7.25 inches

SOUTHERN MARTIN
Progne elegans
Length 7 inches

BAHAMA SWALLOW
Tachycineta cyaneoviridis
Length 5.75 inches

ROCK WREN
Salpinctes obsoletus
Length 6 inches

BEWICK'S WREN
Thryomanes bewickii
Length 5.25 inches

NORTHERN WHEATEAR
Oenanthe oenanthe
Length 5.5–6 inches

VARIED THRUSH
Ixoreus naevius
Length 9.5 inches

SAGE THRASHER
Oreoscoptes montanus
Length 8.5 inches

CURVE-BILLED THRASHER
Toxostoma curvirostre
Length 11 inches

SPRAGUE'S PIPIT
Anthus spragueii
Length 6.5 inches

BLACK-THROATED GRAY WARBLER
Dendroica nigrescens
Length 4.75–5 inches

GOLDEN-CHEEKED WARBLER
Dendroica chrysoparia
Length 4.75–5 inches

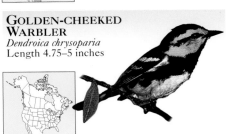

TOWNSEND'S WARBLER
Dendroica townsendi
Length 4.75–5 inches

KIRTLAND'S WARBLER
Dendroica kirtlandii
Length 5.5 inches

MOURNING WARBLER
Oporornis philadelphia
Length 5.25 inches

MACGILLIVRAY'S WARBLER
Oporornis tolmiei
Length 5.25 inches

BANANAQUIT
Coereba flaveola
Length 4.5 inches

WESTERN TANAGER
Piranga ludoviciana
Length 7.25 inches

WESTERN SPINDALIS
Spindalis zena
Length 5.8–6.75 inches

YELLOW-FACED GRASSQUIT
Tiaris olivacea
Length 4.25 inches

BLACK-FACED GRASSQUIT
Tiaris bicolor
Length 4.5 inches

GREEN-TAILED TOWHEE
Pipilo chlorurus
Length 7.25 inches

SPOTTED TOWHEE
Pipilo maculatus
Length 7–7.5 inches

LARK SPARROW
Chondestes grammacus
Length 5.75–6.75 inches

BLACK-THROATED SPARROW
Amphispiza bilineata
Length 5.5 inches

LARK BUNTING
Calamospiza melanocorys
Length 7 inches

FOX SPARROW
Passerella iliaca
Length 6.75–7.5 inches

HARRIS'S SPARROW
Zonotrichia querula
Length 6.75–7.75 inches

GOLDEN-CROWNED SPARROW
Zonotrichia atricapilla
Length 7 inches

LAPLAND LONGSPUR
Calcarius lapponicus
Length 6–7 inches

CHESTNUT-COLLARED LONGSPUR
Calcarius ornatus
Length 5.75–6.5 inches

SNOW BUNTING
Plectrophenax nivalis
Length 6.25–7.25 inches

BLACK-HEADED GROSBEAK
Pheucticus melanocephalus
Length 7–8.5 inches

LAZULI BUNTING
Passerina amoena
Length 5.25–5.75 inches

TAWNY-SHOULDERED BLACKBIRD
Agelaius humeralis
Length 7.5–8.5 inches

WESTERN MEADOWLARK
Sturnella neglecta
Length 9–11 inches

YELLOW-HEADED BLACKBIRD
Xanthocephalus xanthocephalus
Length 8.75–11 inches

BREWER'S BLACKBIRD
Euphagus cyanocephalus
Length 8.75–10.25 inches

BRONZED COWBIRD
Molothrus aeneus
Length 6.5–8.75 inches

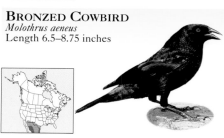

BULLOCK'S ORIOLE
Icterus bullockii
Length 7–8.25 inches

RED CROSSBILL
Loxia curvirostra
Length 5.5–6.5 inches

EVENING GROSBEAK
Coccothraustes vespertinus
Length 7.75–8.5 inches

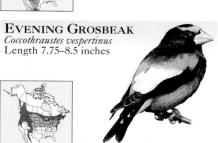

GLOSSARY

• **AERIE**
A nest located on a cliff or high place, usually built by a raptor, a bird of prey.

• **AGAVE**
A desert plant with a spikelike flower, similar to a Yucca plant.

• **AIR SAC**
A series of thin-walled sacs, typically eight or nine (but ranging from six to fourteen, depending on the species) that in conjunction with the paired lungs comprise the bird's respiratory system.

• **ALAR BAR**
A contrasting line (bar) of plumage beginning in the alar region of the wing (where the wing bends at the wrist and on the leading edge) and running from that point at an angle toward the bird's body, stopping where the back of the wing joins the body. The effect is a patch or line of feathers that differ from the color of the wing feathers around it, thus producing a visible bar on the top of the wing. Sometimes the bar runs from the alula to the base of the wing on the front side (leading edge).

• **ALTERNATE PLUMAGE**
See Breeding Plumage.

• **ALTITUDINAL MOVEMENTS**
(Vertical migrations) A bird's regular seasonal vertical movement, often from the mountaintops in summer to lower regions or valleys during winter, with a return to higher elevations the following spring.

• **ALTRICIAL**
Term for young birds that hatch in a helpless state, usually naked with eyes closed, and are totally dependent on the parents.

• **ALULA**
A small group of feathers that protrude from the outermost joint of the wing. It has its own group of muscles and moves independently from the flight feathers. By adjusting the angle of the alula, the bird is able to regulate the air flow over the top of the wing, allowing it to alight or land at slower speeds without stalling.

• **ANHEDRAL**
The downward curve of a bird's wings when in flight.

• **ARBOREAL**
A tree-dwelling bird.

• **AURICULARS**
Feathers along the sides of the ears, often called ear coverts or ear patches.

• **AXILLARIES**
Rigid feathers along the underside of the wings where they connect to the body, corresponding to the underarm area in a human.

• **BASIC PLUMAGE**
See Winter Plumage.

• **BREEDING PLUMAGE**
(Alternate plumage) Seasonal alterations in appearance to attract birds of the opposite sex, such as changes in color or the addition of ornamental ruffs. This is accomplished by a feather molt from the basic, or winter, plumage.

• **CAMBIUM**
Plant tissue near the inner bark of a tree that produces lateral growth.

• **CATKIN**
A spike of flowers such as those found on a willow or birch tree.

• CERE
The fleshy area on top of the base of the upper bill that contains the nostrils. Present on the bills of some bird species, particularly among birds of prey.

• CLUTCH
The total number of eggs laid during a single nesting period; some birds lay several clutches in a nesting season.

• COLONIAL
The pattern of nesting close together with birds of the same species. Sometimes only a few nests packed close together constitute a colony, but some may hold hundreds or thousands of nesting pairs.

• CONSPECIFIC
Birds that are members of the same species.

• CONGENERS
Distinct bird species that are related to one another by being in the same genus.

• COVERTS
A covering of feathers overlaying the upper and lower part of the wings, covering the bases of the flight feathers (wing coverts); also on top of the tail feathers (uppertail coverts and undertail coverts).

• CRECHE
An aggregation of hatchlings of a nesting colony, living together while they are in a dependent state and fed and tended by the adult birds.

• CREPUSCULAR
Birds that feed and are active during twilight hours.

• CRISSUM
Feathers covering the base of the undertail, usually a different color from the rest of the underparts. Also called undertail coverts.

• CROP
Where food is stored in the esophagus for later digestion, or to be regurgitated and fed to hatchlings. Some birds, such as pigeons and doves, have a two-chambered crop that produces special milk to nourish their young.

• CROWN
Top of the head between the forehead and the back of the head or occiput.

• CULMEN
Top ridge of the upper mandible, darker on some birds than the side of the bill.

• DABBLING
Method of surface feeding by a relatively short-necked short-legged duck. It tips up the tail and body, then dips its bill and neck into water. These ducks are called dabblers. See Tipping-up.

• DECURVED
Sloped downward, usually referring to the bill.

• DETRITUS
Small particles of dead organic matter.

• DIHEDRAL
Wings held in a shallow V while bird is in flight.

• DISTAL BAND
A strip of color near the end of the tail, end of wing, or on the lower part of the leg.

• DIURNAL
Birds that feed and are active during the day.

• ECLIPSE PLUMAGE
Dull-colored plumage, similar to that of the female, into which many male ducks briefly molt in summer.

• EXTIRPATED
Exterminated or destroyed from a part of a species range.

• **EYE RING**
A circle around the
eye, usually of a
contrasting color.

• **EYE STRIPE OR
EYEBROW**
See Supercilium.

• **FIELD MARKS**
Plumage or anatomical
features of a bird that help
to distinguish it from other
similar species.

• **FLASHMARK**
Color or marking on
plumage that is visible
only when the bird is
in flight.

• **FLEDGE**
The act of a young bird
(nestling) leaving the
nest. Also fledging.

• **FLEDGLING**
A young bird that has
feathers and is old enough
to have left the nest but is
still dependent on adult
birds for care and feeding.

• **GONYS**
A ridge on the lower
mandible of a gull that
causes the midline to
appear angled.
Sometimes shows a red
patch during breeding
season.

• **GORGET**
A small iridescent patch
on the throat of a
hummingbird.

• **GULAR SAC**
A large or small pouch
in the upper throat that
helps a bird regulate
body temperature and
sometimes holds
undigested food. In a
few species, such as
the Magnificent
Frigatebird, the pouch
greatly expands for
courtship display.

• **HAWKING**
The act of catching
prey, usually insects, in
flight. Generally done
with the bill. Typical of
flycatchers.

• **HERONRY**
(Rookery) The colonial
nesting site for herons,
egrets, and ibises.

• **HINDNECK**
The bird's nape or back
of the neck.

• **HUMERAL**
The patch of feathers
overlying the bone near
the upperwing or
shoulder area.

• **JIZZ**
The abstract
combination of a bird's
posture, plumage
pattern, shape, size,
and behavior that
allows an experienced
birder to recognize a
species instantly
without further
examination.

• **LAMELLAE**
Miniature ridges inside
the bill of a duck or
water bird that
resemble the teeth of a
comb and serve as
a strainer during
feeding.

• **LARDER**
A place where a shrike
impales and stores its
prey on sharp branches
or wire.

• **LEK**
A communal gathering
place during breeding
season where males of
some species of birds
display to attract the
females. It contains
numerous territories,
each guarded by a
different male.

• **LORES**
Space between the eyes
and the base of the
upper part of the bill on
the side of the bird's
face.

• **MALAR**
Refers to the cheek area
along the side of the
face. Field mark here is
called malar mark or
malar stripe.

• **MANDIBLE**
The lower half of the
bill. Maxilla is the
upper half; both
halves collectively
are called mandibles.

• **MANTLE**
The feathers covering the back and upperwing coverts; feathers of the back and folded wings.

• **MANUS**
The portion of a bird's wing that corresponds to the hand of a human. The fused bones of the palm and reduced digits bear the primary feathers and the alula.

• **MELANISTIC**
A bird that has a surplus of dark pigment in its plumage.

• **MIMIC THRUSH**
A member of the family Mimidae, which includes thrashers, catbirds, and mockingbirds.

• **MORPH**
When birds of the same species have two or more different colored plumages, that are independent of season, sex, age, or breeding. Color phases may or may not be related to range and climate.

• **NEOTROPICAL**
The New World tropical region that encompasses the northern portion of the Mexican rain forest and the Caribbean islands, and extends to the nontropical regions of South America.

• **NEW WORLD**
Earth's Western Hemisphere; includes North, South, and Central America.

• **NOCTURNAL**
Birds that feed and are active at night.

• **NON-PASSERINE**
Any of the birds that are not Passerines, which are the songbirds or perching birds. Includes loons, waterfowl, owls, shorebirds, hawks, woodpeckers, and doves.

• **NUCHAL PATCH**
A patch of contrasting color located on the back of the bird's neck or nape.

• **OCCIPITAL PATCH**
A patch of color located high on the back of the head. Higher on the head than the nuchal patch.

• **OCCIPUT**
The area on the back of a bird's head between the nape and the crown.

• **OCOTILLO**
A spiny desert shrub with red flower clusters at the tips of its branches.

• **OLD WORLD**
Earth's Eastern Hemisphere: Europe, Asia, and Africa.

• **ORBITAL RING**
See Eye Ring.

• **PALEARCTIC**
Faunal region surrounded by the Atlantic, Arctic, and Pacific Oceans; encompasses Asia north of the Himalayas, Europe, and Africa north of the Sahara desert.

• **PASSERINES**
Any of the birds belonging to the order Passeriformes, which comprise more than fifty percent of the world's birds. Highly evolved, these birds are able to sing and have three forward-pointing toes adapted for perching.

• **PEEP**
Birder's name for a group of small, similar-looking sandpipers; may have been derived from their high-pitched calls.

• **PELAGIC**
Birds that spend most of their time at sea and rarely are seen from shore.

• **PIEBALD**
Plumage that shows two contrasting colors.

• **PISHING**
Sound produced by birders to attract birds; made by clinching the teeth together and

forcing air out through the teeth and lips to create a noise that sounds like *pish-pish-pish*.

• **POLYANDROUS**
When female bird has two or more mates; female often larger, has brighter plumage, and defends her territory. Male of the species usually incubates and tends young.

• **POLYGYNOUS**
When a male bird takes two or more mates.

• **POLYGAMOUS**
When both male and female of a species may take two or more mates.

• **POSTOCULAR STRIPE**
A line that leads from behind the bird's eye to the auricular or ear patch.

• **PRECOCIAL**
Term for young birds that hatch with their eyes open, are down-covered, and are able to leave the nest within two days of hatching. These hatchlings may be either partially or not at all dependent on the parents for care and feeding.

• **PRIMARIES**
One of two sets of flight feathers, or remiges, located distally to the

secondaries and joined to the manus of the wing.

• **PROMISCUOUS**
Birds, male or female, that come together solely for mating purposes and leave within a few hours to mate with other birds.

• **PYRIFORM**
Pear-shaped; often used to describe shape of egg.

• **RAPTORS**
A name applied to birds of prey – the hawks, falcons, eagles, kites, and owls.

• **RECTRICES**
The principal feathers that make up the tail. They range in number from eight to twenty-four, but the average in songbirds is twelve.

• **REMIGES**
Refers to flight feathers – primaries, secondaries, and tertials.

• **RIPARIAN**
Located on or near a river bank, stream bank, or other body of water.

• **SCAPULARS**
Feathers joined to the shoulder area of the bird and covering the top of the folded wing.

• **SECONDARIES**
One of two sets of flight feathers located between

the body and the primaries and joined to the part of the wing that corresponds to the forearm of a human.

• **SEMIALTRICIAL**
Term for young birds that hatch with eyes either open or closed, are down-covered, and are incapable of leaving the nest; fed by parents.

• **SEMICOLONIAL**
Nesting pattern in which several birds of the same species nest close to one another, often within sight of each other's nests and do not behave aggressively toward one another.

• **SEMIPRECOCIAL**
Term for young birds that hatch with eyes open, are down-covered, and able to leave the nest soon after hatching, but remain in nest and are fed by parents.

• **SKYLARKING**
Elaborate territorial display flight given by a male songbird. It sings and often flutters in circles before swooping back to earth.

• **SPATULATE**
A long rounded spoonlike shape; sometimes used to describe bill or tail.

• **SPECULUM**
A small area of contrasting iridescent feathers located on the secondary feathers of the wings. Often seen in ducks.

• **SQUEAKING**
Sound produced by birders to attract birds; made by pursing the lips tightly together and sucking air in to make a high-pitched sound. This can be amplified by placing the lips on the back of the hand and sucking in a kissing fashion.

• **SUPERCILIUM**
Line above each eye; an eyebrow. Also called a superciliary stripe.

• **SUPERSPECIES**
Closely related species that are often separated from each other by geographic barriers. Without these barriers the two species probably would interbreed and become one.

• **SYMPATRIC**
Birds that inhabit the same range but remain distinct and separate species.

• **TAIGA**
Subarctic coniferous forests.

• **TARSUS**
The top of the foot behind the toes, often called the shank. Usually either bare or covered with scales, plates, or sometimes feathers.

• **TERTIALS**
The group of secondary feathers that are closest to the body; often a contrasting color.

• **TIPPING-UP**
Method of surface feeding by a duck, goose, or swan in which it raises its tail and dips its bill, head, and neck into the water. See Dabbling.

• **TOTIPALMATE**
All four toes joined together by webbing.

• **TYMPANI**
(Tympaniform membranes) Valves in the vocal organ of a bird that produce sound.

• **UNDERPARTS**
The plumage and coloring on the breast, belly, sides, flanks, and undertail coverts.

• **UPPERPARTS**
The plumage and coloring on the nape, back, shoulders, rump, and upper part of tail.

• **VANE**
Contoured flight feather that acts as a propeller. It consists of a central shaft surrounded by an inner and outer web.

• **VENT**
The opening of the cloaca, or anus; sometimes refers to a contrasting patch of feathers in this area.

• **WATTLE**
Fleshy piece of brightly colored skin that hangs from the lower bill; associated with turkeys and some chickens.

• **WILDTYPE**
A biological term based in genetics that describes the form that most individuals in a wild population take; description includes shape, color, patterns, and size.

• **WINGSTRIP**
A distinct line on the wing, usually of a contrasting color.

• **WINTER PLUMAGE**
(Basic plumage) Seasonal alteration in a bird's appearance produced by the fall molt.

INDEX

A

Accipiter
　cooperii 117
　gentilis 373
　striatus 116
Accipitridae 109–23
Actitis macularia 156
Aechmophorus occidentalis 371
Aegolius acadicus 377
Agelaius
　humeralis 384
　phoeniceus 355
Aimophila aestivalis 330
Aix sponsa 86
Ajaia ajaja 78
Alaudidae 253
Albatross, Yellow-nosed 371
Alca torda 375
Alcedinidae 225
Alcidae 36
Alle alle 375
Amazilia yucatanensis 377
Ammodramus
　caudacutus 340
　henslowii 337
　leconteii 338
　maritimus 341
　nelsoni 339
　savannarum 336
Amphispiza bilineata 383
Anas
　acuta 94
　americana 88
　bahamensis 372
　clypeata 93
　crecca 95
　cyanoptera 372
　discors 92
　fulvigula 91
　penelope 372
　platyrhynchos 90
　rubripes 89
　strepera 87
Anatidae 83–108
Anhinga 62
Anhinga anhinga 62
Anhingidae 62
Ani
　Groove-billed 376
　Smooth-billed 212

Anous
　minutus 199
　stolidus 198
Anser albifrons 371
Anthus
　rubescens 289
　spragueii 381
Aphelocoma coerulescens 250
Aphriza virgata 373
Apodidae 222
Aquila chrysaetos 123
Aramidae 139
Aramus guarauna 139
Archilochus
　alexandri 377
　colubris 223
Ardea
　alba 67
　herodias 66
Ardeidae 64–75
Arenaria interpres 161
Asio
　flammeus 377
　otus 376
Athene cunicularia 216
Auk, Great 36
Avocet, American 151
Aythya
　affinis 100
　americana 97
　collaris 98
　marila 99
　valisineria 96

B

Baeolophus bicolor 262
Bananaquit 382
Bartramia longicauda 157
Basileuterus culicivorus 325
Bittern
　American 64
　Least 65
Blackbird
　Brewer's 384
　Red-winged 355
　Rusty 357
　Tawny-shouldered 384
　Yellow-headed 384
Bluebird, Eastern 276
Bobolink 354
Bobwhite, Northern 129

Bombycilla cedrorum 290
Bombycillidae 290
Booby
　Brown 55
　Masked 54
　Red-footed 56
Botaurus lentiginosus 64
Brachyramphus perdix 376
Brant 372
Branta
　bernicla 372
　canadensis 85
Bubo virginianus 215
Bubulcus ibis 72
Bucephala
　albeola 103
　clangula 104
Budgerigar 207
Bufflehead 103
Bulbul, Red-whiskered 272
Bunting
　Indigo 351
　Lark 383
　Lazuli 384
　Painted 352
　Snow 383
Buteo
　brachyurus 120
　jamaicensis 121
　lineatus 118
　platypterus 119
　regalis 122
　swainsoni 373
Butorides virescens 73

C

Cairina moschata 372
Calamospiza melanocorys 383
Calcarius
　lapponicus 383
　ornatus 383
Calidris
　acuminata 374
　alba 163
　alpina 169
　bairdii 374
　canutus 162
　ferruginea 374
　fuscicollis 167
　himantopus 170
　maritima 374

Calidris (cont.)
  mauri 165
  melanotos 168
  minutilla 166
  pusilla 164
Calliphlox evelynae 377
Calonectris diomedea 44
Calypte anna 378
Campephilus principalis 35
Canvasback 96
Caprimulgidae 218–221
Caprimulgus
  carolinensis 220
  vociferus 221
Caracara, Crested 124
Caracara cheriway 124
Cardinal, Northern 348
Cardinalidae 348–53
Cardinalis cardinalis 348
Carduelis
  pinus 367
  tristis 368
Carpodacus
  mexicanus 366
  purpureus 365
Catbird, Gray 284
Cathartes aura 81
Cathartidae 80–81
Catharus
  bicknelli 279
  fuscescens 277
  guttatus 281
  minimus 278
  ustulatus 280
Catoptrophorus semipalmatus
  155
Certhia americana 266
Certhiidae 266
Ceryle alcyon 225
Chaetura
  pelagica 222
  vauxi 377
Charadriidae 142–148
Charadrius
  alexandrinus 144
  melodus 147
  montanus 373
  semipalmatus 146
  vociferus 148
  wilsonia 145
Chat, Yellow-breasted 326
Chen
  caerulescens 84

  rossii 371
Chickadee, Carolina 261
Chlidonias niger 197
Chondestes grammacus 383
Chordeiles
  acutipennis 377
  gundlachii 219
  minor 218
Chuck-will's-widow 220
Ciconiidae 79
Circus cyaneus 115
Cistothorus
  palustris 271
  platensis 270
Clangula hyemalis 373
Coccothraustes vespertinus 384
Coccyzus
  americanus 210
  erythropthalmus 209
  minor 211
Coereba flaveola 382
Colaptes auratus 232
Colinus virginianus 129
Columba
  fasciata 376
  leucocephala 202
  livia 201
  squamosa 376
Columbidae 37, 201–06
Columbina passerina 206
Contopus
  cooperi 378
  sordidulus 378
  virens 234
Conuropis carolinensis 37
Coot, American 138
Coragyps atratus 80
Cormorant
  Double-crested 60
  Great 61
Corvidae 249–52
Corvus
  brachyrhynchos 251
  ossifragus 252
Coturnicops noveboracensis 130
Cowbird
  Bronzed 384
  Brown-headed 361
  Shiny 360
Crane
  Sandhill 140
  Whooping 141
Creeper, Brown 266

Crossbill, Red 384
Crotophaga
  ani 212
  sulcirostris 376
Crow
  American 251
  Fish 252
Cuckoo
  Black-billed 209
  Mangrove 211
  Yellow-billed 210
Cuculidae 209–12
Curlew, Long-billed 159
Cyanocitta cristata 249
Cygnus columbianus 372
Cynanthus latirostris 377

D
Dendrocygna
  autumnalis 371
  bicolor 83
Dendroica
  caerulescens 300
  castanea 308
  cerulea 310
  chrysoparia 381
  coronata 301
  discolor 306
  dominica 304
  fusca 303
  kirtlandii 382
  magnolia 298
  nigrescens 381
  palmarum 307
  pensylvanica 297
  petechia 296
  pinus 305
  striata 309
  tigrina 299
  townsendi 381
  virens 302
Dickcissel 353
Dolichonyx oryzivorus 354
Dove
  Common Ground- 206
  Eurasian Collared- 203
  Key West Quail- 376
  Mourning 205
  Rock 201
  Ruddy Quail- 376
  White-winged 204
  Zenaida 376

Dovekie 375
Dowitcher
Long-billed 172
Short-billed 171
Dryocopus pileatus 233
Duck
American Black 89
Harlequin 372
Long-tailed 373
Masked 373
Mottled 91
Muscovy 372
Ring-necked 98
Ruddy 108
Wood 86
Dumetella carolinensis 284
Dunlin 169

E

Eagle
Bald 114
Golden 123
Ectopistes migratorius 37
Egret
Cattle 72
Reddish 71
Egretta
caerulea 69
rufescens 71
thula 68
tricolor 70
Eider
Common 372
King 372
Elaenia, Caribbean 378
Elaenia martinica 378
Elanoides forficatus 110
Elanus leucurus 111
Emberizidae 329–47
Empidonax
alnorum 378
flaviventris 378
minimus 236
traillii 378
virescens 235
Empidonomus varius 379
Eremophila alpestris 253
Eudocimus
albus 76
ruber 371
Euphagus
carolinus 357
cyanocephalus 384

F

Falco
columbarius 126
peregrinus 127
sparverius 125
Falcon, Peregrine 127
Falconidae 124–27
Finch
House 366
Purple 365
Flamingo, Greater 82
Flicker, Northern 232
Flycatcher
Acadian 235
Alder 378
Ash-throated 379
Brown-crested 379
Fork-tailed 380
Great Crested 238
La Sagra's 379
Least 236
Olive-sided 378
Scissor-tailed 242
Sulphur-bellied 379
Variegated 379
Vermilion 379
Willow 378
Yellow-bellied 378
Fratercula arctica 376
Fregata magnificens 63
Fregatidae 63
Frigatebird, Magnificent 63
Fringillidae 365–68
Fulica americana 138

G

Gadwall 87
Gallinago gallinago 173
Gallinula chloropus 137
Gallinule, Purple 136
Gannet, Northern 57
Gavia
immer 40
pacifica 371
stellata 39
Gaviidae 39–40
Geothlypis trichas 321
Geotrygon
chrysia 376
montana 376
Gnatcatcher, Blue-gray 275

Godwit
Bar-tailed 373
Black-tailed 373
Hudsonian 373
Marbled 160
Goldeneye, Common 104
Goldfinch, American 368
Goose
Canada 85
Greater White-fronted 371
Ross's 371
Snow 84
Goshawk, Northern 373
Grackle
Boat-tailed 359
Common 358
Grassquit
Black-faced 382
Yellow-faced 382
Grebe
Eared 371
Horned 42
Least 371
Pied-billed 41
Western 371
Grosbeak
Black-headed 383
Blue 350
Evening 384
Rose-breasted 349
Gruidae 140–41
Grus
americana 141
canadensis 140
Guiraca caerulea 350
Gull
Band-tailed 375
Black-headed 375
Bonaparte's 181
Franklin's 374
Glaucous 375
Great Black-backed 185
Herring 183
Iceland 375
Laughing 180
Lesser Black-backed 184
Little 374
Ring-billed 182
Sabine's 375
Thayer's 375

H

Haematopodidae 149
Haematopus palliatus 149
Haliaeetus leucocephalus 114
Harrier, Northern 115
Hawk
  Broad-winged 119
  Cooper's 117
  Ferruginous 122
  Red-shouldered 118
  Red-tailed 121
  Sharp-shinned 116
  Short-tailed 120
  Swainson's 373
Helmitheros vermivorus 314
Heron
  Great Blue 66
  Green 73
  Little Blue 69
  Tricolored 70
Himantopus mexicanus 150
Hirundinidae 254–60
Hirundo rustica 260
Histrionicus histrionicus 372
Hummingbird
  Anna's 378
  Black-chinned 377
  Broad-billed 377
  Buff-bellied 377
  Calliope 378
  Ruby-throated 223
  Rufous 224
Hydrobatidae 49–51
Hylocichla mustelina 282

I

Ibis
  Glossy 77
  Scarlet 371
  White 76
  White-faced 371
Icteria virens 326
Icteridae 354–64
Icterus
  bullockii 384
  galbula 364
  pectoralis 363
  spurius 362
Ictinia mississippiensis 113
Ixobrychus exilis 65
Ixoreus naevius 381

J

Jaeger
  Long-tailed 179
  Parasitic 178
  Pomarine 177
Jay
  Blue 249
  Florida Scrub- 250
Junco, Dark-eyed 347
Junco hyemalis 347

K

Kestrel, American 125
Killdeer 148
Kingbird
  Cassin's 379
  Eastern 240
  Gray 241
  Loggerhead 379
  Tropical 379
  Western 239
Kingfisher, Belted 225
Kinglet
  Golden-crowned 273
  Ruby-crowned 274
Kite
  Mississippi 113
  Snail 112
  Swallow-tailed 110
  White-tailed 111
Kittiwake, Black-legged 375
Knot, Red 162

L

Laniidae 243
Lanius ludovicianus 243
Lapwing, Northern 373
Laridae 176–200
Lark, Horned 253
Larus
  argentatus 183
  atricilla 180
  belcheri 375
  delawarensis 182
  fuscus 184
  glaucoides 375
  hyperboreus 375
  marinus 185
  minutus 374
  philadelphia 181
  pipixcan 374

  ridibundus 375
  thayeri 355
Laterallus jamaicensis 131
Limnodromus
  griseus 171
  scolopaceus 172
Limnothlypis swainsonii 315
Limosa
  fedoa 160
  haemastica 373
  lapponica 373
  limosa 373
Limpkin 139
Longspur
  Chestnut-collared 383
  Lapland 383
Loon
  Common 40
  Pacific 371
  Red-throated 39
Lophodytes cucullatus 105
Loxia curvirostra 384

M

Mallard 90
Martin
  Cuban 380
  Purple 254
  Southern 380
Meadowlark
  Eastern 356
  Western 384
Melanerpes
  aurifrons 378
  carolinus 227
  erythrocephalus 226
Melanitta
  fusca 372
  nigra 102
  perspicillata 101
Meleagris gallopavo 128
Melopsittacus undulatus 207
Melospiza
  georgiana 344
  lincolnii 343
  melodia 342
Merganser
  Common 106
  Hooded 105
  Red-breasted 107
Mergus
  merganser 106

Mergus (cont.)
  serrator 107
Merlin 126
Mimidae 284–87
Mimus
  gundlachii 286
  polyglottos 285
Mniotilta varia 311
Mockingbird
  Bahama 286
  Northern 285
Molothrus
  aeneus 384
  ater 361
  bonariensis 360
Moorhen, Common 137
Morus bassanus 57
Motacillidae 289
Murre, Thick-billed 375
Murrelet, Long-billed 376
Mycteria americana 79
Myiarchus
  cinerascens 379
  crinitus 238
  sagrae 379
  tyrannulus 379
Myiodynastes luteiventris 379
Myiopsitta monachus 208

N

Night-Heron
  Black-crowned 74
  Yellow-crowned 75
Nighthawk
  Antillean 219
  Common 218
  Lesser 377
Noddy
  Black 199
  Brown 198
Nomonyx dominicus 373
Numenius
  americanus 159
  phaeopus 158
Nuthatch
  Brown-headed 265
  Red-breasted 263
  White-breasted 264
Nyctanassa violacea 75
Nycticorax nycticorax 74

O

Oceanites oceanicus 49
Oceanodroma
  castro 51
  leucorhoa 50
Odontophoridae 129
Oenanthe oenanthe 381
Oporornis
  agilis 320
  formosus 319
  philadelphia 382
  tolmiei 382
Oreoscoptes montanus 381
Oriole
  Baltimore 364
  Bullock's 384
  Orchard 362
  Spot-breasted 363
Osprey 109
Otus
  asio 214
  flammeolus 376
Ovenbird 316
Owl
  Barn 213
  Barred 217
  Burrowing 216
  Eastern Screech 214
  Flammulated 376
  Great Horned 215
  Long-eared 376
  Northern Saw-whet 377
  Short-eared 377
Oxyura jamaicensis 108
Oystercatcher, American 149

P

Pandion haliaetus 109
Parakeet
  Carolina 37
  Monk 208
Paridae 261–65
Parula americana 295
Parula, Northern 295
Parulidae 36, 291–326
Passer domesticus 369
Passerculus sandwichensis 335
Passerella iliaca 383
Passeridae 369
Passerina
  amoena 384
  ciris 352

  cyanea 351
Pelecanidae 58–59
Pelecanus
  erythrorhynchos 58
  occidentalis 59
Pelican
  American White 58
  Brown 59
Petrel, Black-capped 43
Petrochelidon
  fulva 259
  pyrrhonota 258
Pewee
  Eastern Wood- 234
  Western Wood- 378
Phaethon
  aethereus 53
  lepturus 52
Phaethontidae 52–53
Phalacrocoracidae 60–61
Phalacrocorax
  auritus 60
  carbo 61
Phalarope
  Red 374
  Red-necked 175
  Wilson's 374
Phalaropus
  fulicaria 374
  lobatus 175
  tricolor 374
Phasianidae 128
Pheucticus
  ludovicianus 349
  melanocephalus 383
Philomachus pugnax 374
Phoebe
  Black 378
  Eastern 237
  Say's 379
Phoenicopteridae 82
Phoenicopterus ruber 82
Picidae 35, 226–33
Picoides
  borealis 231
  pubescens 229
  villosus 230
Pigeon
  Band-tailed 376
  Passenger 37
  Scaly-naped 376
  White-crowned 202
Pinguinis impennis 36

Pintail
Northern 94
White-cheeked 372
Pipilo
chlorurus 382
erythrophthalmus 329
maculatus 382
Pipit
American 289
Sprague's 381
Piranga
ludoviciana 382
olivacea 328
rubra 327
Plectrophenax nivalis 383
Plegadis
chihi 371
falcinellus 77
Plover
American Golden- 143
Black-bellied 142
Mountain 373
Piping 147
Semipalmated 146
Snowy 144
Wilson's 145
Pluvialis
dominica 143
squatarola 142
Podiceps
auritus 42
nigricollis 371
Podicipedidae 41–42
Podilymbus podiceps 41
Poecile carolinensis 261
Polioptila caerulea 275
Pooecetes gramineus 334
Porphyrula martinica 136
Porzana carolina 135
Procellariidae 43–48
Progne
cryptoleuca 380
elegans 380
subis 254
Protonotaria citrea 313
Psittacidae 37, 207–08
Pterodroma hasitata 43
Puffin, Atlantic 376
Puffinus
gravis 45
griseus 46
lherminieri 48
puffinus 47

Pycnonotidae 272
Pycnonotus jocosus 272
Pyrocephalus rubinus 379

Q

Quiscalus major 359
Quiscalus quiscula 358

R

Rail
Black 131
Clapper 132
King 133
Virginia 134
Yellow 130
Rallidae 130–38
Rallus
elegans 133
limicola 134
longirostris 132
Razorbill 375
Recurvirostra americana 151
Recurvirostridae 150–51
Redhead 97
Redstart, American 312
Regulidae 273–74
Regulus
calendula 274
satrapa 273
Riparia riparia 257
Rissa tridactyla 375
Robin, American 283
Rostrhamus sociabilis 112
Ruff 374
Rynchops niger 200

S

Salpinctes obsoletus 381
Sanderling 163
Sandpiper
Baird's 374
Buff-breasted 374
Curlew 374
Least 166
Pectoral 168
Purple 374
Semipalmated 164
Sharp-tailed 374
Solitary 154
Spotted 156
Stilt 170

Upland 157
Western 165
White-rumped 167
Sapsucker, Yellow-bellied 228
Sayornis
nigricans 378
phoebe 237
saya 379
Scaup
Greater 99
Lesser 100
Scolopacidae 152–75
Scolopax minor 174
Scoter
Black 102
Surf 101
White-winged 372
Seiurus
aurocapillus 316
motacilla 318
noveboracensis 317
Selasphorus rufus 224
Setophaga ruticilla 312
Shearwater
Audubon's 48
Cory's 44
Greater 45
Manx 47
Sooty 46
Shoveler, Northern 93
Shrike, Loggerhead 243
Sialia sialis 276
Siskin, Pine 367
Sitta
canadensis 263
carolinensis 264
pusilla 265
Skimmer, Black 200
Skua, South Polar 176
Snipe, Common 173
Somateria
mollissima 372
spectabilis 372
Sora 135
Sparrow
Bachman's 330
Black-throated 383
Chipping 331
Clay-colored 332
Field 333
Fox 383
Golden-crowned 383

Sparrow (cont.)
 Grasshopper 336
 Harris's 383
 Henslow's 337
 House 369
 Lark 383
 Le Conte's 338
 Lincoln's 343
 Nelson's Sharp-tailed 339
 Saltmarsh, Sharp-tailed 340
 Savannah 335
 Seaside 341
 Song 342
 Swamp 344
 Vesper 334
 White-crowned 346
 White-throated 345
Sphyrapicus varius 228
Spindalis, Western 382
Spindalis zena 382
Spiza americana 353
Spizella
 pallida 332
 passerina 331
 pusilla 333
Spoonbill, Roseate 78
Starling, European 288
Stelgidopteryx serripennis 256
Stellula calliope 378
Stercorarius
 longicaudus 179
 maccormicki 176
 parasiticus 178
 pomarinus 177
Sterna
 anaethetus 195
 antillarum 194
 caspia 187
 dougallii 190
 forsteri 193
 fuscata 196
 hirundo 191
 maxima 188
 nilotica 186
 paradisaea 192
 sandvicensis 189
Stilt, Black-necked 150
Stork, Wood 79
Storm-Petrel
 Band-rumped 51
 Leach's 50
 Wilson's 49
Streptopelia decaocto 203

Streptoprocne zonaris 377
Strigidae 214–17
Strix varia 217
Sturnella
 magna 356
 neglecta 384
Sturnidae 288
Sturnus vulgaris 288
Sula
 dactylatra 54
 leucogaster 55
 sula 56
Sulidae 54–57
Surfbird 373
Swallow
 Bahama 380
 Bank 257
 Barn 260
 Cave 259
 Cliff 258
 Northern Rough-winged 256
 Tree 255
Swan, Tundra 372
Swift
 Antillean Palm- 377
 Chimney 222
 Vaux's 377
 White-collared 377
Sylviidae 275

T

Tachornis phoenicobia 377
Tachybaptus dominicus 371
Tachycineta
 bicolor 255
 cyaneoviridis 380
Tanager
 Scarlet 328
 Stripe-headed. *See*
  Spindalis, Western
 Summer 327
 Western 382
Teal
 Blue-winged 92
 Cinnamon 372
 Green-winged 95
Tern
 Arctic 192
 Black 197
 Bridled 195
 Caspian 187
 Common 191

 Forster's 193
 Gull-billed 186
 Least 194
 Roseate 190
 Royal 188
 Sandwich 189
 Sooty 196
Thalassarche chlororhynchos 371
Thrasher
 Brown 287
 Curve-billed 381
 Sage 381
Thraupidae 327–28
Threskiornithidae 76–78
Thrush
 Bicknell's 279
 Gray-cheeked 278
 Hermit 281
 Swainson's 280
 Varied 381
 Wood 282
Thryomanes bewickii 381
Thryothorus ludovicianus 267
Tiaris
 bicolor 382
 olivacea 382
Titmouse, Tufted 262
Towhee
 Eastern 329
 Green-tailed 382
 Spotted 382
Toxostoma
 curvirostre 381
 rufum 287
Tringa
 flavipes 153
 melanoleuca 152
 solitaria 154
Trochilidae 223–24
Troglodytes
 aedon 268
 troglodytes 269
Troglodytidae 267–71
Tropicbird
 Red-billed 53
 White-tailed 52
Tryngites subruficollis 374
Turdidae 276–83
Turdus migratorius 283
Turkey, Wild 128
Turnstone, Ruddy 161
Tyrannidae 234–42

Tyrannus
  caudifasciatus 379
  dominicensis 241
  forficatus 242
  melancholicus 379
  savana 380
  tyrannus 240
  verticalis 239
  vociferans 379
Tyto alba 213
Tytonidae 213

U

Uria lomvia 375

V

Vanellus vanellus 373
Veery 277
Vermivora
  bachmanii 36
  celata 293
  peregrina 292
  pinus 291
  ruficapilla 294
Vireo
  Bell's 380
  Black-whiskered 248
  Blue-headed 246
  Philadelphia 380
  Plumbeous 380
  Red-eyed 247
  Thick-billed 380
  Warbling 380
  White-eyed 244
  Yellow-green 380
  Yellow-throated 245
Vireo
  altiloquus 248
  bellii 380
  crassirostris 380
  flavifrons 245
  flavoviridis 380
  gilvus 380
  griseus 244
  olivaceus 247
  philadelphicus 380
  plumbeus 380
  solitarius 246
Vireonidae 244–48
Vulture
  Black 80
  Turkey 81

W

Warbler
  Bachman's 36
  Bay-breasted 308
  Black-and-white 311
  Black-throated Blue 300
  Black-throated Gray 381
  Black-throated Green 302
  Blackburnian 303
  Blackpoll 309
  Blue-winged 291
  Canada 324
  Cape May 299
  Cerulean 310
  Chestnut-sided 297
  Connecticut 320
  Golden-cheeked 381
  Golden-crowned 325
  Hooded 322
  Kentucky 319
  Kirtland's 382
  MacGillivray's 382
  Magnolia 298
  Mourning 382
  Nashville 294
  Orange-crowned 293
  Palm 307
  Pine 305
  Prairie 306
  Prothonotary 313
  Swainson's 315
  Tennessee 292
  Townsend's 381
  Wilson's 323
  Worm-eating 314
  Yellow 296
  Yellow-rumped 301
  Yellow-throated 304
Waterthrush
  Lousiana 318
  Northern 317
Waxwing, Cedar 290
Wheatear, Northern 381
Whimbrel 158
Whip-poor-will 221
Whistling-Duck
  Black-bellied 371
  Fulvous 83
Wigeon
  American 88
  Eurasian 372
Willet 155

Wilsonia
  canadensis 324
  citrina 322
  pusilla 323
Woodcock, American 174
Woodpecker
  Downy 229
  Golden-fronted 378
  Hairy 230
  Ivory-billed 35
  Pileated 233
  Red-bellied 227
  Red-cockaded 231
  Red-headed 226
Woodstar, Bahama 377
Wren
  Bewick's 381
  Carolina 267
  House 268
  Marsh 271
  Rock 381
  Sedge 270
  Winter 269

X

Xanthocephalus xanthocephalus 384
Xema sabini 375

Y

Yellowlegs
  Greater 152
  Lesser 153
Yellowthroat, Common 321

Z

Zenaida
  asiatica 204
  aurita 376
  macroura 205
Zonotrichia
  albicollis 345
  atricapilla 383
  leucophrys 346
  querula 383

ACKNOWLEDGMENTS

The author would like to dedicate this book to his father, Fred J. Alsop, Jr., and thank his wife, Cathi Alsop, for her support during the writing of this book and for editing the final proofs of the range maps.

Southern Lights would like to thank: Ron Austing for photo coordination; Kristi Tipton for research on species profiles and range maps; Sandra Porter, Kristy Cuccini, Kelly Buford, and Anne Esquivel for species profile research; Jenny Cromie and Nina Costopoulos for editorial assistance; Holly Cross and R. Clay White for copyediting; Denise McIntyre and Rebecca Benton for proofreading; Marianne Thomas, Melissa Givens, George Griswold III, Jim Larussa, Will McCalley, Rick Tucker, and Christana Laycock for graphic assistance; Catherine O'Hare, Michelle Boylan, Taylor Rogers, Brad Reisinger, and Beth Brown for administrative support; and Charles (Chuck) Hunter of the US Fish and Wildlife Service, John C. Sterling, and Joseph DiCostanzo of the American Museum of Natural History for manuscript review and commentary.

Picture Credits
Plumage illustrations: Simone End, Carl Salter. Silhouettes: Terence Clark/Housewren 22–23.
Profile illustrations: Svetlana Belotserkovskaya 36t & b, 37b, 357f, 358f, 379-lc-4, 380-lc-5, rc-4, 382-lc-4, rc-4. Ernie Eldredge 12t, 13c, 43, 44, 50, 376-lc-2, 377-rc-2. Alice Pederson 14t, 14b, 15t, 200, 376-lc-1, 377-lc-3, rc-3, 380-rc-5, 384-rc-1.

Abbreviations: b = bottom, t = top, c = center, l = left, r = right, m = male, f = female.

Accidental species are credited left column 1–5 (lc-1) and right column 1–5 (rc-1). Inside photographs: Fred J. Alsop III 24bl, 25t, 25b, 29tr, 63m, 78, 204, 367, 374-rc-4. Ron Austing 25c, 28tl, 28tr, 28b, 29cl, 30t, 32c, 33t, 33c, 53, 54, 62f, 64, 65f & m, 66, 67, 68, 70, 71, 72, 73, 75, 76, 79, 80, 84, 85, 86f & m, 88m, 89f & m, 92m, 94m, 96f & m, 97f & m, 98m, 100m, 103f & m, 104f & m, 105f & m, 106f & m, 107f, 108f & m, 109, 110, 115f & m, 116, 121, 125f & m, 126f & m, 128f & m, 129f, 133, 134, 135, 138, 139, 140, 143, 144f & m, 145, 146, 148, 149, 151, 154, 155, 156, 157, 158, 159, 161, 167, 174, 180, 182, 183, 185, 188, 189, 194, 201, 209, 210, 213, 214, 215, 216, 217, 218, 220, 221, 222, 223f & m, 224f & m, 225f & m, 226, 227f & m, 228, 229, 230, 232, 233f & m, 234, 235, 236, 238, 243, 244, 246, 247, 249, 250, 251, 253, 255, 256, 260, 261, 262, 263f & m, 264, 267, 268, 270, 271, 274f & m, 275m, 276f, 277, 280, 282, 283f & m, 284, 285, 287, 288, 290, 291,

293, 294, 295, 296f & m, 297f & m, 298m, 299m, 300f & m, 301f & m, 302m, 303m, 304, 305, 306, 307, 308m, 311, 313f & m, 314, 316, 318, 319, 321f & m, 322f & m, 324f & m, 326, 327f & m, 328f & m, 329f & m, 331, 332, 333, 334, 335, 336, 337, 343, 344, 346, 347f & m, 348f, 349f & m, 350f & m, 351m, 352f, 353m, 354f, 355f & m, 356, 359f & m, 361f & m, 362f & m, 364m, 365f & m, 366f & m, 368f & m, 369f, 371-lc-2, rc-3, 372-lc-3, 4, rc-2, 3, 4, 373-lc-2, 374-lc-3, 376-rc-5, 377-lc-4, rc-1, 5, 378-lc-3, 5, 380-lc-2, 3, 381-lc-4, rc-3, 382-lc-1, 5, rc-1, 383-lc-1, 3, 4, rc-1, 2, 384-lc-3, 5. **Rick & Nora Bowers** 176, 258, 259, 348m, 352m, 371-lc-5, 372-lc-2, 373-lc-1, 376-lc-5, 378-lc-4. **Cornell Laboratory of Ornithology**/Allen Brooks 37t; L. Page Brown 119; B. B. Hall 363; George Sutton 35. **Mike Danzenbaker** 45, 55, 61, 107m, 173, 184, 303f, 371-lc-3, 373-lc-3, 4, 374-lc-1, 375-lc-1, 376-rc-1, 2, 378-lc-1, rc-3, 379-rc-4, 381-rc-2. **DK Picture Library**/ 207; Dennis Avon 129m, 205, 272; Simon Battersby 12b; Peter Chadwick 29cr, 30b, 31tr, 31cl, 31cr; Mike Dunning 114; Frank Greenaway 123, 127; Cyril Laubscher 74, 81, 124, 150, 208, 369m; Karl & Steve Maslowski 237, 240, 266, 273f, 276m, 345, 354m; Jane Miller 137; Kim Taylor 90f & m. **James R. Fisher** 82. **Frank Lane Picture Agency**/ S. C. Brown 195; Steve McCutcheon 320f; Mark Newman 141; R. Van Nostrand 377-lc-2; Martin Withers 376-rc-4. **Kevin T. Karlson** 42, 52, 63f, 77, 87m, 91, 92f, 93f & m, 95f & m, 98f, 99f & m, 102f, 112f & m, 113, 117, 118, 132, 152, 153, 171, 177, 191, 196, 198, 199, 202, 203, 212, 219, 241, 252, 273m, 286, 289, 292f & m, 298f, 299f, 317, 338, 342, 360f & m, 372-rc-1, 375-lc-2, 4, 376-lc-3,

378-rc-2, 379-lc-3, rc-5, 380-lc-1, rc-1, 3, 382-rc-2. **Brian E. Small** 46, 49, 59, 60, 62m, 69, 87f, 88f, 94f, 100f, 122, 130, 131, 142, 147, 160, 163, 164, 165, 166, 169, 170, 193, 206, 211, 245, 248, 254f & m, 257, 265, 275f, 278, 302f, 308f, 309f & m, 310f & m, 312f & m, 315, 323m, 330, 339, 341, 351f, 358m, 364f, 371-rc-1, 5, lc-4, 372-lc-5, 373-rc-2, 3, 5, 374-lc-4, 5, rc-1, 375-rc-2, 377-lc-1, rc-4, 378-rc-1, 379lc-1, 2, 5, rc-2, 3, 380-rc-2, 381-lc-1, 3, rc-4, 5, 382-lc-2, 3, 383-lc-2, rc-3, 4, 5, 384-lc-1, 4, rc-3, 4. **Tom Vezo** 39, 40, 41, 56, 57, 58, 83, 101f & m, 102m, 111, 136, 162, 172, 175f & m, 178, 179, 181, 187, 190, 192, 239, 242, 269, 281, 323f, 340, 371-rc-1,2,4, 372-lc-1, rc-5, 373-rc-1, 4, 374-lc-2, rc-5, 375-lc-3, 5, rc-3, 5, 378-lc-2, rc-5, 379-rc-1, 381-lc-2, rc-1, 382-rc-5, 383-lc-5, 384-lc-2, rc-2. **Vireo**/ B. Chudleigh 118f; Rob Curtis 320m; R. & S. Day 353f; J. Dunning 376-lc-4; H. & J. Eriksen 375-rc-1; M. Gage 374-rc-2; C. H. Greenewalt 197; T. Laman 51, 279; M. Lockwood 381-lc-5; S. Maka 231; A. Morris 357m; J. P. Myers 168; R. L. Pitman 48; D. Roby & K. Brink 375-rc-4; F. K. Schleicher 186; D. Tipling 47, 374-rc-3; F. Truslow 378-rc-4; Tom Vezo 373-lc-5; Doug Wechsler 325, 376-rc-3, 377-lc-5, 380-lc-4, 382-rc-3; B. K. Wheeler 120. **Kenny Walters** 7b, 29b, 31b, 34b.